Britain's strategic nuclear weapon carriers, 1955-69: the V-bombers Avro Vulcan (in the lead), flanked by the Vickers Valiant (to port) and Handley Page Victor

Crown copyright photo

The RAF
Strategic Nuclear Deterrent Forces:
their origins, roles and deployment
1946-1969
A documentary history

by

Humphrey Wynn

Ministry of Defence

Air Historical Branch (RAF)

1994

London: HMSO

Applications for reproduction should be made to HMSO
First published 1994

ISBN 0 11 772778 4

iii

FOREWORD

by Air Chief Marshal Sir Kenneth Cross KCB CBE DSO DFC
Air Officer Commanding in Chief Bomber Command
1959-1963

This history records the circumstances and events that led to probably the greatest change in British defence policy in peacetime, and its implementation by Bomber Command of the Royal Air Force. It is an account of courage, determination and devotion, beginning with the decision by a small number of Ministers in 1947 to develop an atomic bomb. It then takes us through the brilliant work of our scientists and engineers in designing Blue Danube, the first operational weapon, the foresight and planning of the Air Staff resulting in the specification and building of the 'V' bombers – Valiant, Vulcan and Victor, the best aircraft of their type anywhere in the world at the time, and the final execution of the deterrent policy by Bomber Command.

The task given to the Command was immense. It was to prepare and maintain for instant retaliation against an attack more than 180 'V' bombers and 60 Thor intermediate-range ballistic missiles. The maintaining of this force at virtually war readiness called for a sustained effort by all ranks in the Command and considerable sacrifice in the private lives of commanders, staffs, air and ground crews. That these sacrifices were made willingly was a measure of their belief in the Command's role and its importance in deterring war.

This account also tells of the remarkable partnership between Strategic Air Command of the United States Air Force and Bomber Command of the Royal Air Force. These two Commands alone provided the Western deterrent in the nineteen fifties and sixties; theirs was a great working partnership based on a common aim, a mutual respect for each other's professional capabilities and, as time went on, personal friendships at all levels.

It is excellent that all this history should be recorded now whilst many of the participants are still alive and their memories can so usefully supplement the official papers.

INTRODUCTION

This is an "official" history in the sense that it has been written from official records, to which the author has had unrestricted access and from which he has quoted extensively: many of them, having been subjected to the reviewing process and consequently "weeded", now only exist in this form.

The history covers a period of 24 years, 1945-69, from the ending of the Second World War and the contemporary Chiefs of Staff considerations of the possibility of future war and the weapons that might be employed, to the handing-over by the RAF to the Royal Navy in mid-1969 of responsibility for British strategic nuclear deterrence – the so-called QRA (quick reaction alert) standby duties, representing the highest state of operational readiness ever achieved by UK forces in peacetime, then transferred from bombers to submarines.

Initially there had been considerable debate, in 1945-46, as to whether Britain should manufacture nuclear bombs at all. Once that decision had been taken by a group of senior Ministers, not by the Government, early in 1947 – and it cannot be stressed too greatly how crucial was the role of the former Chief of the Air Staff, Lord Portal, in influencing that decision (as will subsequently be described) – the rest followed: the issue by the Air Staff of Operational Requirements for an atomic bomb and for aircraft capable of delivering it; plans for the training of aircrew and the preparation of suitable airfields; a test of the first atomic warhead and the consequent production of nuclear bombs; the build-up and deployment of a jet bomber force; further development of both aircraft and weapons, including thermonuclear bombs; the introduction of a guided bomb and the proposed introduction of entirely new weapons like the Blue Streak MRBM and TSR.2 (tactical strike/reconnaissance) aircraft – cancelled projects whose "rise and fall" form the themes of chapters in this history.

While two of the three atomic-capable medium bombers which were produced were developed into more powerful (B.1A and B.2) versions and the kiloton-range nuclear bombs they originally carried were succeeded by megaton-range weapons, the means of delivering nuclear warheads only changed twice during this period from the traditional free-fall bomb technique: with the introduction of Blue Steel air-launched guided bombs in 1962-63, and with the deployment in Britain of American Thor intermediate range (1,500-mile) ballistic missiles from 1958 to 1963, manned by RAF Bomber Command crews. Plans to build and deploy a British medium range (2,000-mile) ballistic missile, Blue Streak, were abandoned in 1960 in the expectation that the RAF would be supplied with the 1,000-mile range American ALBM (air-launched ballistic missile) Skybolt for its B.2 Vulcans, but this weapon was cancelled at the end of 1962; and TSR.2, which was to have replaced Bomber Command's Canberras and Valiants in the 1960s and would additionally have had a low-level strategic role, was cancelled in 1965.

The development of RAF jet bombers – Canberras, Valiants, Vulcans and Victors – and of the British nuclear weapons the V-bombers carried[1] are described in separate, self-contained chapters in this history, which has been written from an impartial viewpoint, to give future researchers and historians a clear and consecutive account of each stage of development during the RAF strategic nuclear deterrent period.

In those years, Bomber Command made its most massive effort since the Second World War, building-up and deploying 32 Canberra[2] and 15 V-bomber squadrons and embodying the UK policy of deterrence with QRA (quick reaction alert) and dispersal techniques. What might be called the Canberra period began in 1951 when the first squadron was equipped, while the V-bomber period began in 1955 when the first Valiant squadrons were formed, giving the Command a nuclear weapon delivery capability.

Its Commanders in Chief at these most significant stages in its history were Air Marshal (later Air Chief Marshal) Sir Hugh Pugh Lloyd, who had distinguished himself as Air Commander in Malta when the island was desperately defending itself against attack and who during his term as AOC in C (1950-53) "saw in" the first Canberras after his Command had had to borrow B-29s from the United States to keep up its long-range capability until its Lincolns could be replaced; Air Marshal G H (later Sir George) Mills, whose term of office (1953-56) covered the arrival of the Valiants and who sponsored a "blueprint" for the Air Staff covering every aspect of the setting-up of the V-bomber force[3]; Air Chief Marshal Sir Harry Broadhurst (1956-59), who with vast wartime experience of fighter and tactical air operations behind him introduced a "fighter-pilot type" mentality into V-force aircrew (whose aircraft were having to get off the ground as quickly as Spitfires and Hurricanes had done in the Battle of Britain), and who initiated close co-operation with the USAF Strategic Air Command; and Air Marshal Sir Kenneth Cross (1959-63), who had formerly been AOC No 3 Group in Bomber Command and whose period as AOC in C saw the RAF strategic nuclear deterrent forces rise to the greatest height of their destructive powers, with thermonuclear-weapon-armed V-bombers supplemented by American Thor missiles with megaton warheads, who fostered the close Bomber Command/SAC co-operation and who infused V-force personnel with a dedicated sense of discipline and purpose, during 1962 introducing an all-the-year-round QRA standby, which was maintained until the transfer of strategic nuclear deterrence to the Royal Navy's Polaris-armed nuclear submarines in mid-1969.

Bomber Command had had a difficult time in the years following the

---

[1] The interdictor Canberras, the Valiants of the TBF (Tactical Bomber Force) and some of the Vulcans and Victors carried US nuclear weapons, held under USAF custodianship.

[2] Six Canberra squadrons were subsequently formed in Germany, four in Cyprus and one in the Far East.

[3] *A Review of the 'V' Force* – 7 March 55 (AHB IIH/272/3/48).

Second World War, not only because of the obsolescence of its piston-engined aircraft but also because of official and public reluctance to acknowledge the great contribution it had made to victory in Europe, and with Fighter Command maintaining popular esteem through the annual Battle of Britain displays – evocatively named though portraying the whole of the RAF. Further, the vast numbers of aircraft and personnel involved in the wartime bombing offensive had melted away: the mighty force which had been able to put up 700/800 heavy bombers nightly over Germany was reduced to a few squadrons of Lancasters/Lincolns and Mosquitoes, and most of its highly skilled aircrew and groundcrew had returned to civilian life. When the 'Cold War' began in 1947 and the Soviet Union became a potential enemy the RAF had no bombers with sufficient range to reach significant targets there: the Lincolns would scarcely have been able to penetrate beyond the Russian frontiers. In 1948 the Chief of the Air Staff (Lord Tedder) said that "if war comes we must fight as best we can with what we have got"[1], and in 1952 his successor (Sir John Slessor) admitted that if a Russian attack came earlier than 1957 "we should have to do the best [we could] with what we had"[2].

Because of the lack of a long-range bomber the loan of B-29 Superfortresses from the United States was arranged: they were named Washingtons in RAF service; and production orders for Canberras (to be used as tactical day bombers in the event of a Warsaw Pact advance across Europe – hopefully with more success than the ill-fated Battles in the 1940 "blitzkrieg") and for Valiants were accelerated to fill the bomber "gap" until the arrival of the Vulcans and Victors originally ordered by the Air Staff.

The Air Staff had drawn up its requirements for new bombers and an atomic weapon in 1946, and these were implemented once the crucial nuclear bomb policy decision had been taken early in 1947. But while there seemed to be no particular problems about developing the bomb, apart from its uniqueness (given the high-level impetus and impressive technical skill devoted to it), the aircraft, owing to their advanced configurations, took a long time to develop: the Valiant seven years, because of its comparatively straightforward design to a less demanding specification, the Vulcan nine and the Victor ten years. Bomb delivery, because of the much higher operating altitudes and speeds of the turbojet bombers compared with their piston-engined predecessors, raised the problem of guidance to ensure accuracy of results: an initial concept, Blue Boar, for a TV camera in the bomb and a joystick control in the aircraft, was abandoned in favour of a powered guided bomb – Blue Steel, to be launched from the V-bombers and fly on a parabolic course to its target 100 miles away.

---

[1] Note for the Chiefs of Staff on the Modernisation of the Strategic Bomber Force.
[2] Minute to S of S for Air (Lord De L'Isle and Dudley VC) on 10 March 52.

But aside from the airborne "hardware", much planning had been going on for the V-force[1], the first comprehensive summary of which had been sent to the Air Staff in early 1955[2], just as the first Valiants began to appear on RAF stations.

This *Review of the V-force* was a remarkable blueprint for the future – British strategic nuclear deterrence in RAF terms. Its premises were as unambiguous as mathematical equations. The force would have to be one that a would-be aggressor "must reckon with" if resorting to hostilities to gain his ends. It would pose a threat of retaliation "of such consequence" as would "negate the advantages of conquest by destroying the aggressor industrially, administratively and economically".

If Russia, as a would-be aggressor, contemplated challenging the Western nations to a trial of armed strength, she would seek ways of forestalling British retaliation from the outset – with a strong probability that her first hostile act might be to attempt to destroy the V-force on its bases by surprise. Therefore, "we must ensure that the Force can deliver its first, and strongest, retaliatory blow within the time limits of warning we can rely upon" – the genesis of the early-warning system and QRA (quick reaction alert); and "the Force must be deployed in such a way that Russia will need to expend the largest possible number of her own nuclear weapons in order to be sure of destroying it" – the origin of the dispersal plan, aimed at getting as many as possible of the V-bombers off the ground and ensuring that the V-force presented as widely dispersed a target as possible.

From these basic parameters all the rest of the planning followed. The V-force was to be based on ten Class 1 airfields, each with a single 9,000ft runway of LCN 60 or above weight-bearing capacity[3] and each with three squadrons of eight aircraft UE (unit establishment), ie a total force of 240 V-bombers[4]. These main bases, defended by Bloodhound surface-to-air missiles, were to be equipped with major support facilities – an electronics centre, ring mains for fuel and power, ILS (instrument landing system) and ACR7 surveillance radar for recovery of aircraft, synthetic training and briefing equipment and weapon storage areas (the principal weapon being the Mk 1 atomic bomb, plus 1,000lb HE

---

[1] This term seems to have originated in 1952. At an Air Council meeting on 2 October the CAS (Slessor) said that A V Roe were anxious that their version of the B.35/46 Specification should be named Ottawa – in line with Wellington and Canberra; but it would not be in line with Valiant, and "his own inclination was to establish a 'V' class of medium jet bombers". An unsigned note in a file on Aircraft Nomenclature (ID3/94/8 (Pt 1)) says: "Decided Oct 1952 that the A V Roe version of the B.35 should be named Vulcan, following Valiant and preceding Victor, thus making a 'V' class of medium bombers. Thus a break from tradition of naming bomber aircraft after towns in Commonwealth or those associated with British history".

[2] *A Review of the 'V' Force* – BC/TS.84435, 7 March 1955.

[3] Providing for aircraft weighing up to 160,000lb.

[4] This was the total originally hoped for, but subsequently whittled-down to 184, as will be described.

weapons and pyrotechnics). An enormous amount of new ground equipment had to be provided for the V-bombers, like Douglas Tugmaster heavy tractors, 2,500 gal pressure refuellers, bomb-hoisting gantry cranes[1], servicing and power conversion trailers and air cooling and cabin testing trolleys, plus a wide range of less important items. Operational flight trainers (simulators) were an essential and costly facility on all main bases, specifically designed for each type of V-bomber.

Apart from the "hardware" – the capital investment in main bases and their installations – there was a large and high-quality human investment in aircrew and groundcrew for the 33 new squadrons (30 bomber, two photographic reconnaissance and one "special signals") expected to form, and these men were going to be "screened" from the normal postings machinery so that they stayed in the V-force for at least five years.

Training for pilot and navigator aircrew was mainly to be done at the Canberra OCU and high qualifications were required for acceptance on the V-bomber squadrons. Pilots[2] had to have had 2,000 hr experience as first pilots, plus Canberra experience, or experience on multi-engined jets, though it was recognised that the 2,000 hr criterion would in course of time have to be relaxed. From the Canberra OCU they would go to a V-force OCU for captains' or second pilots' courses. Navigators were of two categories, plotter and bomb aimer, the latter being responsible for the very complex NBS (Navigation and Bombing System Mk 1), equipment, on which – and on its operator – the success of the bombing mission ultimately depended. It was estimated that bomb aimers and navigators needed at least 100 hours' operating experience on NBS – the core of which was the H2S Mk 9 radar – before they could be considered operationally proficient. Signallers, as fifth crew members, were to be responsible for operating the long-range air communications equipment, tail-warning radar and RCM (radio countermeasures) set.

As far as the V-bomber aircrew were concerned, there were two significant differences between their mode of operating and that of their Second World War predecessors: the crew members were all together, within sight and touching distance of each other, in a pressurised cabin; there was no isolation, like that of tail gunners in the wartime bombers. Secondly, they had no guns to fire; the V-bombers carried no self-defensive armament: their protection lay in their radio countermeasures and tail-warning radar equipment, plus tactical routeing and manoeuvres.

The same high standards of qualification, and the same mandatory five-year tour, applied to groundcrew on the V-force squadrons because

---

[1] With special application to the Valiants, whose bombs were loaded-in from above.
[2] The cost of training a V-bomber pilot was estimated to be £55,000 (US of S, in answer to a Parliamentary question, 16 May 56).

of the complex aircraft and equipment they were going to have to service and maintain. The *Review of the V-force* instanced the fact that "a V-bomber base, with 24 UE (unit establishment) aircraft, requires 1093 items of radio test equipment of 270 different types, of which approximately half are for NBS". At Gaydon, the first V-bomber OCU, there was a Valiant servicing school; technicians also attended manufacturers' courses, and in view of the high standard of maintenance of complex equipment required, a policy to screen trained technicians for at least five years was regarded as imperative.

The V-bombers which had to be maintained by these technicians housed a complex mass of equipment and systems to make them into self-contained atomic weapon carriers. In addition to their primary NBS/H2S navigation and bombing equipment they had Green Satin/GPI dead reckoning navigation system, Mk 10 autopilot, a wide range of communications equipment (20-channel VHF and H/F RT and WT), tail warners giving active and passive warning, RCM equipment – mainly jammers on a wide range of frequencies, facility for in-flight loading of the Mk 1 atomic bomb, a flight-refuelling capability, and IFF Mk 10 for identification of friendly/enemy aircraft.

Thus the V-bombers, apart from being the most dramatic individual designs of big aircraft ever created by the British aerospace industry, were the most comprehensively equipped machines ever put into the air by the RAF; and the plans for their deployment – as a unique airborne deterrent force within Bomber Command – were reminiscent of the Independent Force created on the Western Front in 1918 for the prime purpose of bombing strategic targets well beyond the German lines and inside Germany itself.

In addition to its main deterrent role, however, the V-force had other operational tasks – deployment overseas (in the years before Britain's withdrawal from bases east of Suez) and, if required, shipping strikes and minelaying. V-bombers operated from Cyprus and from Singapore; they made increasingly long long-distance flights – eventually non-stop from the UK to Australia; they flew off singly eastwards and westwards (Lone Rangers and Western Rangers) carrying a crew chief to demonstrate their self-sufficiency when away from base; they were constantly on the move – exercises to test squadrons' readiness might be called at any hour of the day or night, and if dispersal was involved their aircraft would fly off to any of the 36 nominated dispersal airfields throughout the country. At all times throughout its existence the V-force had to be "on its toes".

Only once, however, did it drop bombs "in anger" – during the Suez operation of October/November 1956 (described in Chapter X of this history) – and only the Valiant squadrons were involved, in a conventional role, with Canberras also bombing and acting as target-markers. The experience was not a happy one for Bomber Command, especially as its Valiants were not then as fully equipped as they should have been: some of the NBS equipment had not been fitted, so the crews had had no real experience of it. In the *Review of the V-force* of March 1955 the fear had been expressed that the supply of NBS and its associated components might be delayed, with the comment that "it would be a tragedy if aircraft and airfields are ready but the use of operational equipment" was "prohibited" by delays.

The V-force was to be dogged by other delays, and cancellations, during its 14-year history: a delay in bringing the Blue Steel stand-off bomb into service; cancellation of the Skybolt ALBM (air-launched ballistic missile) which was to succeed it; and cancellation of the Blue Streak MRBM (medium-range ballistic missile) which would have taken up the experience gained in operating the American Thor IRBM (intermediate-range ballistic missiles). These events are fully recounted in the chapters which follow.

What cannot be recounted, or even estimated, is whether the force would have been successful had it been called upon to exercise its deterrent power; whether all the training, all the skill, all the courage, would have got it off the ground in the face of a missile attack upon the United Kingdom, and whether if it delivered its bombs, it would ever have been able to return to its bases in the face of nuclear devastation and fall-out. The fact that it was never called upon to operate in earnest can be adduced as success for the deterrent threat it posed. That it was created and trained and exercised in earnest, in co-operation with its American counterpart the USAF Strategic Air Command, should be evident from the pages which follow.

ACKNOWLEDGEMENTS

This history has been written in the Air Historical Branch of the Ministry of Defence and the author has received much help from many individuals, both in the MoD at large and the AHB in particular, and in other Government Departments such as the Cabinet Office, Procurement Executive and the Public Record Office – individuals who have displayed patience, courtesy and conscientiousness in dealing with requests for documents and affording facilities for studying them.

Referring first to colleagues in the AHB, the Head of the Branch when this project was initiated was Gp Capt E B Haslam: to him and to his successors, Air Cdre H A Probert and Gp Capt I Madelin, especial thanks are due, as they are to the following members of the staff: G R Gately, D C Bateman (in particular for obtaining photographs), Mrs L R Robinson, J P McDonald, J Whittuck, Miss V L R Shrubsall, H H Edmonds, S H Bostock, J Spottiswood, E H Turner, Mrs K P Cummings, L Howard, Mrs M Higgs, Sqn Ldr F W J Davies (who compiled the sketch-maps and chronology) and Sqn Ldr P H R Singleton for liaison with HMSO and Nova Graphics and additional photographic requirements.

For records obtained from MoD sources the assistance of the following is gratefully acknowledged: Mrs F Goodwin, D Lock and G Morris of OS9 (Archives); J C Marshall and R Scott of CS(R)2a (Zodiac Control); Mrs J Church of OS9A (Hayes); P Raymond, R Estlick and G A Bay of PTCAn1; and W C Wood of RDT3, PE(MoD).

For Cabinet Office papers, thanks are due to J Cheatle, D J Woodhams, J Robertson, R Pullen and C Smith.

The assistance of Professor Margaret Gowing, the Atomic Energy Authority's official historian and author of *Britain and Atomic Energy 1945-1952* and subsequent volumes, and of her research assistant Mrs Lorna Arnold on matters relating to the British nuclear energy programme is gratefully acknowledged: no-one who writes on this subject can fail to be indebted to their massive and authoritative work.

Help with questions about, and papers on, Blue Steel development by A V Roe was kindly provided by M D Baxter of Hawker Siddeley Dynamics and G R Wrixon of the Royal Aeronautical Society.

The following retired RAF officers generously gave their time to be interviewed, or provided written material, on subjects with which they had been associated: Air Mshl Sir John Rowlands GC (RAF assembly of the first British nuclear device); AVM G Silyn-Roberts (V-bomber development); Gp Capt K G Hubbard (Grapple Trials); Gp Capt D Roberts (Blue Danube Trials); Gp Capt U L Burberry (Valiant and Victor operations); Wg Cdr R D Alexander (Valiant TBF): and Sqn Ldr R K Collyer (Thor squadron). Mr R P ("George") Pedley, ex-Airwork, provided invaluable first-hand information on the construction of the first atomic bomb.

The assistance of the librarians in the MoD Air Library, Adastral

House, should also be acknowledged, successively of F White, H Milton, Mrs M Deighton, Mrs V Brooke, Mr R Wafer, Mrs J Lane and Mr A Vine; of the Royal Air Force, for its hospitality at Wittering (when Gp Capt J G Whitaker commanded the Armament Support Unit there) and Waddington; and of the RAF Museum, during a visit to Henlow to see the Blue Steel example there. The audio-typing of classified documents was ably undertaken by Mrs M E Meighan and her staff in OS23B. Col I T C Wilson, RE(Ret), kindly made available a copy of Chapter X The Nuclear Test Programme of Vol X of the *History of the Corps of the Royal Engineers*.

Finally the author express his thanks to Messrs Edward Johnson and Les Pettet of HMSO Print Procurement, who have proved themselves to be the most capable, understanding and co-operative of publishers.

February 1991.   H.W.

CHAPTER I

ORIGINS OF THE BRITISH ATOMIC BOMB AND NUCLEAR DETERRENT STRATEGY

THE IDEA OF an atomic bomb and its effect upon warfare had been germinating in British military and political consciousness since well before the end of the Second World War, and steps had been taken to acquire such a weapon before the Americans dropped their A-bombs on Japan.

In November 1944, with the war in Europe far from won and victory in the Far East even further from being achieved, the UK Chiefs of Staff asked their Technical Warfare Committee to look into the future: it was to investigate the potentialities of weapons of war and make a report on them[1]. In the Chiefs' own words:—

"Among the most important factors affecting the future defence of the British Empire are the likely development of existing weapons of war, the further development and improvement of weapons now in the experimental stage, and the development of entirely new weapons and methods which though considered practicable in theory have not yet been attempted in practice...

"The Joint Technical Warfare Committee, availing themselves of the best scientific advice available, are required to review the position and to forecast to the best of their ability developments in weapons and methods in each important field of warfare during the next ten years, having regard both to theoretical possibilities and also to the practical limitations at present foreseeable".

What the JTWC did was to set up an *ad hoc* scientific committee under the chairmanship of Sir Henry Tizard, he and his distinguished fellow scientists[2] producing a report which came to bear his name.

Although the Tizard Committee was denied access to any information on atomic bomb developments – "we have been given no information", its report said, "on what has been and is being done in America, nor have we been informed of the policy of the British Government" – it nevertheless, in discussing atomic energy, sowed the seeds which were to burgeon into future government policy.

The Tizard Report of 3 July 1945 urged that the Government should encourage large-scale research into atomic energy; it foresaw the

---

[1] COS(44)360th meeting (O), 7 Nov 44.
[2] J D Bernal, P M S Blackett, C D Ellis and G P Thompson. This Committee on Defence Research Policy was the post-war successor to the pre-war Committee for the Scientific Survey of Air Defence, also chaired by Tizard (see Ronald W Clark's *Tizard* – Methuen & Co, 1965).

1

devastating effects of atomic weapons[1]; it envisaged the development of jet bombers able to cruise at 500 mph at 40,000ft, carrying a bomb load equivalent to that of the Lancaster; and it also postulated the idea of nuclear deterrence. If the atomic bomb were perfected (it said) and could be produced without prohibitive cost, sudden attacks could be made without warning, though it was unlikely that tests could be kept secret because of earth shocks. "Assuming the worst", the committee concluded, "the only answer that we can see to the atomic bomb is to be prepared to use it ourselves in retaliation. A knowledge that we were prepared, in the last resort, to do this might well deter an aggressive nation".

Thus the Report spelt out the main parameters of British strategic defence policy in what the scientists foresaw as the nuclear age: the production of atomic energy for nuclear purposes; the design and manufacture of very fast, very-high-flying jet-powered bomber aircraft; and a preparedness to use atomic bombs against a possible aggressor – the idea subsequently enunciated by the Chiefs of Staff as the nuclear deterrent philosophy.

When the Report first appeared the war in Europe had been won but no-one could foresee how long the Far East conflict would go on; and although the Allies had gained victory in the West a giant shadow loomed on the European horizon – that of the Soviet Union, now with a foothold in Western Europe and emerging from the Second World War as one of the Great Powers, unlikely to disarm or withdraw when victory had been won at the cost of fearful losses[2]. The other Allies – particularly the Americans – were anxious to re-group their forces against the Japanese or to demobilise.

In a telegram to President Truman on 12 May 1945[3] after Germany had been defeated, Prime Minister Winston Churchill had set down his views on the state of Europe after more than five-and-a-half years of warfare:—

"I am profoundly concerned about the European situation. I learn that half the American Air Force has already begun to move to the Pacific theatre. The newspapers are full of the great movements of the American armies out of Europe. Our armies also are, under previous arrangements, likely to undergo a marked reduction. The Canadian

---

[1] "If atomic energy can be released explosively, the character of war...will be completely changed...
"There is...a possibility that some practical method may be found to release atomic energy explosively. The total energy involved...is about two million times that released by the explosion of an equal weight of TNT. Even allowing for a low efficiency, and for the probable need of elaborate and heavy gear to release the energy, we conclude that a single bomber could do an amount of damage equal to that of a thousand bombers using normal bombs". *Cf* the attacks on Hiroshima and Nagasaki by single B-29s with the RAF 1,000-bomber raids on Cologne, Essen and Bremen in 1942.
[2] The German invasion and subsequent defeat cost the Russians 20 million casualties.
[3] The so-called "Iron Curtain" telegram, quoted in Churchill's *The Second World War Vol VI Triumph and Tragedy* (Cassell & Co, 1954), pp 498-499. "Of all the public documents I have written on this issue", he said, "I would rather be judged by this".

Army will certainly leave. The French are weak....Anyone can see that in a very short space of time our armed power on the Continent will have vanished, except for moderate forces to hold down Germany.

"Meanwhile what is to happen about Russia?...I feel deep anxiety because of their misinterpretation of the Yalta decisions,[1] their attitude towards Poland, their overwhelming influence in the Balkans, excepting Greece, the difficulties they make about Vienna[2], the combination of Russian power and the territories under their control or occupied, coupled with the Communist technique in so many other countries, and above all their power to maintain very large armies in the field for a long time. What will the position be in a year or two when the British and American Armies have melted and the French have not yet been formed on any major scale...and when Russia may choose to keep two or three hundred divisions on active service?

"An iron curtain is drawn down upon their front. We do not know what is going on behind..."

This was a global statesman's view of a Western Europe devastated and debilitated by war, a Europe into which a new World Power had entered whose potentiality was greater than that of the defeated Germany, and whose credo was worldwide domination – by political, economic or military means. If there were to be a military clash in a few years' time, the Western Powers by themselves could not withstand the overwhelming forces of the Soviet Union; nor could they automatically rely on American aid.

The Churchill telegram – hardly a victory salutation, more a cry of despair – was sent to Truman only four days after the German surrender on 8 May 1945. In the following month, on 26 June, the United Nations charter was signed in San Francisco by 50 countries – leading to the formal emergence of the United Nations Organisation on 24 October 1945. Here was a hope for the future – an organisation in whose Assembly all nations had a voice, and in whose Security Council the major Powers could act in concert to deter aggression.

But the emergence of the atomic bomb (the possibility that the Tizard Committee had foreseen – the release of atomic energy explosively) so soon after the UN Charter had been signed – the first one tested on 16 July 1945, the second and third dropped on Japan on 6 and 9 August – created a dangerous imbalance among the world Powers, so recently allied for the defeat of Germany and Japan. The United States had a monopoly of the most potent weapon yet devised, and had shown that the use of it could destroy an enemy's resistance overnight; the Soviet Union, having greatly extended her territory and her area of influence, had nevertheless been placed in a position of inferiority as a non-nuclear Power; and the United Kingdom, having contributed to the

---

[1] On broadening the Polish Government to include all parties, and on ensuring that free elections were held and democratic governments established in countries occupied by Allied armies.

[2] Austria did not regain her independence until 27 July 1955.

original knowledge leading to atomic bomb development[1], was now in a three-sided dilemma: she could not willingly acquiesce in an American monopoly of nuclear weapons, yet could not see the new United Nations Organisation being strong enough to enforce international control of atomic energy development; she knew that the scientific and industrial capability to make an atomic bomb existed in Britain, subject only to Governmental authority to proceed; and she realised that the possession of atomic bombs would be an effective deterrent to Russian domination of Western Europe.

The AOC in C RAF Bomber Command (Air Chf Mshl Sir Arthur Harris) had referred at the end of March 1945, when victory in Europe was at last in sight, to the problem of defeating the Japanese and the part bombing might play in bringing about victory in the Far East. At the end of a long letter to the Deputy CAS (Air Mshl Sir Norman Bottomley) on 29 March he had commented:—

"Japan remains. Are we going to bomb their cities flat – as in Germany – and give the Allies a walkover – as in France and Germany – or are we going to bomb only their outlying factories, largely underground by the time we get going, and subsequently invade at the cost of 3 to 6 million casualties? We should be careful of precedents"[2].

These were the comments of a strategic bomber force commander who had been able to launch between 500 and 1,000 aircraft per night against targets in Germany, made on the basis of his Command's contribution to the war in Europe. Having propounded the thesis that an all-out bombing campaign would lessen the horrific casualties likely to be incurred in landings on Japanese soil, Sir Arthur could hardly have foreseen that Japan would be defeated by bombing attacks on two cities, each made by one aircraft carrying a single bomb. Such were to be the stark, simple statistics of nuclear warfare.

On 18 August 1945 the distinguished RAF bomber pilot Gp Capt G L Cheshire VC, who had done more than a hundred operations over Europe, made a report on the USAAF atomic bomb attacks on Hiroshima and Nagasaki[3]. Of the Hiroshima operation he wrote:—

"Zero hour was timed for 0915, August 6th, Tinian time[4]. There were three particular aircraft – one to drop the bomb, the second to make

---

[1] "The early British work embodied in the 1941 Maud Report was decisive in getting the American atomic bomb project off the ground" (*Independence and Deterrence Britain and Atomic Energy 1945-1952 Vol 1, Policy Making*, by Margaret Gowing, assisted by Lorna Arnold (Macmillan, 1974). In her earlier work, *Britain and Atomic Energy 1939-1945* (Macmillan, 1964) Prof Gowing commented that "Without the work of the Maud Committee...the Second World War might well have ended before an atomic bomb was dropped". This committee on the uranium bomb was set up in London in mid-1940 in the Ministry of Aircraft Production: its first Report (July 1941) was on the use of uranium for a bomb.

[2] Quoted in *Bomber Harris – The Authorised Biography*, by Dudley Saward (Cassell Ltd and Buchan & Enright Publishers Ltd, 1984).

[3] Quoted as Appendix 9 in *The Atomic Bomb An Account of British Policy in the Second World War*, by John Ehrman (Cabinet Office, London SW1, 1953).

[4] Tinian was the Pacific island from which the USAAF B-29s flew to drop the atomic bombs.

4

scientific observations, the third to photograph the explosion. To my surprise the operation was executed as planned, the bomb being dropped within one minute of zero hour with both the observation plane and the photographic plane in its correct position. On the explosion of the bomb the two leading aircraft had turned on a reciprocal course and were thus free from danger, while the photographic aeroplane was flying directly towards the target at a distance of some 25 miles. Two severe shock waves were felt which all aircraft interpreted as flak and consequently started taking evasive action. The scientific observations were successfully made and after watching the spectacle for a short time the aircraft returned to base. No defences of any sort were encountered".

On the 9 August attack against Nagasaki he reported:—

"The plan for this operation was exactly as that for the previous one. The three aircraft were to rendezvous over Yakushima, south of Kyushu, at 0915 and proceed in formation to the target, the primary target being Kokura and the secondary Nagasaki. Weather reconnaissance was carried out one hour prior to the attack so that the attacking aircraft could be diverted to whichever of the two targets was clear. In point of fact both targets were reported wide open.

"On arrival at the rendezvous point the three aircraft failed to make contact, which did not surprise me in the least, since instead of orbiting Yakushima in a tight circle, they flew around in dog legs some 40 miles long at varying heights. There being no adequate arrangements in the event of contact not being made and the leader not being willing to break radio silence although there was no conceivable reason why he should not, the three aircraft continued to orbit for an hour and ten minutes. The pilot of the photographic aeroplane, in which both Penney and myself were riding[1], then proceeded to fly around the approaches of Kokura wondering what he should do. Eventually, almost two-and-a-half hours after we had arrived at the rendezvous point, we noticed the explosion of the bomb some 80 miles to the west. The pilot said he was unable to go up to observe it since he was short of petrol. On my pointing out that we could always land at Okinawa he agreed to fly up and circle the target. We reached the target some ten munutes after the explosion at a height of 39,000ft. At this time the cloud had become detached from the column and extended up to a height of approximately

[1] Dr W Penney and Gp Capt Cheshire were the only British observers. One of the victims of the Nagasaki bomb was Cpl R F Shaw, RAF, who had been captured by the Japanese when with No 84 Sqn in Java in 1942. When the city was attacked he was working in Fukuoka camp, being trapped and killed by falling masonry (AHB5 correspondence D/AHB(RAF)/ P375879/42, 10 Jul 84). Gp Capt Cheshire subsequently published his recollections in a book called *The Light of Many Suns The Meaning of the Bomb* (Methuen, 1985). In *Britain and Atomic Energy 1939-45* (Macmillan 1964) Prof Margaret Gowing comments that "Cheshire, with his great experience of bombing attacks on Germany, was not impressed with the organisation of the operation; but it must be remembered that the organisation of raids on Germany had been brought to a high pitch of efficiency by hard experience, whereas the atomic weapon sorties from Tinian were the first operation of their kind".

60,000ft. From the bomb aimer's compartment I had an excellent view of the ground and could see that the centre of the impact was some four miles north-east of the aiming point and that the city proper was untouched.[1] Fortunately however the bomb had accidentally hit the industrial centre north of the town and consequently had caused considerable damage. Had it exploded in any other direction it would have fallen in open country....

"From subsequent interrogation of the crew it transpired that three unsuccessful attempts had been made at bombing Kokura and that the aircraft had then proceeded to Nagasaki and had dropped the bomb on its first run, although the crew realised that it was not an accurate run. By this time the crew must have been tired and a little wrought up and I do not think that any blame can be attached to them for the gross error in aim...."

The British official history of the war against Japan has commented that the damage at Nagasaki, a town with 270,000 inhabitants, was "not so great as at Hiroshima since the bomb did not explode over the centre of the target area, but 23,753 of the inhabitants were killed and 43,020 wounded. It is perhaps interesting to reflect that, in the big fire raid on a small area of Tokyo on the night of the 9th/10th March, 84,000 were killed and over 40,000 wounded. The view expressed that the use of the atomic bomb against Japan, though it might cause almost complete local destruction, would save far greater and widespread destruction elsewhere was not far from the mark".[2]

It was against this background of scientific advice about nuclear energy altering the character of warfare, of Russian armies potentially capable of marching across Europe, of American exploitation of atomic bombs to defeat Japan and of a new United Nations Organisation only just brought into being, that Britain's leaders – political and military – had to decide whether her future defence policy should be based on the possession of nuclear weapons, and if so, how these were to be acquired and operationally deployed.

The development of a British atomic bomb, eventually to be carried by the V-force aircraft of RAF Bomber Command, was based on an Air Staff Operational Requirement (OR1001) issued on 9 August 1946 and on a Government decision, made on 8 January 1947, to authorise research and development work on atomic weapons. But these major steps were taken only after several high-level expressions of opinion, from 1945 onwards, had created an "atomic climate" favourable to British design and manufacture of A-bombs. The Royal Air Force did

---

[1] *Ruin from the Air The Atomic Mission to Hiroshima*, by Gordon Thomas and Max Morgan Witts, published in the UK by Hamish Hamilton in 1977, says: "the atomic bomb missed the Aioi Bridge" – the aiming point – "by 800ft..." The attack on Hiroshima therefore seems to have been much more accurate than the subsequent one on Nagasaki.

[2] *History of the Second World War The War against Japan Vol V*, by Maj-Gen S Woodburn Kirby with Brig M R Roberts, Col G T Wards and AVM N L Desoer (HMSO, 1969). This view has subsequently been challenged: see *Hiroshima The Strange Myth of Half a Million American Lives Saved*, by Rufus E Miles Jr in *International Security*, Fall 1985.

not initiate this atomic policy; it reflected official – that is, military, political and scientific – thinking. But because the weapons were to be delivered by aircraft – no other means of delivery being practicable at that time – the Air Staff took the responsibility for setting-down the parameters (derived from the predicted size of the warhead) of the bomb to be carried by high-speed, high-altitude aircraft to be designed for that purpose.

On 5 July 1945 a UK General Election had brought a Labour Government to power; and following the Japanese surrender on 10 August, hastened by the American bombs which British scientists had played a part in developing, the new administration had to consider – along with many other urgent matters – what Britain's post-war atomic energy policy should be. During the war, Prime Minister Churchill "had vigorously insisted that knowledge of the atomic bomb be kept to the smallest possible circle of Ministers and advisers. About seven Ministers in the wartime coalition had been involved in the bomb project in varying degrees and at varying times but only two of them, Sir John Anderson and Lord Cherwell, knew continuously and in detail about the whole business"[1].

On 10 August, the day after the second American atomic bomb had been dropped on Japan, a committee of senior Ministers known as Gen 75 – which became a "forum for decision-making on atomic energy policy"[2] – held its first meeting and was told by Prime Minister Attlee that an Advisory Committee on Atomic Energy (ACAE) was to be set up, to ensure continuity of knowledge and to advise on future policy. On the 21st he announced its formation, with Sir John Anderson as chairman. Its most numerous regular members were scientists – Sir Edward Appleton, Professor P M S Blackett, Sir Henry Dale and Sir George Thomson; its other members were from the Services (Lord Alanbrooke and Lord Tedder) and the Civil Service (Sir Alan Barlow and Mr Nevil Butler). Other scientists who attended its meetings were Sir James Chadwick, Sir Robert Robinson and Sir Henry Tizard, while the Services and the Civil Service had other representatives from time to time. The ACAE's terms of reference were twofold: "to investigate the implications of the use of atomic energy and to advise the Government on what steps should be taken for its development in this country for military or industrial purposes"; and "to put forward proposals for the international treatment of this subject". It was "responsible for making the recommendations which led to the first decisions on the shape of Britain's atomic programme and the attitude to international control"[3].

---

[1] The seven Ministers were Sir John Anderson, Lord Cherwell, Mr R A Butler, Colonels J J Llewellin and J T C Moore-Brabazon, Mr Anthony Eden and Lord Hankey. See *Independence and Deterrence Britain and Atomic Energy 1945-1952*, by Margaret Gowing, assisted by Lorna Arnold; Macmillan, 1974.

[2] Ibid.

[3] *Independence and Deterrence*, by M Gowing: see previous reference.

At its first meeting, on 21 August under the chairmanship of Sir John Anderson, it discussed the effect of the atomic bomb on future methods of warfare and set down a number of questions to which it required answers.

At the Gen 75 committee's second meeting, on 29 August, the Prime Minister circulated a memorandum on The Atomic Bomb. It began unequivocally:–

"A decision on major policy with regard to the atomic bomb is imperative. Until this is taken, civil and military departments are unable to plan. It must be recognised that the emergence of this weapon has rendered most of our post-war planning out of date".

Probably the first British leader to expound a policy of nuclear deterrence, Mr Attlee then gave historical perspective – in uncompromising terms – to the idea which subsequently became embodied in the philosophy of strategic nuclear deterrence:–

"We recognise, or some of us did before this war, that bombing would only be answered by counter bombing. We were right. Berlin and Magdeburg were the answer to London and Coventry. Both derive from Guernica[1]. The answer to an atomic bomb on London is an atomic bomb on another great city".

He also propounded the irresistible conclusion that any attempt to keep atomic bomb technology in American and British hands would be useless:–

"Scientists in other countries are certain in time to hit upon the secret[2]. The most we may have is a few years' start. The question is, what use are we to make of that few years' start?".

Attlee's Memorandum was discussed by the Gen 75 Ministers (those who would eventually take the decision to authorise A-bomb R & D) at their meeting on 29 August, when they also considered a Memorandum by the ACAE, which eight days earlier had discussed the effect of the atomic bomb on future methods of warfare.

At the same time the Chiefs of Staff had reacted to the immense change which had affected the military scene with the emergence of this new weapon, and on 20 September instructed their Technical Warfare Committee to revise the Tizard Committee report on Future Developments in Methods of Warfare – referred to at the beginning of this chapter – in the context of this change. Meanwhile, a powerful individual opinion had been expressed from the United States – that of

---

[1] Bombed on 26 Apr 37 by German aircraft co-operating with the Nationalist Government in the Spanish Civil War.

[2] The Russians exploded their first atomic device on 29 Aug 49. (See *The Advisers Oppenheimer, Teller and the Superbomb*, by Herbert F York; W H Freeman & Co, 1976). In 1945 Attlee had hoped that the USA, UK and the USSR would collectively declare that the new invention had made it essential to end wars; he declared that America and Britain were "responsible as never before for the future of the human race". But within a year or so his Government had to abandon its hopes for world peace through the United Nations Organisation.

Sir James Chadwick, who had been closely involved in Anglo-American atomic energy relationships during the last two years of the war[1]. On 10 September he sent a telegram to London saying that the military applications of atomic energy made a production plant "of our own" essential for the defence of the United Kingdom and Commonwealth. "I believe there can only be one opinion on this question", he said. His telegram[2] was seen by the Advisory Committee on Atomic Energy at its second meeting on the 20th.

The Chiefs of Staff expressed their views quite unequivocally on international control of atomic energy and – if that should be impossible to achieve – on possession of the means of retaliation, in a minute to the Prime Minister on 10 October[3]. Replying to his request for comments[4] on Sir John Anderson's Memorandum on the International Control of Atomic Energy[5], the Chiefs of Staff agreed that "we must aim at international control – it is probably the only alternative to mutual destruction". But in their opinion it was "of vital importance that any international agreement into which we enter should include the most unequivocal and comprehensive rights of inspection". It seemed to them that "the whole conception of international control . . . stands or falls on the efficacy of the arrangements for such an inspection". Their minute continued:–

"Russia is a country which appears to have both the natural resources and the remote areas for the secret development of atomic weapons. There is the obvious danger that we and the Americans might be led to agree not to produce atomic weapons while the Russians secretly carried out their research and production in the remote areas of the Soviet Union. The right of inspection will provide no security unless it is completely comprehensive. How this is to be achieved under the present Soviet system is the crux of the problem.

"The Chiefs of Staff recommend therefore that, before entering into international discussions about control of atomic energy, it should be our policy to make an agreement with the Americans to ensure that in any international agreement the right of inspection will be insisted upon and fully exercised in respect of the Soviet Union".

The last paragraph of the CoS minute contained a crucial enunciation of their views on the possession of atomic weapons and on nuclear deterrence:–

"It is clear that in the event of failure to secure an international agreement, possession of atomic weapons of our own would be vital to our security. The best method of defence against the new weapon is likely to be the deterrent effect that the possession of the means of

---

[1] Gowing, *Independence and Deterrence Britain and Atomic Energy 1945-1952.*
[2] Ancam 412.
[3] COS 1449/5.
[4] Minute D.7/45 of 6 Oct.
[5] Dated 2 Oct 45 (GEN 75/5)

retaliation would have on a potential aggressor. The Chiefs of Staff therefore consider that we should press ahead in the field of research and that it is essential that British production of atomic weapons should start as soon as possible. To delay production pending the outcome of negotiations regarding international control might well prove fatal to the security of the British Commonwealth".

"Means of retaliation" comprehended both the weapon and its delivery system, and there was never any question in the Tizard Report – which the Chiefs of Staff accepted – that the means of delivery would be manned aircraft, which "for the next ten years" (in the view of its authors) were "likely to be the only practical means of delivering atomic or biological weapons to ranges of over 400 miles".

On 12 October the CoS Committee had considered a memorandum by Sir Henry Tizard on "Central Direction of Scientific Effort", which opened with the words: "The atomic bomb has vividly impressed upon us all the tremendous influence of scientific progress on every aspect of national and international life . . . . The broad problems of war can no longer be separated from those of peace". He proposed the appointment of a Scientific Adviser with a small planning staff, saying that he had been convinced that "far more time and continuous thought, by scientists of considerable authority in the heart of the Government machine, would alone ensure that the Chiefs of Staff get scientific advice reliable enough to guide their strategic decisions. . . ." The Chiefs concurred: on the 26th they expressed themselves "in general agreement" with the Tizard memorandum, and on 1 November they asked for a draft report, "containing their views on the Central Direction of Scientific Effort, including the terms of reference and composition of the proposed Defence Research Policy Committee".

When the Gen 75 Ministers met again on 16 October 1945 to discuss the international control of atomic energy they decided to ask for a Report by Officials, "presenting a summary of the problem and setting-out the alternative lines of policy which might be adopted"[1], and this was produced within two weeks. Like the CoS Minute to the Prime Minister, it recommended that the United Kingdom should produce atomic bombs.

Dated 29 October, the Report by Officials[2] was a ten-page printed document entitled "International Control of Atomic Energy". No authors' names were appended to it. On the same date, the Prime Minister had told the Commons[3] that an establishment was to be set up at Harwell to engage in research on all aspects of atomic energy. He said that, following a recommendation from the Advisory Committee on Atomic Energy,

"the Government have decided to set up a research and experimental

[1] GEN 75/5th mtg.
[2] GEN 75/10.
[3] Hansard Vol 415, Cols 38-39.

establishment covering all aspects of the use of atomic energy. Accommodation is being provided for the establishment at Harwell airfield near Didcot. . . . It has further been decided that in view of the importance of this work to the Service Departments, responsibility for research on this subject which has hitherto rested with the Department of Scientific and Industrial Research should be transferred to the Ministry of Supply. The Tube Alloys Directorate (which is the name by which the technical organisation dealing with these matters has hitherto been known)[1] will accordingly become a part of that Ministry. . . ."

When asked whether the change of control to a Department more closely associated with the Services meant that the Government were more concerned "about the weapon value of atomic energy than about its production value" the Prime Minister replied:–

"No, not at all. It can hardly have escaped the Hon Gentleman's[2] notice that the Ministry of Supply is also engaged on civilian production. It is a mistake to suggest that it is entirely concerned with weapons".

The Report by Officials was considered by the Gen 75 Ministers on 1 November.[3] Its recommendations as to what should be done were clear and forthright. One of them was that "the United Kingdom Government should itself undertake the production of atomic bombs as a means of self-defence as soon as possible"; another, that "in the course of his forthcoming conversations with the President, the Prime Minister should inform him that "we intend to proceed as rapidly as possible with the large-scale production of bombs for defence purposes". One of the Report's Conclusions was that "the Advisory Committee [on Atomic Energy] should be given an indication of the Government's views in regard to the relative importance of (i) the production of bombs as quickly as possible; (ii) the development of atomic energy for industrial purposes; and (iii) research and development on new and more powerful types of bomb. The Prime Minister should issue a directive that priority is to be given to the first of these objectives.

When the Ministers discussed this conclusion, they felt that further information was needed on the nature of the choice involved, and decided to ask the ACAE to submit a report on the technical factors which might make it necessary to lay down an order of priority between the three suggested courses.

ACAE's report, Large Scale Production, dated 10 December 1945, was circulated to Ministers and considered by them on the 18th. Signed by the committee's chairman, Sir John Anderson, it pointed out that "for military applications, in the present stage of development,

---

[1] Wartime code name for the atomic energy project.
[2] Mr James Maxton, ILP.
[3] GEN 75/7th mtg.
[4] The Truman-Attlee-Mackenzie King meetings were held 10-15 Nov 45.

11

plutonium is greatly superior to U235"[1] and that "for industrial applications, the position is not so clear, but it is probable that plutonium will prove superior to U235." ACAE's first recommendation was that "either one or two piles should be constructed on a suitable site in this country for the production of plutonium". In discussion on the report, the Prime Minister said that how many piles should be built in the UK for the production of plutonium "depended in part on the output of bombs which the Government thought necessary". The Ministers therefore decided to ask the Chiefs of Staff to submit a report on requirements for atomic bombs, and on the possibility of making consequential reductions in other forms of armament production. They also gave approval to the building of one pile on a suitable site for the production of plutonium – work which was to be treated as of "the highest urgency and importance".

When the Chiefs of Staff, at their meeting on 17 December, discussed the large-scale production of atomic energy[2] in response to the Prime Minister's request for their views on the ACAE report, Lord Portal (who was in the chair) handed-round a graph showing the cumulative total of bombs which the major Powers might be able to produce during the next 15 years, emphasising that these estimates were entirely conjectural. The comments he then made can be seen now as the genesis of the British strategic nuclear deterrent force.

On the assumption (he said) that it were decided to "insure" against the failure of the United Nations Organisation, and the breaking of the agreement not to use atomic weapons, it seemed to him that the UK ought to manufacture as many bombs as it could and take all practicable steps to develop means for delivering them to targets. In the event of a future outbreak of unlimited warfare, it seemed likely that the conflict would be largely waged on the capital of bombs accumulated in peacetime. The UK would therefore be well advised to "build up and disperse" stocks in the hope that such action would tend to act as a deterrent to a possible aggressor[3].

The Chiefs of Staff made their own report in the form of a Minute to the Prime Minister, dated 1 January 1946. Signed by Lords Alanbrooke, Cunningham and Portal, it urged the construction of a least two atomic piles. "Until the United Nations Organisation is proved"[4], they said, "we require as quickly as possible the greatest capacity to make atomic bombs that economic factors and the supply of raw materials will allow". In three key paragraphs, they expressed the hope of future world

---

[1] Separation of the fissile material from natural uranium involved complicated and expensive physical processes. Plutonium had to be manufactured from uranium using a 'pile'. The bomb dropped on Nagasaki ('Fat Man') contained plutonium, as did the prototype US atomic bomb tested at Alamogordo on 16 Jul 45. 'Little Boy', dropped on Hiroshima, contained U235.

[2] *Ie* as opposed to small-scale production for, say, medical purposes.

[3] COS (45) 285th Mtg, Confidential Annex.

[4] It had formally come into existence on 24 Oct 45: see previous reference.

security through UNO but put their faith in a national nuclear deterrent:—

"While we hope that our future military security will be assured by the United Nations Organisation, that organisation has not yet been proved. From a military point of view, therefore, we must consider the position should the UNO fail and a potential aggressor be in possession of atomic bombs.

"We are convinced that the best method of defence against the atomic bomb is likely to be the deterrent effect that the possession of the means of retaliation would have on a potential aggressor. We must be prepared for aggressors who have widely dispersed industries and populations. This means that in order to be effective as a deterrent we must have a considerable number of bombs at our disposal. It is not possible now to assess the precise number which we might require but we are convinced that we should aim to have as soon as possible a stock in the order of hundreds rather than scores.

"It is evident, therefore, that in the next ten years the output of one pile would be comparatively insignificant against a determined aggressor. Although we cannot say that two piles will produce sufficient bombs at an early date, clearly two piles are better than one and in the number of bombs we have will lie our strength."

The Chiefs added that starting the construction of two piles now did not commit Britain to the manufacture of atomic bombs:—

"The decision whether to devote the output of atomic piles to industrial development or to atomic bombs need not be taken until the fissile material is produced from the pile, which need not be until the fifth year after construction has started".

When the GEN 75 Ministers considered the CoS report, and a paper from the Minister of Supply, on 23 January 1946 they decided in the light of what the latter advised that work should proceed on the building of the first pile and on setting-up the research establishment at Harwell and that the production programme should be reviewed in three or four months' time. The stage was therefore set, by the beginning of that year, for British R&D work on A-bombs, and one of the leading actors in the scenes which were to follow was shortly to make his appearance in a new role – as Controller of Production of Atomic Energy. One of Lord Portal's final acts as Chief of the Air Staff had been to sign the CoS report on Production of Atomic Energy, and on 29 January the Prime Minister announced his appointment as CPAE and that of Professor J D Cockcroft as director of the research establishment at Harwell, which would "require fissile material for its work. The Government have accordingly had under consideration the most suitable organisation for the production of such material. . . . The object in view will be to make available as speedily as possible material in sufficient quantity to enable us to take advantage rapidly of technical developments as they occur, and to develop our programme for the use of atomic energy, as circumstances may require. The production of these materials will be a responsibility of the Ministry of Supply and the appropriate organisation is being set up within that Department.

"The choice of a suitable head for this organisation is clearly a matter of supreme importance, and for this new post the Government have been fortunate in securing the services of Marshal of the RAF Lord Portal of Hungerford. . .".[1]

When the Prime Minister's announcement about the appointments of Lord Portal and Professor Cockcroft was being finalised, some notes for possible Supplementary Questions were drafted:—

"The Prime Minister may be asked whether the Government have decided to produce atomic bombs in this country, or whether the fact that the late Chief of the Air Staff is to be the head of the new organisation implies that the Government attach more importance to the military than to the possible industrial uses of atomic energy.

"To a question of this sort, he might reply that the step which the Government are now taking follows naturally upon the decision to set up a Research and Development Establishment, and means that we shall still be in a position to produce in this country the material which is indispensable. . . for any future development of the use of atomic energy. Our programme will be flexible and the use which we make of the material we produce will depend upon circumstances. The fact that we are setting-up this organisation, and that the first head of it is a man who has done such great service to the country in organising and directing one of the three armed Services, in no way implies that the Government are looking at this matter primarily from the standpoint of military preparation".

Some years later the then Minister of Works, Sir David Eccles, put the matter rather more bluntly. Speaking in the Commons on 10 December 1953 on "Atomic Energy – Ministerial Responsibility"[2] he said:—

"The House will remember the history of the United Kingdom atomic energy programme; how during the war it was placed under the Lord President, Sir John Anderson (as he than was), because he had great personal qualifications, and also because the Lord President was the Minister responsible for scientific matters arising out of Government policy. After the war the project was transferred to the Ministry of Supply.

"As I understand it, there were two reasons for that. First, the armament programme was being rapidly run down and therefore the Ministry of Supply had spare capacity and, secondly – perhaps more important – at that time the over-riding aim of the atomic energy project was to produce a British bomb. That is the key to the arrangement which was then made.

---

[1] His appointment was Controller of Production (Atomic Energy) at the MoS (Commons Hansard 29 Jan 46, Col 683).

[2] Commons Hansard, Cols 2314-5.

"In 1946, when the Act was passed placing the project under the Minister of Supply, the United States knew how to make an atomic bomb. We did not, although our scientists, as the US President said in his most significant speech last Tuesday [8 December], had made great contributions to knowledge of nuclear fission. But the Americans, for reasons which we understand but nonetheless regret, felt unable to share with us all the secrets of the production process. Therefore, the Labour Government – and Her Majesty's present Ministers think they were right – determined to make a bomb here; and, with this their chief object, it was natural to give the job to the Minister responsible for the manufacture of weapons. From 1946 to 1951, £100 million or more was spent by the Ministry of Supply on this project, and in the last two years further great sums have been laid out for the same purpose".

One anomaly which resulted from Lord Portal's new appointment was that Sir John Anderson's Advisory Committee on Atomic Energy was still in existence: it advised the Prime Minister and the Gen 75 Ministers on atomic energy policy. Since a full-time Controller of Production of Atomic Energy had now been appointed, and the United Nations Commission on Atomic Energy had been set up – with a consequential increase of business for the Government to handle, it was felt that the machinery for inter-Departmental consultation on atomic energy matters should be overhauled. A serious disadvantage was that the chairman of the ACAE did not attend Ministerial meetings, whereas CPAE did attend those of the Gen 75 Ministers discussing atomic energy policy. A further reason for a new arrangement was that Lord Portal needed the support and advice of a technical committee, such as he was planning to set up in the Ministry of Supply.

The result of these feelings, stemming from the new situation which had come about, was that the Atomic Energy (Official) Committee was set up in August 1946 "to consider questions in the field of atomic energy which call for discussion between Departments" – adding in parenthesis, to take account of the *status quo*, "other than those questions appropriate to the Committees presided over by Sir John Anderson and Lord Portal" –, "to make recommendations to Ministers, and to settle questions on which reference to Ministers is unnecessary".

These terms of reference were set out in a note by the committee's chairman, Sir Edward Bridges, Secretary of the Cabinet, on 1 August 1946. Departments represented on the committee were the Cabinet, Foreign and Dominions Offices, the Chiefs of Staff, Treasury and Ministry of Supply. When its first meeting was held, on 25 September, Lord Portal attended and Sir James Chadwick and Sir George Thomson were also present.

Early in his appointment as CPAE, Lord Portal wrote to the Chiefs of Staff about security at the atomic energy plants which were to be built, and his letter was considered at a CoS meeting on 8 March – Lord Alanbrooke pointing out that there were two aspects to the problem, defence against enemy action in time of war, and sabotage and leakage of information. In thus bringing this matter to the attention of the Chiefs of Staff, the value of Portal's prestige in relation to them was demonstrated, for the benefit of the atomic energy programme – which, during 1946, was beginning to take organisational shape, although no Governmental decision about weapon development had as yet been made.

In May of that year CPAE visited the United States, where although he was received with great friendliness and shown the main atomic energy establishments it was made clear to him that it would be useless to enter into any further negotiations at that juncture. Then shortly after his return to the UK the McMahon Bill was introduced into, and passed by, the US Senate. If this became law (as it subsequently did on 1 August 1946) it would effectively prevent the US Government from disclosing any information of a secret character to Britain[1]. Portal's conclusion, after his American visit, was that if Britain were not to lag hopelessly behind the United States for many years in nuclear energy achievement she would have to "think big, take chances and above all translate into reality the priority which HMG have accorded to the project".[2]

An inhibiting factor, however, was the country's economic situation; and the question inevitably asked later during that year (when the senior Ministers concerned met on 25 October) was whether the Government could afford to divert from civilian consumption and the restoration of the balance of payments the economic resources required for a project of this scale, since the country might find itself faced with an extremely serious economic and financial situation in two or three years' time. On the other hand, the United Kingdom could not afford to be left behind in a field of such revolutionary importance, from an industrial as well as a military point of view. The country's prestige in the world, and her chances of securing American co-operation, would suffer if she failed to exploit to the full a discovery in which from the outset she had played a leading part.[3]

In the meantime, during the momentous post-war autumn and winter when the key decision to set up an organisation for the production of atomic energy had been taken, and when the Chiefs of Staff had expressed themselves unequivocally in favour of Britain making atomic bombs, the Tizard Committee Report on Future Developments in Weapons and Methods of War was being revised at their request,[4] to take account of the existence of atomic bombs – to

---

[1] The McMahon Act, which got its name from Senator Brien McMahon, chairman of the US Atomic Energy Committee, "destroyed general Anglo-American collaboration in nuclear energy" (*Britain and Atomic Energy 1939-1945*, by Margaret Gowing; Macmillan, 1964).

[2] Quoted in *Independence and Deterrence Britain and Atomic Energy 1945-1952, Vol I Policy Making*, by M Gowing assisted by Lorna Arnold (Macmillan, 1974), p 178.

[3] Gen 75/15 ministers meeting: see Gowing and Arnold, Vol I, pp 178-179.

[4] COS (45) 229th Mtg, 20 Sep 45.

which the original Report had referred only in hypothetical terms.

This revision was done by the Joint Technical Warfare Committee of the CoS Committee, and the revised report was ready on 1 July 1946. It contained conclusions and recommendations and a long annex dealing with facts about new weapons, targets and requirements for them, resultant changes in the nature of war, and consequent problems for civil defence and for defence research. In sum, the revised report provided a comprehensive initial guide to atomic warfare.

Its first conclusion expressed the total effectiveness of a small number of atomic bombs in accomplishing the defeat of a nation without the need for a land or sea invasion, as had been the case of Japan in August 1945:–

"Given sufficient accumulation in peace and adequate means of delivery, atomic and biological weapons might achieve decisive results with relatively small effort[1] against the civil population of a nation without a clash between the major military forces and too rapidly to permit either the building-up of military forces or the exercise of sea power".

On the means of delivery of such weapons, the report said:–[2]

"The development of high-performance long-range aircraft for offensive purposes must proceed on the highest priority concurrently with methods of accurate navigation, preferably automatic...."

In these two conclusions alone, and their subsequent implementation in terms of atomic bombs and jet bombers to carry them, can be seen the origins of the RAF strategic nuclear deterrent force.[3]

In its recommendations the JTWC said that should the Chiefs of Staff accept its conclusions they should "invite the Deputy CoS Committee (or the proposed Committee on Defence Research Policy[4]) to consider the tasks in respect of naval land and air weapons given in Annex I, paragraph 51". This part of the Annex was headed "Main Problems for Defence Research" and listed (though not in an order of priority) atomic and biological weapons, high-performance manned aircraft capable of carrying atomic bombs to the range required and supersonic pilotless aircraft and/or rockets capable of carrying atomic and biological warheads to ranges required, plus fully automatic means of navigation, interference-free.

On 8 July the Chiefs of Staff recommended[5] that the Cabinet Defence Committee should accept the conclusions of the revised Report as a basis for planning and should approve its recommendations; and at its meeting on the 22nd the CDC made three decisions: it accepted the

---

[1] In its attacks on Japan from Tinian Island, the USAAF used three B-29s each time – one to drop the bomb, a second to make scientific observations and a third to take photographs.
[2] Paragraph 7.
[3] See Appendix (1) for full text.
[4] Eventually set up, under the chairmanship of Sir Henry Tizard, in Jan 47.
[5] Their report to the Cabinet Defence Committee was signed by MRAF Lord Tedder, CAS; Admiral J H D Cunningham, CNS; and Lt-Gen F E W Simpson, VCIGS.

conclusions contained in paragraphs 7 and 8[1] of the JTWC sub-committee report attached to the CoS report "as a basis for planning"; invited the Chiefs of Staff "to arrange for consideration to be given" to the tasks "in respect of naval, land and air weapons given in Annex I, paragraph 51"; and authorised the Chiefs to set up a joint inter-Service, civil and scientific staff to maintain a continuous study of future developments in weapons and methods of warfare.

This Cabinet-level approval of plans for new weapons, in the context of atomic developments[2], meant that the way was now clear for the Air Staff to issue its first requirement for an atomic bomb – OR1001, dated 9 August 1946, for "the development of a bomb employing the principle of nuclear fission". This object is stated in the second issue of the OR (dated 17 August 1948), no copies of the original issue being now in existence. The weapon envisaged was not to exceed 10,000lb in weight, 290in (24ft 2in) in length and 60in (5ft) in diameter[3]. It had to be suitable for release at all heights between 20,000ft and 50,000ft and at speeds of between 150kt and 500kt. Ballistically, it had to have a TV (terminal velocity) suitable for accurate aiming at these heights and speeds, "with bombsights now under design". Because it would only just fit into the bomb-bays of the aircraft whose configurations were being sketched at that time, the new bomb would have to have flip-out fins, extending after its release.

Thus by mid-1946 the Chiefs of Staff had recommended that a stock of atomic bombs be built up; an atomic energy production organisation had been formed and a controller of production and director of research appointed; an Atomic Energy Bill had been published, putting the Minister of Supply in charge of development; the Americans had started peacetime testing of atomic weapons, had given Strategic Air Command the responsibility for delivering them and had passed the McMahon Act, designed to secure a US monopoly of atomic weapons until international control of them could be achieved; the Cabinet had accepted CoS proposals for the inclusion of atomic weapons, and the means of delivering them, in Britain's future military plans; financial provision for atomic energy R&D had been approved;[4] and the Air Staff had written down its requirement for an atomic bomb. Yet the Government had not yet authorised the development of atomic weapons, and it was not until early 1947 that they did so. The final

---

[1] See Appendix (1).

[2] By that date, the United States had exploded its fourth atomic bomb, on 1 July, dropped on ships by a B-29. On 25 July, three days after the CDC met, a fifth weapon was exploded 60ft under water. British observers were present at these trials and wrote a detailed report on them – *1946 Atomic Bomb Trials (Operation Crossroads) Report of the British Service Observers at Bikini Atoll – Parts I & II and Appendices.*

[3] A Defence Research Policy Committee Report on the Strategic Aspects of Atomic Energy (22 March 48) explained that the diameter (for a plutonium bomb) was a non-decreaseable dimension.

[4] DO (46) 17 (Revise), 12 Feb 46. The sum was £5.9m.

impetus for this decision was provided by two key figures in British atomic energy development, Dr William Penney and Lord Portal.

At that time (the latter half of 1946) Dr Penney did not have an official position in the British atomic energy programme; he was Chief Superintendent of Armament Research in the Ministry of Supply. Yet he knew more than any other man in Britain about atomic weapons, having been involved in the development of the American bombs and having only recently participated in the Bikini trials. During Lord Portal's visit to the US in May, Sir James Chadwick had spoken with him about work on the explosive aspect of atomic energy, and had written to Penney about Portal that "he seems to be very willing it should be put in your charge with final responsibility devolving on him".[1] Later that year, CSAR and CPAE met, and the former – perhaps as a result of their discussions – began to plan an Atomic Weapons section in his Armament Research branch. Subsequently he sent these plans to Portal, observing the utmost secrecy, with a hand-written note covering a document he had typed himself. The note referred to a meeting on the following Monday and also suggested where atomic weapon design work might be located. Dated 1 November 1946, it said:–

"Here are the results of my efforts. I hope to see you on Monday 4th Nov in your office at 3 p.m.....

"I have looked at Whitchurch carefully. There is no doubt in my mind that it is *not suitable*.... Only if we were prepared at great expense to run the place as a highly inconvenient temporary measure would I agree to go there. We can do much better at Woolwich and Halstead".

The typed document, headed "Proposals for an Atomic Weapons Section in the Armament Research Department Written and typed by Dr W G Penney, CSAR[2]", said in its Introduction:–

"The manufacture of atomic bombs of present design naturally falls into two parts. First, there is the production of the active material; and second, there is the ordnance part which is briefly the manufacture and assembly of the components causing the explosion of the active material. Without any doubt, it is possible to begin and carry the second part of the work to completion without any necessity at any stage of using fissile material. Formally, but not with a clear conscience, it could be maintained that the whole of the second part of the work was conventional armaments reserarch. The implications of this fact are profound and must properly be taken into account by all schemes purporting to 'control' atomic energy. The purpose of the present memorandum, however, is not to comment on the difficulties of International Control, ...but rather to suggest how the ordnance part of the manufacture of atomic bombs and other atomic weapons could be carried out, if it were decided in the National interest that such work should proceed.

---

[1] Gowing and Arnold, *Britain and Atomic Energy 1945-1952* (previously referred to).
[2] Chief Superintendent of Armament Research.

"The assumptions are made that the Ordnance parts of the atomic weapons must be complete in the fourth year, that the highest priority will be given to certain modest building requirements, and that some loss of performance elsewhere in Armaments Research will be accepted".

The proposals then went into detail about the organisation of work on atomic weapons, the numbers of personnel – both scientific and industrial – required, and its location at Fort Halstead and Woolwich. In sum, the document[1] formed a blueprint for British atomic weapon design and development.

Referring to Broad Groupings of the Work, Dr Penney wrote:–

"The present designs of atomic weapons using plutonium are such that the main problem on the ordnance side is the production of explosive lenses with the correct performance. It is proposed to call the group which makes the lenses the 'Explosives Branch'. There will be two main groups servicing the Explosives Branch, namely the Engineering Branch and the Physics Branch. The chief function of the Engineering Branch will be the preparation of working drawings of well-designed moulds for casting the lenses, to the requirements of the Explosives Branch as advised by the Physics Branch, and the making of these moulds either in the workshops of the Engineering Branch or elsewhere. The chief function of the Physics Branch will be to test and advise on the performance of the lenses, made by the Explosives Branch. Special high-speed photographic and electronic recording apparatus must be designed and built by the Physics Branch in order to carry through its assigned section of the work.

"Besides the three main groups of work mentioned above, there must be several smaller groups, perhaps attached to one or other of the three main groups. For example, there is the group which designs, tests and provides the firing mechanism of the weapon. Another group must study the ballistic problems associated with delivery. A most important group must consider all aspects of performance of atomic weapons both for offense and defence, and this group must certainly be prepared to advise on strategic planning".

As to the number of personnel involved, Penney estimated a total scientific staff of about 90, and from the skilled industrial class – mainly highly skilled fitters – also about 90. "The lens mould job alone", he said, "will need the full-time services of about 20 highly skilled fitters of the tool-making or instrument-making class. Clearly, a first-rate Superintendent for the Engineering Branch is needed immediately...".

Referring to the locations of the different kinds of work, Penney said:–

"The proposal is made that the Explosives Branch be placed on ARD ground at Woolwich... ; that the Physics Branch be placed at Fort

---

[1] In LO.351 (Aldermaston file) – Development of Atomic Weapon Policy.

Halstead...; and that the Engineering Branch be placed partly at Woolwich and partly at Fort Halstead. Small-scale field tests are to be made both at Woolwich and Fort Halstead, but the heavier firings are to be made at the ARD range at Shoeburyness,..."

After his meeting with Penney and first-hand appraisal of these proposals, Portal met the Chiefs of Staff on 13 November[1], when he said that he wished to consult them on two questions: the secrecy governing British manufacture of the atomic bomb, and the allocation of responsibility for this. If they agreed that British manufacture should proceed under a Top Secret categorisation, it would be unwise to allow the subject to be dealt with by the normal departmental machinery for weapon development. He would be prepared to accept responsibility for development and manufacture of the atomic bomb. This would provide a convenient link between the CoS and MoS, and he would be assisted in the latter by an adjustment in the position of Dr Penney.

Questioned by the CAS (Lord Tedder), Portal explained the method of cover which would govern the manufacture of the bomb in the UK. There were three ways in which allocation of responsibility for manufacture could be made: by an official mandate from the Prime Minister; by unofficial mandate whereby, after explaining the position to the PM, nothing would be recorded but authority would be given to proceed with manufacture under his responsibility; or, by allowing details of manufacture to be discussed by the normal departmental machinery for weapon development.

The Chiefs of Staff agreed in discussion that Portal should approach the Prime Minister and, after explaining the position, state that they agreed with his recommendation that the most appropriate method of proceeding would be to authorise him to assume responsibility for manufacture of the atomic bomb; and that details of the production procedure for the bomb should be kept outside the departmental machinery for weapon development. On the question of secrecy, the CoS would endeavour to suppress any reference to details of the manufacture being raised officially in their Ministries; but it would be necessary to inform Sir Henry Tizard, chairman-designate of the DRPC (Defence Research Policy Committee), of the background to the arrangements decided upon.

Six days after this meeting, on 19 November, Portal sent a note to the Prime Minister saying that he considered that a decision was required about the development of atomic weapons in the United Kingdom. It concluded with the words: "I...ask whether it is your wish that I should take responsibility for initiating and supervising research and development work on atomic weapons. If so, I suggest that I should report periodically to the Chiefs of Staff, and on matters requiring Ministerial authority (including the actual construction of a weapon

---

[1] COS (46) 167th Mtg.

when this becomes possible) to yourself or to the Minister of Defence". On this note, which was at once a bridge between the CoS meeting of 13 November and the Gen 163 meeting of 8 January 1947 and also a catalyst for Government action, the Prime Minister wrote: "I want a meeting of the Atomic Bomb Cmte on this. CRA". Subsequently the words "Atomic Bombe Cmte" were amended in the Secretary's Memorandum to "Ministerial Atomic Energy Committee".

The Prime Minister's reaction had been extremely prompt, for later that same day Portal wrote a note for the file that "the PM had decided to bring the matter before a meeting of Ministers, including the Minister of Supply". Some changes to the draft had apparently been suggested, and Portal recorded: "I promised him a new note *via* the Minister here and this is enclosed...."

It was the Minister of Supply (Mr John Wilmot), therefore, whose memorandum – "I forward for the consideration of Ministers a note by the Controller of Production of Atomic Energy" – introduced a forceful document by Lord Portal to a Meeting of Ministers at 10 Downing Street on 8 January 1947[1] which took one of the most momentous British Government decisions in the 20th Century, to develop atomic weapons.

The note this meeting had before it was the one originally sent on 19 November 1946 to the Prime Minister. It shows clearly that Portal's persuasion brought the Government to a decision on a military atomic energy programme. He conveyed his views quite unequivocally:–

"I submit that a decision is required about the development of atomic weapons in this country. The Service Departments are beginning to move in the matter[2] and certain sections of the Press are showing interest in it.

"My organisation is charged solely with the production of 'fissile material', *ie* of the 'filling' that would go into any bomb that it was decided to develop. Apart altogether from producing the 'filling', the development of the bomb mechanism is a complex problem of nuclear physics and precision engineering on which some years of research and development would be necessary.

"I suggest that there are broadly three courses of action to choose from:
  (*a*) Not to develop the atomic weapon at all;
  (*b*) To develop the weapon by means of ordinary agencies in the Ministry of Supply and the Service Departments;
  (*c*) To develop the weapon under special arrangements conducive to the utmost secrecy.

"I imagine that course (a) above would not be favoured by HM Government in the absence of an international agreement on the subject.

"If course (b) is adopted it will be impossible to conceal for long the

---

[1] Gen 163/1st Mtg: changed from Gen 75 – as the meetings of Ministers concerned with atomic theory were known – to ensure secrecy.
[2] Presumably a reference to the Air Staff's Operational Requirements for an atomic bomb and aircraft to deliver it.

fact that this development is taking place. Many interests are involved, and the need for constant consultation with my organisation (which is the sole repository of the knowledge of atomic energy and atomic weapons derived from our wartime collaboration with the United States) would result in very many people, including scientists, knowing what was going on.

"Moreover, it would certainly not be long before the American authorities heard that we were developing the weapon 'through the normal channels' and this might well seem to them another reason for reticence over technical matters, not only in the field of military uses of atomic energy but also in the general 'know-how' of the production of fissile material".

So, having argued forcefully against two of his suggested courses of action, CPAE came with remorseless logic to persuade the Government to accept his third suggested course – to develop the atomic bomb in great secrecy:-

"If, for national or international reasons, the special arrangements referred to in (c) above are thought desirable, we are at present well placed to make them. The Chief Superintendent of Armament Research (Dr Penney) has been intimately concerned in the recent American trials[1] and knows more than any other British scientist about the secrets of the American bomb. He has the facilities for the necessary research and development which could be 'camouflaged' as 'Basic High Explosive Research' (a subject for which he is actually responsible but on which no work is in fact being done). His responsibilities are at present to the Army side of the Ministry of Supply, but by special arrangements with the head of that Department he could be made responsible also to me for this particular work and I could arrange the necessary contacts with my organisation in such a way as to ensure the maximum secrecy. Only about five or six senior officials outside my own organisation need know of this arrangement.

"I have already discussed this matter with the Chiefs of Staff, who authorised me[2] to say that they are in agreement with me in strongly recommending the special arrangements outlined in paragraph 6 above[3]. If these were adopted, the Chiefs of Staff would see to it that security was not prejudiced by enquiries from the Service Departments. (The chairman of the Defence Research Policy Committee[4] would of course be informed).

"I therefore ask for direction on two points: first, whether research and development on atomic weapons is to be undertaken; and if so,

---

[1] Bikini Atoll, July 1946.
[2] At their meeting on 13 Nov 46.
[3] Ie, beginning "If, for national or . . .".
[4] Sir Henry Tizard.

23

whether the arrangements outlined... above are to be adopted".

Such were the terms of CPAE's 'ultimatum' presented to the Government *via* the Minister of Supply's memorandum of 31 December 1946.

Lord Portal referred again to the matter of secrecy when he spoke at the meeting on the afternoon of 8 January 1947[1]. The Chiefs of Staff, he said, "were naturally anxious that we should not be without this weapon if others possessed it. About three years' work would be needed to solve the problems of nuclear physics and engineering involved in developing the bomb mechanism. If this matter were handled through the ordinary agencies responsible for weapon development, the result would inevitably be that a large number of persons in the Service Departments and in the Ministry of Supply would be made aware of what was being done. The alternative would be to make special arrangements whereby research could be carried on by the Chief Superintendent of Armament Research (Dr Penney)", who would set up a special section at Woolwich, the work of which would be described as "basic high explosive research". He would be responsible for this work to Portal, who would arrange for the necessary contacts with the Atomic Department in such a way as to ensure maximum security.

The Foreign Secretary stressed the international implications of developing the new weapon. In his view, it was important that Britain should press on with the study of all aspects of atomic energy; she could not afford to acquiesce in an American monopoly of the new development. Other countries might develop atomic weapons. Unless an effective international system could be set up under which the production and use of the weapon could be prohibited, Britain must develop it. The Minister of Defence agreed with this and said that in his view the arrangements suggested by Lord Portal should be effective in securing the greatest possible secrecy. The Minister of Supply commented that a considerable amount of work would have to be done, particularly on the engineering side. In two years' time, the staff of all grades being employed would amount to about 180 people.

The meeting

> (1) Agreed that research and development work on atomic weapons should be undertaken;
>
> (2) Approved the special arrangements for this purpose, outlined in paragraph 6 [beginning "If, for national or international reasons"] of the memorandum circulated by the Minister of Supply.

So, at the beginning of 1947, the decision was made from which depended the subsequent development and deployment of the British

---

[1] Those also attending were the Prime Minister, Foreign Secretary (E Bevin), Lord President of the Council (H Morrison), S of S for Dominion Affairs (Lord Addison), Minister of Defence (A V Alexander), Minister of Supply (J Wilmot), Sir Edward Bridges (PS, Treasury), N Butler (Foreign Office) and G Barnes (Downing Street).

airborne strategic nuclear deterrent force – a decision which, in the view of the atomic energy project historian,

"had not been a response to an immediate military threat but rather something fundamentalist and almost instinctive – a feeling that Britain must possess so climacteric a weapon in order to deter an atomically armed enemy, a feeling that Britain as a Great Power must acquire all major new weapons, a feeling that atomic weapons were a manifestation of the scientific and technological superiority on which Britain's strength, so deficient if measured in sheer numbers of men, must depend...[1]".

That secrecy had been well maintained was shown by a Minute sent to VCAS (Air Mshl Sir William Dickson) by ACAS(TR) (AVM J N Boothman) on 7 January 1947, the day before the Meeting of Ministers authorised R&D work on atomic weapons. Showing that even the Air Staff had been kept in the dark, Boothman wrote:–[2]

"I am very worried about the lack of information which exists or is indeed given to us about our own progress in the atomic field. As you know, we stated a requirement to the Ministry of Supply last September for an atomic bomb.[3] CS(A)[4] immediately got in touch with the Department of Atomic Energy and discussed the whole matter with them. It now transpires that there is no organisation in GB to develop the military side of atomic energy and in the opinion of individuals in the Dept of Atomic Energy, there is not likely to be such an organisation for some time to come.

"The Air side of the MoS have also been told that they will be ill advised to finalise the dimensions of the bomb-bays of our future bombers until they obtain officially the probable dimensions of the bomb. In view of the fact that there is no organisation to do development on the bomb, things have now reached a complete 'impasse'.

"I also understand that Professor Penney, who is the only technical authority in this country on the design of atomic bombs (which he gleaned during his work in America) is in honour bound not to give away his information to anybody.

"We have therefore arrived at the Gilbertian situation in which we have asked for long-range bombers and atomic bombs to go inside them, but the one individual who is able to satisfy the major part of our demand is unable to start things going because there is no Government organisation which can produce the necessary items, and also because of some wartime promise.

"In view of the fact that all our appreciations on future strategy

---

[1] *Independence and Deterrence Britain and Atomic Energy 1945-1952*, by Margaret Gowing, assisted by Lorna Arnold (Macmillian, 1974), Vol 1, chapter 6, page 184.
[2] 939/ACAS(TR) in Atomic Weapons – ID9/518 (Pt 4).
[3] OR1001, issued in August 1946.
[4] Air Mshl Sir Alec Coryton.

hinge on the atomic bomb and on the dates when they will be available in quantity to ourselves and other Powers, I would therefore ask your guidance as to the next step to take....

"The information which I have given above is all hearsay and I am at a loss to know what steps to take in order to get things moving. My own view is that possibly the best line would be for the Chiefs of Staff to make a firm request for a statement of progress to the Ministry of Defence...".[1]

In fact, much more had been going on in the second half of 1946 than ACAS(TR) realised and it could be said that by the end of that year – following the US ban on atomic information of 1 August (the McMahon Act) – the framework of a British atomic energy organisation had been erected. The Official Committee on Atomic Energy had met for the first time on 25 September; Dr Penney had sent Lord Portal his proposals for atomic weapon development (1 November); Sir Henry Tizard had told the Chiefs of Staff (6 November) that he would be willing to chair the newly formed Defence Research Policy Committee from 1 January 1947; and on the 6th also the Atomic Energy Act had become law, providing for "the development of atomic energy and the control of such development" and giving the Minister of Supply the duty of "promoting and controlling" this development.

With the Governmental decision of 8 January 1947 to authorise R&D work on atomic weapons, and the issue on the previous day (by coincidence) of the specification for jet bombers to carry them, the beginning of 1947 marked the start of the development and manufacturing programme which was to lead, nearly a decade later, to the RAF V-force with a stock of Blue Danube atomic bombs. Both aircraft and weapon development, therefore, started at about the same time; but there was a remarkable difference in the way each proceeded. V-bomber development followed well-established procedures – Air Staff OR, Operational Requirements Committee, MoS Specification, tenders by aircraft companies, etc. Weapon procurement was quite different, because of the uniqueness of the A-bomb (only the Americans had previously built them) and because the whole programme was shrouded in secrecy, knowledge of it being limited to those people actually involved[2].

Bomb design and production was a familiar activity for the RAF, the Ministry of Supply (or its predecessor) and the British armaments industry, which had turned out bombs by the million during the Second

---

[1] CoS meeting on 22 Mar 48 Conclusions say that ACAS(TR) had been appointed CoS representative on the Atomic Energy (Defence Research) Ctte which was under the chairmanship of Sir H Tizard (43rd(48) mtg).

[2] It was as a result of the atomic weapons programme that PV (positive vetting) security clearance was introduced for RAF personnel.

World War[1]. Atomic bomb R&D and production was another matter.

It should be added that the first report by the newly formed Defence Research Policy Committee set up in January 1947 under the chairmanship of Sir Henry Tizard, its report on Future Defence Research Policy, published on 30 July 1947, added to the "atomic climate" to which reference has already been made. It said that the first of the fundamental requirements which had been assumed by the committee "to meet our initial strategic aims" was "an effective bomber force" and added: "Furthermore we have kept in mind the views of the Chiefs of Staff that one of the essential measures required in time of peace to give us a chance of survival and victory in the event of war is 'to increase and exploit our present scientific and technical lead over our potential enemies, especially in the development of weapons of mass destruction'".

The report further said, under the heading 'Atomic War', that "for atomic weapons to be a useful deterrent, we must hold a stock, of the order of 1,000, of such bombs, and we must have the means of delivering them immediately on the outbreak of war". Referring to 'Long-range strategic bombardment', it commented: "We do not believe that for the next ten years, and possibly much longer, either the very-long-range parabolic rocket or the unmanned bomber will have been developed sufficiently to replace the manned bomber as the main instrument of our strategic bombardment. Moreover, we do not think that a manned supersonic bomber with the requisite characteristics will be achieved within ten years or, indeed, within a much longer period". Its conclusion on the means of delivery was:–

"We consider therefore that the main operational requirement in this field is a fast subsonic manned bomber capable of high-altitude flying and delivering atomic and other bombs at a radius of the order of 2,500 miles. . . . Whether such a radius is practicable remains doubtful[2] at present and a radius of the order of 2,000 miles would be acceptable as an intermediate aim. Full advantage should be taken of the increasing bias in favour of the Offence and we thus regard it as reasonable to accept an unarmed bomber for this purpose, a decision which would probably be forced upon us in any case by reason of the range/load requirements".

---

[1] Even so, the supply position had been critical at times during the height of the bomber offensive – eg average monthly Allied production from August to December 1944 was 49,250 1,000lb bombs and 320,000 500lb bombs, but average monthly expenditure by the RAF and USAAF for June and July 1944 from UK bases only was 59,000 1,000lb bombs and 290,000 500lb bombs (draft letter from DCAS to AOC in C Bomber Command on Weapon Policy (CS.22930/DCAS, in Bombing Policy – Enemy-occupied Territory, AIR 20/3248). On 14 Dec 44 the D/C in C Bomber Command reported to Air Ministry that stocks of 1,000lb bombs were running very low and the allocation of American bombs to the Command had been falling off, the only other sources of supply being the total UK production of about 17,500 bombs per month. AM were requested to take immediate action, as attacks on close-support targets for the Army required 1,000lb bombs (Bomber Command ORB, July-Dec 1944 (AIR 24/307)).

[2] OR230 asked for a 2,000nm radius of action, OR229 for 1,500nm.

A "big advance in bombing accuracy" compared with wartime standards was necessary to achieve "true economy of force":–

"Therefore, in the associated fields the main emphasis of R&D should be directed to improving navigation methods and instruments, bomb-sights, high-altitude ballistics, and bomb control, the aim being that by 1957 a bridge will be considerd a suitable target for individual blind bombing from high altitude".[1]

Here were foreshadowed all the elements of the eventual V-bomber force – small in numbers compared with its wartime predecessor but capable of inflicting mass destruction: its stock of kiloton- and then megaton-range nuclear weapons; its quick-reaction (QRA) alert posture; its high-flying, fast subsonic unarmed bombers; their navigation and bombing systems ensuring accurate delivery of bombs; and the bombs themselves so designed as to fall accurately from high altitudes. There was no case at that time, the committee considered, for the rocket delivery of nuclear warheads: the Royal Air Force would have the same basic equipment with which it fought the 1939-45 strategic bombing campaign – aircraft and free-falling bombs, but both of immeasurably greater power and capability.

As to the development of atomic bombs in the UK, the report commented that contemporary effort on atomic weapons was "extremely small, less than 0.1% of the total scientific effort" and was "directed mainly to research on the material effects of, and protection against, atomic weapons". It recommended that "the effort on atomic weapons should be increased as rapidly as possible and, in the first instance, should be concentrated on the development to the stage of a sealed design of an atomic bomb based on present knowledge".[2]

---

[1] RAF bombs were successfully dropped from 30,000ft in trials at Muroc, California, in mid-1957. Similarly successful results were obtained in the Farge (near Bremen) trials that year.

[2] However, the Defence Research Policy Committee "did not directly concern itself with the development of nuclear weapons, a situation which was curious if not ludicrous" (*Tizard*, by Ronald W Clark; Methuen & Co, 1965).

CHAPTER II

DEVELOPING THE BOMB

The only man in Britain in 1946–47 with first-hand experience of designing, building and testing atomic bombs was Dr Penney (although there were "five former inhabitants of Los Alamos at Harwell"[1]); and when the Gen 163 Ministers approved R&D the work was done by a Royal Air Force team under his aegis at the Armament Research Establishment, Fort Halstead, Kent. This team had a two-headed chain of command, in that AVM E D Davis, an armament specialist of great experience who after retiring from the RAF in 1946 had been given a special atomic energy appointment at the Ministry of Supply, was responsible for the nuclear weapon programme not only to Lord Portal[2] but also to the Vice-Chief of the Air Staff (Air Mshl Sir Ralph Cochrane) as "customer" for the finished product. From 1942 to 1945 AVM Davis had been AOC No 25 Group. When formed in 1934 this was the Armament Group, but during the war it was transferred to Flying Training Command and assumed responsibility for observer and air gunner training and also for bomb disposal.

One of AVM Davis's first tasks in 1947, at the Department of Atomic Energy in the Ministry of Supply, was to pick a Royal Air Force team who could not only design an atomic bomb to the requirements of OR1001 – the first priority – but also work out methods of handling, storage and training in readiness for its introduction into service. He chose as leader of this team the then Sqn Ldr J S Rowlands, serving at Farnborough, who had been an armament specialist since 1940 and had been awarded the George Cross in August 1943 for "conspicuous courage" on bomb disposal duties[3]. He was interviewed at Farnborough in July or August 1947[4] and when his appointment to work on the bomb had been approved (by VCAS and AVM Davis) he and the latter went to "P" staff at the Air Ministry and picked the rest of the team – nine more members – with the aid of a Hollerith computer. These were all "good quality technical men – brought in from all over the world". In other words, whatever their current posting or career state, the need for them on the atomic bomb programme had overwhelming priority[5]. They were

---

[1] *Britain and Atomic Energy 1945–1952*, by M Gowing, Vol II, p 445.
[2] "A special officer had been appointed to Lord Portal's staff with non-secret responsibilities as a cover, whose real job was to act as a focal point for this work. All contact between Penney's team and the outside world took place through him, and the connection between Penney's work and the Atomic Energy Division in the Ministry of Supply was hidden" (ibid, Vol I, p 210).
[3] Royal Air Force Awards No 618 (Pt 3), AMB No 11086, 10 Aug 43. His appointment to Fort Halstead was approved at VCAS level.
[4] This and subsequent information on the atomic bomb programme has been based on interviews with Air Mshl Sir John Rowlands GC KBE RAF (Ret) in Dec 73–Jan 74.
[5] "Everybody wanted these chaps with good degrees". When the Hollerith computer was used, "the same names kept dropping out" (ibid).

the first RAF personnel to be subjected to PV (positive vetting) security clearance, introduced into the atomic in advance of the military field. With two exceptions – Sqn Ldr J H Hunter-Tod and J P Prior – they were all Flight Lieutenants: C S Betts, A H Bullock, D W Densham, H Durkin, D Mercer, P E Mitchell and M E Pulvermacher.

The RAF team worked at Fort Halstead under the aegis of Dr Penney, to design a warhead for the atomic bomb for which the Air Staff had issued their OR1001 requirement. This had specified a diameter of 60in, so that parameter determined the size of the spherical warhead which could go inside it[1]. A simple description of a plutonium bomb[2] says that "a number of wedge-shaped pieces of plutonium, which together will build into a sphere, are arranged at equal intervals around a neutral source. Explosive charges of exactly equal weight are placed behind each wedge and all are detonated together. The wedges shoot towards the centre and touch each other at the same moment. This technique was used for the second American bomb, which was dropped on Nagasaki".

Only the Americans, with Dr Penney as a member of the team, had previously designed and built an atomic bomb. The RAF team was starting from scratch, but had the benefit of Penney's knowledge and experience in the oversight of their work. Wg Cdr Rowlands' task was "to see that everything we were making could be put together in one case"; he controlled the ARE building where the team assembled the prototype warhead.

Fort Halstead, where the team worked on their calculations and designs, was only one site in a complex chain of establishments whose work produced the Blue Danube atomic bombs for Bomber Command. Chief link in this chain was the MoS Establishment at Aldermaston, which was responsible for assembling the bombs for delivery to the RAF. The fissile material came from the MoS factories at Springfields (the uranium metal factory near Preston, Lancashire) and at Windscale, Cumberland, site of the plutonium-producing pile; metallurgical work to the RAF team's designs was done at ARE Woolwich, one of the Fort Halstead stations; RAE Farnborough were reponsible for ballistic design of the bomb carcass; and Hunting Aircraft, the only non-Government concern involved, under contracts from HER and RAE, were responsible for making the whole of the Blue Danube centre-section, including the sphere with its "lenses" and the supercharge – although they did not themselves handle any explosives, using inert

---

[1] In a Report on the Strategic Aspects of Atomic Energy dated 22 March 1948 the Atomic Energy Sub-committee of the Defence Research Policy Committee gave the dimensions of a plutonium bomb as 10,000lb in weight, 60in in diameter and 11ft in length, and said that "the dimension that cannot be decreased (except possibly by a few inches) is the diameter. The weight can hardly be decreased; the lengths are fixed simply by ballistic and carrying considerations" (AES(48)1 (Final)).

[2] *How it Works* – A Marshall Cavendish Encyclopaedia, Pt 1.

replicas instead[1].

This form of weapon procurement, with a Royal Air Force team being responsible for design of the explosive part, with Government agencies and one civilian contractor contributing materials and hardware, and with a former Chief of the Air Staff controlling the whole project through his nominated representative in the Ministry of Supply, was probably unique in RAF history. In the interests of secrecy, the normal channels had been avoided. As Lord Portal had remarked in his submission to the Gen 163 meeting of Ministers on 8 January 1947, "to develop the weapon by means of the ordinary agencies in the Ministry of Supply and the Service Departments" would have meant that it would be "impossible to conceal for long the fact that this development is taking place. Many interests are involved, and the need for constant consultation with my organisation... would result in very many people, including scientists, knowing what was going on"[2]. Hence "the proposal for the Portal–Penney arrangement, with Portal as the channel for communication for the Chiefs of Staff and Penney's work camouflaged under a misleading name such as 'basic high explosive research'"[3]. Thus "a third and largely independent kingdom was added to the atomic empire, under the loose suzerainty of Lord Portal, as Dr Penney took up office alongside Dr Cockcroft and Mr Hinton [in charge of atomic industrial organisation]. Britain was now going in for independent deterrence in earnest"[4].

Surprisingly, Dr Penney did not know of the Gen 163 meeting in January, nor of its momentous decision, and was not given a go-ahead on the atomic weapons programme until the following May. In June 1947, the historian of the Atomic Energy Authority records, "Penney invited a carefully selected group of 34 scientists and engineers mainly from Fort Halstead and Woolwich, both establishments of the Armaments Research Department, with a few from some of the other ARD establishments, to a lecture in the library at Woolwich. He told them they were going to make an atomic bomb"[5]. Penney "had only one immediate and specific task – to develop and test a nuclear 'device', that is, a bomb without its ballistic case; the device would be made of plutonium and be similar to the bomb that had destroyed Nagasaki. The device was to provide proof of British capability in nuclear deterrence"[6].

---

[1] Interview with R P Pedley Esq, who was research engineer in the Hunting Aircraft research department when the Fort Halstead and RAE contracts were placed, and subsequently became research manager of the weapons research division then technical director of Hunting Engineering when that company was formed in 1957.

[2] One leading scientist who probably "did not in fact know of the decision to make an atomic weapon" was Sir Henry Tizard, newly appointed chairman of the Defence Research Policy Committee (Gowing, Vol 1, p 181, footnote).

[3] Ibid, p 181.

[4] Ibid, p 183.

[5] Gowing, Vol 2, p 442.

[6] Ibid, p 443. "On 11 Aug 48 Portal told the Chiefs of Staff "Our own programme was... directed to the development of the Plutonium type bomb as used at Nagasaki"(48)11.

The time-scale for development of the nuclear device which was to be the prototype of the warhead for the Blue Danube atomic bomb was dictated by three factors: the worsening international situation in 1948–49, which gave a greater impetus to defence preparations; the production of plutonium, from 1951 onwards; and plans for the first British test explosion.

While work on developing the atomic bomb and the V-bombers was going on, the "iron curtain"[1] descended across Europe: the Communists took over Czechoslovakia (22 February 1948) and from the beginning of April the USSR inhibited Western access to Berlin. On 17 March the five Western Powers (Belgium, France, Luxembourg, the Netherlands and the UK) had signed a self-defence treaty in Brussels, and USAF Strategic Air Command B-29 Groups were deployed to Europe[2]. In these circumstances when "the East–West disagreements and disputes of 1946 and 1947 hardened into the Cold War of 1948" the Government made its first public admission that atomic bomb development was going on, the Minister of Defence (Mr A V Alexander) saying in answer to a Parliamentary question on 12 May that "all types of modern weapons, including atomic weapons", were being developed[4]. When on 29 August 1949 the USSR exploded its first atomic bomb – ending the US monopoly of nuclear weapons – there was shocked reaction in the UK, where those concerned with the military atomic energy programme had confidently expected that Britain would be the second Power after the United States to possess them. On 20 September the Prime Minister said in a minute to the Minister of Supply that R&D on atomic weapons and the means of delivering them were projects to which he attached the highest importance – reinforcing his directive early in 1949, when the atomic energy production programme was expanded by the addition of a third pile and a low separation plant, by commenting: "I attach to this expanded programme the same high degree of importance and urgency as I attached to the original. . . . I hope nothing will be allowed to interfere with its realisation and that you will let me know at once if any difficulties are encountered. . . ."[5]

---

[1] In a speech at Westminster College, Fulton, Mo, on 5 March 1946 Mr Winston Churchill said that "from Stettin in the Baltic to Trieste in the Adriatic, an iron curtain has descended across the Continent. . . ."

[2] "A ready air atomic striking force was becoming a major instrument of US policy, and although the Strategic Air Command (SAC) with its B-29 Superfortresses as yet had few atomic bombs, it did seem to offer some kind of deterrent to aggression"(*United States Air Forces in Europe and the Beginning of the Cold War*, by Walton S Moody; *Aerospace Historian*, Summer/June 1976 issue).

[3] Gowing, Vol 1, p 214.

[4] Commons Hansard, Col 2117 in Vol 450.

[5] Gowing, Vol 1, p 224. See also Vol 2, p 474: "The Americans and the Russians had acquired a plutonium bomb much faster. Even though the British started with so much knowledge from the American project, Penney could not, with the resources at his disposal, have achieved an earlier date: for example, even if work on design problems had started earlier, the plutonium core and the polonium would not have been available before 1952 and the shortage of electrical experts would have prevented earlier production of the firing circuit".

While the international situation gave increased urgency to the military atomic energy programme, its real pace-maker was the supply of plutonium. This did not become available until about March 1952 – the members of the RAF team who were to take the test device out to Monte Bello for the 3 October explosion had not seen any plutonium up to six or eight weeks before the test took place.[1] Referring to the "limiting factor" in the date of the availability of the first atomic weapon, Lord Portal had told the Chiefs of Staff on 8 August 1949[2]:–

". . . it may well be that the limiting factor is now the date by which plutonium can be produced. The CoS will be aware that, apart from the construction of the piles themselves[3], plutonium production requires an elaborate and novel plant for its separation from the uranium and from the fission products generated in the pile. The design of this plant must depend upon data supplied by research and pilot-scale work, and this has had to be done almost entirely in Canada because of the lack of facilities in this country. The research facilities here were to have been provided in the 'hot laboratory' at Harwell, and the MoW, who are building it, have been about a year late with the first part of the programme. The Canadian establishment is also about equally late in their research and pilot-scale work on this matter.

"The production organisation, unable to wait any longer for the full data, has been compelled to design and start to build the plutonium separation plant without it, so this great plant must be regarded as experimental, and the date when it will come into operation, the efficiency with which it will work and the output to be expected from it are all uncertain. . . ."

Almost a year later, on 14 June 1950, the Chiefs of Staff noted that "production of plutonium at Windscale . . . starts in 1951, and by the end of 1952 appreciable quantities would be available[4]. . . ."

The historian of the atomic energy project has recorded that "development of the non-radioactive components of the bomb had started early. On two of the radioactive components, plutonium for the core and polonium for the initiator, only preliminary work could be undertaken by G L Hopkin and his staff until the materials themselves were available – at the very end of 1951 in the case of plutonium and a little earlier for polonium"[5].

The third parameter for work on the atomic bomb project was the date of the test, for which the prototype warhead had to be ready; and associated with this was a decision on its location. On 10 August 1950

---

[1] "The date for the production of the plutonium shapes for 'Hurricane' was 1 August 1952; despite the short time available after the delivery of the plutonium from Windscale, this date was met" (Gowing, Vol II).

[2] Memorandum by the Controller of Production of Atomic Energy, MoS.

[3] At Windscale – "our only plutonium producting plant", it was noted at the time of a visit by Air Ministry/Paymaster General representatives in July 1952.

[4] COS/738/14/6/50.

[5] Gowing, Vol II, p 466. Hopkin, a metallurgist, was a divisional head in the ARE.

Lord Portal had written to Air Mshl Sir William Elliot, Chief Staff Officer to the Minister of Defence and Deputy Secretary (Military) to the Cabinet[1], to say:–

"I wish to put before you our latest thoughts on the trial of the first British atomic weapon.

"As you know, we told the Chiefs of Staff in May that we must know by 1 July 1950 whether and on what conditions the Americans would allow us to use their range. We are still without any answer except that they invite us to make a formal request and Lord Tedder informed us on 27 July that he was making such a request.

"Failing to get a reply from the US by the necessary date, we have been thinking of alternatives to the use of an American range[2].

"A site in northern Canada has been considered, and at first sight appeared to have attractions, but it is now losing favour on closer examination.

"Our thoughts then turned to a site off the west coast of Australia where it might be possible to arrange the prototype trial to represent an attack on a port by a ship with an atomic bomb concealed in it. This is a type of attack which presumably must be taken into account as a possible form of 'bolt from the blue', but its effects have not yet been studied by the Americans. The Strategic Aspects Committee of the DRPC have endorsed our view that the effects of such an attack should if possible be investigated. . . .

"Preliminary enquiry by the Admiralty shows that a suitable site probably exists in the Monte Bello Islands (approximately latitude 20°S, longitude 115°E), some 50 miles off the north-west coast of Australia and 700 miles north of Perth. These islands are uninhabited, though seasonally visited by shell or pearl fishermen. They include a channel about six fathoms deep close in-shore. . . .

"It is thought that the main HQ of the expedition could be shipborne, and that a temporary tented camp could be erected to accommodate the range party for the preparatory period of about three–six months.

. . . .

"Dr Penney has envisaged a force of about 150 to 200 scientists and about 250 working party.

. . . .

---

[1] Ref 330/207/1/1. On 8 September 1949 he had put a paper to the CoS Cttee headed Operation "Hurricane" (COS(49)292) which began: "Lord Portal of Hungerford has written to suggest that it is not too early to start thinking about the problem of testing our first atomic bomb".

[2] ". . . since Anglo-American military collaboration was flourishing, it was hoped that testing could be dealt with as a purely military, not an atomic, topic. With the Prime Minister's approval Lord Tedder approached the American Chiefs of Staff, who were encouraging. An official request was therefore made to them, but it posed difficult political and practical problems for the Americans and an official reply was long delayed" (Gowing, Vol 2, p 476).

"Whatever may be the final American reply to our enquiry, I think that it will be most desirable to have this proposed alternative available"[1].

This assumption by Lord Portal proved prescient, for in the autumn of 1950 it became clear that the United States was unable to loan facilities to the United Kingdom for an atomic bomb test[2], and on 23 January 1951 he suggested to the Chiefs of Staff that approval should be sought to hold the trial at the Monte Bello Islands site[3]. At their meeting on 15 February 1951 the CoS Committee approved in principle the idea of holding a trial there in October 1952, and put a paper to the Ministerial Committee on Atomic Energy recommending that the approval of the Australian Government should be sought for this. Subsequently both Ministerial and Australian approval was given, the former for the initiation of preparations for the trial, the latter for its being held at Monte Bello[4].

At a meeting in Washington on 27 August 1951 the Americans had turned down UK proposals for collaboration on a weapons test, the Secretary of State (Mr Dean Acheson) saying that they would lead to the disclosure of US atomic energy Restricted data and therefore be contrary to the McMahon Act[5].

The long telegram reporting this meeting (ANCAM 463) ended by quoting a "highly placed State Department official" (who was not named) as saying that "if he were English and were faced with the American counter-proposals he would turn them down flat, would proceed to carry out the British test in Australia and that this would be the best possible thing for Britain, the British Empire and indirectly for the USA" – views with which Portal, in a letter of 29 August to the Chief of the Air Staff (MRAF Sir John Slessor), said coincided with his own and with which Slessor agreed.

The American counter-proposals were carefully considered, and Dr Penney went to Washington for discussions with US officials and scientists; but at their meeting on 24 October 1951[6] the Chiefs of Staff agreed that on balance it would be preferable "to carry out the test of

---

[1] Plans for this trial had been initiated on 16 Aug 49 when the MoS had submitted a paper to the Chiefs of Staff. Monte Bello was first suggested to the CoS as a suitable site by the MoS in a paper of 10 August 1950, following an Admiralty investigation. The planning staff started forming under Rear Admiral A D Torlesse in April 1951 (Operation Hurricane – AHB II/127/4/20). AVM E D Davis had sent a comprehensive report on the Monte Bello Islands to CS HER (Penney) on 3 Jan 51 saying "I am of opinion that . . . the site would prove suitable for the trial" (ID3/190/1 Pt 1).

[2] The US was "not in a position to consider the loan of facilities to the United Kingdom" (telegram from Lord Tedder to Sir William Elliot, 17 Oct 50, in Atomic Bombs – Testing (ID3/190/1)).

[3] Paper by Controller (Atomic Energy) Ministry of Supply – Testing of United Kingdom Atomic Weapon (Ibid).

[4] "Ministers have now approved the initiation of preparations for a trial of the atomic weapon in the Monte Bello Islands . . ." (telegram from McLean to Tedder, 21 Mar 51) and "Menzies has now agreed to our proposals for Monte Bello tests" (telegram from Cabinet Office to BJSM Washington, 16 May 51) (ibid).

[5] Telegram, BJSM Washington/Cabinet Office in Atomic Bombs – Testing (ID3/190/1).

[6] COS (51) 70th Mtg.

35

our atomic weapon under our own arrangements at Monte Bello rather than with the US Government in Nevada", and this view was conveyed to the Atomic Energy (Official) Committee for submission to Ministers. On 20 December the Cabinet Office informed BJSM Washington[1] that "Ministers have now decided to proceed with arrangements for test in Australia". A test in Nevada, it was pointed out, "would have the disadvantage that it would not provide a shallow water explosion, which from the United Kingdom point of view would give the most useful results"[2].

The proposal for a test site in the Monte Bello Islands thus turned out to be not an alternative but the location of the first British atomic explosion on 3 October 1952 in Operation Hurricane. From its start to that successful conclusion, the programme took just over five years – as far as the RAF were concerned, from the day in the summer of 1947 when Sqn Ldr J S Rowlands had been picked to lead the design team.

During that time, Rowlands and his nine-man team had made their calculations and drawn up their designs for "a bomb employing the principle of nuclear fission", as required by the Air Staff – a weapon of which few in the UK had any previous practical knowledge, notably Dr Penney, civilian head of the project[3]. Although the RAF team was numerically small compared with the overall manpower involved at the various establishments, they were at the heart of the programme, they were involved in design leadership, they were responsible for seeing that an Air Staff requirement was met and – looking beyond the design and building of the prototype – for a production weapon that could be handled, transported[4], stored, serviced and loaded by their colleagues in Bomber Command. Their part, as both makers and ultimate users of the production Blue Danube Mk 1 atomic bomb, was crucial to the success of its development.

A memorandum of 31 May 1949[5], describing work in progress at that time, gave a very good indication of the technical problems and challenges facing the team:–

1. The final processing of all radioactive components.
2. The design and manufacture of numerous internal parts of the weapon mechanism.
3. The design, method of manufacture, testing and proving of

---

[1] Telegram CANAM 356.

[2] The text of this and the other 1950–51 telegrams relating to plans for the first British atomic test are in the file ID3/190/1 – Atomic Bombs – Testing. There was "much correspondence between London and Washington concerning the possible use of American ranges . . . but to no avail, owing to restrictions imposed by the McMahon Act and similar legislation" (Operation "Hurricane" file – II/127/4/20).

[3] "Britain had had a strong wartime team at Los Alamos. . . . Her nineteen scientists had been spread through various departments there so that they had obtained a very good coverage of the work. . . ." (Gowing, Vol 2, p 456).

[4] Transport was specially designed.

[5] Aldermaston file 0023. Quoted in *Independence and Deterrence: Britain and Atomic Energy 1945–1952, Vol 2, Policy Execution,* by Margaret Gowing; Macmillan, 1974.

the components, *ie* the fissile core, the initiator, the tamper and the lens and supercharge, leading up to the manufacture of components for the field test of the prototype weapon.

4. The design, proof and manufacture of detonators.
5. The design, proof and manufacture of firing circuits.
6. The design, proof and manufacture of a fuse to give the required air-burst performance.
7. The design, proof and manufacture of secondary firing and fuse circuits should the main ones fail.
8. The research, design and production of a large number of exceptionally high-performance photographic and electronic instruments needed for the field trials of individual components and of the prototypes.
9. The nucleus of a team for conducting the field trial of the prototype, including the assembly.
10. Research on the climatic storage of individual components.
11. Research on the methods of gauging of all components.
12. Research and design problems to minimise the time of assembly.
13. The nucleus of a team to assemble every weapon and mate the components together in the best way, and then disassemble for storage.
14. Training RAF officers to undertake the assembly of weapons for operational use.

Considering that, during the following year (1950), a date in October 1952 was fixed for Operation Hurricane, the atomic bomb test in the Monte Bello Islands, and considering that membership of the team was limited by technical qualifications and by the need to ensure secrecy, it is striking proof of the team's determination, devotion to its task and applied skills that the development stage of the project was successfully completed. The object of Hurricane was to blow off the prototype warhead, so painfully designed and precisely constructed, to see that it worked. If it did, the production warheads for Blue Danube Mk 1 would follow the pattern set.

What the team at Fort Halstead were designing was a plutonium bomb, similar in principle to that which the Americans had dropped on Nagasaki: this followed the decision, taken in 1945, to produce plutonium in Britain rather than U-235, which had been used for the first American A-bomb dropped on Hiroshima. As the historian of the atomic energy project described it[1]:–

"An implosion design had been chosen, in which the mass of high explosive, surrounding a sphere containing both the fissile material and a tamper, was so arranged as to produce a shock wave travelling rapidly inwards and thus compressing the material. This design had the advantages of high velocities, which reduced the chance of pre-deto-

---

[1] Gowing, Vol 2, p 457.

nation despite the many background neutrons present in plutonium; at the same time, the material was compressed to such density that supercritical conditions were obtained with comparatively little material. It had been realised at Los Alamos that performance would be improved by using explosive lenses to turn the divergent waves, which started from detonators, into parts of a common spherical wave converging on the centre of the sphere.

"The main components of the gadget can be listed, working from the outside to the centre. First came the detonators, which operated by an impulse from a firing device and involved other auxiliaries like safety switches and arming circuits. The detonation had to be started simultaneously in all the lenses; the lenses themselves were carefully calculated shapes[1], containing a combination of fast and slow explosive so that transit from the detonator to every point on the inner spherical surface of the lens was simultaneous. The detonation from the lenses then reached a spherical shell of homogeneous high explosive called the supercharge. Within the supercharge was the tamper, which converted the convergent detonation wave into a convergent shock wave, reflected some of the neutrons back into the fissile material and generally increased the efficiency of the explosion. Within the tamper was the plutonium and within that the initiator. This last component was necessary because, although the implosion resulted in a powerful compression of the fissile material and the surrounding tamper, the material would stay compressed only for a few microseconds and would then expand again very quickly. It was therefore essential to make sure that the chain reaction started at the right moment. This could be done by creating at the centre of the fissile material an intense neutron source"[2].

It is clear from their "work sheet", and from the nature of the nuclear device, that a knowledge of physics, mathematics, chemistry, metallurgy and telemetry was required, in varying degrees, from the members of the team at Fort Halstead, so that they would know what would happen as a result of their designs, and so that they were in a position to check the hardware produced at other establishments. For example, the high-explosive lenses – a term derived from focusing, because they had to fit so perfectly together – were matched with a tolerance of one-tenth of a millimetre[3]. The original moulds, or shapes, for the lenses were

---

[1] There were 32 lenses, 20 of them irregular hexagons and 12 regular pentagons, and 32 detonators.

[2] "Nuclear weapons consist in general of a large quantity of conventional HE which is detonated to compress a mass of fissile material, either plutonium or U-235, into a critical shape" (Nuclear Weapons – Safety and Handling Note by DCAS, in Strategic Aspects of Atomic Energy – ID6/R.13 Pt 6).

[3] "A much higher accuracy was required, both in dimensions and in uniformity of composition, than ever before, especially in explosive stores where a dimensional accuracy of the order of one thousandth part of an inch was essential" (Gowing, Vol 2, p 462).

made at Chatham Dockyard; and the prototype lenses, and the supercharge for the Hurricane weapon, at Woolwich, one of the Atomic Research Establishment stations. Wg Cdr Rowlands' task was "to see that everything we were making could be put together in one case". He also, at the same time, got together a team who were to write the RAF training manual on the Mk 1 atomic bomb.

Meanwhile, ballistic work on the design of the case was going on at RAE Farnborough. There was not quite the same urgency on this, however, as there was on the prototype warhead – because of the date fixed for its test, the number of people going out to Monte Bello for that purpose and the flotilla of Royal Navy ships transporting them and their equipment. But there was nothing that could be done to speed up the development work: the team were dependent on getting the plutonium out of Windscale and the manufacturing process there could not be hurried – it was "a matter of Kilowatt hours and days"[1]. Nevertheless, the fact that a UK atomic test was to be held "at a site in Australia" was announced on 18 February 1952[2].

Although the Royal Engineers who were to build roads and jetties and to erect buildings for the test had sailed from Portsmouth on 19 February[3] and the party of scientists[4] left in April, it was not until during August that the first plutonium was delivered from Windscale via Aldermaston; and the way in which the fissile core for the test explosion was carried out to Monte Bello by Wg Cdr Rowlands and two of his colleagues gave Operation Hurricane a tense last-minute drama before its scientifically triumphant conclusion.

HMS *Plym*, the Naval frigate which was to be destroyed in a lagoon in the Monte Bello Islands in Operation Hurricane, was loaded with the seeds of her destruction in the Thames Estuary on 5 and 6 June 1952 – the No 1 assembly having been taken out from Shoeburyness on the first day, the No 2 being loaded on the following day. These grim spheres had been transported to the jetty by open lorry, under a tarpaulin. Aboard ship, they were held in place by a ring made by Hunting Percival Aircraft; this was a highly successful and appropriate assembly, similar to that which would hold the warhead in place in the Blue Danube bomb, for which the company made the whole of the centre-section. This warhead weighed approximately three tons – that is, two-thirds of the total weight (10,000lb) of the bomb. As *Plym* made her way out to Australia and her ultimate doom off the Western

---

[1] Windscale – the plutonium production pile – "attained its scheduled production only weeks before the Monte Bello explosion" (R N Rosecrance, *Defense of the Realm, British Strategy in the Nuclear Epoch;* Columbia University Press, 1968).

[2] ID3/190/1 (Pt 2) Atomic Bombs – Testing.

[3] See *History of the Corps of Royal Engineers,* Vol X, Chapter X – The Nuclear Test Programme (Institution of Royal Engineers).

[4] ". . . staff required for the first trial would be 200 scientists, 50 technicians and 100 industrial workers" (Gowing, Vol 2, p 477). Their main base was the former aircraft carrier HMS *Campania*, which sailed in April, her voyage lasting "just over eight weeks".

Australian coast, the key ingredient in the Monte Bello test, the plutonium for the fissile core, was arriving from Windscale for fabrication at Aldermaston, to be carried out to the test site by air by Wg Cdr Rowlands, accompanied by Sqn Ldr P E Mitchell of the RAF team, and W J Moyce, an explosives expert from Aldermaston. Wg Cdr Rowlands had written the Movement Order for the journey to Australia.

This began with a road convoy from Aldermaston – two green furniture vans (one of them a back-up vehicle, in case of a breakdown), a car with the RAF officers in civilian clothes and an escort of RAF Police – to RAF Lyneham, whence they were to fly out by Hastings of Transport Command to Singapore. The plan[1] was then for the officers, with their "two small loads of special equipment", to transfer to Sunderlands of the Far East Flying Boat Wing and be flown direct to the test site in the Monte Bello Islands[2]. For this reason the Hastings was diverted to Seletar airfield when in the circuit of Changi, Singapore, to facilitate transfer to the flying-boats, Seletar being the base of the Far East Flying Boat Wing (Nos 88, 205 and 209 Squadrons).

The plutonium – a "darkish metal" – was hermetically sealed in an extremely strong metal container, 18in deep and 18in in diameter. This had a flotation collar, in case of a forced landing in the sea, either by the aircraft or by the three officers – who were supplied with parachutes. They were also given fireproof boxes, "made like safes", to protect the plutonium from fire. Wg Cdr Rowlands "signed for the stuff going out – and had to certify that it had been destroyed".

The first Sunderland flight from Seletar to Monte Bello was made on 10 September 1952 and the second on the 18th: the Royal Navy had provided facilities for flying-boats in the islands and at Onslow, 70 miles south-west.

When the three officers touched down on the lagoon with their cargo of radioactive material, last link in the chain of Britain's first atomic test, they would have seen HMS *Plym*, the vessel which was to be blown up by the device placed below her water-line – with an explosion equivalent to 10,000 tons of TNT, anchored off the western shore of Trimouille, one of the four main islands. Control centre for the test was on another of the four, Hermite (to the south-west); and HMS *Campania*, the former aircraft carrier which served as floating headquarters for the scientific and Naval personnel, lay some four miles to the south-east. What Wg Cdr Rowlands and his colleagues had to do was to put the fissile core into the device which they had designed and assembled, which was now suspended inside the frigate's hull. This was the very opposite procedure to the wartime work which he had done –

---

[1] Loose Minute, Operation Hurricane, 23 May 1952 (CMS.2056/2653).
[2] The ORB of No 88 (MR) Squadron for September 1952 says that "Flt Lt Houtheusen with specially selected crew, and including the Officer Commanding, Far East Flying Boat Wing (Wg Cdr MacKenzie), were engaged on Top Secret transit trip to Australia in connection with the Monte Bello atomic tests".

removing fuses from unexploded bombs.

During assembly aboard HMS *Plym* they wore protective clothing and rubber gloves. In addition to the plutonium, they had to put in the polonium/beryllium initiator and the "urchin" – so-called because its shape resembled that of a sea urchin: it was a standard neutron source. This work of arming the device was done in the last few hours before the test, on 2 October 1952, and after it had been completed the men concerned left the ship for H1 (the main camp and laboratories) or by launch for HMS *Campania* – a rough ride across the open sea in the early hours of the morning of the 3rd.

At 0930 hr local time on that day the device was exploded by cable from the island of Trimouille, 400 yds off whose shore the frigate lay, and 23 microseconds after the explosion the fireball was observed by Kerr cell camera "as a faint segment of a circle on the water-line of *Plym*"[1]. This fireball grew vaster; after about 0.1 sec water was observed emerging from it, its column increasing and forming a mushroom shape. "The diameter of the column reached a maximum of 1,150ft after which fall-out and the effect of the wind began to obliterate the clear-cut outline"[2]. The top of the cloud rose up to about 1,800ft at 1 sec and reached a maximum of about 10,000ft at four minutes. Nothing remained of *Plym*, and the effects on various other objects, like Spitfire wings and tailplane and Lancaster wings and fuselage section[3], were carefully measured. Britain's first atomic test had been a complete success.

On 10 October Dr Penney – to whom Prime Minister Winston Churchill, whose Government inherited the atomic energy programme on their election to office a year previously, had sent a telegram beginning "Well done, Sir William"[4] – left for the UK by Transport Command Hastings from RAAF Onslow. Among the nine other passengers were Wg Cdr Rowlands and Sqn Ldr Mitchell[5].

For the RAF, the test had meant that the principle of an atomic explosion had been successfully put into practice, but the work of incorporating the nuclear device into a weapon for Service use still remained to be done. It was to be just over a year before the first

---

[1] "Scientific Data obtained at Operation Hurricane" (Director's Report).

[2] Ibid.

[3] One object of the test was to discover the effects of an atomic explosion on aircraft on the ground (see file Operation "Hurricane" – II/127/4/20).

[4] The official announcement about the Monte Bello test was made by Mr Churchill in the Commons on 23 October 1952 (Hansard, Cols 1268-1271). "The weapon was exploded in the morning of 3rd October", he said. "Thousands of tons of water and of mud and rock from the sea bottom were thrown many thousands of feet into the air and a high tidal wave was caused." At the same time, 10 Downing Street said that the Queen had approved Dr Penney's appointment to Knight Commander of the Order of the British Empire. In Australia the CAS-designate, Air Mshl Sir William Dickson, on a round-the-world tour, said that Britain had started to make atomic bombs and the aircraft to carry them.

[5] Over whose departure a complication arose, because having arrived by flying-boat on the Monte Bello lagoon they had never booked-in at RAAF Onslow: fortunately an Australian security officer who was on board verified their credentials.

A-bombs were delivered to Bomber Command, in November 1953.

At the end of the latter year the Minister of Works (Sir David Eccles) summed-up in Parliament what had been achieved[1]:–

"The House will remember the history of the United Kingdom atomic energy programme; how during the war it was placed under the Lord President, Sir John Anderson (as he then was), because he had great personal qualifications, and also because the Lord President was the Minister responsible for scientific matters arising out of Government policy. After the war the project was transferred to the Ministry of Supply.

"As I understand it, there were two reasons for that. First, the armament programme was being rapidly run down and, therefore, the Ministry of Supply had spare capacity; and, secondly – perhaps more important – at that time the overriding aim of the atomic energy project was to produce a British bomb. That is the key to the arrangement which was then made.

"In 1946, when the Act was passed placing the project under the Minister of Supply, the United States knew how to make an atomic bomb. We did not, although our scientists . . . had made great contributions to knowledge of nuclear fission. But the Americans, for reasons which we understand but nonetheless regret, felt unable to share with us all the secrets of the production process. Therefore, the Labour Government – and Her Majesty's present Ministers think they were right – determined to make a bomb here; and, with this their chief object, it was natural to give the job to the Minister responsible for the manufacture of weapons. From 1946 to 1951, £100m or more was spent by the Ministry of Supply on this project, and, in the last two years, further great sums of money have been laid out for the same purpose."

Sir David added that "enormous though the expenditure on the atomic energy establishments[2]" had been, the results had been "equally enormous. The bomb has been made and has been exploded, and that achievement has greatly increased the defensive power of this country and the help and comfort we can bring to our allies. . . ."

Before referring to the introduction of atomic bombs into the RAF, however, it is appropriate to describe the development of the aircraft which were to carry them – the V-bombers, and also of the Canberra, the first British jet bomber.

---

[1] Atomic Energy – Ministerial Responsibility (Commons Hansard – 10 Dec 53, Cols 2314-5).

[2] Harwell, Risley, Windscale, Calder Hall, Capenhurst, Springfields and Aldermaston, AERE Harwell was concerned with research; MoS Factory, Risley, with design for fissile production; MoS Factory, Windscale, with fissile production; MoS Factory, Springfields, with uranium extraction; MoS Establishment, Aldermaston, with HER design, assembly, etc. Other establishments were ARE Fort Halstead and ARE Woolwich Common, both concerned with HER design; ROF, Chorley, with HERE, HE production; ROF, Cardiff, with HER mould production; and HER (RAE) with electronic design.

CHAPTER III

V-BOMBER AND CANBERRA DEVELOPMENT

One of the recommendations of the Tizard Committee had been that "the development of high-performance long-range aircraft for offensive purposes must proceed on the highest priority concurrently with methods of accurate nevigation, preferably automatic. Once the latter has been achieved, supersonic pilotless aircraft and/or rockets may well replace manned aircraft, but we do not consider this latter development likely within ten years...."

It was the two post-war Chiefs of the Air Staff, Marshals of the RAF Lord Tedder (1946–50) and Sir John Slessor (1950-54), who firmly linked the idea of the nuclear deterrent with the assumption of its being delivered by high-flying, long-range jet bombers. In a Note for the Chiefs of Staff on "Modernisation of the Strategic Bomber Force", written early in 1948[1], the former said that "in the furtherance of the supreme aim of our defence policy – namely, to prevent war – the air striking force will play a role of such paramount importance that I am sure my colleagues will wish to be informed of the present programme for its development and of the earliest date at which we can expect it to constitute an effective deterrent to a potential aggressor". He continued:–

"It has been appreciated that the risk of war between now and 1952 must be accepted and that, if war comes, we must fight as best we can with what we have got. Thereafter the risk will greatly increase until about 1957, by and after which date it will become really serious. As stated by the Minister of Defence[2], we must place emphasis on 'those sections of our Armed Forces which have an obviously deterrent effect'; and 'the RAF must provide a striking force equipped with strategic bombers capable of reaching and hitting all the principal targets in Russia, and the gravity of the risk in 1957 may be materially reduced if we can build up a strong deterrent force before that date'"[3].

Sir John Slessor, writing early in 1952[4], was even more forthright about the importance of air-delivered nuclear deterrence in Western defence plans. As he put it:–

"I have always been sceptical about the popular conception of World War III. I believe the supreme need is to prevent it, and that we can prevent it. But if it came, I do not believe the Red Army could be stopped by the Divisions and Tactical Air Forces which Nato can in fact build up without busting Europe and UK economically – which may well be the Russian game. I believe the only really sound course would be to build up a completely overwhelming British/American bomber

---

[1] The draft was dated 3 Apr 1948.
[2] DO(48)2, para 6.
[3] Ibid, para 14.
[4] In reply to a Minute of 5 Mch 1952 from S of S for Air.

force with the A-bomb, capable of pulverising Russia itself and eliminating the Red Air Force at its bases".

Slessor pointed out that "since 1947 the Chiefs of Staff and HM Government had adopted for planning purposes (including research and development) the assumption that a Russian attack might come in 1957, and that if it came earlier (which was not considered likely) we should have to do the best [we could] with what we had". He expressed the view that there had been, and still was, "a tendency to go far too fighter-minded. The Western Union Commanders-in-Chief had produced a plan which in my view seriously neglected the bomber, and at a meeting in Paris the previous August I had succeeded in getting a considerable increase in the proportion of bombers to fighters in the plan which was subsequently adopted by SHAPE. The RAF were the only people (apart from the Americans) who could make any serious bomber contribution to NATO.... The Valiant had not flown, but we placed a small order off the drawing-board[1]. The only other bet was the Canberra, and we ordered as many as we could get to build up a first-line force... in the UK, all for the support of SHAPE"[2].

The account which follows traces the development of the RAF medium bombers – Vulcan and Victor to the B.35/46 Specification, Valiant to B.9/48 – and a subsequent chapter that of the Canberra light bomber, whose origins were rather more complex, as will be explained.

Early in 1946 the Air Staff had drafted a requirement for a long-range bomber, unarmed and with a 2,000nm radius of action. Although this OR remained in draft form, it is interesting as showing the trend of Air Staff thinking on a high-altitude, high-speed bomber, very much on the lines later formulated in the ORs which led to the Valiant, Vulcan and Victor.

This long-range bomber requirement (OR230) asked for a landplane capable of carrying one 10,000lb bomb – that is, an atomic bomb[3] – to a target 2,000nm from a base situated anywhere in the world. This aircraft would be required to attack targets at great distances inside enemy territory; assuming that it would be plotted by radar and other means for a large part of its flight, it had to be capable of avoiding destruction by making attack from ground- and air-launched weapons difficult. In order to achieve such comparative invulnerability, it had to have a high cruising speed (500kt was envisaged), manoeuvrability at high speed and high altitude (cruising at heights from 35,000 to 50,000ft) and capacity for carrying adequate warning devices to detect the approach of ground-launched weapons and opposing aircraft, and

---

[1] The initial Valiant order, for 25 aircraft, was placed on 9 Feb 51. The Vickers 660 prototype made its first flight on 18 May that year from Wisley.

[2] Canberras were not deployed to Germany until the latter half of 1954, when the build-up of the Canberra force in the UK was nearing its peak.

[3] OR1001 (see previous chapter) specified that the bomb was not to exceed 10,000lb in weight.

defensive apparatus like proximity fuse exploders and missile jamming devices. Maximum all-up weight of the bomber was not to exceed 200,000lb.

There were several drafts of this requirement, which was issued in December 1946. The Ministry of Supply at first refused to accept it, considering it too difficult, but at least one manufacturer thought it could be met and was given a contract to build an experimental half-scale model to investigate aerodynamic problems. These, however, were not the only difficulties. It was estimated that the resultant aircraft would require a 2,000yd take-off run to clear a 50ft barrier, thereby posing problems of runway length.

Although OR230 was not proceeded with, because its requirements were found unacceptable at the time[1], its importance lay in the fact that the practicability of jet bombers was accepted. "In 1946, the choice that lay before the Air Staff was one of deciding between an armed piston-engined bomber, operating at relatively low altitudes and relatively low speeds, and an unarmed very-high-flying, high-speed jet bomber. The decision was a difficult one to make. After prolonged and careful consideration, however, the Air Staff decided in favour of the unarmed jet bomber. . . ."[2]

The Operational Requirement which led to the RAF V-bombers, OR229, was first circulated in draft form on 7 November 1946. Broadly, it differed little from OR230 except in the all-important aspects of range and weight. "The Air Staff [it said] require a medium-range bomber landplane capable of carrying one 10,000lb bomb to a target 1,500nm from a base which may be anywhere in the world". Further, "it must be possible to operate this aircraft from existing HB (heavy bomber) type airfields and the maximum weight when fully loaded ought, therefore, not to exceed 100,000lb. The Air Staff is to be informed if this weight will be exceeded"[3].

Although OR229 was specifically envisaged as the carrier of an atomic (10,000lb) bomb, it was to be capable of carrying a 20,000lb load of conventional high-explosive bombs of 10,000lb, 6,000lb or 1,000lb sizes. Thus, if a decision had not subsequently been taken to develop and produce atomic bombs in Britain, the new bomber could have gone into service as a carrier of conventional bombs. The 10,000lb "special" bomb had larger dimensions than its HE equivalent – a length of 24ft 2in and a maximum diameter of 5ft as against the same length but a maximum diameter of 3ft 4in.

---

[1] It was eventually cancelled on 17 September 1952, the DOR(A) notice commenting that it had been "in abeyance for some time".

[2] Paper on Policy for Bomber Development (DRP(49)58), 6 May 1949. "The RAF did not wait to hear whether Attlee's inner Cabinet had ratified the decision that the UK should 'go nuclear', before it started to lay plans to build aircraft as 'delivery vehicles' for nuclear bombs. As a result, three new V-bombers were being readied for deployment by the end of the 1950s" (Solly Zuckerman – *Monkeys, Men and Missiles: An Autobiography 1946–88;* Collins, 1988).

[3] All-up weight of the Lincoln – which the jet bombers were to replace – was 82,000lb.

The new bomber differed from its wartime predecessors in four chief ways: it had jet instead of piston engines; it had no guns for self-defence; its five-man crew were all accommodated close together; and their compartment was pressurised for high-altitude flying. Another completely new idea was that this crew cabin should be jettisonable, "provided with parachutes to reduce the falling speed to a value at which the occupants will be unhurt when hitting the ground while strapped in their seats". This emergency escape requirement was not in fact fulfilled, and the alternative added that "if such a jettisonable cabin cannot be provided the seats must be jettisonable"[1].

OR229 was discussed by the Operational Requirements Committee on 17 December 1946, when the Committee also had OR230 before it. The chairman (Air Mshl Sir William Dickson, VCAS) and the chief MoS representative (Mr S Scott-Hall, P/DTD[2]) explained the significance of the two requirements, and also what was envisaged as to their practical realisation. Thus VCAS said that while modifications to the requirements might be found necessary as a result of detailed examination, the Air Staff would prefer that they should go forward, accepting such delay as might arise owing to the necessity of developing flying scale models.

In fact, OR230 did not go forward, only OR229 being put out as a Specification by the Ministry of Supply. What P/DTD said at the meeting on both requirements proved to be exceptionally prescient – that after a good deal of discussion in the Ministry "the conclusion had been reached that the long-range bomber, the all-up weight of which would be in the region of 200,000lb, and have swept-back wings[3], represented too great an advance in design to be entertained at the present juncture. Considerable research and development would be necessary – including, in all probability, the construction of half-scale flying models. He therefore recommended that consideration should be given to the medium-range aircraft, holding the long-range requirements in abeyance for a time".

He added that his remarks regarding the long-range aircraft were to some extent true of the medium-range bomber, but a more conventional type of aircraft could be designed, at some sacrifice in performance, as an insurance against failure to develop suitable aircraft to meet the full medium-range requirements. He explained that what he had in mind was a three-phase development. Firstly, what he would call the insurance type, which would replace the Lincoln; then the medium-range bomber, which he referred to as the long-term project; and thirdly the long-range bomber which he regarded as a very long-term project.

In the event, four types of jet bomber were built to Specifications based on OR229: Shorts' B.14/46, which did not proceed beyond the

---

[1] In the event, only the pilots' seats were.

[2] Principal Director of Technical Development (Air).

[3] OR230 made no mention of this design feature.

prototype stage, only two aircraft (named Sperrin) being built; Vickers' B.9/48 "interim class" Valiant, first of the V-bombers to be ordered and the first to enter service with RAF Bomber Command; and the Avro Vulcan and Handley Page Victor versions of B.35/46.

After OR229 had been discussed by the Operational Requirements Committee on 17 December 1946 the approved OR was issued on 7 January 1947, and on the following day – by coincidence the day when the Gen 163 Ministers decided to authorise the development of atomic weapons (8 January 1947) – the Ministry of Supply started to send out letters to various companies inviting them to submit tenders. These went from Mr S Scott-Hall, P/DTD(A) (Principal Director of Technical Development) (Air), MoS, to technical directors and chief designers – Mr R S Stafford (Handley Page) on the 8th, Sir John Buchanan (Shorts), Mr J Lloyd (Armstrong Whitworth), Dr A E Russell (Bristol) and Mr R Chadwick (Avro) on the 9th, and Mr W E W Petter (English Electric) on the 15th[1]. Subsequently, on the 24th, four companies – Avro, Armstrong Whitworth, English Electric and Handley Page – were invited to tender for the supply of prototype aircraft to MoS Specification B.35/46, based on the Air Staff Operational Requirement OR229 for a medium-range bomber. Six companies – the four just mentioned plus Shorts and Vickers-Armstrongs – prepared technical brochures to Spec B.35/46.

The four companies – Armstrong Whitworth, Avro, English Electric and Handley Page – were invited to tender by 30 April, and on 28 July a Tender Design Conference was held[2]. This recommended that an order for a prototype of the Avro version of Spec B.35/46, and for a flying model, should be placed; and, additionally, that either the Armstrong Whitworth or the Handley Page version should be ordered, with a flying model, after further investigation by the Royal Aircraft Establishment, Farnborough. This investigation would include high-speed wind tunnel tests of Handley Page's crescent-wing design – "following which a choice" would "be made between this and the Armstrong Whitworth design"[3].

At the Operational Requirements Committee meeting on 17 December 1946, when ASR No OR229 for a medium-range bomber was discussed, Mr Scott-Hall had said that a more conventional type of aircraft – one with straight instead of swept-back wings – could be designed, at some sacrifice in performance, as an insurance against failure to develop suitable types to meet the full medium-range requirements. In fulfilment of this "insurance" policy another Specification, No B.14/46, was issued by the Ministry of Supply on 11 August 1947.

This specification was based on Air Staff Requirement No OR239 for

[1] As it happened, the letters which went to the two ultimately successful contenders both began, "My dear...".
[2] On 25 July Sir Frederick Handley Page had written to Mr Scott-Hall a letter headed "Crescent and Delta Wings", giving reasons why his company "considerd but turned down the delta wing".
[3] The AWA tailless design was subsequently ruled out as unacceptable.

47

a Medium Range Bomber "Insurance" Aircraft, issued in January 1947, which began as follows: —

"The Air Staff have set out in their Requirement No OR229 the details of a medium-range bomber which they would like to have. This requirement, however, is a severe one and will necessitate an aircraft with swept-back wings and other features which are at present somewhat unconventional and not proved[1]. The Air Staff therefore require an additional aircraft built as nearly as possible to Requirement No OR229 but constructed on more or less conventional lines, so that it could go into service in the event of the more exacting requirement being held up or delayed an undue length of time.

"This requirement for an 'insurance' aircraft should therefore be read in conjunction with OR229, which provisions should be met in all respects except as follows…"

These exceptions referred to weight (to be kept down to 140,000lb or if possible 120,00lb when fully loaded, to enable the aircraft to operate from exis ing heavy-bomber airfields); speed (maximum continuous cruise at 435kt at heights of 35–50,000ft); climb and ceiling (ability to reach 45,000ft after flying 1,500 miles – references to heights of 50,000ft in OR229 were to be taken to read 45,000ft); and also to take-off performance and flight with one or two engines stopped.

Even as early as August 1947, however, doubts were being expressed in the Ministry of Supply as to the ability of the Shorts' bomber to meet even the OR239 requirements. On the 18th DMARD (Director of Military Aircraft Research and Development) (Mr J E Serby) wrote to ACAS(TR):–

"It has been apparent for some months now that the Short B.14/46 design will not quite meet the performance requirements written by DOR in OR239 and incorporated by us as the Appendix B in Specification B.14/46. The advisory design conference on this aeroplane was held on 10 July and we are now fairly clear on the probable extent of the deficiency….

"I consider that Shorts have made the best job they can of this design, and it is no discredit to them that they have fallen a little short on performance. DOR, however, is feeling rather conscious of these shortcomings and, at the ADC, somewhat naturally declined to revise

---

[1] The first operational swept-wing aircraft were the Soviet and US fighters the MiG-15, which first flew in the latter half of 1947, and the North American Sabre (F-86) which first flew on 1 Oct 47. The first successful British operational swept-wing type, the Hawker Hunter, made its maiden flight on 20 Jul 51. The Supermarine Swift, ordered as an "insurance" against the failure of the Hunter, first flew on 5 Aug 51: it proved unsuccessful as an intercepter. The US equivalent to the British V-bombers, the six-engined swept-wing Boeing B-47, made its first (prototype) flight on 17 Dec 47. "The XB-47 was the first large jet-propelled aircraft to be fitted with swept-back wings and tail surfaces" (*Jane's All the World's Aircraft, 1953–54*). The USSR first flew a four-engined jet bomber, the Il-22, which had a high-mounted tapered wing and podded engines, on 24 Jul 47, but only the prototype was built. The Soviet contemporary of the V-bombers was the Tu-16 "Badger", first seen during 1955.

his written performance requirements.... On our side we feel that we should make the position perfectly clear that there are these differences, ... that the aeroplane is the best we can offer at the moment, and that ... we are going ahead with our order for prototypes on this basis."

When the Air Council considered a report on future defence research policy[1] at its meeting on 8 September 1947 the comment was made on Specification B.14/46 that "when OR229 was sent to the Ministry of Supply they warned us that the high speed would involve much research work and that there might be long delays in getting satisfactory aircraft flying. They therefore advised us to write a requirement for an aircraft with a top speed of 435kt and a lower ceiling so that a more conventional straight-wing design could be used. This design would be completed as an 'insurance' against delays in the B.35/46 type, but would only be put into production if these delays became serious. Prototype should fly about 1951/53".

The main differences between Specs B.14/46 and B.35/46, affecting the type of aircraft to be designed, lay in the height and speed requirements. B.35/46 had to be able to cruise at maximum continuous cruising power at heights of from 35,000 to 50,000ft at a speed of 500kt; it had to cruise at 50,000ft with a full load less two-and-a-half hours' fuel. B.14/46 had to be able to cruise at maximum continuous cruising power at heights of from 35,000 to 45,000ft at a speed of 390kt; it had to cruise at 40,000ft with a full load less one hour's fuel. In other respects, like range, radius of action and bomb load, the requirements of the specifications were identical.

Three companies – Avro, Handley Page and Shorts – were given ITPs (Intention To Proceed, marking the official contractual start of design work, although this had already been going on for some months) by the Ministry of Supply in December 1947 – Shorts for the B.14/46 "insurance" bomber and Avro and Handley Page for the B.35/46. There seemed to have been more confidence, at the time, in Avro's delta-winged version of the advanced requirement; for a Ministry of Supply meeting in November 1947 recommended that they should be given financial cover, while official approval was not forthcoming for the Handley Page crescent-winged design until an Advisory Design Conference on 23 December 1947. In that month it was forecast that A V Roe could start production by mid-1955 and Handley Page by mid-1956.

On 17 September 1947 P/DTD(A) (S Scott-Hall) and DOR(A) (Air Cdre T G Pike) had visited Vickers-Armstrongs at Weybridge, Surrey,

---

[1] DRP(48)98 – Future Defence Research Policy – Report to the Minister of Defence – Brief Summary of Research and Development Projects now included in the Operational Requirements which have been put to the Ministry of Supply (Folder ID9/520(Pt 2) on Science and Defence). Four types of bomber were listed: OR229 (B.35/46), OR230, OR239(B.14/46) and OR199(B.3).

and a report signed by the former gave this account of their visit:[1]–

"In preliminary discussions DOR(A) and I had agreed that inasmuch as the long-range bomber is by far the most important item in our future programme we should re-examine the possibility of proceeding with interim types to Spec B.35/46 to take a place in the programme between the Short B.14/46 and the advanced types envisaged, such as the HP crescent wing and the Avro delta wing B.35/46. We agreed that this would be in line with the policy proposed by DRPC.[2]

"We accordingly discussed with Edwards[3], who considers the difficulties of a delta or crescent wing will be very great. Vickers have now made an examination of such a project and their work fully endorses Edwards' views.

"We asked Edwards to reconsider his B.35/46 proposals[4] on the following basis:

1. Avon or Metro Vickers F9s[5] instead of the Napier T.2/46 which it was agreed would probably not be developed in time for an interim bomber even if it is ordered. . . .

2. All-up weight 115,000lb *but* with tandem wheel arrangement (4ft wheel centres) on the understanding that this allows existing heavy bomber runways to be used.

3. Total bomb load limited to 10,000lb (third 600lb bomb eliminated).

4. Cabin jettisoning not required[6].

5. The discarding of any items of 'luxury' equipment which cause special embarrassment such as cloud and collision warning.

"Edwards will submit new proposals on these lines.

"DOR and I agreed that Petter of English Electric should be invited to resubmit his proposal on the same lines."

These thoughts were conveyed in a letter to G R Edwards on 7 October 1947 from DMARD (J E Serby). English Electric (W E W Petter) were also asked for a statement on further studies of the B.35/46 requirement.

Thus by the end of 1947 three medium bomber types based on OR229/239 were in the design stage; but the Air Staff were clearly not happy about the procurement situation, and this disquiet was expressed by the VCAS (Air Mshl Sir William Dickson) when he summarised the position in September 1947:–

---

[1] From MoS files 7 Aircraft 1505 Medium-range Bomber Long-term Design Technical Policy Pt I.
[2] Defence Research Policy Committee report of 30 July 1947 – "one or more intermediate types . . . may well be necessary".
[3] G R (later Sir George) Edwards, then chief designer at Weybridge.
[4] Vickers were one of the six companies which submitted technical brochures.
[5] The development of this engine was taken over in 1948 by Armstrong Siddeley Motors and it became the Sapphire.
[6] The original requirement, for the complete pressurised crew cabin to be jettisoned in an emergency and to float to the ground under parachutes, was abandoned owing to the design and constructional difficulties it involved.

"...we have set the Ministry of Supply two main tasks in the production of replacements for the Lincoln [he wrote to the CAS, MRAF Lord Tedder]. The first is a long-term replacement...a bomber which will have the approximate performance of 3,350nm range at 45,000ft at 500kt. In our specification we have said that it is desirable that the all-up weight of this type should not exceed 100,000lb and we have stressed that this aircraft should be able to operate from existing heavy-bomber airfields[1]. To meet these requirements it is inevitable that we must venture into revolutionary changes in aerodynamics. In other words the delta wing. At the current rate of research and devlopment it is unlikely that an aircraft of this performance will be ready for production inside eight years. Tenders are...to be placed with Handley Page and Avro.

"As an insurance against the possibility that the firms in question will not be able to solve the aerodynamical problems involved in the production of this new type of bomber, we have asked the Ministry of Supply to build a bomber of conventional design with a reduced performance of not less than 3,350nm at a height of 40,000ft and a speed of 435kt. While this reduced requirement is less than we think to be essential, we cannot afford not to have a replacement for the Lincoln which is already obsolescent if not obsolete.

"To meet our requirements for this 'insurance' bomber, the Ministry of Supply have already placed an order with Shorts. We are not at all happy about this, because from what we know, the Short design is very unimaginative and its estimated performance is already dropping below the Air Staff figures I have quoted above. From our knowledge of the work of this firm it is probable that the performance will drop still further, which is very serious bearing in mind that we do not expect to get even this 'insurance' type into production inside 6–7 years. We also know that since the Ministry of Supply have placed this order..., two further designs have been submitted for this 'insurance' specification; one from English Electric[2] and the other from Vickers. From what the Air Staff know these designs are superior to that of Shorts. On the other hand, these two alternative designs are based on a new jet engine, which is still on the drawing board, whereas the Short design employs an engine which is much further advanced in design..."[3]

Such uncertainties about the medium bomber programme led to its being thoroughly reviewed towards the end of 1947. In the October–November issue of the Air Ministry Quarterly Liaison Report, reflecting the situation in (say) early September, the summing-up had been

---

[1] VCAS's comments covered papers of 21 Aug 47 by DRPS(Air) (AVM R Ivelaw-Chapman) on "Limitation in all-up weight of landplane aircraft for the Royal Air Force" and "Limitation on length of runways".

[2] EE were already engaged in developing the B.3/45 (Canberra) high-altitude bomber.

[3] In the event, both the Short SA.4 Sperrin (B.14/46) and the Vickers Valiant (B.9/48) had Rolls-Royce Avons, although the second prototype Valiant was originally due to be powered by Armstrong Siddeley Sapphires.

complacent, though there was an implication that all was not well:–

"The Short bomber B.14/46 is proceeding according to plan. The mock-up conference has now been held and also the Advisory Design Conference. Orders have also been given to proceed with the Avro bomber of delta wing design, and also with the Handley Page crescent wing design. The Handley Page design was subjected to wind tunnel tests at the RAE and these proved quite satisfactory. Work is now proceeding on the design of both these bombers.

"In view of the great importance of the bomber, however, the Air Staff are now considering a contract for yet one more version of the same specification…".

In the next (January–March 1948) AMQLR this fourth – "insurance" – version of the medium-bomber requirement made its appearance, as a result of re-thinking by the Air Staff:–

"As mentioned in the last Report a complete review of the Bomber Programme has been made in view of its great importance. It has been decided that another type of bomber should be built to bridge the gap between the conventional medium-range bomber – the Short B.14/46 – and the two more advanced types which have been ordered from Handley Page and Avro – the B.35/46. Design studies were received from a number of firms and that of Vickers has been judged to be the most promising and a contract is about to be placed for prototypes of this aircraft. The Vickers medium-range bomber will have a still air range of 3,350nm carrying a bomb load of 10,000lb at a speed of about 465kt and height of about 45,000ft. It will weigh approximately 110,000lb and this will be distributed on a multi-wheel undercarriage. …The aircraft will be powered by four Rolls-Royce Avon engines and will start with an initial sweep-back of 20° on the outer-plane with the possibility of increasing this in future development to 30° and later 42°. The inner section of the wing is swept back to 42° initially[1]."

Further comment on the Vickers design was made in the 1949 (2nd) edition of SD573 (Future Aircraft and Equipment), where it was stated that "since the first issue of this publication (September 1947) it has been decided to order prototypes of a third bomber to the B.35/46 specification. The general features are not so advanced as the Handley Page and Avro versions. By accepting some reduction in performance it is hoped to avoid the lengthy period of development associated with the advanced designs. The anticipated performance, however, should be better than the 'Interim' Class bomber B.14/46".

Vickers received a prototype ITP (intention to proceed to the construction of prototypes) contract from the Ministry of Supply in

---

[1] When on 6 Jan 48 the DRPC (Defence Research Policy Committee) held its first meeting it "endorsed the proposals for accelerating and strengthening the heavy bomber programme". One of the suggestions made was that Canada might be invited to undertake the production of an interim bomber prototype to Spec B.35/46 (File on Future of the Long-range Bomber – 1158).

April 1948 and a contract to build two prototypes – delivery to be made "as early as possible" – in February 1949. A specification for the Vickers version of OR229, Specification No B.9/48, was issued on 19 July 1948.

Shorts, however, only received an order for two prototypes, which they built and flew. They had originally been invited to tender for the design and manufacture of these on 18 January 1947 and started design work in March of that year. By September they had a sizeable work force engaged on the programme and on 11 December 1947 received an ITP from the Ministry of Supply. This was followed by a contract on 19 February 1948 for the design, manufacture and supply of two prototypes – the first of which flew on 10 August 1951 from Aldergrove airfield, Northern Ireland.

While the Short SA.4 Sperrin (as it was known) was being developed, however, the Vickers B.9 version – two prototypes of which had been ordered in February 1949 – had been taking shape and the Air Staff considered that it would have a better performance than the Sperrin.

Summing-up the medium bomber situation in the autumn of 1949, ACAS (TR) (AVM C B R Pelly) gave the following comparative figures[1]:–

	B.14	B.9
Cruising speed	430kt	445kt
Still air range	2,900nm (3,350nm with tanks when cruising speed is 420kt and height over target 37,600ft)	3,350nm (4,350nm with overload tanks; speed and height not affected)
Height over target	40,000ft	43,700ft
Speed over target		465kt

He went on to say that

"in examining the research and development programme of the Ministry of Supply, with a view to imposing financial cuts[2], it was suggested that the B.14/46 could be abandoned now in view of the progress made with the B.9 and its improved performance over the B.14....

"The Air Staff has...been asked to state its views on the possible abandonment of the B.14. At a meeting held at the Ministry of Supply on 11 October, I said that we could do without the B.14 for the following reasons. If the long-term planning dates to which the whole of our programme is aimed are still valid...there is every reason to hope that one of the B.35 designs will be available in time, but...we still need one earlier type with which to re-equip Bomber Command, to practise the techniques involved in long-range operations at such high altitudes and

---

[1] Minute to VCAS (LM/TS6/ACAS(TR)) of 14 Oct 49.
[2] Ibid.

to be ready at the same time as the special bomb. Nevertheless, only one type of aircraft would be required, and I feel sure that the B.9, in view of its performance, offers a far better solution to our problem, the only disadvantage being that it is six months behind the B.14. Although the B.9 is of more advanced design than the B.14, the increased knowledge gained lately on swept-back wings and other high-speed complications leads to the belief that no major troubles need to be expected with the B.9 and, therefore, production of that aircraft could start early in 1953 if need be and would, I understand, match up with the production of the special bomb."

ACAS(TR) said that he had told CS(A) (Air Mshl Sir Alec Coryton) that "we can agree to stopping all further development on the B.14" and asked for confirmation of this policy.

In the event, no production order was placed for the Sperrin, which made its first public appearance at the SBAC Flying Display at Farnborough in September 1951. Subsequently, both prototypes were used for various trials, including ballistic trials of the Blue Danube atomic bomb in April 1953 from RAF Woodbridge. The first prototype, VX158, was eventually scrapped in 1958; the second, VX161, had been scrapped the previous year.

The Vickers bomber built to Spec B.9/48, the Valiant, like all the V-bombers, had a distinctive design: a shoulder wing (in which the engines were housed) with compound sweepback, and a tailplane mounted halfway up the fin. Internal fuel, in the fuselage and wings, could be supplemented by large under-wing tanks. The aircraft was powered by four Rolls-Royce Avon RA.28 Mk 204 turbojets, each giving 10,000lb (4,540kg) static thrust; and take-off could be assisted by two de Havilland Super Sprite liquid-propellant rocket motors in jettisonable pods under the wings[1].

Four Valiant variants were produced and entered service: the B.1, the bomber version; the B(PR).1 for bombing or photographic reconnaissance; B(K).1 flight-refuelling receiver aircraft for bomber or tanker roles; and B/PR(K).1 flight refuelling receiver aircraft for bomber, PR or tanker roles. As will be seen, Valiants were the initial equipment of the V-force and pioneered and performed all its roles apart from the carrying and launching of powered bombs. They were used for the air-dropping tests of Britain's atomic and hydrogen bombs and they equipped the TBF (tactical bomber force) committed to Saceur (Supreme Allied Commander, Europe).

The Valiant was the most quickly produced of the three V-bomber types. From the issue of an ITP (intention to proceed) to Vickers on 16 April 1948 and their receipt of a production order for 25 aircraft on

---

[1] RATO (rocket-assisted take-off) was originally considered to be a requirement for the V-bombers, particularly for operations from dispersed airfields; but when the thrust of their engines was doubled (from 11,000lb in the Vulcan and Victor B.1s to 20,000lb in the B.2s) the requirement was curtailed (Air Council meeting No 17 (59), 23 July 59).

9 February 1951 to the arrival of the first B.1 for No 138 Squadron at Gaydon on 8 February 1955, the whole process took just two months under seven years, partly due to the fact that the aircraft was ordered "off the drawing board"[1]. It was also the only one of the three medium bombers for which no flying scale models were built, and Vickers were unique in maintaining good relations with their customer, whereas at times those between the Royal Air Force and their other contractors – particularly over alleged delays – became acrimonious[2].

Avro and Handley Page had received an official go-ahead for their designs to the B.35/46 Specification during November 1947. Writing on 8 December of that year in a note headed "B.35/46 – Avro and HP designs", DMARD (Mr J E Serby) recorded that "ITPs have now been issued to both Avro and Handley Page to enable them to go ahead with the design of prototype aircraft as well as flying models. This is the official contractual start of the design...". What had led up to it was recalled in some briefing notes prepared for ACAS (OR) (Air Cdre H V Satterly) when he visited Avro's factory on 16 May 1952:–

"The draft OR229 for a medium-range bomber was circulated on 7 November 1946. The ORC (Operational Requirements Committee) was held on 17 December 1946 and the approved OR was issued on 7 January 1947. Armstrong Whitworth, English Electric, Handley Page and A V Roe were invited to tender by 30 April. The Tender Design Conference was held on 28 July. This conference recommended that an order for the prototype of the Avro design of the B.35/46, and a flying model, should be placed. Additionally, either the Handley Page or the Armstrong Whitworth should be ordered with a flying model, after further investigation by RAE. Nothing much happened until a meeting at the Ministry of Supply in November 1947. This meeting recommended that financial cover should be given to A V Roe's. An ADC (advisory design conferencee) was held on the Handley Page version on 23 December and by 9 January 1948 we were advised that token sums of money had been granted to cover ITPs issued to A V Roe's and Handley Page. In the same month it was forecast that A V Roe's could start production by mid-1955 and Handley Page's by mid-1956".

Armstrong Whitworth's proposal was rejected because of the company's absorption at that time in the AW52 tailless designs, and because the MoS did not seem confident of its ability to tackle an operational requirement. The English Electric proposal had been turned down because that company was already fully committed on the B.3/45 (Canberra) specification.

[1] Writing in 1952, the then CAS (MRAF Sir John Slessor) recalled that when defence expenditure was dramatically increased after the December 1950 meeting of the North Atlantic Council in Brussels, new types of aircraft were ordered in quantity. "The Valiant had not flown, but we placed a small order off the drawing board....".

[2] About half the cost of Valiant procurement was paid for under the US Military Assistance Programme.

It was on 19 November 1947 that the MoS sent Handley Page a contract for two prototypes, and on the 27th it was agreed that an ITP should be issued to A V Roe to cover their design of the B.35/46 bomber and two flying models (Avro 707s). The forecast of dates for when the two companies could start production proved to be pessimistic; in fact the Vulcan came into RAF service during 1956 and the Victor during 1957 – the former nearly nine years, and the latter nearly ten years, after the initial contracts were issued. MoS Aircraft Specification No B.129P for the Vulcan B Mk 1, to cover production of the type, was issued on 25 September 1952, and a reprint (incorporating amendments) on 1 September 1954.

Two aspects of the original design requirements for the V-bombers[1] which were later to cause controversy were the exclusion of self-defensive armament and the attempt to provide a comprehensive crew escape system.

OR229 in its first version (published as an Appendix to Specification B.35/46) said unequivocally: "The aircraft will rely upon speed, height and evasive manoeuvre for protection against interception. It will not carry orthodox defensive armament, therefore, but will be equipped with early-warning devices to enable effective avoiding manoeuvres to be made, radar countermeasures to deflect a beam on which a controlled weapon may be launched against it, and equipment to cause premature explosion of proximity-fused weapons". However, in the second issue of OR229, dated 19 January 1953, this requirement was modified to read: "When a suitable installation becomes available the aircraft may need to be equipped with rear armament. Therefore basic structural and aerodynamic provision is to be made for its retrospective fitment...." Then the third issue of OR229, dated 2 June 1954, reverted to the original policy; it simply said: "No provision need now be made for rear defensive armament"[2].

This change in the requirement had undoubtedly been made in deference to opinion on the Air Staff which did not like the idea of crews being sent over enemy territory without any guns to counter-attack intercepting fighters. Such feelings were reflected in a paper of 6 May 1949 by the Director of Operational Requirements (Air Cdre G W Tuttle)[3] in which, writing about the "Basis of Unarmed Bomber Decision", he said:–

"In 1946, when the Air Staff examined the policy for future bombers, the practicability of jet bombers was firmly established and a decision had to be made between continuing to use piston-engined bombers or

---

[1] Which got their names in 1952: "Decided Oct 1952 that the A V Roe version of the B.35 should be named Vulcan, following Valiant and preceding Victor, thus making a 'V' class of medium bombers...." (Unsigned pencilled note in file on Aircraft Nomenclature – ID3/94/8 (Pt 1)).

[2] OR1116 – Rearward Defensive Armament for Bombers – was cancelled in 1953.

[3] "Policy for Bomber Devlt" (DRP(49)58).

adopting jet bombers. Whichever type was decided on, each would have to be capable of the same range. This meant that the jet bombers would be compelled to fly very high and fast. Piston-engined aircraft would, by comparison, only be capable of much lower speeds and heights, and could not therefore rely upon evading fighter attacks. They would thus have to be heavily armed. On the other hand, no form of armament then existed or appeared possible to develop which could be fitted to jet bombers that could not (by added weight and drag) so greatly reduce their performance (unless they were made very large) as to make them wholly incapable of achieving the required minimum range.

"Thus, in 1946, the choice that lay before the Air Staff was one of deciding between an armed piston-engined bomber, operating at relatively low altitudes and relatively low speeds, and an unarmed, very-high-flying, high-speed jet bomber. The decision was a difficult one to make. After prolonged and careful consideration, however, the Air Staff decided in favour of the unarmed jet bomber....

"While the Air Staff are convinced of the correctness of the decision, it cannot be regarded as satisfactory to send our bombers over enemy territory without any form of armament whatever. This is a question which is under constant discussion in the Air Staff. Until recently, however, the chances of successful evasion have been thought to be very high and the possibility of developing any form of armament for the bomber that would not unacceptably reduce its performance has appeared remote. A little while ago, however, it was concluded, from investigations that were being made into the problems of developing a supersonic fighter, that the possibilities of doing so before 1957 were distinctly better than they were at first thought to be. While this may bring some comfort to us from the point of view of our own air defence, it has increased the Air Staff's latent uneasiness about the future bombers having no means of self-protection. The Air Staff could not, therefore, ignore so significant a change in one of the principal factors involved in bomber development policy. Consequently the matter was re-opened with the Ministry of Supply to see whether any developments had occurred since it was first decided to adopt jet bombers, which might make it possible to give these bombers some form of self-protection, which would not have such an adverse effect upon their performance....

"In the light of these new factors, it is the view of the Air Staff that research into the possibility of arming a jet bomber without prejudicing its primary function should be vigorously pursued, and that, should a possible solution to this problem emerge, they would attach great importance to the rapid development of prototype equipment...".

In the event, no guns for self-defence were ever fitted to the V-bombers, although there were strong feelings in the Air Staff about arming them. In a minute of 7 April 1949 ACAS(TR) (Air Vice-Marshal C B R Pelly) had put forward arguments for continued research "into the possibility of arming a bomber without prejudicing its primary function", as a matter of Air Staff policy. In this (and also in advocating target-marker versions of the B.14, B.9 and B.35) he was supported by ACAS(Ops) (AVM C E N Guest) and also by DCAS (Air Mshl Sir Hugh Walmsley), who said on 13 April: "I have never been happy about the unarmed bomber policy, nor do I consider that this policy should be accepted as final". He was supported, in a minute of the following day to PS/VCAS, by the Scientific Adviser to the Air Ministry (Dr R Cockburn) who considered that "research on . . . defensive armament must . . . continue"[1].

The other problem, that of emergency escape for crew members, particularly at low level, was never satisfactorily solved and was to cause controversy throughout the whole period of V-force operations, particularly when accidents occurred in which the two pilots were able to escape by means of their ejection seats but the rear crew members were unable to get out of the aircraft.

When OR229 was approved, and issued early in 1947 with the Specification No B.35/46, it said unequivocally under the heading "Emergency Exits":–

"The complete pressure cabin must be jettisonable. Such a cabin must be provided with parachutes to reduce the falling speed to a value at which the occupants will be unhurt when hitting the ground while strapped in their seats. If such a jettisonable cabin cannot be provided the seats must be jettisonable".

However, in the second issue of OR229 (19 January 1953) this original requirement had been modified and now read:–

"When jettisoned, the canopy above the pilots' seats [ie ejector seats] must leave the aircraft under all conditions of accelerated flight and fall free without damage to the remaining aircraft structure. A separate emergency battery must be provided for the escape facilities which are dependent in the first instance on electricity.

"The crew members other than the pilots are to be provided with an escape exit which protects them, during the process of abandoning the aircraft, from the blast of the airflow".

The reason for this change was that the manufacturers had found it impossible to fulfil the original requirement for a jettisonable pressure cabin. When an advisory design conference on the B.9/48 was held on 4 June 1948, the difficulty of developing a completely jettisonable cabin in time for the prototype was discussed and Vickers' chief designer, Mr G R Edwards, said[2] that the structural difficulties in providing ejection seats for all the crew were too great; the extra space required would prejudice the design of the cabin canopy. As a result, the requirement was re-worded: Specification B.9/48 for the Valiant, dated 19 July 1948, said: "A completely jettisonable cabin is desired. If this is not

---

[1] File on Air Staff Policy for Future Bombers (ID9/A.10).
[2] Minutes (7 Airft 3458).

58

practicable, arrangements should be made for good emergency escape means for the crew". Avro's chief designer, Mr W S Farren, wrote to DMARD early the following year (8 February 1949): "there is no doubt that the provision of [cabin jettisoning] in a manner which we feel could command both your confidence and that of those who would use the aircraft, is very difficult, and would certainly involve a considerable increase in complexity and in structure weight. . . . I am . . . concerned at the real difficulty of solving a problem of such a novel kind at the same time as the many other problems which are vital to the success of the project. . .". Design development by Handley Page of a jettisonable crew cabin for the Victor continued, however, until 1951. On 10 May, DDOR wrote[1]: "we wish the development of the jettisonable cabin on the Handley Page B.35/46 to continue. On the other hand we would not wish [its] development to delay the second prototype". Eventually, even the Handley Page effort in this direction was abandoned.

Unfortunately, the problem of emergency escape from the V-bombers was highlighted by accidents early in the careers of these aircraft. When the Valiant prototype (WB210) caught fire during engine relight trials on 12 January 1952 and the crew abandoned it, the pilots ejected and the rear crew members baled-out through the hatchway. The co-pilot, Sqn Ldr B H D Foster, Bomber Command liaison officer at Vickers, was killed as a result of striking the fin after ejecting – the aircraft was in a descending turn. The other crew members landed safely.

During 1951 there had been criticism of the pilots' ejection seats in the Valiant as being uncomfortable. On 13 August the AOC in C Bomber Command (Air Chf Mshl Sir Hugh Lloyd) had written to the Air Ministry (ACAS (OR)) to say that a pilot's endurance on them was "something of the order of one-and-a-half hours". At that time, as was pointed out in a reply to him on the 30th, the jettisonable cabin was still "under development". One of those who attended a meeting at Martin Baker Ltd on 3 September, to discuss the comfort of ejection seats, was Sqn Ldr Foster. His successor as liaison officer after the Valiant accident, Sqn Ldr R G W Oakley, substantiated his opinion that the pilots' seats were "very uncomfortable".

The first RAF Valiant to be lost – indeed the first V-bomber in service to be destroyed in an accident – was WP222 of No 139 Sqn, which on take-off from Wittering on 29 July 1955 suffered a runaway aileron trim actuator and struck the ground in a steep descending turn. One member of the crew (the signaller, Plt Off A R Lyons) baled out through the entrance door, which had been jettisoned, but was killed. In its report the Court of Inquiry recommended that "further investigation be conducted into the general problem of abandoning Valiant aircraft when the aircraft is in an unusual attitude, as in this case; also to see if the arrangements for the crew cannot in some way be improved. At

---

[1] Ref C.40004/49.

present the fact that it is so difficult for the crew to abandon aircraft to some extent negatives the provision of ejector seats for the pilots".

The second Vulcan to be delivered to the RAF (XA897) crashed on an approach to London Heathrow on 1 October 1956 at the conclusion of what had been a most successful "showing the flag" visit to Australia and New Zealand, code-named Tasman Flight. The two pilots (Sqn Ldr D R Howard and Air Mshl Sir Harry Broadhurst, AOC in C Bomber Command) ejected successfully but the four rear crew members were killed, as the aircraft was at such a low altitude there was insufficient time and airspace for them to get out through the exit hatchway and use their parachutes. Controversy over the provision of emergency escape facilities for V-bomber rear crew members continued until the late 1960s, as will be seen in subsequent references.

At the heart of the V-bombers was their navigation and bombing system – NBS Mk 1, which in the 1952 issue of TSD 573 was described in the following terms:–

"This navigation and bombing computer is an electronic computer of groundspeed and drift, and ground position. Its purpose is to take the load off the navigator by performing continuous automatic dead-reckoning of position, and to improve the accuracy of blind and visual bombing, making use of the navigational information so obtained.

"It obtains the information on wind speed from any available navigational source including H2S . . ., and its output is bombing data on the radar display or on a visual sighting head, and navigational data in the form of ground position in latitude and longitude.

"The visual sighting head is capable of giving vector or tachometric solution of the bombing problem. The complete equipment, less cabling, is expected to weigh approximately 800lb."

Because of the sophistication of their equipment – the NBC system (as it became known – navigation/bombing computer), pressurisation, turbojet powerplants, radar self-defence, all-weather landing aids and aerodynamic design for operations at great heights and airspeeds – the V-bombers took a long time to develop and get into service: no wonder, considering the complications of their design and construction; but there was never any move on the part of the Government to cancel them, as there was with its missile projects. They were a quantum leap in technology compared with their predecessor the Lincoln, a development of the Lancaster. Gone were the propellers and gun-turrets, gone the isolation of individual crew members, gone the tailwheel undercarriage: the nosewheel, so grudgingly adopted by the British compared with the Americans – indeed, apart from the Armstrong Whitworth Albemarle, not at all until jet engines became the norm, was an understood feature of the Operational Requirement for the V-bombers. The wings were swept back to cope with much higher speeds and altitudes and the wing area greatly increased: indeed the delta-winged Avro Vulcan was described as having "virtually no fuselage"[1].

To assist them in overcoming aerodynamic problems in hitherto unexplored areas of flight, both manufacturers of the more advanced (B.35/46) types of V-bomber – Avro and Handley Page (who went for a crescent wing shape) – built flying scale models: Avro built and flew four 707s and Handley Page the HP88, which unfortunately crashed, killing the test pilot – as did one of the 707s. But in general neither the Vickers Valiant, nor the Avro Vulcan and Handley Page Victor, encountered serious problems in development, a tribute to the Air Ministry/MoA supervision and to the manufacturers' responses and skills.

One problem which arose during development was that of weight – the new four-jet bombers were going to be very much heavier than their wartime predecessors, and a ceiling of 100,000lb was set if Bomber Command's new types were to operate from existing heavy-bomber airfields. "I cannot help feeling", CAS wrote to VCAS on 19 September 1947, "that the trend towards very large and heavy aircraft is an extremely dangerous one…; …by accepting these proposed increases in weight we tie ourselves to long and very heavy concrete runways, of which we can only hope to have a very limited number, and in so doing gravely limit the mobility of our striking force[2].…"

As will be seen, however, this mobility was never limited – as a result of the dramatic contribution made by the aero-engine manufacturers to the V-bomber programme.

During development the powerplant of the V-bombers – a crucial feature in giving them the range, height, speed and take-off performance which were required – increased greatly in thrust from that originally specified. Thus the B.9/48 Valiant first flew with Rolls-Royce Avon RA.3s of 6,500lb thrust but went into service with Avon RA.14s of 9,500lb thrust. The prototype B.35/46 Victor had Armstrong Siddeley Sapphires of 8,000lb thrust but production versions had Sapphire Sa.7s of 11,000lb thrust. Similarly, the prototype B.35/46 Vulcan flew with Rolls-Royce Avon RA.3s of 6,500lb thrust (like the first Valiant), but from the second prototype was powered by Bristol Olympus engines of 9,750lb – increasing in power on production versions to Olympus 101s of 11,000lb thrust, 102s of 12,000lb or 104s of 13,000lb thrust, all in the Vulcan B.1s. These engines were all newly developed: the Avon, in different versions, was used in other military aircraft like the Canberra, Hunter and Scimitar, and in civil airliners like the Comet and Caravelle; Sapphires were used also in Gloster Javelins, and the Olympus was the progenitor of Concorde's powerplant.

In mid-1952 the B.35 programme was accorded special priority,

---

[1] DCAS to S of S, after the Vulcan accident at Heathrow on 1 Oct 56.

[2] Tedder/Dickson correspondence in Folder (1158) on the Future of the Long-range Bomber. AMQLR for Jan–Mar 51 reports on "medium bomber airfields…now in progress of construction" as "being provided with a runway of 9,000ft length by 200ft width with an overrun at either end of 1,000ft".

along with that for Gloster F.4 Javelin all-weather fighters, the Cabinet deciding on 12 June that – subject to detailed Treasury approval – an order for 50 should be placed[1]. However, a decision on the grant of special priority to the B.35 programme (as the Minister of Supply had urged) was postponed until after the review which was to be made of the defence production programme[2].

During the latter half of 1954 the number of Victors and Vulcans on order was substantially increased: the Air Ministry Quarterly Liaison Report for July–September 1954 noted that "orders have been placed for a further 32 Victors and 32 Vulcans, bringing the number of each type on order to 57".

When the Air Council discussed progress with the V-bombers at its meeting on 20 January 1955[3] DCAS (Air Mshl T G Pike) reported that the Valiant had now been released; two were awaiting collection, the next three would be available in March and thereafter delivery would be at the rate of three per month. The first Vulcan was expected to be available in a year's time and the Victor in 18 months.

Referring to the two latter types, CA (Air Chf Mshl Sir John Baker) said that the Victor "still needed a great deal of assessment". While he felt that aerodynamically it would prove a success, Handley Page were "showing a good deal less enterprise than were A V Roe with the Vulcan". Avro were "making substantial progress" and "displaying marked willingness to develop well-thought-out improvements and to enlarge the scope of their development work". He commented that in the MoS this was felt to be "psychologically a valuable opportunity of illustrating to the industry the importance, in relation to the price factor and the need to avoid time-lags in production, of the rewards and penalty principle by placing an order for ten or 12 Vulcans additional to those already ordered". The Council agreed that CA should explore this possibility further with DCAS.

On 21 October 1955 S of S (Lord De L'Isle and Dudley VC) approved a proposal that orders should be placed for an additional 24 Vulcans and 18 Victors[4]. By mid-1956, according to papers prepared in the Air Ministry at the request of the Minister of Defence for submission to the Chiefs of Staff[5], the numbers of the three types of V-bomber ordered were 92 Valiants, 75 Victors and 89 Vulcans (plus 18 sets of long-dated materials). At that time, according to an Air Ministry

[1] CC(52)59th Conclusions, Min 5 (in VCAS Defence Programme 1952/55 – AHB file ID9/11/4, Pt 1). See also AUS(A)/CAS minute, 27 Jun 52, in ID3/942/5, Pt 2 – Victor/Vulcan (B.35) Development & Production.

[2] CC(52)59th Conclusions. "By July 1952, although neither of the prototypes had flown, a production order was placed for 25 each of the B.35 series aircraft…" (Some notes on the Avro Vulcan… – Brief for ACAS(OR)'s visit to the firm in Jan 53.) The Vulcan flew for the first time on 30 Aug 52 and the Victor on 24 Dec 52.

[3] Air Council Conclusions 2(55). Review of the Air Staff Research and Development Programme – November 1954 – AC(54)73. Note by DCAS.

[4] AHB file ID3/942/5 Pt 2 Victor/Vulcan (B.35) Development and Production.

[5] COS(56)26 4 and 5. See ID3/901/6 (Pt 2) Medium Bomber Force – Size & Composition.

Note of 11 July 1956 on the Size of the Deterrent, the ultimate size of the MBF was to be 200 instead of the 240 origionally planned[1]. Subsequently the total was 184, including a front line of 120 Mk 2 Vulcans and Victors. These figures were to be the subject of many papers and much debate between the Services and the Ministries in the mid- and late-1950s[2].

The three types of V-bomber which emerged from Vickers, Avro and Handley Page were arguably the most impressive and beautiful military aircraft ever designed in Britain and gave splendid service to the RAF. Although the Valiant was in service for less than ten years it was metal fatigue, not any design failure, which caused its withdrawal from operational use and the scrapping of every aircraft except one – XD818, which dropped the first British thermonuclear bomb on 15 May 1957 in the Operation Grapple trials from Christmas Island and has been preserved. The Vulcans and Victors continued in RAF service for over 30 years, long after the role for which they had originally been designed – strategic nuclear deterrence – had been handed over to the Royal Navy.

These three aircraft had two design features in common – wing sweepback and "buried" (as opposed to "podded") engines, giving them all exceptionally clean lines. Because the Valiant was produced to a less demanding specification – B.9/48 – as has already been described, its aerodynamic shape was not as dramatic as that of the Victor and the Vulcan. Its wing leading edge had compound sweepback, and the wingtips and trailing edge were both straight. The four jet exhaust pipes of its Avon engines protruded above the trailing edges of the wings and the tailpline was set clear of the efflux, halfway up the fin.

The Victor and Vulcan can be directly compared as both were designed to the same Specification, B.35/46, Handley Page adopting a crescent-wing and Avro a delta-wing configuration. This led to marked differences elsewhere in the shapes of these two aircraft. The Victor's leading-edge sweepback was compound, like that of the Valiant, but its wingtips were rounded and the wing trailing edge had a backward sweep, the only straight portion being where the jet pipes protruded. The fin and tailplane added to the dramatic appearance of the Victor design, for the tailplane – repeating, both fore and aft, the sweepback of the main wing and itself as large as a jet fighter[3] – was set right on the top of the fin.

By contrast, the Vulcan was a pure delta shape, like a huge paper dart, with no fuselage to speak of, only the pressurised crew compartment protruding in advance of the wing area – which housed engines, weapons and fuel. Its leading-edge sweepback was graduated, coming to a point at the trailing edges, which were straight, apart from the protrusions of the jet pipes. Control surfaces – ailerons and elevators –

---

[1] and [2] See ID3/901/6 (Pt 2) Medium Bomber Force – Size & Composition.
[3] Span of the Victor tailplane was 32ft 8in, the wingspan of the Hawker Hunter 33ft 8in.

were incorporated in this trailing edge as "elevons"[1], so the fin was entirely uncluttered, giving the Vulcan a remarkably clean aerodynamic shape.

When the design of the V-bombers, which had the benefit of jet engines and carried no gun turrets, is compared with that of their predecessor the Lincoln the contrast is remarkable: the bomber had at long last become a match for fighters and had been designed to over-fly missile defences – at least those of the foreseeable future.

Canberra Development

Side-by-side with the medium bombers, another bomber was being developed – like them, capable of high speed at high altitude, turbojet-powered, pressurised, unarmed, but twin-engined and with only a two- or three-man crew and a range of 1,500nm. A product of the English Electric Co and subsequently named Canberra, it was not designed to deliver atomic bombs, nor could it operate – like the medium bombers – against targets in the Soviet Union from bases in the UK. It played an important part in the development of the RAF airborne nuclear deterrent force, because the original V-bomber squadrons all initially operated Canberras and their crews received their first jet-flying experience on the type; but at the time of its inception there seems to have been no clear idea of the operational requirement for a high-altitude light bomber. In fact, the company appear to have taken the initiative in putting the idea into the minds of the Air Staff, by showing them a mock-up and brochure description of the proposed machine. This followed discussions between English Electric and the Ministry of Aircraft Production in 1944 on a design project for an experimental high-speed bomber.

The company had been building Hampdens, Halifaxes and Vampires during the war; they wished to produce their own aircraft again and a design department set up under Mr W E W Petter started work on a high-speed, high-altitude, unarmed strategic bomber referred to as a "Mosquito replacement", notwithstanding the fact that the operational scenario for which that aircraft had been designed no longer existed. In February 1945 the firm sent formal proposals on this to the MAP, requesting a design contract. The Ministry responded by writing to both English Electric and to de Havilland, manufacturers of the Mosquito, suggesting that they might like to design a successor to it.

During June, English Electric submitted a preliminary brochure on a single-engined, high-speed, high-altitude bomber and this was passed to the Air Ministry. The company were given a contract for a design study and the manufacture of mock-ups.

Discussions between the Air Ministry and MAP led to comments on the proposals being sent to English Electric during July, expressing

---

[1] In the Mk 2 Vulcans, which had four full-span elevons in place of the outboard ailerons and inboard elevators of the Mk 1.

general approval but recommending certain alterations. A major change was the decision to use two engines (Rolls-Royce Avons) instead of the large single centrifugal compressor engine originally envisaged, and the firm issued a new brochure embodying the changes.

In July also the Director of Operational Requirements (Air Cdre A R Wardle) visited English Electric to discuss the proposals, a visit which was referred to in a letter from Mr Petter to ACAS(TR) (AVM J N Boothman, who had recently taken up the post) on 3 August, in which he said:–

"You may have heard that since joining this company to start up a design organisation with a view to continuing permanently in the aircraft business, we have been working on a high-altitude bomber (nominally a Mosquito replacement although in fact much larger). I have discussed this with Breakey" – AVM J D Breakey, Boothman's predecessor as ACAS(TR) – "and DOR who recently came up here to see a preliminary mock-up and I should like, if possible, to take an opportunity when next in town of running briefly over the layout with you".

ACAS(TR) responded on the following day by saying that he could see Petter on the suggested date (23 August), but that he might forestall him by paying a flying visit to English Electric before then.

As a result of these meetings and discussions between the company and members of the Air Staff and OR Directorate an Air Staff Requirement was drafted – ASR No 199, for a high-speed, high-altitude bomber. Based on the English Electric brochure, it envisaged an aircraft capable of cruising at not less than 440kt at 40,000ft with a range of not less than 1,400nm in still air. Received at the MAP during September, this draft ASR represented the first official Air Staff thinking on the aircraft which became the Canberra, and it resulted from the English Electric initiatives of 1944–45. "The Canberra project began as a design project of our experimental high-speed bomber in discussions between the firm and the Ministry", it was stated in a Procurement Executive document (Draft Outline of MoS Procedure for Planning Aircraft Development and Production for the RAF, with special reference to the Canberra B.1 and B.2); "it was not related to an OR until a later stage".

In November 1945 the MAP drafted Specification E.3/45 (later B.3/45), based on ASR No 199, and an advisory design conference was held; and in December the Ministry issued a contract for the design and construction of four prototypes to Spec E.3/45, based on the English Electric brochure of July and the draft OR (ASR No 199). Then on 3 January 1946 the Operational Requirements Committee, bringing together representatives of the Air Ministry, MAP and Bomber Command, discussed the requirements for a high-speed, high-altitude bomber (ASR No 199) and approved details of OR No 199 which was issued in March 1946 and resulted in the Canberra.

This chronology clearly shows that the Canberra stemmed from an

English Electric initiative, fostered by the Ministry of Aircraft Production, leading to an Air Staff Operational Requirement. In fact, after the OR had been issued[1], ACAS(TR) wrote to the AOC in C Bomber Command, on 29 March 1946[2], to explain the reasons for it and to put it into the perspective of the bomber programme: —

"...the aircraft under discussion [he explained] is being built by the English Electric Co, not as a private venture, but in response to a MAP specification based on requirements prepared by the Air Staff. It was evolved as an operational aircraft and the requirements were not based entirely on technical considerations as you suggest, although of course the employment of jet propulsion, while offering considerable advantages in speed, did impose limitations in the range performance for which we could ask[3].

"The suitability of the E.3/45 specification should be examined in relation to the bomber fleet as a whole; it must not be regarded as an aircraft intended for the whole sphere of bomber employment. It appears impracticable, and it would certainly be uneconomical, to cover every role of our bomber forces with one type of aircraft, and our intention is to provide two types – a long-range bomber, the primary feature of which will be long range at very high cruising speed, and a much smaller bomber with a relatively modest range but a very high cruising speed.

"The long-range bomber is likely to be an aircraft capable of 5,000 miles' range in still air at a speed of 500 mph or more and a bomb capacity of 20,000lb or less. Such requirements are likely to produce an aircraft of well over 100,000lb gross weight, and although such a type may be the primary bomber of the RAF, it would obviously be uneconomical to employ it for the many tasks at shorter ranges which will undoubtedly be required. A smaller aircraft is therefore indicated, even though only a small proportion of the total force may be equipped with this type. It then becomes possible to take advantage of the smaller size and shorter range to obtain even a higher speed than is possible with the larger aircraft[4].

"...Air Staff requirements for the E.3/45 bomber have deliberately limited the role for which the prototype is being designed to high-altitude operations and completely 'blind' bombing in order to concentrate technical effort on the most difficult problems for which

[1] On 8 March ACAS(TR) had written to the Controller of R&D, MAP, to say that "the Air Staff have formulated operational requirements for a high-speed, high-altitude bomber".

[2] In reply to a letter of 7 Feb 46 from C in C Bomber Command which unfortunately seems to have been destroyed.

[3] At the ORC meeting on 3 Jan 46, when the Deputy Director of Bomber Operations (Gp Capt W C Sheen) commented that for strategic bombing the range fell short of requirements by approximately 1,000 miles, the chairman (AVM Boothman) said that the aircraft was intended to be a Mosquito replacement and that long-range bombing would be a requirement of the new bomber to be discussed later.

[4] In the event, not only were the Canberras more numerous than the V-bombers, but the latter were faster than the Canberras.

solutions are required....

"The range requirement in the E.3/45 specification is a minimum; as the design progresses it is apparent that this one can be very appreciably increased".

After further remarks on possible different roles for the type, ACAS(TR) concluded his letter in terms which suggested that the AOC in C had complained that Bomber Command had not been consulted in the drafting of OR199, for he assured him that they would be consulted in the drafting of the medium bomber requirement (OR229):–

"Outline requirements for the long-range bomber will shortly be ready and this will be fully discussed with you before any order for a prototype is placed with MAP. With the rapid advance in the development of turbine engines it is difficult to choose the appropriate moment for establishing a specification; requirements which were regarded as impossible of attainment three months ago are quite practicable today, and the advance still goes on....

"The high-speed bomber must be regarded as complementary to the long-range bomber and judgment as to its value in relation to the long-range bomber and the place it shall take in the long-range bomber fleet of the Royal Air Force must be reserved at least until the specification for the long-range bomber is completed. The E.3/45 will in any case, as you suggest, be useful for the study of the many tactical and technical problems involved in the great advance in performance which will be obtained by the employment of turbine engines".

The final sentence of this letter from ACAS(TR) about the usefulness of the Canberra "for the study of . . . many tactical and technical problems" was remarkably percipient, in that the type provided training and experience in jet bomber operations before the advent of the Valiants, Vulcans and Victors, V-force squadrons of which were nearly all initially equipped with Canberras.

Originally B.3/45 (as the E.3/45 specification became known) was envisaged as a "blind" bomber; OR199, on which it was based, stated clearly under Bomb Sighting: "The aircraft is to be laid out for bomb aiming by radar and other mechanical vision systems and for the use of guided projectiles".

Unfortunately the equipment which was to give the Canberra this capability, H2S Mk 9, failed to keep pace with the aircraft in development. The AMQLR for July–September 1949 noted:–

"H2S Mk 9 was originally required for use in the B.3/45. It has now been decided not to put H2S into this aircraft and the Mk 9 will be used for experimental purposes. . . . The same basic equipment, however, is being developed for use with larger bombers than the B.3 and incorporating a larger scanner. This is now known as H2S Mk 9A...".

On 13 May 1949 the first Canberra prototype, the English Electric A.1, made its maiden flight; but the B.1 version (the "blind" bomber, built to Spec B.3/45) was not given a CA Release and no production order was placed for it. The delay in the development of blind bombing equipment made it necessary to proceed with development and production of the tactical day bomber version (B.2), leaving the blind-bombing role to the V-bombers. On 12 July DOR (Air Cdre G W Tuttle) wrote to DMARD (Director of Military Aircraft Research and Development, Mr J E Serby) about the English Electric Blind Bomber (B.3/45):–

"VCAS has decided that in view of the fact that H2S for the above aircraft could not be ready before that for the B.9 [ie the Valiant] without delaying the H2S for the B.9, the B.3/45 is no longer an Air Staff requirement and therefore the Air Staff will not require production of this model of the English Electric blind bomber.

"He has asked me to request that you will ensure that any effort released on the abandonment of the B.3 should be applied to the development of the B.9 and its equipment".

Referring to the operational role of the Canberra before it entered service (in May 1951), VCAS (Air Chf Mshl Sir Ralph Cochrane) commented in a note to CAS (MRAF Sir John Slessor) on 29 January about a conference which had been held at HQ Bomber Command on the 25th–26th:–

"There was . . . a tendency to look upon the Canberra as a long-range, high-flying bomber, and to press for equipment to enable it to undertake this role. At the end, however, it was generally accepted that the Canberra is a short-range tactical bomber, that there is no equipment which will enable it to hit a small target from 45,000ft, and that it must therefore come down to a height from which it can achieve results. . .".

The change in Air Staff thinking from the original 1945 concept of a high-speed, high-altitude bomber (OR199) able to operate at 40,000ft and with radar bomb-aiming equipment, to the tactical day bomber requirement (OR235) which resulted in the Canberra B.2, reflects a more realistic appreciation of the original English Electric concept of an unarmed bomber to replace the Mosquito[1].

OR235 did not ask for the aircraft to carry a 10,000lb bomb load (as OR199 had done), but to deliver a 7,500lb weight of bombs – in addition to other kinds of weapon, up to a maximum of 8,000lb – and to operate at 15–20,000ft with a ceiling of 40,000ft, rather than cruising at 40,000ft with a ceiling of 50,000ft, as had been required by OR199. In other

---

[1] "The requirement for this high-speed, high-altitude, unarmed light strategic bomber was issued in January 1946. It was the intention that this type of aircraft should be an interim replacement for the Main Force bombers held by Bomber Command, pending the introduction of the medium-range bombers, viz B.9 and B.35.

"In July 1949, an examination showed that the H2S Mk 9/NBC Mk 2 equipment was delayed to a date when it would be required simultaneously by both the Canberra B.1 and Vickers B.9/48. . . . As only one type of blind bomber was required and since the production date of the B.9/48 compared favourably with that of the fully equipped Canberra B Mk 1, the development effort for the H2S/NBC was devoted fully to the B.9/48 and further development of the Canberra B Mk 1 was cancelled." (File on Aircraft Production and Repair – AHB ID/53/1/465 D of Policy (AS) 411/5.)

words, requirements for the aircraft which eventually entered service as the first Canberra, the B.2 version, had been considerably scaled-down from the initial concept. Its bomb-aiming equipment was also simpler. Instead of H2S Mk 9 plus NBC Mk 2 or Gee-H Mk II which had originally been requested (and which, at the design stage, had been found to add considerably to the all-up weight and therefore to affect performance adversely) the aircraft was to have Gee-H Mk II. This of course limited its bombing range, by contrast with that of the V-bombers, to the effective available Gee coverage.

OR235, for a tactical day bomber version of the B.3/45, was issued in February 1947, and the stages leading to a prototype contract occurred during that year. In August, an advisory design conference was held; in October, a mock-up conference. Then on 12 November the Ministry of Supply issued Specification No B.5/47, for a tactical day bomber version of the B.3/45, and in April 1948 placed a contract with English Electric for one prototype. By that date the first RAF jet bomber, the Canberra B.2, was within sight of becoming an operational reality.

These different versions of the Canberra caused confusion, however, even at Bomber Command. On 20 September 1950 the AOC in C (Air Mshl Sir Hugh Lloyd) expressed "serious concern" about the new bomber. Telling the CAS (MRAF Sir John Slessor) that they were "drifting into a mess" over it he said that there had originally been three versions – the B.3/45 high-speed, high-altitude bomber, the B.5/47 tactical day bomber and the PR.31/48 PR version. The B.3/45 had been given first priority, but because "the essential blind navigation and bombing equipment would not be available in time, there was no point in completing the special nose for the H2S scanner" so "the tactical version came ahead". As a result, it was intended to use the B.5/47 "in this Command for operational flying at great heights and speeds whilst we waited for the future four-engined types". While this "was admirable in every way", from that concept the Canberra had developed "from being not only a replacement for the light marker Mosquito (B.22) but latterly even as a replacement for the Main Force aircraft – and now, so it seems, to about two-thirds of the total planned main force[1]. I feel, therefore, it is as well to know what we are in for".

Adding that CAS was "aware of the magnificence of its speed, height and range", the AOC-in-C went on to point out that, navigationally, the Canberra's only aid was Gee – it was "a hostage to Gee cover", a comment which was remarkably percipient in view of what happened in the Suez operations of October 1956[2]. He added that it was possible "to

<hr>

[1] This was an accurate reflection of the policy described by CAS in a minute to S of S for Air in 1952 (see page 44) when he said that, in 1951–52, "the RAF were the only people (apart from the Americans) who could make any serious bomber contribution to Nato. The Valiant had not flown, but we placed a small order off the drawing-board. The only other bet was the Canberra, and we ordered as many as we could get to build up a first-line force . . . in the UK . . . for the support of SHAPE".

[2] See Chapter X.

go beyond Gee cover by DR and visual fixes", though "above the overcast and at altitude at night" this would "not be worth very much". The navigator could only get fixes "by leaving his seat, divesting himself of all his equipment and . . . crawling through an exceedingly small tunnel into the prone position" – a journey which was "so exhausting" that some navigators had been "unable to get out when in" and had had to be "hauled out by their feet".

Commenting that there was "no planned blind-bombing method" for the B.2, the AOC in C concluded his Personal and Top Secret letter to CAS[1] by pointing out what he considered to be "the grave risks . . . being taken in replacing the Lincoln as a main force aeroplane with the Canberra", which was "too ill-equipped at present to perform its task".

---

[1] Air 8/1518 file.

The Aircraft

All photographs are Crown Copyright

English Electric Canberras were Bomber Command's first jet aircraft - precursors of the V-bombers. This B.2 of No 9 Sqn shows the type's manoeuvrability

Graceful lines characterised the Canberra: a B.2 of No 12 Sqn

Aerobatic bombers: the No 231 OCU team of four T.4s in 1956, led by Sqn Ldr F P Walker

Vickers Valiant, first of the V-bombers: a plan view showing compound sweepback of the wing leading edge

Another view of the Valiant, showing shoulder-high wing and tailplane mounted halfway up the fin. In white anti-flash paint, this No 49 Sqn aircraft had been specially modified for the Operation Grapple series of megaton weapon trials flown from Christmas Island during 1957–58

A Valiant of No 214 Sqn at Marham being towed past Bloodhound SAMs, deployed for low-level defence of the V-bomber airfields

Enter the Avro Vulcan: B.1s of No 230 OCU at Waddington, with Canberras (training aid for the V-force) in the background

Vulcan B.1 at take-off, with another behind it on the runway and a third taxying

Vulcan B.1
airborne, showing
its delta-wing
planform

Head-on aspect of the Vulcan, which had "virtually no fuselage"

Vulcan underside view, showing the heat flaking on the jet pipes, the huge wing area and the size of the bomb-bay

Four Vulcan B.2s on an ORP (operational readiness platform), one of the features of the QRA policy

Low-level camouflage: Vulcan B.2 XM647 of the Akrotiri Strike Wing (Nos 9 and 35 Sqns) over Cyprus in 1969

Crescent-winged V-bomber with a high-set tailplane: the Handley Page Victor B.1

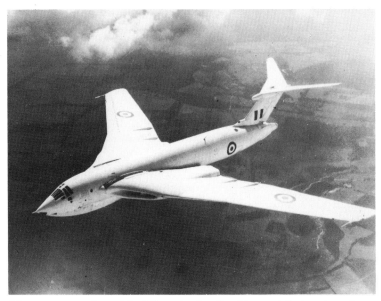

Three-quarter view of the Victor in the all-white anti-flash paint scheme

On the climb: Victor B.1 of No XV Sqn

Camouflaged Victor K.2 XL513 of No 55 Sqn on the ORP, with four
white Vulcans in the background

Victor B.2 of No 139 (Jamaica) Sqn armed with an Avro Blue Steel
stand-off bomb

CHAPTER IV

PLANS FOR THE MEDIUM BOMBER FORCE

The Statement on Defence 1954, published on 18 February[1], had said: "the primary deterrent...remains the atomic bomb and the ability of the highly organised and trained United States strategic air power to use it. From our past experience and current knowledge we have a significant contribution to make both to the technical and to the tactical development of strategic air power. We intend as soon as possible to build up in the Royal Air Force a force of medium bombers capable of using the atomic weapon to the fullest effect"[2].

The statement went on to emphasise the importance of the part the RAF had to play in current defence policy, saying that "the Air Force has the major deterrent role". In referring to the production of atomic weapons in the UK and delivery to the forces, it said that much attention had been paid during the past year in the UK and in Nato to the problems of tactics and training which the advent of new weapons would create, and to their effect upon the size and shape of the forces, adding: "With all these considerations in mind, the Government have concluded that a gradual change should be brought about in the direction and balance of our defence effort. Still greater emphasis will have to be placed on the Royal Air Force because of the need to build up a strategic bomber force and because of the importance of guided missiles in air defence".

The importance which the RAF attached to the creation of the medium bomber force was made clear when the Air Council considered the implications of setting it up. During November 1954, at two meetings, the Council considered a paper by the VCAS (Air Chf Mshl Sir Ronald Ivelaw-Chapman) in which he said: "one thing that is clear in all the uncertainties about our strategy is the overriding importance of the medium bomber force. In peace it is the force which can provide the necessary power behind our voice in international affairs and in war it is the one force with which we could strike a worthwhile blow against our enemies. It can fill neither of these roles unless and until it is highly efficient. It is well worth our while therefore to make sacrifices in other fields in the interest of this force.

"All experience, including the experience of the US Strategic Air

---

[1] Cmd 9075.

[2] The V-bombers also had a conventional bombing capability. In a Directorate-General of Engineering report on Valiant Aircraft – Bombing-up and Armament Acceptance (in AMSO's Quarterly Liaison Report No 33 – Quarter ending 31 Dec 54) reference was made to "a bombing-up demonstration . . . held at Wisley in October 1954 during which alternative loads of (a) 21 x 1,000lb MC Mk 6 bombs, (b) one x 10,000lb HC bomb and (c) ten x 2,000lb A Mk 9 mines were loaded into a Valiant bomb-bay. . . ." The Memorandum accompanying the 1959–60 Air Estimates (Cmd 673) said that "it is not only in the nuclear role that the V-bombers are so valuable. If need be they can be used, together with other aircraft of Bomber Command, to deliver a very heavy weight of conventional bombs. . . ."

Command, shows that to bring the efficiency of a force of this sort to the standard necessary will need a very great deal of effort and will take time. The Americans have brought their Strategic Air Command to a high pitch of efficiency, but only after several years[1], during which they have lavished upon it massive human and material resources. Unless we take special measures we shall not get value from the capital we are spending. We certainly shall not achieve our object of having a force which commands the respect of our friends and our potential enemies."

VCAS outlined several areas in which a maximum effort of organisation was required – personnel, particularly in the selection of commanding officers for stations and squadrons; equipment – in the sense of supporting hardware being introduced for the aircraft for which it was required, and the proper phasing of ground and bomb-handling equipment and vehicles, etc, and spares; and works services, particularly for the Class 1 airfield programme. He commented: "we have become used (as our experience with the Canberra force, for example, shows) to a situation in which units do not get all they need for operating efficiency until some years after a type has been introduced", adding: "We cannot afford this with the medium bombers"[2]. He recommended that the officers particularly concerned – the Air Members for Personnel and for Supply and Organisation, and the Controller of Aircraft – should report on the specific measures they thought should be taken to ensure the efficiency of the medium bomber force.

In its discussions on this force during 1954, the Air Council agreed that special measures would be necessary for its creation and that the progress of its development should be specially watched. For this purpose the normal machinery provided by the Expansion and Re-equipment Policy Committee, the Air Council Standing Committee and the Council itself should be used.

The Chief of the Air Staff (Air Chf Mshl Sir William Dickson) expressed the view that everything should be done short of giving a special priority to the medium bomber force, but that any explicit declaration of such an intention should be avoided. In agreeing with this, VCAS said that the importance of the force had been stressed in the Defence White paper and it would soon become clear to the Service, without any declaration in so many words by the Air Council, that special attention was being given to it. The Secretary of State (Lord de L'Isle and Dudley VC) felt that it was impossible for the council to decide whether or not to give special priority to the medium bomber

---

[1] Strategic Air Command had been established on 21 March 1946 as one of the three major combat commands of the US Army Air Forces (see the booklet *Development of Strategic Air Command 1946–1976*, dated 21 March 1976 and published by the Office of the Historian, HQ Strategic Air Command. See also *The History of the US Air Force*, by David A Anderton (Crescent Books, New York, 1981), pp 135ff.).

[2] However, it did occur in the case of the Valiants; see subsequent chapter on the Suez operation.

force until it had had an opportunity to consider the specialised reports from the members responsible. But he thought that the principle to adopt was one under which staffs at all levels concerned with work directly or indirectly connected with the force should give their first attention to matters concerning it, subject to this causing the minimum of distraction from their other tasks. It would probably be as well for the council to avoid making any statement of policy: they should let their actions speak for themselves.

The sort of problems the council considered in 1954, and asked for reports upon, were those of personnel – getting the right men in the right place; for example, first-class Group AOCs should be chosen and effective teams built up under them – and training, particularly the matter of keeping aircrew together for a considerable length of time without disruption by postings for any reason, including promotion. As far as groundcrew were concerned a great deal had already been done, in co-operation with Bomber Command, towards screening technical ground staff. On this point, CAS stressed that the council "should be quite clear that they were concentrating on the medium bomber force and not on Bomber Command as a whole".

As far as equipment was concerned, the council considered that extraordinary measures – particularly in the provision of spares, for example – and "extraordinarily expensive measures" should not be considered unless the situation itself became extraordinary.

In his paper, VCAS said that although Government approval had been given only for an establishment of 144 medium bombers plus 16 PR aircraft, and a firm decision on the total numbers to be purchased was not expected in the immediate future, the Air Staff must continue to plan for the size of force outlined in Plan "K". This was a revised plan for strengthening the RAF, superseding Plan "H" of 1952; it was aimed at preserving the spirit and ideas of the "global strategy" concept[1] despite cuts in defence expenditure. Under it, the Air Staff hoped there would be 200 medium bombers by the end of 1957 and that they would ultimately reach a strength of 240[2].

Referring to equipment, VCAS said that Treasury approval had been given[3] for the purchase of 229 aircraft, including both bomber and PR versions, 115 of them – 90 bombers and 25 PR versions – being Valiants. Any reduction in final size of the planned force of 240 aircraft would mean that it would contain a higher proportion of Valiants, which had a poorer performance than the Vulcans and Victors. He said that all three types had suffered from development troubles, and there would also be

---

[1] The Chiefs of Staff Report on Defence Policy and Global Strategy (Annex to COS(52)361), approved by the Cabinet Defence Committee on 9 July 1952, had propounded the doctrine of nuclear deterrence.

[2] A total never in fact achieved, as will be shown.

[3] On 9 Sep 1954 the Chancellor of the Exchequer (Mr R A Butler) had agreed to the placing of orders for a further 32 Vulcans and 32 Victors (Medium Bombers – Future Requirements (ID3/942/9 Pt 1)). 25 of each type had already been ordered.

delays in production of some items of equipment, such as the NBC (navigation and bombing computer) Mk 2/H2S Mk 9, Red Garter tail-warning device, autostabiliser and autopilot, VSA (visual sighting attachment) and radio countermeasures equipment. With one or two exceptions, like test gear for the NBC/H2S, the provision of ground equipment for the medium bombers was satisfactory.

VCAS expressed some reservations about the supply of bombs; he said that by January 1955 the Valiant would be cleared to carry "only the 10,000lb HC, the 1,000lb MC[1] and 100lb practice bombs", and of these only the last-named would be available. The 10,000lb MC bomb[2] which the Valiant would be cleared to carry by the same date was "far from ideal in its present form" and had "many undesirable features"; it should be transportable over any distance by surface and air[3] and be able to remain on an aircraft for at least 48 hours without inspection.

He also expressed concern about the provision of synthetic operational flight trainers; the Service had little experience of the use of them, but the "vastly increased capital and operating costs of new types of aircraft" made them an obvious requirement. They were expensive – approximately £150,000 each. Three Valiant OFTs had been ordered but were a long way behind scheduled delivery; the prototype was expected to be installed at Gaydon by the end of February 1955 and a further three to six months would be required for initial adjustments and for training instructors. Prototype Vulcan and Victor OFTs had been ordered[4].

Complaining of a lack of effort and insufficient priority, VCAS said that the medium bomber force had been accepted by the Chiefs of Staff as the "primary weapon in the national armoury", but it had not been accorded the necessary priority to enable it to reach an efficient operational state as quickly as it could. Many of the delays in design and development of items of aircraft equipment could "presumably be avoided if sufficient effort were devoted to them"; there was a shortage of scientific personnel and money for R&D.

Referring to the high standards set by Bomber Command for aircrew – particularly pilots and bomb-aimers – in the MBF, VCAS commented that the pilot requirement could be met initially by taking the best pilots already in the command; later, calls would have to be made on other commands. As for bomb-aimers, 75 navigators who were bomb-aimers had been selected for the MBF; all had previous experience of H2S, and from their number the instructors would have to be drawn. The balance would have to be made up as far as possible from bomb-aimers

---

[1] High capacity and medium capacity.
[2] *ie* Blue Danube.
[3] OR1001 had specified "use in any part of the world".
[4] HQ Bomber Command informed HQ 3 Group on 11 Dec 1953 (BC/S.85837/Trg) that the synthetic trainer establishment for Gaydon would be one Valiant OFT Mk 1, two Link Trainers Type D4 Mk 2 (Jet), one H2S Mk 9/NBC Mk2 Trainer Type 418, two Gee-H Trainers Type 99A, one AMBT Mk 5 and one DR trainer Mk 3.

who had completed a tour on Canberras. Provision and training of navigators should not be a formidable problem, he said; it was planned to take them as far as possible from the Canberra force. Radio officers, responsible for the aircraft electrical systems, RCM and communications, were a new category; a scheme for the provision of suitable personnel was required[1].

If the MBF were to be really efficient, stability of aircrew postings was essential, VCAS considered. It had been proposed that "combat" and "select" crews should do $5\frac{1}{4}$- and $7\frac{1}{4}$-year tours respectively, the length of these tours easing the training commitment and raising the standard in the Command; the subject was currently being examined. He thought that the highest state of morale should prevail in the MBF, as training would be hard, domestic problems sometimes acute and tour lengths long. Some way should be found of bringing home to the public the fact that Bomber Command had fought the Second World War continuously from start to finish, and by so doing to restore the spirit of prestige and greatness in the Command. Referring to groundcrew, he considered that there would be no major difficulties apart from the Service-wide shortage of some skilled trades; the complexity of some of the equipment in the medium bombers would demand a very high standard of ability and training among the tradesmen.

While the original plans for the MBF envisaged its operating from ten Class 1 airfields, the development of the Soviet long-range air force, rapid increases in the power of atomic weapons and the fact that the initiative was certain to lie with the Russians had made it obvious that the force was extremely vulnerable to surprise attack – so dispersal was essential[2], and that raised a series of problems, such as the availability of suitable airfields, the facilities and servicing to be provided at them, and the possible use of overseas bases.

Other problems outlined by VCAS were the protection of the MBF by countermeasures, should it be called upon to operate by day; the possible production of unmanned "spoof" aircraft; and whether the V-bombers should be equipped with wing nacelles, at about £40,000 per pair, to increase their conventional bomb-carrying capacity. He also expressed concern about delays in development of the MBF, because no special machinery had been set up to ensure progress. Much preliminary work remained to be done to provide a sound foundation.

That was the situation as reported upon towards the end of 1954, and the points made by VCAS form an instructive basis for comparison with the first V-force summary of progress[3], a copy of which was sent to CAS

[1] An entirely new groundcrew trade, Aircraft Servicing Chief, was introduced in the V-force; he was responsible for the operational serviceability of a particular aircraft.

[2] "With the deployment of the first V-bomber squadron at Wittering during July, urgent attention is being directed towards drawing up detailed plans for the dispersal of the Medium Bomber Force in war, or during times of international tension (AMSO Qtly Liaison Report No 36 – Quarter ending 30 Sep 55 – A232030/55).

[3] A Review of the 'V' Force – BC/TS 84435, 7 Mch 55, referred to in the Introduction.

by the AOC in C Bomber Command (Air Mshl Sir George Mills) on 15 March 1955. "Broadly speaking", he commented, "the report shows that, within the limits set by the late arrival of the aircraft and of essential equipment like NBC, all concerned are getting together well in starting training and in the build-up itself".

At the time of this report the V-force, which got its name from a remark made by the CAS (MRAF Sir John Slessor) in 1952[1], had two Valiant B.1s at Gaydon and a small stock of atomic bombs at Wittering. By mid-March 1955, six of the 12 Class 1 airfields[2] from which it was to operate were virtually complete; these were Gaydon, Wittering, Wyton, Marham, Honington and Waddington, and the aim was to have the remaining six[3] available by the end of 1957. Aircrew training had begun at No 232 OCU, Gaydon, where first Valiant and then Victor crews would be trained. Preparations were being made to convert the first Vulcan squadron and to form the Vulcan OCU at Waddington.

Referring to aircrew requirements, the report said that the successful manning of the MBF depended to a great extent on the willingness of the Air Ministry to direct the best flying officers in the RAF to it. An uninterrupted tour of five years in V-bomber squadrons was mandatory, though a clear policy on this had yet to be stated. The Canberra OCU (No 231, at Bassingbourn) would "indirectly bear the brunt of V-force crew training". All its pilots must have Canberra experience and must therefore complete the OCU course; disbandment of Canberra squadrons had to be "slotted in" with the build-up of MB squadrons; ". . . a great deal of latitude is required", the report commented, "in overbearing establishments by ranks in both Canberra and V-bomber squadrons. The disbandment of Canberra squadrons must be coincident with the peak requirements of the V-force". There was an urgent need for training aircraft equipped with NBS; bomb-aimers and navigators would require at least 100 hours' experience with this equipment before they were operationally proficient and reliable – training on H2S in Lincolns alone was not enough.

NBS components, the report commented, noting that early Valiant squadrons would "suffer from delays in production and Service clearance of airborne equipment", would not be available until early 1956. The first squadron, already formed[4], was "unable to use Green Satin, NBS, ILS or the radio equipment for one of the above reasons". RCM/ECM would not be available in effective strength before 1959, with the exception of Window launchers, already being fitted; the forecast date for delivery and fitting of RATOG (rocket-assisted take-off gear), the use of which had been emphasised by the decision to operate from

[1] When names for the B.35/46 were being discussed by the Air Council (AC64 (52)) CAS said that his own inclination was "to establish, so to speak, a 'V' class of medium jet bombers".
[2] An increase on the ten originally proposed.
[3] Coningsby, Finningley, Cottesmore, Scampton, Bassingbourn and Watton.
[4] No 138.

dispersed airfields[1], was the end of the first quarter of 1956.

Omitting no detail of requirements for V-force operations ("we have tried to gather together all the salient points into one document", the AOC in C said in his covering letter to the CAS), the review went on to refer to the setting-up of electronics centres, where NBS equipment would be serviced, and which would not be ready to service a full squadron until early in 1956; to the "present opinion of MBF strategy" that each aircraft was to be considered as an atomic weapon carrier, and that therefore production should be adequate to allow maximum effort for the first and second strikes; to the need for approach aids in both directions to the main runway – at present the force was committed to the use of ILS in an east–west direction only; to the establishment of aircrew leaders; and to the "serious thought" that had to be given to Bomber Command reorganisation to ensure that the operational force could be effectively controlled at all times – particularly when dispersed.

Referring to operational planning and tactics, the review said that a study of suitable strategic targets was being made; this would not be complete until agreement had been reached to integrate target planning with Strategic Air Command of the USAF[2]. Target material and briefing procedures were being prepared; crews would be allotted targets in advance and the bulk of their training would be devoted to procedures for attacks on these. As for the tactics to be employed, these were dictated by the rigid flight profile of the aircraft and had to be pre-planned; there might be limited tactical routeing for the Vulcan and Victor, but the Valiant's radius of action allowed practically no flexibility. For self-protection over "the vast expanse of enemy territory" the force had to depend on RCM/ECM. Trials of V-bombers and fighters were planned for the latter half of 1955, to determine the most effective defensive manoeuvres to be used with tail-warning devices. Problems of recovery on return from operations were also being studied; these were extremely complex, including rapid let-down and landing arrangements, which had to be flexible to permit diversions in the event of enemy attack on home bases.

Other aspects of operations being considered were overseas commitments, which it was thought that Valiants could fulfil more suitably than Canberras; anti-shipping strikes, which V-force aircraft could be used for with Green Cheese[3] as a weapon against surface craft, or with their radar reconnaissance capability employed for search, location and identification; and minelaying – though there was no weapon which could be dropped accurately from normal medium-bomber heights and speeds.

---

[1] See map.

[2] Talks between the RAF and USAF on integrated atomic operations were initially held at the Air Ministry on 15 June 1955.

[3] A special anti-ship weapon under development. It was a joint Air Ministry/Admiralty project for a 4,000lb fully active homing bomb based on a Red Dean head and a Blue Boar body (ref ID3/946/6 Development and Production of Anti-Ship Weapon – "Green Cheese").

In his covering letter of 15 March 1955 to CAS, the AOC in C Bomber Command said that there were two important subjects which "overshadowed everything": one was dispersal; and the other, training of air and ground crews. On the former, he said that the Command hoped to submit a plan setting-out requirements up to 1957/58; this was based on a maximum holding of "four atom carriers on one airfield", but he regarded this as too many – "we look on the plan as the basis for getting down to pairs at the most". Extremely wide dispersal was a "must" and could not be limited by financial or establishment constraints; if need be, a token £10m or £20m must be asked for in advance of detailed estimates[1].

As to air and ground crew training, the AOC in C wanted it to be set out as firm policy that aircrew and ground crew must remain in the V-force for at least five years or possibly more. "We cannot", he said, "afford any of the usual drain away because people are promoted and wanted for overseas or for staff colleges...If we heed these calls we will not build up and what we do get will not be efficient". He expressed the view that the summary of the Review "might form the basis for an ERP (Expansion and Re-equipment Policy) Committee[2] meeting to discuss progress, which I think might be useful before long".

That such a development indeed occurred was confirmed by a Note to the Air Council dated 3 June 1955 by VCAS on Deployment of the V-bomber Force[3], in which he said at the outset that "the ERP Committee has been made responsible for progressing the development of the V-bomber force". While, therefore, not proposing to report to the Council about all the questions which came before the committee, he sought endorsement of a number of the more important decisions it had taken – relating to dispersal of the force. He invited the Council to agree that deployment in a period of tension should provide for dispersal over ten Class 1 airfields and 45 other airfields, and to endorse the committee's decision that planning for the force should proceed on the following assumptions: that the airfields needed a 2,000yd runway and LCN[4] of 40; that there would be three sorties by a diminishing force; and that there would be a period of tension, not exceeding 30 days, when the force would be deployed and ready to operate at 1½ hours' notice. Also, to approve these proposals as a basis for planning and long-term costing, and to agree that action to implement them should

---

[1] On 11 Nov 60 the Treasury approved estimates totalling £2.1m for works services at 36 Bomber Command dispersal airfields (2-DM126/127/06).

[2] Originally formed during the war and reviewed in 1950 (Air Council Standing Committee Conclusions 17(50), Para 14). Its terms of reference (ERP Committee – Constitution and Proceedings, ID3/90/4) were "to progress and co-ordinate action on the programme for increasing the fighting power of the Royal Air Force".

[3] AC(55)26.

[4] Load classification number. Another factor in dispersal plans was the support of other Commands: "The majority of Commands at Home will be called upon to provide basic deployment facilities for elements of the Force" (AMSO Quarterly Liaison Report No 36, Quarter ending 30 Sep 55).

proceed progressively to match the build-up of the force.

As far as synthetic training on the V-bombers was concerned, CAS asked whether a Valiant flight simulator was being considered. The Controller of Aircraft confirmed that it was in hand and that synthetic training plans were well advanced. On the matter of works – the problems involved in modifying airfields to appropriate standards, the question was asked whether the Council still thought that a minimum of ten V-bomber main bases would be wanted – excluding those necessary for the PR squadron and the OCU. The Council considered that ten represented the absolute minimum necessary if a medium bomber force as then conceived was to be able to operate at all.

S of S raised the question of dispersal. He thought that the V-bomber airfields would represent first priority targets for enemy attack, and posed the question as to whether the force was going to be concentrated at too few airfields. It would be an immense advantage, he thought, if it could operate – even accepting certain limitations – from airfields other than those designed for the V-bombers. CAS pointed out that length of runway was not the only consideration to be taken into account in dispersal airfields; runway strength and the existence of refuelling facilities were also relevant. Plans for dispersal airfields, bearing in mind the additional expenditure involved, were to be considered and any proposals clarified. One further point made, by the Air Member for Supply and Organisation (up to 30 April 1954 Air Chf Mshl Sir John Whitworth Jones, succeeded by Air Mshl Sir Donald Hardman), was that changes in the forecast all-up operating weight of the V-bombers had recently come to his notice: these might well mean reconsideration of airfield plans and a great deal of additional expense.

It is interesting to note that, at this stage, dispersal of the V-force, which later became an integral part of its operations, was considered as something additional to the ten designated Class 1 airfields. The importance of dispersal was stressed by the AOC in C Bomber Command (AM Sir George Mills) when he wrote to CAS (MRAF Sir William Dickson) on 15 March 1955 forwarding a copy of *A Review of the 'V' Force*. "I am more than ever convinced", he said, "that we can never be a true deterrent force until we can really disperse. Nor can we wait until our build-up is nearing completion; we must match our dispersal plans to our build-up. . .".

When the Air Council considered these V-force deployment proposals at its meeting on 23 June 1955[1] it agreed that plans should provide for dispersal in a period of tension over ten Class 1 and 45 other airfields in the UK, subject to two conditions: a review of the number of dispersal airfields in the light of later information about the ultimate size of the force; and the development of the dispersal plan being geared to the build-up of the force. It also endorsed the ERP Committee decision that

---

[1] Air Council Conclusions 11(55) (Special).

planning should proceed on four assumptions: that dispersal airfields required "extensible" 2,000yd runways; that subject to further discussions, these airfields should provide for LCN 40; that there would be three sorties by a diminishing force; and that, subject to review, there would be a period of tension not exceeding 30 days during which the force would be deployed and ready to operate at 1½ hours' notice. The Council also agreed that planning should provide for the deployment being completed within 72 hours, and – subject to points made in discussion – approved the proposals put forward by VCAS as a basis for costing and long-term planning.

Thus dispersal became an integral part of plans for the MBF from its inception; as VCAS had said in his Note on deployment, "the V-bomber force is being built up primarily as a deterrent and one of the main objects of the deployment plan is to ensure that the enemy realises that the Force cannot be wiped out by ten bombs on ten Class 1 airfields". The Air Council did not disagree with this principle; the question was, how many dispersed airfields would be required; and the ultimate number depended on two factors – the final size of the force[1] and the cost of its dispersal[2] in relation to overall expenditure on the RAF. As the S of S for Air (Lord De L'Isle and Dudley VC) said during the Air Council discussion, it was necessary "to weigh the risk that too lavish an expenditure on the dispersal of the V-bomber force might reduce our ability to spend money in other highly necessary and important directions".

In fact, the overall cost of the V-force – its aircraft, weapons, training, support equipment, airfields[3] and dispersal – was to be a major, and sometimes controversial, element in British defence policy during the 1950s and '60s.

Writing of the potential tasks of the V-bomber force, the Secretary of State for Air said in 1955[4]:–

"The strategic air offensive must be an Anglo-American operation. The role of the V-bomber force will be to join with the USAF Strategic Air Command in (i) striking immediately and in overwhelming strength at the arteries of Russian life – her centres of Government, production and communications; (ii) limiting the Russian nuclear offensive by

---

[1] At that time a force of 240 V-bombers was envisaged; but under the revised Plan K (Star) Government approval had so far been given for a front-line UE of 144 medium bombers (Air Council Conclusions 3(55) – 3 Feb 1955).

[2] The VCAS Note quoted the costs of a Bomber Command dispersal scheme as £25m and of an ERP Committee scheme as £19m.

[3] On 2 Apr 54 the Treasury approved an estimate of £982,000 to bring Marham up to Medium Bomber standard, this expenditure including hardstandings, domestic and technical facilities (£528,000), bomb stores (£290,000), approach lighting (£10,000) and an HF/DF station (£998) (A 42992/50, Pt II Marham, Bomber Command (VHB) Works Services). An additional bulk fuel installation (to bring storage capacity up to 504,000 gal) was to cost £138,000 and a pressure refuelling system £122,000.

[4] Letter to the Minister of Defence (Harold Macmillan) on 23 March 1955, covering a paper on the size of the V-bomber force (Defence Review – Medium Bomber Force Private Office No 1922 Pt V).

destroying her airfields and nuclear potential; (iii) reducing the sea power of the enemy at source and supporting the war at sea; (iv) acting in support of the Allied front in Europe and the Middle East. The force must be capable of surviving a surprise attack and of penetrating the Russian defences."

Referring specifically to the offensive against airfields, S of S said that there were about 150 in the Soviet Union and her satellites from which nuclear attacks could be launched against the United Kingdom. "The primary objective of the British bomber force", he concluded in the summary of his paper, "must be the airfields from which nuclear attack on this country can be launched. In the face of the thermonuclear threat[1] the destruction of these airfields must be immediate. It must be our aim to achieve this in the first sortie." Looking to a future situation, he added: "When the threat of a ballistic rocket develops, the only effective counter will be an immediate and overwhelming attack upon the internal organisation of Russia; and unless by then we have developed our own ballistic rockets in sufficient numbers and with sufficient range, bombers will still be required."

It was against this strategic background, and its operational implications, that S of S concluded that a force of 240 medium bombers was "the minimum required", and made a recommendation to that effect to the Minister of Defence.

---

[1] From 1954 onwards.

CHAPTER V

THE UK POLITICAL BACKGROUND, 1947–1955

The years during which the V-bombers and their weapons were under development, 1947–1955, were marked by great difficulties for Britain in both home and international affairs. So much so that it is remarkable that such a big military undertaking as the creation of the V-force should have been carried through with such steady determination to a successful conclusion – because the possession of an independent nuclear deterrent capability was a cornerstone of British post-war defence policy.

The difficulties, both economic and political, arose directly from the Second World War. On the one hand, more than five-and-a-half years' sustained conflict had left Britain's economy in a debilitated state; on the other, the war had seen the rise of the Soviet Union to World Power status and her advance into Europe. Both these factors combined harshly in the post-war years, when the economy needed to recuperate under peaceful conditions; for instead, new strains were placed upon it by dangerous international circumstances – the threat of a third world war was never far away in the late 1940s/early 1950s. It was a case, for Britain, of 'Qui desiderat pacem, praeparet bellum'[1] – certainly from 1948 onwards, after the formation of the Western Union defensive alliance; and this saying, in fact, could aptly summarise the philosophy behind the creation of the V-force.

Economic difficulties were reflected in the continuance of wartime restrictions and regulations, like the rationing of some foods and of petrol; in fact, an 'austerity plan' was announced by the Prime Minister (C R Attlee) in August 1947. There was a fuel crisis in January of that year, during an exceptionally cold winter; and for young men of military age there was conscription, under the National Service Act of July 1947. In fact, many of the things which people longed for with the successful conclusion of the war – freedom from authority, unrestricted supplies of food and fuel, the ability to live in an individual and unregulated way, and security of existence – had not come to pass. Life at home was hard and difficult, and there were dark clouds on the international horizon. The wartime Allies, having defeated one major enemy in Europe, now faced another one of greater potential and even more sinister character, armed with more terrible weapons; for to the ambitions and intransigence of the Soviet Union in the post-war world had to be added her possession of nuclear capability from 1949 onwards, and between then and 1955 both the USA and USSR advanced into the thermonuclear weapon era.

The other major political factor in these years was the return of the

---

[1] Flavius Vegetius Renatus (c AD 386), *De Re Militari*. Alternatively, 'Si vis pacem, para bellum'.

United States to Europe – unlike after the First World War, when following the Versailles Treaty she withdrew into isolation. In the post-Second World War period, however, the circumstances were quite different; the emergence of the Soviet Union as one of the victor nations was allied to her ambitions as the leading Communist Power, ambitions which were strengthened by the foothold she had gained in countries of Eastern Europe never before subjected to Communism. It was not therefore surprising that, with all to gain and nothing to lose, the Soviet Union under Marshal Stalin proved an intractable 'ally' when the drafting of peace treaties was discussed with the three Western Powers, Britain, France and the United States. Even as early as 1947 the peacetime gulf which had opened up between the wartime allies was all too evident. "For all practical purposes the Moscow conference of 1947 [to discuss the drafting of peace treaties] marked the end of post-war co-operation between Russia and the democratic countries", wrote Lord Ismay in his history of Nato[1]. The United States, by the promulgation of the Truman Doctrine and initiation of the Marshall Plan in that year – the former pledging support for peoples resisting subjugation and the latter offering economic aid to war-shattered European countries, widened rather than narrowed the rift between Communist and democratic ideologies by these imaginative and humanitarian measures. When Poland, for example, reacted enthusi-astically to the idea of Marshall Aid she was quickly pulled back into line by the USSR and her representatives forbidden to participate in the Paris conference on the Plan. The "iron curtain" which Winston Churchill referred to in the previous year[2] had been effectively pulled down between western and eastern Europe.

The original dependence on American nuclear deterrence, and the need for Western Europe to combine in self-defence, were emphasised by Lord Ismay. During 1947 (he wrote)

"the danger to the Western democracies was not only economic. Russia had paralysed the work of the United Nations Security Council by the abuse of her power of veto. She had armed forces amounting to some $4\frac{1}{2}$ million men on a war footing and equipped, for the most part, with the latest weapons. In addition, she was engaged on organising the armies of her satellites on Soviet lines, despite the fact that to re-arm Roumania, Bulgaria and Hungary was a direct violation of the Peace Treaties signed with those three countries in 1947. Finally, the Soviet armament industries were working at high pressure.

"In face of this threat, the armed forces of the West were weak, unco-ordinated, and drastically short of modern equipment. There was, in fact, nothing – except America's possession of the atomic bomb

---

[1] *Nato: The First Five Years 1949–54.*
[2] In a speech at Westminster College, Fulton, Missouri, on 5 March 1946 when the ex Prime Minister said that "from Stettin in the Baltic to Trieste in the Adriatic, an iron curtain has descended across the Continent…".

– to deter the Soviet from over-running Western Europe. The only hope of beginning to restore the balance of power lay in the free European countries combining together, not only for the sake of economic recovery, but also for the defence of their hearths and homes"[1].

Worse was to come, for 1948 saw open confrontation between the Soviet Union and the Western Powers, with the Communist take-over in Czechoslovakia and the Russians' closure of Berlin to traffic from the West. In the face of these events the countries of Western Europe retaliated with the Western Union Treaty, binding them into a five-power defensive alliance (Belgium, Britain, France, The Netherlands and Luxembourg)[2] which formed the basis of Nato; and, even more dramatically, with the Berlin Airlift – which brought the United States back into active military participation in Europe, for the transport aircraft deployed for it were supported by F-80s in Germany and by B-29s, based in Germany and the United Kingdom as a deterrent force.

It is pleasant to record that, in those cheerless days of the Cold War, when the Berlin Airlift was in full swing to keep the beleagured city supplied, when Palestine was becoming a crisis area for Britain, when the Malayan Emergency occurred, when a State of Emergency had been declared in Britain itself because of a dockers' strike, and when USAF bombers were back on English soil as they had been only a few years previously in the strategic offensive against Germany, that – amidst "wars and rumours of wars" – the first post-war Olympic Games should have been held in London, symbolising reassurance in the present and faith for the future.

The immediate future, however, saw little respite from the tense international situation – rather, a drawing of demarcation lines between East and West with the formation of Nato and the Warsaw Pact; a beginning of nuclear rivalry between the USA and USSR; and the threat of world – or even nuclear – conflict through the escalation of the Korean War, the first conflict to involve the still-new United Nations Organisation.

The North Atlantic Treaty Organisation effectively came into force on 24 August 1949, following signature of the Treaty in Washington on 4 April. Its first Council meeting was held there on 17 September, but of more significance to Britain was its Council meeting in Brussels a year later (on 15 September 1950) which resulted in the biggest-ever UK peacetime defence programme – costing £3,600 million over three years, a figure later increased to £4,700 million. Later, meeting in New York, the Council decided that an integrated force should be created for the defence of Nato European countries, to be placed under a Supreme Commander appointed by Nato. That decision was implemented when,

---

[1] "In December 1947...Ernest Bevin decided to seek a military relationship with Western Europe that would eventually include the United States" (*Defense of the Realm: British Strategy in the Nuclear Epoch*, by R N Rosecrance; Columbia University Press, 1968).
[2] The Brussels Treaty, 17 March 1948.

on 19 December 1950, General Eisenhower was appointed Nato Supreme Commander. At the same time, the Council took the first steps to bring about West German participation in Nato. After only four years, General Eisenhower was back in Europe heading the military forces of the Western Allies; but unlike the 1944 situation, the enemy of those days was becoming an ally and the former ally in the East was officially designated an enemy. This Nato framework was to set the pattern for British military defence planning for future years, as were the SEATO and Baghdad Pact treaties, entered into respectively in July 1954 and March 1955.

Behind these defensive alliances lay the great shadow of nuclear rivalry between the United States and the Soviet Union, which by 1953 had progressed to thermonuclear dimensions. The first Soviet atomic explosion, near Semipalatinsk on 29 August 1949, was significant not only as a scientific achievement but also as ending the American monopoly of nuclear knowledge.

When the United States decided to proceed to the production of hydrogen bombs[1], and exploded her first thermonuclear weapon experimentally at Eniwetok on 15 November 1952 – just six weeks after the first British atomic test in the Monte Bello islands, there may have been hopes of a new monopoly with this infinitely more powerful and devastating weapon. But the Soviet Union was not far behind, with her first thermonuclear detonation on 12 August 1953. And with the United States' thermonuclear weapon tests in the Marshall Islands in March 1954, the hydrogen bomb could be said to have entered the military inventory. Its advance, Winston Churchill told the Commons on 1 December 1954, "has fundamentally altered the entire problem of defence".

The nuclear background gave the Korean War, which started with the invasion of South Korea on 25 June 1950, a triply-significant importance. First, there was the significance of conflict between Communist and non-Communist forces; secondly, of possible war between China and the United States; thirdly, of the possibility of atomic bombs being used in war for the second time by the Americans – with the prospect of nuclear retaliation. Yet another significant feature of the war for the Western military world was the emergence of the Russian-built swept-wing MiG-15 fighters – only effectively countered by the American F-86A Sabres.

The Cold War, the Korean War, continuing operations in Malaya, a State of Emergency in Kenya, the British nuclear test and the American and Russian thermonuclear tests, the emergence of Nato and the Middle and Far East alliances, marked the early 1950s as times of crisis and sinister portent; and against this strategic background, with a

---

[1] Not without an agonising and terrible debate, for a brilliant account of which see *The Advisors: Oppenheimer, Teller and the Superbomb*, by Herbert York (W H Freeman & Co, San Francisco, 1976).

rearmament programme imposed upon an already weak economy, the new RAF bomber force – an important element in the Nato armoury – was steadily brought into being. "The creation of the British nuclear deterrent force", wrote the American historian Alfred Goldberg,

"required almost 15 years of effort and the expenditure of £1,000m. It resulted from a conjunction of military, technological, political, economic and psychological currents in 1952 that persuaded the Churchill Government, newly returned to power, to adopt the nuclear deterrent strategy and accept the consequences. The evolutionary span of 15 years falls into two periods of approximately equal length, with the year 1952 as the watershed between the two. During the first period – from 1945 to 1952 – the foundations of the nuclear deterrent force were laid and the basic decisions arrived at. The second period – from 1953 to 1960 – saw the production of nuclear and thermonuclear weapons and the V-bombers...."[1]

---

[1] Article in *International Affairs*, October 64 (Vol 40 No 4).

CHAPTER VI

THE INTRODUCTION OF ATOMIC BOMBS

The keynote of the Air Staff Requirement (OR1001) for the first British atomic bomb was simplicity. The Air Staff, said the second issue of the requirement (17 August 1948 – superseding the first of 9 August 1946), "are prepared to reconsider any of the military characteristics if by so doing simplicity of design, manufacture and maintenance can be achieved". Later, "the bomb must be designed for use in any part of the world by Service personnel who have been given adequate training in maintenance and assembly, and to this end must be made as simple as possible".

The weight of the weapon had been specified in the OR – it was not to exceed 10,000lb; its dimensions had also been specified – to fit into the aircraft bomb cell it was not to be more than 290in long and 60in in diameter (only on diameter was flexibility allowed – it could be, and in fact was, 62in)[1]; it had to be capable of being dropped at heights of between 20,000ft and 50,000ft and at speeds of between 150kt and 500kt; and because accommodation in the bomb cell was so tight it had to have flip-out fins – an entirely new feature.

Several working parties were involved in designing the non-atomic part of Blue Danube[2] – that is, the approximately 3,500lb worth of structure which was to enclose the nuclear sphere and carry it down to a target. One working party was concerned with installation in the aircraft, another with the fuse, another with handling and transportation, and another with the ballistic case and supporting structure. Long before the Monte Bello test, at a meeting on 11 May 1948, design of the ballistic casing was the subject of preliminary discussion – how to enclose a sphere of 57½in diameter and two cylinders, each about 3ft in diameter and 1ft long, weighing about 6,500lb in a casing giving good ballistic performance[3]. This design work was done by RAE Farnborough and a report by its Armament Development Division on 26 September 1950[4] referring to full-scale ballistic trials said that 11 ballistic models had been dropped, from altitudes of between 28,000ft and 35,000ft. These early dropping trials were done from a

---

[1] In a letter to Gp Capt C H B Bullock, DDOR2, on 2 Jul 51 Dr Penney wrote: "As you know, RAE and ourselves have recently examined the possibility of reducing the diameter of the Mk 1 bomb. It was found that even a small reduction in diameter – considerably less than 2in – would prove technically difficult and the advantages that would accrue from such a small reduction in diameter would be of doubtful value. It has therefore been decided that the diameter of the Mk 1 bomb will remain at 62in".

[2] Also referred to as Smallboy.

[3] Working Party "C", File No AF/CX 31/66.

[4] ARM.1775/F/SAH/98. When HER Working Party "C" held its first meeting at Fort Halstead on 28 Sep 50 and assembly of the bomb was discussed, Wg Cdr Rowlands said that it had to be possible to hold the ball during assembly and that one lens had to be removable for insertion of the inner component. Other Working Parties discussed Aircraft Installations ("A"), the Fuse ("F"), and Handling and Transportation ("H").

Lincoln[1]; the first dropping trials from a Valiant did not start until November 1954, after the first production weapons had been delivered to Bomber Command.

High explosive for the atomic bomb was manufactured by the Royal Ordnance Factory at Chorley in Lancashire, and HER placed a contract with Hunting Aircraft, who were to handle the explosive elements and assemble the sphere[2]. This was prior to the first ball being built, but the system had been determined. The company had two contracts, one with Woolwich (via Fort Halstead) and the other with RAE, and made the whole of the Blue Danube centre section. They did not themselves, however, handle explosives, but used inert replicas.

Royal Air Force planning for the introduction of atomic weapons had begun in 1948. On 14 June that year Lord Tedder told a Chiefs of Staff Committee meeting that he had received a suggestion from the Ministry of Supply that training should begin in the RAF on the handling and storage of atomic weapons. In its discussion, the committee agreed that the slight risk to the security of information involved in carrying out training under these two headings should be accepted, and agreed that the RAF should proceed with such training.

Subsequently, a committee was set up to discuss and decide upon all matters relating to the introduction of atomic weapons into the RAF. Known as the Herod Committee[3], it met under the chairmanship of VCAS and consisted of all the senior officers responsible for the use and handling of such weapons, like the C in C Bomber Command, DGMS, ACAS(Ops) and DGM, etc, plus AVM E D Davis from the Ministry of Supply, and its first meeting was held on 22 November 1948. At one of its subsequent meetings, when storage and explosive risks of atomic bombs were being discussed, the comparative risks were outlined of the component parts – HE charge, fissile material, urchin (a standard neutron source – so-called apparently because its shape resembled that of a sea-urchin), electronic components and fuse, and detonators. It was expected that the prototype weapon would be ready for test by midsummer 1952, and that the issue of bombs to the RAF would start in 1953[4], and one matter discussed by the committee at its first meeting was whether Lincolns could be modified to carry the A-bomb, should the B.9 (Valiant) not be in service when the first was delivered. The finding was that the Lincoln could be so modified[5], though it was not possible to give an answer to this question until the modifications necessary for

---

[1] Which were to be modified to carry atomic bombs operationally, should the V-bombers not be available.
[2] Author's interview with R P ("George") Pedley of Airwork (ex-Hunting Aircraft) on 22 Jan 74.
[3] This code name stood for "High Explosives Research Operational Distribution" (letter from AVM E D Davis to D of Weapons, 30 April 1951).
[4] Memorandum on RAF Assembly Teams for atomic weapons (undated).
[5] Minute from D of Wps to ACAS(Ops), 9 April 1951. Conversion of Washingtons for this purpose would have had to have been done in the US.

ballistic trials had been completed – in fact, until 1950, when notes on the modificaton necessary were circulated to Herod Committee members[1].

At its meeting on 24 January 1951 the committee agreed that planning for the accommodation of nuclear weapons should proceed in respect of Wittering and Marham[2]. Later that year, on 11 June, it made the important decision that in-flight insertion of the tube containing the fissile components and corresponding sections of the metallic and explosive layers (replacing the lens assembly procedure) should be an Air Staff requirement – for safety reasons[3].

In the two-day defence debate of 14–15 February 1951 the Opposition (in the person of its Leader, Winston Churchill) took the Government to task for its "inability . . . to produce any atomic bombs of our own in the five-and-a-half years which have passed since the war". The Prime Minister (Clement Attlee) retorted that it was "utterly untrue" to suggest that there had been a failure to develop the atomic bomb in Britain; there had been successful development[4].

During September 1951 the Air Staff was able to report confidently to the Secretary of State for Air on progress with plans for the introduction of atomic weapons into the RAF. Writing about what had been achieved, VCAS said[5] that Ministry of Supply development of a British atomic bomb was now nearing fruition; active steps were being taken to ensure that the RAF was in a position to accept the new weapons and employ them effectively. Project work was directed through the Herod Committee, whose membership was restricted to heads of sections of the staff directly involved from the Service point of view.

Referring to differences between the British and American bombs, VCAS said that as the bomb-bays of the British aircraft were larger than those of the US ones, a somewhat longer bomb had been designed. It would be more efficient ballistically than the American version; its intrinsic efficiency should be high, and its power greater than that of the bomb dropped on Nagasaki.[6] The policy was to use the new jet medium bombers, initially the B.9, for carrying the bomb – which was likely to be ready before the aircraft.

Under the aegis of the Herod Committee, plans were well advanced for storage of the weapons, for the design of the buildings required, for maintenance and for security; a training scheme was being developed to provide the numbers of personnel needed to handle the weapons from

---

[1] VCAS/154 of 24 July 1950.
[2] Minutes, CMS 1074/D of Wps.
[3] Minutes, ibid.
[4] Commons Hansard, 15 Feb 1951, Cols 630–631. On 31 Oct 51 a Conservative Government came into power.
[5] Draft Minute to S of S, through CAS, in Herod Committee Papers (AF/CMS 999/66 Part II).
[6] Also a plutonium bomb.

delivery to the RAF to their despatch on an operational mission. A training establishment was to be set up in Bomber Command, to start work in about March 1953, although a nucleus of Service personnel – including instructors – would be trained by the Ministry of Supply prior to that date, in fact at Fort Halstead from the beginning of 1953.

In November 1951 the Herod Committee considered two important matters, the location of the RAF Atomic Weapon School and aircrew training on atomic weapons. It was decided to locate the school at the first medium-bomber airfield where the weapons were to be stored, namely Wittering[1], and as this base eventually housed the first Valiant squadron (No 138) and before that the Valiant Trials Flight (No 1321), it could be described as the birthplace of what became the V-bomber force.

When the committee discussed aircrew training on atomic weapons, at a special meeting on 16 November 1951[2], they agreed on certain main principles – such as, that a practice bomb should be the same size as a real one, of the same weight and ballistic characteristics, and should incorporate in-flight loading; also that lead crews (as they were referred to)[3] should drop three practice bombs each year.

By the spring of 1952, plans for the introduction of atomic weapons into the RAF, with all their implications – transport, storage, handling, training and location – had been fully laid down: at a meeting of the Herod Committee on 29 April 1952, attended by Dr Penney (who had been invited by VCAS in August 1951 to attended Herod meetings and to see the committee's papers), all these aspects were discussed and also – with especial reference to his design and production knowledge – the questions of in-flight arming of weapons and their state of readiness (governed by the supply of initiators).

On 29 August 1952, Penney wrote to VCAS to advise him as to when the RAF might expect to receive its first atomic weapons. He said that assuming the Monte Bello explosion – now just over a month ahead – was successful, "we have then to prove fully airworthy (a) ballistic case, (b) radar fuze and contact fuzes, (c) firing circuits, (d) in-flight loading. The programme has been tight, not only on the weapon side, but also on the Valiant. It would be optimistic to assume that we shall have a completely proven weapon in service before mid-1954. This, however, does not mean that HER will not be handing over weapons to the RAF until then".

Expressing confidence in the capabilities of the Royal Air Force,

---

[1] Honington had originally been chosen as location for the Armament Training School, when it was planned to be the first station operating Valiants, but Wittering was subsequently chosen for both purposes (letter from DofO to DDO1, 9 Jan 1953).

[2] Minutes, D of Weapons, 21 November 1951.

[3] Referring to training after Valiants were introduced, Bomber Command said in July 1952 that it would be the aim to qualify all medium bomber crews as Lead Crews and to classify a limited number of specially selected crews as Senior Lead Crews or "A" Bomb Crews (letter from C in C to D of Wps on the subject of practice bombs: BC/TS81/AIR of 18 July 1952).

Penney commented:–

"My philosophy is that the RAF has handled aircraft for a long time, and can fly Valiants as soon as they come off the production line. But the RAF has not yet handled atomic weapons. Therefore, we must get some bombs to the RAF at the earliest possible moment, so that the handling and servicing can be practised and fully worked out. . . ."

Weapons delivered, Penney said, might well "be the same as those which are fully proved later on"; they would not need much modification. "The sort of modification which might have to be made is the cap of the cartridge. At the very worst, if the IFI[1] needs some modification, and if you have to use the first few bombs in 1954, you may have to load the cartridge just before take-off instead of in-flight loading."

Describing the work of the Herod Committee, the Director of Operations (B & Recce) wrote to DCAS on 15 January 1953 that it was "formed in 1948 for the explicit purpose of introducing the atomic bomb into the service and examining all associated training, personnel, equipment, storage and works problems". He said that, in addition to AVM Davis of the Ministry of Supply, Dr Penney or his representatives usually attended meetings; and that the scope of the committee's work could be judged from the items that it had considered: selection of Bomber Command airfields as A-bomber bases; determination of the type of storage, both at airfields and at depots; phasing of the production of weapons with aircraft availability; training of ground personnel and setting-up the armament school; the provision of training weapons and laying-down of the scale of reserve; and co-ordination of the overall security plan.

Another committee, known as the Salome Committee, was set up to deal with all technical and supply aspects of the introduction of atomic weapons into the RAF[2], and held its first meeting on 1 April 1953. This committee ruled that the armament training school at Wittering must open on 1 August 1953, the first course being scheduled for 1 October[3]. The training manual was being prepared to Fort Halstead, where servicing techniques were also being developed.

By mid-1953, preparations were well advanced for the receipt and storage of atomic weapons at four medium-bomber airfields. A report to ACAS (Ops) on 27 August 1953[4] said that the present policy was to have two bomb clutches at each MB airfield and that construction had started at Wittering, Marham, Honington and Waddington – the first

---

[1] Presumably in-flight initiation, referred to by the RAF as IFL (in-flight loading). From mid-1953, Penney's title was changed from CSHER (Chief Superintendent, High Explosive Research) to DAWRE (Director, Atomic Weapons Research Establishment).

[2] CMS 1074/48/DDOps(B), Note on the Formation of the Herod Committee, 10 April 1953.

[3] "Note on Progress towards Acceptance of the Atomic Bomb into the Royal Air Force", prepared for the Herod Committee meeting on 20 July 1953 (CMS 1074/48/DofOps(2)).

[4] Aide-memoire for ACAS (Ops) Special Weapons – Atomic. CMS.1074 27 Aug 1953.

should be ready by 1 November and the second by 1 January 1954. A bomb depot at Barnham, Norfolk, should be ready by 1 May 1954[1]; the Training School at Wittering was in position, the first course starting on 1 January 1954[2]. Ancillary aircraft equipment for the first 100 V-bombers, and 50 training weapons, were being provisioned. The report said that what it called "day-to-day detailed problems associated with the introduction of the bomb into the RAF" were being tackled by the Salome Committee: these were listed as packaging; transportation equipment; servicing and preparation; safety, disposal and transport regulations; training; and supply procedure and supply security.

AOC in C Bomber Command was told in October 1953 that the Ministry of Supply expected to deliver the first atomic weapon to his Command on 1 November 1953 and that five weapons would be delivered during the year, three in November and two in December[3]. Despite the fact that at that time the RAF had no aircraft capable of carrying them, DCAS was keen for political reasons that the new bombs should be accepted into service as soon as possible[4].

In fact, the first atomic bombs for the Royal Air Force were delivered to the Bomber Command Armament School at Wittering on 7 and 14 November 1953. The unit's Operations Record Book said of their arrival: "One complete set of Smallboy weapon components was delivered to the BCAS on the nights 7th and 14th November. Subsequently, one centre section and four tail sections arrived direct off production. . . ." Summing up that momentous period, the ORB remarked: "November 1953 has been a historic month for this unit, and indeed for the Royal Air Force and the country. During this month the first atomic bombs have been delivered to the Royal Air Force, and they are now held by this unit. These bombs will raise the striking power of Bomber Command to an order completely transcending its power hitherto.

"The arrangements for storing and servicing these bombs have been left entirely to the unit, reliance being placed on the knowledge and experience of the staff."

BCAS had been formed at RAF Wittering on 1 August 1953; its first CO was Wg Cdr J S Rowlands, who had led the design and assembly team at Fort Halstead and who later echoed the words of the ORB about the "knowledge and experience of the staff" (the first members of which reported for duty on 4 August) when he said that they had "the confidence of knowledge[5]". With the advice and help of those civilians, like Dr Penney, who had been involved in the American atomic bomb project, they had worked out everything themselves from scratch; they

---

[1] There was another one at Faldingworth, Market Rasen, Lincolnshire.

[2] The first courses at BCAS were being trained before the end of 1953 (ORB).

[3] Two seem to have been delivered during November 1953; subsequent numbers were not disclosed.

[4] Loose Minute, Ops(B)3 to DofOps(2), 14 Oct 1953.

[5] Interview with Air Mshl Sir John Rowlands GC KBE BSc CEng, 19 Dec 1973.

had written the RAF training manuals and drafted the movement orders. Fittingly, the two officers who had taken the plutonium out to the Monte Bello test accompanied the second convoy to arrive at Wittering from AWRE Aldermaston on the Saturday night of 14 November 1953. According to the ORB account, this "conveyed, *inter alia,* the radioactive materials. At the request of SASO No 42 Group[1], Wg Cdr J S Rowlands, OC, BCAS, and Sqn Ldr P E Mitchell, Arm 2, BCAS, travelled with this convoy, since they had previous experience of the transport and handling of radioactive materials during the Monte Bello trials. . .".

Initially, the task of the Bomber Command Armament School was defined as "providing instruction for servicing personnel in advanced forms of armament equipment", and its original staff numbered seven officers and 11 airmen. That it clearly had no illusion about its unique function was shown by the compiler of its first Form 540 (ORB) entry, who wrote:–

"The first atomic bombs are expected to be delivered to the Royal Air Force on 1st October 1953 and it will be necessary to train personnel in their custody, storage, servicing, transportation and use. This will be done at the Bomber Command Armament School (BCAS). The RAF has no experience in dealing with atomic weapons, and it was therefore decided to staff BCAS largely with RAF personnel who had experience in the design and development of atomic weapons at the AWRE."

The compiler was also clear, however, about BCAS having more than a training role – sited as it was on what was to be the first of the V-bombers' operational bases. Describing the unit's functions, he said that it had been established for training purposes only, but that "from casual discussion it is clear that Air Ministry and HQ Bomber Command intend to place extensive additional tasks on the unit and, so far as can be gathered, its functions, *inter alia,* will be as follows:–

  (*a*) To train RAF personnel of all ranks and branches on atomic weapons and associated matters.
  (*b*) To train selected Naval, Army and civilian Government personnel on atomic weapons.
  (*c*) To accept the first atomic bombs delivered to the RAF, and to be responsible for the custody, storage and servicing of these bombs.
  (*d*) To develop and formulate the servicing procedures relating to atomic bombs.
  (*e*) To prepare the full servicing procedures relating to atomic bombs.
  (*f*) To write the Air Publication relating to atomic bombs.
  (*g*) To carry out trials as required for Air Ministry and the Atomic Weapons Research Establishment".

---

[1] Maintenance Command Group controlling the ammunition depots.

At the start, BCAS had visits from the AOC-in-C and SASO, Bomber Command (Air Mshl G H Mills and AVM G D Harvey); Wg Cdr Rowlands himself visited MoS factories at Windscale, Springfields and Capenhurst[1], accompanied by Gp Capt D A Wilson of the Directorate-General of Medical Services, Air Ministry; and several of the School's officers went on temporary duty to AWRE Fort Halstead, in connection with the provision of test and training equipment, and the transfer of security-classified documents. Meanwhile, bomb stocks were accumulating at Wittering – the ORB recording that the build-up "is proceeding in accordance with the AWRE policy of delivering components to the RAF immediately they are produced. BCAS is the only unit in the RAF which is, at present, capable of holding atomic bombs, and the atomic bomb storage depots in Maintenance Command will not be completed for some months[2]. In the meantime, BCAS must hold all atomic bombs delivered to the Royal Air Force. . .".

Training had also begun at BCAS, the unit's ORB for December 1953 recording that "the training of the first courses on atomic weapons has continued satisfactorily during the month[3]. . . ." No 1 Aircrew Course was held during 2–15 December 1954. However, the weapon had still to be matched with the aircraft which was to carry it, and although there were hopes that trials would begin during 1954, these did not in fact start until 1955 because the first Valiant which could be provided for them, WP201, a B.1 of the first batch ordered, was not delivered to Wittering until 15 June 1955. This was the third production aircraft, and it was flown in by Sqn Ldr D Roberts and his crew – Flt Lts R MacA Furze (co-pilot), K L Lewis (navigator/observer), T E Dunne (nav/plotter) and J H Sheriston (signaller) – of No 1321 Flight.

This unit has been formed at Wittering in April 1954 to carry out MoS (AWRE and RAE) Trial 248/54 – that is, trials of the ballistics and internal working apparatus of the 10,000lb Blue Danube bomb, thus proving the design and assembly work which had been done at Farnborough and Fort Halstead. MoS Valiant WP201 was used, the crew having started their work more than a year before (prior to the formation of BCAS) at Vickers-Armstrongs' Wisley test airfield[4].

Sqn Ldr Roberts went there on 20 April 1954 from Binbrook, where he had been commanding No 617 Sqn (Canberra B.2s), for a three-week Valiant conversion course; instead he stayed there for 15

---

[1] Windscale produced the fissile material, Springfields was concerned with uranium extraction and Capenhurst was a gaseous diffusion plant.

[2] Initially there were to be atomic bomb clutches at Wittering, Marham, Honington and Waddington airfields and special storage depots at Barnham and Faldingworth.

[3] Referring to Aircraft Loading Procedure, a Progress Report for Nov 53 said that the erection of a Valiant Model Bomb Bay had been completed and also a crew cabin console. A supply of aircraft control boxes, snatch plugs etc from AWRE was awaited "before the model can be utilised as an efficient training aid".

[4] "It is proposed to run trials on atomic weapons at Wittering. These . . . will involve drops of training weapons for AWRE and RAE to check the bomb ballistics and the performance of electrical and electronic bomb components" (BCAS ORB, May 1954).

months, until he went to Wittering on 15 June 1955 in command of No 1321 Flight[1]. The RAF liaison officer at Wisley at that time was Sqn Ldr R G W Oakley (successor to Sqn Ldr B H D Foster, killed in the accident to the prototype Valiant on 12 January 1952), who was subsequently to command the first Valiant squadron, No 138. Vickers' test pilot Mr Brian Trubshaw had dropped some bomb shapes from a Valiant, the RAF crew built up their experience on the type, and a trials team which had been formed at Wittering began work in preparation for the tests which were to prove the Valiant/Blue Danube combination as a viable weapon-system.

The trials team prepared servicing schedules and gained ground handling experience using a BCAS practice store. It received equipment for transportation trials, including five complete stores, during October 1954 and in the following month did the first phase of these trials. Two AWRE stores were each taken on 20-, 40-, 80- and 100-mile runs, then broken down and examined. In a second phase (December-January 1954-1955) these trials were completed using three stores; then in February the trials ended and the equipment was returned. During March-April 1955 preparations were made for the first airborne trial: equipment was accepted, a site prepared and servicing platforms made, and the stores serviced. For the whole of May, Valiant WP201 was at RAE Farnborough for tests and equipment preparatory to the ballistic trials, while the crew remained at Wisley for further Valiant flying experience.

Then on 15 June they flew WP201 to Wittering to start the MoS trials programme and on 6 July ballistic store B.1 was successfuly dropped from 12,000ft. V-bomber and A-bomb were at last starting to come together. At Gaydon (as will be described later) the first RAF Valiant B.1, WP206, had been delivered to the first Bomber Command squadron to operate the type, No 138, on 8 February 1955.

Two kinds of trial were being conducted at Wittering under the collective title MoS Trial 248/54: ballistics, which were the concern of RAE Farnborough, and involved the performance of the bomb shape at differing speeds and altitudes; and monitoring of the internal equipment, designed and assembled by AWRE, to see that it worked in its operational environment.

The No 1321 Flight Valiant was parked about 200 yards from the Bomber Command Armament School and shrouded by canvas screens during the bomb loading. Like the American B-24 Liberator, the Valiant stood low off the ground and its bomb doors opened upwards inside the fuselage, on the roll-top-desk principle. The bomb, comparable in

---

[1] Interview with Gp Capt D Roberts DFC AFC RAF on 15 February 1974. In a report to OC Bomber Command Development Unit, dated 14 August 1956, when he was OC No 49 Sqn, he had recalled that "in April 1954 No 1321 Flight was established at Wittering to undertake armament trials with a Ministry of Supply Valiant on behalf of AWRE and RAE, known as BC Trial 248/54. There was a delay in releasing the aircraft and operations at Wittering started on 15 June 1955" (ref 49/S.100/1/AIR).

dimensions to those of the 22,000lb Tallboy of the Second World War (though of less than half its weight), was loaded upwards from underneath the Valiant, hauled up into the bomb-bay by a rod with a hook on the end of it, lowered from an arm or gantry.

The B.1 trials ('B' for ballistics), the first of which was flown on 6 July 1955, were designed to check the bomb's ballistic performance and to determine its accuracy for aiming purposes. This first release, from 12,000ft at 330kt over the Orfordness bombing range, was successful; but on 22 July, when the first F.4 ('F' standing for internal workings) trial was flown, it proved to be abortive, the first successful F.4 drop being achieved on 28 July. Another achievement on that day was "the first-ever assembly and dismantling of live radioactive components within the Royal Air Force"[1].

On the following day (29 July) Bomber Command lost its first Valiant when WP222 of No 138 Squadron, which had moved to Wittering from Gaydon on 6 July, crashed shortly after take-off with the loss of all its crew – Sqn Ldr E R Chalk, Flt Lt A G Allen, Fg Off T S Corkin and Plt Off A R Lyons. This accident is referred to later in the chapter on the introduction of Valiants into the Command.

From Wittering (where No 138 Squadron was now engaged in its working-up programme[2]) the No 1321 Flight Valiant flew a "race-track-like" course to and from the Orfordness range on the Blue Danube dropping trials, first reaching the required altitude, then positioning for its "bombing" run at the designated speed and height. WP201's track was monitored in a hut on the ground, being checked like the "crab" in a Link trainer making its chinagraph line across a transparent plastic surface. Flying, along a beam, had to be very accurate; Sqn Ldr Roberts found the Valiant "a very stable bombing platform". The trials had to be done in clear weather because the weapon's trajectory was followed visually by theodolite. Blue Danube's ballistics were found to be so good that when released, it might "fly" beneath the tail area of the Valiant. To counter this, strakes were fitted to the underside of the fuselage, forward of the bomb-bay: these created an initial disturbance of airflow which had the effect of giving the bomb a push downwards. In the trials, a bomb-sight was not used as the weapon was released on instructions from the ground; at the same time, however, a visual bomb-sight was being developed[3]. When a Blue Danube was dropped, it was not recovered; the navigator, Flt Lt (later Wg Cdr) K L Lewis, probably knew whether it had fallen into the water or on land. In order to save weapons[4], an effort was made to combine different types of trial

---

[1] BCAS ORB entry for July 1955.
[2] Including, during August, concentrated practice for the SBAC Display at Farnborough in the following month.
[3] This was the T.4, later used in the atomic bomb trials over the Maralinga range in South Australia (Operation Buffalo) and in the Suez operations.
[4] It was estimated in 1952 that the cost of a practice bomb would be £4,750 (D of Wpns draft paper, Provision of Practice Bombs, 29 August 1952 (CMS.1074/D of Wpns)).

on the same drop. After the initial tests of B.1 and F.4 during July 1955 there was a gap in the trials until September, when F.4 stores were again dropped, successfully, at high altitude/high speed (from 45,000ft at Mach 0.73) and at a lower altitude/lower speed (12,000ft at 175kt). Then in October two ballistic stores were successfully dropped and an F.4 from high altitude at a comparatively low speed (46,000ft/194kt). During November the activity of the preceding months was doubled, and included a drop from 47,000ft at 184kt. The new weapon was thus being thoroughly put through its paces, and in recalling work done during the trials programme Gp Capt Roberts paid a retrospective tribute to No 1321 Flight's "marvellous groundcrew", whose crew chief was Chf Tech Small. From 23 January 1956, after its trials role had been completed, the flight became "C" Flight of No 138 Squadron, whose "B" Flight had joined the squadron from RAF Gaydon on 16 November 1955, its aircraft flying to Wittering two days later. By the end of January 1956, therefore, the first V-force squadron was complete – with eight Valiant B.1s – and the force's atomic weapon had been exhaustively test-dropped, although it was not released in its live form until 11 October 1956 in the Operation Buffalo tests[1].

On 8 February 1956 a conference was held at Bomber Command HQ to discuss the programme preparatory to Operations Buffalo and Grapple. It was then that No 1321 Flight was re-named "C" Flight of No 138 Squadron, six specially modified Valiants being established, including two for Operation Buffalo. The RAE ballistic trial was to be discontinued and the AWRE series called the "F" Series Trial. Then on 1 May "C" Flight of No 138 Squadron became No. 49 Squadron,[2] "equipped and manned for work on the 'F' Series Trial and in process of being equipped and trained for a trial code-named 'Grapple'".[3] The squadron was commanded until 3 September 1956 by Sqn Ldr Roberts, then on the 4th command was taken over by Wg Cdr K G Hubbard OBE DFC.

Operation Buffalo, based on Edinburgh Field, South Australia, in September-October 1956, included the first airborne trial of a British atomic bomb. The whole operation lasted from July to November but the Rounds were fired on 27 September 4, 11 and 22 October – that on the 11th being air-dropped from a Valiant of No 49 Squadron captained by Sqn Ldr E J G Flavell, as will be subsequently described in more detail. The Air Ministry Quarterly Liaison Report for October-December 1956 commented that Round No 3 (on 11 October) was "the first occasion on which the Royal Air Force had dropped an atomic bomb".

---

[1] From 15 June to 25 November 1955 eight 10,000 stores Type F.4 and one Type F.6 were dropped at Orfordness for AWRE and five 10,000lb ballistic stores for RAE (No 49 Sqn 'F' Series Trial – Reports IIH1/1 1/1 Pt. 1)
[2] Progress Reports – "F" Series Trials in IIH1/176/1/1 No 49 Squadron "F" Series Trial – Reports (Pt 1).
[3] No 49 Sqn ORB, Nov 56.

It could be said, however, that the Royal Air Force had an atomic bombing capability from July 1955 onwards – with the conjunction of the Bomber Command Armament School, No 1321 Flight and No 138 Squadron at Wittering.[1] On the 6th of that month the squadron had arrived there from Gaydon and the flight had made its first drop of a ballistic store; on the 25th the school had loaded a fully assembled atomic bomb on to a modified Queen Mary transporter and then removed it, as an exercise; and on the following day it was re-loaded and taken to HQ Bomber Command, where it was viewed by the AOC in C and Staff Officers on the 27th, being returned to BCAS on the same day. Then on the 28th, to quote the school's ORB:–

"The first-ever assembly and dismantling of live radioactive components within the Royal Air Force was carried out . . . in accordance with procedures which had been previously approved by representatives of the Air Ministry (Armament Engineering)".

The ORB further noted that "this assembly was done by Sqn Ldr D G Beal and Flt Lt J G Whitaker. Previously the only other Royal Air Force personnel who had handled live materials were Wg Cdr J S Rowlands and Sqn Ldr P E Mitchell during the first trials done on the British atomic bomb at Monte Bello in 1952".

The ORB added the rider that "the mishandling of fissile materials could have catastrophic consequences, and the success of this assembly by Service personnel, following Service procedures, is of vital significance to the Royal Air Force.

"BCAS have urged that live assemblies be done, as soon as possible, by all appropriate personnel trained at BCAS and this live assembly was the first step towards implementing this policy. Live assemblies were recommended because there is a great psychological difference between handling live and dummy fissile materials, and it was felt that personnel who will be expected to assemble these materials in an emergency should become accustomed to doing so".

Since Wittering held a stock of atomic bombs, since BCAS was the repository of RAF knowledge about them and experienced in handling them, and since the first Valiant bomber squadron and the atomic weapon trials flight were based on the airfield, there was an A-bomb capability there which, had an emergency arisen in mid-1955, could have been deployed operationally by the RAF.[2]

At the same time, however, as the RAF was introducing its A-bombs into service – bringing the new weapons and their carrier aircraft together at Wittering – the Government was deciding to proceed with

---

[1] SSAs (Supplementary Storage Areas) for the storage of nuclear weapons were originally sited in 1955: see ID9/R.2-30C (Pt 2) A, B & CW, Explosives, Weapons – Atomics Project 'E' – Security (Storage of Nuclear Weapons).

[2] The Statement on Defence 1954 (Cmnd 9075) had said that "atomic weapons are in production in this country and delivery to the forces has begun", and "we intend as soon as possible to build up in the Royal Air Force a force of medium bombers capable of using the atomic weapon to the fullest effect".

the development of thermonuclear bombs.

Britain was a generation behind the United States and the Soviet Union in nuclear weapon achievement: within six weeks of the first British atomic test at Monte Bello the Americans had exploded their first two thermonuclear devices at Eniwetok and about ten months later the Russians too entered the H-bomb age by successfully testing a thermonuclear device on 12 August 1953. Early in 1954 the Americans again exploded thermonuclear weapons, in the Marshall Islands; on 1 December that year the Prime Minister (Sir Winston Churchill) said in Parliament that "the advance of the hydrogen bomb" had "fundamentally altered the entire problem of defence"; and the following February, in its Statement on Defence,[1] the Government set out its policy on the second generation of nuclear weapons and their effect on the means of delivery, first recalling that

"in the Statement on Defence, 1954 (Cmd 9075), HM Government set out their views on the effect of atomic weapons on UK policy and on the nature of war. Shortly afterwards the US Government released information on the experimental explosion at Eniwetok, in November 1952, of a thermonuclear weapon many hundred times more powerful than the atomic bombs which were used at Nagasaki and Hiroshima in 1945. On 1 March 1954 an even more powerful thermonuclear weapon was exploded in the Marshall Islands. There are no technical or scientific limitations on the production of nuclear weapons still more devastating.

"The US Government have announced that they are proceeding with full-scale production of thermonuclear weapons. The Soviet Government are clearly following the same policy; though we cannot tell when they will have thermonuclear weapons available for operational use. The United Kingdom also has the ability to produce such weapons. After fully considering all the implications of this step the Government have thought it their duty to proceed with their development and production.[2]

"The power of these weapons is such that accuracy of aim assumes less importance; thus attacks can be delivered by aircraft flying at great speed and at great heights. This greatly increases the difficulty of defence. Morever, other means of delivery[3] can be foreseen which will, in time, present even greater problems".

This was the world nuclear weapon situation, and the Government's defence policy reaction to it, in 1955 when RAF Bomber Command was matching its newly acquired Valiants to its Blue Danube Mark 1 atomic bombs at Wittering.

---

[1] Cmd 9391.
[2] "If the noble Earl, Lord Attlee, had not taken what I believe to be the courageous and seminal decision to set about making the atom bomb; and if, in his turn, Sir Winston Churchill had not decided to initiate the manufacture of the nuclear fusion weapon, we should have been miles behind, both industrially and militarily" (Viscount De L'Isle and Dudley VC, former Air Minister (1951-55), in the Air Estimates debate, House of Lords, 7 May 1958 (Lords Hansard, Vol CCIX, Col 47)).
[3] Ie, by missile, either land- or undersea-launched.

CHAPTER VII

CREATION OF AN RAF JET BOMBER FORCE

During December 1950 the Bomber Command Jet Conversion Flight was formed at RAF Binbrook, north-west of Louth, in the Lincolnshire Wolds; it had two Meteor 7 two-seat trainers and two Meteor 3 single-seaters. Reporting this, the Air Ministry Quarterly Liaison Report for January-March 1951[1] said that "during that period under review the first Bomber Command pilots detailed for Canberra conversion have been trained in the techniques of high-altitude, high-speed jet flying. When the Canberra re-equipment programme commences the Jet Flight will be responsible for the conversion of the squadrons concerned on to the Canberra."

Binbrook was at that time (early 1951) one of six heavy-bomber stations in the Command; it had four Lincoln squadrons – Nos 9, 12, 101 and 617. There were three other stations with Lincoln squadrons – Hemswell (Nos 83/150 and 97), Waddington (Nos 61/144 and 100) and Upwood (Nos 7/76, 49/102, 148 and 214) – and two stations with B-29 Washington squadrons: Coningsby (Nos 15/21, 44/55 and 149) and Marham (Nos 57/104, 90 and 115/218). The work of transforming the Command into a jet-bomber force was continuous; the first four Canberra squadrons to be created were formed from the Lincoln squadrons at Binbrook, which was the original repository of knowledge and experience on Canberras in the RAF, as Gaydon was later for Valiants and Victors and Waddington for Vulcans.

The first Canberra for the Royal Air Force, a B.2,[2] WD936, was delivered to Binbrook, to No 101 Squadron, on 25 May 1951, appropriately by Wg Cdr (Ret) R P Beamont, the English Electric chief test pilot whose brilliant flying had contributed greatly to the successful development of the new bomber. The squadron ORB recorded on that date: "Today has been a day of note for Bomber Command. This squadron has received the first of the Command's jet bombers. Wg Cdr Beamont flew in a Canberra, WD936. Before lunch he gave a talk about the aircraft to pilots and navigators who will be flying this type. The aircraft is now on acceptance checks by the Technical Wing."

A Meeting on Canberra Policy, held on 9 January 1951,[3] had had before it a brief which said that "the Canberra B Mk 2 is designed as a short-range day bomber. Owing to its navigation limitations it cannot effectively be operated outside Gee cover except in visual conditions. Its role in Bomber Command has therefore been defined as bombing in

---

[1] Issue No 18.

[2] There was no B.1, as explained earlier, as the original concept for a high-altitude strategic bomber had been abandoned. The B.1 would have needed H2S/NBC equipment required for the Valiant.

[3] Annexure B (C.37724/48), Appreciation of Navigation Requirements for a Medium-range High-altitude Canberra Bomber/Marker.

support of the land battle within 250 miles of the frone line. . . .[1]"

This brief went on to stress the importance of marking targets which were beyond the range of ground-based aids. It said that means of accurate blind bombing beyond the range of such aids "were not yet in sight. From high altitudes, target identification makes visual day bombing difficult. For accurate bombing therefore, there is a continuing need both by day and by night to be able to mark targets accurately. There will therefore be a requirement for an aircraft to mark visually for a medium-range Canberra force".

The implication was that, provided the Canberras operated over Europe, where they could use Gee, they could bomb effectively. Outside of Gee cover, they needed a marker force. This was dramatically demonstrated in the Suez operations towards the end of 1956 (31 October-6 November) because over Egypt the Canberra squadrons operating from Malta and Cyprus did not enjoy the benefit of ground-based aids and there was only one target-marking squadron (No 139 (Jamaica) Squadron), target-marking having been officially abandoned some time previously in a change of policy.[2]

Reports written after the Suez operations, commenting on the difficulties, said that "the Canberra aircraft forming the bulk of the forces deployed [were] equipped only with Gee-H as a blind-bombing device and it was not possible to position ground beacons to give coverage for this equipment over Egypt. . . . It was considered that it would be prudent for the early attacks to be made at night, and this necessitated a reversion to the marking techniques successfully used in the Second World War. . . .[3]" Another report commented that, in 1956, Bomber Command "was geared to a 'radar' war in Eastern Europe and was not constituted nor organised for major operations overseas".[4]

In 1951-52, however, when the Canberra force was being built up, its prime task was operations over Europe in support of Shape. Although the build-up was slow at first, with only one squadron in existence by the end of 1951 (in the seven months after the Canberra's introduction into service only nine aircraft were delivered), 1952 saw a rapid increase in the size of the force – to eight squadrons (seven bomber and one reconnaissance).

On 13 March 1952 the Cabinet had decided to accord "Super

---

[1] Following a conference on Bomber Command held at the Command's HQ on 25-26 January 1951, VCAS minuted CAS on 29 January (VCAS file No VCAS/4505): ". . . There was . . . a tendency to look upon the Canberra as a long-range high-flying jet bomber, and to press for equipment to enable it to undertake this role. At the end, however, it was generally accepted that the Canberra is a short-range tactical bomber, that there is no equipment which will enable it to hit a small target from 45,000ft, and that it must therefore come down to a height from which it can achieve results. . . ."

[2] In the summer of 1955, when it was decided to eliminate the marker squadrons (HQ BC Report on Operation Musketeer – BC/S. 87926). But the decision was reversed, marker trials were completed in the spring of 1956 and one squadron re-established.

[3] The Techniques Used and the Results Achieved by Bomber Command during Operation Musketeer.

[4] Musketeer Report (both in AHB IIH/272/3/4OA).

101

Priority" to the production of the most up-to-date jet aircraft, including the Canberra,[1] and (reported the Minister of Supply (Mr Duncan Sandys) in a memorandum to the Cabinet on 10 June),[2] output was building up steadily and the type gave "no cause for concern".

There was as yet no formal operational conversion on to the Canberra – that was to come later, when No 231 OCU was established at Bassingbourn; at Binbrook, Bomber Command was learning as it went along, while No 101 Squadron re-equipped with the new type. Some aircrew had gained experience earlier in the year with the English Electric Co; in its issue of 15 February 1951 *Flight* had published air-to-air photographs of "Canberra B.2 three-seater tactical bombers . . . flown by English Electric pilots, . . . carry[ing] RAF personnel for 'acclimatisation'". The caption named the "much-envied RAF crew . . . – the first operational crew to man a Canberra" as Wg Cdr T G Mahaddie DSO DFC AFC and Flt Lt E Cassidy DFC (pilots), and Flt Lt R A G Barlow (navigator). The magazine also said that an RAF-manned Canberra was shortly to fly to the USA, "where it will demonstrate the qualities which have led the US Government to order quantity production in their own country." This flight was made on 21 February by a crew from A&AEE Boscombe Down – Sqn Ldr A E Callard DFC (pilot), and Flt Lts E A J Haskett (navigator) and A J R Robson DFC (signaller) – and by it Canberra WD932 became the first jet-propelled aircraft to make a direct unrefuelled Atlantic crossing. At Baltimore, Maryland, the aircraft was demonstrated by Wg Cdr R P Beamont and the Glenn L Martin Co there subsequently produced the type as the B-57A under contract from the USAF.

By the end of June 1951 No 101 Squadron had two Canberras and on 5 July experienced the first Canberra accident in the RAF with an electrical power failure on the second aircraft, WD938, during a practice overshoot. Despite the loss of both engines as a result, the pilot, Flt Lt Thomas, managed to make a wheels-up landing on the airfield. Neither he nor the squadron commander, Sqn Ldr E Cassidy, who was instructing him, nor the navigator, Sgt Dix, were injured; nor was the aircraft seriously damaged. The Canberra was not flown again until 24 July.

The squadron, which ended its association with Lincolns during July 1951 when the last Lincoln B.2 4A departed, built up its Canberra strength slowly. Authorised to have ten B.2s, it still had only three by the end of August, four by the end of September, six by the end of October and nine by the end of the year, when it was still the only Canberra squadron in Bomber Command. But from the start, it operated its aircraft intensively on Service trials and operational training.

What was the role of the Canberra squadrons considerd to be?

---

[1] CC(52) 30th Conclusions, Min 5.
[2] C(52)187.

The first four of these – Nos 101, 617, 12 and 9 – were all formed (in that order) at Binbrook; the fifth – No 109/105 – at Hemswell; the reconnaissance squadron – No 540 PR (MR), which did not in fact receive its first PR.3 until December 1952 – at Benson; the seventh – No 50 – at Binbrook; and the eighth – No 139 – at Hemswell. The AOC in C Bomber Command (Air Mshl Sir Hugh Lloyd) had expected to have ten Canberra squadrons by the end of 1952. Referring to the expansion plan in a letter to US of S on 4 October 1951 he said; "Plan 'H' shows my Command as being equipped with ten Lincoln, eight Washington and ten Canberra squadrons by December 1952. My Lincolns will be equipped with H2S Mk 4A,[1], my Washingtons with APQ 13[2] and the Canberras with Gee-H. These are all radar methods of bombing. . . ."

In a directive from CAS on 20 March 1950 the AOC in C had been told: "Your principal effort is likely to be directed against targets within 250 miles of the Rhine so that full advantage can be taken of maximum bomb-loads and navigational aids to bombing"; and in a note of 1 March 1952 on British Bomber Policy[3] CAS said that "the ultimate build-up of the [bomber] force under Plan H (extended) aims at the provision of 560 light bombers and 152 medium bombers.[4] All the light bombers are committed to the support of Saceur and in fact constitute the main part of his striking force". He described the Canberra as "a good modern light bomber for tactical use at night and in bad weather against airfields, communications, etc". The Chiefs of Staff, in their Report on the Size and Shape of the Armed Forces over the Three Years beginning 1951/52, dated 12 October 1950[5], said that most of the 36 squadrons to which Bomber Command's front line would be increased by the end of 1953/54 would be equipped with the Canberra – "which can only carry 7,500lb over a radius of 500 miles; and its hitting power will be small in relation to its commitments in support of the defence of the UK and the land battle in Europe"[6].

---

[1] Mk 4A (or IVA) was one of the variants of radar bomb sight, in the Lincoln Mk 2.

[2] APQ 13 was the American version of the British H2S radar.

[3] Described in a covering note to VCAS as "CAS's counterblast to the PM's doubts about the need for a bomber force". After the loss of the prototype Valiant on 12 January 1952 Winston Churchill had minuted S of S for Air on the 17th: "I suppose we have lost a quarter of a million pounds. This is a heavy blow to all that line of Air thought who argue that Britain should plunge heavily on the largest class of Air bombers. The Americans will do this and also have the things to carry. We should concentrate *not entirely* but far more on the fighter aircraft we need to protect ourselves from destruction. I am not at all comforted by the assertion that you are going to make a lot more Valiants. . . ".

[4] The terms "light" and "medium" followed the USAF categorisation referring to radius of action – light, less than 1,000nm; medium, 1,000-2,500nm.

[5] COS(50)409, in VCAS folder Defence Expenditure – Size and Shape (AHB ID9/11/1 Pt 1).

[6] The medium bomber force was also likely to be involved. "Although the Canberra Light Bomber Force is part of RAF Bomber Command", VCAS wrote to S of S on 20 January 1956, "it is wholly assigned to Saceur except for the Marker Squadrons. The Medium Bomber Force is retained under HMG's control but the Minister of Defence agreed on 17 December 1953 that one of its primary tasks in war would be retardation operations designed to assist Saceur" (file on US/UK strike plans, in AHB ID9/240/16 – Co-ord of UK/US Strategic Bomber Force).

The build-up of the Canberra light bomber force directly reflected the pledge made by Britain to the North Atlantic Council at its meeting in Brussels in December 1950 "to strengthen the defences of the free world", as the Prime Minister (Mr C R Attlee) put it in a statement on the defence programme in the Commons on 29 January 1951[1]. Writing to S of S for Air (Lord De L'Isle and Dudley VC), who had asked him about the assumptions on which the projected size and shape of the RAF in 1955 were based, CAS (MRAF Sir John Slessor) had said on 10 March 1952 that the RAF were "the only people (apart from the Americans) who could make a serious bomber contribution to Nato". Because the Washingtons and Lincolns were obsolescent and the Valiant had not flown (though a small order had been placed "off the drawing board") and "the only other bet was the Canberra", "we ordered as many of them as we could get to built up a first-line force of 560 in the UK, all for the support of Shape. . . ."[2] (This figure, however, "plus 64 in the Middle East where we had nothing but 16 obsolescent Brigands", he subsequently said would be reduced "to provide for the new mediums").

Thus from its inception the RAF Canberra force was committed to the defence of Europe[3]. Initially all its main force squadrons were based in the UK; not until August 1954 were the first Canberras deployed to Germany, and even so, they were still operationally controlled by Bomber Command. A full list of Canberra squadrons, showing when they were formed and what aircraft they operated previously, is given in one of the Appendices.

By the end of 1952 there were six bomber and one PR Canberra squadrons. By the end of 1953, an impressive year for the Canberra force, there were 17 bomber and three PR squadrons; and by the end of 1954, 24 squadrons (all bomber except for one PR squadron) in the UK and three in Germany, the latter being described as "under overall policy control of Bomber Command but under day-to-day operational control of 2nd TAF". The Canberra LBF reached its zenith at the end of April 1955, with 305 on hand, equipping 23 squadrons in the UK and four in Germany. Until June 1954 the force had been entirely composed of B.2s, but on the 11th of that month No 101 Sqn, which had been the first to be equipped with Canberras, collected its first B.6 – a mark which had more powerful Rolls-Royce Avons and greater fuel capacity.

No 101 Squadron's original conversion on to Canberras had taken a

---

[1] Commons Hansard Col 579.

[2] The Plan H expansion programme for the RAF.

[3] "The light bomber component of your force will be operated wholly in support of the Supreme Allied Commander, Europe, and controlled by you on his behalf" (Command Directive from the CAS (Air Chf Mshl Sir William Dickson) to the AOC in C Bomber Command (Air Mshl G H Mills), 13 May 1953 in Medium Bombers – Future Requirements (ID3/942/9 Pt 1)).

long time because there were delays in production of the aircraft[1]. Thus although they received their first B.2 in May 1951 it was not until the end of that year that they completed re-equipment with ten aircraft and crews. The administration of the jet conversion flight at Binbrook was then handed-over to No 617 Squadron, the second squadron to be converted. The crews, originally planned as three-man, became two-man during 1951. This followed a decision by the AOC in C Bomber Command (Air Mshl Sir Hugh Lloyd) in June of that year. On the 22nd he wrote to CAS (MRAF Sir John Slessor): "Thank you for your letter of 13 June . . . in which you asked me to consider the two alternatives, *ie* two or three in a crew for a Canberra. I accept the recommendation that we should plan for a crew of two."[2]

It was in the early years of the Canberra LBF, also, that the decision was made to classify crews into select, combat or non-combat categories. In a directive of 4 July 1952 to his two AOCs, AVM D A Boyle (No 1 Group) and AVM W A D Brook (No 3 Group), the AOC in C said that, so that he might be informed of the Command's state of readiness, he desired that all crews should be classified as select, combat or non-combat from 1 July. An Appendix to the directive described the qualifications for these categories, qualification being for a crew as a team. Select crews were to hold their classification for six months and were authorised to land anywhere outside the UK; combat crews were to hold their classification for four months and could land in the UK and Germany only; non-combat crews could land only in the UK. Squadrons with less than four select or combat crews were to be regarded as non-operational. Qualifications for captains of select crews included a current green IR (instrument rating) and, for Lincoln and Washington captains, 250hr on any four-engined aircraft, of which 125hr had to be at night; and for Canberra captains, 100hr on type, of which 50hr had to be at night. Other crew members had to have comparable qualifications.

A Crew Classification Scheme issued by HQ Bomber Command on 30 December 1953[3] revised a previous scheme of 14 September. It outlined the Air Qualification for Combat and Select Canberra, Lincoln and Washington bomb aimers, and combat and select standards for pilots and navigators in low-level marker squadrons with Blue Shadow (sideways-looking-search) radar.

---

[1] AMQLR for July-September 1951 (No 20) reported that "five Canberra aircraft have been delivered to RAF Binbrook and the service trials of this aircraft are now under way. The formation date of the first Canberra OCU [the original plan was to have two OCUs, but this idea was subsequently abandoned] has been postponed until January 1952 due to delays in Canberra production".

[2] Although No 231 OCU seems to have trained three-man crews and initially No 101 Sqn had them (see subsequent references) two-man crews became standard on the squadrons. In announcing a revised policy on Gee-H bombing on 11 Dec 53 HQ Bomber Command (BCS.84547) said that two navigators were to be carried on all details involving the release of practice or live bombs, the second being there "solely for monitoring purposes".

[3] BC/S.8426/Trg.

During 1951, No 101 Squadron had not only been engaged in converting pilots to the Canberra but also in carrying-out intensive flying trials "covering the complete operational range and performance of the aircraft", as well as testing a completely new range of flying clothing[1]. When the squadron had been fully re-equipped with aircraft and crews, the Air Ministry organised a Press visit to Binbrook in January 1952 and *The Aeroplane* reported[2]:–

"The introduction of the Canberra is more than a re-equipment programme, and marks the start of the general expansion of Bomber Command. Selected crews from existing Lincoln, and later, from Washington, squadrons will convert on to Canberras to form new squadrons, but the piston-engined bombers will remain in service with Bomber Command until the introduction of the Vickers Valiant multi-jet bomber. In the case of No 101 Squadron, commanded by Sqn Ldr E Cassidy DFC, its Lincoln crews were strengthened by experienced pilots from Bomber Command, many of whom had been flying instructors.

"No wireless operator is carried in the Canberra B.2, which has a crew of three – pilot, navigator/plotter and observer, each with a Martin-Baker ejection seat. The observer acts as an assistant navigator, and as bomb aimer when the target is reached. With the re-introduction of the observer category into aircrew, the wheel has turned a full circle, now that bomber crews are being reduced in size and individuals must specialise in more than one task".

Referring to the intensive flying trials, the magazine reported that in accordance with a recent Air Ministry decision, IFTs of an entirely new character "are to be made with all new aircraft in the future, as soon as the first squadron is equipped" – a procedure which was later followed in the cases of the Valiant, Vulcan and Victor squadrons. "With the Canberra", the report continued, "No 101 Squadron is flying at two or three times the intensity of normal peacetime squadron routine. When an aircraft is in large-scale production, it is preferable that any changes found necessary under intensive operations should be incorporated as soon as possible on the production line, rather than made retrospectively on a large number of aircraft in general squadron service. This system of intensive flying trial should assist in accelerating the re-equipment of RAF squadrons with aircraft ready for immediate and effective operational employment.

"The Canberra, however, has proved exceptionally easy to service and maintain, even though the squadron aircraft have been used on intensive training and conversion. There have been very few snags or

---

[1] An article in *Air Clues* for January 1977 on "25 Years with the Canberra at No 231 OCU" commented that students on the courses there, "coming as they did mostly from piston-engined squadrons . . ., particularly the navigators, felt a little like space cadets when confronted with pressure-breathing equipment, bone domes, pressure cabins and ejector seats".

[2] In its issue of 18 January 1952.

defects in a total flying time during which six Rolls-Royce Avon engines have completed their overhaul life. In the large number of take-offs and landings, there were no brake failures or hydraulic snags, and the turnaround time between sorties compared favourably with that of jet fighters".

In its operational training No 101 Squadron, doubtless setting a precedent for the subsequent Canberra squadrons, concentrated on the use of Gee-H equipment. In doing so it had to contend with some unserviceability. It should be remembered that the new jet bomber force was being built up in many ways on a framework left over from the wartime force of Lancasters, Halifaxes and Mosquitos. On 20 April 1951 a note on Gee-H, the results from which were said to be "very bad" and the equipment "quite frightful" – according to a letter from the AOC in C Bomber Command to the Vice-Chief of the Air Staff (Air Chf Mshl Sir Ralph Cochrane) on 30 March 1951, was sent to VCAS. This commented that

"When the Gee-H organisation was disbanded at the end of the war, the skilled operators and computers were lost to the Service or absorbed in other jobs. Most of the equipment was put into store. We are now suffering from the inevitable difficulties which arise in trying to get the organisation re-started.

"As regards the technical aspect, CEE (Controller of Engineering and Equipment) is working closely with Bomber Command, and are giving the matter their close attention. CEE appears to be sanguine that, as the defects due to long storage are progressively removed, the reliability and technical accuracy will steadily improve".

However, a more hopeful note about Gee-H was sounded by VCAS later that year when in a minute of 21 September 1951 to ACAS(OR) he said: "My own feelings are that Gee-H has surprised us by the accuracy which can be achieved, now that crews know how to use the set; but that the serviceability is bad and will never be good, but with growing experience will undoubtedly get better. Nevertheless, we must consider seriously how quickly we can replace it by a better equipment".

During 1952, Bomber Command formalised Canberra training by opening a Canberra OCU (Operational Conversion Unit), No 231 OCU, at RAF Bassingbourn.

No 231 OCU was authorised to form by a Headquarters Bomber Command Organisation Memorandum No 54/51 of 1 December 1951; it succeeded No 237 PR OCU, which was disbanded, and the official title of the new unit was No 231 OCU RAF Bassingbourn. In its ORB for December 1951 its title and task were set down as "Bomber Command Operational Conversion Unit. Training pilots, navigators and radar operators to reinforce PR and light bomber squadrons at home and overseas". Initially the unit operated with Mosquito and Meteor trainers and PR aircraft. In January 1952 its ORB reported that "most of the flying carried out in Meteor 7 aircraft this month has been devoted to instrument flying and standardisation of instruction preparatory to Canberra flying". During February the unit carried out acceptance checks on its first two Canberras. In March (the ORB reported) the conversion of instructional staff on to Canberras continued satisfactorily; a high aircraft utilisation figure of 89hr 50min on the two Canberras was achieved. During April, Canberra familiarisation flying continued, all the instructors completing one night solo. The unit's aircraft establishment was to be 26 Canberra B.2s and four PR.3s. In May, further intensive Canberra flying was carried out, providing experience for the instructional staff, and day visual bombing exercises were completed.

By June 1952 No 231 OCU had gone into business with its first two Canberra courses, the first of which assembled on 27 May and the second on 24 June, and the number of B.2s on the unit had risen to 14. The first course, totalling five crews, passed out on 26 August; by that time, with the aircraft establishment still at 26, there were 21 B.2s at Bassingbourn. The second course (nine crews) passed out on 17 September, and at that time the OCU was still converting crews to Mosquitos. The Mosquito task, however, gradually diminished and by July 1953 there was only one T.3 left on the unit. By that date there was an establishment for 30 Canberras; there were 30 B.2s on strength plus a T.4 trainer and ten Meteor 7 trainers. The unit's flying task put considerable pressure upon the engineering staff and the groundcrew – particularly the latter, who,

"largely National Service and poorly paid, worked in primitive conditions from unheated, poorly lit and unsanitated dispersal huts. They were under constant pressure to produce serviceable aircraft for the intensive flying effort. . . .

"Shortage of components and inadequate stock control necessitated frequent 'robbing' of items from one aircraft to make another serviceable for the flying programme. For example, bomb racks were so scarce that if an aircraft became unserviceable before flight, the crew had to wait for a second aircraft to be armed from scratch with the bomb rack from the first".[1]

No 231 OCU seemed to have been operating the three-member crew configuration – one pilot and two navigators – during 1952 and 1953, certainly from the sad statistics of the fatal accidents which occurred on the unit. On 19 December 1952 a Canberra crashed just after take-off and all three crew members were killed, the aircraft being destroyed. On 16 February 1953, at night, a Canberra crashed at Croydon Hill, again with the loss of its three crew members. On 7 April 1953 a Meteor crashed during local night flying and the pilot was killed. These accidents may well have been due to the comparative inexperience of crews passing through OCU compared with the aircrew who formed the

---

[1] "25 Years with the Canberra at No 231 OCU", by Flt Lts A D Cloag and C M F Webster (*Air Clues*, January 1977).

first Canberra squadron at Binbrook.[1]

On the other hand, the good flying characteristics of the Canberra were illustrated in an accident to a B.2 from Bassingbourn on 11 August 1953 when both engines cut at 15,000 feet after steep turns (according to the ORB). The pilot was unable to relight the engines and the aircraft was force-landed near Debden without injury to its crew members. The accidents which occurred should be set against a monthly flying total by the OCU of approximately 1,000hr. By the end of 1953, 23 Canberra courses had been completed on the unit.

While the Canberra was noted for amiable aerodynamics, however, it suffered from runaway actuator trim problems from mid-1953 onwards. The first incident of this kind occurred on 26 July that year, and there were subsequently 50 reports[2] of serious actuator faults, 14 of the incidents resulting from runaway tail trim – seven of them occurring on Mk 2 Canberras with single-speed actuators and the others on aircraft with two-speed actuators (Mks 4, 6 and 7). Five of the accidents were fatal, and subsequently all Canberras with single-speed actuators were grounded.

In one incident of this kind which occurred to a B.2 of No 231 OCU on 26 September 1955[3], three of the four crew members survived after the tailplane actuator moved to the fully nose-up position and the aircraft become uncontrollable. But by rolling it into a steep turn the instructor "regained partial control until the two navigators had ejected and the student pilot had escaped through the entrance hatch. He then made a safe ejection himself, but was slightly injured during the descent when his parachute became tangled with the ejection seat. The student navigator's body was found still strapped into his seat; the remaining two crew members landed without injury".

One feature of the introduction of new jet bomber aircraft into the RAF was that they were taken on trips abroad as soon as possible after coming into service. This occurred with the Canberra, and later with the Valiant and Vulcan. Thus during 1952 the AOC in C Bomber Command, Air Mshl Sir Hugh Lloyd, flew to the United States in a Canberra on 18 April and returned on 9 May; then on 28 September he went to Nairobi by the same means, in 9hr 55min. But the first impressive show of strength overseas was put on by four B.2s of the newly reformed No 12 Sqn, which left Binbrook on 20 October on a

---

[1] "It says much for the expertise of the flying instructors that the accident rate was not higher in conditions which today would be considered unacceptable", commented the article on No 231 OCU in *Air Clues* (previously quoted), pointing out that "on the flight safety side, airfield and area radar had not yet appeared at Bassingbourn and landing aids were primitive. The circuit normally included a mixture of piston and jet aircraft, with a wide range of skill and experience in both the aircrew and ground controllers." The authors conclude that "perhaps inevitably the accident rate was high, with contributions both from handling errors and serious technical defects."

[2] See MoA file BU/96/02 Aircraft Accidents – Policy, which contains a complete list of these 50 incidents.

[3] No 1 Gp ORB, Sep 55.

24,000-mile goodwill tour of South America led by the AOC No 1 Group, AVM D A Boyle.[1] The third Canberra squadron to form, No 12, had begun its conversion from Lincolns in March 1952. In August its ORB noted: "All crews are now qualified in Gee-H bombing with one exception. This crew is expected to qualify shortly". During that month the squadron had dropped 200 25lb practice bombs – 140 by Gee-H and 60 visually. By the time of Exercise Round Trip, the South American goodwill tour, the newest Canberra squadron was operationally qualified.

Each aircraft had a three-man crew (pilot, plotter and observer – though the AOC had a second pilot and a plotter) and on the outward flight AVM Boyle set up an unofficial record on 23 October of 4hr 27min for the South Atlantic crossing from Dakar to Recife. The squadron ORB devoted five pages to a complete description of Round Trip and subsequently *Flight's* American correspondent reported[2] that it had been very good for British prestige in Latin America, which meant much in terms of goodwill and trade. He also made the point that in some of the smaller Central American states the aircraft were described locally as being American, because it was believed that only the United States made jets; and he further commented that it was not considered necessary to send out any spare Avon engines for the Canberras – nor did they need any, and he regretted that this fact was not publicised.

In addition to the prestige accruing from it, such an overseas trip was useful in proving the new aircraft over long distances, and giving their crews the experience of flying and navigating over foreign territory. It was also a test of servicing the Canberras away from their home base.

After No 12, No 9 became the next squadron to be converted to Canberras, receiving the first three of its new aircraft on 2 May 1952. This meant that RAF Binbrook became the first station in Bomber Command to house four Canberra squadrons – Nos 101, 617, 12 and 9.

Another station in No 1 Group, Hemswell, then began to re-equip with Canberras. In its case, however, the change was not from Lincolns but from Mosquito B.35s – the two squadrons concerned, Nos 109/105 and No 139 (Jamaica), making up the Bomber Command Marker Force. The former started its conversion on to Canberras in August 1952 and completed it during September. No 139 received its first Canberras during November 1952, was somewhat delayed in its conversions by bad weather – especially during January 1953, but in its February ORB was able to record: "All crews are now converted to Canberras". The compiler went on to comment that "the general opinion seems to be that the Canberra handles well on instrument approaches and its single-engine performance is exceptionally good". Both squadrons subsequently took up their original role with the new

[1] Later CAS (1956-59) as Air Chf Mshl Sir Dermot Boyle KCVO KBE CB AFC.
[2] Issue of 17 Apr 53.

type, forming a marker force in Bomber Command exercises.

A fifth squadron formed at Binbrook during August 1952. This was No 50 and its first four crews came direct from No 231 OCU at Bassingbourn, a fifth coming from No 101 Sqn; another came from No 12 Sqn on 15 September and two more came from No 231 OCU on the 18th. The squadron's first Canberra B.2 had arrived on 18 August.

Towards the end of 1952, No 540 (PR) Sqn, part of the Bomber Command Strategic Photographic Force and originally equipped with Mosquito Mk 34As, received its first Canberra PR Mk 3 at its base, Benson in Oxfordshire. The squadron ORB for December 1952 recorded that "the first Canberra PR Mk 3 has been delivered. It is not equipped with the necessary mountings for cameras and photographic trials cannot yet be carried out. However, aircrew and groundcrew conversion and familiarisation is proceeding". Thus by the end of 1952 Bomber Command's Canberra force consisted of five Main Force light bomber squadrons, two marker squadrons and the beginnings of a Canberra photographic reconnaissance squadron. Official totals at the end of the year were 70 B.2s authorised and 48 on hand, plus eight PR.3s authorised and one on hand. AMQLR for Oct-Dec 1952 reported:–

"The five Canberra squadrons at RAF Binbrook, Nos 9, 12, 50, 101 and 617, are now equipped to eight UE and are carrying out full operational training. The two Light Marker Force squadrons, Nos 109 and 139, at RAF Hemswell have been equipped to eight UE and 109 Sqn crews are carrying out operational training; some of the 139 Sqn crews are still undergoing conversion training by the Jet Conversion Flight".

During 1952 RAF Bomber Command experience of high-level jet operations was increased when a special reconnaissance flight, known as the Special Duties Flight, was formed at Sculthorpe (then a USAF base) with three North American RB-45C Tornados, reconnaissance version of the B-45 (four General Electric J-47-GE-3 turbojet engines), whose prototype the XB-45 had been the first American multi-jet heavy aircraft to fly, on 17 March 1947 at Muroc[1]. The RB-45C was the high altitude photographic reconnaissance version, with a crew of three (pilot, co-pilot and photo-navigator) and five camera stations capable of carrying ten different types of camera. The aircraft were equipped for flight refuelling and the three RAF RB-45Cs were supported by six USAF B-50 tankers. The loan of them had been offered by General Hoyt S Vandenberg, Chief of Staff, USAF, in early 1951 to give the RAF an experience of reconnaissance flying above 40,000ft, and the flights made in them in 1952 – on 17-18 April and 12-13 December – were the fastest and longest high-level sorties flown by the RAF in jet aircraft up to that time. The captains were Sqn Ldrs J Crampton (flight commander) and W Blair and Flt Lt G Kremer; the sorties were flown at

---

[1] *Jane's All the World's Aircraft*, 1952-53 edition.

32,000-42,000ft, and their objectives were to obtain radarscope photographs of potential targets in Western Russia – *ie* to obtain target information for the V-force. Three routes were planned, one to cover targets in the southern area and two to cover those in the northern area; and when the crews were briefed they received three separate weather forecasts for each route – a genuine one and two bogus ones, one for their Sculthorpe "cover story" and the other for possible Russian interrogators (who were to be told they were on a met reconnaissance – of the Black Sea in the case of the southern route and of the Gulf of Bothnia in the case of the northern ones) should misadventure occur and capture follow. In the event, all went well, and the first flights were deemed to have been successful in their results, although weather and engine troubles delayed their return to Sculthorpe; for about 20 minutes before the first aircraft (Sqn Ldr Blair) was due there low stratus started to roll in from the North Sea, so he had to divert to Manston. Sqn Ldr Crampton arrived during a temporary break in the fog, so got in successfully; but Flt Lt Kremer, who had had to go into Copenhagen because of engine trouble (icing-up of the fuel filters), had to divert into Prestwick. The later flights were not so successful, and after them the AOC in C (Air Chief Mshl Sir Hugh P Lloyd) wrote on 16 December 1952 to the Commander, 7th Air Division (Maj-Gen John P McConnell), to say: "I am only sorry that the operation ended as it did – without the answers".

1953 was an interesting year in the build-up of the Canberra LBF, because for the first time squadrons began to be formed which had not previously operated Lincolns. For example, at the beginning of the year No 10 Squadron, whose previous existence had been in a transport role (Halifaxes), was re-formed at Scampton, on 15 January. Its ORB recorded that "the squadron commander, Sqn Ldr D R Howard DFC, was posted in from RAF Binbrook where he had completed a tour of duty as flight commander on No 101 Squadron. Eight crews, two from RAF Binbrook and six from No 231 OCU, assembled at Scampton". During the year the run-down of the B-29 Washington force and the re-equipment of its squadrons with Canberras started. The AMQLR for January-March 1953 noted that "the run-down of the Washington Force began on 1 March 1953. No 44 Squadron was the first to start conversion training prior to re-arming with Canberras, and will be followed by Nos 149, 57 and 15 Squadrons".

No 44/55 (Rhodesia) Squadron, which during the Second World War had been the first Bomber Command squadron to convert completely to Lancasters (and which with No 97 Squadron made the daring daylight attack on Augsburg[1] on 17 April 1942), became non-operational during January 1953 owing to its conversion to Canberras; and during that month its Washingtons were offered for

---

[1] Out of a force of 12 aircraft only five returned, the CO of No 44 Squadron (Wg Cdr J D Nettleton) being awarded the VC.

disposal among the other Washington squadrons of Bomber Command. During the following month it concentrated on jet conversion flying in Meteors, and got its first Canberra B.2s in April, when it also became the first Canberra squadron at Coningsby airfield near Lincoln. No 149, the second Washington squadron to be converted to Canberras, was not far behind. In January 1953 its ORB noted: "The squadron has completed its operational commitment on Washington aircraft and as from 4 February will commence its re-arming with the English Electric Canberra". Its pilots went to Hemswell for a short Meteor course and thence to Bassingbourn; its navigators went to Bassingbourn via RAF Lindholme, the Command Bombing School. The compiler of No 149's ORB had been a little optimistic as to dates. On 5 February he recorded that "after flying two Washingtons on Exercise King Pin on the night of 5 February all flying on the squadron ceased and the remainder of the month was taken up with transferring the aircraft to other squadrons, dealing with postings-out and preparing in general for the arrival of the Canberra aircraft, crews and equipment". The Canberras, however, had to be modified at Binbrook and the first did not reach No 149 at Coningsby until 17 April, three more arriving during that month. In May two more Washington squadrons began to re-equip with Canberras, No 57 receiving its first two B.2s on the 12th and No 15 its first on the 29th.

The Canberra bomber build-up, which reached its peak in Apr 1955 when there were 390 of both marks on hand at bases, including those in Germany, was comparable with that of Bomber Command in the Second World War; for by then 27 squadrons had been formed – the bomber aspect of the RAF part of the British rearmament programme instituted after the Brussels meeting of the North Atlantic Council in December 1950. Thus by the time the second stage of Bomber Command's re-equipment began, with the appearance of the Valiants, considerable experience in the operation of jet bombers had already been gained by its flying and engineering personnel.

With its low wing loading and docile flying characteristics, the Canberra was a well-liked aircraft: as the first jet bomber in the RAF, it gave Bomber Command a pride and prestige it had lost in the years following the Second World War, when its aircraft became slow and obsolescent. It carried a 6,000lb conventional bomb load; not until 1958 were Canberras armed with nuclear weapons, as will subsequently be described. Powered by two Rolls-Royce Avons, the Canberra was manoeuvrable enough for a formation aerobatic team to be formed (in 1956) with four aircraft, and for the LABS manoeuvre employed by the interdictor (B(I).8) squadrons in RAF Germany, as will subsequently be mentioned. But the Canberras' role was tactical: they were visualised as battlefield-support weapons, had the Warsaw Pact forces embarked on a land invasion of Western Europe; though whether they would have fared better than the Blenheims and Battles of 1940, considering the generous target area and large radar profile they presented, is an arguable question. In the context of this history, which is concerned with the RAF strategic nuclear deterrence role, they represented a stepping-stone in the build-up of the V-bomber force, particularly in providing high-altitude and jet experience for the crews to be converted on to the Valiants, Vulcans and Victors in 1955-6-7.

By the end of 1955 there was a reduction in the Canberra B.6 force, from six to five squadrons: as the AMQLR for Oct-Dec 1955 put it, "in order to relieve accommodation problems at Hemswell and Binbrook and to permit the timely formation of the H2S attack wing of the Bombing School. . . ."

CHAPTER VIII
V-BOMBERS' ENTRY INTO SERVICE:
THE VALIANT SQUADRONS

Wittering has already been referred to as the home of the Bomber Command Armament School and the repository of the first Blue Danube atomic bombs in November 1953. The airfield was also to be the site of the initial Valiant flying in Bomber Command, for a special unit, No 1321 Flight, already referred to, was formed there on 3 August 1954 to conduct trials of the Valiant on behalf of the Ministry of Supply. Thus Wittering, as far as both weapons and aircraft were concerned, played a pioneer part in the origin of the V-force.

Gaydon had a similar pioneer role, for on 1 March 1954 authority was given for the opening-up of the airfield there[1] as the base for No 232 OCU, where the first purely RAF flying on Valiants was to be done and the first squadron (No 138) formed, before it moved to Wittering. The role of the OCU was to train Valiant crews. Unlike the Canberras, squadrons of which were formed before an OCU was started, the V-bombers were introduced at OCUs where training began contemporaneously with the arrival of the aircraft. Squadrons were then formed as soon as enough crews had been trained; but it had been a matter for debate whether a Valiant OCU or a squadron should be formed first[2]. In the case of the Valiants at Gaydon, the first squadron was formed before the OCU, by a matter of weeks: No 138 was established with effect from 1 January 1955 and got its first aircraft on 8 February; No 232 OCU was established on 21 February. The latter's task was to convert crews to the new type, from that date onwards, and also to conduct intensive flying trials with the Valiant.

While the V-force crews were formed at Gaydon, and later at Waddington, their members had received initial training in their roles elsewhere. As AVM S W B Menaul, who as a Group Captain had commanded the Bomber Command Bombing School at Lindholme from 1957 to 1959, put it in his book *Countdown: Britain's Strategic Nuclear Forces:*–[3]

---

[1] Originally completed in 1942, it had been a satellite for RAF Chipping Warden, base of No 12 OTU which trained crews for Wellington IIIs. From September 1942 it was controlled by RAF Wellesbourne Mountford and used by Nos 22 and 6 OTUs. In July 1945 part of the airfield was used by No 3 Glider Training School in Flying Training Command, then it was reduced to inactive status until March 1954, when revived and developed on a large scale to receive the first V-bombers.

[2] There was considerable Air Staff discussion as to whether the first Valiant unit to be formed should be a squadron or an OCU. A meeting held by DCAS (Air Mshl Sir Ronald Ivelaw-Chapman) on 26 June 53 decided in favour of a squadron, as far as nomenclature was concerned; but its function would have to be combined with that of a development unit and of a training unit.

[3] Robert Hale Ltd, 1980. AVM Menaul later became SASO at HQ Bomber Command, 1961-65.

"To support the front line, there was a large training organisation including the Bombing School, the Operational Conversion Units . . . and a nuclear weapons school. . . ."

Earlier, he said that

"the Bombing School at Lindholme, in Yorkshire, where young aircrew were trained in the complex radar, navigation and bombing equipment they would have to use on joining an operational squadron in Bomber Command, was a very important link in the training organisation. On completion of the course at Lindholme, crew members went to Gaydon or Waddington (later Finningley) where they joined captains and co-pilots for the remainder of their training as complete crews. Lindholme had been specially prepared and equipped to fulfil its important role in training the bomb aimers and navigators, and as the build-up of the V-force gathered momentum, it worked at very high intensity turning out the crews needed for newly formed squadrons. Although the course was already long and demanding, it was decided to add to it elementary instruction on nuclear weapons and their effects,[1] so that navigators and bomb-aimers, in addition to mastering the intricate equipment of their trade, would also have a good working knowledge of nuclear weapons. After all, they might one day have to drop them in anger".

Referring to the part played by Lindholme in the training of V-force aircrew, *A Review of the V-force*, issued in March 1955 (previously quoted)[2], said that Valiant aircrew training began in earnest at Gaydon in February 1955 and that "preparatory training on NBS and H2S" was "in progress at the Bomber Command Bombing School, Lindholme, and in the H2S training squadrons at Hemswell".

From the beginning of 1955 onwards Gaydon had as significant a role to play in the development of the V-force as Binbrook had had in the creation of the Canberra force and Waddington was to have from 1956 onwards in the build-up of Vulcan squadrons – although no operational squadrons were based at Gaydon, as at the other two airfields. After the first Valiant (WP206) had been delivered there on 8 February 1955 the first course on the type – of four crews who were to form the first flight of No 138 Squadron – began on the 21st. Meanwhile, the Aircraft Servicing Flight did a Primary Star Servicing on WP206, and the same on the second Valiant (WP207) which had arrived on the 19th.

During its first full month of operation (March 1955) No 138 Squadron flew 58hr 40min with its two Valiants, two QFIs being converted to the new type and the conversion of "A" Flight crews started. At the same time, courses for airframe, electrical and armament mechanics were being given in the Valiant Servicing School, and the Intensive Flying Trials team were hard at work in the first three months,

---

[1] The first Nuclear Weapons Course at Lindholme was held from 8 to 12 Sep 58.
[2] BC/TS 84435 7 Mch 55.

when approximately 400hr flying was completed.

In April, No 138 got four more B.1s – WP213, 212, 211 and 215 – and did 52hr flying, during the course of which two "A" Flight crews went solo; armament, instrument, electrical and radio instruction continued in the Servicing School; and the IFT team produced detailed and searching reports on aircraft performance.

One more Valiant (WP217) arrived at Gaydon during May and was "temporarily allocated to No 138 Squadron pending re-allocation to No 543 Squadron" (as the ORB put it). No 543 was shortly to be formed,[1] as the second Valiant squadron, the No 2 Valiant Conversion Course – which began on 2 June – becoming its "A" Flight. Its role was to be photographic reconnaissance, with B(PR).1s. During July "A" Flight got its full establishment of four aircraft – WP217, 219, 223 and 221 – and its four crews did their first solo on the type. In August the total of Valiants at Gaydon increased to 11 and No 3 Conversion Course, which began on the 25th, consisted of "B" Flights of Nos 138 and 543 Squadrons. About half the hours flown during this month were devoted to practice formation for the SBAC Display at Farnborough in September: "training suffered severely", the ORB commented, quoting the flying hours' totals as 44hr training and 43hr formation. In the latter month there was an even larger imbalance: out of 169hr total flying, 87hr was spent in formation, 55hr on training and 27hr on "other" flying.

It was not until 16 November that "A" Flight of No 543 and "B" Flight of No 138 Squadrons left for their respective operational bases, Wyton and Wittering.

No 138 Squadron had moved to Wittering on 6 July; this is recorded in the squadron ORB, but not in that for RAF Gaydon/No 232 OCU – though the latter does record that "B" Flight of 138 Squadron started its conversion training on 25 August, in No 3 Valiant conversion course.

On 11 December "B" Flight of No 543 Squadron, their conversion training complete, left Gaydon for Wyton; and by that month over 500 pupils had passed through the Servicing School for courses in airframe, electrical equipment, engines, armament, instruments and radio. These inevitably rather dreary dates and figures do indicate, however, the logistic problems involved in introducing into RAF service the most complex type of aircraft it had so far operated – the Valiant, first of the V-bombers, which was to be used over the next ten years in the bombing, strategic reconnaissance and tanker roles, and also to test-drop the British atomic and hydrogen bombs.

The three stations where the Valiants were first based – Gaydon, Wittering and Wyton, all in No 3 Group of Bomber Command – formed the foundations for the V-force which started to come into being during 1955. By the end of that year the first two squadrons, Nos 138 and 543,

---

[1] Its official date of formation was 1 Apr 55 (AMSO Qtly Liaison Report No 35 – Quarter ended 30 May 55).

had been inaugurated at Gaydon, where Valiant intensive flying trials were done and where No 232 OCU was in full swing training air and ground crews.

At Wittering, No 138 was established as the first operational Valiant squadron; and there too was the Bomber Command Armament School, possessor of all knowledge and experience of atomic bombs in the Royal Air Force and holder of existing stocks of weapons, the Bomber Command Development Unit – whose functions (as has already been stated) were to undertake trials of aircraft and ancillary equipment and to study tactics and operating procedures – and No 1321 Flight, engaged on Blue Danube trials.

At Wyton, with the establishment of No 543 Squadron there, a long-range element had thus been added to Bomber Command's photographic reconnaissance capability. When the squadron was in the course of working-up at Gaydon its ORB had recorded (during October) that it was "part of Main Force Bomber Command Strategic Reconnaissance Photographic Wing". Its move to Wyton was mainly made during November, though the four crews of "B" Flight moved there in December when their conversion at No 232 OCU had been completed. Squadron strength increased gradually during 1956. With an establishment of eight Valiant B(PR).1s, it had seven by March – a month during which one of its aircraft did NBS/H2S clearance trials – and ten by April.

When No 138 Squadron made the move from Gaydon to its operational base, Wittering, its first four Valiants flew in there on 6 July, having been preceded by an advance party to set up the administrative headquarters. At Wittering, No 138 encountered the genesis of the Bomber Command V-force – the Command Armament School, repository of RAF knowledge of atomic bombs; the Command Development Unit; and No 1321 Flight, engaged on Blue Danube trials.

As has been mentioned in an earlier chapter the new squadron lost one of its Valiants, and all the crew aboard, in an accident at Wittering only three weeks after arriving there. On 29 July at 0917 hr Sqn Ldr E R Chalk and three other officers (Flt Lt A G Allen – the squadron engineering officer who was acting as co-pilot, Fg Off T S Corkin – navigator, and Plt Off A R Lyons – signaller) took off on a cross-country flight. Soon after becoming airborne their Valiant B.1, WP222, went into a left-hand turn, which continued through 300°, in a descending attitude, until the aircraft struck the ground at a speed estimated as about 300kt only some three minutes after take-off. During this descending turn the aircraft door was jettisoned and though one crew member, Plt Off Lyons, baled out he unfortunately did not survive.

A Court of Inquiry expressed the "firm opinion . . . that the accident was due to the aileron trim tab being in the fully up position, and that this was caused by a runaway actuator". It recommended that "the aileron trim tab setting should be limited so that, when flying in power, the aircraft can be controlled up to its maximum design speed". The Court made a further recommendation about emergency escape from Valiants – that "further investigation be conducted into the general problem of abandoning the Valiant aircraft when the aircraft is in an unusual attitude, as in this case; also to see if the arrangements for the crew cannot in some way be improved. At present the fact that it is so difficult for the crew to abandon aircraft to some extent negatives the provision of ejector seats for the pilots".[1]

This was the first RAF Valiant to be lost – the prototype, WB210, had been lost three-and-a-half years earlier on a test flight on 12 January 1952 when an engine fire developed during relight trials. On that occasion all the crew abandoned the aircraft – the rear crew members through the doorway and the two pilots by ejection – but the co-pilot, Sqn Ldr B H D Foster, was unfortunately killed when he struck the fin of the Valiant after being shot out of his cockpit, because the aircraft was in a descending turn.

The provision of escape facilities in the Valiant, Vulcan and Victor was to cause controversy later in the history of the V-force.

During the first half-year of its existence at Wittering, to the end of 1955, No 138 Squadron was chiefly engaged on engine proving trials: the first Valiants had Rolls-Royce Avon 20101s – developed from RA14s of 9,500lb s.t. These were known as "Gold Seal" engines in the context of the trials[2]. Far more hours were flown during this period on these trials than for any other purpose, except for Operation Too Right, a proving flight to the Far East. Thus as the end of October the ORB reported that 58hr 48min had been flown on Trial 270 (the engine trials), 37hr 02min on other sorties and 145hr 55min on Too Right, which was concluded on 6 October. During November, 172hr were flown on Trial 270 and 54hr on other sorties; and in December, 159hr on Trial 270 and 54hr on other sorties – including, for example, "continuation training, ILS, GCA, etc". To give an even better idea of the ratio, during this last month of 1955, out of a total of 48 sorties flown, 31 were on Trial 270.

Operation Too Right demonstrated how, from its inception, the V-force practised mobility. Its aim was "to provide a proving flight of two aircraft to the Far East". Valiants WP206 and WP207 left Wittering on 5 September for Habbaniya, Iraq, groundcrew having previously been positioned along the route[3]. They flew thence to Negombo, Ceylon (WP206 having to have No 3 engine changed at Sharjah), with a refuelling stop at Karachi; from there to Changi, Singapore, then to Australia – which WP207 reached on 10 September, two days ahead of its delayed partner. In Australia, both Valiants took part in displays at

---

[1] Court of Inquiry proceedings.
[2] Interview with Gp Capt U L Burberry, OBE, RAF (Ret), on 18 Nov 76.
[3] Report on Operation Too Right, App No 36 to No 138 Sqn ORB for October 1955.

Sydney, Melbourne, Canberra, Hobart (Tasmania) and Adelaide, and on 19 September flew to New Zealand. There they gave demonstrations – over Christchurch and Wellington – then returned to Australia on 26 September, demonstrating over Brisbane and Amberley. Three days later both Valiants left for Changi, and after primary inspections began their homeward flight on 2 October. Flying via Negombo and Karachi (for refuelling) they reached Abu Sueir, Egypt, on 4 October. The intention was for them to fly direct from there to Wittering: WP206 did this and arrived back on 6 October, but WP207 developed a fault in the transfer tank feed, diverted into El Adem and after refuelling reached Wittering some three hours after WP206.

During this operation the Valiants were supported by a four-Hastings transport force (two aircraft from No 24 (Commonwealth) Squadron and two from No 47 Squadron), and the report said that it showed that the Valiant was "capable of flying to high intensity, in a variety of climates, without the immediate backing of a static base". Also that, as it developed, the thoughts of the aircrew became globally rather than parochially inclined – suggesting that operations away from the UK were "an essential part of the V-force aircrew's education".

The Operation was a very useful proving flight for the Valiant, its engines and equipment. The diary noted that "of the components and equipment carried in the aircraft the modified Avon engines, Green Satin and STR18B2 probably provide the most interest, and the general results, in spite of unserviceabilities in WP206 [which had the engine change at Sharjah], are sufficiently complete to prove the efficiency of all three". As to aircraft performance, "half-hourly recordings were made on all flights and have been forwarded to the Bomber Command Development Unit for analysis". Green Satin, the main navigational aid used, became unserviceable in WP206 after the first 53 hours' flying, but in WP207 "behaved magnificently throughout the flight". Likewise, STR18B2 radio equipment "was used continuously throughout the operation with good results" in the latter aircraft, but in WP206 became unserviceable after being used continuously during the first 20 hours of the operation.

Although the experience gained in Too Right could not be said to read across directly to V-force operations from UK bases, it was valuable in giving the Valiant a long work-out under varied climatic conditions and also in demonstrating what kind of support was required at bases along the route to the Far East – thus providing information on provisioning for future overseas deployments. The Royal Air Force, and Bomber Command, also gained kudos from the publicity given to the appearance of the first of its V-bombers in Australia and New Zealand. The report noted that "the press gave very good coverage and were particularly understanding about Security Regulations governing the disclosure of detailed information". *Flight* recorded during the visit (30 September 1955) that the Valiants' first public appearance in Sydney "aroused considerable interest", and the AOC in C Bomber Command, Air Mshl Sir George Mills, went out to Australia at the same time in one of the support Hastings and met the No 138 Squadron crews there. They were led by Sqn Ldr R G Wilson, OC "A" Flight.

Early in 1956 three more Valiant squadrons – Nos 214, 49 and 207 – came into being and another Class 1 airfield, Marham, was added to the V-force bases: until then it had housed four Canberra squadrons, Nos 35, 90, 115/218 and 207. No 214 Sqn, based there, collected its first B.1 on 15 March from Gaydon; its CO, Wg Cdr L H Trent VC DFC, captained the delivery flight. On the 28th he participated, flying one of 214's three Valiants, in a formation fly-past – with aircraft from Wyton – for visiting Soviet Ministers. The new squadron's role was to form part of the Main Force of Bomber Command.

The fourth Valiant squadron to form – No 49, at Wittering – had a different, specialist role to play: that of carrying-out 'F' Series Trials (Operation Grapple, the first live drop of British atomic bombs at Christmas Island in the Pacific). Its first CO was Wg Cdr K G Hubbard OBE DFC, who took over in September 1956 from Sqn Ldr D Roberts DFC AFC, who had commanded No 1321 Flt which did the Blue Danube aerodynamic trials from Wittering during 1955. The first sortie recorded in the re-formed squadron's ORB[1] was in Valiant WP201 which had been No 1321 Flight's aircraft. No 49 therefore took on No 1321's trials role and immediately started on preparations for Operation Grapple[2].

No 207's formation was the first instance of the conversion of a Canberra into a Valiant squadron: until February 1956 it had been operating Canberra B.2s from Marham. Towards the end of May it re-formed there as part of the Main Force, Bomber Command, and in June began Valiant flying – its first five sorties being three delivery flights and two continuation training exercises.

Two more Main Force Valiant squadrons came into being before the end of 1956, both converting from Lincolns – No 148 forming at Marham, on 1 July, its CO (Wg Cdr W J Burnett DSO DFC AFC) and his crew collecting their first B.1 from Wisley on the 26th; and No 7 at Honington – another of the Class 1 airfields – on 1 November, its CO (Wg Cdr A H C Boxer DSO DFC) and his crew delivering their first Valiant at the end of that month[3].

Thus by the end of 1956 the V-force had seven Valiant squadrons – six in the bomber and one in the reconnaissance role, which was to be its total complement of this type. These Valiants occupied four Class 1

---

[1] It had been operating Lincolns.

[2] During its first month's existence the ORB records meetings at the Air Ministry and with Vickers-Armstrongs to discuss the operation.

[3] No 7's ORB records that "the first Valiant was collected from No 49 Sqn at Wittering by Wg Cdr A H C Boxer DSO DFC and crew on 30 Nov. The arrival of this aircraft was to have been the occasion for a small ceremony at which the AOC No 3 Group, AVM K B B Cross CB CBE DSO DFC was to have been present but the aircraft proved to be unserviceable...."

airfields in No 3 Group – Gaydon (the OCU), Wittering, Marham and Honington.

During 1956 also, Vulcans made their first appearance with the V-force – on Operational Reliability Trials (see Chapter XI).

No 138 Squadron had another commitment during late 1955, in addition to the engine trials and Operation Too Right – practising for, and performing, fly-pasts during that year's SBAC Display at Farnborough. Its ORB for August reported that "flying for the month was almost entirely spent on fly-past practice for the SBAC Show"; and at the end of September the ORB noted that there had been a dress rehearsal for the fly-past on the 5th (opening day of the Show), two further fly-pasts being performed on the 6th and the 10th. Subsequently, on the 13th, No 138 was visited by the Prime Minister (Sir Anthony Eden), for whom a fly-past was organised; and on the 21st the squadron's CO (Wg Cdr R G W Oakley) demonstrated the Valiant at Marham to the Netherland's War Minister (Mr Cornelis Staf) and other Dutch visitors, who were accompanied by the Under-Secretary of State for Air (Mr George Ward).

Dispersal was an aspect of operations which was stressed very early in the existence of the V-force. Referring to "dispersal of the Medium Bomber Force in war", the AMSO Quarterly Liaison Report for the quarter ending 30 September 1955[1] said that "with the deployment of the first V-bomber squadron at Wittering during July, urgent attention is being directed towards drawing up detailed plans for the dispersal of the MBF in war, or during times of international tension. The plan is intended to give full effect to HM Government's declared defence strategy based on the deterrent value of the V-force. The majority of Commands at home will be called upon to provide basic deployment facilities for elements of the force"[2]. The full implications of dispersal are described in Chapter XVIII of this history.

---

[1] No 36 – A 232030/55.
[2] In the event there were 27 dispersal airfields, belonging not only to home-based RAF Commands but in some cases to the Royal Navy and the MoA, in addition to the ten main V-bomber bases.

CHAPTER IX

CANBERRA LIGHT BOMBER
FORCE DEPLOYMENTS

During 1954, as has been noted, the Canberra light bomber force grew towards its final size and shape; and on 25 August that year the first Canberra squadron was deployed to Germany: this was No 149, which went initially to Ahlhorn. By the end of the year there was a total of 24 squadrons, Main Force Canberras totalling 214, 19 of which were B.6s, more powerful and with greater range than the B.2s. The first stage of Bomber Command's post-war re-equipment programme with jet aircraft had thus been completed and preparations were well under way for the next stage – setting-up the medium bomber force. That year's *Statement on Defence*, published on 18 February[1], had been quite unequivocal in its forecasts. "We intend as soon as possible", it said, "to build up in the Royal Air Force a force of medium bombers capable of using the atomic weapon to the fullest effect"; and it added: "atomic weapons are in production in this country and delivery to the forces has begun". The Canberras, however, constituted a conventional bombing force. It was not until 1958, in Germany, that they were given a nuclear capability with American weapons.

By 1954, when the V-force was about to receive its first aircraft, Bomber Command had built up a considerable body of experience and operational knowledge of jet aircraft with its Canberras: it was from this force that aircrew for the V-bombers were largely to come. The Air Ministry Quarterly Liaison Report for October-December noted that "captains and navigators for the first Valiant squadron have been selected and are now undergoing training with Messrs Vickers-Armstrong" and that "bomb aimers for the first Valiant squadron have been selected and are now undergoing intensive electronics and radar bombing training at the Bomber Command Bombing School at RAF Hemswell".

Another important development during this year in planning for the future was that on 24 August authority was given for the formation of the Bomber Command Development Unit at RAF Wittering, its main tasks being to undertake trials of aircraft and equipment as directed, and "to study tactics and operating procedures and make recommendations which will assist the C in C to fulfil his operational tasks with the resources at his disposal". At about the same time and on the same station, No 1321 Flight was formed "for the purpose of conducting special trials on the Valiant aircraft on behalf of the Ministry of Supply". Bomber Command was thus now urgently preparing for the build-up of its jet medium bomber force, armed with nuclear weapons.

---

[1] Cmnd 9075.

The light bomber force of Canberras reached its peak size in 1956, when there were 24 squadrons (five of B.6s and 19 of B.2s) with a total UE of 230 aircraft[1]. Describing its capabilities in a report to S of S[2] in March of that year, VCAS said that the Canberras were equipped for visual bombing from heights of up to 43,000ft; their only radar bombing aid was Gee-H – "a ground-based aid liable to jamming"[3]. VCAS's report went on to refer to a chain of stations in north-west Europe extending to about 200 miles east of the Rhine, and said that provided seven days' warning could be obtained, plans existed to position equipment at certain forward sites, extending this coverage.

The Canberras' main radar navigational aid was Gee Mk 2, but again the cover this provided was restricted (to the UK, France and Germany up to a line Rostock-Magdeburg-Munich). Additional navigational aids were Rebecca – fitted to all aircraft – and the radio compass, with which a small number of Canberras were fitted for operations overseas. But all these aids, like Gee-H, were liable to jamming. Two of the B.6 squadrons were also fitted with Blue Shadow, a sideways-looking search radar. None of the Canberras currently had any RCM equipment, but could carry Window; a dispenser was being developed, but could not be in squadron use before mid-1957.

Referring to the Canberras' atomic potential, VCAS said that the development of Red Beard [a tactical nuclear bomb] was going ahead; current estimates indicated that the first weapon would be available to the Service at about the end of 1957. He added that English Electric were working on a full trial installation of an American weapon[4] and dropping trials from a partially modified Canberra were due to begin shortly at RAE. It was proposed to modify the B(I).8 version first, as the modification was simpler on this aircraft and would provide "an atomic capability in the shortest possible time".

Canberras were deployed to the Middle East theatres during 1957 by the re-equipment of Venom squadrons – Nos 32, 73/6 and 249 in MEAF and No 45 in FEAF – with B.2s[5]. The ME deployment stemmed from a Baghdad Pact planning decision in May 1956 that the UK should declare four light bomber squadrons to the organisation's forces[6] and

---

[1] Most of the squadrons had a UE of ten aircraft.
[2] In VCAS file Operational Readiness of the RAF (ID9/90/18 (Pt 1)). S of S was then Mr Nigel Birch and VCAS was Air Chf Mshl Sir Ronald Ivelaw-Chapman.
[3] The reliance of the Canberras on Gee-H limited their effectiveness during the Suez operation later in 1956, when Pathfinder Force techniques were re-introduced.
[4] Presumably the US Mk 7 weapon, with which Canberras were equipped from 1958 onwards (initially the squadrons in RAF Germany), is referred to here.
[5] See Conversion of MEAF and FEAF Squadrons to Canberras – AHB IIH/272/3/12 Pts 1 and 2. The first of four B.2s for No 45 Squadron arrived at RAF Tengah, Singapore, on 13 December 1957; one was delayed at Katunayake with a technical defect and two collided when about five minutes away from the airfield, only two of the aircrew (Squadron Leader C C Blount, the squadron commander, and his navigator Flying Officer F N Buchan) surviving (ORB, RAF Tengah, Dec 57). (See also page 127).
[6] Baghdad Pact – Planning (ID3/440/2 Pts 1–2).

the Far East deployment followed-on from the detachment of UK-based Canberra B.6 squadrons from 1955 onwards during the Malayan Emergency[1].

The Baghdad Pact (Cento) Treaty had been signed in March 1955 when the United Kingdom acceded to the Turco-Iraqi Pact; then Pakistan and Persia joined, making the Pact a five-power organisation, and a permanent Council was established. In 1956/57 the United States became a member of the Pact's Economic and Military Committees. Following the Iraqi coup on 14 July 1958 and the fall of its Government that country withdrew from the Pact, in March 1959, and on 20 August the Pact's name was charged to Central Treaty Organisation, the Secretariat-General and the Military Planning Staff moving their HQ to Ankara in October.

When the Baghdad Pact had been formed the UK was the only member country[2] which (as in the case of Nato in 1950–51) could provide a bomber contribution, and in November 1955 the plans were for two Canberra B.2 squadrons – totalling 16 aircraft – to form in the Middle East Air Force at the end of 1956. It was considered that they would then, or shortly afterwards, be capable of carrying nuclear weapons[3]. At the end of 1955, however, this view was modified to one that "a real nuclear potential" could not be produced in MEAF before 1959[4], and this more realistic appreciation was confirmed in early 1956[5].

It was in May of the latter year that the idea of four light bomber squadrons as part of the UK commitment to the Baghdad Pact was considered and approved by the UK Chiefs of Staff[6], and in July that intention was confirmed: two fighter/ground-attack squadrons were to be re-equipped in the near future and "at a later date two further squadrons with Canberras". This was the origin of the re-equipment of the Venom squadrons previously mentioned – Nos 32, 73, 6 and 249 – with B.2s. This committal of four light-bomber squadrons to the Pact was approved by the CoS on 13 July 1959.

The deployment of the first two Canberra B.2 squadrons, Nos 32 and 73, was mounted from Weston Zoyland, the base of two Canberra squadrons, Nos 76 and 542[7], and the first two B.2s sent to Cyprus, WH870 and WK103 of No 32 Sqn, reached Nicosia on 3 March 1957 (subsequent flights were routed to Akrotiri). Two more B.2s arrived on the 7th; on the 19th the squadron completed its move from Nicosia to Akrotiri; and by April it had been equipped with eight aircraft. Its ORB

---

[1] See *The Malayan Emergency 1948–1960* (MoD Jun 70).
[2] The US was never a full member.
[3] Brief for the CIGS in ID9/4/38 (Pt 1).
[4] ACAS (P) Baghdad Pact Appreciation of the Military Situation, 23 Dec 55.
[5] JPS 18 January 56.
[6] COS(56) 270.
[7] No 76 was involved in the Christmas Island (Operation Grapple) trials and No 542 was a PR(MR) squadron.

for February had commented:–

"No clearly defined operational policy exists at the moment, but a preliminary directive from AHQ Levant lays down that crews are to become familiar with ME air routes and are to attain a high standard of visual bombing as soon as possible. A shallow dive marker element is to be trained within the unit".

No 73 Sqn flew out its first four aircraft to Akrotiri on 19–20 March 1957 and another four at the end of the month, completing the Canberra move from Weston Zoyland. In its first month (April) of operations from Akrotiri the flying had been "quite varied" (the ORB noted) and included flights to El Adem, Malta, Aden and Teheran, "giving experience to the crews . . . of their operational area".

The other two MEAF light bomber squadrons, Nos 6 and 249, formed and flew out from Coningsby in the summer and early autumn of 1957: No 6 arrived at Akrotiri in two flights, 'A' on 15 July and 'B' on 1 August. No 249's departure from the UK was held up, however, first by the fact that its Venoms were involved in Oman so consequently its ground crews might not be back in Cyprus for the originally planned arrival dates there in September, and secondly by non-receipt of a signal in the Air Ministry and by fog in Lincolnshire: it eventually arrived at Akrotiri on 16 October, its two flights having left Coningsby on the same day with a two-hour interval between them[1]. Its arrival meant that the station then housed five Canberra squadrons (four bomber and one PR – No 13).

The B.2s' role was a conventional bombing one, and although in 1958 references were already being made to "the theatre nuclear strike force" in Air Ministry comments on Baghdad Pact air defence[2] it was not until the squadrons had been re-equipped with B.6s in 1960 and a tactical nuclear bomb (Red Beard) became available that the Akrotiri Canberra squadrons achieved a strike capability.

While the Canberras sent to the Middle East represented a new element in that theatre, those sent to the Far East confirmed an existing element, the presence of Canberras in the offensive air support forces of Operation Firedog from 1955 onwards[3]. These were B.6s of Nos 101, 617, 12 and 9 Squadrons detached from the UK to RAAF Butterworth in northern Malaya for Operation Mileage, from March to August 1955. Canberra B.2s were then based in Malaya from the end of 1957 onwards, with the arrival of the first aircraft for No 45 Squadron at

---

[1] File IIH/727/3/121 Conversion of MEAF and FEAF squadons to Canberras.
[2] File Baghdad Pact – Planning ID9/440/2 (Pt 7), the comments being made in May of that year in reference to CMPS (Combined Military Planning Staff) paper on Air Force Requirements for the Baghdad Pact Area "Not Limited by existing potentials".
[3] See *The Malayan Emergency 1948 – 1960* (MoD, June 1970).

Tengah on 13 December[1], its re-equipment (from Venoms) being followed during 1958 by the re-equipment of Nos 2 (B) RAAF and 75 RNZAF Squadrons. As the official history of the Malayan campaign[2] puts it:–

"The potential air-strike force received considerable reinforcements in the second half of 1958 with the build-up of the Commonwealth Strategic Reserve in Malaya but only a small part of this force was actually required for the remaining offensive air support commitments in Operation Firedog[3]. The Venoms of No 14 (RNZAF) Squadron were replaced at Tengah by the Canberras of No 75 (RNZAF) Squadron on 1 July 1958, while Nos 2(B) and 3(F) Squadrons of the RAAF, equipped with Canberras and Sabres respectively, arrived at Butterworth on 11 November, where a small detachment of Bomber Command Valiants was also deployed for short periods of two weeks at three-monthly intervals (Operation Profiteer). The arrival of these forces at Butterworth restored the ability of the air forces to respond quickly to bids for strike action in Northern Malaya, that had been affected by the withdrawal of No 45 Squadron to Tengah in November 1957, but such action was hardly ever required at this stage in the campaign . . .".

The re-equipment of No 45 Squadron was completed with the arrival of its second flight at Tengah on 9 January 1958, but its B.2s were not used in Firedog operations until March, continuing until they made their final strike in August 1959[4]. The historian of the campaign expressed scepticism about the Canberras' operational value in Malaya, saying[5] that they were "too elaborate for the task they were required to carry out" and adding:–

"They carried half the bomb load of Lincolns and their cruising speed of 250kt at the optimum bombing height required more elaborate navigational aids and made map-reading impracticable and visual bomb-aiming difficult. The pilot had a poorer visibility than in a Lincoln and the Canberra could not be flown at night or in close formation and could not be employed in a strafing role. They suffered, in common with all jet aircraft in the tropics, from a serious limitation in their endurance at low level, which precluded the possibility of postponing or delaying an air strike once they were airborne. This was a serious disadvantage in the uncertain weather conditions of Malaya, especially in 1958 when Canberras were operating in the northern part

---

[1] Unfortunately an ill-fated arrival, a FEAF Press Release dated Friday, 13 Dec 57, stating: "Two of three RAF Canberra twin-jet aircraft on a ferry flight from the UK to a Royal Air Force station in Singapore this afternoon collided in dense cloud near Kulai in the Pontian district of Johore. Each of the aircraft carried a crew of three. Two of the occupants, the pilot and navigator, of the leading aircraft parachuted to safety...". (See also page 124).

[2] See note [3] on page 126.

[3] The campaign against Communist terrorists in Malaya lasted from June 1948 to July 1960.

[4] FEAF News Service Release of Oct 60 in IIJ50/140/4/7 (Pt 1) Command Information Office – RAF Tengah No 45 Sqn.

[5] In *The Malayan Emergency 1948–60*.

of the country far from their parent base at Tengah near Singapore, and was reflected in an increase in the rate of abortive air strikes when they replaced Lincolns. When flown at their normal speed at low altitudes the swirl vanes of Canberra engines suffered badly from metal fatigue in the hot, turbulent air which also made flying conditions difficult for their pilots. For those Canberras that were not fitted with Godfrey air coolers, sun canopies, cooling trollies and external compressed air supplies had to be employed to combat the danger of loss of bodyweight through sweating which could amount to as much as 3lb per sortie.

"Both from the point of view of maintenance and flying conditions Lincolns were preferable to Canberras in the type of campaign that prevailed in Malaya...".

The Canberra squadrons at Akrotiri encountered different environmental problems during 1958 – those of internal security during the EOKA campaign and of a Middle East crisis centred on Jordan and the deployment of British forces there. From that year onwards, as a bomber wing they took part in MEAF, Cento and Nato/Mediterranean exercises. In 1959-60 two of the squadrons, Nos 6 and 249, were given a target-marking capability by being re-equipped with B.6s with Blue Shadow sideways-looking radar; then in 1961 the re-equipment of the squadrons with B.15s (Nos 32 and 73) and B.16s (Nos 6 and 249) began: these were conversions of the B.6 for NEAF and FEAF, equipped to operate in the tactical nuclear or conventional bombing roles, or as ground-attack aircraft; and in November of that year Akrotiri achieved its nuclear storage capability for this B.15/16 force when on the 28th its Supplementary Storage Area was "taken over and occupied"[1]. The Strike Wing, as the Canberra squadrons then became, was operational from the station until early 1969, being succeeded in March of that year by two Vulcan B.2 squadrons, Nos 9 and 35, as will be described in a later chapter.

---

[1] Station ORB.

Weapons

All photographs are Crown Copyright

'Fat Man' - the American plutonium bomb dropped on Nagasaki, killing 23,753 inhabitants and wounding 43,020. It had no ballistic streamlining and was described by aircrew of the B-29 which dropped it as 'just a huge iron cask'

'Little Boy', the U-235 bomb dropped on Hiroshima: like 'Fat Man', an unstreamlined weapon

Blue Danube, the first British atomic bomb (employing U-235), produced after the successful Operation Hurricane test in the Monte Bello Islands in October 1952 and issued to the Bomber Command Armament School, Wittering, from November 1953

A sectioned model of Blue Danube: note the ballistic streamlining and how the "ball" determines the size of the case

The first RAF thermonuclear weapon - Yellow Sun Mk 1, the "interim" megaton bomb designed after the Operation Grapple tests and issued in 1958

Yellow Sun Mk 2, the definitive British free-fall megaton-range bomb, seen here on a Type L trolley

Yellow Sun Mk 2 in a dissassembled state

Red Beard, the 'tactical nuclear bomb', on a Type J trolley

Another view of Red Beard, giving an indication of its size

A Symonds Hoist, used for loading Red Beard (2,000lb) into a Victor
B.1 of No 100 Sqn - denoted by its skull-and-crossbones badge

Red Beard on a Type J trolley for lifting into a Vulcan

WE177B 950lb retarded low-level weapon on an O trolley

US Project 'E' weapon, the Mk 43 (2,100lb), on a Type J trolley

Another view of the 2,100lb Mk 43 US bomb

Loading an inert Yellow Sun Mk 2 bomb during a Nato Exercise Unison

Conventional (1,000lb) bombs being loaded: the Victor could carry 35 of these in its capacious bomb-bay

A thermonuclear
explosion
photographed by
a Canberra PR.7
of No 58 Sqn
after a drop by
Valiant XD825
of No 49 Sqn on
8 November 1957
during the
second series of
Grapple trials

Vulcan B.2 depicted with two Douglas Skybolts, the US ALBM which
would have extended the QRA role of the V-force: instead, this was
taken over by the Royal Navy's submarine-launched Polaris missile

Avro Blue Steel being carried by a Vulcan B.2 of No 617 Sqn

A Blue Steel-armed Victor B.2, XL158, of No 139 (Jamaica) Sqn

Low-level Blue Steel carriage by Vulcan B.2 XM572 of No 9/35 Sqns

Mating Blue Steel to its carrier: the Vulcan procedure

Victor/Blue Steel mating - with limited ground clearance

Blue Steel being lowered on to its trolley for Victor arming

Vulcan B.2/Blue Steel weapon system

Victor B.2/Blue Steel, the kneeling figures showing close ground clearance

A Blue Steel being unloaded on to a trolley from an AEC Mandator ten-ton guided missile transporter

A Blue Steel being refuelled in the HTP (high test peroxide) bay at Scampton, base for the Vulcan/Blue Steel force

Blue Steels in the servicing and storage bay at Scampton, their exposed rear ends showing the Bristol Siddeley Stentor rocket engine which powered them to the apogee of their flight path

Another view of the Blue Steel refuelling procedure: note the protective clothing worn by the airmen

CHAPTER X

THE SUEZ OPERATION

Although the compiler of the No 7 Squadron ORB had noted that its aircrew "were warned to stand by for flying duties in connection with operations in Egypt", the newest Valiant squadron was not in fact called upon to participate in Operation Musketeer (31 October to 6 November 1956). It could only have made a nominal contribution, however, unless the operation had gone on longer, since at the time it only had one aircraft and three crews.

Four of the six other Valiant squadrons participated – Nos 138, 148, 207 and 214, all of them Main Force squadrons. The other two, Nos 49 and 543, had specialist roles – nuclear weapon trials and strategic reconnaissance respectively. In addition to the Valiants there were ten squadrons of Canberras in Operation Musketeer: Nos 9, 12, 101 and 109 (all with B.6s) flew from Malta and Nos 10, 15, 18, 27, 44, 61 and 139 (all with B.2s except for No 139 which had B.6s and operated in a marker role) from Cyprus. The Valiants' sorties over Egypt were the first, and only, time these V-bombers ever bombed "in anger".

Before referring to the exhaustive report made on Operation Musketeer, the squadrons' own comments – made at the time in their ORBs – are worth noting.

Summarising its activities for October 1956, No 138 Squadron recorded that

"the important event of this month has been the detachment of the squadron to Luqa, Malta, and the subsequent bombing attacks on airfields and military barrack areas in Egypt. On 31 October six crews were briefed to carry out an attack on Cairo West airfield. Led by the squadron commander, these crews took off during the afternoon but after roughly one hour's flight all aircraft were recalled, as it was believed that American civilians were being evacuated by air from that airfield. After burning off fuel, all aircraft brought back their bombs and landed safely. Later that evening two crews, captained by Sqn Ldrs Wilson and Collins, carried out an attack on the airfield at Abu Sueir. Both crews dropped proximity markers and 11,000lb of bombs and both marking [techniques similar to those used in the Second World War being employed] and bombing were observed to be extremely accurate. No enemy opposition, either by fighters or anti-aircraft fire, was encountered by either crew.

"The squadron groundcrew were flown out to Luqa in Shackleton aircraft and worked extremely long hours in a cheerful manner to keep all aircraft serviceable. Before operations commenced, two aircraft took part in an exercise from Luqa and two other aircraft carried out bombing details at Filfla Island".

No 138 was the only squadron to have its full strength of eight

Valiants at Luqa; Nos 148 and 207 each had six and No 214 only four. The three latter squadrons told their operational stories in ORB entries for October 1956, No 148 noting that on the 31st it "became the first V-force squadron to take part in operations by leading the attack against Almaza airfield". This was made "by five Valiants of No 148 Squadron and one from 214, four Canberras of No 109 Squadron and three of No 12 operating from Malta. The visual marking was done by Canberras operating from Cyprus[1]. Canberras from Cyprus also carried out bombing on the same target. Little opposition was encountered. There was light flak around the target area but it was sporadic and well below the attacking aircraft . . . . Intelligence reports stated that there were ten Vampires, ten MiG-15s, ten Il-28s, nine Meteors and 31 twin-engined transports on the airfield . . . ."

Nos 207 and 214 Squadrons' ORBs both referred to Operations Goldflake and Albert – the former being a deployment to Malta as a measure against a Pearl Harbour-type attack on Cyprus by Egyptian forces, and the latter, sorties against Egyptian targets, – and the compiler of No 214's operational record[2] provided a vivid vignette of the squadron's experience in Malta when he wrote:–

"For the record, it is interesting to note that in spite of every endeavour, it was impossible to discover throughout the long period of standby at Marham just who the future enemy was likely to be.

"Crew-room diplomats and students of Middle East history were of the opinion that Fighter Command and Jordan[3] would be arraigned against Bomber Command and Israel. Other well-informed crew members had little doubt that we were standing by to assist Egypt against Israel.

"The looks and expressions of surprise can only be imagined when, within two hours of landing at Luqa, all crews gathered in the Bomber Wing Operations briefing room for the first operational briefing and the curtains were drawn aside to reveal Egyptian airfields as the targets.

"Targets in Phase 1 were the Egyptian airfields operating Russian-built Il-28 bombers and Mig-15 fighters and at dusk on 30 October operations commenced.

"Airfields attacked by the squadron were Almaza near Cairo (on 30 October) and Abu Sueir (on 31 October). The aiming-points were the runway intersections and crews were briefed to avoid the camp areas. Further instructions were given that bombs were not to be jettisoned 'live' in case Egyptian casualties were caused".

During Operation Musketeer the airfields on two Mediterranean islands, Malta and Cyprus, were crowded with RAF bombers. On the

---

[1] Presumably by No 139 (Jamaica) Squadron with Canberra B.6s, the only target-marker squadron at the time of the Suez operations.

[2] Flying Officer R A C Ellicott.

[3] At the time of the Suez operations No 32 Squadron, with Venom FB.1s, was based at Mafraq in Jordan.

former, Luqa had 24 Valiants (the entire commitment of the V-force to the operation) and seven Canberra B.6s of No 109 Squadron; Halfar had 22 Canberra B.6s of Nos 9, 12 and 101 Squadrons. On Cyprus, a 59-strong Canberra force was concentrated at Nicosia – consisting of Nos 10, 15, 18, 27, 44 and 61 Squadrons with eight B.2s each and No 139 (the target-marking squadron already mentioned) with 11 B.6s.

Operations against targets in Egypt, for the six-day period (31 October – 5 November) during which 131 sorties were flown from Malta and 264 from Cyprus and 942 tons of bombs dropped, proved to be a disappointing experience for Bomber Command – whatever excitement there was at the time among the crews, either those with Second World War operational tours behind them or those without wartime memories, at the prospect of "live" bombing. In fact there were more hazards in recovery to the island airfields than when over Egypt, where very little opposition was encountered.

Abu Sueir, Almaza, Cairo West, Fayid, Kabrit, Kasfareet and Luxor airfields were the chief targets, in addition to Almaza and Huckstep barracks, El Agami Island (where a submarine repair depot was believed to be located) and Nifisha marshalling yards. One of the many reports written subsequently commented: "The operations over Egypt met little opposition and the targets bombed were large and distinctive . . ."[1].

The chief themes of these reports were that the bomber force was not geared to this kind of operation, and that its navigation/bombing equipment was either not suitable or non-existent – not yet having been fitted in some of the Valiants.

The Musketeer Report[2] said bluntly that "in July 1956 Bomber Command was ill-prepared to undertake a Musketeer-type operation . . . . The Command was geared to a 'radar' war in Western Europe and was not constituted nor organised for major overseas operations . . . . The majority of the Valiant Force had neither NBS nor visual bomb-sights and were not cleared for HE stores . . . ".

As for the Canberras, "the Canberra aircraft forming the bulk of the force deployed are equipped only with Gee-H as a blind bombing device and it was not possible to position ground-based beacons to give coverage for this equipment over Egypt . . . . It was considered that it would be prudent for the early attacks to be made at night and this necessitated a reversion to the marking technique successfully used in World War II . . . "[3].

Bomber Command nevertheless had to perform the tasks it was called upon to undertake with the aircraft currently available, even though the Canberras needed Gee coverage for efficient operation and many of the Valiants were not fully equipped. Lincolns, which no doubt would have

---

[1] Appendix 'C' to 1395/S1/2/Air dated 16 Nov 56.
[2] AHB file IIH/272/3/40A: Musketeer Reports, which contains all the reports quoted from here.
[3] The Techniques Used and the Results Achieved by BC during Operation Musketeer.

done the job effectively (although vulnerable to jet fighters), had been retired from front-line service by the end of 1955.

The Musketeer Reports commented critically on the bombing and navigation equipment in the Valiants and Canberras at that time[1]. For bombing, Valiants had NBS1/Gee-H and T2 sighting head and Canberras (both B.2s and B.6s) the T2/T3 bombsight and Gee-H. "Of these equipments [Annex 'G' comments], it is understood that the NBS initially had a fairly high unserviceability rate[2] mainly due to the difficulties of servicing a new equipment away from the parent base, and that serviceability later improved. Gee-H could not be used as there were no Gee-H beacons in the Middle East. Thus the bombing capability was reduced to visual bombings of target indicators in good weather only with, in the case of Valiants, fixed sighting angles at all heights, and in the case of Canberras the T2/3 bombsight, capable of visual bombing at all operational heights . . .".

For navigation, equipment in the Valiants was NBS, Green Satin/GPI(iv),[3] VHF, ILS and periscopic sextant; and in both marks of Canberra, Gee-H, Rebecca Mk 4 and ("in some aircraft") radio compass. The Annex comments that "of these equipments, Gee and Gee-H could not be used as there are no stations or beacons in the theatre. Some Valiants had serviceable NBS. The range of Rebecca Eureka was limited to 80 and 90 miles. This meant that the Valiants were still capable of accurate navigation with Green Satin when sea states were suitable and when NBS was serviceable, and of reasonably accurate timing by monitoring the Green Satin by astro. The Canberras, however, had to rely entirely on DR (dead reckoning) navigation monitored by visual pinpoints and in a few cases by radio compass bearings. This was a handicap to the Malta Canberras operating at ranges near their operational radius of action at night, but navigation of Nicosia-based aircraft on their relatively short sorties was not seriously affected".

Two further observations, on recovery of aircraft by their island bases and on weather during the operations, as well as a general recommendation for any future "limited war" bomber operations, were made in Annex 'G' to the Musketeer Reports.

On "the landing problem", it commented that "with no accurate navigation system covering the operational area and the landing bases, it was not practicable to operate large forces from either base, as all aircraft had to be brought overhead to establish position before they could be separated for landing; this restricted the operational radius of action of the Malta Canberra and Valiant forces".

As to weather, "the . . . conditions prevailing in Cyprus and Egypt were

---

[1] Annex 'G' to ATF/TS.11/56 of 11 November 1956.
[2] On the first sortie, against Almaza airfield, two out of the five No 148 Sqn aircraft reported that their NBS was "unserviceable" and "not functioning properly".
[3] Green Satin was the code-name for a navigation computer, operating on the Doppler principle, providing a continuous and automatic measurement of drift and groundspeed.

excellent throughout the period of operations. At Malta, local weather conditions were sometimes bad and three raids had to be cancelled...".

In conclusion, the report recommended that "if 'limited war' bomber operations are again to be mounted it is considered essential that the force should have an all-weather bombing and navigation capability...."

Bomber Command itself produced a 15-page report, with eight appendices, on the Suez operation[1], from which it is clear that this had been an experience which led to much hard thinking about organisation, techniques, equipment and training. When the crisis occurred, the Command "was capable of operating the two Alacrity squadrons[2] in the Middle East at 96 hours' notice". For many reasons, the rest of the Command "could not undertake such operations" pending the positioning of the necessary equipment and supplies, the preparation of additional marker aircraft and crews to enable the force to operate independently of Gee-H, clearance of the Valiant for HE bombs, the fitting of an improvised bomb sighting head to the aircraft and training crews in visual bombing, recovery of the "temporary leeway in Canberra visual training caused mainly by the grounding of B.2s for actuator modifications and by the formation practice for the Royal and Russian visits to Marham", and the exercise of the whole force in marker techniques.

On marking, the report said that no up-to-date photographs and intelligence on targets were available for briefing marker crews; marking equipment was inadequate – no flare clusters were available and old type flares had to be used; the flare carriage system was devised and produced on the initiative of Bomber Command. Nevertheless, "the marker technique was successful and 50 per cent of all bombs plotted fell within 650yd of the target".

Referring to aircraft recovery from sorties, it commented that this was effected proficiently, GCA proving invaluable in Malta, where "the prevailing weather. . . and . . . lack of an alternative overshoot airfield equipped with a landing aid reduced the recovery rate". In operations from both Malta and Cyprus, "the bomber forces involved displayed a very high degree of training and proficiency in operating at intensive rates from congested airfields without an accident or incident".

Among its recommendations for future limited-war operations, the report suggested that the necessary overseas base, supply and servicing communications facilities be provided; that suitable air-transportable equipment should be developed; that Canberra effectiveness should be improved "by the installation of navigation and bombing aids which are

---

[1] HQ Bomber Command Report on Operation Musketeer – BC/S.87926.
[2] Alacrity referred to two Canberra squadrons being on standby to reinforce MEAF.
[3] A major cause of Canberra fatal accidents attributable to technical reasons in the 1952-56 period was malfunction of the tailplane operating electrical system, resulting in runaway tail trim actuators.

independent of ground stations", that adequate air transport should be provided to airlift personnel and equipment in support of overseas deployments, that "Command diversionary commitments such as fly-pasts be strictly controlled and – when unavoidable – should not involve unproductive flying",[1] and that overseas reinforcement squadrons should "undertake regular deployments to, and training in, areas in which they may be required to operate".

---

[1] A clear references to the "formation practice for the Royal and Russian visits to Marham" referred to earlier. Four Valiants of No 138 Squadron had flown past the Queen at Marham in July.

CHAPTER XI

FIRST VULCANS AND VICTORS; THE IMPROVED (B.1A) VERSIONS

As Gaydon had been the alma mater for all Valiant crews (and later was to be so for Victor squadron personnel) so Waddington was the centre for Vulcan knowledge. There, at No 230 Operational Conversion Unit, the second of the V-bombers was introduced into service. Preparations for this started in 1955, but because the Vulcan operational reliability trials were done at A&AEE (Aeroplane and Armament Experimental Establishment) Boscombe Down, the OCU did not receive its first aircraft until January 1957. Some of the frustration felt by the unit's staff at the delay in getting its work going is conveyed by entries in the Operations Record Book, which also voices criticism of the way things had been done at Gaydon (No 232 OCU) in introducing the Valiant.

No 230 OCU had trained Lincoln crews at Upwood until January 1955, then in the middle of that year moved to Waddington and there began to get organised for its new task – setting-up office accommodation, refurbishing the ground school block, drawing-up syllabi, drafting lectures and holding dummy courses attended by members of the resident Canberra squadrons (Nos 21 and 27). The unit's new CO, Wg Cdr F L Dodd DSO DFC AFC, arrived on 19 October and subsequently a Memorandum on the Formation of the Vulcan OCU at Royal Air Force Waddington was prepared (dated 5 November) in which the unit's aim was described as: "To train crews to operate the Vulcan efficiently to its limits". Copies of this paper were sent to the Headquarters of No 1 Group and of Bomber Command. It criticised the procedure followed at Gaydon: "At the Valiant OCU an attempt was made to train crews for the first squadron concurrently with staff for the OCU. This method inevitably delays the date by which the OCU is ready to undertake its proper task; and in the haste to form a squadron, or part thereof, it is possible that the OCU does not have the time to discover the full capabilities, and limitations, of the aircraft on which it is supposedly responsible for the teaching. This is a risk which must be taken in war but may be difficult to justify in peace". As to the flying syllabus at Waddington, "it is proposed to take advantage of the greater range of the Vulcan by including grid navigational trips to high latitudes, as well as routine Mediterranean trips . . ."; while as to ground training, ". . . the Vulcan itself, compared with the Valiant, is simpler in that it has an automatic fuel cycling system, and is devoid of tailplane, flaps and manual reversion . . .".

The Vulcan was given its Service release on 31 May 1956, as DOR(A) (Air Cdre H J Kirkpatrick) informed PS to CAS in a minute of 4 June[1], a

---

[1] In AHB file ID3/942/5 (Pt 2) Victor/Vulcan (B.35) Development & Production.

release which, he said, "clears the Vulcan for speeds up to 0.98 indicated Mach number. It also permits flying at up to 167,000lb all-up weight. This is the weight with full internal fuel plus a 10,000lb bomb load...". As it happened, the official formation date for No 230 OCU coincided with the Release: "Authority is now given", said a postagram from the Air Ministry to Bomber Command on 23 March, "for the formation of No 230 OCU at RAF Waddington, equipped with 10 UE Vulcan B.1, with effect from 31st May 1956"[1]. It was later agreed that the unit should also have three Canberra T.4s.

The decision to base the Vulcan trials at Boscombe Down had been taken in mid-1956. A letter from SASO, Bomber Command, on 23 June said:[2]–

"It has been decided that Operational Reliability Trials for the Avro Vulcan are to take place at A&AEE Boscombe Down.

"Vulcan XA895[3] is to be detached from Waddington to Boscombe Down for the duration of the trials, which call for 150 flying hours".

SASO (AVM S O Bufton) added that the trials were to be carried out "as intensively as possible", with a minimum of 30hr per week as the target. This trials flying was also to be "utilised fully by No 230 OCU for the conversion of flying instructors".

At the same time, the OCU was keeping a sharp eye open at Waddington on what was going on at the A&AEE. The unit's ORB for April 1956 recorded that "heartening news was received from Wg Cdr F L Dodd after a visit to Boscombe Down about the progress of our first production aircraft, now undergoing acceptance trials with the Boscombe Handling Squadron". Then in May, pre-dating what SASO said in his letter, the ORB quoted the Operation Order for the trials:–

"It has been decided that the Operational Reliability Trials for the Avro Vulcan, involving about 200 hours' flying, are to be carried out on Vulcan VX895[4] at A&AEE Boscombe Down. All aircrew and servicing personnel are to be provided by No 230 OCU".

Before the new delta-wing V-bomber was in service, enthusiastic plans were being made to show it around the world. In July the ORB recorded:–

"The unit has been involved in the planning for two special flights to be made by the AOC in C (Air Mshl Sir Harry Broadhurst) in a Vulcan. One is a flight to the USA in company with two Valiants to observe the SAC Bombing Competition, and the other is a trip to Australia and New Zealand to participate in the Battle of Britain celebrations in these two countries".

Everything possible was to be done to speed the preparations:–

"As well as paper planning [the ORB recounted] a certain amount of

---

[1] OS9A file No A177010/53 No 230 OCU – Establishment of.
[2] BC/87949 in A225139/55 Pt I Intensive Flying Trials Vulcan Aircraft.
[3] XA895, seventh production aircraft, was allotted to the OCU on 16 Aug 56.
[4] This should be XA895: see subsequent reference.

physical help has been given. A team of groundcrew from the station, many of whom belong to this unit, has been detached to A V Roe Ltd at Woodford to assist the firm in the fitting of Column 9 equipment[1] [Green Satin ARI5851, NBS (H2S Mk IX and NBC Mk II), Blue Devil[2], Gee Mk III ARI5186, Marconi radio compass, radio altimeter, radar altimeter, AMU Mk IV, AMI, periscopic sextant Mk II and mounting, STR18 and ILS] to XA895 and XA897. This will considerably reduce the period required by the technicians for the aircraft to be on the ground after their delivery to the RAF. Also at the works is one airman who has been painting station and unit crests and the C in C's markings on the two aircraft. . . ."

These two Vulcan B.1s were, in fact, the first two of their type to be delivered to the Royal Air Force – allotted to No 230 OCU but initially operated from A&AEE Boscombe Down. The ORB for August 1956 expressed some frustration at having two Vulcans on the unit strength but not being able to fly them from Waddington, commenting: "The drawback of having to operate the aircraft at Boscombe Down still remains a major problem, particularly administratively, but it is one which we must accept until the Operational Reliability Trials are completed".

September 1956 saw the first substantial amounts of flying by Vulcans in the RAF. On the 9th, the planned trip to Australia and New Zealand – Operation Tasman Flight – began (the other planned overseas sortie, to the USA, had been postponed in August); and on the 20th, operational reliability trials on XA895 began at Boscombe Down, 46hr 50min flying being completed by the end of the month. No 230 were obviously pleased about this achievement; as the ORB recorded: "When it is considered that two Primary Star and one Primary inspection had also been carried out during this ten-day period, it is obvious that a very high utilisation rate indeed has been achieved. Although this reflects favourably on the aircraft's inherent serviceability it is largely due to the unremitting efforts of the groundcrew, who have worked long hours under difficult conditions to keep the aircraft flying."

Operation Tasman Flight, in Vulcan XA897 which had been painted with the station and unit crests and C in C's markings, had as its aim route-proving and survey to Australia and New Zealand. Aboard the Vulcan were the AOC in C Bomber Command, Air Mshl Sir Harry Broadhurst, flying as second pilot; four Squadron Leaders – D R Howard (captain), E J Eames (navigator), J G W Stroud (observer and spare pilot) and A E Gamble (air electronics officer); and a civilian, Mr F Bassett, representing A V Roe the manufacturers. Accompanying the

---

[1] *Ie*, equipment enabling the aircraft to fulfil its assigned task.

[2] A minute of 20 Jan 55 from DMARD(RAF) to DOR(A) refers to "the question of adopting Blue Devil in place of VSA for the V-bomber visual sight" and "an estimate of the time required by the three firms to complete a trial installation of Blue Devil equipment". This was the T.4 bomb-sight to OR/3041 (file B.35/46 Medium-range Bomber – Type Requirements. OR/299 – Vulcan (C48971/52/Pt IV)).

137

Vulcan and under command of the AOC in C were three Coastal Command Shackletons carrying technical support teams and equipment, and a Canberra PR.7 flown by the PSO to the AOC in C, which the latter would use as emergency transport to keep to the planned itinerary should the Vulcan become unserviceable. In addition, Vulcan XA895 at Boscombe Down was held in reserve to fly out in case XA897 became unserviceable for a long period. This did not occur, XA897 being "able to adhere precisely to its planned itinerary over a period of 23 days"[1] (the 9 September–1 October duration of Tasman Flight).

The Vulcan flew from Boscombe Down to Aden (Khormaksar) in 7hr 20min on the first day and on the second from Aden to Singapore (Paya Lebar) in 8hr 20min. On 11 September it arrived in Melbourne (Avalon), having flown from Singapore in 7hr 35min, and subsequently visited Sydney (Mascot) and Adelaide (Edinburgh Field). At Sydney the Vulcan did fly-pasts over RAAF Richmond and Bankstown, as well as over the city and Mascot airfield; at Edinburgh Field a great deal of servicing assistance was given by the ground crew of the Operation Buffalo Task Force[2].

On 18 September, XA897 went on to New Zealand – to Christchurch (Harewood); and after departing from there on the following day for RNZAF Ohakea it did a low-level tour of the South Island, flying at 2,000ft over the towns *en route* at precise times – which had been announced in advance by local radio stations. On 19 September it flew low level over towns in the North Island, achieving all its ETAs within one minute. When the Vulcan landed back at Ohakea its tail parachute was streamed "by popular request", to make up for the disappointment caused when this was not done on the first arrival there.

With its departure from Ohakea on 22 September for Brisbane (Amberley), XA897 was homeward bound, flying on to Darwin the next day and thence to Singapore (Changi). The report made an interesting comment on the Vulcan's landing at the last-named airfield: "Changi runway is only 2,000yd[3] so it was decided to stream the parachute. No difficulty was experienced and without harsh use of brake the aircraft was stopped in about 900 yd. . . ." On the outward flight XA897 had landed at Singapore's civil airport, Paya Lebar.

Landing in Ceylon on 27 September was not, however, quite so straightforward: "Because Negombo runway is only 2,000yd with difficult approaches, it was decided to stream the tail parachute . . . but as soon as it developed it immediately jettisoned, necessitating fairly strong braking to bring the aircraft to a stop. The Vickers release unit was found to be burnt out, which caused the parachute to jettison". The

---

[1] Report on Operation Tasman Flight (BC/S89168/Ops. HQ Bomber Command, February 1957).

[2] Operation Buffalo was code-name for the atomic bomb dropping trials in which Valiants of No 49 Squadron were involved.

[3] Compared with the 3,000yd, plus overruns, available at Class 1 airfields in the UK.

report also commented that "during the flight to Negombo it was hoped to make contact and speak to CAS by HF R/T. The necessary arrangements were made".

The hope was that these would result in a successful air-to-ground conversation during the flight to Aden on the 30th; but the attempt was abortive: "Contact was made with Farnborough by HF R/T, but before arrangements could be made for the AOC in C to talk to CAS, conditions deteriorated and further contact was arranged for the following day".

This was 1 October, the final day of Operation Tasman Flight, and the report recorded:

"The aircraft was loaded to 168,000lb and take-off conditions were much the same as they had been on 10 September.

"Contact with Farnborough was soon made on HF R/T and the AOC in C had a conversation with CAS.

"Instruction to land at London Airport[1] had been received at Aden, together with the procedure to be adopted. The flight was uneventful until another Vulcan (XA895, Wg Cdr Dodd) made contact over Sardinia and kept in company to the French coast.

"Vulcan XA897 crashed while doing a GCA approach at London Airport."

In the accident, which resulted from the aircraft touching-down short of the runway during its ground-controlled approach, the four rear-crew members lost their lives and the two pilots ejected safely. After a Court of Inquiry had considered the circumstances and prepared a report[2], the Secretary of State for Air (Mr Nigel Birch) made a statement in the House of Commons on 20 December 1956[3] clearly describing the circumstances of the disaster and detailing subsequent investigations into its causes. The Vulcan, he said,

"had left Aden at 0250hr GMT where the captain had been given forecasts of landing weather at London Airport and certain other airfields to which he might need to divert. He obtained later information en route, including further forecasts for London Airport. The last of these was given to him when he was over Epsom. This forecast, which indicated broken low cloud, heavy rain and little wind, with visibility at 1,100yd, proved an accurate description of the weather actually experienced".

The Minister continued:–

"The aircraft had ample fuel to divert, and Air Marshal Broadhurst emphasised to the captain that he should divert if he was dissatisfied with the weather conditions prevailing. The captain decided to make

---

[1] Where a VIP reception had been arranged for the Vulcan crew; see *The Aeroplane* for 5 Oct 56: "Unhappily, the disaster occurred while the distinguished party gathered . . . to welcome the aircraft home was waiting in the VIP enclosure".
[2] DFS Accident File XA897; in 90/29 Aircraft Accident Vulcan XA897 (London Airport).
[3] Commons Hansard 20 Dec 1956 Cols 1476–1479. Although the Court of Inquiry Report had been prepared by 17 Oct 1956 there were some dissentient views on its findings.

one attempt to land at London Airport. At about 1000hr, at a height of 1,500ft and about 5nm from touch-down, and with both altimeters correctly set, the aircraft began its descent under the control of the Talkdown Controller at London Airport. The captain set his 'break-off height' at 300ft. That is to say, he intended to come down under the talkdown control until his altimeter stood at 300ft and, if he then found that it was not possible to make the landing, to overshoot at that height. The GCA talkdown instructions were followed, with some undulation relative to the glidepath and some corrections in azimuth, up to a point about three-quarters of a mile from touch-down, when the pilot was informed that he was 80ft above the glidepath. At this point the weather was at its worst. The pilot received no further information on elevation, and at a point about 1,000yd from the touch-down point and 700yd from the threshold of the runway, the aircraft struck the ground. Both main undercarriage units were removed, and the elevator controls[1] were damaged. Subsequently the aircraft rose sharply to a height of 200–300ft, when it was found to be out of control. The captain then gave the order to abandon the aircraft and himself used his ejector seat. The co-pilot repeated the order and after trying the controls also ejected. Within seconds of the order being given the nose and starboard wing of the aircraft dropped and the aircraft crashed to the ground. The remaining three members of the crew and the passenger were killed instantly on impact."

Referring next to subsequent investigations, the Minister said:–

"The Royal Air Force Court of Inquiry, which assembled the following day, found nothing to suggest any technical failure in the aircraft which could have contributed to the accident. They concluded that the captain of the aircraft was justified in deciding to make an attempt to land at London Airport but it considered that, in the circumstances, he made an error of judgment in setting himself a break-off height of 300ft and also in going below that height. The Court drew attention, however, to the facts that though the GCA controller informed the pilot about seven seconds before the aircraft first hit the ground that he was 80ft above the glidepath, he did not subsequently advise him that he was below it, and that after the aircraft had hit the ground he continued his talkdown as if the approach had been normal. The Court concluded that, since the aircraft was under GCA control, the failure of the controller to warn the captain that he was going below the glidepath was the principal cause of the accident."

Having given the main finding of the RAF Court of Inquiry[2], the Minister went on to refer to the inquiry into the GCA system. He said:–

"On receipt of the Report, I referred the passages relating to the GCA

---

[1] The Vulcan B.1 had four trailing-edge control surfaces on each wing, the outer pairs acting as ailerons and the inner pairs as elevators (A V Roe brochure SB.10 Issue 1, Jul 54).

[2] With which Captain V A M Hunt, Director of Control and Navigation, MTCA, dissented, issuing a separate statement.

aspect to my right hon Friend the Minister of Transport and Civil Aviation[1], who immediately arranged for an inquiry into the operation of the GCA system to be undertaken by Dr A G Touch, the Director of Electronic Research and Development at the Ministry of Supply.

"In a report which he submitted last week[2], Dr Touch concluded that there was no evidence of technical failure or malfunctioning in the GCA equipment. His investigation confirmed that the pilot was not warned by the GCA unit of his closeness to the ground, but despite a detailed and exhaustive examination of various possibilities, Dr Touch was unable to establish the reason with certainty. He thought that the most likely explanation was that throughout the approach the controller concentrated too much on azimuth at the expense of information on elevation. He felt, however, that there were extenuating circumstances connected with the unusual speed of the aircraft and the number of corrections in azimuth. He also considered that even if a warning had been given in the final five or six seconds of the ten seconds which, in his opinion, elapsed after the pilot was told that he was 80ft above the glidepath, it would have been too late.

"My right hon Friend the Minister of Transport and Civil Aviation and I have given most careful consideration to these findings. We are agreed that there was an error of judgment on the part of the pilot in selecting a break-off height of 300ft and in going below it, and also that the GCA controller did not give adequate guidance on elevation during the descent and, in particular, that he was at fault in the concluding stages in not warning the pilot that he was below the glidepath and therefore dangerously close to the ground. The apportionment of responsibility is difficult. I accept the conclusion of the Royal Air Force Court, but neither I nor my right hon Friend feel able to define the degree of responsibility precisely.

"It would be unjust to the pilot and co-pilot were I not to make it clear in conclusion that it was their duty to eject from the aircraft when they did. The Court of Inquiry were satisfied on the evidence put before them that there could have been no hope of controlling the aircraft after the initial impact. In these circumstances, it was the duty of the captain to give the order to abandon the aircraft and of all those who were on board to obey if they were able to do so. Both the pilot and co-pilot realised when they gave their orders that, owing to the low altitude, the other occupants had no chance to escape and they considered that their own chances were . . . negligible.

"The House will wish to join with me in expressing regret that so successful a flight should have ended so tragically and in tendering sympathy to the bereaved."

The last point the Air Minister made in his statement, about the

---

[1] Mr Harold Watkinson.
[2] MTCA Report of the Special Investigation by Dr A G Touch into Certain Aspects of the Accident to the RAF Vulcan . . . XA897 at London Airport on 1 Oct 56; HMSO '57.

ejection of the two pilots from the Vulcan, was the only aspect of the Heathrow accident which had a bearing on future operations by the V-bombers – for means of escape for rear-crew members in emergency at low altitude continued to be a matter for debate throughout the life of the V-force.

On the day after the loss of Vulcan XA897 the Air Minister asked the Air Staff to set out their policy on ejection seats, and DCAS (Air Mshl G W Tuttle) replied on 15 October 1956 with a minute describing the design arrangements for escape from the V-bombers. He recalled that when they were "originally conceived between 1946 and 1947

"it was the intention that each of them would have a jettisonable pressure cabin which would separate from the aircraft and then do a parachute-stabilised descent. As design and development proceeded it became clear that this facility could not be provided, and agreement not to have a jettisonable cabin was reached in the case of the Valiant in June 1948, the Vulcan in May 1949 and the Victor in October 1952.

"In all three bombers the layout of the cabin, which was operationally very satisfactory, made it impossible, for structural reasons, to produce ejection facilities for aircrew other than the pilots. It was, however, agreed to provide ejector seats for the pilots so that they could remain with the aircraft longer and help the other crew members to escape. Facilities for the other crew members were provided by means of side doors in the Valiant and Victor and through an underneath hatch in the Vulcan, which has virtually no fuselage.

"The result of this is that all three bombers and the developments of them will, according to present planning, have ejector seats for the pilots and escape by door or hatch for the three other crew members. A trained crew takes approximately 20sec from the time the order to jump is given until the last man leaves the aircraft, but it is important to remember that it is unlikely that the three non-pilot crew members would escape in conditions where high G forces are being applied through battle damage or loss of control, when the aircraft is at a low level. On the other hand, when the first Valiant had a fire in the air all five members of the crew got out of the aircraft successfully at high altitude – unfortunately the second pilot was killed by striking the fin[1].

"I have discussed a possible modification plan for the V-bombers with Mr James Martin[2] and with the Ministry of Supply, and am of the opinion that it is certainly not impossible to incorporate ejection facilities for the three non-pilot members of the crew of the V-bombers …but the implementation of such a policy would naturally raise very grave issues.

"The first issue is whether or not we would rather be right to go in for such a policy, and the second issue is whether we could afford to do so, both in terms of money and effort as well as in the delay of the V-force

[1] See page 59.
[2] Of the Martin-Baker Aircraft Co, makers of ejection seats.

build-up... A retrospective modification programme would naturally be an immense undertaking but it is not technically impossible, and if we do not go in for it we must realise what may be involved. My own view is that we should not attempt to adopt such a policy...".

At No 230 OCU, regret was expressed on both professional and personal grounds at the loss of such highly skilled crew members. Its ORB for October 1956 noted sadly:–

"Overshadowing all things this month has been the disaster to Vulcan XA897 on 1 October, which crashed at London Airport whilst landing on its return from Tasman Flight, with the loss of four lives. The captain, Sqn Ldr D R Howard DFC AFC, and second pilot, Air Mshl Sir Harry Broadhurst KCB KBE DSO DFC AFC, escaped from a low altitude by using their ejection seats. Sqn Ldr J G Stroud, pilot[1], Sqn Ldr E J James AFC, navigator, Sqn Ldr A E Gamble, air electronics officer, and Mr F Bassett, A V Roe's representative, were killed in the crash. Their loss is deeply felt by all members of the unit, and in one blow the OCU lost the Senior Flight Simulator Instructor, the Chief Navigation and Weapons Instructor, and the Senior Air Electronics Officer."

The Air Staff had made it clear that the accident did not affect plans for forming Vulcan squadrons, which would go ahead as fast as deliveries permitted[2].

During October, operational reliability trials continued on XA895 at Boscombe Down, and most of the No 230 OCU flying instructors were converted to type on this aircraft by the CFI, Wg Cdr C C Calder DSO DFC. On 8 November, the latter visited A V Roe's at Woodford to get up-to-date forecasts on the delivery of subsequent Vulcans to the unit; and during December, with the ORTs completed, XA895 returned to Waddington.

It was during January 1957 – "the best month that the unit has had since its formation", to quote the ORB – that No 230 OCU really got into its stride. "On the 18th . . . both XA895 and XA898 became available to the unit for flying and at 0920hr on the 19th the first aircraft took off on the first sortie of the Intensive Flying Trials. . . . On the 29th a conference was held on the station to decide . . . future . . . policy in respect of the participation of the Strategic Air Command Bombing Competition, the training of our courses and the Intensive Flying Trials. . .". It was decided that the order of priority should be: the SAC Bombing Competition, training the first course, and the IFTs. The competition commitment "had priority over all others in respect of the Vulcan in Bomber Command".

---

[1] In the RAF Proceedings of the Court of Inquiry into the Vulcan accident Sqn Ldr Stroud's crew duty is given as "2nd Nav" and his hours on type and hours on all types entered as "Not known". But he was a qualified Vulcan pilot with a Master Green rating. (See *V-force, The History of Britain's Airborne Deterrent*, by Andrew Brookes; Jane's 1982).

[2] Minute, DCAS/S of S, 5 Dec 1956.

1957 might well be described in Bomber Command history as the year of the Vulcans and Victors (the Valiants, whose activities will be described later, had come up to full strength by May 1957 with 59 aircraft in seven squadrons)[1]. The first two Vulcan squadrons, Nos 83 and 101, were formed and at the end of the year the Victor entered service with No 232 OCU.

Vulcan activity during 1957, which was to culminate in the new bomber's participation in the SAC Bombing Competition at Pinecastle AFB in Florida during October[2], was centred on No 230 OCU at Waddington where the first two squadrons were formed. The spirit of that unit, now it was beginning to operate its own Vulcans, was epitomised by an ORB entry for January which said: "This has been the best month that the unit has had since its formation. The commencement of really serious flying has had a wonderful effect on the morale and spirit of all our personnel, despite the 24hr-a-day seven-day-a-week work which has been involved. As we have always believed, our aircraft is inherently serviceable and with reasonable luck our commitments can be met without any undue trouble".

On 20 February No 1 Course on the Vulcan, consisting of 25 students – ten pilots, ten navigators and five signallers (one of them an AEO), began conversion; their three months' training included a month's ground school, two weeks' ILS flying and lectures, and six weeks' flying (captains were expected to do 31hr day and 20hr night) – with 15 May as target date for completion. The ORB commented: "After 18 months of planning, talking, organising and not a little frustration, we have now begun the task for which we are primarily established. It is upon the training which we give to this course and its successors that the efficiency of Bomber Command and hence the hitting power of the Royal Air Force very largely depends...".

During March three more Vulcan B.1s arrived at Waddington – XA896, XA901 and XA900; but (commented the ORB), "although there are [now] five Vulcans on the station, the combination of a large modification programme and normal periodic servicing has meant and will continue to mean that we can rarely hope to have more than one aircraft flying at any time. This places an appreciable limitation on the amount of training which can be carried out".

No 1 Course at No 230 OCU graduated during May and on 21 May the first Vulcan squadron, No 83, was formed at Waddington with graduates of the course as crews – these five five-man crews being commanded by Wg Cdr A D Frank DSO DFC and the squadron

[1] Last of these to form was No 90, on 1 January 1957, although it did not receive its first Valiants until March. There were also an SR (No 543) and an ECM (No 199) Squadron.

[2] "After an absence of several years, the Royal Air Force entered the competition with two Vulcan and two Valiant aircraft and crews" (*The Development of Strategic Air Command 1946–1971*, HQ SAC brochure). An invitation had been extended by the USAF in 1956 but it was "reluctantly decided" to decline it (RAF Participation in SAC Bombing Competition (AHB file ID3/921/62, Pt 1)).

(formerly flying Lincolns at Hemswell) having an establishment of four Vulcan B.1s. Unfortunately, it did not have any aircraft as yet; as its ORB said, in reporting its royal inauguration: "On the day of the formation of the squadron, the station was honoured by a visit from HRH the Duchess of Kent, who watched the first take-off by a squadron crew at 1445hr that day, flown by Sqn Ldr Staff on a practice bombing mission. It was unfortunately abortive, owing to unserviceability of the radar bomb sight. Since no squadron aircraft had arrived, all flying was by courtesy of No 230 OCU".

During June 1957 two crews of No 83 Squadron, captained by Wg Cdr Frank and Sqn Ldr D R Howard, competed in the Bomber Command Bombing Competition, winning it and carrying off four out of the six prizes awarded. Then in July the squadron got its first two Vulcans – XA905 delivered on the 11th and XA904 on the 16th – its ORB recording that "both aircraft are finished in white and have the new Olympus 102 engines"[1]. Two more were collected from A V Roe's at Woodford during August and in that month there was practice flying for the SBAC Display in September and the SAC Bombing Competition in October. To quote the ORB: "Sqn Ldr F R C Staff and crew and Flt Lt P M Woodward and crew did several practice formation fly-pasts with two Valiants from Wittering in preparation for the SBAC Show at Farnborough. On Friday, 30th August, the three crews for the SAC Bombing Competition did a practice formation fly-past. This was in preparation for the ceremonial fly-past to coincide with the arrival of HM the Queen at the Jamestown celebrations[2]. This is believed to be the first three-Vulcan formation. . .".

The two crews selected to take part in the SAC Competition, captained by Wg Cdr Frank and Sqn Ldr Howard, left Waddington on 26 September together with a crew from No 230 OCU. Their destination was Pinecastle AFB, Florida, and their first leg was flown to Goose Bay, Labrador, which was reached in 5hr 10/15min despite a 130kt headwind over part of the route. Meanwhile, No 2 Course at the OCU had completed their training in August and No 3 in September – the latter being the first course to be posted off the station, to Finningley, to form the first flight of the second Vulcan squadron, No 101.

The two Vulcans and the two Valiants which formed the RAF entry for the SAC Bombing Competition represented the first Vulcan and Valiant squadrons, Nos 83 and 138, and their two parent formations – Nos 1 and 3 Groups. A total of 90 crews took part, making up 45 teams, each of two aircraft. In the team results for blind bombing and navigation combined, the Valiants were placed 27th and the Vulcans 44th. One of the Valiant crews achieved the second-best blind bombing

---

[1] Of 11,000lb s.t.
[2] The Festival celebrating the 350th anniversary of the founding of Jamestown, first English-speaking settlement in America.

score and was placed 11th in the final analysis of the 90 individual crew results; this was the crew captained by Sqn Ldr R W Payne of No 214 Squadron, representing No 3 Group. Overall, however, the results were disappointing for the RAF and for the V-force crews making their first appearance in the competition.

The AOC in C Bomber Command, Air Chf Mshl Sir Harry Broadhurst, who was at Pinecastle, commented that "the results have rather hinged on the experience of the ground crews in maintaining the equipment rather than the aircrews using it". As to the malfunctioning of some electronic equipment, he said that "the humidity has been affecting the Vulcan more than anything else"[1]. A leading article in *Flight* for 15 November 1957, headed "Back in the Nuclear Club", referred to the C in C's comments and added some pertinent ones of its own:–

"…The Valiants and Vulcans failed to do well: not through lack of effort or skill, but mainly through a combination of adverse circumstances – malfunctioning of electronic equipment; operations at an altitude much lower than the V-bomber crews prefer[2]; and, in the case of the Vulcans, comparative unfamiliarity of crews with their machines.

"Yet Sir Harry rightly stresses the benefits of the contest. The RAF crews and their USAF counterparts have become 'mentally integrated to an extraordinary degree'; SAC has been informally invited to take part in the RAF competition next year; and a satisfactory exchange of information exists between the two Commands. All to the good; for what matters above all is the high standard set by the Americans and the experience gained by the V-bomber crews of working overseas. Suez gave Valiant crews a taste of this, and the tropical atmosphere of Pinecastle[3] has provided an even stiffer lesson.

"Sir Harry summed up one aspect of the competition when he said, 'We are back in the nuclear club'. But the technical implications must now be taken to heart by his Command. Much remains to be done before it becomes a wholly effective nuclear force."

On the 12th the Prime Minister had himself expressed concern about the poor showing of the V-bombers at Pinecastle. In a minute to S of S for Air[4] Mr Macmillan commented:–

"We do not seem to have done very well in the bombing competition in Florida. I remember that we used to take pride in surpassing the Americans at navigation and bomb-aiming.

"I see that the Valiants were 27th (out of 45), and that the Vulcans

---

[1] Report in *The Aeroplane* for 15 Nov 1957.

[2] Bombing runs were made at a height of 34–35,000ft (Operational Research Branch, Bomber Command, Memorandum No 185 Results of the SAC Bombing & Navigation Competition 1957).

[3] Near Orlando, Florida, where the competition was held 30 Oct – 5 Nov. On 9 October the detachment commander, Gp Capt John Woodroffe DSO DFC, who was station commander at Wittering, was killed in an accident to a B-47 in which he was flying with Col Michael N W McCoy, USAF, 321st Wing Commander.

[4] PM's Personal Minute, M.560/57.

(which are, after all, supposed to be much better) were very much worse. "I am sure there is a good explanation for all this. ...."

Replying on the 13th, Mr Ward expressed disagreement with the Prime Minister, saying: "I don't think we did at all badly" and that next year the RAF would have longer squadron service with their aircraft, and pointing out that it was "the culmination of the year's training" for SAC, the two best crews from each of its 43 Bombing Wings being selected to take part. Its B-47s had been in squadron service for six years and the B-52s for nearly two, compared with 2½ years for the Valiants and nearly a year for the Vulcans. One of the Valiants had recorded the second best individual bombing score (25 yards) and finished 11th overall. The "primary advantages" of the Vulcan – speed, range and height over target – could not be fully used in the competition, in which the bombing height was 36,000ft – the limit of some of the American aircraft but "well below" that at which the V-bombers regularly practised. In brief, S of S concluded, the RAF crews had shown that they could hold their own with the best SAC crews[1].

While the Vulcan/Valiant teams were participating in the SAC competition the first Victors were coming into service. On 25 April 1957 a minute referring to Victor B Mk 1 Operational Reliability Trials[2] said that "arrangements have been made with the Ministry of Supply for the operational reliability trials of the Victor aircraft to be carried out at A&AEE Boscombe Down....The aircraft used will be XA930 and Bomber Command crews will be participating in these trials". The debut of the third type of V-bomber was officially made with its Air Ministry Initial Release to Service on 29 July 1957. This said that "subject to the observance of the limitations defined in subsequent paragraphs[3], the Victor B Mk 1 is released for Service use by day and by night in temperate climates only". Describing this latest addition to the V-force, the Release said: —

"The Victor B Mk 1 is a crescent-wing medium bomber powered by four Sapphire 7 Mk 202 engines. A crew of five, comprising two pilots, two navigators and an air electronics officer, is accommodated in a single pressure cabin. Power-operated flying controls are incorporated; these have sub-divided or duplicated components as safety measures. There is no manual reversion."

The CA Release of the Victor for Service use, dated 29 July 1957[4], was subject to many limitations – eg, airframe and engine anti-icing systems were not to be used, nor was the autopilot – and an Appendix listed ten pages of modifications as the minimum to the standard of production aircraft before delivery to the RAF.

It may be that the number of modifications which had to be

---

[1] RAF Participation in SAC Bombing Competition – AHB file ID3/921/62 (Pt 1).
[2] Ops(B)2 – C.62164/DDOps(B).
[3] Eg, maximum take-off and emergency landing weight, 160,000lb.
[4] AH/521/01.

incorporated accounted for the delay – over two months – before the first Victor B.1 (XA930) arrived at A&AEE Boscombe Down on 9 October for operational reliability trials. (Boscombe Down had had the first production Victor for preliminary assessment in June 1956, when 13hr flying was done. It was reported that the new type "showed promise" in its primary role as a medium bomber, but that defects which A&AEE had listed had to be rectified before Release to Service could be recommended. Problems which had arisen were "probably no greater than" those experienced at a similar stage with the Vulcan[1].)

Meanwhile, preparations had been made at what was to be the first Victor unit – No 232 OCU, Gaydon, which had introduced the Valiant – for ground instruction on the new type. During May 1957 the Victor flight simulator there was given final trials prior to acceptance; in June the ORB reported that "a staff Victor ground school course was . . . completed . . . , attended by 27 instructors and simulator operators of this OCU and three officers from HQ BC, BCDU and RAF Defford[2]. Flt Lt E Protheroe and FS Brown designed and constructed working models of the Victor hydraulic and power control systems. These demonstration models greatly assisted the instruction during the course". In August the Victor simulator was put to good use – the target was 75hr, of which 67hr were achieved, eight hours being lost through unserviceability. "All the training hours used", the ORB reported, "were taken up by the simulator and flying instructional staff". In September the simulator was used for 60hr 30min, giving continuation training to its staff and to the "A" Squadron QFIs. The ORB recorded somewhat plaintively in October that "the Victor simulator is still awaiting the first Victor course. However, training of instructors continues". The Victor/Valiant ground training school had 49 personnel on its electrical, airframe, engine, armament, instrument and radio courses on the Victor. In November the first Victor aircrew course, and the first Victor aircraft, arrived – the ORB reporting that "No 1 Victor course commenced ground school on 21 November", and that "at 1536hr on 28 November, Victor XA931 landed safely at RAF Gaydon. This was the first Victor aircraft to be delivered by the makers, Handley Page, to the RAF". The ORB added that on the following day the AOC No 3 Group, AVM K B B Cross, "visited RAF Gaydon and flew a one-hour demonstration detail in the Victor".

So, ten years after the prototype contract for it had been placed, the

---

[1] Minute, DOR(A)/PS to CAS (C.82117/OR1, 30 June 56). That the date 9 Oct did not mean that XA930 was ready for trials is indicated by Report No 1 (AH/311/03) dated 18 Dec 57, which said that the Victor arrived at A&AEE on 9 Oct "but was not handed over to the Establishment by the firm, Messrs Handley Page Ltd, until the afternoon of 14 Nov .... During this time a firm's working party was engaged in modifying the aircraft up to Standard No Victor 1/Y/2...". The Release to Service had cleared the Victor for speeds up to 330kt below 35,000ft or MO.95 indicated above it and a maximum auw of 160,000lb.
[2] Base of the MoS Radar Research Flying Unit.

Victor – last of the three V-bombers – entered RAF service[1]. But no kind of exhilaration attended its debut at No 232 OCU, no enthusiasm comparable with that which had marked the Vulcan's entry into service at No 230 OCU in the previous January, and the excited anticipation which had preceded it. Possibly because No 232 OCU had been "in business" with Valiants since the beginning of 1955, when the first squadron had been formed before the OCU itself, the Victors might have been regarded rather as successors to the Valiants – though like the Vulcans they were the embodiment of the B.35/46 Specification, whereas the Valiants were a less complex interim type which had been got into service more quickly.

A second Victor B.1, XA924, reached Gaydon on 27 January 1958 and during that month Operational Reliability Trials continued with XA930 at Boscombe Down. On 21 January the three types of V-bomber now in service – a Valiant from Marham and a Vulcan from Waddington joining one of the Gaydon Victors – had "posed" for Air Ministry photographers flying in two Javelins and a Meteor.

In the early months of 1958 the Victor ORTs continued at Boscombe Down, where there was a two-crew detachment for this purpose, while at Gaydon the new type increased in numbers – there were five by the end of February – and aircrew and ground training courses continued. On 15 March the Air Ministry approved the formation of the first Victor squadron, No 10 (formerly operating Canberra B.2s from Honington but disbanded there in January 1957), wef 15 April.

During April, the No 232 OCU ORB noted, the strength of Victors at Gaydon "decreased to five; Victor XA924 and XA925 left the unit with No 1 Course for RAF Wyton". The latter station was the base of two PR squadrons, Nos 543 (Valiants) and 58 (Canberras). No mention was made in No 543's ORB of the arrival of the Victors or of No 1 Course from the OCU.

No 10 Squadron received its first Victor B.1, XA935, at Cottesmore on 9 April; it was flown in there by the CO, Wg Cdr C B Owen DSO DFC AFC. He subsequently made two further deliveries from the Handley Page airfield at Radlett – of XA927 on 16 April and XA928 on 5 May. In June, this first squadron with the new type noted in its ORB that it was "part of Main Force, Bomber Command" and that it had an establishment of eight Victor B.1s with six on strength. During July, with the arrival of two new crews, the squadron achieved a total of six crews. Meanwhile, IFTs (intensive flying trials) of the Victor had been going on at Gaydon; by the end of June, 694hr 25min had been flown on these, and the target – 1,000hr – was reached on 29 July.

Later that year a second Victor squadron, No XV, was formed at Cottesmore, on 1 September. Its first aircraft, XA941, was collected from Radlett on the 16th by the CO, Wg Cdr D A Green DSO OBE DFC and his crew.

---

[1] The Ministry of Supply had sent Handley Page an ITP (Intention to Proceed) – a contract to build two prototypes – on 19 November 1947.

149

As a third Vulcan squadron, No 617, had been formed at Scampton in May, the V-force consisted by the end of 1958 of seven Valiant bomber squadrons, plus one PR and one ECM squadron with Valiants, three Vulcan and two Victor bomber squadrons. At 31 December there were 82 V-bombers on hand and 104 crews.

Having V-bombers on stations, however, did not necessarily mean that they were fully operational – in terms of equipment or crews. In a letter to CAS (MRAF Sir Dermot Boyle) on 2 June 1958 the AOC in C (Air Chf Mshl Sir Harry Broadhurst) made the startling comment: "Although we have had V-bombers in the Command for over three years it was not until last year that we had a single aeroplane complete to operational standards. We had no groundcrew, aircrew or staff officers with any experience of the equipment and its associated problems...". Nearly two years later, in a minute of 16 May 1960 to the Minister of Aviation (Mr Duncan Sandys), the Minister of Defence (Mr Harold Watkinson) commented:

"I have just returned from a visit to a V-bomber station, where I was surprised to learn that the Victor 1 bombers . . . there had no auto-pilots. I was assured that the Victor 1As and 2s would be supplied fully equipped in this respect."

His minute had been annotated with the note:

"There is an auto-pilot installed. But it is not cleared for use pending modification (re-positioning) of pitot static head. The aircraft are being modified now."

Referring in May 1958 to the cost and capabilities of the V-bomber force, the Earl of Gosford, Joint Parliamentary Under-Secretary of State for Foreign Affairs, said in a House of Lords debate on the Air Estimates[1]:

". . . even allowing for research and development on aircraft, bombs and ballistic missiles, less than one-tenth of the Defence Estimates this year is being devoted to the strategic nuclear deterrent – that is, the V-bomber force and the ballistic missiles with which it will be supplemented. . . . Much of this expenditure fulfils a double purpose. The V-bomber force is fully capable of being used in the conventional role with high-explosive bombs. The same is true of the reconnaissance squadrons of the V-bomber force. Therefore, to say that this force is entirely for deterrent purposes only is not strictly accurate".

In opening the debate, Lord Balfour of Inchrye had said that "out of some £1,500 million defence expenditure we are spending about 7½ per cent on the deterrent and another 7½ per cent on the protection of the deterrent. That is to say, out of a total of some £1,500 million about £250 million is spent on the deterrent and its protection in the form of Fighter Command, radar chains and other protective measures . . ."[2].

---

[1] House of Lords Hansard, 7 May 1958, Col 50.
[2] Ibid, Col 32.

While the Valiants were not developed beyond the B Mk 1 version the Victors and Vulcans were improved to a B Mk 1A standard in a programme which began during 1959, these changes reflecting a reaction to the strategic situation and also to the availability of much greater engine power. Referring to the development of the Vulcan B.1A, AVM D B Craig said in 1980[1] that Intelligence estimates during 1957 about improved Soviet air defence capabilities led the Air Staff to press for improvements to the Vulcan B.1s, and their efforts were rewarded in two ways:–

"First, from 1959 until March 1963 some 29 B.1s were individually withdrawn from the front line for conversion to B.1As. This involved fitting ECM equipments in order to improve the ability to penetrate enemy air defences safely. The bulk of the kit was carried in an enlarged, extended tail cone, and a flat ECM aerial plate was mounted between the two starboard jet pipes. Flight-refuelling equipment in the receiver role was also installed. The first Mk 1A (XH500) went to No 617 Squadron on 29 September 1960.

"Secondly, a dramatic increase in engine power became available as a result of further work by Bristol on their Olympus. The Mk 1 aircraft had only 11,000lb s.t. per engine (Mk 101), and during 1957-58 plans had been prepared to provide rocket-assisted take-off (RATO) for the MBF to ensure adequate runway performance at the smaller dispersal airfields. By mid-1959 these plans were abandoned in the light of engine developments", following a decision to introduce the uprated Olympus 301.

At the same time a Victor B.1 improvement programme was under way, as described by the historian of Handley Page[2], who comments that

"The Air Staff had declined a suggestion in 1959 to re-engine Victor B.1s with 10,000lb s.t. Rolls-Royce Avon RA.28s, but gave full priority to rapid conversion of the last B.1s to a new standard incorporating ECM, using equipment developed by trials in XH587; the modified aircraft were to be known as Victor B.1A and XH613 was allotted for trial installation of the retrofit modification…which entailed revisions to the crew stations as well as the ECM equipment itself[3]. In the event XH617 was written-off, after damage on 19 July 1960, so only 24 Victors were converted; the first, XH613, was flown in from No XV Squadron to

---

[1] Chadwick Memorial Lecture at the Manchester Branch of the Royal Aeronautical Society, 19 March 1980 by AVM D B Craig, AOC No 1 Group (subsequently VCAS, then AOC in C Strike Command and CAS as Air Chief Marshal Sir David and subsequently CDS), whose RAF career had been closely associated with the Vulcan – as CO of a squadron (No 35) and station commander at Akrotiri when the two B.2 squadrons of the NEAF Bomber Wing were based there.

[2] C H Barnes, *Handley Page Aircraft since 1907* (Putnam, 1976).

[3] "During 1959 the basic Victor B.1 underwent several important changes; these included the provision of a flight-refuelling probe, the fitting of drooped leading-edges, tail-warning radar, new ECM equipment under the nose and in the rear fuselage, and the strengthening of the pressure cabin. This modified aircraft emerged as the Victor B.1A…" (*V-bombers*, by Robert Jackson; Ian Allan 1981).

Radlett soon after the last new B.1, XH667, had been delivered from Colney Street on 31 March 1960. It completed its flight tests in May and was prepared for the final ECM conference on 28 June, by which date the second B.1A, XH618, was also ready for despatch...."

XH613 arrived at Cottesmore, where Nos 10 and XV Squadrons were based, on 22 July 1960. As the first Vulcan B.2, XH558, had been delivered to No 230 OCU on 1 July it becomes clear, as AVM Craig pointed-out in his lecture, "when we consider the parallel work on B.1s and B.1As, that there was no clear-cut switch from procurement of the...Mk 1s to the Mk 2s". He was referring to the Vulcan programme but the same was true of the Victors: "The fortieth B.1, XH619, [was] completed at Colney Street in May [1959] with the second B.2, XH669, close behind[1]". He went on to comment that

"as Bomber Command received its new marks of V-bombers into service, conversion courses, IFTs[2] and the formation and re-formation of squadrons were telescoped into a very tight time-scale....Bearing in mind the parallel introduction of the Mk 1 and Mk 2 Victors, there was clearly great urgency and determination to develop and maintain the credibility of our contribution to the West's deterrent strategy of massive nuclear retaliation in the event of an attack by the Warsaw Pact..".

---

[1] C H Barnes, *Handley page Aircraft since 1907*.

[2] "The differences between the Mk 1 and 2 variants were...sufficiently great to justify holding further in-service intensive flying trials, although previously it had not been usual to hold IFTs on new marks of existing in-service aircraft" (AVM D B Craig lecture on *The Vulcan in Service*, previously referred to). By October 1959 all 45 Vulcan B. Mk 1s had been completed (DCAS Progress Report on Weapon Systems up to 31 Oct 59 – AC(59)88).

CHAPTER XII

VALIANT ROLES:
FLIGHT REFUELLING, NUCLEAR TESTS,
SR AND ECM

While the Vulcans and Victors were in the throes of being brought into service the Valiants had been active in six different types of operation – bombing (their part in the Suez operation has already been referred to, and before other V-force squadrons were formed they were the spearhead of Bomber Command's Main Force); strategic reconnaissance (the second V-bomber squadron formed was No 543 (PR) with Valiant B(PR).1s which worked-up in the second half of 1955); dropping tests of the first British atomic bombs in 1956; ECM (electronic countermeasures), equipping No 199 Squadron from 30 September 1957 onwards; flight refuelling, which No 214 Squadron pioneered from February 1958; and Blue Steel trials, which will be referred to subsequently. Thus the Valiants not only made up a complete strategic force, with bomber, SR and ECM elements; they also had the special roles of introducing jet tanking to the RAF, and air-dropping the atomic bombs.

Commenting on the countermeasures requirement, the Air Ministry Quarterly Liaison Report for April–June 1952 had said: "It has now been agreed that a specialist RCM aircraft is required to operate with, and in support of, bomber forces. Consideration is being given to the suitability of the Canberra or the Comet for this role as a short-term measure. It is proposed to meet the long-term requirement by a suitably equipped Valiant." During 1956 a Signals staff minute, referring to the rearming of No 199 Squadron with Valiants, described it as "a specialist RCM squadron whose role is to meet the RCM training requirements of Fighter Command and other formations", adding that it was "at present equipped with Lincoln aircraft, but . . . being rearmed with seven Valiants".

Flight refuelling, by contrast, did not have an easy introduction into the post-war RAF. There had been pre-war experiments and successful transfers of fuel, but the system had never been developed operationally. There seems to have been some official scepticism as to its operational value, and it was largely through the determined persistence of Sir Alan Cobham in the 1945–60 period that the idea came to be accepted. He kept up a "slow bombardment of letters" (as the AOC in C Fighter Command, Air Mshl Sir William Elliot, described Cobham's epistolary offensive), with the then ACAS(TR) (AVM J N Boothman of pre-war Schneider Trophy fame) as his chief initial target.

That official scepticism existed about the operational value of IFR was indicated by an item in the AMQLR for January–March 1947, which announced: "The Air Ministry have come to the conclusion that flight refuelling on future types of aircraft is not a paying proposition. Since FR fittings have already been ordered for the Shackleton, it has been decided to complete these and test the equipment on one aircraft. Thereafter it is not proposed to continue any further development of flight-refuelling equipment, but to rely on the aircraft carrying internal fuel for the ranges required."

However, views changed. On 8 January 1954 DCAS (Air Mshl T G Pike) reported to S of S (Lord De L'Isle and Dudley) that the Air Staff had decided that all Vulcans and Victors should be capable of flight refuelling and that it was "desirable" that the Valiants should be similarly capable. Later that year, on 29 October, ACAS(OR) (AVM H V Satterly) told CAS (Air Chf Mshl Sir William Dickson) that the "overall policy" was that "as many V-bombers as possible" should be capable of flight refuelling in the double role of tanker or receiver. In *A Review of the 'V' Force* which the AOC in C Bomber Command (Air Mshl Sir George Mills) sent to CAS on 15 March 1955 there were two references to flight refuelling, one saying that "about half the Valiants and all Victors and Vulcans will be capable of accepting fuel in flight. It is also possible to convert the aircraft into tankers"; the other that "flight refuelling for 80 of 117 Valiants will begin to be available at the end of the first quarter of 1956. Flight refuelling will be available to all Vulcans and Victors for the RAF". However, there was no mention of a tanker force in the *Review.* But a month later an Air Staff Requirement – No OR3580 for an Electronic Positioning System for Flight Refuelling – was issued, which said at its outset: "V-class bombers are to be fitted to enable them to carry out flight refuelling." The OR quoted from the ASR as follows: "It should be noted that, with the exception of some early Valiants, all V-class aircraft will have fixed fittings to enable them to be operated as either tankers or receivers. No aircraft will, therefore, be designed solely for use as tankers." The ASR concluded with a reference to a target date: "The Air Staff require this equipment first in the V-class aircraft. It should therefore be in service as soon as possible and not later than 1957."

Although the principle of in-flight refuelling had been accepted for the V-force and preparations made for it, by mid-1955 there were no aircraft to spare for it. All the 84 Valiants ordered in 1954–55 were to form front-line squadrons, and it was not until the Vulcans and Victors came into service that Valiants could be spared to form tanker squadrons; there was no question of an order being placed for additional Valiants to perform the flight refuelling role – those aircraft so designated were withdrawn from the Main Force, and care had to be taken to ensure that its striking power was not diminished. The range and extent of arguments which had to be marshalled to make a case for the provision of FR capability from the resources of the V-force can be seen in papers prepared for the Air Council towards the end of 1957. So complex was this matter, involving the total number of V-bombers and the assignment of bomber forces to Saceur, that Treasury agreement to a Valiant tanker force was not finally obtained until early in 1959. In a minute of 3 December 1957 to CAS (Air Chf Mshl Sir Dermot Boyle), DCAS (AVM G W Tuttle) commented that everyone had "underestimated the size and difficulty of the problems in developing FR equipment for the RAF at heights and speeds hitherto not attempted", and there had been "doubt in the minds of the Treasury and those responsible for development regarding the size and shape of the bomber force and its method of operation".

A paper prepared early in 1957[1] set out the plan for the V-force as envisaging a total of 184 aircraft UE made up of 120 Mk 2 Vulcans/Victors, 40 Mk 1 Vulcans/Victors and 24 Valiants. As to tankers, it went on to say that no aircraft were included in the plan specifically as tankers; bombers would be used as necessary and "suitably fitted Valiants and Vulcans Mk 1 could be kept as tankers when they disappear from the front line". As to the physical capability of the three types of V-bomber in the flight refuelling role, in the case of the Valiants 42 would be fitted as tankers and receivers and 32 sets of tanks for the tanker version had been ordered (if there were no technical hitches, it was hoped that these 32 sets would be delivered by March 1958). Vulcans from the 16th aircraft onwards would be fitted as receivers, and from the 26th aircraft onwards would have fixed fittings as tankers – tanks had been designed but none had yet been ordered. All Victors had been fitted for receiving fuel but none had yet been equipped as tankers[2].

Another paper, dated May 1957, set out the reasons – including the flight-refuelling role – for retaining the Valiants and Mk 1 Vulcans and Victors in addition to the 120-strong Mk 2 Vulcan/Victor force. Unattributed, but nevertheless indicative of Air Staff thnking at that time[3], it delineates two of the roles eventually performed by Valiants – support for Saceur and flight refuelling. It gives as chief reason the size of an attacking force – the larger this is, the greater will be the percentage that will get through the defences – and lists "the main tactical methods of employing the Mk 1 aircraft": in support of the deep penetration force (ie the Mk 2s), attacking fringe targets, in support of Saceur – "if, as seems likely, it is necessary to detach medium bombers for this purpose" – and in the flight refuelling role, "for which there are several possible uses, including routeing some deep penetration raids far round the flanks of the enemy defences".

Towards the end of 1957 the VCAS, Air Mshl E C Hudleston, prepared a Note for the Air Council on Deployment of Valiants in 1961 and the Provision of Flight Refuelling Capability after 1961[4]. Dated 6

---

[1] In Medium Bomber Force – Size and Composition (ID3/901/6 (Pt 2)) – AHB.
[2] The subsequent role of the Victors, when they succeeded the Valiants as tankers in 1965, could not then have been foreseen.
[3] In Medium Bomber Force – Size and Composition (as above – Pt 3).
[4] Air Ministry File No CMS.2228/53; Air Council paper No AC(57)92.

December 1957, this set out the requirements for flight refuelling, principally that "as the Russian air defences improve it will be essential for the medium bomber force to be given the maximum tactical freedom in routeing in order to maintain the viability of the deterrent". Flight refuelling would give this tactical freedom by increasing the force's radius of action.

In global war, the Note went on, the greater range obtainable could be exploited in various ways: more diversionary routeing would be possible so as to reduce penetration distance (and hence aircraft losses), to avoid heavily defended areas, to achieve a measure of tactical surprise and to exploit the inherent advantages of the powered bomb; further, especially important targets such as nuclear stockpiles, beyond normal operational range, could be attacked. In limited war and in peace, the greater flexibility conferred by flight refuelling could be exploited in several ways: deploying overseas more quickly by making longer stage-lengths possible, flying around territories which might become unfriendly, ensuring the safe use of short-runway airfields (especially when HE loads were carried) by refuelling after take-off, and "basing our bombers beyond the radius of action of any enemy air force yet within our own increased radius".

As to the size of tanker force needed, VCAS said that HQ Bomber Command estimated that four squadrons would meet the requirement; but after careful study, and bearing in mind the financial implications, it was recommended that there should be two Valiant tanker squadrons plus a "shadow" tanker squadron which would be formed in the Bomber Command Bombing School. In addition to these two tanker squadrons VCAS recommended that three squadrons of Valiants should be formed in 1961 to replace the Bomber Command Canberras assigned to Saceur, who had "repeatedly stated his requirement for a blind bombing capability and also his dislike of ground-based aids to achieve this capability". None of the solutions proposed for modifying the Canberras to meet this requirement were really satisfactory; the best solution would be to re-arm the assigned Canberra squadrons with surplus V-bombers, annual running costs of three Valiant squadrons at 24 UE being approximately the same as those for four Canberra squadrons at 64 UE. Valiants "to build and support five squadrons in addition to those patterned for the . . . training units" would become surplus in 1961.

After VCAS's paper about the employment of surplus Valiants in new roles after 1961 had been circulated, the Treasury asked for an assurance that any aircraft used in the tanker role would be found within the agreed UE and backing for the V-bomber force, and that if they agreed to expenditure on completing the development of Valiants as tankers, the Air Ministry would not seek future authority to develop the Vulcan or Victor for the same role.[1]

When the Air Council considered VCAS's Note on 20 December 1957, they agreed[2] that Saceur should be asked to accept that the Canberras assigned to him should in due course be replaced by a smaller number of Valiants, and also that there was a requirement for Valiant tankers. They further decided that representations should be made to the Treasury for authority to resume work immediately on Valiant tanker development.

At the Air Council meeting on 9 January 1958[3] the PUS (Sir Maurice Dean) said that the Treasury had given authority for Valiant tanker development work to go ahead on a hand-to-mouth basis until the end of the month; it was therefore difficult for him to approach them on this question until the Air Council were ready to state proposals for a tanker force, and he suggested that a study of logistic and financial implications of VCAS's proposals was required – to which the Council agreed. The Treasury subsequently insisted that any aircraft used as tankers had to be found "within the agreed UE and backing" for the V-force, and that if the Valiant was used as a tanker the Air Ministry would not seek to develop the Victor or Vulcan in the tanker role.

On 22 December 1958 the Chancellor of the Exchequer (Mr D Heathcot Amory) told the Minister of Defence (Mr Duncan Sandys) that he had no objection to 24 V-bombers being provided for Saceur in replacement for 64 Canberras, but he considered that room had to be found for a tanker force "within that part of the front-line strength of 144 aircraft which it has been agreed shall not be equipped with Mk 2 aircraft".

The Air Ministry disputed the Chancellor's contention, emphasising that a force of not less than 144 Vulcan/Victor bombers was the minimum necessary to provide a viable deterrent, and that the requirement for tankers should be considered on its own merits – it did not depend solely on support for V-bomber operations: flight refuelling would be essential to any overseas reinforcement by Fighter Command in limited war or peace, and might also be essential to the deployment of tactical transport aircraft[5].

As the Chancellor of the Exchequer had expressed his views to the Minister of Defence, a reply had to come from the latter, and the Air Ministry were anxious that it should convey their determination to form a Valiant tanker force. When, after several weeks, no such reply was forthcoming, the Air Minister (Mr George Ward) wrote to the Minister

[1] Brief for CAS (ACAS(P)), 19 Dec 57. But time had its revenge, for when the Valiants had to be withdrawn from service in 1965, Victors succeeded them in the tanker role.

[2] Air Council Conclusions, 28(57).

[3] Conclusions of Meeting 1(58).

[4] Minute to CAS/PUS from DUS II, 17 Jan 58, in ID9/94/8 (Pt 3) Flight Refuelling of Aircraft, Jun 55-Dec 62.

[5] Letter DUS I/MoD (DUS I/5791) of 7 Jan 59.

of Defence on 1 April 1959:–

"I should be grateful for your assistance in resolving one outstanding issue affecting the Royal Air Force's front line.

"In spite of your approval last November of proposals for the formation of the Valiant tanker squadrons, the Chancellor in his letter to you of 22 December contended that these squadrons should be within and not additional to the approved bomber front line. I do not think that the Chancellor's contention can be sustained for reasons stated in a letter from the Air Ministry to the Ministry of Defence dated 7 January last[1].

"I should be grateful for your continued support since our detailed deployment planning for the bomber force is delayed pending acceptance of the proposals which you have approved."

The Minister of Defence did not have time to write to the Chancellor before leaving for a SEATO meeting, so discussed the matter with Sir Richard Powell, Permanent Secretary, MoD, who took it up with his opposite number at the Treasury, Sir Roger Makins, setting out the merits of the proposed tanker force in a letter of 6 April 1959[2]. He said that it would give increased flexibility to match the growing effectiveness of enemy defences; that in some areas it would be possible to concert tactical plans more closely with the USAF Strategic Air Command; that in limited war loaded V-bombers could take off from short runways and refuel immediately afterwards, increasing their ability to reinforce overseas Commands; that the ferry range of the P.1 (Lightning) could be extended, allowing it to be deployed overseas, and the new AW660 tactical freighter could also be flight-refuelled; and that the tanker force could provide a means of recovering other aircraft which might be caught in bad weather without adequate fuel for diversion.

All these capabilities advanced for two squadrons of Valiant tankers seemed to have alarmed, rather than impressed, the Treasury; for on 16 April Sir Roger Makins replied cautiously:–

"Our understanding is that a front-line strength of 16 tankers would add some £2.8 million a year to the running costs of the V-force. This is a fairly substantial addition to current defence expenditure; but our main concern is about the potential refuelling commitment outlined in your letter. (I gather that, in addition to the aircraft which you mention, the TSR.2 may also have to be made capable of refuelling in flight.)

"Does not all this amount to a very formidable task for a tanker force of 16 aircraft? Are you satisfied that the Air Ministry's immediate proposal will not be the forerunner of a plan to establish a much larger tanker force?

---

[1] Quoted above (page 157). In addition the letter said it was essential "to consider the requirement for tankers on its own merits since it does not depend solely on the value of tankers to support V-bomber operations".

[2] RRP/404/59.

"If we are thinking in terms only of the force of 16 tankers, the cost of their operation as an addition to the V-bomber force might be acceptable. If however there is any question of a substantial build-up to a larger force, perhaps we should together consider now whether the Air Ministry should be asked to find compensating reductions elsewhere. . . ."

In a reply on 20 April[1] Sir Richard Powell assured the Treasury that, while he could not rule out the possibility that at some later date a proposal to increase the size of the tanker force beyond 16 might be put forward, there were no current plans of that kind. He hoped that the Treasury would be able to agree to the immediate establishment of a tanker force of 16 converted Valiants.

This approval was forthcoming on 27 April, though the Treasury added a word of caution about possible future expenditure:–

". . . In the light of your assurances [Sir Roger Makins wrote] we can now agree to the establishment of a tanker force of converted Valiants with a front-line strength of 16 aircraft in addition to the agreed front-line V-bomber strength of 144 aircraft.

"There remains one point of uncertainty. It appears that within a few years a large part of the total front-line strength of the RAF will be equipped to refuel in flight. The cost of this must be considerable. Has thought been given to the question whether flight refuelling facilities should be provided only for a smaller proportion of the front-line strength so that the number of aircraft so equipped may bear a closer relationship to the tanker force? . . ."[2].

Preparatory work for the use of Valiants in flight refuelling had begun more than a year previously, in February 1958. During that month CA (Controller of Aircraft) Release was given for both the B(K). Mk 1 and B(PR.).K. Mk 1 versions to be used – subject to certain conditions – in the tanker role in day or night flight refuelling, in the receiver role "to take on fuel from Valiant Tanker by day and night up to the maximum quantity of transferable fuel", and in the training role as tanker/receiver for day and night training. This Release followed joint trials by Vickers-Armstrongs and A&AEE, and in a covering note to OR1, Air Ministry, on 24 February 1958[3] AD/RAF/B.2 commented that "A&AEE are particularly concerned over the training of aircrew for this type of flying. They recommend at least 30 satisfactory 'dry contacts' should be achieved before a crew attempt fuel transfer". The note added that "pilots from Vickers-Armstrongs and A&AEE are available to give instruction on both tanker and receiver techniques. Tanker panel operators from Flight Refuelling[4] can be made available for their

---

[1] RRP/464/59.

[2] All this correspondence is in CAS file on Use of V-bombers in Tanker Role (ID3/901/11 (Pt 1) – AHB).

[3] AH/369/036 and AH/491/02 in file Vickers Valiant Release to Service (AF/CT5537/64 Pt II).

[4] Flight Refuelling Ltd, Tarrant Rushton airfield, near Blandford, Dorset, the firm of which Sir Alan Cobham was managing director.

technique instructions".

The last paragraph of the note indicated that it would be some time before Valiants could be modified as tankers up to CA Release standards, but that training could proceed:–

"As regards the actual aircraft used, whilst it is appreciated the Service require fitment of outstanding modifications prior to return, the time lost could be an important factor. We would not expect to see these aircraft up to full standard before September. You may wish to look into the possible use of the tanker before then either for crew training or even for development of other receiver aircraft."

In fact, preparations for the tanker role had begun even earlier in the Valiant squadron at Marham – No 214 – which pioneered jet flight refuelling in the RAF, a task which does not seem to have been welcomed by personnel of a Main Force squadron. Its ORB for December 1957 recorded "A general reshuffle of aircraft between the flights. . . . 'B' Flight now have all the under-wing tank aircraft[1] and 'A' Flight are preparing to do the initial work converting the whole squadron to the tanker role, a gloomy and unpopular prospect"[2].

At the beginning of 1958 – in January – Sqn Ldr J H Garstin and his crew were detached to A&AEE Boscombe Down to gain experience in air-to-air refuelling, while three 'A' Flight crews were detached to Flight Refuelling Ltd at Tarrant Rushton for a week's course on the equipment, in preparation for the squadron's forthcoming role. At Marham, the ORB noted, "flight refuelling equipment is building up in the hangar and it is possible that the first training flights will take place towards the end of February".

Progress was indeed made in the latter month, when (the ORB reported) "'A' Flight crews began the indoctrination of flight refuelling. No 'hook-ups' have been made as yet; to date, experience is being given in practice trailing. . . . Valiants XD869 and XD870 are now equipped with flight refuelling hose drum units; the remaining 'A' Flight aircraft are to be equipped as facilities permit".

It was in March 1958 that formal trials began for the new role – when, to quote again from the ORB, "Phase 'A' of Trial 306 – Flight Refuelling commenced. . . . This . . . involves training of 'A' Flight crews in positioning of aircraft and making and maintaining dry contacts by day. Crews are being trained in both the 'tanker' and 'receiver' roles. During the initial training Sqn Ldr P Bardon from A&AEE and Mr B Trubshaw, deputy chief test pilot of Vickers-Armstrongs Ltd, assisted in the conversion of crews." Ground training was concerned with the operation and servicing of the new equipment, Mr K Wickenden of Flight Refuelling Ltd giving lectures and Mr Trubshaw a talk on flying techniques. An Interim Report drawn up by the squadron on Trial No

[1] These tanks held 1,650gal each, giving 9,440gal total fuel.
[2] No 214 had four aircraft modified as tanker/receivers and four as receivers only for the Service trials of the in-flight refuelling system.

306 (dated 30 June) included a recommendation that a flight refuelling ground school should be established at Marham "as soon as possible", and this was approved by HQ Bomber Command on 1 August.

No 214 Squadron, however, with their Valiant B(K).1s, were still part of the Main Force of Bomber Command; and on 6 June 1958, during Exercise Full Play, they were visited at Marham by a representative of *The Times* who wrote an article on the V-force – based on his talks with squadron personnel and a flight in one of the Valiants – which was published on the 9th. In it he said that the force "in some three years of operation, have worked up first in their Valiants and now also in the Vulcans and Victors, into a formidable weapon in their own right, well able to press home their attacks with superb efficiency".

Describing V-force aircrew as "the élite of the Service", the article commented that the "overriding impression" to an outsider was "the extent to which the policy of avoiding war by being capable of waging it better than their opponents is the mainspring of the force".

Saying that "automation has come to the bombers", the writer described the V-force crews as "qualified technicians", with salaries in the £1,500–£2,000 a year bracket, living in £3,000–£4,000 houses[1]. Most of them could be "something in the City" – except for an "unmistakable air of quiet confidence and pride of Service in their bearing". This "air of self-effacement" was deceptive, however: "top-level British policy is based on the premise that there would be a period of warning in any future war and, therefore, crews are not in constant battle readiness as are their colleagues in SAC".

On a three-hour sortie with Sqn Ldr F Furze and his crew – "a mere 2,000-mile flight which covered the English Channel, Devon, Scotland, the tip of Northern Ireland, the Shetlands and the north-east coast" – the *Times* correspondent felt that "there is no sense of flying; . . . simply the subdued hum as in a power station, and three men sitting quietly, two of them watching radar screens and dials which give position, height, speed, courses and 'who won the Test match'. Occasionally the aircraft trembles slightly, but there is nothing to indicate movement. Even in the cockpit the bomber seems suspended in space, with hundreds of miles of cloud stretching far away below".

Making a comparison of the V-force with the American airborne deterrent, the writer said that "Strategic Air Command circles the world, and it is their boast that somewhere they have an aircraft in the sky every minute of the day and night, they are the embracing shield of the free world, and if at times they seem fanatical in their approach to ensuring peace[2], they nevertheless have reached a superb degree of skill. But Bomber Command's V-force – smaller and run on less lavish lines than SAC – is served by men and aircraft who are the equal of any, but who are still past masters at the art of hiding lights under bushels".

---

[1] At mid-1958 prices.
[2] SAC's motto, adopted in 1957, is "Peace is our Profession".

Only a month earlier an assessment of the V-force had been made in the Air Estimates debate in the House of Lords by the Earl of Gosford, Joint Parliamentary Under-Secretary of State for Foreign Affairs, on 7 May, when he said that the last year had "seen a further increase in the hitting power of the V-bomber force – making the deterrent effort, I hope, even more effective as a deterrent. The proportion of Vulcans has steadily increased[1]. Deliveries of the Victor have begun, and the build-up of the bomber force itself has been accompanied by the build-up of its stockpile of weapons. The growing stock of kiloton weapons is now beginning to be supplemented by megaton bombs[2]. The range of the Valiant, which continues to provide a very powerful element in our V-bomber force, will be increased by refuelling in flight. This is important, not only because it will expose new targets but also because it will allow the aircraft a wider choice of routes and so increase the task of the enemy defences. We are now planning refuelling trials with the Vulcan and Victor in the receiver role"[3].

During September 1958 the first public demonstrations of jet aircraft flight refuelling were given by No 214 Squadron at the SBAC Flying Display at Farnborough (1–7 September) and at the Battle of Britain Displays at Cottesmore, Honington, Marham and Upwood, although the system was not yet operational. The squadron was still part of the Main Force of Bomber Command, and at Marham one of its Valiants demonstrated a "scramble" take-off, getting airborne in 3½ minutes. No 214's dual role at this time was evidenced in an ORB entry for this month, which said: "In the time remaining after the SBAC and Battle of Britain fly-pasts, normal bombing training and some flight refuelling training were carried out." During October, in preparation for the squadron's forthcoming role, crew training started in the flight refuelling simulator at Marham; this was now fully operational and procedures could be practised.

1959 was the year in which some twelve months of training and practices came together and No 214 Squadron began to show what could be achieved by flight refuelling. In January the first transfers of fuel in the air took place, the ORB reporting: "Trial 306:– Two tanker aircraft were modified up to the standard required for day and night fuel transfer. The first transfers of fuel in the air (wet hook-ups) were carried out [on 23, 26 and 27 January] by crews captained by Sqn Ldrs J Garstin and S Price and Flt Lt B Fern. Between 26 January and the end of the month these crews completed 26 day and 17 night wet hook-ups." Then, in February, "the first long-range sorties of 12 hours' duration were carried out by Wg Cdr M J Beetham [the squadron CO – later to

---

[1] By the end of April 1958 there were two Vulcan squadrons and a third, No 617, formed at the beginning of May 1958.

[2] The first megaton warhead (Violet Club) started to enter Bomber Command service in March 1958.

[3] House of Lords Hansard, 7 May 1958, Cols 56–57.

become Chief of the Air Staff from 1 August 1977] – and crew on the 23rd and Sqn Ldr Price and crew on the 24th". Gradually No 214's role was changing: "Emphasis this month was placed on flight refuelling training and little bombing and navigation training was carried out. . . . The AOC in C Bomber Command and AOC No 3 Group visited the squadron on the 26th to discuss the progress of the flight refuelling trial and the programme of the long-range flight-refuelled flights."

The first of these long-range flights were made in April 1959, the month in which Treasury approval was given for the establishment of a tanker force of 16 Valiants. Not only were the flights successful; they were well publicised, with Press, TV and news-reel coverage. No 214 Squadron's ORB tells the story, recording what was still part of Trial 306:–

"Three long-range flight-refuelled flights were carried out this month, two to Embakasi and one to Salisbury, Southern Rhodesia. Sqn Ldr S Price and crew flew to Embakasi on 6 April followed by Flt Lt B Fern and crew on the 7th. . . . Flt Lt Fern and crew set up an unofficial record for the England–Nairobi flight with a time of 7hr 40min, an average speed of 567mph. On both the outward and return flights the aircraft was refuelled by No 214 Squadron tankers over Malta.

"For the third long-range flight, to Salisbury, Southern Rhodesia, tankers were based at Idris for the outward flight and at Nairobi and Idris for the return: on 16 April Wg Cdr M J Beetham and crew flew from Marham to Salisbury in a record time of 10hr 12min – an average speed of 522mph. This flight of 5,320 miles is the longest non-stop flight by a jet aircraft yet undertaken by the Royal Air Force....RVs and flight refuelling...took place over Idris on the outward flight and over Lake Victoria and Idris on the homeward flight....

"On 15 April, the day previous to the squadron commander's flight to Salisbury, a Press conference was held at Marham to explain the purpose of, and the techniques to be used on, the flight to representatives of the national and local Press, BBC and ITN television news services and Pathé News. On the following day the hook-up over Idris was filmed for TV and news-reel use from a PR Canberra from Wyton[1]. Details of the flight then appeared in the Press and films were shown on TV and cinema screens. The details of the flight also became the basis of an article in *Flight* magazine."

In the magazine article[2] Wg Cdr Beetham was quoted as saying, after arriving at Salisbury, that "the purpose of these flights, which will continue to increase in range, is to perfect operating procedures, especially rendezvous techniques and signals communications". The article commented that this underlined what he had said at Marham

---

[1] From No 58 Squadron, flown by Flt Lt P Major, photography being done at 40,000ft.
[2] 24 April 1959 issue.

some 24 hours previously, and commented that "what emerged, too, was the amount of versatility and team-work required and how 214 have achieved an efficient synthesis of the various factors involved – their aircraft, in both the giving and receiving roles; the relevant crew techniques; and the equipment developed by Flight Refuelling Ltd". The AOC No 3 Group, AVM K B B Cross, was quoted as saying that the squadron were training to do air refuelling in any part of the world; it would be a requirement for fighter aircraft such as the Lightning, though at the moment its use was confined to Bomber Command. At present No 214 had the dual function of being both a bomber and tanker squadron.

During 1959, No 214 Sqn gradually increased the non-stop distances flown by Valiants to over 6,000 miles (later this was to be increased to 8,000 miles – the distance of a Far East (UK – Singapore) deployment). On 18 June Wg Cdr Beetham and his crew set up an unofficial UK – Johannesburg record, over-flying Jan Smuts airfield 11hr 3min after leaving Marham – a distance of 5,845 miles covered at an average speed of 529mph. The squadron's ORB for that month proudly recorded that "this was the first-ever non-stop flight to South Africa and beat the previous record set up by a de Havilland Comet in 1957 by two hours". In July, an even better distance and speed were achieved: on the 9th Wg Cdr Beetham and his crew again went to South Africa, setting up two more unofficial records – "flying from overhead London Airport [to quote from the exuberant ORB report] to D F Malan Airport, Capetown, a distance of 6,060 miles in 11hr 28min at an average speed of 530mph and returning from D F Malan Airport to overhead London Aiport in a time of 12hr 20min at an average speed of 491.5 mph. These times beat the official records held by an RAF Canberra by 53min on the outward flight and 56min on the return flight". On this flight to Capetown, and on those to Johannesburg and to Salisbury, Southern Rhodesia, in June, refuelling was undertaken over Nigeria by No 214 Sqn tankers based at Kano.

Of perhaps even more significance than the long-range flights – impressive though those were – was the start which No 214 Sqn made in October 1959 on refuelling practice with Vulcans. The ORB reported that on the 28th one of 214's tanker Valiants "rendezvoused with a Vulcan of No 101 Sqn and a start was made on converting Vulcan crews to the receiver role. Sqn Ldr B E Fern flew as a co-pilot in the Vulcan to check out the pilots. Owing to adverse weather and the unavailability of Vulcan aircraft, no further Vulcan conversion flights were carried out during the month but these flights will be resumed in November". No 101 Squadron, based at Finningley, reported the event briefly in their ORB: "The squadron's first flight refuelling dry hook-up was today carried out by Flt Lts W S Green, AFC, and I N Wilson in XA910. A rendezvous with a Valiant tanker from No 214 Sqn at Marham was made and a successful [   ][1] completed."

Taking-in two other flight-refuelling trials en route (T.306A was an evaluation of the Rebecca/Eureka rendezvous aid and T.306B the evaluation of NBS as a flight-refuelling positioning aid – and on 24 August Sqn Ldr S Price and crew "were detached to Boscombe Down with an aircraft from the squadron to test a new type of probe and drogue, the Mk 8, which gives a higher rate of flow and standardises with the USAF") No 214 were able to announce in their ORB that "with the publication of the Final Report on the Flight Refuelling Trial dated 30 November 1959, Trial 306, which has occupied the major portion of the squadron effort since January 1958, came to an end". It could be said, then, that from November 1959 the V-force had an operational flight-refuelling capability.

No 214 Squadron had also maintained its bombing role. On 1 September two of its Valiants were on Sunspot detachment at RAF Luqa, Malta, this number being doubled in the 16–22 September period for Exercise Crescent Mace when eight successful sorties were made against the US Navy's 6th Fleet. The detachment ended on 7 October, and during that month (its ORB recorded) "the squadron flew 25 flight-refuelling training sorties as part of the programme for the training of new crews and the continuation training of experienced crews. A total of 76 day and 15 night wet contacts were carried out during these sorties. In addition . . . 15 bombing and cross-country details were carried out as part of the normal squadron bombing and classification training".

On 28 November 1960 VCAS (Air Mshl Sir Edmund Hudleston) gave his approval to an operation which was to be a spectacular demonstration of RAF ability in flight refuelling – a non-stop UK–Australia flight by a Vulcan which had been proposed by the AOC in C Bomber Command (Air Mshl Sir Kenneth Cross). In a letter to the C in C, VCAS agreed that planning should go ahead for a flight in June of the following year.

It was in fact on 20/21 June 1961 that a Vulcan Mk 1A of No 617 Squadron, captained by Sqn Ldr M G Beavis[2], flew non-stop from Scampton to Sydney in 20hr 5min supported by Valiants of No 214 Squadron. The Vulcan refuelled over Akrotiri, Karachi, Singapore and 500 miles south of Singapore, nine tankers being involved along its route. The operation triumphantly justified the C in C's claim for it in his original proposal as "an advertisement of our deterrent potential"[3].

The first large-scale flight-refuelling achievement by Valiants had been Operation Dyke (or Dyke Tankex, as it was also referred to) in

---

[1] Word missing.
[2] Later Air Mshl Sir Michael.
[3] Letter to VCAS, 24 Oct 60, in Flight Refuelling of Aircraft (June 55 – Dec 62) (ID9/94/8, Pt 3). Total distance was 11,600sm and average ground speed 500kt (575mph), with four fuel transfers.

October 1960 when four Javelin FAW.9s, plus two "spares" pre-positioned at Mauripur, Pakistan, of No 23 Sqn were supported out to Singapore by No 214 Sqn in a Far East emergency reinforcement exercise. This went off "without any serious incident or major unserviceability" (in the words of No 23's ORB compiler) and VCAS formally congratulated the AOCs in C of the three Commands involved – Bomber, Fighter and Transport (which provided Hastings and Britannia support).

No 214 Sqn had previously (in May 1960) flight-refuelled itself out to Singapore. On the 25th/26th Valiant WZ390 captained by Sqn Ldr J H Garstin took off from Marham at 1638hr and reached Changi at 0813hr(Z), covering 8,120sm[1] in 15hr 35min at an average speed of 520mph. This was the longest non-stop point-to-point flight made by any RAF aircraft up to that date and it was supported by tanker Valiants operating from Akrotiri, Cyprus and Mauripur.

In April 1959 the Treasury had given its agreement to a tanker force of 16 Valiants[2] and it was decided to form a second squadron as soon as possible. "The demands for refuelling are clearly increasing beyond the capability of one tanker squadron", VCAS wrote to D of Ops (B and R) on 27 June 1961[3]. "Please let me know the implications of converting a second Valiant squadron to the tanker role in September 1961."

However, D of Ops (B and R) replied on 13 July[4] that Bomber Command were of the opinion that a second squadron could not be fully effective until about 1 January 1962, and recommended that this date be accepted for the change of role, to which VCAS agreed. Bomber Command were advised of this on 31 July and also told that plans for a third tanker squadron were "still fluid" – that its conversion might have to be postponed for a few months[5].

The designated second Valiant tanker squadron, No 90 at Honington, was told in August that there was a requirement for it to be fully operational in the tanker role by the end of 1961. "All the training of air and ground crews will be done by No 214 Sqn in conjunction with the Flight Refuelling Ground School", its ORB recorded. On 1 October No 90 relinquished its commitment to the Main Force bombing role and in December – by which time it had three B(K).1s – did its first FR exercise, supporting Javelins to Malta.

In a minute to VCAS on 31 October 1961, D Air Plans said that he had been "endeavouring to obtain financial approval" for a third tanker squadron "since Plan 'O' was agreed by the Air Council at the

---

[1] This is the figure (given also as 7,052nm/452kt) quoted in a minute of 26 May 1960 from D of Ops (B, BM and R) to ACAS(Ops). No 214 Sqn give a distance of 8,110sm out to Singapore in their ORB and 7,805sm back from Butterworth to Marham, flown in 16hr 17min at an average speed of 479mph.
[2] Makins, JPS, Treasury, to Powell, PS, MoD, 27 Apr 59.
[3] In Flight Refuelling of Aircraft (ID9/94/8, Pt 3).
[4] Ibid.
[5] ACAS(Ops)/AVM Menaul, Air Staff (Ibid).

beginning of the year".

This agreement had been given on 22 December 1960[1] when a Note by VCAS[2] on Front-line Strengths of the RAF over the next ten years had been discussed, the section relating to flight refuelling saying that the patterns "include a third Valiant tanker squadron in addition to the two for which Treasury approval had been given in April 1959". VCAS explained that the Treasury had made it clear that they would expect an offset elsewhere if a third squadron were later proposed, and that the reduction from 144 in the V-bomber front line constituted such an offset. A third squadron was needed "to give the strategic striking force a reasonable air alert capability" and to facilitate overseas reinforcement operations. In its conclusions the Council invited AMSO to issue the proposed squadron pattern "as Plan 'O', as at 1 January 1961".

In his minute, D Air Plans explained to VCAS that the case for a three-squadron Valiant tanker force rested "as much on its use in support of transports as on its use for bombers and fighters"; but in view of further possible delays he suggested that the provision of a third Valiant tanker squadron should be given "absolute priority over tentative development ideas for transport aircraft".

Subsequently, DD Air Plans was asked to prepare a paper for the Air Council giving "a comprehensive picture of the place of flight refuelling in the RAF" and resolving the tanker requirement[3]. This paper eventually came before the Air Council on 1 March 1962[4] as a Note by VCAS on Tanker Force Requirements[5]. As a result, the proposal for a third tanker squadron was approved in principle, and VCAS was invited to initiate a design study of the Victor Mk 1 in the tanker role. He had said that this type was a "better choice" than the Valiant; it had a longer fatigue life and its performance was more compatible with that of the Lightning 3. In the 1961 Defence Review £0.6m had been allowed for converting a third single-point Valiant squadron; he estimated that conversion costs for a Victor 1 tanker squadron would be about £1m, and the extra £0.4m would be more than offset by the Victor 1's longer life. In the event, a third Valiant tanker squadron was never formed; and on 22 November 1962 the Air Council decided that the Victor should replace the Valiant in the tanker role, and that a third tanker squadron should be formed "as soon as possible".[6]

On the day before this meeting, some of the Valiant's shortcomings in the tanker role had been pointed out to VCAS in a minute from D Air Plans[7], who said that "the overriding one" was the fact that its fatigue life finished in 1968; this alone ruled out its continued use in the role. Also,

---

[1] Conclusions 20(60), Top Secret Annex 'A'.
[2] AC(60)68.
[3] DD Air Plans 1/73.
[4] Conclusions 3(62), Top Secret Annex.
[5] AC(62)9.
[6] Conclusions 16(62), Secret Annex 'B'.
[7] D Air Plans/6760 in ID9/94/8 (Pt 3) Flight Refuelling of Aircraft (June 55 – Dec 62).

it had "a relatively small transferable fuel load", necessitating the use of two tankers to one fighter on some of the longer stages; with mono-point refuelling, there was the inherent disadvantage that the transfer operation might be abortive; its performance was not strictly compatible with that of some of the aircraft which needed refuelling; and it had insufficient speed to refuel TSR.2.

Figures supporting these arguments were that the Valiant had 45,000lb total transferable fuel compared with an estimated 98,500lb for the Victor 1; that its maximum refuelling height and speed were 32,000ft at Mach 0.74 compared with 40,000ft/MO.91 for the Victor – whose weakness in the tanker role, the D Air Plans minute added, was "its relatively poor take-off performance".

These criticisms were drastic, but were made in the context of a staff paper arguing the case for a more advanced type of V-bomber to supplant an earlier type in the flight-refuelling role. Despite their limitations, Valiants of Nos 214 and 90 Sqn gave sterling service in the FR role for two years (1962-64) before Valiants were grounded in December 1964 and finally withdrawn from operations at the beginning of 1965. Both squadrons jointly supported the three-Vulcan non-stop Waddington to Perth, Western Australia, flight by No 101 Sqn (Operation Walk About) in July 1963; they jointly or severally supported eastward reinforcements by Javelins, Lightnings, Victors and Vulcans, did a trial for an airborne alert by Vulcans, co-operated with Royal Navy Sea Vixens and Scimitars and tested Airborne Command Post communications with Main Force V-bombers[1]. One operation which had to be planned and executed with even more care than usual was Operation Chive in March 1964 when Valiants of both the tanker squadrons supported four Javelin Mk 9Rs, en route from Binbrook to Butterworth, across the Arabian Sea and Indian Ocean from Aden to Malaysia. No 90's ORB noted that the operation "was of particular interest from the FR aspect, as the legs Khormaksar-Gan and Gan-Butterworth were over the sea and diversion airfields, Masirah and Katunayake, long distances from the routes. Refuelling plans had to be carried out with great accuracy to ensure that, in the event of an emergency, the aircraft would have sufficient fuel to reach the diversion".

It was not any inherent inability that ended the Valiants' role as tankers, but their withdrawal through main spar fatigue problems and the better performance offered by the Victors – not only in capacity, range, height and speed but also in the two- and then three-point refuelling capability they possessed. The Valiants had pioneered the role in the RAF: the combination of their intrinsic soundness and reliability as aircraft, the equipment which had been designed and

[1] Exercise Hallstand (amended from Hallmark III) in April 64, designed to test communications between ACP and exercise aircraft. It followed BC Trial No 490 in the previous month.

developed by Flight Refuelling Ltd, and the skill and devotion of the aircrew who established and practised the techniques, ensured that in-flight refuelling became an accepted part of bomber and fighter operations. Like helicopters, whose introduction was marked by scepticism and prejudice but which came to be taken for granted, the jet tankers have become an integral part of the operational scene – though their area of deployment shifted to the Nato theatre with the ending of Britain's east-of-Suez commitments, and Victor K.1s of No 214 Sqn (finally disbanded in January 1977) were succeeded by the more capacious and powerful K.2s of Nos 55 and 57 Sqns. The introduction of Victors into the FR (later known as AAR) role is described in a later chapter.

As in the development of flight refuelling by jet tankers, so in the air testing of atomic bombs, Valiants played a unique role. Reference has already been made to the work of No 1321 Flight at Wittering, doing ballistic trials with the 10,000lb Blue Danube atomic bomb during 1955. The Flight concluded its work in this role at the end of January 1956, then becoming part of No 138 Sqn; but the trials were continued, leading up to the first air-drop of an atomic bomb, and for this purpose a new Valiant squadron – No 49 – was formed.

Its first CO was Sqn Ldr D Roberts DFC AFC, who had commanded No 1321 Flight, and its task was quite unequivocally set down in its first ORB entry, for May 1956. Listing three Valiants and three crews on strength, backed by ground-staff technician teams for first-line servicing and for the trials, the ORB stated: "No 49 Sqn was re-formed[1] at RAF Wittering under the command of Sqn Ldr D Roberts DFC AFC, on 1 May . . . to carry out 'F' Series trials."

Perhaps the clearest idea of how these trials fitted into the pattern of British atomic weapon development can be gained from the Bomber Command Development Unit's first report on the "F" Series Trials, which put them into historical perspective[2]. It recalled that "No 1321 Flight was established at Wittering in April 1954 to undertake armament trials with a Ministry of Supply Valiant aircraft on behalf of AWRE and RAE and known as Bomber Command Trial No 248/54. There was a delay in releasing the aircraft and operations at Wittering started on 15 June 1955. Between that date and 25 November 1955,

"eight 10,000lb stores Type F.4 and one Type F.6 were dropped at Orfordness for AWRE. Ballistic information was obtained where possible from the AWRE stores and this was done on three occasions. In addition, five 10,000lb ballistic stores were dropped for RAE. A number of flights were made over the bombing range and without stores loaded in order to test special equipment.

---

[1] It had previously been a Lincoln Mk 2 squadron, ceasing to operate as such on 1 August 1955.

[2] Bomber Command Development Unit, "F" Series Trials Progress Report No 1, 16 Aug 56 (Witt/S.4064/Air).

"From 25 November 1955 to 8 March 1956 the Valiant, WP201, underwent a minor inspection and the modification state was brought up to date.

"On 8 February 1956 a conference was held at HQ Bomber Command to discuss the programme preparatory to Operation Buffalo[1] and Operation Grapple[2]. No 1321 Flight was then re-formed as 'C' Flight of No 138 Sqn and six Valiants, specially modified, were established, including two for Operation Buffalo. The RAE ballistic trial was discontinued and the AWRE series became known as the 'F' Series Trials. On 1 May 1956 'C' Flight of No 138 Sqn became No 49 Sqn[3]".

As there was no equivocation about the new squadron's description of its role, so there was no delay in getting down to it. The diary records on the day of No 49's re-formation: "Visit by Air Cdre C T Weir DFC of Air Ministry and Wg Cdr J R Moir of Bomber Command to discuss Operation Buffalo. Flt Lt R N Bates carried out practice runs at Orfordness." Then, on the following day, 2 May: "Sq Ldr D Roberts, Flt Lt K L Lewis [his navigator/radar] and Flt Lt T E Dunne [nav/plotter] visted Wisley to discuss Operation Grapple with Sqn Ldr R T Duck of Air Ministry and Mr B Trubshaw of Vickers-Armstrongs."

Operation Buffalo was to involve the first air drop of a British atomic weapon – by No 49 Squadron on 11 October 1956. Describing the purpose of the operation, the commander of the Air Task Group, Gp Capt S W B Menaul DFC AFC, said later in the introduction to his report on the air operations[4]:

"A series of scientific and operational experiments was carried out by British, Australian and Canadian Service and civilian staffs at the Ministry of Supply's new atomic range at Maralinga, in South Australia, between July and November 1956. The trials were designed primarily to advance research and development and to carry out proof tests of atomic weapons. At the same time measurements were made to elucidate more clearly the basic effects of nuclear explosions in terms of air and ground disturbances, heat and nuclear radiations and residual radioactivy, to assess the capabilities of atomic weapons for attack and to devise methods of defence against such weapons, or of reducing

---

[1] Operation Buffalo was the code-name for atomic trials held at Maralinga, South Australia, Jul–Nov 56.

[2] Operation Grapple was the code-name for megaton weapon trials at Christmas Island in the mid-Pacific Ocean in 1957–58.

[3] "The work of AWRE in preparation for overseas trials involves a substantial number of flight trials made in this country. Generally these are carried out by No 49 Sqn of Bomber Command stationed at Wittering. Both carry-over and dropping trials are made at the Orfordness Bombing Range where the general manning of the range, including control of the aircraft, is an RAE responsibility. Facilities have been given to No 49 Sqn to carry out training of aircrews over Orfordness Range to familiarise themselves with the technique of bombing under the conditions of the trial and further facilities have been given to the RAE for the training of aircraft controllers for the overseas trials programme." (Report ARM.NW 1/57 RAE Apr 57).

[4] In Operation Buffalo Report on the Atomic Trials held at Maralinga, South Australia, July – November 1956 by Air Cdre C T Weir DFC, Task Force Commander.

the magnitude of the damage likely to be suffered in atomic warfare. "Two nuclear devices were exploded on steel towers, one on the ground and one was dropped by a Valiant aircraft of the RAF. This was the first nuclear weapon to be dropped from the air by Britain."

This operation was the task towards which No 49 Squadron directed its main energies and efforts during the summer and early autumn of 1956; it was not, like four of the other Valiant squadrons, involved in bombing attacks on Egyptian targets in Operation Musketeer at the end of October–beginning of November. Training for Buffalo was task enough in the time available before the atomic tests, even if everything had gone according to plan – which it did not, as the report again makes clear[1]:

"The Valiants arrived at [RAAF] Edinburgh having completed part of a bombing training programme in the UK. It was planned to complete their training in Australia using the range facilities at Maralinga or Woomera as required. The main reason for the non-completion of training in the UK was the late delivery of aircraft and the lack of flight clearance for certain items of equipment, notably the bombing system, the automatic pilot and the radar altimeter. Unsuitable weather and difficulties in obtaining bombing ranges also added to the delays.

"Both aircraft were fitted with a T.4 bombsight which had been modified by the incorporation of drift smoothing. The system had never been tested in a Valiant type aircraft, however, until 5 June 1955. A&AEE gave temporary clearance for the installation after a six-bomb detail had been completed from 19,000ft. During the training which followed, ten practice 10,000lb bombs and 60 x 100lb bombs were dropped in the UK by the two Valiant aircraft. The 10,000lb bombs were primarily to prove the weapon and aircraft systems and the 100-pounders to prove the accuracy of the T.4 bombsight, particularly in the hands of inexperienced crews. On completion of this training programme in the UK, the results of which were not entirely satisfactory, it was decided that the standard obtained, considering the time available, was adequate and the aircraft and crews were prepared for fly-out to Australia. Technical defects discovered during the UK training phase were corrected, and modifications to the bombsight sighting head and the Green Satin output improved the system and gave considerably better bombing results at a later date. The whole of the training programme in the UK could have been considerably improved if more emphasis had been placed on overseas operations."

In their preparation for Operation Buffalo, which because it was the first British atomic weapon trial to include an air drop[2] marked the

---

[1] Page 25, paras 81–82.

[2] In Operation Hurricane (Monte Bello Islands, 3 Oct 52) the device had been exploded in a frigate; in Totem (Emu Field, 300m NW of Woomera), there were two tower bursts, 14 and 26 Oct 53; and in Mosaic (Monte Bello Is) there were likewise two tower bursts, on 16 May and 19 June 56. In Buffalo there were two tower and one surface burst in addition to the air drop, which was of a low-yield bomb (The Effects of Nuclear Weapons, US DoD 6).

culmination of the work which began in 1947 when Ministers decided that an atomic bomb should be developed, No 49 Sqn worked hard to perfect bombing techniques. The ORBs from May to early August, when two Valiants left Wittering for Australia, contain records of dropping "stores" (as the ballistic models were called), conferences and discussions, tests of special equipment and bombing practices at different ranges. At the same time the squadron was training, and making preparations, for Operation Grapple – the trials of megaton-range weapons at Christmas Island which were to follow. The two aircraft for Buffalo, Valiants WZ366 and WZ367, left for Australia on 5 August captained respectively by Sqn Ldr E J G Flavell and Flt Lt R N Bates. It can be seen, then, in view of the comments made in Gp Capt Menaul's report, that these two crews had only had three months in which to prepare for the trials. The two Valiants, with WP201 (veteran of No 1321 Flight), had formed the original equipment of No 49 Sqn; they were painted white, as protection against radiation, and their equipment included a Mk 10 autopilot, T.4 bombsight, Bhangmeter, accelerometer and thermal recorder.

The Operation Buffalo Air Task Group Commander, Gp Capt S W B Menaul, said in his report on air operations at Maralinga that despite some delays and disappointment "the whole operation . . . was extremely successful. New and improved techniques were practised, many more air and ground crews were indoctrinated in the effects of atomic weapons, and 11 October became an historical day in the annals of the Royal Air Force – and, indeed, of the country – as the day on which Britain dropped her first nuclear weapon from an aircraft". On that day, as the report describes,

"At 1400 hours . . . Valiant WZ366 took off from Maralinga airfield with the live nuclear weapon on board. The crew consisted of Sqd Ldr Flavell (captain), Gp Capt Menaul, Flt Lts Ledger and Stacey, Flg Off Spencer and Plt Off Ford. The aircraft climbed to 38,000ft in a wide arc, avoiding the range area until it reached the emergency holding area. The bombsight was levelled, contact was established with the air controller on the ground by VHF and HF, and the aircraft then descended to 30,000ft ready to begin the fly-over sequences, using precisely the same drills and procedures as in the concrete and HE drops[1]. At 1425hr the first fly-over, Type 'A', was successfully completed, with all equipment, both in the aircraft and on the ground, working satisfactorily. Types 'B' and 'C' fly-overs were then completed in turn, and by 1500hr all was in readiness for the final Type 'D' fly-over and the release of the nuclear weapon. The final 'D' type fly-over was completed according to plan with all equipment functioning perfectly, and the weapon was released at 1527hr. Immediately after release a

---

[1] The Valiants had done four telemetered test drops – one with an inert and three with HE rounds.

172

steep turn to starboard on to a heading of 240° true was executed in order to position the aircraft correctly for the thermal measuring equipment to function. During this turn 1.9 G was applied. The weapon exploded correctly and the aircraft, after observing the formation of the mushroom cloud, set course for base, where it landed at 1535hr. The operation had gone smoothly and exactly according to the plans drawn up during training. The bombing error was afterwards assessed at 110yd overshoot, and 40ft right. . . ."

Also in the air at this momentous time was the second No 49 Sqn Valiant, WZ367, flown by Flt Lt Bates, which

"took off at 1415hr for Bhangmeter tests only, and took up position on the predetermined race track orbit without aid from the ground radars . . . which were fully occupied with the dropping aircraft. The second Valiant was at 35,000ft and 5nm west of the target. At 2¼ minutes before detonation, the aircraft turned on to a heading of 250° true, the bomb doors were opened and the system primed. On detonation the clock stopped as expected and was removed from its mounting. The Bhangmeter equipment on this aircraft also worked satisfactorily[1]."

The CAS (Air Chf Mshl Sir Dermot Boyle) got his first news of the nuclear weapon drop in a Note from his PSO (Wg Cdr F D Hughes) on 11 October. This reported that "the signal we have received says no more than 'device successfully exploded' ".

A week later, on 18 October, a signal reached Bomber Command HQ which said:

"For Commander in Chief and ACAS (Ops) from Commander Task Force Buffalo [Air Cdre C T Weir DFC]:–

"On the departure of the Valiants of 49 Squadron for the United Kingdom I would bring to your attention the industry and care displayed by Sqn Ldr Flavell, his two crews and the ground staff in preparing for the first atomic air drop.

"The operation was carried out with skill and precision and above all without fuss.

"It was an honour to have the detachment under my command."

Subsequently, DCAS (Air Mshl G W Tuttle) gave details of the drop in a Note of 24 October to S of S for Air (Mr Nigel Birch). Saying that the Minister would "have seen Press reports of the dropping of an atomic device from a Royal Air Force Valiant on the 11th October", he went on:–

"The weapon, a Blue Danube round with modified fusing, in-flight loading and with the yield reduced to 3–4 kilotons, was dropped from the Valiant aircraft at 30,000ft. The weapon was set to burst at 500ft and telemetry confirmed that the burst occurred at between 500 and 600ft.

---

[1] Report on Air Operations, page 38. In his personal account of Operation Buffalo – *Maralinga – Field of Thunder* – Sq Ldr W E Jones described the No 49 Sqn participation as a "first class bombing exercise".

The bomb was aimed visually after a radar-controlled run-up. . . ."

One of the RAF officers present at the test, Sqn Ldr W E Jones, said in his book *Maralinga – Field of Thunder*[1] that "the burst had occurred about 100yd to port with an undershoot of 60yd from the target . . . . There was nothing to be seen of the triangular marker".

Another Bomber Command squadron which took part in Operation Buffalo was No 76, equipped with Canberra B.6s and based (when in UK) at RAF Weston Zoyland in Somerset, an experienced participant in atomic trials since it had been given a new role – cloud-sampling – at the end of 1955 as the Canberra Element of 308.5 Task Group. It had taken part in the third series of trials – Operation Mosaic, in the Monte Bello Islands during May and June 1956, being based at RAAF Pearce, near Perth, Western Australia – and on this occasion its ORB graphically recorded that on 16 May 1956

"No 76 Sqn sampled the first atomic explosion of Britain's third series of atomic trials, Operation Mosaic on the Monte Bello Isles. This was the culmination of six months' hard effort by both ground and air crews.

"The explosion took place at 0351(Z)hr. At that time four Canberras of No 76 Sqn, in line astern battle formation, were flying at 45,000ft and at a range 40nm south of the firing site. Prior to the firing the aircrews had listened-out to the count-down, the pilots with their seats lowered and the navigators with their window screened. For a period of six seconds beginning at minus three seconds before firing, the aircrew closed their eyes to protect them from the brilliant flash. On opening their eyes the aircrew saw the atomic burst, relatively small from altitude[2], yet still impressive and awe-inspiring.

"The aircraft orbited clear of the cloud as it ascended at phenomenal speed, forming the typical mushroom top associated with these explosions. At 0354hr under orders from the Air Controller, the aircraft descended, breaking into two sections, and they assessed the top and bottom heights of the cloud and passed this information to the Controller. The cloud was sampled on a given direction and altitude, the backers-up turning away before entering cloud in order to avoid contamination. Previously, these aircraft had taken photographs of the primary samplers and the atomic cloud as the final run was made.

"All the cloud-sampling equipment operated successfully and orders were given for the aircraft to return to base independently, the samplers at all speed, the backers-up at normal cruising conditions. The samplers landed at Pearce at 0550hr and the backers-up approximately 15min later. After taxying the primary aircraft to the 'Active Area' the samples obtained were removed by the scientific staff who soon confirmed that these were just what the 'doctor' had ordered. However, the squadron

---

[1] Unpublished. See footnote on p173.
[2] The two tower bursts in Operation Mosaic had yields in the kiloton range.

task did not finish there.

"The atomic cloud had to be tracked to ensure that any fall-out was not contaminating populated, or other, areas of life. This task was also successfully completed and by midday on 17 May 1956 the last aircraft had returned to base.

"So ended the first sampling and cloud-tracking tasks of Operation Mosaic. No 76 Sqn thus held the honour of being the first Royal Air Force squadron to be employed on atomic trials and to have the first squadron crews and aircraft to enter an atomic cloud. That the whole operation went smoothly and successfully is attributable to careful planning and the unreserved enthusiasm and co-operation of all ranks."

The squadron's primary upper sampler aircraft, WH978, was flown by the CO, Sqn Ldr J N B Boyd, with Flg Off J Love as navigator and Gp Capt S W B Menaul, the Task Group Commander, aboard as observer. Their backer-up and photographic Canberra, WH979, had Flg Offs B H Newton (pilot) and E R Broadbank (navigator) as crew with Flg Off D H King as observer. The primary lower sampler aircraft was WH976 (Flt Lt I C B Brettell and Flg Offs P N Phillips and J R Digby) and their backer-up and photographic aircraft was WH962 (Flg Offs K D Bretherton, P K Fernée and J H Wilson).

No 76 Sqn performed the same role in Operation Buffalo, as part of the Air Task Group[1], and the commander's report recorded that "new sampling techniques were developed and proved successful. . . . All Canberra crews on Operations Mosaic and Buffalo carried out at least one sampling sortie, either as primary sampler or secondary sampler/backer-up, and at least one tracking sortie. On all the sampling sorties good samples were obtained and delivered safely to the scientific laboratories. Although some of the equipment failed, there were no operational failures from the flying standpoint. Every crew saw one or more atomic weapons exploded, and learnt at first hand what nuclear explosions are, what they do, and how certain precautions to minimise the effects of the explosion can be taken. They also learnt at first hand the amount of work involved in mounting one of these operations, which are extremely costly, and which demand meticulous planning, exact timing and good discipline, both on the ground and in the air"[2].

The squadron's own account of its part in the operation was much more prosaic that its record of participation in Mosaic:–

"During the month of October [its ORB recorded for October 1956 at Edinburgh Field] the squadron was actively engaged in Shots 2, 3 and 4 of Operation Buffalo. Five crews, aircraft and supporting groundcrew were detached to RAF Maralinga for each shot, Shots 2, 3 and 4 being fired on October 4, 11 and 22 respectively. The squadron was employed

---

[1] Which in addition to Valiants and Canberras included Varsities, Hastings.
[2] Report, page 45.

175

in the same roles as on Shot 1 [on 27 September]. All the tasks given to the squadron were carried out successfully. The last few days of the month were spent preparing for the return of most of the aircrews and groundcrews to the UK in November, Operation Buffalo having been brought to a successful conclusion."

The Canberras and their crews returned to Weston Zoyland, as did the two Valiants of No 49 Sqn, to Wittering, its ORB summing-up the tasks in Buffalo as "target reconnaissance; simulated radar bombing runs at Woomera and Maralinga; telemetry checks including one concrete 10,000lb special weapon drop under radar survey with visual release; two 10,000lb live special weapon drops on Kite target; Bhangmeter (flash) measurements on the three phases of ground-fired atomic explosions with a thermal flux measurement on Phase Three; and the 10,000lb atomic weapon drop on 11 October 1956". The two aircraft, the ORB added,

"were used in all phases of the atomic explosion trials to carry equipment capable of measuring the atomic bursts. During this time training for the Air Burst progressed with telemetry checks, bombsight checks and practice special weapon drops, all of which culminated in the Atomic Drop by Sqn Ldr E J G Flavell being bhangmetered by Flt Lt R N Bates on 11 October. After which the detachment returned to Edinburgh from Maralinga, the forward flying base, and thence to the UK where they joined the squadron on 27 October at Wittering".

At Wittering, exercises, trials and training were going on for the squadron's part in Operation Grapple, the trials of a megaton-range weapon − the first hydrogen bomb for the RAF − to be held in the Christmas Island area, in the middle of the Pacific Ocean, during May and June 1957, and described in a later chapter.

The other two specialist roles performed by Valiants, in addition to flight refuelling and nuclear weapons trials, were strategic reconnaissance[1] and electronic countermeasures. That reconnaissance was of high importance to the V-bomber force was emphasised by the fact that the second Valiant squadron to be formed, with Mk 1 B(PR) aircraft, had this role − operating from Wyton, the centre of Bomber Command reconnaissance activity, already housing four Canberra PR squadrons. As mentioned earlier, the new squadron, No 543, came into

---

[1] In this role, "Valiants were particularly useful because of the number of cameras they could carry. . . . The RAF installed fans of cameras to provide horizon-to-horizon cover, an expedient which reached an extreme in the Valiant B(PR).1 which carried a camera crate in the bomb-bay capable of holding a fan of eight F96s with 48in lenses and four F49 survey cameras": *Photo Reconnaissance The Operational History*, by Andrew J Brookes; Ian Allan Ltd, 1975). Noting the structure of RAF PR at that time, he says that "in response to Suez, and to meet the need to evolve new reconnaissance techniques to cope with the jet age, the RAF decided once more to combine all its UK strategic reconnaissance forces into one Group. Thus the Central Reconnaissance Establishment (CRE) came into being at Brampton on April 1st, 1957, to control JARIC [the Joint Air Reconnaissance Centre] and the successor to the PRU, the UK Reconnaissance Force, whose PR element following disbandment of 82, 540 and 542 Sqns comprised 58 Sqn and 543 Sqn, the latter having re-formed in 1955 with Valiant B(PR).1s".

being after No 138 at No 232 OCU, which was responsible for the introduction of, and initial training on, Valiants; and its ORB thus described its inception:–

"No 543(PR) Sqn was formed at RAF Gaydon as a Main Force photographic reconnaissance squadron on 1 June 1955 and should have moved to RAF Wyton on 24 September, when all crews of 'A' Flight would have completed conversion training at No 232 OCU.... Due however to insufficient accomodation and lack of technical backing, RAF Wyton was unable to accept the squadron during September and the date of the move to that station was postponed until 26 October. Wg Cdr R E Havercroft AFC took command ... on 1 August and the squadron started operating independently as a lodger unit at RAF Gaydon as from 24 September."

No 543's move to Wyton was not in fact accomplished until November, and even then there were delays: "owing to weather it was not possible to fly the two serviceable aircraft from Gaydon as had been planned, but they were later flown into Wyton on 21 and 22 November". These were WP217 and WP221. With a current strength of four out of an establishment for eight Valiants, the ORB reported that "WP223 was at Vickers-Armstrongs for rectification and ... was collected from Wisley and brought to Wyton on 28 November. WP219 is still at Gaydon undergoing a minor inspection". With the move to its proper base achieved, the ORB recorded that "No 543 Squadron is part of the Main Force Bomber Command Strategic Reconnaissance Photographic Wing". During December 1955 the aircraft strength increased to five (with the loan of a Valiant from Marham) to expedite training, as WP219 was still at Gaydon and as the new squadron's "B" Flight had arrived from there, its four crews having completed their conversion course at No 232 OCU.

It was at the beginning of 1956, therefore, that No 543 Sqn really got down to training – though still with only enough Valiants for its "A" Flight, and having to continue borrowing one from Marham and to send a crew to Wittering for flying training on a 138 Sqn aircraft. Not until 9 February was the squadron able to make a serious contribution to V-force activity, when it

"took part in a Bomber Command V-force Interception Trial, providing two Valiant aircraft out of a force of seven Valiants and 18 Canberras. The purpose of the trial was to conduct a study of V-force penetration and interception problems and to observe the degree of success that the fighters and radar defences achieved in dealing with the penetration. Both of the aircraft provided completed the briefed route, according to plan"[1].

In this trial, No 543 was simply contributing two bombers; it was not yet qualified to act in a reconnaissance role, but only emerging from the

---

[1] No 543 Sqn ORB.

OCU stage. For example, during March "the squadron carried out normal continuation training. . . . For the first time a Continental cross-country was included in the navigation exercises". In April, when its strength was up to ten Valiants, a sortie to Iceland and return was included in the cross-country exercises. During May, No 543 was again used in the normal bomber role: taking part in the Bomber Command Exercise Rejuvenate – the purpose of which was to give Fighter Command aircraft interception practice in the sector covering the north-west approaches to the UK – the squadron "flew three night sorties on the 5th and three day sorties on the 6th. . . . All six sorties were completed as planned".

A Bomber Command Operational Research Branch report on Exercise Rejuvenate[1] made an interesting comment on the Valiant crews' awareness (or otherwise) of interception. Giving figures for the number of raids intercepted, it said that

"the source of data is mainly the raid reports submitted by bomber aircraft after each sortie with the exception that in the case of the Valiant raids the fighter claims (as supplied by Fighter Command) have had to be used. By day, Canberra admissions have agreed very well with fighter claims and the use of bomber admission data enables valid conclusions to be drawn on interception rates. However, the Valiant admissions in this exercise and in a minor exercise previously have been appreciably less than the fighter claims. Whereas this difference applies to three small raids only and is not statistically significant, there is a strong possibility that Valiant crews are not aware of a fighter's presence with the near 100% certainty that applies to Canberras".

During June 1956 the new SR squadron was able to spread its wings abroad for the first time – one of its Valiants, captained by the CO (Wg Cdr Havercroft), flying to Idris in Libya on the 24th to participate in Excercise Thunderhead, designed to test Nato defences in the north-eastern Mediterranean. The ORB noted with pride that with the return of WZ394 to Wyton on the 28th, the squadron's first Lone Ranger sortie[2] was completed successfully without incident and that "the participation of an aircraft in Exercise Thunderhead . . . was a noteworthy feature in the squadron's short history". At this time, one of No 543's Valiants was doing flying trials with H2S Mk 9 Yellow Aster. This was a non-scanning radar system which had resulted from an Air Staff OR for equipment which would make it possible to carry

---

[1] Memorandum No 173 Interception of Bomber Aircraft during Exercise Rejuvenate – May 1956.
[2] Lone Rangers were single-aircraft deployments overseas, designed to test mobility and self-sufficiency away from base.

out reconnaissance in all-weather conditions[1]. To meet this requirement, Yellow Aster Mk 1 was produced as an interim measure. These trials continued during June, July and August 1956.

The squadron had still not operated in its specialised reconnaissance role, the reason apparently being that its Valiants were not yet suitably equipped; but the picture was begining to change towards the end of the year. Reporting in November 1956 on training the ORB said that flights had been "severely restricted, due to the absence of several aircraft at Vickers-Armstrong Ltd, Weybridge, and Marshall's Ltd, Cambridge, for major modification and servicing"; but it added: "now that fully modified aircraft are becoming available, a series of seven-hour cross-countries has been initiated, for general research into flight planning, fuel loading and aircraft performance".

From 9 October to 29 December 1956 a detachment from No 543 Sqn, with two Valiants, was at RCAF Namao, near Edmonton, Alberta, on Operation Snow Trip – a Ministry of Supply/Bomber Command joint project to assess the effect of winter conditions on airborne radar equipment[2]. Further phases of this exercise followed during early 1957. Not until May of that year, however, was No 543 able to demonstrate its true role. The ORB recorded:–

"This month the squadron took part in its first operational reconnaissance during Exercise Vigilant. The first four sorties that were flown were very successful, all the allocated targets being covered". Referring to the exercise (24 to 27 May) in more detail, the ORB said that "two crews were to fly each night . . . to carry out radar targeting raids. The flights on the night of the 24th were cancelled owing to weather conditions, but two flights were completed on each of the nights of the 25th and 26th . . .". No 543's Valiants were still undergoing modification, and for the first half of May only five aircraft were available.

The technique of radar coverage of target areas was well exercised in Canada, Phase III of Operation Snow Trip taking into consideration late winter, thaw and early spring conditions and all the flying being "directly concerned with the radar coverage of the various target areas . . . obtained from various heights and with both radial and sidescan radar". In summing-up the influence of Snow Trip, the ORB commented that the squadron's detachment "gained considerable experience of cold weather conditions and returned to the United Kingdom with a host of data which will undoubtedly advance the squadron's operational role".

[1] A note on Yellow Aster Mk 1 (OR3578) in MoD Defence Research Policy Committee paper DRP/P(58) of 26 Feb 58 began: "The primary requirements of air reconnaissance have hitherto been met by high-level photography by day and night. Its limitation to visual conditions is unacceptable, and there is an urgent need for equipment which will make it possible to carry out reconnaissance in all weathers".
[2] "A survey of the DEW (distant early warning) radar chain across the Canadian Arctic border" (*Vickers Aircraft since 1908*, by C F Andrews; Putnam & Co, 1969).

Proof of its reconnaissance capability came in a visit by two of its Valiants to Malta during June 1957 to give a presentation of radar reconnaissance equipment and techniques to AFMED (Allied Forces, Mediterranean), several special Sidescan sorties being flown before the presentation. At this time, too, the first two 543 crews to be declared "combat" were classified – Wg Cdr Havercroft and his crew at the end of May, and Sqn Ldr G D Cremer and his crew during June.

It can be seen that, with modification of aircraft and training of crews, with the detachments to Canada, with Lone Rangers, and with practices for special events like the Battle of Britain "at home" display in 1956 and the Queen's Birthday Flypast in 1957, plus participation in a NATO Reconnaissance Symposium at Lahr in Germany, it was 18 months from the beginning of 1956 – when the squadron had settled-in at Wyton – before it became operational as part of the Bomber Command Strategic PR Wing. It then became involved, from 18 August 1957 onwards, in the Antler series of nuclear weapon trials at Maralinga.

No 543 Sqn had two aircraft (Valiants B (PR) Mk 1 WZ391 and WZ392) on detachment to RAAF Edinburgh Field, South Australia, for these trials as part of Air Task Group Antler – "a composite force of approximately one thousand men, operating eight different types of aircraft, carrying out a series of nuclear tests at Maralinga Range" (to quote from the squadron ORB). The detachment's task was to "carry out radar reconnaissance before, during and after" each of the three nuclear explosions – on 14 and 25 September and 9 October 1957, both of the Valiants participating on each occasion, doing both radar and photograhic reconnaissance. Two of the three kiloton-range test shots were exploded on towers and the other was suspended from a series of balloons.

According to the report by the detachment commander, Sqn Ldr G D Cremer, the PR Valiants and their crews did all that was expected of them, although several sorties had to be aborted, because of cancellations due to meteorological conditions on the range. "On the postponement of a shot firing, aircraft and crews reverted to standby. As the Valiants were operating from 450 miles away, it happened they would be airborne before the cancellation was announced" – which meant a loss of 2½ hours' flying as the aircraft reduced their fuel load to a safe landing weight. "On one occasion the cancellation was received when the aircraft were at the take-off point with ten seconds to take-off" – two highly disappointed crews having to return to dispersal.

On this detachment the Valiants also did radar reconnaissance (three sorties) for the Weapon Research Establishment's Blue Steel project, to gather data. From departure from Wyton on 18 August to return there on 22 October, the detachment lasted just over two months, and in the words of Sqn Ldr Cremer was "most successful . . . both from the point of view of the transit flights and the operations carried out at

Edinburgh Field".

In the electronic countermeasures role, Valiants and their crews did not form a new squadron but re-formed an existing one – No 199, whose Lincolns were then given the status of a flight. The squadron ORB noted the change baldly but succinctly: "With effect from 2359hr on 30 September 1957, No 199 Sqn re-formed at Royal Air Force Honington on Valiant aircraft. The unit at Hemswell flying Lincoln aircraft becoming 1321 Flight".

No 199 had been engaged in ECM operations during the war, from mid-1944 onwards, in No 100 Group, as No 199 (BS – bomber support) Sqn, its Stirlings and the Halifaxes which succeeded them operating on radio countermeasures with Window (metallised strips to confuse enemy RDF) and Mandrel (airborne jamming equipment). The squadron was disbanded in July 1945 but re-formed in the same role during October 1951 as part of the Central Signals Establishment at Watton, flying Lincoln Mk 2/4As and Mosquito NF.36s. But on 17 April 1952 it was transferred from No 90 Group to Bomber Command, becoming a squadron in No 1 Group. The operational flying task it was given on 9 May specified 88hr per month initially, divided among Fighter Command (39hr), Anti-Aircraft Command (20hr), Bomber Command (18hr) and the Royal Navy (11hr). Lincoln pilots were to be converted to Mosquito NF.36s so that they could fly both types; Mosquitoes were held on the squadron to make good the deficiency in Lincolns and would be disposed of when the Lincoln establishment had been filled. It was not until early 1954, however, that the Mosquitoes disappeared, and the squadron gained one Canberra B.2 in addition to its nine Lincolns – the latter providing the main RCM effort for Bomber Command and the other Services until the arrival of the first Valiants in 1957.

No 1321 Flight, to which the Lincolns were then assigned after the re-formation of No 199 Sqn, had previously been engaged in Ministry of Supply ballistic trials at Wittering but had completed this task early in 1956. As an ECM unit, it operated with Lincolns at Hemswell from 1 October 1957 until 31 March 1958, when it had two Lincoln B.2s.

No 199 Sqn, at Honington, operated a Canberra as well as Valiants from January 1958 onwards, the latter being equipped with APT-16A, ALT-7, Airborne Cigar, Carpet-4, APR9 and APR4, and Window Dispensers[1].

A letter from Bomber Command to Air Ministry in July 1957 explained the complexity of the numbering and locations of No 199 Sqn and No 1321 Flight.[2] It said that owing to the modifications to be

---

[1] No 199 Sqn ORB for February 1958. These equipments were, respectively, jamming transmitters (APT-16A and ALT-7), jammers (Airborne Cigar and Carpet-4) and search receivers (APR9 and APR4) and foil dispensers.

[2] HQ Bomber Command to US of S (DDO2), Air Ministry, on 2 July 1957 (BCS.86485/Admin Plans).

installed in the Valiants before they would be fit for squadron service, the re-arming of No 199 was to cover a minimum period of nine months. "During this period an increasing Valiant element will be based at Honington and a decreasing Lincoln element at Hemswell". It continued:–

"It is considered that difficulties are bound to arise in the administration and operational control of this squadron operating with two different types of aircraft from two different airfields for such a lengthy period. It is proposed, therefore, that the Valiant and Lincoln elements of No 199 Squadron should be given independent status . . . .

"It is requested that approval be given for the re-organisation of No 199 Squadron on this basis and that a Flight number plate be allocated to the Lincoln element based at Hemswell with effect from 1 October 1957 . . . ."

This proposal was agreed to; subject to there being no increase in establishment, the Lincoln and Canberra Flight at Hemswell to be No 1321.

At about the same time, the need for RCM in the V-bombers was acknowledged and defined by the Air Ministry, which said in a Note:–

"RCM, radio countermeasures, are means of upsetting those elements of the enemy's defence system that are based on radar or radio devices. Radar detection depends on picking-up and isolating a very low-powered signal; RCM, by emitting a large number of random signals over a wide range of frequencies, prevents an accurate bearing being taken on the signal generated by the radar echo, thus seriously embarrassing the defenders.

"The RCM installation which is planned for the V-bombers consists of a three-fold system to jam both active and passive radar systems, as well as disrupting the enemy communications radio. It will be effective against radar-guided missiles as well as ground radar systems".[1]

At the end of 1956 a paper had been prepared in the Operational Requirements Branch on "ECM Policy for V-class Aircraft",[2] and this also spelt out what was needed to counter enemy defences. Referring first to the requirements for countermeasures, it said that

"An effective deterrent cannot be maintained unless the force has the manifest ability to penetrate the defences to deliver its weapons. The V-class bombers face Russian defences which are becoming increasingly effective against sub-sonic bombers. It is predicted that these defences will become extremely lethal to the V-force in three or four years' time unless methods of reducing their efficiency are devised and the aircraft appropriately fitted.

"Some increase in safety can be achieved if the aircraft are developed

---

[1] AM Note of 1957 on RCM in V-bombers, in file Working Papers Only RCM in V-bombers – Policy (RD/37/048).

[2] OR18, 28 Dec 56/C.46548. In AF/CT1373/65 Pt I V-force RCM Co-ordinating Meetings ARIs 18074/18075/18076/5919/18105.

to give improved performance – in speed and height in order to stretch the interception procedures and in range to give the opportunity to employ evasive routeing where possible. There is, however, a limit to these improvements which is set by basic aircraft design parameters and therefore other expedients must be employed to keep down the loss rate. It is generally accepted that defensive armament is not profitable in present concepts where air-to-air and surface-to-air weapons will ultimately constitute the most serious threat to the bombers.

"All defence systems are dependent on some sort of control and reporting organisation. The basis of this . . . is a ground radar network with a radio link to its fighters in the conventional concept; at a later stage the fighters may be replaced or supplemented by a SAGW system. This form of defence, however, would still depend on a ground radar system. The ground radar and communications links are vulnerable to jamming and suggest the most promising method of reducing the effectiveness of the defences and thereby reducing the forecast of the loss-rate of the bomber force".

The paper then went on to describe Russian defensive radar, saying that

"The principal ground radar in the Russian C and R (control and reporting) system is the Token centimetric (S band) equipment. It is a multi-beam, continuous height-finding radar operating on five or seven frequencies between [   ] and [   ] mc/s. It is backed up by a chain of metric stations, most of which are now of the Kniferest type operating on 65 to 75 mc/s with apparently the additional ability to operate on frequencies up to about 104 mc/s as an anti-jamming measure. The Russians seem clearly aware of the vulnerability of these radars to jamming.

"The Russian fighter control operates in the conventional VHF band between 100 and 156 mc/s. The aircraft equipment is a simple four-channel set which rather restricts the flexibility of control. This suggests that the control may be fairly vulnerable to countermeasures despite the possibility of using a substantial high-power transmitter on the ground as a countermeasure step".

Describing British development of ECM equipment, the writer said:-

"With this general background of Russian defences, three jammers have been developed for the V-class aircraft. These are

OR3618 Centimetric jammer ARI 18076
OR3520 Communications jammer ARI 18074
OR3521 Metric jammer ARI 18075.

"Although it is realised that alternative frequencies ground radars can be used to supplement the Token and Kniferest stations, it would take a considerable time for even the Russians to provide comprehensive cover on new frequencies. In any case, it would be very difficult to cloak such intentions from our intercept service; the same considerations apply, but to a lesser degree, to a possible change from

VHF to UHF fighter communications.

"This brings out two principles of ECM philosophy: firstly that ECM policy must not remain static but must take account of enemy development; and secondly, the threat of ECM invokes a strategic requirement for the continued development of ground radar and communications with a consequent expenditure of effort and money."

To show what this expenditure meant in terms of equipment fitted into the V-bombers, the following was the fit in a Valiant in October 1957:[1]

(i)   A passive warning receiver system. This warns the crew when they are locked-on by enemy ground radar.

(ii)   An active tail warner, with a special radome. This warns the crew when the aircraft is being followed by an enemy fighter.

(iii)   A system of jamming transmitters. At present these are contained in nine separate cylindrical drums, each being approximately 3ft high, 18in in diameter and 200lb in weight. These cover the metric and centimetric wave bands and are intended to block the enemy's ground radar, and air-to-air radio and radar.

(iv)   The jamming apparatus demands a system of water/glycol cooling. This is an elaborate system of pipes, connected to a special air intake and heat exchanger. (This is the most intricate part of the airframe installation. . . .)

(v)   A turbo-alternator to provide the AC power necessary to operate the jamming apparatus.

(vi)   Five separate sets of aerials connected with the RCM apparatus. These are situated in the nose, tail, both wing-tips and beneath the fuselage.

"The whole of the apparatus described . . . has had to be fitted into the fuselage of an aircraft which was not designed to receive it. The jamming system, with its cooling tubes and electrical connections, is elaborate and extensive and occupies almost the whole of the rear half of the fuselage. . . ."

It should be noted here that V-bomber countermeasures were both active and passive. In March 1959 Air Staff Targets were issued for IRCM (infra-red countermeasures) designed to protect the V-bombers from the guidance to enemy missiles provided by infra-red emissions from the bombers' jet engines. These ASTs were Nos OR 3604-6, respectively Airborne Detection System for Warning of the launch of AAGW; Infra-red Decoy Flares; and Infra-red Screening for Aircraft[2]. AST OR3606 was cancelled on 13 April 1961, but a Specification for a system for dispensing rapid blooming Window and/or Infra-red Decoy

---

[1] Note of a visit to Vickers-Armstrongs, Weybridge: AirB2(a), 25 Oct 57, in file RD/37/048 RCM in V-bombers Finance and Policy.

[2] File C152386/62 Infra-red Suppression in V bombers, Pt II.

(OR3605) was produced in May 1961 by Microcell Ltd[1].

In fact, Valiants had not been designed either for ECM equipment nor for carrying fuel as tankers, though their role in photographic reconnaissance had been envisaged from their inception – and they could carry more cameras than any other RAF aircraft up to that time, and on longer sorties. In performing these roles, and as bombers and additionally as nuclear weapon trials vehicles, they proved themselves to be the most versatile of the three types of V-force aircraft.

---

[1] See note[2], page 184.

CHAPTER XIII

BLUE STEEL: ORIGIN, DEVELOPMENT AND DEPLOYMENT

At the Air Council meeting on 19 September 1955[1], when the V-bombers were being discussed[2], DCAS (Air Mshl Sir Thomas Pike) said that measures to extend their operational life and to increase their effectiveness against developments in Russian air defences by 1960 included "a powered guided bomb which was being developed for Service use by 1960. This would have a range of 100 miles and a speed of Mach 2". Thus when the first of the V-bombers had only just entered squadron service, and when their original weapon, the free-falling Blue Danube nuclear bomb, had not yet been finally proved in live dropping trials, plans were being made for a bomb which would be launched from V-aircraft and fly to its target, thus decreasing the bombers' vulnerability to enemy missile defences.

The idea of a guided bomb had been examined in 1946-47. During 1946 the Air Staff had stated a requirement for a guided bomb "with the object of improving the accuracy of bombing from high altitude at high speed with high-explosive bombs"[3]. Explaining the original work on this project, code-named Blue Boar, ACAS(OR) recalled in 1953 that consultation with the Ministry of Supply had revealed that "television/command control was the only practicable system of guidance which could be undertaken at that time". But "the operational limitations of the system were well known"; however, it was considered necessary to build up teams and experience both in industry and the MoS establishments, to deal with all the problems involved in control, guidance and the aerodynamic performance of bombs. "There was promise that when a more operationally suitable system of guidance became practicable, much time could be saved by having available a controllable vehicle in which to install it. . . ." Disadvantages of TV guidance were that visual conditions were required by day, the system had not been proved feasible at night, and "the addition of radio and TV equipment to the . . . mechanical complexity of an atom bomb will reduce its reliability, with no compensating . . . increase in accuracy, due to weather limitations". ACAS(OR) considered that, on such grounds, the development of TV guidance as an operational weapon could not be justified.

Studies of a guided bomb had continued through the late 1940s-early 1950s. When the Air Council considered a report on current R&D

---

[1] AC Conclusions 17(55) (Special).
[2] Review of the Air Staff Research and Development Programme – August 1955 – AC(55)43 – Note by DCAS.
[3] ACAS(OR) to SoS (through DCAS) on Blue Boar – Policy, DCAS/3872, 1 Sep 53.

projects on 8 September 1947[1] they learned that "work was proceeding" on a guided bomb (OR1059). The Council's Memorandum for that year[2] included a progress report by the Scientific Adviser to the Air Ministry[3] which said that a study had recently been started "with a view to determining the need for a guided bomb. A proposal for the control of guided bombs by means of a tachometric bombsight has been investigated and is considered to be technically feasible".

In the March 1949 issue of an Air Ministry publication on Future Aircraft and Equipment[4] there was a drawing of a controlled bomb called Blue Boar. This had a TV head, an explosive head and flip-out wings with control surfaces. Capable of being released from altitudes of up to 60,000ft and at speeds of up to 600kt, it was controlled by a joystick for some distance after launch, then fell free, a TV camera in its nose scanning a 65° area. A little later that year, the Air Ministry Quarterly Liaison Report for April-June 1949 contained an item headed OR1089 – Control of Bombs – Television, which stated that "the probable usefulness of the television bomb Blue Boar is being investigated. It was feared that weather conditions at the target might severely limit this usefulness, but it now appears that the limiting factor in using the bomb may be the sustained rate of effort of the aircraft and not the state of the weather at the target". Only one bomb could be controlled from any one aircraft at a time, and Blue Boar required large space and power facilities in its parent bomber.

Air Staff Requirement No OR1089, entitled Control of Bombs – Television, was issued on 11 October 1949, superseding OR1059, as its introduction explained:–

"The Air Staff Requirement OR1059 for a controlled bomb to improve bombing accuracy under blind conditions is no longer considered capable of early solution, and has been re-issued as an Air Staff Target AST1059.

"However, the Air Staff are prepared to exploit any system which offers improvement of bombing accuracy, even in limited operating conditions, and believe that a controlled bomb using a television intelligence system will afford such an improvement over a free-falling bomb aimed from high altitude that a very material saving of effort in bomber operations will result . . . ."

The object of a TV-controlled bomb was thus stated:–

"The Air Staff require the development of a bomb capable of displaying to a parent aircraft by television, the target in relation to the flight path of the bomb. They further require a system of control of the flight path of the bomb . . . whereby apparent errors may be progressively eliminated to such a degree that a very high standard of

---

[1] AC Memoranda, Nos 31-72, Jun-Dec 1947
[2] and [3] Ibid, No 21(48).
[4] SD573 PtII.

bombing accuracy will be attained".

At the end of the first issue of OR1089 the Air Staff noted that "to maintain continuity" they would "prefer that the code name Blue Boar be retained for this specific requirement". In the second issue of the OR, for a television/command control bombing system and an associated 5,000lb HC missile, the Air Staff stated that "the bomb and its associated equipment is required to be produced to be in Service use in 1956". A contract for the project had been placed with Vickers-Armstrong in June 1950 and early in 1959 a contract had been placed with EMI Ltd for television research.

While Blue Boar was still an active requirement, the Scientific Adviser to the Air Ministry commented on the importance of such a weapon in the airborne deterrent force armoury[1]. "The trend towards greater heights and speeds", he said, "makes accurate bombing by conventional methods increasingly difficult. Development of the guided bomb is therefore of the first importance, and research into methods of guidance capable of operating in all-weather conditions by day and night must be actively pursued".

The need for a guided bomb was not disputed; the question was, the means of guidance, whether TV-controlled or inertial. Some of the arguments against the former have already been quoted; others were that it required a cloud base not lower than 10,000ft for its efficient operation, and that at night the target had to be illuminated by a 5,000lb flare[2]. But there were doubts about the wisdom of stopping the development of Blue Boar because of the absence of a suitable alternative weapon. However, in June 1954 the decision to cancel the project was finally taken[3], S of S for Air agreeing on the 17th that it should be omitted from the R & D programme.

As a result of the anticipated introduction of surface-to-air guided weapons into the enemy's defensive system around major vulnerable areas, however, by 1960, it was considered necessary to initiate development of a stand-off weapon for the V-bombers. This would be self-contained, able to proceed independently to a target once it had been launched from the parent bomber. As will be mentioned later, the company which eventually built the weapon which emanated from this Air Staff thinking, Blue Steel[4], regarded it as an aircraft.

Referring to the limitations of Blue Boar and putting forward arguments for an alternative air-launched bomb, ACAS(OR) said in a paper of 15 June 1954:

"In the light of the future requirement, it is proposed to produce a

---

[1] A Note by the Scientific Adviser on the Trend of Air Warfare, 29 Apr 53, in AC Memoranda as AC(53)31.

[2] ACAS(OR) paper, Blue Boar – Policy, in Development of Blue Boar Guided Bomb (ID3/946/2).

[3] Ibid, Min DCAS/CGWL of 24 Jun 54.

[4] A V Roe were the prime contractors.

weapon carrying an atomic warhead capable of being launched at ranges up to 100nm from the target and using an inertia guidance system. This...system is the outcome of a programme of development resulting from a previous attempt to couple inertia control to the Blue Boar missile.... The completion date for the weapon into service is 1960".

ACAS(OR) went on to say that the completion of Blue Boar by 1958 would result in a weapon of limited operational use and one whose Service life might be extremely short – to 1960. The proposed new propelled, inertia-controlled missile "should result in an extension of the useful life of the V-bomber force and should also enable more accurate bombing of targets...by the utilisation of the best radar offset aiming point within the range of 100nm. This weapon should be available by 1960".

The Operational Requirement for this weapon (OR1132 – A Propelled Air-to-surface-Missile for the V-class Bombers) was issued on 3 September 1954 and accepted by the Ministry of Supply in November of that year – on the understanding that the probable date of introduction into service would be 1961/62, as against an Air Ministry requirement for service in 1960 when the Mk 2 V-bombers were to be available. The OR asked simply for "a propelled controlled missile for use with the V-class bombers[1]". It was to be capable of being launched at ranges of up to 100nm from its selected target, and only one missile was required to be carried by each aircraft. Associated equipment in the parent bomber, which together with the missile would form the bombing system, would be NBS Mk 1, suitably modified for aiming the missile – that is for determining, in conjunction with available reconnaissance data, bearing and distance of the target from the release point; Green Satin Doppler equipment for determining ground speed and drift; and an accurate heading reference. The missile's guidance system and weapon fuze were also to be shielded as far as possible from enemy countermeasures.

Two things are clear at the outset in the history of Blue Steel development and its entry into service. First, that the idea of a guided bomb dated from 1946 when it had become evident that the new jet bombers were going to fly much faster and higher than their piston-engined predecessors, but that the plan for TV guidance was abandoned in 1953[2] and succeeded in 1954 by an OR for a self-guided bomb[3]. Secondly, that the achievement of a successful weapon of this

---

[1] Carriage by Valiants was deleted from the Requirement in 1958 (Min DCAS/ACAS(OR) of 9 June 58).

[2] "The official position regarding Blue Boar is that no requirement exists, as it was removed from the R&D programme when [it] was reviewed by the DRP Programmes Sub-Committee. The removal was confirmed in a Minute from DCAS to CGWL dated 24 March 1953" – introduction to a paper from ACAS(OR) to DCAS, 15 June 1954 (CMS1879/ACAS(OR)/3250).

[3] Which was also referred to (in the minutes of a Treasury meeting on 22 Nov 55) as a "powered megaton bomb" (Blue Steel (OR1132) Financial Aspects file – ID/47/296 (Pt 1)).

kind was going to be difficult, particularly as no prior experience existed.

Blue Steel was the product of a Government/industry programme; responsibility was divided between the Ministry of Supply and the design company, Weapons Research Division of A V Roe Ltd. On the Government side, departments at the Royal Aircraft Establishment, Farnborough, acted as design authorities for the guidance, firing and fuzing systems; RAE was technical adviser to DAArm (Director of Air Armament), the approving authority; and RAE Aberporth gave technical assistance to Avro's on specific problems. "Work at the firm [said an RAE paper of April 1957][1] is "mainly concerned with design of the missile structure and of the systems and services contained in it. Apart from the continuing model tests in wind tunnels and free flight to obtain aerodynamic data, the 2/5th scale model programme releasing an inert vehicle from a Valiant is scheduled to begin in January 1957 at Aberporth. . . ."

Referring to the scale models used in the first series of flight trials, when they were dropped from a Valiant, the former chief engineer of the Weapons Research Division of A V Roe & Co Ltd, Mr R H Francis, said in a Royal Aeronautical Society lecture on 6 November 1963[2] that the model itself was, "by British standards of 1957, a missile of quite substantial size . . . fabricated in a stainless steel to gain experience with design and manufacture of steel airframes". The model was carried inside the Valiant's bomb-bay and dropped in the same way as a ballistic bomb; the first trials objectives were "substantially achieved" by the end of 1958[3].

Putting Blue Steel into an historical perspective, Mr Francis said that it could be regarded "not only as a step in the evolution of the steel, high-supersonic-speed aircraft, but also of the two-stage aircraft. . . . Its predecessors were the Porte Baby fighter of the First World War, the Mayo composite flying-boat of the 1930s, the Vickers supersonic dropped model experiments in the UK in 1946 and the US Rascal missile of the early 1950s. Related missile projects were the ground-launched Navaho and its X-10 model flight test vehicle and Blue Boar".

Mr Francis recalled that during 1954 there were some studies at RAE and A V Roe of the possibilities of stand-off bombing, which led to the placing of a contract with A V Roe for a design study of a stand-off bomb suitable for the V-bombers. From this study came a proposal for a missile "which is, in substance, the present Blue Steel".

---

[1] Report ARM.NW 1/57.
[2] Astronautics and Guided Flight Section; published in *RAeS Journal*, May 64 (Vol 68, No 641,).
[3] Two Valiants on charge to the Controller of Aircraft, WP199 and WP206, were used for Blue Steel trials.

A development contract was placed with A V Roe by the Ministry of Supply in March 1956, and there were three other main contractors: Elliott Brothers (under RAE design authority) for the inertial navigation system; de Havilland Engines for the power supply turbines and also for some of the special propulsion motors to be used in the early test vehicles; and Armstrong Siddeley for the Stentor propulsion motors. Armament Department, RAE, were responsible for the armament system; and A V Roe for all other equipment and the airframe, also being co-ordinating contractors.

In the second phase of development, when full-scale test vehicles of various degrees of complexity were flown, the problems encountered were more complicated than those in the first phase, Mr Francis said. "The development of techniques of manufacture of stainless-steel airframes took longer than expected, and more development was found necessary on some of the internal systems than had been planned". Also a number of components were found to need special manufacture to meet the Blue Steel reliability requirement. Among the many that had to be made specially for the missile were "silicon diodes and tran-sistors, tantalum capacitors, rate gyros, position gyros, accelero-meters, servo motors, hydraulic servo valves, explosive valves, hydraulic accumulators, electrical relays, printed circuit board materials and so forth".

The final phase of development was flight trials of the operational type Blue Steel, and the missile was accepted into service in December 1962.

Mr Francis's remarks in his paper need to be borne in mind, as representing the company's point of view, when Air Staff criticisms of A V Roe & Co for delays in developing Blue Steel, voiced in 1960-61, are mentioned subsequently. It should also be remembered that Blue Steel, both in size and in the number and complication of its control systems, was virtually an aeroplane – in fact the company regarded it as such. It was 35ft long, with small delta-shaped moving foreplanes, half the span of its rear-mounted 13ft wing, and rear-mounted upper and lower fins. Powered by a hydrogen-peroxide[1] – kerosine rocket motor (DH Double Spectre in the test vehicles, Armstrong-Siddeley Stentor in the operational version), it was guided by inertial navigation and its flight control and trajectory decision-making were purely automatic; its power supply was by hydrogen peroxide turbine driving a hydraulic pump. Once launched from a Vulcan or Victor, it had to accelerate through the transonic speed range and "perform various manoeuvres at supersonic speed" before reaching its target.

---

[1] High test peroxide (HTP), an energy-rich material used as a motor propellant in missile propulsion units and rocket motors: a solution of hydrogen peroxide and water, it looked like clear water but had to be very carefully handled to avoid the risk of fire or an explosion.

A description of Blue Steel and its warhead by the Royal Aircraft Establishment[1] is relevant here. This said that the weapon was "being developed to meet the Air Staff Requirement OR1132 which asks for a propelled controlled bomb capable of delivering a megaton warhead. It is intended for carriage in the V-class bombers and to have a range of 100 miles after release. The weight of the bomb fully fuelled is expected to be about 17,000lb and it is intended to attain speeds of about M2.5 and heights approaching 75,000ft after release to obtain a high degree of immunity from the target defences. Guidance is to be effected by inertia navigation". The Blue Steel missile "forms part of an overall bombing and navigation system combining the following sub-systems: GP1 Mk 6 and associated equipment, NBS Mk1A, Green Satin, inertia navigator and associated equipment"[2].

The launch weight of Blue Steel included about 400gal of HTP fuel and 80gal kerosine, and its flight path after being released from a V-bomber at 40,000ft involved first a dive to 32,000ft, when the engine started; then a climb to 59,000ft, where speed increased to M2.3, followed by a cruise/climb to 70,300-70,500ft, where burn-out occurred. From that altitude the weapon would dive on to its target.

As the sketch[3] on the following page shows, the fuselage of the missile was divided into nine different compartments – each housing a separate component or fuel – by a series of bulkheads. From the pitot head rearwards these were: the flight rules computer (FRC); the autopilot; the navigator; the kerosine and forward HTP (some 400gal) tanks, which fed the kerosine and two peroxide pumps; the warhead (store); the main fuel tank; the alternator and electrical power control unit (EPCU); and the Stentor rocket motor which provided the power in free flight.

---

[1] Report ARM. NW 1/57 Royal Aircraft Establishment April 1957. Ref Arm 3399/11A Third Progress Report on the Contribution of the RAE to the Nuclear Weapons Programme July 1956-January 1957.

[2] Minute, Tech Serv Plans/D of M2, 16 May 1961 (files on Devlt of Victor – C127845/60, Pt III).

[3] Copied by the author at RAF Henlow, during research for this history, looking at a Blue Steel stored there for forthcoming display at the RAF Museum, Hendon.

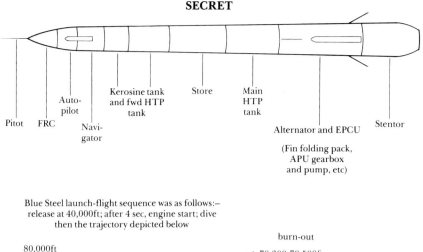

Pitot FRC Auto-pilot Navi-gator Kerosine tank and fwd HTP tank Store Main HTP tank Alternator and EPCU (Fin folding pack, APU gearbox and pump, etc) Stentor

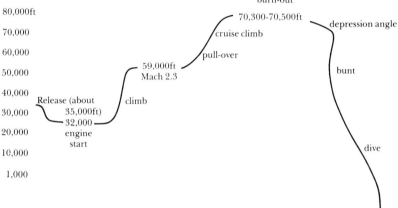

Blue Steel launch-flight sequence was as follows:–
release at 40,000ft; after 4 sec, engine start; dive
then the trajectory depicted below

Referring to Blue Steel's guidance and control system, Mr Francis said in his RAeS lecture that this consisted of three parts: the navigator (supplied by Elliotts), the flight rules computer and the autopilot (both by A V Roe). "The navigator computes the present position of the missile; the flight rules computer determines the flight plan, and the autopilot commands the control movements necessary to obtain the desired path, including the short-term stabilisation. Pitot pressure [the pitot head was in the nose of Blue Steel] was chosen as the most suitable and readily available measure of the aerodynamic environment by which the control parameters could be selected. . . . It was felt that Blue Steel was more similar to an aeroplane than to the early generations of intercepter missiles. . . ."

The RAE description of Blue Steel said that it would carry the Green Bamboo warhead. This was being developed at the AWRE (Atomic Weapons Research Establishment) and it was common to the Yellow Sun free fall weapon – the first British bomb with a yield in the megaton range, chief armament of the Vulcans and Victors before Blue Steel came into service.

An overall contract for the design and development of a missile to meet the requirements of OR1132 was given to Messrs A V Roe & Co on 9 March 1956, and the greater part of the work was carried out at their Weapons Research Division at Woodford, Cheshire[1].

In his RAeS lecture on Blue Steel, Mr Francis said that most of its development was done in the laboratory – not in flight. But during the planning of the development in 1955 – when, as he said later, most of the decisions about the missile's aerodynamics were made – "there seemed to be a number of problem areas where the information necessary to finalise the missile design could be obtained only by free flight trials. Also there was the need to build up a flight trials organisation which, when eventually presented with the operational Blue Steel, would be able to conduct proving trials efficiently and safely. For these reasons it was planned that two series of air-launched free flight test vehicle trials should precede trials of the operational Blue Steel".

This reference to a "flight trials organisation" appears to be to No 4 JSTU (Joint Services Trials Unit), formed in September 1956 "for the purpose of familiarisation with the Blue Steel weapon and weapons system prior to carrying-out joint MoS/Service acceptance trials"[2] and based initially on the A V Roe factory at Woodford (later at Scampton as No 18 JSTU with an Australian element at RAAF Edinburgh). It had four main functions: "to maintain at the missile contractors' works and at other establishments specified by DAArm, a detachment of officers and ORs for familiarisation and training on the missile and its associated equipment, and to represent Service aspects at the earliest possible time in the development stage; to gain flying and firing experience with the missile; to assist in planning the acceptance trials; and to conduct joint MoS/Service acceptance trials of Blue Steel in accordance with the directives and programmes approved and issued by the Blue Steel Trials Panel"[3].

A full report by the Avro Weapons Research Division on Blue Steel[4] described the flight trials programme as being

"based on a series of some 140 test vehicles of increasing sophistication leading up to a final vehicle, W.100A, intended to be a Service weapon meeting the requirements of OR1132. The first batch of these test vehicles (Type No 19/15) are geometrically approximate 2/5th scale models of the proposed weapon. Most of them are powered and controlled and they were planned primarily to provide an early pilot experiment to uncover difficulties likely either in the manufacture of steel missiles or in the conduct of air-launched trials, but they also gave

---

[1] Blue Steel, MoS and No 4 JSTU Early Organisation – AHB No VB/154/13.
[2] Ibid.
[3] Ibid.
[4] Blue Steel Weapon Plan Vol 1 Programme of Development and Manufacture for Pre-flight and Flight Trials. Avro Weapons Research Division May 1958.

aerodynamic and equipment environmental data. Overlapping with the later stages of this pilot experiment are the full-scale trials, starting with unpowered and uncontrolled vehicles (W.102) followed by vehicles (W.103 and W.103A) which are powered and controlled but differ from the final weapon by being built with aluminium alloy and, in some cases, by having simpler equipment, and then by steel missiles (W.100) which carry most of the proposed operational equipment apart from the warhead system. There are then two other batches of steel missiles which will have provision for the warhead system, and will include some changes already found desirable since completion of the W.100 design and also include many modifications deriving from the W.100 trials. Some of the last batch (W.100A) will be offered for Service acceptance trials".

Referring to the programme's time-scale – and bearing in mind that the Air Staff had asked in OR1132 for "the missile and its associated equipment . . . to be in service by December 1960" – Avro admitted that even by early 1958 there was some slippage in schedule:–

"It is of interest", they said, "to compare some of the forecasts of the present Plan with those of its predecessor of September 1955. The latter expected the pilot experiment to be completed 'late in 1958', while we now expect it to overrun into the early months of 1959. The full-scale trials were expected 'to start at Aberporth[1] in January 1958' while, in fact, they did not start until May 1958. In general, therefore, the project seems at present to be running some four to six months behind the forecasts of September 1955."

Bearing in mind the facts that Avro had had no previous experience of designing and manufacturing missiles, and that the operational demands of the Blue Steel requirement posed some particularly difficult problems which involved a long and complicated test programme, the four-and-a-half years available from the date when the contract was placed to that when it was required to be in service did not seem an unduly long period – especially when compared with a seven or ten-year time-cycle for manned aircraft.

Nor were the delays necessarily all on the contractor's side; there were some hold-ups in availability of test-bed Valiants. On 30 December 1957 DCAS (Air Mshl G W Tuttle) wrote to the Controller of Aircraft (Air Chf Mshl Sir Claude Pelly) about Valiant WP199 which was to be used for the first stage in flight-testing the inertia system being developed by Elliott Bros for Blue Steel. He said[1] that the aircraft had been at Marshalls of Cambridge for over a year for refurbishing and modification, which was scheduled to be finished by October 1957. "This seems to be a very long time", he commented, "but even so, it would have allowed over a year to carry out the inertia navigator trials in preparation for the first guided Blue Steel air test. The current official

---

[1] DCAS 5888/57.

date for delivery is 31 December 1957, but I understand that the aircraft will not in fact be available until April 1958 or even later. If this is so, it is difficult to see how a corresponding slippage in the remainder of the Blue Steel programme can be avoided".

CA replied on 16 January 1958[1] with some comments about the difficulties of finding suitable trials aircraft:–

"...we, too, have been very concerned about the progress of Valiant WP199 for inertia navigation trials and we have recently cancelled work on this aircraft in favour of using another Valiant, WP206. I hope that this latter will be available in April for the start of the IN trials...".

CA went on to point out that the troubles experienced with the IN trials Valiant "emphasise the difficulties that we run into when we have to rely on aircraft in the CA fleet which may not be entirely suitable for the work that they have to do. WP199, an early production non-standard aircraft[2], is a good example of this; even standard Valiant modification kits had to be specially re-designed to allow them to be embodied".

Earlier (16 December 1957) DCAS had written to CA about the Blue Steel Trials Organisation, insisting that the RAF should have ultimate authority. He recalled that the main object in setting-up the JSTU organisation for GW trials was (from the Air Staff point of view),

"to ensure that the earliest possible Service experience was obtained with each weapon. For this reason we have always insisted that overall functional control of the JSTUs should be vested in ACAS(OR), although DGWT[3], in effect, exercises day-to-day control of the units in carrying-out the instructions of the Trials Panels (of which he is chairman and on which all the appropriate Service and Ministry of Supply interests are represented).

"In practice, this arrangement has worked admirably from our point of view. We have a very close liaison with DGWT and through him with the JSTUs in Australia and with the Range authorities. DGWT and his staff have, over a period of years, established excellent relations with the various departments and establishments concerned at home and overseas by regular visits and in the process of ironing-out the many practical difficulties which have arisen. We have found...that this personal relationship is a most important factor in the...running of GW trials 12,000 miles away.

"In short, I believe that DGWT's organisation, which was expressly set up in the Ministry of Supply to run GW trials in Australia, is meeting our requirements well and I think it would be logical for DGWT to run the Blue Steel trials, acting as agent for D(RAF).B....

---

[1] AH/783/019 CA/3/5/4.
[2] It had been with CA since production on 18 December 1954 as the first Valiant of the first 20 ordered to be delivered.
[3] Director of Guided Weapons (Trials) (Air Cdre B A Chacksfield).

"I fully realise that A&AEE...also have an indispensable contribution to make from their own experience...and I believe this could be fully utilised through the existing medium of the Trials Panel as with other GW".

CA replied to this on 23 January enclosing an appendix headed "Blue Steel Acceptance Trials Organisation" – which, as agreed to with one amendment incorporated, read as follows:—

(1) Acceptance trials of Blue Steel will produce clearance for the Mother Aircraft and for Blue Steel. The final clearance will be for the weapon system as a whole.

(2) Joint Trials Panel under the chairmanship of D(RAF).B includes DOR(C), DGWT, the Project Officer and co-opted members such as A&AEE and the contractor.

(3) No 4 JSTU is an Air Ministry RAF unit which includes aircrew and maintenance personnel and has attached to it a scientific element responsible to MoS.

(4) A&AEE will produce a draft Trials Programme in conjunction with the MoS Development Project Officer, the Air Staff Project Officer, HQ Bomber Command, No 4 JSTU, the Contractor, RAE and other interested parties. The programme will be approved by the Joint Trials Panel under the chairmanship of D(RAF).B. Arrangements for using the range in Australia will be made in consultation with DGWT.

(5) Trials will be run under the joint control of OC, No 4 JSTU and the Senior Officer in charge of the Scientific element which will be supplied by A&AEE. OC, No 4 JSTU will have direct access to DOR(C) as well as the project organisation in MoS. Scientific staff associated with No 4 JSTU will be responsible to the Commandant, A&AEE.

(6) Detailed functional control of the trial will rest with D(RAF).B as chairman of the Joint Trials Panel. ACAS(OR) will retain overall functional control of No 4 JSTU.

(7) Reports on the acceptance trials will be made to the Joint Trials Panel, by No 4 JSTU and the Scientific Staff on their respective aspects.

(8) Final clearance for the weapon system will be given by CA.

With so many exacting authorities, with the problems of new technology (a supersonic flying bomb had never before been produced in Britain) and with the elaborate planning necessary for every trials weapon (each had its own lengthy documentation, consisting of a specification and trials instruction), it is no wonder that the Blue Steel programme got behind schedule – making the Air Staff hopes of an introduction into service in 1960 ever less realisable, and the MoS estimates of 1961/62 ever more realistic.

Early in 1958 DCAS reported on the situation and mentioned ways in which development might be speeded-up in order to come nearer to meeting the Air Staff requirement. He said that a joint Air Ministry/ MoS paper had been submitted to the DRPC (Defence Research Policy Committee)

"recommending that Blue Steel should be engineered for production because the weapon is essential for maintaining the deterrent power of the V-force in the early 1960s. The current development progress of Blue Steel is running about six months behind the firm's present development programme. However, the firm have now produced a more detailed programme which is being examined with the Ministry of Supply. This aims at completion of production of all R&D and Acceptance missiles (a total of 109) by November 1960 and completion of firing trials six months later. The possibility of compressing the R&D and Acceptance firings still further is being examined with the object of trying to get a few early missiles into the hands of Bomber Command for preliminary training by the end of 1960".

The Air Staff's anxiety to get Blue Steel into service resulted from an Intelligence appreciation of the increasing effectiveness of Soviet ground-to-air and air-to-air defences, making V-force penetration to targets with free-falling bombs less and less operationally feasible. Not only was a stand-off bomb urgently required, but one of greater range than the 100nm promised by Blue Steel. Long before the latter had come into service the Air Staff were thinking of a guided missile which could fly up to ten times as far, and on 28 May 1958 DDOR9 put out an Air Staff Requirement to this effect – No OR1159 for an extended-range air-to-surface guided missile. The introduction to it embodied this forward thinking on the operational prospects facing the V-bombers, and the use that could be made of experience gained with Blue Steel: —

"By 1963 it is expected that the Russian SAGW and the fighter defences will be so improved and expanded that the V-bombers, even with Blue Steel and RCM, will find it increasingly difficult to penetrate to many of their objectives.

"In order to maintain an effective deterrent during the period commencing with the decline in effectiveness of Blue Steel and continuing during the build-up of the RAF ballistic missile force, it will be necessary to introduce a replacement for Blue Steel having a range sufficient for attacking…targets from launching points outside the enemy defence perimeter. It is envisaged that V-bombers equipped with this missile should be able to supplement the ballistic missile deterrent for several years[1].

"Studies have shown that by making maximum use of the knowledge gained in the Blue Steel programme, the development, production and

---

[1] 1958 was the year in which Thor IRBMs (to which separate reference will be made) were deployed in the UK, supplied by the United States and manned by RAF personnel; and at this time the Blue Streak MRBM was under development.

deployment costs can be minimised for a new weapon with a range capability of at least 600 nautical miles...".

The aim was, therefore, to have "an air-to-surface guided missile by the beginning of 1963 with a range of at least 600nm" – or more; for the requirement went on to state that "a missile range of 600 nautical miles will be acceptable as an initial operational capability but a range of 1,000nm is desirable". However, in 1960 the Minister of Aviation (Mr Duncan Sandys) was to stress that the "first requirement" was "to ensure that the maximum effort" was "put behind Blue Steel Mk 1" and that nothing should be done "which might distract Avro's attention from the need to get this weapon into service as quickly as possible"[1]. The Minister of Defence had told him, in a letter of 18 May[2],

"Both the Secretary of State for Air and I are extremely worried about Blue Steel. We are committed to the statement that Blue Steel Mk 1 will be available as the weapon for the Mk 2 V-bombers as they come into service. At the moment, there seems no hope at all that it will in fact be ready for the Vulcans as they begin to come in next year."

This resulted from a meeting on that date between the Minister of Defence and S of S for Air and their advisers, which decided that the former should write to the Minister of Aviation asking him to "consider urgently how the work on Blue Steel Mk 1 could be accelerated"[3].

In his reply, the Minister of Aviation said that Blue Steel was "planned to start to come into service in mid-1962". At his request, the company had taken action to increase the effort on Blue Steel Mk 1 by deploying on it some of the resources released by the cancellation of OR1159 and Blue Streak.[4]

There was also considerable pressure on R&D at Government Establishments with the number of weapon projects under way in the 1950s. In a Foreword to the AHB history *Defence Policy and the Royal Air Force 1956-63* by T C G James[5] the former DUS, MoD, Sir Frank Cooper, commented that "one of the most striking facts related in the text is the blunt statement reportedly made by Sir William Strath of the Ministry of Aviation, during the debate about the future of Blue Streak and Blue Steel, that the resources of the RAE and the RRE were insufficient to achieve two Marks of Blue Steel...as well as TSR.2. Over-stretch was universal".

---

[1] Minute to Minister of Defence, 16 May 60, in TS 407/101/024/63 – Possible Future Nuclear Deterrent Weapon System (British Nuclear Deterrent BND). In June, Treasury approval was given for a production order for 75 Blue Steels (Devlt & Production of Power-guided Bomb (BS) – ID3/946/8(S), Pt 2).
[2] ID9/194/4 Blue Steel.
[3] Ibid.
[4] Ibid.
[5] Air Historical Branch (RAF) 1987.

During 1958, 1959 and 1960, trials of what was to be the Mk 1 Blue Steel weapon continued. In his RAeS lecture on the development of Blue Steel (already referred to) Mr R H Francis said that the objectives of the first series of trials, using 2/5th scale models dropped from a Valiant, were "substantially achieved by the end of 1958". Main objectives of these trials were to check the firm's estimates of flight dynamics, to develop the range safety procedure and to train personnel in the techniques of large air-launched missile trials.

The second series of trials, of full-scale stainless-steel test vehicles to be launched from Valiants and Vulcans, were "regarded as an essential preliminary to the development of the operational type Blue Steel". Their purposes were to gain information on the supersonic environment, with a realistic trajectory; to check conditions inside the missile when carried by aircraft at high altitude; to confirm the adequacy of a simple release system; and to examine the interface between aircraft-borne and missile-borne equipment in a realistic environment.

Because Avro found difficulty in getting these trials started, largely owing to the time spent in learning the techniques of manufacturing in steel, it was decided to insert a number of full-scale aluminium-alloy test vehicles into the test programme. Their auxiliary power was provided by hydraulic reservoirs and batteries instead of hydrogen peroxide turbine, and they had a minimum of aircraft-to-missile connections. The first two of these vehicles – inert dummies – were launched during 1958, and during 1959–60 some powered test vehicles in this series were launched.

"These flight trials of rudimentary full-scale test vehicles went a long way to meeting the first three of the objectives listed", said Mr Francis, referring to the purposes of the trials, "but not, of course, the fourth", *ie* examining the interface between aircraft-borne and missile-borne equipment. "For this we still had to await the originally planned and more sophisticated steel test vehicles.

"These now had Stentor engines and towards the end of the programme approximated . . . much more closely to the operational missile than had originally been planned, thus partly atoning for their late appearance. In fact, the last few...were very nearly the operational type Blue Steel"[1].

Mr Francis said that because of the extension of the test vehicle programme, "trials of the operational-type missile started with a much greater back-log of development experience than would otherwise have been available. A number of engineering weaknesses revealed by the test vehicles might otherwise have found their way into the operational missile. The result was that a high standard of performance

---

[1] In June 1960 Treasury approval was given for a production order for 75 Blue Steels (Minute of 22 Jun 60, F.6/AUS(S) in ID9/194/4 Blue Steel). On 28 Jul 60 Sir Roy Dobson, Avro chairman, phoned CAS (Air Chf Mshl Sir T Pike) to say that the first sophisticated W.100 had been flown at Aberporth (ID/47/296/Pt 2) – Blue Steel (OR1132) Financial Aspects).

and functioning reliability was achieved from the start of these trials, and compensated for the previous pains and tribulations".

However, lengthening the trials programme meant that there was no hope of the Air Staff's original aim of having the new weapon in service by the end of 1960 being achieved – although when the operational requirement was issued they were probably being over-optimistic in allowing six years for the design, development and acceptance of an entirely unique weapon, in fact a robot aeroplane. Justifiably, the Ministry of Supply had been less optimistic and considered an in-service date of 1961/62 more likely. But as time went on, mid-1962 looked to be the earliest date by which Blue Steel Mk 1 would reach the Mk 2 Vulcan and Victor squadrons. On 28 April 1961 the Minister of Aviation (Mr Peter Thorneycroft), reporting to the Cabinet Defence Committee, recalled that

"Blue Steel was accepted as a requirement in January 1956. It was then thought that the first delivery of missiles would be made to the RAF in 1961/62. By the end of 1960, however, it had become apparent (owing to delays in the development programme) that the number of trial firings that could be expected to have been made by early 1962 would not be sufficient to enable the first deliveries of missiles to the RAF to be approved for normal operational use. It is however expected that by mid-1962 the functioning and safety of the weapon (including its warhead) will have been sufficiently proved to enable the missile to be used in an emergency, if required, thus providing a deterrent capability. Further trials will continue during the succeeding months to enable approval to be given for normal operational carriage and use of the missile."

The Minister said that although the trials had not gone as well as was hoped, "the programme allows some margin for delays, and there is no reason at this stage to conclude that approval to use the missile in an emergency could not be given by mid-1962". He commented that "development of a complex weapon of this type may reveal two kinds of difficulty. Firstly, a basic fault in the concept, entailing major re-design – costly in both time and money; nothing of this sort has yet appeared in Blue Steel. . . . Secondly, detailed engineering faults and problems. These we are encountering; they are a normal part of the development process, and may be expected to continue". To achieve the earliest possible in-service date, orders had been placed for 57 missiles.

This total was made up of 48UE operational rounds (W.105) plus five backing rounds and four proof rounds. In addition there were 16 training rounds (W.103A), ten with light-alloy and six with steel carcasses.

The Minister of Aviation's report to the Cabinet Defence Committee on Blue Steel, like the public statements made on the weapon – for example the bold assertion by the Air Minister (Mr George Ward) in the Commons on 8 March 1960 that "Blue Steel is to be in service next

201

year", glossed-over some of the difficulties which surrounded its procurement – its delayed entry into service, increasing costs of development, and disenchantment felt by the customer for the contractor. There can be few major British defence contracts which caused such bitter feelings. These were probably aroused by the fact that, even in 1956, A V Roe were talking of a developed Blue Steel with a range of 1,000 miles – Mr Ward's predecessor Mr Nigel Birch having been told on a visit to the firm in March of that year that they could produce such a developed weapon by 1961/62, yet by 1961 they were unable to deliver the goods in the shape of a 100-mile-range Blue Steel. During those five years the Air Staff had watched the development of Soviet missile defences and realised that if the V-bomber force were to continue to be viable, not only was an operational capability with Blue Steel required but there also had to be a successor to it with much greater range. Yet the longer the trials continued the greater was the delay before the stand-off bomb entered service; and the feeling must have been that if the chosen contractors could not perfect a bomb to fly 100 miles, how could they perfect one with ten times that range? Such a feeling, aroused by a realisation of the immensity of the operational task and frustration at the lack of equipment with which to perform it, can be deduced from the criticisms and recriminations which became common parlance in Blue Steel records from 1960 onwards.

Thus, a report to the Air Minister on 20 October 1960 made reference to "grave shortcomings in the project management" which had "dogged development progress" and said that if the history of the system might be taken as a guide, it was difficult to envisage full CA clearance being given by the last quarter of 1962. During that month the Minister was informed that the estimated cost of Blue Steel had gone up from £150,000 per missile (exclusive of warhead) to £250,000, and that the current estimate for R&D expenditure was £60m compared with an October 1958 estimate of £35m.

The Air Staff agreed "reluctantly" to reduce the number of proving missiles by two and decided that the training missiles should be of cheaper construction, estimated to cost £200,000 as against £250,000. On this basis, financial approval for an expenditure of £21.2m was given by the Chancellor of the Exchequer in November 1960. The production order, placed in December, was for 57 W.105 operational rounds (48 UE, 5 backing rounds and 4 proof rounds) and for 16 W.103A training rounds (10 with light alloy and 6 with steel carcasses).

In a particularly scathing minute to DCAS on 21 October 1960, headed "Further Blue Steel Phantasies", Air Cdre S W R Hughes, DRPS (Air), referred to "an entirely new proposal" by A V Roe made to the Minister of Defence when he visited them on the 14th – adding a "boost variant" to Blue Steel to give it a range of 850 miles from an aircraft or a ground-launched range of about half that. It would soar to 100,000ft during flight and achieve a speed of M6.5. The Minister "could do no less than suggest" that the firm presented their proposals formally to the MoA; no doubt "shining brochures with a CEP embracing at least MoA and MoD" were "likely to be fired within the next week".

The writer went on to suggest that there was "quite enough jinx in Blue Steel to keep us busy, without letting anyone worry about a proposal of this nature at this stage", and he recommended that "every pressure should be brought to bear to ensure that Blue Steel Mk 1" was delivered on time and up to specification, adding that "no encouragement should be given to the firm to divert effort or thought on any other project until they have shown that they are capable of producing this relatively simple 100-mile weapon *before* we take delivery of the 1,000-mile range Skybolt"[1].

The Avro proposals were subsequently discussed at a joint AM/MoA presentation in the Ministry of Defence on 7 November[2].

When the Parliamentary Under-Secretary, MoA, Mr Geoffrey Rippon, reported on Blue Steel progress to the Minister of Defence (Mr Harold Watkinson) on 19 January 1961 he referred to the late in-service date for Blue Steel – initial release to service in May 1962, with final release in 1963, compared with a projected in-service date of 1961/62 – and concluded with these unequivocal comments:–

"Even allowing for the fact that Blue Steel broke entirely fresh ground, A V Roe's past performance has not been satisfactory. They have been left with no delusions about the effect of continued delays. They have thoroughly overhauled their organisation and other resources of the Hawker Siddeley Group have been brought in to assist. There is no room for complacency, and everything now hangs on the success of the Australian trials. We know of no further measures which could reasonably be taken to improve their chances"[3].

The reaction of the Air Minister (Mr Julian Amery) to this letter, a copy of which had been sent to him, was to ask for DCAS's advice "as to whether there is anything that the Air Ministry can usefully do to improve the situation", and for any comments he might offer to the Minister of Defence on the report[4].

Some blunt comments came from ACAS(OR) (AVM R N Bateson), who referring to Mr Rippon's letter in a minute to PS/S of S on 27 January said that it "substantially confirms the long-expressed opinion of the Air Staff that A V Roe programmes have been unrealistic". He went on:—

---

[1] ID/47/296 Pt 2 Blue Steel (OR1132) Financial Aspects.
[2] Ibid.
[3] In AF946/8(S) Pt 2 Development and Production of Power-guided Bombs (Blue Steel).
[4] PS/SofS to PS/DCAS on 23 Jan 61.

"There is plenty of evidence of a weak management structure in the missile division at A V Roe and this may need yet further overhauling.

"The Air Staff have always regarded the firing of the first navigated round as an essential demonstration of a progressive and logical development plan. It is therefore all the more regrettable that this first attempt to prove the missile in free flight should be more than a year behind schedule.... It is my view that the first navigated round constitutes an essential milestone, which must be passed successfully before we can have any real confidence in the promise of an Initial Operational Capability within the next twelve months."

Clearly there was a crisis situation on Blue Steel at the beginning of 1961, and the Air Staff were being asked what was to be done. VCAS (Air Mshl Sir Edmund Hudleston) was advised by DCAS (Air Mshl R B Lees)[1] that the Minister of Defence was "likely to ask whether anything can be done by the RAF to give Blue Steel some sort of operational capability earlier than the 'emergency' release of June 1962. This would be on the basis that aircraft, plus weapon, plus warhead must add up to something better than a free-fall bomb even if the weapon is not adequately tested and is of uncertain performance". DCAS added that the view of the ACAS (Ops and OR) staffs was that, "while this might not make very much operational sense, it would be worth looking carefully into the possibilities in view of the Parliamentary and Press history of Blue Steel"[2].

The Minister of Defence wrote to both the Air Minister and the Minister of Aviation about Blue Steel at the beginning of February, stressing the importance of being able to declare an initial operational capability with the weapon at the earliest possible date.

Mr Watkinson told the Air Minister (on 1 February) that "it would be helpful if we could have even one squadron with an initial operational Blue Steel capability, say in January 1962"; and he told the Minister of Aviation (on the 8th) that "we must keep up the heaviest pressure on the firm".

In his reply to the Minister of Defence, on 23 February, the Air Minister said that deliveries of aircraft modified to carry Blue Steel were due to build up from September 1961. He understood that the MoA expected that sufficient aircraft and test equipment would have been delivered by January 1962 to support one squadron of Mk 2 Vulcans; by then, too, there should be sufficient trained air and ground crews. But the position on missiles and warheads was less straightforward.

On present forecasts, he said, "we shall have enough missiles. The question is, whether we shall be in a position to claim with confidence that they would work". Trials in Australia had already fallen behind

---

[1] PS/DCAS to PS/VCAS on 24 Jan.
[2] For example, on 1/2 May 1960 there were newspaper reports of a "major row" between the Government and the RAF over the preference for Skybolt over Blue Steel Mk 2 as a V-force weapon.

schedule and the first fully-navigated round had still to be fired. He regarded it as an essential condition of any claim to operational capability that the MoA should give a firm assurance, based on completion of not less than 20 trial firings, that the missile would work. He believed that this assurance should be possible before January 1962.

The Minister added that the proper warhead for Blue Steel[1] was not due to become available before March 1962. But it would be possible to equip missiles before then by the interim use of Yellow Sun warheads[2]. He understood that the MoA considered that the operational reliability of the latter in Blue Steel could not be fully guaranteed, but believed they would be entirely safe in the air or on the ground. "If the MoA can confirm this", he concluded, "it should be possible to claim an emergency operational capability for Blue Steel with the Yellow Sun warhead"[3].

The difficulty, however, as the Minister of Aviation explained to the Minister of Defence in his reply (on 2 March), lay not in the warhead but in the weapon. The real question was "whether we will know that Blue Steel will work by January 1962. The answer appears to be 'No'".

"The real difficulty", he explained, "is with the weapon itself. The truth about any plans to bring forward its operational capability is that we are trying to speed up a programme which has already slipped. It is impossible to be dogmatic now about the number of trial firings required to establish whether the weapon will work. But, on any realistic assessment of the development firing programme, we cannot expect to have proved Blue Steel even to the very minimum standard by January 1962. I am convinced that it would be unwise to expect before June 1962 the emergency capability which the Air Ministry desire...".

The Minister added that the firing of navigated rounds could now be carried out more effectively in Australia than at Aberporth, and that round 6 – which was to have been fired at Aberporth – would not now be fired. He said that the firing of a longer-range round – "from which we expect to derive more and better information" – was planned to take place during March in Australia.

At this disclosure the Minister of Defence expressed dismay, and his further comments (in a note of 15 March) reflected the annoyance and impatience which Blue Steel development seems to have engendered at this time. He said he was "disturbed" to learn about the non-firing of round 6 – "the first navigational round, which was scheduled for July 1960 and was to be an important milestone in development". He recalled that he had sent minutes "enquiring about its progress" on 18 October and 24 November 1960 and on 8 February 1961, and added sharply: —

---

[1] Red Snow.

[2] Yellow Sun Mk 1 was in service 1960–63 and Mk 2 in service 1961–66. Both were free-falling megaton bombs of approximately 7,000lb weight.

[3] Meanwhile, RAF training had gone on in preparation for the new weapon: the first aircrew Blue Steel course was completed at BCBS, Lindholme, in September 1961.

"I should like to know more of the reasons for the decision to abandon this round and to substitute a firing at Woomera. Does this mean a further slippage? When will this firing take place? Is there any danger that it too will be delayed? As you know, I have been closely questioned in the House of Commons about Blue Steel in the past year and we must both expect further questions in due course. I should therefore like to be kept closely in touch with any changes in its progress. . .".

The Minister of Aviation did not reply until a fortnight later (on 15 March), when he explained that round 6 was not fired at Aberporth because this would have delayed the departure of an aircraft to Australia and held up the trials programme there. An unnavigated round fired in Australia on 24 March had been only partially successful; records on it had to be more fully analysed before further firings – including that of a navigated round, which had been due to take place on 28 March. He "shared the anxiety" of the Minister of Defence about Blue Steel.

As a result of this situation, the Minister of Defence asked the Minister of Aviation to put a paper to the Defence Committee on Blue Steel[1]. This paper has already been referred to (see page 201); at the end of it, the Minister suggested alternative courses to the CDC: to abandon Blue Steel and to accept a gap in the credibility of the deterrent, which would leave the Victors (which would not carry Skybolt)[2] without a stand-off weapon; or "to continue with the development and production of Blue Steel, recognising and accepting the risk that it may come into service somewhat later and cost more than at present estimated". He invited the committee to approve the second alternative.

At the CDC meeting, on 17 May 1961, Blue Steel was clearly put into context as the V-force's second-generation weapon – with free-falling bombs as the first and Skybolt as the third. To quote the minutes[3]:–

"The Minister of Aviation said that Blue Steel was a fully navigated cruise-type missile with a range of 100nm designed for launching from Mk 2 Victors and Vulcans. It was intended to provide the main deterrent weapon between the time when bombers equipped with free-falling bombs were likely to become less effective against enemy defences, and the introduction of Skybolt. Its cost was currently estimated at £60m for R&D and £21m for production; of this total, some £44m had been spent or committed. Trial firings had proved disappointing in some respects, but it appeared that the difficulties were caused by teething troubles rather than by any basic fault which might invalidate the

---

[1] In a minute of 17 April, AUS(A) (Mr R C Kent) commented (AUS(A)/136) that the paper had been "inspired by the knowledge that the *Daily Telegraph* were to publish an article suggesting that Blue Steel was so behindhand that it would have to be cancelled (Richard Brett-Smith, *Daily Telegraph*, 15 April)".

[2] Whether they could or could not, or should or should not, was much debated: see later references, when the proposed procurement of Skybolts is discussed.

[3] D(61) 7th Meeting, minutes dated 24 May 1961.

concept of the weapon. Further trials were proceeding at Woomera and it should be possible to make a comprehensive review towards the end of the year."

The Minister of Defence summed up the meeting (at which the Air Minister and CAS were present) by saying that, although progress had been below expectations, the delay in development would not be critical unless the fully-instrumented trials – due to be held towards the end of the year – proved ineffective. There were no grounds for considering abandoning the project at this stage.

The committee agreed that work on Blue Steel should continue as planned, and invited the Minister of Aviation to report progress towards the end of the year.

In fact, long before the end of 1961 the Minister of Defence was again asking the Minister of Aviation where the Blue Steels were, when they would start coming into service, and whether things could not be hurried up at Boscombe Down and Woomera. "I regard it as most desirable", he wrote to the Parliamentary Secretary, MoA, on 5 July (in the absence of the Minister, who had left on a tour),

"to lose no time in getting some production weapons into the RAF, so that they can begin familiarising themselves with them, even before everything is ready for the warheads to be installed. I would hope that they could start reaching the RAF by October".

He enquired whether it might be possible to quicken the trials procedures:–

"As to Boscombe Down, I would be grateful if you would let me know what is being done to minimise the time that Blue Steel takes there, in accordance with the top priority which Mr Thorneycroft told me he had arranged for the project. For example, is work going on on Saturdays and Sundays? As to Woomera, I think it might help if I were to write to Mr Townley.[1] . . . As I understand it, the problem is to get the maximum flexibility in the allocations at Woomera so that tests can be carried out without delay as soon as a round is ready".

In his reply, on 14 July, Mr Geoffrey Rippon advised the Minister that the main hold-ups were at the manufacturers:–

"The Blue Steel rounds planned for delivery to the RAF later this year are not production weapons but the W.100A pre-production version. They are closely representative of the production rounds which will emerge in 1962 and will enable the RAF to start handling and maintenance trials, but [they] will not be operational. Recent setbacks, primarily in the build of W.100As at A V Roe, make it unlikely that these trials can start in October, though we are examining with the Air Ministry the possibility of making special arrangements to get one W.100A to the RAF in October . . . to allow familiarisation and other preliminary work".

---

[1] Mr Athol Townley, Australian Minister of Defence.

Referring to the Minister's comments about Boscombe Down and Woomera, he commented that

"the chief holding factor in the development of Blue Steel is not the capacity available at Boscombe Down and Woomera, but A V Roe's ability to build and fire missiles . . . . Boscombe Down is not delaying the programme nor is it likely to do so, and the introduction of weekend working would not expedite matters. At Woomera, A V Roe are being given top priority and are . . . getting all the range time they can use. . . . Some further improvement in the arrangements is still undoubtedly possible . . . but I should counsel against your writing to Mr Townley at this stage".

On 24 July the Minister of Aviation reported on the Blue Steel situation, and what he had to say provoked an almost despairing reply from the Minister of Defence. The former said that information received since his PS's minute of the 14th

"showed that the development and firing programme was not proceeding as fast as we had hoped and that the production programme might be slipping back. I therefore invited Sir Roy Dobson and Sir Harry Broadhurst[1] to come and see me in order that I might impress on them once again the importance of maintaining the programme and satisfy myself that everything possible was being done to that end.

"We had a full and frank discussion. The firm cannot guarantee that delivery of production missiles will start in June 1962. They will make every effort to achieve this, but advised me that deliveries might be a month or two late. The programme was tight to begin with but this means that practically all the contingency margin in it is used up and it is now very tight indeed. Nevertheless by altering our plans and fitting warheads to the pre-production missiles which the RAF will have been using for handling and maintenance trials, it should still prove possible to maintain the emergency release in June 1962. I have instructed my officials to explore this urgently with the Air Ministry....

"A V Roe are putting everything they can into the programme and are deploying on it the full resources of the Hawker Siddeley Group. Sir Roy assures me that everything that could be done is being done...".

To this, the Minister of Defence replied on the 26th with a note of weary resignation. "I am afraid", he said,

"this is the same story that you and I have heard so many times before. The firm really cannot seem to live up to any kind of delivery promise that they make. I think we should look at this again in September; perhaps when we all have to be about for the Farnborough Air Show. Perhaps then the three of us who have political responsibilities for this could have a meeting and decide whether we ought to take steps to make it plain that present undertakings given by all three of us in the House of Commons are unlikely to be kept".

---

[1] Respectively chairman and managing director, A V Roe & Co Ltd.

During August, a report on Blue Steel progress was prepared[1]; it was sent to DCAS on the 31st[2]. It said that the dates in which the Air Staff was most interested were (a) that on which an assurance could be expected that the weapon had something like a 60 per cent reliability, and (b) that on which the Scampton complex could be expected to be equipped with eight operable and supported aircraft/missile combinations. The report's conclusions were that

"in spite of the top priority awarded to Blue Steel by all concerned since October 1960, the time scale for this project is still going back.

"The project is now in such a state that the Air Staff feel that it is impossible to make a firm forecast of the date on which we can expect an initial operational capability. This situation is likely to obtain until the flight trials of Blue Steel start to show some reasonable measure of success. Although, therefore, the MoA are now forecasting that we might expect an IOC in about June 1962, all the available evidence and past experience point to an IOC not being likely before late in 1962 or early 1963."

The three Ministers – of Defence, Aviation and Air – concerned with Blue Steel had a meeting about it on 26 September 1961; this followed a discussion between the Defence and Aviation Ministers, for which the latter had sent the former a brief (dated the 14th) on the W.100/100A trials in Australia. This said that, although two faults had been outstanding – failures of the auxiliary power unit and malfunctioning of the rocket motor, neither was expected to be fundamental. Nothing in recent firings had thrown doubt on the weapon's ultimate capability. The programme had slipped by four/five months since the end of 1960, but "subject to the outcome of our present discussion with the Air Ministry on the details of the release to be offered, it should be possible to provide emergency capability in June 1962, linked to the use of the 16 pre-production rounds being delivered to the RAF. Indications were that the first production missile would not be available to the RAF until August 1962. The first W.100A was due to reach Scampton in January of that year, with RAF trials and training starting in February/March – four/five months later than planned.

When the three Ministers met on 26 September[3] the Minister of Defence said he had called the meeting to consider the position they should take on Blue Steel when Parliament reassembled; it would be important to adopt a common line. The Minister of Aviation said that though A V Roe's programme had slipped by about four months in the last year and there was probably still a certain optimism in their

[1] CMS. 2485/OR26a.
[2] CMS.2485/9300.
[3] MM 53/61, 29 Sept 1961. In ID9/194/4 – Blue Steel Jan 1961 to June 64, in which many of these papers recur, there is a Minute of 22 Dec 1961 from the Minister of Aviation to the Minister of Defence telling him that a W.100 "travelled the full range" on 12 Dec.

forecasts, recent trials had gone better, the system looked like working and it seemed probable that by June 1962 an emergency operational capability would be achieved.

The Ministers decided that it was important in public statements not to go beyond what had been already said, that progress should be reviewed in January 1962, that care must be taken that public statements about Blue Steel did not cast doubt on Skybolt (or vice versa) and that, as more became known about Soviet SAGW point defences, criticisms of the viability of the V-force with free-falling bombs might be expected.

The Air Ministry took the opportunity provided by this last point to make an assessment of the V-force's current capability against known Soviet defences, sending it to the Minister of Defence on 28 September with the comment that "after our meeting on Blue Steel...you mentioned your concern at the latest reports which showed that the Russians are likely to achieve full SAM coverage of their major cities by the end of this year. I have since discussed the implications of this situation with the Air Staff". His note continued: —

"There is no doubt that the high priority given by the Russians to SAM has made it more difficult for our bombers to penetrate to their targets. This may mean that in the period before we get Blue Steel we should not be able to achieve quite the same level of destruction as we expected a year or eighteen months ago. For reasons given below, however, we do not believe that the reduction in the effectiveness of the V-force will be very serious.

"The JIC, in the recent examination of the air defence of the Soviet Union up to 1965 (JIC(61)8 final, issued in May 1961), forecast that Soviet city defences would be complete by 1961. Bomber Command has thus been able to make its plans in the light of this assessment for several months. In particular they propose to reduce the effectiveness of SAM defence by the following methods: —

(i)   The use of ECM. By the end of the year the bulk of the V-force should have an ECM capability.
(ii)   Tactical routeing to avoid known SAM sites. This has been greatly assisted by the latest report.
(iii)   Increasing the number of aircraft allocated to the more important and heavily defended targets.

"Bomber Command are also studying the operation of the V-bombers at low level to take advantage of the reduced efficiency of the Russian SAM at heights below 5,000ft. Our difficulty here is that the low-level nuclear weapon which is being designed for the TSR.2 is not yet ready.

"There is the further consideration that the Russian SAM crews are only now receiving their operational equipment, and that it will be some time before they can work up to peak efficiency.

"I spoke yesterday to the Commander in Chief, Bomber Command, who is well aware that the high priority given by the Russians to their SAM defences has made his task more difficult. He is, however, quite confident that the medium bomber force, even operating without the Americans, is still in a position to destroy the greater part of the targets at which it would be launched. In an operation with the Americans there should be no reduction in our joint ability to reach the targets, though of course Russian SAM capability would necessarily impose heavier casualties on both of us.

"None of this in any way lessens the need to press on with Blue Steel as fast as possible. But I thought you might like to have this assessment of our present capability, which is on the whole reassuring, and which I am satisfied is sound."

Blue Steel difficulties were not confined to the missile but involved the aircraft as well, some indication of the complexity of the programme of bringing the eight IOC Vulcan B.2s up to full operational Blue Steel standard being conveyed in a minute of 29 November to DCAS from Gp Capt D T Witt, who commented that "the need for this programme was forced on us for three main reasons: (a) failure of the structural test specimen giving rise to several strengthening modifications essential for Blue Steel carriage, too late for these to be embodied in production; (b) numerous minor aircraft modifications resulting from late modifications to the missile; and (c) the Air Staff policy, which has been followed (without much success) since mid-1960, of refraining from asking for any modification which would delay delivery to service of these eight aircraft . . . ".

When progress on Blue Steel was reviewed at the beginning of 1962 the Cabinet Defence Committee, meeting on 12 January[1], learned from the Minister of Aviation that the firing of the W.100A rounds – closely representative of the final production version, and to be used to prove the Blue Steel system in Mk 2 Vulcans and Victors – was about to start[2]. He explained that the future programme depended critically on achieving greater success with the W.100As than had been achieved with the experimental rounds. By August or September, he said, "we should have obtained enough preliminary information from launchings to enable the Air Ministry to assume an emergency capability". The CDC invited him to report again in March, when the results of further trials were known.

In fact, the Minister's next report was made in early April[3], when he said that since the reopening of the Woomera range at the end of January four further missiles had been fired. "Two of these, of which one was the first representative pre-production W.100A round, hit the target over the full range of approximately 100nm. The third failed to achieve its planned trajectory and was destroyed after 75 miles . . . . On the fourth missile the engine failed to start because the wire lanyard between the aircraft and missile broke on launching and did not release the engine starting safety lock. . .".

[1] Minutes of D.(62) 1st meeting.
[2] Memorandum, D.(62)2, 3 Jan 62.
[3] D.(62)19.

He added that clearance of the weapon for safe carriage, with warhead, by the RAF might go back from June to July 1962; but the Air Ministry should still be able to assume an emergency capability in August or September. The start of full-scale trials at Scampton had been further delayed by a set-back in completion of operational test equipment. "However, by using development test equipment and with the assistance of skilled contractor's staff at the airfield, we expect to be able to start some of the trials in the very near future. . . . The first inert training round is now with the RAF and will shortly be cleared for carriage in flight."

The Minister concluded that the case for Blue Steel had not changed – a conclusion with which the CDC, at its meeting on 13 April[1], concurred; though it emphasised in discussion the embarrassment that would be caused to the Government if the Blue Steel emergency capability were not achieved by the autumn – though the accuracy displayed by the weapon in the Woomera trials was encouraging.

In a memorandum accompanying his report the Minister said that Blue Steel was "essential to the credibility of our deterrent until Skybolt is introduced in 1965/66 and it will be available thereafter in Victors to supplement Skybolt".

Meanwhile, the threads of policy, materialising in Ministerial statements and CDC meetings, were being joined by the warp and woof of Bomber Command personnel experience – at station and squadron level – with the new weapon that was soon to be introduced into service. In August–September 1961 the first Blue Steel training courses were held at the Bomber Command Bombing School, RAF Lindholme, and during the latter month one of the NBS trainers there was converted into a Blue Steel trainer. Early in the following year (as the Air Ministry Quarterly Liaison Report for January–March 1962 noted) the first Victor Blue Steel ground trainer was accepted from the contractors at BCBS – on 6 February; and the first of the Blue Steel training rounds was delivered to No 18 Joint Services Trials Unit at Scampton – during March.[2]

In July 1962 a production-model Blue Steel was successfully air-launched at Woomera[3] and in September the long-awaited clearance was given – for Bomber Command to carry operational Blue Steels on its Vulcans in an emergency. On the 25th the Minister of Aviation (now Mr Julian Amery) wrote to his successor as Air Minister, Mr Hugh Fraser:–

---

[1] D.(62) 6th meeting.

[2] AMQLR for Jul–Sep 62 reported that "the second NBS/Blue Steel Procedural Trainer for use by operational aircrews was accepted into service at RAF Wittering on 11 Sep".

[3] On 3 July the following signal was received in London: "Thorneycroft Woomera. Julian Amery London. Greetings from Woomera. Have just witnessed completely successful air launching of production model Blue Steel".

"I am glad to be able to inform you that Sir George Gardner[1] has today forwarded to DCAS a CA Release for Blue Steel to be carried on Vulcan aircraft, complete with its operational warhead, in a national emergency.

"The clearance does not specifically authorise the launching of the missile because the required trials to prove the safety of the systems are not yet complete. However, no difficulties have been experienced up to date which affect the safety after launch and we are confident that further trials will provide the necessary proof. We expect to issue the operational launch clearance in December 1962.

"We have issued the present clearance on the understanding that, should a national crisis occur which warrants the carriage of the operational Blue Steel with its warhead, limitations as to its use could be overridden.

"In effect this means that you could declare an operational capability with Blue Steel as soon as you consider that you are in a position to do so"[2].

The first V-force squadron to have Blue Steel was No 617 – appropriately, in view of the pioneer role for which it had originally been formed, in 1943[3] – which had Vulcan B.2s at Scampton; and two pertinent questions discussed by the Air Staff in the latter part of 1962 were as to when an operational capability should be declared, and when a Press visit to the first BS squadron should be held.

The idea of a Blue Steel Press facility, the date for which would have to be dependent on the declaration of an operational capability with the weapon, had been mooted by the then Air Minister (Mr Julian Amery) during May 1962. He said he would like to make a presentation to the Press towards the end of July, though realising the importance of being able to show a more complete weapon system, which might be easier a month or so later – adding that he "did not wish to lose valuable publicity for Blue Steel by putting-off a presentation until September when public interest would have shifted to the Skybolt trials". He asked DCAS (Air Mshl Sir Ronald Lees) to consider the question of timing.

This proposal was further discussed on 28 May, when DCAS told the Minister that he would prefer August or September for a Press visit to Scampton, and it was inevitably bound up with the prior achievement of an operational capability with Blue Steel. However politically desirable the publicity might be, in view of the delays which had occurred in the programme it was unwise to seek it until any claim that might be made could be seen to be soundly based. This was the tenor of the minute DCAS wrote on 12 October, advising deferment of a Press facility until there were sufficient tested missiles in service – in fact a further

---

[1] Controller of Aircraft, MoA.
[2] In AHB ID3/946/8, Pt 1 Development of Blue Steel.
[3] The attack on the Mohne, Eder and Sorpe dams, 16/17 Aug 43. No 617 had been re-formed on 1 May 58 as a Vulcan B.1 squadron; it got Vulcan B.2s from Sep 61 onwards and in July 62 received its first Blue Steel training rounds.

postponement, for at a meeting on 16 July S of S had accepted his advice that a Blue Steel Press facility should be "delayed until the autumn". In his minute DCAS recalled that the Minister of Aviation had written to S of S on 25 September to say that a limited CA clearance had been issued on Blue Steel and that the RAF could declare an operational capability as soon as they were in a position to do so. He went on:–

"The clearance given by the MoA says, in effect, that missiles – complete with operational warheads – may be carried on Vulcan Mk 2s but not launched. The restrictions which remain will be lifted one by one as soon as the MoA trials to prove the safety of the system are completed. Nevertheless CA makes it clear to me in a covering minute [of 24 September, in which CA had said that the weapon had been cleared for and could be flown in a fully 'warlike' configuration and was capable of being launched] that the trials have progressed sufficiently far for the Air Ministry to . . . take the risk of launching the missiles should a national crisis justify our overriding the prohibitions which remain. We have examined the clearances given and are satisfied that by cutting certain corners and taking certain risks we could, if necessary, use Blue Steel in an emergency."

DCAS then entered into details of what was involved in getting the new weapon – which was quite different from anything which Bomber Command had ever operated before – into its initial squadron service, and stressed the need for sufficient numbers, saying that the principal factor preventing the declaration of an emergency operational capability was the rate of build-up of missiles and associated equipment: the numbers of available aircraft, trained aircrew and warheads should present no difficulty. The first operational missile, he added,

"should be available and fully tested by about mid-October. Subsequently the rate of build-up will be such that four fully tested missile/aircraft combinations can be available by mid-November; six by mid-December and eight (a full squadron's worth) during January 1963".

He commented that the emergency capability of these systems would be limited by the following factors: a four-hour generation time would be needed to get an aircraft/missile combination ready for a sortie; the aircraft would lack rapid take-off capability, even after a four-hour generation period[1]; once missiles had been fuelled with high-test peroxide they could remain on aircraft for a maximum period of approximately seven days, because of uncertainty over the life of HTP in the missile tanks; and after fuel had been removed a missile had to be dried out before it could be refuelled, but drying-out facilities would not

---

[1] A large instructional handbook, "RAF Wittering Blue Steel Generation", contains 42 photographs and descriptive captions.

be available for some time to come. DCAS added the recommendation that

"we should wait until at least we have a full squadron capable of emergency operation before claiming to have an emergency operational capability. We have always contended that a squadron is the minimum size of force necessary to substantiate an initial capability. Nevertheless I recognise that public statements have been made to the effect that Blue Steel would be operational this year and that it could be politically embarrassing to defer a declaration until next year.

"If you consider that the possibility of political embarrassment demands an earlier capability, then it would be possible to claim an emergency capability with six missiles in mid-December, or even with only four in mid-November. I should recommend that we do not declare the capability until at least six missiles are operational.

"I recommend that we do not make a special public announcement about this capability, and that the Press facility at Scampton should be deferred until we have sufficient tested missiles to claim an emergency operational capability, at which time an appropriate statement could be made."

At a meeting with CAS and DCAS on 29 October, the Air Minister agreed with DCAS's reasoning; it was decided that, when at least six missiles were operational, an appropriate statement should be made – perhaps in connection with the proposed Press facility – indicating that Blue Steel was in squadron service.

However, Bomber Command HQ had reservations about the advisability of a Press visit to Scampton at all, as the Air Ministry's Chief Information Officer[1] indicated in a minute[2] of 18 January 1963, when he suggested "some time early in February" as "the earliest practicable date":–

"I have . . . been waiting for an assurance from Bomber Command that Blue Steel as now supplied to No 617 Squadron, and its supporting ground environment at Scampton, are sufficiently well developed to be able to present them safely to the Press as a viable going concern. Headquarters Bomber Command have now confirmed that this is so but have entered reservations as to the wisdom of having a facility at all.

"Whilst I agree that it would be unwise to present Blue Steel at a time which might suggest that the RAF is supporting the exaggerated claims that have recently been made for it, this can be avoided by proper handling and timing. Such a facility should be based on the original concept of Blue Steel coming into squadron service as planned, and the assessment that the weapon will be effective until some time in the second half of the decade, dependent upon the development of Soviet defence systems. If we can stick to our original ground in this matter, I do not see any particular hazards. . . ."

---

[1] Air Commodore J Barraclough.
[2] CIO/17350/9493 to PS/SofS.

CIO added that if the Press facility were delayed much longer, "we will be departing from precedent in these matters and inviting suspicion"; and at a meeting on 25 January the Secretary of State agreed to the holding of a Press facility at Scampton in mid-February. But the AOC in C Bomber Command still had reservations, which he expressed in a letter to DCAS on 7 February[1]:–

"You will I know appreciate that the withholding of clearance to put acceptance rounds on aircraft for the purpose of bringing them to readiness does, to an unpredictable extent, prejudice the Blue Steel Press facility.[2]

"To me 'an operational capability' means bringing an aircraft to 15 minutes' readiness for operational take-off, and that is why I asked for clearance, so that we could show this aspect.

"Of course the fact that now no aircraft at readiness will be shown does not mean that the facility will not be successful. . . . Nevertheless we are running a risk, slight though it may be, that this subject will come up. . . .

"I have already expressed my preference for the Press facility at a later date; but nevertheless I believe we have already done enough, and have enough at Scampton, to provide a successful Press facility on Blue Steel. . . ."

The Press visit to No 617 Squadron at RAF Scampton on 14 February 1963 provided public proof that the V-force was now armed with a stand-off bomb of 100nm range; but in the meantime, at the end of 1962 its intended successor, the American GAM-87 Skybolt with ten times greater range, had been cancelled by President Kennedy and his proffered alternative of submarine-launched Polaris missiles had been accepted by Prime Minister Macmillan at the Nassau conference of 18–21 December 1962[3].

In a leading article on 21 February entitled "The Weapon that Never Was", *Flight International* commented that the Press facility "provided the first official statement by Bomber Command after the demise of Skybolt" and that it "was by way of a fanfare marking the introduction of Blue Steel into RAF service". The article commented that

"throughout his briefing the C in C made not a single reference to Skybolt, the Command's Weapon That Never Was. He concentrated entirely on a Bomber Command with Blue Steel as principal weapon, carried in Vulcan B.2s and, subsequently, Victor B.2s. . . . Bomber Command have now buried the past and look to the future – with a British air-launched missile that will last for 'quite a number of years' and which (in the Command's view) gives the United Kingdom a credible nuclear deterrent defence force".

---

[1] BC/126/CINC.

[2] Withholding clearance did not prevent missiles being loaded into aircraft but prevented live warheads being put into missiles.

[3] Bahamas Meetings December '62 Text of Joint Communiqués, Cmnd 1915.

At the Scampton briefing the AOC in C said that his Command had "learned about Blue Steel as it was tested". Two units had been responsible for bringing it into service – No 18 Joint Services Trials Unit at Scampton and No 4 JSTU at Edinburgh Field, Australia. There had been firings from Vulcan B.1s and B.2s, flown by both Service and civilian pilots, and there had been "many successes" as well as some failures. It was hoped to fire training rounds at Woomera later in the year. In addition to No 617 the two other Vulcan squadrons at Scampton were to be equipped with Blue Steel: No 27's training was well advanced and No 83's would follow. The next Blue Steel station would be Wittering (Victor B.2s), where facilities already existed.

No 139 (Jamaica) Squadron there did not, however, start their conversion to the role with modified aircraft (B.2Rs) until October 1963: their first sortie with a training missile was flown on the 24th. A year earlier the AOC in C had complained to DCAS that Handley Page had "fallen down badly in the production of the Victor Mk 2 Blue Steel". Originally there were to have been six Blue Steel squadrons, three of Vulcans and three of Victors; but the delay in getting the Victor B.2Rs into service led to an Air Council decision on 10 February 1964 to allot the third Victor B.2 squadron to the strategic reconnaissance role.

VCAS (Air Mshl W H Kyle) explained to the Council that because of a slippage in production, resulting in the third Blue Steel Victor squadron not being in service until May 1965, the operational benefit of a third squadron would be enjoyed for less than a year, since it was planned to withdraw one of the squadrons in the first quarter of 1966 for conversion to the PR role to replace the Valiants of No 543 Squadron. In a Note to the Council he said that in view of the expenditure and effort involved in converting a Mk 2 Victor squadron to the Blue Steel role it was difficult to justify so short an effective period at the originally planned strength; the plan had therefore been reviewed.

The alternative proposed was that only two Victor B.2 squadrons would be equipped to carry Blue Steel and that the third squadron should proceed direct to the strategic reconnaissance role in 1965. There would be economies if such a decision were taken quickly – possibly £100,000 in not carrying out Blue Steel modifications, plus some £200,000 on fuel and repair costs which would not be required for the Valiant PR squadron. The Air Council Standing Committee endorsed VCAS's proposals, and on 24 February 1964 CAS told them that S of S had given his approval.

By early 1963, therefore, Blue Steel was firmly in service with the Vulcan squadrons[1]; and on 21 August an Air Ministry Nuclear Weapon

---

[1] On 17 January DCAS told the Air Council (Conclusions 1(63)) that of the 13 Blue Steel missiles so far delivered, six had still to complete their acceptance tests; and on 28 March he reported (Conclusions 5(63)) that six acceptance missiles at Scampton could be used operationally in an emergency.

Clearance for its use on QRA Standby was issued, although the weapons were to be unfilled and unfuelled except in an emergency: it was not until 16 April 1964 that CA gave clearance for "a filled and fuelled operational Blue Steel weapon to be used with the Vulcan B Mk 2 Quick Reaction Alert".

However, with the cancellation of Skybolt, which had originated from a joint USAF/RAF requirement in 1959 for a 1,000-mile-range air-launched ballistic missile, the Air Staff now had to find means of extending the operational life of the Mk 2 V-bomber/Blue Steel combination until the introduction of the Royal Navy's Polaris missiles. The effects of Skybolt's cancellation, and the eventual return to free-falling bombs as prime armament of the V-force, will be described in Chapter XXIV. The implications of this new situation were succinctly stated in the Air Ministry Quarterly Liaison Report for January–March 1963, which said that "since the last report was prepared, Skybolt has been cancelled and Polaris substituted, with the result that Bomber Command will have to maintain the independent deterrent without Skybolt for longer than was foreseen. To improve their chances of penetrating enemy defences it has been decided to give the aircraft a low-level capability by

(a)   providing a nuclear weapon which can be released from very low altitude.

(b)   modifying Blue Steel to enable it to be launched from below 1,000ft[1].

(c)   improving the performance at low level of the bombing and navigation fit of the V-bombers".

The problem of modifying Blue Steel was compounded by the fact that it was still at that time being introduced into service; and only a month before he handed over the command of the bomber force to his successor Sir John Grandy (on 1 September 1963) Sir Kenneth Cross expressed scepticism as to the weapon's reliability and readiness potential. Writing to CAS (MRAF Sir Thomas Pike) on 30 July[2] he said that the chances of a missile being fit for powered launch at the launch point were no better than 40% and the probability of a missile reaching the target after launch was about 75%. This meant that "of, say, six weapons on Readiness, two or at the most three will be launched and the

---

[1] VCAS (Air Mshl Sir Ronald Lees) told the DRPC on 8 May 63 that the modifications necessary, which concerned the flight rules computer and the arming and fuzing mechanism, were "comparatively slight" (DRP/P(63)31). To reduce radiation risks in the event of an accident during MoA/Air Ministry Blue Steel trials, natural uranium was substituted for fissile material in the warheads and the HTP was diluted with water.

[2] ID9/194/4 Blue Steel Jan 61-Jun 64.

remainder will have to be carried over the target and dropped free fall. Of those launched, one will probably fail to reach the target". He added that although there was as yet no experience of maintaining Blue Steel aircraft on Readiness, it was evident that the frequency of changing the aircraft/missile system would be appreciably greater than with a free-fall weapon. Considered in the context of a full-scale generation of 75% of the Blue Steel force during an alert, he concluded, "the low reliability implies that on present assessment only 14 missiles out of 36 could actually be launched, and 11 would reach the target"[1].

Sir Kenneth went on to say that it was already evident that the time needed to generate a Blue Steel weapon system could not be reduced much below seven hours even when no defects arose, and might take between ten and 15 hours; so steps were being taken to maintain some missiles permanently in a partly generated state. What concerned him more, however, was the time it would take to recover from either a full-scale exercise or an emergency generation of weapons. Owing mainly to the need to dry out missiles after draining the HTP (high-test peroxide), with only one drying unit being scheduled for each station, the time could be "as long as 15 days for a station to recover its normal peacetime preparedness". His prognostications for the future were equally gloomy:–

"The reliability of the weapon may of course improve with more experience but I am doubtful if we can expect anything significant, particularly in view of its future role at low level, and the dependence for serviceability on the performances of so many associated equipments in the aircraft.

"No doubt improvement in performance will occur as with other equipments in the past, but there are so many basic faults in Blue Steel from a readiness aspect that it is very doubtful whether they can be overcome".

CAS commented in reply (on 9 August) that the conclusions had been based on "a small sample of R&D firings and the experience gained so far from the trials at Scampton"; it was to be hoped that when modifications had been embodied in production missiles there would be "a noticeable improvement in performance and generation time".

In August 1963 the Ministry of Aviation gave clearance for the use of unfilled and unfuelled Blue Steels on QRAs with Vulcan B.2s, and on 4 October the new AOC in C visited Scampton, where he saw a demonstration loading of a Blue Steel missile and a QRA exercise. Subsequently he wrote to S of S for Air (Mr Hugh Fraser), after the latter has visited Scampton on 18 November, to tell him what was required "if we are to have an efficient and viable weapon system by next

---

[1] The RAF bought 57 Blue Steels, four or them for in-service proof firings (Bombers – Powered Bombs Blue Steel – Post Acceptance Trials (ID9/B. 18-11)).

year[1]". Authority was required, he said, to fuel missiles at readiness on aircraft with warheads fitted; to fit thermal batteries into readiness missiles and to leave them there, so obviating the system of last-minute loading; and to fly missiles with warhead loaded, and fuelled, from main bases to dispersals so as to test the weapon systems' capability to withstand long periods of readiness on dispersals[2].

However, four months later the AOC in C wrote to VCAS (Air Chf Mshl Sir Wallace Kyle) to say that no decision had been made on "the most important recommendations" in his letter of 19 November 1963 — that thermal batteries should be left in the missiles on QRA and that armed missiles on QRA should be fuelled.

Approval for a "wet" QRA involved the Nuclear Weapons Safety Committee, and a long paper was prepared in the Air Force Department for their consideration and that of the MoA[3], the NWSC discussing it on 14 July 1964.

Early reasons militating against the use of Blue Steel as a quick-reaction weapon had been set out long before it came into service, in a minute from DCAS (Air Mshl R B Lees) to CAS (Air Chf Mshl Sir Thomas Pike) on 22 July 1960[4]. These were, in the case of the warhead, whose design included thermal batteries which various British Safety Committees considered should not be stored permanently in the warhead capsule but inserted at the last possible opportunity before take-off, this insertion probably taking as much as 30 minutes; and in the case of the electric power control unit, which "as currently designed" would take approximately 20 minutes to stabilise the electrical power to the quality required by the missile. It was considered then that, as Blue Steel was late coming into service, items such as these which denied it "a really rapid reaction capability" could be rectified before operational missiles became available.

[1] "Service environmental trials ended at Scampton on 31 December 1963 and Blue Steel is now fully in the hands of Bomber Command" (AMQLR for October-December 1963).
[2] Correspondence in ID9/194/4 Blue Steel – January 1961 to June 1964.
[3] Ibid.
[4] In Development & Production of Power-guided Bomb (Blue Steel) ID3/946/8(S), Pt 2.

CHAPTER XIV

THE GRAPPLE TRIALS

Britain's thermonuclear weapon tests over the Pacific Ocean in 1957–58 were a major scientific and tri-Service operation, with the Army – who did all the engineering work at Christmas Island, the Royal Navy and the RAF playing leading parts in support of the Atomic Weapons Research Establishment trials. The RAF were to drop the test weapons which, in production form, they were later likely to have to use: they were therefore participating in the Grapple tests as potential customers for the scientists' products. The Valiant crews dropping the weapons would have the unique experience of bombing with the weight of destructive power other V-force crews would subsequently be enabled to deploy.

Planning for these megaton weapon trials had begun in 1955, the Air Council receiving their first intimation in a note by DCAS[1] in which he said:–

"The Director of the Atomic Weapons Research Establishment is planning a series of atomic weapons trials in 1956/57. The first of these is Operation Mosaic and is planned for Monte Bello in the spring of 1956. The second is Operation Buffalo, which will include an air drop from a Valiant aircraft of the Mk 1 weapon and the trial of the prototype of a tactical weapon[2]; in addition there will be two or three experimental explosions. This operation is planned for Maralinga in the autumn of 1956. The final operation is Green Bamboo. The venue for this is not yet firm but the spring of 1957 is the most probable date."

DCAS added that DAWRE had so far asked the RAF to provide air support for Mosaic and Buffalo; similar tasks would "almost certainly" have to be undertaken for Green Bamboo[3].

A month later, a brief for the Secretary of State for Air gave more specific details of the proposed Operation Gazette (as Grapple was then called). This said that the Director, AWRE, wished to test a thermonuclear weapon (Green Bamboo) in the spring of 1957. The only likely area where such a test could be carried out was the south-west Pacific, and there were four possible methods of mounting the trial, one of which was a drop from a V-bomber to give an air burst over an uninhabited island. Preliminary investigation had shown that the most suitable area appeared to be Malden Island, but there was to be a photographic survey of a number of islands – Malden, Penrhyn, Christmas, McKean, Palmyra and Aitutaki – to find an airstrip where the Task Force could be based, and a target area.

---

[1] Air Council paper AC(55)37 dated 19 Jul 55 (CMS.2680/55).
[2] The air drop was of a Blue Danube round; the other trials were tower bursts.
[3] This was the original code-name, changed to Gazette and then to Grapple.

Towards the end of 1955 the Chiefs of Staff Committee had been given a full briefing on the requirement for megaton weapons in a report – the British Megaton Warhead Trial Series – by the Atomic Energy Sub-Committee of the Defence Research Policy Committee[1]. This recalled that the Government, in the 1955 Defence White Paper, had announced their decision to develop and produce megaton weapons[2]. The DRPC commented: "The earliest possible achievement of a megaton explosion is necessary to demonstrate our ability to make such weapons, as part of the strategic deterrent against war." Referring to the increasing political pressure against further megaton trials[3], it said that since they might become politically unacceptable after the planned UK ones, "it is essential that this first series should be planned in such a way as to safeguard the future by obtaining the greatest possible amount of scientific knowledge and weapon design experience as the foundation of our megaton weapon development programme".

The committee said there were four needs for megaton warheads – for the free-falling and the powered guided bomb for the V-force, for the medium-range ballistic missile[4] and for a multi-megaton warhead. The free-falling bomb should be in service in 1959 if the 1957 trials were successful; a megaton warhead for the powered bomb (Blue Steel) would involve restrictions in its shape and size, though the same basic design could be used as for the free-falling bomb; although the ballistic missile would not be in service for about ten years, it was essential to know as early as possible whether a warhead small and light enough to fit it could be developed, because of the severe design problems; and it was necessary to demonstrate that the UK "knows how to make multi-megaton weapons" – the US and USSR had successfully detonated such assemblies.

Explaining that UK scientific knowledge of megaton warhead design was currently "entirely unsupported by experimental evidence", the report said that the most certain way of producing a trial megaton explosion in 1957 was to use a large pure fission assembly in a Mk 1 case with enough fissile material to ensure a megaton yield. Such a device would be "big, heavy and extravagant in fissile material"; its military application could only be as a free-falling bomb.

Referring to the different types of warhead tested in the Grapple trials, the DRPC sub-committee mentioned Green Granite – an experimental assembly involving the only economical way of achieving multi-megaton warheads by 1957; Green Bamboo – a megaton-boosted fission assembly, the principle intended for use in the

---

[1] COS(55)336, 13 Dec 55 (Operation Grapple file, AF190/22(S) – AHB No ID3/190/22(S) Pt 2).

[2] "The United Kingdom . . . has the ability to produce such weapons. After fully considering all the implications of this step the Government have thought it their duty to proceed with their development and production" (February 1955 – Cmd 9391).

[3] *Ie* after those held by the Americans in 1952 and 1954 and by the Russians in 1953.

[4] Blue Streak.

free-falling bomb and powered guided missile; and Orange Herald – of pure fission assembly, a small light megaton warhead, essential basis of the long-range ballistic missile programme. An experiment with a boosted kiloton Mk 1 weapon was also proposed; this was not directly connected with the megaton programme, but for safety reasons the test of such a warhead could not take place in Australia.

Justifying the proposed test explosions, the DRPC sub-committee report went on to say that the Green Bamboo experiment was essential to provide for the development both of a free-falling and of a powered bomb for the medium bomber force; that the Orange Herald experiment was "the essential basis of our long-range missile programme"; and that Green Granite was "the most economical way of achieving a multi-megaton explosion" – it was "exceedingly important both from the scientific and the military point of view that an experiment of this nature should be carried out as soon as possible".

The report added that AWRE estimated that they could provide the effort necessary to prepare all these experimental assemblies in time for a trial in the early part of 1957, and it strongly recommended that the Establishment be instructed to prepare them with a view to testing them at that time; provision had already been made for the fissile material necessary for them in the weapons programme submitted to the Chiefs of Staff[1]. By the time the Mosaic tests had taken place[2], it might be "advisable to reconsider the inclusion of certain items in the series or the order in which they are fired" – that is, to amend the programme according to the results achieved. In fact, as will be seen later, the weapon drops by No 49 Squadron reflected closely the programme originally outlined in 1955.

The DRPC sub-committee report concluded with a very clear brief for the Chiefs of Staff as to the location and logistics of the megaton weapon trials. It explained that reconnaissance had shown that a satisfactory trial could be mounted by using Christmas Island in the South Pacific as a base, dropping the assemblies from a Valiant taking off from that island, to burst in the vicinity of Malden Island, 400 miles to the south. A very large effort by the Royal Navy and RAF would be required to mount this trial, but this was inevitable "if we are to implement the decision to develop and produce atomic weapons".

"To achieve a trial early in 1957" (the report explained) "it is vital that full authority should be given in the very near future to commit the necessary expenditure, and also that the number of shots to be planned for should be confirmed, since this affects very largely the aircraft effort and the logistic support necessary for it." So that Ministerial sanction might be obtained for further planning, the DRPC sub-committee recommended that the Chiefs of Staff should agree that (a) a series of

[1] COS(55)322.
[2] Operation Mosaic was held in the Monte Bello Islands from January to June 1956. It involved tower bursts.

megaton trials should take place as early as possible, based on Christmas Island; (b) AWRE should prepare the following assemblies: (i) Green Bamboo, (ii) Orange Herald, (iii) Green Granite, (iv) a pure fission assembly in a Mk 1 case and (v) a boosted kiloton fission weapon. Ministers "should be informed that although all these assemblies should be prepared, No (iv) should not be fired except as a reserve".

This report has been referred to in great detail because it is seminal to an understanding of the practical implications of the British decision to develop and produce hydrogen bombs – and in particular to an understanding of the Grapple trials in which Bomber Command aircraft played such an important part, and which proved to be a highly successful operation, leading to the achievement of megaton weapon capability by the V-force.

On 16 December 1955, ACAS(Ops) and ACAS(OR) jointly recommended that CAS should support the DRPC Atomic Energy Sub-committee proposals at the Chiefs of Staff meeting on 20 December – when the recommendations were approved, the CoS inviting the Minister of Defence to "take the necessary action to obtain the approval of Ministers", and also agreeing that a senior Service officer should be appointed operational commander for the tests[1].

Initially, the Chiefs of Staff decided to appoint an admiral, but at the end of January 1956 changed their minds; the post was to be filled by a Royal Air Force Officer[2], and in February Air Cdre W E Oulton was appointed, with the rank of air vice-marshal[3]. A directive approved by the Chiefs of Staff on 21 February laid down the chain of command for the Grapple trial. It said that "on the authority of the Prime Minister, responsibility for the planning and execution of Operation Grapple has been placed, at Ministerial level, with the Minister of Supply. This responsibility is discharged on his behalf by the Atomic Trials Executive, of which the chairman is the Controller of Atomic Weapons in the Ministry of Supply." It told the newly appointed Task Force Commander that

"with the approval of the UK Chiefs of Staff, you have been appointed to command the Operation as a whole in accordance with the policy laid down by the Atomic Weapons Trials Executive. You will be assisted in the discharge of your duties by a staff comprised of representatives of the three Services and of the Atomic Weapons Research Establishment. You will be responsible to the Controller of Atomic Weapons for the planning and execution of the operation as a whole and for co-ordination of all agencies taking part. . . . The Chiefs of Staff have decided that you will be in operational command of all forces taking part in the operation. Subject to your responsibilities as above, you will

[1] COS(55)105th meeting.
[2] COS(56)13th meeting, on 31 January 1956.
[3] See his own detailed account of the Grapple trials, *Christmas Island Cracker An account of the Planning and Execution of the British Thermonuclear Bomb Tests 1957* by Wilfrid E Oulton CB CBE DSO DFC (Thomas Harmsworth Publishing).

conduct the operation to meet the technical requirements of the Scientific Director".

The Air Council were informed of the projected tests in a Note by DCAS (Air Mshl Sir Thomas Pike) dated 11 April 1956,[1] which began:–

Operation "Grapple" 1957

The Government have agreed that plans should be made for a series of nuclear test explosions in 1957. The weapon used will be a high-yield (megaton) weapon. The explosions will take place in the vicinity of Malden Island in the South Pacific. The advance air base for the operation will be Christmas Island, where a good deal of rehabilitation will be needed[2]. A main base will also need to be set up in Australia. The weapons to be tested will have to burst in the air to minimise fall-out problems. They will be released from a Valiant aircraft flying at about 43,000ft and will burst at 8,000ft.

The Ministry of Supply will be responsible for the tests. The Task Force Commander will be provided by the RAF. . . .

Later that year, on 5 June, the Cabinet agreed[3] that the Prime Minister should make a Parliamentary statement about the tests, and two days later Sir Anthony Eden told the Commons[4]:–

"In the Statement of Defence, 1955, Her Majesty's Government announced their intention to manufacture thermonuclear weapons. As I have previously stated, the holding of tests is an essential part of the process of providing ourselves with such weapons. The United States of America and the Union of Soviet Socialist Republics have already held such tests and Her Majesty's Government have decided to carry out a limited number of nuclear test explosions in the megaton range.

"These will take place during the first half of 1957 in a remote part of the Pacific Ocean. The explosions will take place far from any inhabited islands and the tests will be so arranged as to avoid danger to persons or property. The tests will be high air bursts which will not involve heavy fall-out. All safety precautions will be taken in the light of our knowledge and of experience gained from the tests of other countries.

"The main base of the aircraft of the Royal Air Force taking part will be Christmas Island, in the Pacific Ocean, and meteorological facilities will be installed there. Her Majesty's Governments in Australia and New Zealand have agreed to make available to the task force various forms of aid and ancillary support from Australian and New Zealand territory. We are most grateful for this.

---

[1] AC(56)24.
[2] The island had originally been surveyed at the end of 1955; it had been occupied by the Japanese during the war, was relieved by the Royal Navy (HMS *Rother*) on 18 October 1945, then continued to be leased to the Christmas Island Phosphate Commission, who had been granted a 99-year lease in 1891. It was reckoned that the main phosphate-bearing area had a deposit of 12m tons awaiting excavation (File Christmas Island A254768/56 – Air 2 13334).
[3] CM(56) 39th Conclusions, Min 3, further discussed on 7 June.
[4] Commons Hansard, 7 June 1956, Col 1382.

"In reaching this decision Her Majesty's Government in the United Kingdom have given full weight to the anxiety which exists about the indefinite continuance of tests of nuclear weapons without control and without limitation. I emphasised on 6th December last year in the House that Her Majesty's Government were prepared to discuss methods of regulating and limiting test explosions which take account of their position and that of other Powers. This remains the policy of Her Majesty's Government. . . ."

Shortly before the Prime Minister's Parliamentary statement had been made, an Air Staff Memorandum of 12 May 1956 issued by the Senior Air Staff Officer, Bomber Command[1], gave details of what the Grapple trials involved for the bomber forces. It referred to the current trials programme leading up to Grapple, saying that this included

"a series of trial drops of inert weapons from Valiant aircraft over Orfordness range. Live tests overseas take place as follows:–

(a)   Operation Mosaic – ground detonated bursts (Monte Bello, May 1956)

(b)   Operation Buffalo – air drop of an atomic weapon (Maralinga, Australia)[2]

(c)   Operation Grapple – air drops of nuclear weapons (Pacific Ocean)".

The memorandum said that the principal bomber forces involved in these trials would be:–

(a)   No 76 Squadron (Canberra B.6s), already at Edinburgh Field for Mosaic and subsequently to support Buffalo and Grapple

(b)   one squadron of Varsities (accompanying No 76 Squadron for Mosaic and Buffalo only)

(c)   No 100 Squadron (Canberra PR.7s), to support Grapple only

(d)   No 49 Squadron (Valiants), to supply four aircraft for the "F" series[3] (UK) trials, two for Buffalo and eight for Grapple.

During the latter half of 1956 there was a great deal of planning, training, crew selection, operational and administrative preparation for Grapple[4], and at the end of the year Bomber Command issued an Administrative Instruction which set out clearly the extent and size of the air effort involved. It said:

"The third of a series of Atomic Weapons Trials will take place in the South Pacific Ocean between March and June 1957. A Royal Air Force Task Group consisting of No 160 Wing (Home Command) and attached squadrons will be based at Christmas Island, south-west Pacific, to provide the Air Support necessary for the successful conduct of the trials. The Bomber Command element of the Task Group will be

---

[1] AVM S O Bufton; Memorandum No 21/56 Conduct and Organisation of "F" Series Trials.
[2] July–Nov 1956.
[3] Code-name for UK atomic weapons trials for which No 49 re-formed on 1 May 1956.
[4] BC file Operation "Grapple" Policy BC/88983. AVM Oulton's book conveys vividly the magnitude and comprehensiveness of these preparations.

responsible for the Air Drops, Cloud Sampling, High Level Meteorological Reconnaissance and Cloud Tracking, together with limited high-level photography of each burst. Additionally, Cloud Samples will be flown to the United Kingdom in Bomber Command aircraft. Coastal Command will be responsible for low-level meteorological reconnaissance and cloud tracking, Air Burst Photography from low level, and for search and rescue. Transport Command are providing transport support in the area."

Canberras in Operation Grapple were to operate at extremes of altitude – at up to 53,000ft for air sampling and at 2,000ft for reconnaissance. Referring to air sampling procedures, HQ Task Force Grapple told Bomber Command on 18 January 1957 that it was "a firm requirement on Operation Grapple to obtain samples at as great a height as is possible and AWRE have been informed that it is hoped to obtain the samples in the Canberra B.6 in the band 50,000 to 53,000ft ..."[1]. For this task, squadron aircrew were to have special oxygen equipment and flying clothing. In an Operation Order on low-level target reconnaissance, issued on 8 May[2], Task Force HQ said that post-burst reconnaissance of the target area was required, to assist with the immediate assessment of correct weapon functioning; the Canberras' mission was "to reconnoitre Malden Island and ground zero from a height of 2,000ft at H (actual) + 15 minutes". Particular note had to be made of the existence (or otherwise) of a large sea wave and of a base surge; whether there was clear vision or not under the nuclear cloud; what the state of the surface of Malden Island was – *ie* whether there was fire; reading from the radiac instruments[3]; and of other significant facts.

No 49 Squadron began their training for Operation Grapple on 1 September 1956; this followed directives received from HQ Bomber Command on 15 June and 24 August, which were used as a basis for training, begun when the squadron reached its full strength of eight crews. Previously, "considerable experience had been gained by Sq Ldr Roberts and crew who had been engaged on 10,000lb bomb trials since June 1955[4], and by Sq Ldr Flavell and crew and Fl Lt Bates and crew in preparation for Operation Buffalo"[5].

However, the squadron was unable to complete its training programme before leaving the UK, owing to adverse weather conditions; this became clear from a report by the CO, Wg Cdr K G Hubbard, on the training task which had to be completed at Christmas Island before No 49 could begin the trials programme. In an "Interim Progress Report to

[1] GRA/10/6/AIR.
[2] No 12/57.
[3] For measuring radiation.
[4] In No 1321 Flt.
[5] Report on the Training of No 49 Sqn for Operation Grapple (File 49/S.71/5/Ops).

First Live Drop"[1] he said that "the first Valiant of No 49 Squadron, piloted by the squadron commander, arrived on the island on 12 March 1957; the remaining three aircraft arrived during the next few days.

"Since weather conditions in the UK had effectively prevented the visual bombing training programme from being completed . . . there was a preliminary training task to be completed before the squadron was ready to commence scientific drops. The operational drill and flying technique had been perfected in the UK prior to departure.

"The training programme, which was commenced without delay, was completed by 23 April; during this time 114 100lb bombs were dropped using the time delay technique to produce overshoot bombing, and the average error from 45,000ft was 450yd. . . .

"Valiants XD818 and XD823 were prepared for the first live drop of Short Granite, and many hours were spent by the ground crews cleaning the aircraft down to produce the anti-flash effect."

The No 49 Squadron Valiants were white, highly reflective cellulose anti-flash paint having been applied as part of their pre-Grapple trials preparation, and the reason for two aircraft being got ready was, the squadron explained,

"Because at one stage of the operation it was feared that the number of live drops would be reduced, it was decided to put an additional Valiant into the air for every live drop in order to act as a grandstand aircraft; and at the same time give crews experience of flash and blast from a thermonuclear weapon.

"To achieve this, the Valiant was allowed to take off shortly after the dropping aircraft, and made rendezvous at IP on the bombing line. When the dropping aircraft commenced its initial run, the grandstand aircraft positioned itself 2,000ft below and approximately ½-mile behind. On the final bombing run the grandstand aircraft commenced its escape manoeuvre approximately 11sec before the 'bomb gone' signal was given. . . ."

The Valiant which made the first live drop of a British thermonuclear weapon was XD818 on 15 May 1957, captained by No 49 Squadron's commander, Wg Cdr K G Hubbard OBE DFC[2]. His crew members were Fg Off R L Beeson (second pilot) and Flt Lts A Washbrook DFC (navigator), E J Hood (observer) and E Laraway (signaller). The report on their historic flight from Christmas Island, lasting 2hr 20min, was factual, prosaic and concise:–

"The aircraft became airborne at 0900 'V' time and all anti-flash screens were in position prior to the aircraft commencing its first run over the target. After one initial run to check telemetry, the Task Force Commander gave clearance for the live run.

---

[1] In Operation Grapple – Reports and Conclusions (BT 2) (49/S.71/5/Ops).
[2] Whose personal account of the trials can be read in his autobiographical book *Operation Grapple-Testing Britain's First H-bomb* (Ian Allan 1985).

"The bombing run was made at 45,000ft true, and as Green Satin drift was fluctuating badly, the set was put to Memory on an average drift. The bombing run was steady on a course of 203°T and the weapon was released at 1036 'W' time. Immediately after release the aircraft was rolled into the escape manoeuvre which averaged a turn of 60° bank, excess G 1.8 to 1.9, airspeed 0.76M, rolling out on a heading of 073°T. The time taken for this turn was 38 sec, and at the time of air burst of the weapon, the slant range between aircraft and burst was 8.65n/ms.

"Neither crew nor aircraft felt any effect of flash, and the air blast reached the aircraft 2.5 min after release; the effect of the blast was to produce a period of 5 sec during which turbulence alike to slight clear air turbulence was experienced.

"Six minutes after weapon release, all shutters in the aircraft were removed, and after one orbit to see the mushroom cloud effect, the aircraft returned to base and made a normal landing[1].

At the same time, seven other aircraft were airborne in the test area – the 'Grandstand' Valiant of No 49 Sqn, captained by Sqn Ldr B T Millett; five air sampler Canberra B.6s of No 76 Sqn; and a reconnaissance/meteorological Canberra PR.7 of No 100 Sqn. The No 76 Sqn ORB provides a clear, unemotional account of the five B.6s' part in the Grapple trials: —

Sample Controller (Air): For the first time in the squadron's association with nuclear trials there was in attendance at all sampling sorties an Airborne Controller, namely Air Commodore D A Wilson AFC, who had previously flown with the squadron on Shot II of Operation Mosaic. His task on Grapple was to assist the ground controller by obtaining the heights and dimensions of the cloud so that the most advantageous sampling run could be carried out. In addition his was the final decision after ascertaining with radiation-measuring instruments that it was safe for the aircraft to penetrate the cloud.

Radio Link and Target Recce: Owing to the possibility of a failure in ground communications, one aircraft was situated approximately half way between Christmas Island and Malden Island prior to the Valiant take-off, so that, if necessary, messages between HMS *Warrior* and Joint Operations Centre could be passed by VHF. Once the Valiant had commenced its initial bombing run the aircraft proceeded to an orbit 76 miles from the target, where it remained until 10 sec after the bomb burst, at which time a maximum-rate descent towards Malden Island was commenced. Maintaining 2,000ft, it continued towards the target, where its prime objective was to see whether in fact the bomb had exploded at the correct altitude. This

---

[1] On 16 May the Minister of Defence sent a signal to Task Force HQ which read: "Personal for Air Vice-Marshal Oulton and Mr Cook from Minister of Defence. Well done, indeed. Warmest congratulations to all members of the expedition on an historic achievement." (Strategic Aspects of Atomic Energy – ID6/R13, Pt 6. William Cook (later knighted) was civilian director of the tests; he was Deputy Director, AWRE.)

it did by looking for abnormal sea waves and fires on Malden Island and taking radiation measurements.

Primary sampler: Took off at approximately 30 min before the drop, so that it arrived at the target area 30 min after the burst. Received the cloud's position and dimensions from the Airborne Controller and the entry point from Mallard, the Ground Controller. It usually made its penetration at bomb burst plus 60 min, taking particulate and gaseous samples until the cumulative dose rate had reached 6 roentgens. To reach the maximum height needed to sample, the fuel carried on this sortie enabled only 3½ hours' flying.

Secondary Sampler: Similar to the Primary Sampler except that all operations were carried out 30 min later.

Reserve Sampler: Required in case of unserviceability or if later samples are needed, and in fact only used on the first operation.

No 100 Squadron with its Canberra PR.7s was responsible for the weather information and for post-burst photography; on the day of the first live drop the squadron CO, Sqn Ldr D A Hammatt AFC DFM, flew with Flt Lt D Andrew as navigator on a target reconnaissance and photography sortie lasting 4hr 40min, from 0730 to 1210hr. The squadron's ORB described what the PR.7 crews had to do – how "during the build-up period before the drops, the unit was required to provide a daily Met flight, taking off at 0700hr local, plus additional flights at the request of the SMO[1]".

There were three rehearsals for the first live drop, and for these, met flights took off at 0330 and 0430hr, followed by a target weather recce and photo sortie which left at 0730hr – the flight which the CO made for the first live drop on 15 May. Its purpose was "to provide up-to-the-minute information on weather and wind velocities over the target up to H-hour, for the use of the Task Force Commander and the dropping Valiant. During the actual drop the crew stood off and took photographs of the development of the atomic cloud, using the two F.24 side-facing cameras. . . ."

On 16 May Sir Frederick Brundrett, Scientific Adviser to the Ministry of Defence and chairman of the Defence Research Policy Committee, the Atomic Energy Sub-Committee of which had outlined the megaton warhead trials in 1955 for the Chiefs of Staff, penned an informal note to the Chief of the Air Staff, Air Chf Mshl Sir Dermot Boyle, from the United University Club. "Having spent most of the day at panic stations", he said,

"preparing speeches to be delivered by either the PM or Sandys on 'the Test', it's only when I got back here for dinner that I have an opportunity to thank you very much indeed for the outstanding co-operation of your people in the Pacific.

---

[1] Senior Meteorological Office (Mr M H Freeman).

"My private advices are to the effect that the performance of your chaps has been simply superb. I am more than grateful for your help, without which we could not succeed.

"So far as I am able to judge from American reports as well as our own preliminary assessments, we have fulfilled expectations – in the circumstances it is an immense achievement of which I think we can all be proud – and as I say, without your splendid co-operation, we could not have done it".

Two days later CAS received a signal from the Grapple Task Force Commander, AVM Oulton, which said: "You will be pleased to know that the air operation went very smoothly and almost exactly according to plan. Both aircrew and ground personnel rose magnificently to the occasion despite very trying conditions. You can be proud of them. I am".

On 20 May, CAS replied to Sir Frederick Brundrett:
"How very kind of you to find the time in the midst of all your other preoccupations to drop me a line regarding the part played by the Royal Air Force in Grapple.

"I hear from every source that the co-operation between all concerned has been first class, and I am sure that at times the conditions have been most trying.

"Reading between the lines – and the code words – I have formed the opinion that probably the first burst has been a success and consequently great things may flow from it. I realise that technically it was a gamble but it seems to have come off, which is a feather in the cap for the scientists".

What CAS probably had in mind when he commented that "technically it was a gamble" was that the Grapple trial combined two things – a first thermonuclear burst with a first air drop. Neither of the other nuclear Powers had done this; both the USA and USSR first ground-burst their thermonuclear weapons, and Britain held three nuclear tests – Hurricane, Totem and Mosaic – before dropping a nuclear bomb in the Buffalo trial. (In a letter to the AOC in C Bomber Command on 2 October 1957 on the nuclear trials programme, Acting ACAS(Ops) (Air Cdre B K Burnett) said that there were "two trials locations, Maralinga and Christmas Island. It is intended basically that kiloton trials shall be held at the former and megaton at the latter but this does not exclude the possibility of inclusion of a kiloton explosion in a megaton series at Christmas Island should it be desirable". He added: "The present atomic weapon trials series, Antler at Maralinga, is scheduled to end early this month. It is intended that Grapple X, Y and Z will follow in November 1957, February and May 1958, respectively, each series being of two rounds and all taking place at Christmas Island...".) What was done at Grapple was to explode a thermonuclear warhead in a nuclear (Blue Danube) bomb case, the ballistic capabilities of which had been already well proved. Thus Grapple was also a trial for

Blue Danube, the original British nuclear deterrent weapon.

Unfortunately the RAF suffered an aircraft loss, not during the Christmas Island trials but associated with them. This was revealed in a letter to CAS from Sir William Penney, Director of the AWRE, on 21 May – six days after the first live drop had been made. "I am writing to let you know", he said,

"how very much I and my senior staff regret the loss of the Canberra off Newfoundland, particularly as the flight concerned was in connection with the return of our samples from Grapple.

"We are all the more distressed by this loss because of the truly admirable effort which your Service has made in connection with these trials.

"I have to write this in confidence because I understand no connection between the accident and the trial is being released".

The Canberra was a PR.7 of No 58 Sqn whose ORB recorded briefly that the accident occurred "during a final approach in inclement weather at RCAF Goose Bay on the 16th May 1957. Plt Off J S Loomes and Flg Off T R Montgomery sustained fatal injuries". The aircraft had apparently arrived over its destination at 48,000ft after a 4hr 22min flight from Namao, near Edmonton, Alberta. Its crew, undoubtedly anxious to get the samples they were carrying back to the UK as soon as possible, had had no proper sleep in the previous 26 hours and no proper meal for the previous 18 hours, and made their landing attempts in extremely adverse weather conditions.

There was, also, a critical situation for a few seconds in Valiant XD822 after the second live drop in Operation Grapple – on 31 May 1957 – though the report by the aircraft captain, Sqn Ldr D Roberts, recounts what happened with a cool professionalism which belies the anxiety he must have felt. For an accident to one of the Valiants at such a time would have been disastrous both in human and technical terms. Fortunately, Sqn Ldr Roberts' experience on the type – he had by then dropped more 10,000lb Blue Danube-type bombs, in the ballistic trials done by No 1321 Flight, than any other captain in the V-force – stood him and his crew in good stead, and the incident was resolved successfully, or as the report puts it in three words: "after regaining control". Prior to that, everything had gone well apart from a brief pre-take-off delay, and the whole report is of interest because of its detail and clarity. Sqn Ldr Roberts began by describing the task and the situation:–

"My crew was detailed to take off at 0900V on 31 May in Valiant XD822 to drop Orange Herald on the target area south of Malden Island. The forecast weather for the target area was one- to two-eighths of cumulus, and wind velocity 090°/20kt at 45,000ft; conditions at base fine. In view of this the fuel load was reduced to 5,000gal in order to give an all-up weight of 99,000lb immediately after release of the bomb.

"The crew reached the aircraft at 0740hr and completed cockpit checks by 0810. AWRE had connected the bomb batteries by the time the crew entered the aircraft at 0840, but then the take-off time was delayed on orders from JOC. At 0900 permission was given to start engines, and we were airborne at 0907".

That reference to AWRE indicates the close and cordial relationship between the Establishment and the RAF on the Grapple trials, which were test-drops of AWRE weapons, flown by the RAF.

Initially all went well on the second live drop, until the short-lived post-drop drama occurred. "The flight to the RV" (the report continued)

"took 50min and was uneventful. Good contact on HF and VHF was established and maintained with the appropriate authorities throughout the flight. The first run over the target was navigation-type and the weather was found to be as forecast. . . .

"After the first run the remaining black-out shutters were fitted, and we went straight round on the initial run. Shortly after completing this, permission was given to carry on with the live run. The run-up was steady, and the bomb was released at 1044, heading 202°T, IAS 216, IMN 0.75. After a slight pause I initiated a steep turn to port at 60° bank. At this stage the second pilot should have started to call readings on the sensitive accelerometer, but on this occasion he was silent for a few seconds. I looked up and saw that the instrument indicated unity. Experience told me to believe the instrument, so disregarding my senses, I increased the backward pressure on the control column. At that instant the second pilot and I realised that the instrument had failed at the time of release; simultaneously, the aircraft stalled, and the bomb aimer, who was making for his seat, returned to the bomb-aimer's well with some force. After regaining control, the manoeuvre was completed in 43sec, using the mechanical accelerometer. This instrument might have been referred to earlier had it not been so far from our normal instrument scan. . . .

"At 53sec by the navigator's count-down a bright white flash was seen through chinks in the blackout screens, and the coloured glass in the first pilot's panel was lit up. At 2min 55sec after release the blast waves were felt, first a moderate bump, followed a second later by a smaller one.

"I waited a further two minutes before turning port to allow the crew to see what had happened. The cloud top at this time appeared to be some 10,000ft above our flight level, and it is a sight which will not easily be forgotten. The symmetry and the colours were most impressive, especially against the dark blue background provided by the sky at that height; as we watched, the upper stem and mushroom head started to glow with a deep peach colour.

"We then set course for base and landed at 1247V.

"After the training that we had received, this was a routine flight. The job of the aircrew is straightforward provided . . . there are no equipment failures..." (report dated 5 Jun 57 in No 49 Sqn ORB Appendices).

As No 49 Sqn spearheaded the operational side of the Grapple trial, the success of which meant that the RAF received its first megaton bombs in 1958 – a year marked by the co-ordination of RAF/USAF nuclear strike plans and by the supply of American nuclear weapons for the Valiants and Canberras, it is worth quoting the squadron's very clear report in its ORB; for this sets out concisely what happened and lists all the bombs which were dropped. Datelined Christmas Island, Pacific, May and June 1957, it says that

"after months of intensive training it was very satisfying when during the month of May 1957 the squadron made history by successfully dropping the first and second nuclear weapons of the megaton range. The build-up prior to each drop followed the same pattern. After a series of HE drops a dress rehearsal involving all units taking part was carried out. On the 15th May 1957 Wg Cdr K G Hubbard OBE DFC and crew in Valiant XD818 dropped the first live weapon (Green Granite). On the 31st May 1957 Sqn Ldr D Roberts DFC AFC and crew dropped the second live weapon. Both operations were described as completely successful....

"The complete list of weapons involved in the trials...were as follows: —

    3 May XD822 1 x 10,000lb HE (OH)
    5 May XD824 1 x 10,000lb HE (GB)
  11 May XD818 1 x 10,000lb HE (GG)
  15 May XD818 1 x 10,000lb Live (GG)
  18 May XD824 1 x 10,000lb HE (OH)
  23 May XD822 1 x 10,000lb Inert (BD)
  23 May XD822 1 x 10,000lb Inert (BD)
  25 May XD822 1 x 10,000lb HE (GB)
  28 May XD822 1 x 10,000lb HE (OH)
  31 May XD822 1 x 10,000lb Live (OH)[1]".

Perhaps the neatest summing-up, from the point of view of the operational crews participating, occurs in the final entry in No 49 Squadron's ORB for June 1957, which says:–

"Operation Grapple is now complete and it can be said that the squadron met its task in every respect. After months of specialised training the squadron occupied a section of a coral strip in the Pacific and successfully dropped the first three 'H' bombs of British design[2].

---

[1] A minute of 5 Jun 57 from PSO/ACAS(Ops) to PS/S of S says that "Orange Herald (megaton warhead for the medium-range ballistic missile) was successfully dropped by a Valiant of No 49 Sqn" and that "a Canberra PR.7 of No 58 Sqn carrying samples landed at Wyton 27hr 40min after...the explosion" (Op Grapple – ID3/190/22S P.)

[2] The third drop was on 19 June, by Sqn Ldr A G Steele and crew. This was of Purple Granite, the last live (and completely successful) drop, made from Valiant XD823, the 'Grandstand' Valiant (XD824) being flown by Sqn Ldr Millett (see *Christmas Island Cracker*, the lively account of the Grapple tests written by the Task Force Commander, AVM W E Oulton).

Throughout the operation an extremely high standard of serviceability has been sustained and coupled with that has been an equally high standard of morale".

What had been the results of the tests in weapon terms? At a Yellow Sun Progress Meeting at St Giles Court on 16 July 1957[1] DAWDP (Mr C W Shaw) said that "whilst Grapple had been successful in providing data on the performance of two different types of megaton warhead, it had not provided sufficient data to enable a firm decision to be made regarding the warhead to be chosen for Yellow Sun. On the evidence of the trials, a Green Bamboo type warhead had been chosen by the Air Staff for use in the interim megaton weapon". Mr Shaw went on to say that it was unlikely that any decision regarding the suitability of the Granite-type warhead for a Service megaton weapon could be made "for some months yet".

Although No 49 Squadron had asserted in its ORB for June 1957 that Operation Grapple was "complete", three further Grapple operations were mounted, in all of which the squadron were involved – 'X' in October-November 1957, 'Y' in April-May 1958 and 'Z' in August-September 1958. For the first of these tests the Task Force Commander was still AVM W E Oulton; for Grapples 'Y' and 'Z' he was succeeded by AVM J Grandy (subsequently CAS, 1967-71)[2].

These were all further megaton weapon trials, and for 'X' No 49 Sqn had four Valiants at Christmas Island, plus a fifth which was used as a courier aircraft; and in its November 1957 ORB the squadron's role was succinctly described:–

"This month heralded the fourth drop of a nuclear device in the megaton range. The drop was made by Sqn Ldr B T Millett (pilot) and Flt Lt F G Corduroy (observer) in Valiant XD825 on 8 November. The results were entirely satisfactory, precluding the necessity for any further tests in this particular phase of Operation Grapple. By the end of the month the entire detachment from Christmas Island had returned to Wittering. . . ."

The main purpose of Grapple 'X', it had been stated in the Air Plan[3], was "the air drop of two thermonuclear weapons with minimum risk to all concerned". A subsidiary task was to "to obtain samples from the radioactive clouds" so that the efficiency of the explosions could be determined. "Owing to the short half life of the fission/fusion products of the explosions the samples need to be flown to the United Kingdom as rapidly as possible". In a signal to the Ministry of Supply after the test the Task Force Commander, AVM Oulton, said that "we used radar-controlled bombing technique for the first time with a live weapon

[1] Minutes (AV/344/02) in file AF/CMS 29/64 Pt III Megaton Bomb OR1136.
[2] At a meeting of the Operation Grapple Atomic Weapons Trials Executive on 4 December 1957 AVM Oulton reported on Grapple X and AVM Grandy gave a progress report on plans for Grapple Y (HQ Task Force Grapple Executive Committee Meetings – IVA/146/2/161 file).
[3] Task Force Grapple Air Plan Pt II (IVA/146/2/165(B)).

and drop was extremely accurate[1]." In a previous signal, referring to the sampling, he had commented: "76 Squadron up to usual form and collected excellent samples". He had added: "Biggest headache in Air Task Group Shackleton serviceability. Nevertheless all sorties asked for were met".

Grapple X, Y and Z were carried out off Christmas Island; Malden Island was no longer used after the May-June 1957 tests. For Grapple X the TFC was still AVM W E Oulton; for Y and Z (in which two were kiloton and two were megaton detonations) he was succeeded by AVM John Grandy. Valiants of No 49 Sqn were responsible for all the air-dropping of weapons in the Grapple trials, in X, Y and Z aiming for an offshore point south-east of Christmas Island about 2-5km from land, the bursts occurring at between 2250 and 2850m. The Grapple X test was on 8 November 1957; Y was on 28 April 1958 and Z later that year: the first balloon system burst on 22 August, the two air-drops on 2 and 11 September and the second balloon burst on 22 September[2]. The intention of these trials was "to get the know-how on the double bomb (Granite type) principle". They were "not directed at any specific weapon because the disappointing results obtained from this type of device in Shots 1 and 3 at Grapple last May have forced the scientists into attacking the problem in a purely scientific manner[3]".

No 49 Sqn had five Valiants (one of them a courier aircraft, surplus to establishment) positioned on Christmas Island, where they were attached to No 160 Wing, by the end of October 1957 for Operation Grapple 'X'. In its ORB report the success of this operation was laconically described:–

"This month heralded the fourth drop of a nuclear device in the megaton range. The drop was made by Sqn Ldr B T Millett (pilot) and Flt LT F G Corduroy (observer) in Valiant XD825 on 8 November 1957. The results were entirely satisfactory, precluding the necessity for any further tests in this particular phase of Operation Grapple. By the end of the month the entire detachment from Christmas Island had returned to Wittering. It is of interest to note that the squadron once again met the rigid error limitations imposed by the scientific section of the Ministry of Supply".

On 6 January 1958 the squadron CO, Wg Cdr K G Hubbard, visited Bomber Command HQ for a conference on training requirements for Operation Grapple 'Y'; and on 12 February the squadron had a visit by the Grapple Task Force Commander, AVM J Grandy, and the Deputy TFC, Air Cdre J F Roulston: by 28 March four Valiants and their aircrew and groundcrew had been positioned on Christmas Island

---

[1] Task Force Grapple Air Plan Grapple Policy (IVA/146/2/160).

[2] AVM Oulton's book *Christmas Island Cracker* (Thomas Harmsworth Publishing, 1987) includes tables prepared in the AWRE setting-out details of UK nuclear weapon tests 1952-58.

[3] Brief for ACAS(OR)'s visit to AWRE on 26 Nov 57 (CMS 2749).

for the third phase of the Grapple tests, Grapple 'Y', which like its predecessor was positioned to the south-east of the island, as the squadron ORB recorded:–

"On the morning of April 28th the Grapple 'Y' nuclear weapon was released visually from Valiant XD824, flown by Sqn Ldr R N Bates and crew. The bomb exploded at its planned height and position, and the scientific records obtained therefrom confirm that the squadron once again accurately fulfilled its commitments in regard to this operation.

"The 'Grandstand' aircraft, Valiant XD822 flown by Sqn Ldr G M Bailey and crew, flew in the racetrack pattern with Valiant XD824, two thousand feet below the latter and approximately one mile behind. Valiants XD818 and 827 maintained an orbit some fifty miles from the ground zero position. Valiant XD818 was flown by Flt Lt T E B Chambers with the crew of Wg Cdr K G Hubbard, as the latter was positioned at Forward Control during the operation, acting as controller of the dropping aircraft. Valiant XD827 was flown by Sqn Ldr E J G Flavell and crew.

"Ground personnel not immediately required for the reception of aircraft on return were evacuated under the overall evacuation plan. Those remaining on essential duty were issued with protective clothing. All four aircraft took off on schedule, completed their details and landed on schedule".

During July 1958 the same four Valiants flew out to Christmas Island for Grapple 'Z' and in August the squadron ORB noted that "due to the decision to accelerate the entire dropping programme for political considerations, the intensity of the high-explosive drops in preparation for the nuclear drop has been increased". Two of the latter took place in September, when the ORB recorded:–

"The month of September brought to fruition all the training for Operation Grapple 'Z' with the dropping of two more nuclear weapons by the squadron. On the 2nd Sqn Ldr G M Bailey and crew in Valiant XD822 dropped the first device of the series. This weapon was the first to be dropped by ground-controlled radar. A 'Grandstand' aircraft on this occasion, Valiant XD818, was flown by Flt Lt S O'Connor and crew.

"On the 11th September Flt Lt S O'Connor and crew, in Valiant XD827, dropped a second nuclear device. This weapon was released on a visual attack. Sqn Ld H A Caillard and crew in Valiant XD824 flew as 'Grandstand'.

"Immediately after the second air drop the aircraft were prepared for the return trip to Wittering".

In commenting on the Grapple 'Z' bombing results in the ORB for September the CO, Wg Cdr Hubbard, said that

"The bombing task on Christmas Island showed a continued improvement in bombing accuracy and for the first time the Mk 7 radar was used as a blind bombing aid for a thermonuclear drop. The bombing error for the blind drop made by Sqn Ldr Bailey in XD822 was

95yd, and for the visual drop of the second weapon by Flt Lt O'Connor in XD827 was 260yd. Both excellent results from 46,000ft".

At the Atomic Weapons Trials Executive meeting on 15 May 1958 AVM Grandy reported that Grapple Y had been a success, for two major reasons: the weapons had been "delivered to the right place and exploded at the correct height, and the measurements obtained were gratifying to AWRE"[1]. In a minute of 3 June to CAS, his PSO had explained that there were two shots in Grapple Y, the first a test of the "trigger" for the second. If both were successful it would mean that "we are a long way down the road towards achieving a megaton bomb weighing no more than one ton which has a warhead immune to the R1 effect"[2].

When he reported on Grapple Z at the 16 October AWTE meeting AVM Grandy said that it too had been "mounted with success", commenting that though the weather had been favourable "it had proved necessary on the first drop to use blind bombing equipment despite some shortcomings of the gear"; and in a reference to the support flying side, remarking that "the Mk 1 Shackletons were on their last legs".

During 1959-60 the Christmas Island base was gradually reduced to a "minimum holding state", following a policy decision in mid-1959 that the United Kingdom would not carry out further nuclear tests, whether in or above the atmosphere, under water or under ground[3]. This decision was taken by the Prime Minister (Mr Harold Macmillan) on the basis of recommendations from the Nuclear Tests Policy Committee forwarded to him by the Minister of Defence. HQ Task Force Grapple was disbanded on 3 June 1960[4].

---

[1] Executive Cttee Mtgs file – IVA/146/2/161.
[2] CAS folder Operation Grapple – ID3/190/22(S) Pt 3.
[3] Minute from DGAW to DCAS, 10 Jul 59 in HQ Task Force Grapple file on Grapple policy – IVA/146/2/160. The Commander, Task Force Grapple, was then Air Cdre J F Roulston.
[4] AMQLR for Apr – Jun 60.

Thor and BMEWS

All photographs are Crown Copyright

Thor arrival: the last of the 60 Douglas IRBMs delivered to the RAF being unloaded from a C-124 Globemaster of the USAF Military Air Transport Service at North Luffenham on 26 April 1960. Like its 59 predecessors, it had been flown in from Santa Monica, California

A Thor being raised to the launch position at RAF Feltwell, where the first of Bomber Command's strategic missile squadrons, No 77 (SM) Sqn, was formed on 1 September 1958

Thor in the launch position, with squadron personnel in protective clothing

Routine Thor practice count-down, with oxidant loading taking place, and showing the support and assembly buildings and high-intensity lighting

The conspicuous "golf balls" at Fylingdales in Yorkshire, the ballistic missile early warning station officially declared operational on 17 September 1963, forming part of the USAF BMEWS system, with radars at Thule in Greenland and Clear in Alaska. Fylingdales significantly increased the warning time for the V-bomber force

Tracking radar - said to be able to "detect an object the size of a door over Siberia" and unceasingly searching - inside the sky-blue honeycomb of the 140ft "golf ball"

CHAPTER XV

MEGATON WEAPONS

Blue Steel had a megaton warhead, Red Snow, which was also used in the Yellow Sun Mk 2 free-falling bomb which the Vulcans and Victors carried. These megaton-range weapons[1] were the physical and operational outcome of the policy enunciated in the 1955 Statement on Defence and of the Operation Grapple tests at Christmas Island in the Pacific during 1957 and 1958. The Statement had said: "The United States Government have announced that they are proceeding with full-scale production of thermonuclear weapons. The Soviet Government are clearly following the same policy. . . . The United Kingdom also has the ability to produce such weapons. After fully considering all the implication of this step the Government have thought it their duty to proceed with their development and production". The first (interim) megaton bomb had been supplied to Bomber Command in March-April 1958. Its developed successor, Yellow Sun, has been described as "the keystone of the offensive deterrent policy".[2]

Clearly, Statements on Defence reflect policies which have been adumbrated, argued about and approved some considerable time previously, and the hydrogen bomb decision was no exception. In mid-1954 the Cabinet Defence Policy Committee had approved a recommendation by the Chiefs of Staff and as a result of this approval an Air Staff Requirement, ASR No OR1136, for a thermonuclear bomb was circulated on 15 July 1954 and issued on 6 June 1955.

This OR asked for a bomb which could be carried internally in Valiants, Vulcans and Victors; it was not to exceed 50in in diameter ("if it can be made smaller it will be an advantage") or 7,000lb in weight and it was to be in service in 1959.

When the Cabinet Committee on Defence Policy, under the chairmanship of the Prime Minister (Sir Winston Churchill) made its decision on 16 June 1954 to authorise hydrogen bomb production, it stipulated that no statement of Government policy in this matter should be made, and that work on the development of the bomb should be carried on as unobtrusively as possible.[3]

The Chiefs of Staff Memorandum which the Cabinet Committee had before it was based on a report by the Working Party on the Operational Use of Atomic Weapons, whose members were Sir Frederick Brundrett (chairman), Sir John Cockcroft, Sir William Penney, General Sir Frederick Morgan, the Deputy Chiefs of Staff and the Scientific Advisers to the three Service Ministries. Their report examined the technical and

---

[1] A yield of 500kr and upwards was classified as a megaton yield.
[2] RAE Progress Report of April 1957: see subsequent reference.
[3] Also that it was "desirable" that the cost should be concealed as far as possible.

military implications of undertaking the manufacture of hydrogen bombs in the UK. They came to the conclusion that there was a choice of three policies: to continue with the present programme (the 62in diameter Mk 1 Blue Danube weapon and a new 30in design), leaving H-bomb development to the Americans; to ask the Atomic Energy Executive to take special steps to increase the AWRE staff and to start work on the hydrogen bomb – "with the object of producing a test explosion in 1958 and a production of Service weapons thereafter" – and to continue with the present programme; or, to continue with the present programme and to add the hydrogen bomb, accepting the delays incurred by competition between the Mk 1, the 30in weapon and H-bombs.

The Working Party's report also concluded that it appeared to be possible for the UK to make a number of hydrogen bombs each year, that new capital expenditure of about £10m would be required and that possession of the H-bomb would "go a long way towards overcoming the difficult problems of terminal accuracy". It added that, whichever course were taken, there would be no effect upon the country's atomic weapon potential until after 1957; that an increase of stocks of H-bombs beyond a certain limited figure did not "confer any corresponding military advantage"; and that a test of a complete H-bomb "would involve certain practical and political problems and consideration of their solution should start at once".

In putting this report to the Cabinet Committee the Chiefs of Staff (whose memorandum was signed by Admiral of the Fleet Sir Rhoderick McGrigor, MRAF Sir William Dickson and Lt-Gen Sir Harold Redman, VCIGS) recalled that in their memorandum on UK Defence Policy they came to the conclusion that this policy must be "to possess the means of waging war with the most up-to-date nuclear weapons". They therefore made four recommendations: that immediate approval should be given to putting in hand a programme for the production of hydrogen bombs annually for five years, starting not later than 1959 and subject to review in the light of developments, and that if a programme were started now and sufficient staff recruited, a test of two weapons should be possible in 1958. Secondly, the present programme for the production of other types of nuclear weapon should proceed as planned – certainly until 1957, but should be subject to review. Thirdly, that the existing R&D programme for the improvement of the Mk 1 bomb and development of the smaller weapon should proceed as planned in addition to work on the hydrogen bomb. Fourthly, that special steps should be taken to enable the Atomic Energy Executive to increase staff at the AWRE, so as to achieve this programme.

The Committee on Defence Policy accepted all the CoS recommendations; it also suggested that an approach might be made to the Canadian Government for a free supply of tritium. (The Working Party Report had said that the AEA had considered the supplies of materials

240

and that "certain of them offer no difficulty, but tritium will involve special measures. To manufacture enough tritium for ten hydrogen bombs a year we would need a new pile. This could be built at Dounreay . . .".) The subsequent Cabinet decision of 26 July 1954 to approve the development of H-bombs[1] was as much a watershed in British military policy, in degree if not in kind, as the original Ministerial decision of 8 January 1947 to authorise R&D work on atomic weapons had been. As in the latter case, the UK had followed the USA (1945) and the USSR (1949) in achieving possession of nuclear bombs, so the UK would be following the USA (1952) and the USSR (1953) in the achivement of thermonuclear weapon potential. (The first US thermo-nuclear explosion was an experimental device in a surface burst, at Eniwetok on 31 October 1952; it was code-named Mike. The first Russian thermonuclear explosion – in the atmosphere – was on 12 August 1953, referred to by the Americans as Joe 4. In his book *The Advisors: Oppenheimer, Teller and the Superbomb*[2] Herbert York says that the Russians claimed that Mike was not a "real hydrogen weapon" – "only a very cumbersome and untransportable structure". Joe 4 was exploded on a tower. The first US air drop of a thermonuclear weapon was on 20 May 1956 at Bikini).

When Sir Winston Churchill made reference to the hydrogen bomb towards the end of 1954, in the Commons debate on the Queen's Speech on 1 December, he did not disclose the momentous decision that had been taken by his Government five-and-a-half months earlier. "The advance of the hydrogen bomb", he said,

"has fundamentally altered the entire problem of defence, and considerations founded even upon the atom bomb have become obsolescent, almost old-fashioned. Immense changes are taking place in military facts and in military thoughts. We have for some time past adopted the principles that safety and even survival must be sought in deterrence rather than defence . . . and this, I believe, is the policy which also guides the United States . . .".[3]

---

[1] The Cabinet "approved in principle the proposal that the current programme for the manufacture of atomic weapons . . . should be so adjusted as to allow for the production of thermonuclear bombs" (Cabinet CC(54) 53rd Conclusions).

[2] W H Freeman & Co. 1976.

[3] Commons Hansard, Col 176 at a Chiefs of Staff meeting on 22 Apr 54 (COS(54)45th Mtg) the CAS (Sir William Dickson) said it was essential that Britain should be able to maintain her influence through the possession of offensive power. For this reason it was of paramount importance "that we should develop the hydrogen bomb".

The Chiefs of Staff decided on 6 April 1955 to develop as first priority a weapon with a yield of about one megaton[1]. The Air Staff Requirement No OR 1136 for a Thermonuclear Bomb was accepted by the Ministry of Supply on 28 July 1955[2]. At the same time the MoS agreed to an in-service date of 1959. This was the start of the programme which led to the Grapple series of tests at Christmas Island in mid-Pacific during 1957 and '58, to the introduction of an "interim" megaton bomb (Violet Club) to RAF service in early 1958 and to the introduction of Yellow Sun Mk 1 – first British bomb with a yield in the megaton range – in 1960.

During March 1956 members of the OR4 and OR19 staffs saw various weapons under development at RAE Farnborough, among them Yellow Sun – drawings and a full-size wooden mock-up were shown to them. Their report[3] said that the first cases were being built; the bomb dimensions were 240in length, 48in diameter, and it had fixed fins – if larger fins were required they would need to be flip-out because of the restricted size of the Valiant bomb-bay – and an extremely blunt nose, "likely to keep the speed within the limits for ballistic stability". The spherical warhead weighed about 3,500lb, giving a completed weapon weight of about 6,500lb. The report added that the firing circuit was considered suitable for trials, though not yet suitable for Service use – more development was required; it would probably be used in the Grapple trials.

The suggestion that an interim megaton bomb might be put into service before Yellow Sun – which in fact occurred with the assembly of Violet Club at Wittering in March 1958 – was first made in October 1956, when it was related to the parallel development of the tactical atomic bomb Red Beard, which was also regarded as a Blue Danube replacement. DGAW[4] had suggested in a note of 11 October[5] that if the Buffalo and Grapple trials were successful, it should be possible to begin deliveries of a form of Red Beard warhead by about January 1958 and a form of megaton warhead at about the same time. If this could be done, it would mean that the warheads would be ready before the bomb bodies being designed to take them. The suggestion was, therefore, that it might be possible to provide interim designs of bomb bodies so that the RAF would have weapons earlier than at present planned. A note commenting on this idea[6] said that a decision on the megaton warhead was needed because apart from the political importance of having a megaton bomb as soon as possible there was the question of using two years' production of U.235, if this were not used until production of the first Yellow Suns in 1959[7].

---

[1] DCAS paper for the Air Council, March 1956, Review of the R&D Programme.
[2] Minute to DOR(A), Air Ministry, on 28 July 1955, ref 7/ARMT/4339(TS.121/1).
[3] OR19(a) of 21 March 1956 in AF/CMS29/64 Pt II file Megaton Bomb – OR1136.
[4] Director-General of Armament and Weapons, MoS.
[5] XY/109/02.
[6] CMS.2327/53.
[7] In Nov 56 an Air Staff Requirement for a Multi-megaton Bomb was drafted, with a yield of 3.5 megaton.

At a meeting held by DGAW on 24 October, attended by Air Ministry representatives, it was stated that if the Grapple results were successful the production of a form of megaton warhead could begin in August 1957. There would be three alternatives, all in a Blue Danube case – Green Granite, Green Bamboo or Orange Herald. The Air Ministry was asked to say whether the principle of having an interim megaton bomb in 1957 was agreed, and if so, which version was required.

A minute sent to DCAS on 2 November 1956 by ACAS(OR)[1], enclosing a copy of this note, suggested that from the political standpoint the RAF ought to accept the interim megaton bombs – probably only getting about ten before the Service weapon, Yellow Sun, was put into production[2].

In a report of April 1957 the Royal Aircraft Establishment described progress with the development of Yellow Sun, discussed the possible alternative warheads and pointed out that the weapon's in-service date depended upon the outcome of the Grapple trials. It said that "the Yellow Sun weapon to meet Air Staff Requirement OR1136 will provide the first British bomb having a yield in the megaton range; as such it is the keystone of the offensive deterrent policy. It is intended for carriage in the V-class bombers and will have a diameter of 48in and a length of approximately 20ft. The weight will be about 7,000lb.

"The weapon is being designed around the Green Bamboo warhead under development at AWRE. The means of making a warhead in this range of yield wholly safe in storage and transport has not been finalised, but all schemes of providing in-flight insertion of some part of the fissile material have been abandoned....

"Consideration has also been give to the alternative warheads Green Granite and Short Granite, which are being tested at Operation Grapple. Both are fission-fusion-fission types and differ only in that Short Granite is smaller and lighter. Neither warhead requires ENI (external neutron initiation). Nuclear safety is ensured by some form of in-flight-insertion.

"Although Yellow Sun is a free-falling ballistic bomb and is stabilised by conventional cruciform fins, it is unconventional in shape in that the nose is flat. This shape has been selected in order to keep the bomb as simple as possible. The nose shape has a high drag and it aids simplicity in two ways. First, it assists in stabilising the bomb, even from the highest altitude, and this permits the use of fixed fins of a span which can be accommodated in the bomb cell and thus avoids the complication of a flip-out tail. Secondly, it keeps the bomb at a subsonic speed in that part of the trajectory where an airburst is required; this greatly simplifies the task of fusing by barometric means . . .".

[1]CMS. 2327/53/ACAS(OR)/827 in file AF/CMS29/64 Pt II Megaton Bomb – OR1136.
[2]During this month (November 1956) an Air Staff Requirement for a Multi-Megaton Bomb was drafted. This became Air Staff Target OR1153, for nuclear warheads with yields of more than one megaton (AF/CMS 89/64 Pt I Multi-megaton Warheads – OR1153).

After referring to the division of responsibilities between RAE and AWRE the Yellow Sun description continued:–

"The Air Staff Requirement calls for the weapon to be in service in 1959. Although full warhead and nuclear safety information has not yet become available, it may still be possible to meet this date, but final information must not be delayed beyond August 1957.

"Preliminary investigation indicates that if after Grapple, Short Granite becomes the preferred warhead, no serious delay should occur, but Green Granite would require a larger and heavier weapon, so that much of the ballistic and fuzing work already well advanced would have to be repeated, and the in-service date would have to be set back at least nine months.[1]

In a Second Progress Statement on Yellow Sun, issued later that year,[2] RAE again referred to the warhead permutations and to the possibility of introducing an interim megaton weapon. It recalled that

"The Operational Requirement (OR1136 Issue 2) calls for the development of a megaton bomb, the type of warhead to be carried not being specified except that it shall be capable of use in both Yellow Sun and Blue Steel. The original requirement was for incorporation of the Green Bamboo warhead and much of the work done has been on the assumption that this warhead will be used. It has however been evident for some time that as a result of the Grapple trials another warhead might be preferred, and preliminary investigations were made at an early stage into the problems which would arise if one of the Granite type of warheads were chosen. These have been followed by further work, especially in connection with the possible use of Short Granite. The general position now is that an early decision as to type of warhead, and information on associated matters such as nuclear safety systems, is essential if development of the weapon is not to be held up".

Recalling that the OR had stated that the weapon was to be carried internally in Vulcans and Victors, the original requirement for carriage in Valiants having been cancelled – though they would continue to be used for development trials until other types became more readily available, the statement said that the aiming system would be NBS, as fitted in the V-bombers – no special development being needed for this, and added:

"Yellow Sun is being developed as a fully engineered weapon to meet the requirements of the OR. The provision of an interim megaton weapon only partially meeting these requirement is planned for introduction into service considerably earlier than Yellow Sun . . .".

Just over a fortnight after the Yellow Sun progress meeting (at which the RAE report was discussed) had been held on 16 July 1957, A/DDOR2

---

[1] Report ARM.NW 1/57 Royal Aircraft Establishment April 1957.
[2] Arm 3450/11/GS Royal Aircraft Establishment, Armament Dept, Bomber Armament Division, 5 Jul 1957.

minuted DDOps(B) on 2 August to say that the RAF had been offered a pre-production version of the bomb in the period June – September 1958 and to ask about the application of these weapons to the Vulcans and Victors which would be available at that time[1]. He added that he could see no reason why the policy which excluded the Valiant should be changed, and DDOps(B) expressed agreement in his reply, commenting that the high-yield weapons should always be reserved for the superior aircraft[2].

Clearly there was some doubt and indecision about the type of warhead to be used in Yellow Sun, and the removal of uncertainties depended mainly upon the results of the Grapple trials. In a paper dated 15 August, entitled Airborne Megaton Weapons, CA Ministry of Supply examined the development of the OR1136 bomb "in relation to the whole programme of airborne megaton weapons". His paper had been agreed by DGAW and AWRE, and the Air Staff had been closely consulted in its preparation[3].

Referring to the October 1956 proposal to introduce an interim megaton weapon[4], he said that

"the object was to give the RAF a megaton capability at the earliest possible moment. It was . . . proposed to base the interim weapon on one of the bombs to be dropped in Operation Grapple and it was stated that the date of introduction to the Service of Yellow Sun would not be affected by the interim missile. . . .

"The results of Operation Grapple were such that none of the rounds dropped was immediately applicable to the interim weapon, but AWRE were satisfied that the principles had been cleared sufficiently for them to offer various alternative warheads to the Air Staff for consideration. The Air Staff, largely on the basis of numbers which could be provided, chose a warhead similar in outside shape to Green Bamboo but having a yield of half a megaton . . . known as Green Grass."

He said that promised deliveries of interim weapons with this warhead were one weapon by the end of 1957, four by April 1958 and 16 by April 1959, and described the weapon as being

"based largely on the present Service weapon, Blue Danube, weighing of the order of 11,000lb with a diameter of 62in. The warhead will be Green Grass with firing circuitry developed for it by AWRE and used at Grapple. . . ."

CA Ministry of Supply commented in critical tones that "throughout the discussions on this interim megaton weapon the general approach has been that, in the interests of providing a megaton capability to the RAF at the earliest possible moment, the Service is prepared to sacrifice rigorous testing, proofing and clearance of the weapon and to introduce

---

[1] Wg Cdr G M Brisbane/Gp Capt Tait (CMS.2467/54 in AF/CMS29/64 Pt III).
[2] DDOps(B)/TS.1095/82A of 9 August 1957.
[3] AV/442/01 and AV/154/01 (draft copy in Megaton Bomb OR1136 – AF/CMS29/64 Pt III).
[4] By DD/AWRE at a meeting chaired by DGAW. See earlier reference.

special maintenance procedures in association with AWRE. Furthermore, the Air Staff were willing for the same reason to discount many of the provisions of OR1136".

Referring to "the weapon to OR1136 – Yellow Sun", he said that "development began in July 1955 of a megaton weapon to Air Staff Requirement OR1136. The bomb, which is 50in diameter and weighs 7,000lb, is being developed by RAE and is progressing well. The agreed forecast date of mid-1959 includes full testing and the normal clearance procedures. . . .

"A re-assessment of the Yellow Sun programme has recently been made primarily to examine the possibility of offering an earlier capability to the RAF in view of the successful progress of the development but also taking into account the desirability of switching-over to the Short Granite type of warhead if and when this is cleared by AWRE. This later type of warhead is very desirable because of the smaller amounts of fissile material needed . . .".

The Limited Approval stage of Yellow Sun with a Green Grass warhead and last-minute safety could be achieved by June 1958 and at that date a few weapons, representing the number of available warheads, could be supplied to the Service. The LA stage of Yellow Sun with a Short Granite type warhead and last-minute loading could be achieved by the end of 1958, provided that a decision to use this warhead were made in the first half of that year.

CA's paper then discussed the proposal that Yellow Sun development should be stopped in favour of the continued Service use of Violet Club – the Interim Megaton Weapon, "conceived to bridge the gap between availability of megaton warheads and completion of development of the weapon to OR1136". If this were agreed, he said, "Violet Club would be the only megaton weapon in service until Blue Steel became available in 1961/62".

Comparing the two weapons – for example pointing out that Yellow Sun was about 3,000lb lighter than Violet Club, thus extra fuel or equipment could be carried; and that YS had been engineered for reliability and met the requirements of OR1136, while VC had been accepted with the minimum of proof and clearance testing and fell short of OR1136 in many respects – CA recommended that development of Yellow Sun to the full provisions of OR1136 should continue; that in mid-1958 at the Limited Approval stage it should be given an initial introduction to the Service; and that the plan for the Interim Megaton Weapon, Violet Club, should proceed until Yellow Sun at the LA stage was available to the RAF. Thereafter, Service use of VC should be discontinued and the warheads transferred to Yellow Sun.

CA's proposal that Stage 1 Yellow Sun should be introduced into service in June 1958 was accepted, with its equipment implications; thus in September 1957 A/DOR(C) minuted D Air Arm:–

"As you know CA is proposing to the DRP (AES) that Stage 1 Yellow

Sun be introduced into service in June 1958. This bomb will be for carriage and release by Vulcans and Victors.

"We shall require by June 1958 at least 18 Vulcans fully modified and equipped. The Victor should be cleared, modified and equipped as soon as possible after the Vulcan, starting not later than September 1958. These numbers should increase at the rate of three a month until all Vulcans and Victors are modified.

"Would you please say whether production and clearance of ancillary equipment will meet this programme....[1]"

On the 27th DCAS minuted DGAW: "We are anxious to get megaton weapons into service as soon as we can. We most certainly think it worthwhile to have even as few as five by the time the Yellow Suns come along. At the same time, we are anxious to get Yellow Sun as soon as we can, because it does not have the serious operational limitations of Violet Club...."

On 28 October 1957 a meeting was held at St Giles' Court to discuss the introduction of Stage 1 Yellow Sun, the chairman[2] explaining that the bringing-into service of this weapon in the following year "had many far-reaching implications. Much of the equipment involved would not have reached the limited approval stage by the time it was necessary for orders to be placed with the contractors concerned. In order to ensure that equipment would be available in time it would be necessary for the MoS and Air Ministry finance branches to decide how equipment, which must be ordered in advance of the LA stage, could be covered financially". He stressed at the end of the meeting that everybody realised that it was necessary to work to a very tight schedule; all possible steps should be taken to prevent the programme slipping.

The Yellow Sun bomb which was to be introduced into Bomber Command service during 1958 differed from its predecessor Blue Danube in being smaller (7,000lb as against 10,000lb) and more powerful (in the megaton range as opposed to the original kiloton-range weapon)[3]. A demonstration and acceptance conference was held at RAE Farnborough on 19 December 1957, when its installation in a Vulcan was shown.

---

[1] LM CMS.2467/54 of 18 September 1957, in AF/CMS29/64 Pt III.

[2] ADAArm 3 – Minutes, Ref AY/344/02 in AF/CMS29/64 Pt IV – Megaton Bomb OR1136.

[3] The number of contractors involved was illustrated by a meeting to review progress on the project held at Hunting Engineering Ltd, Luton, on November 1957 – attended by representatives of the Ministry of Supply, Air Ministry, Kelvin Hughes, Portsmouth Aviation, Southern Instruments, Microcell Ltd, Langham Thompson Ltd and Hunting Engineering Ltd.

Early in 1958 the Armament Department of the Royal Aircraft Establishment issued one of its regular progress statements on Yellow Sun, describing aspects of the work for which it was responsible, as at mid-March.[1] It recalled that the last report had stated that in addition to main development work on a weapon to take the Green Bamboo warhead, some work was also in hand to cover the possibility that, as a result of Operation Grapple, a warhead of the Granite type might be preferred, continuing:–

"In the event, neither the Green Bamboo nor one of the Granite warheads was chosen – Green Grass, a pure fission warhead, being offered instead. This differed from Green Bamboo only in its internal fissile components. . . .

"Following the Grapple trials, the programme of work on Yellow Sun was reviewed and discussed with MoS Headquarters branches and the Air Staff. As a result, it was agreed to plan development on the basis of limited approval and limited introduction to service of the weapon with the Green Grass warhead by June 1958. This early (Stage I) weapon would have last-minute safety. The final (Stage II) weapon would reach the full approval stage by June 1959 and would meet the requirements for in-flight safety. . . .

"In consequence of these decisions, the main effort in the period under review has been devoted to development of the Stage I (Green Grass) weapon for carriage in Vulcan and Victor aircraft. The Valiant . . . has, however, continued to be used in development trials pending the availability of the other V-bombers. . . . Achievement of the Stage I weapon by June 1958 is dependent on the successful outcome of a closely integrated series of dropping trials with these aircraft. . . ."

During March 1958 the first interim megaton weapon for the RAF, Violet Club, was assembled at the Bomber Command Armament School at Wittering. On 24 February ACAS (OR) had written to the AOC in C Bomber Command as follows:–[2]

Interim Megaton Bomb – Violet Club

"I am directed to inform you that the first Violet Club which is now being assembled at Wittering is expected to be completed by the end of the month.

"A total of five of these weapons will be assembled on Bomber Command stations by July of this year, when deliveries of Yellow Sun should commence.

"Violet Club is still in some degree experimental and it will be subject to a number of serious handling restrictions. The extent of these . . . and their effect on operational readiness are still under discussion with the Ministry of Supply.

---

[1] Arm. 3450/11/GSS, 14 April 58.
[2] CMS. 2990/56/ACAS (OR) Kyle/Broadhurst.

"Until Violet Club has been formally cleared by the Ministry of Supply and it is possible to issue specific instructions on storage, handling and transport, the weapon is to remain exclusively in the custody and under the control of the Atomic Weapons Research Establishment.

"It is probable that some such arrangement will continue throughout the life of these weapons as it is intended to replace them with Yellow Sun as early as possible. This will be done as soon as sufficient aircraft are modified to carry Yellow Sun.

"I am to say that the operational limitations of Violet Club, particularly those affecting readiness, are serious. Nevertheless, it provides a megaton deterrent capability several months earlier than would otherwise have been possible".

By March 1958, therefore, Bomber Command had an interim megaton weapon capability; but its possession was hedged-about with a great many limitations and inhibitions. Described in the following terms –[1]

Bomb, A/c HE. 9,000lb – Violet Club

Violet Club is the megaton weapon which is about to be issued to the RAF to provide an interim solution to OR1136....

The weapon is based on the design of an experimental round prepared for Exercise Grapple, with the addition of a nuclear safety device. It consists of an implosion type warhead Green Grass ... and the firing circuit developed for the experimental round, assembled in the Blue Danube carcass ...

– it was subject to restrictions on assembly and carriage. On 21 February 1958 DAWDP, MoS, had written to DOR(C)[2] to say:

"In the course of the next few days we will produce a formal statement giving the conditions under which we recommend the RAF to receive Violet Club.

"The synopsis of these conditions is:–

(a) that Violet Club is basically an experimental weapon which is supplied to the RAF to provide, in emergency, the operational capability of delivering megaton attack. It will have to be prepared for operational use under the guidance of AWRE personnel

(b) because of its experimental nature certain restrictions must be applied to the method of handling this weapon; the most important of these are as follows:

    (i) that it is assembled on the RAF station from which it would be used

    (ii) its road transport is limited to that necessary to convey it from its assembly point to its storage building...."

---

[1] Paper for DOR(C), ref XY/246/01.
[2] XY/246/01.

In a minute to CAS on 3 March,[1] DCAS had said "I think you know that the interim megaton weapon (Violet Club) is rather delicate...."

In appearance, the bomb was much the same as its kiloton predecessor. A paper from DGAW to ACAS(OR)[2] said that it was externally "almost identical with Blue Danube" and that it possessed "the same ballistics, hence it can be used with the same bombing equipment suitably adjusted to cater for the required burst height...." Only a limited number were to be manufactured – five initially, according to the minutes of a meeting at AWRE on 27 February[3] – though more were made, for later in the year Nos 5 to 8 and No 11 were sent to Finningley and Nos 9, 10 and 12 to Scampton[4].

19 March 1958 was the date on which Bomber Command could claim possession of a megaton bomb, for a note on that day from DDOR2 to ACAS (OR) said that the latter "might care to announce [at the VCAS's meeting] that the first British interim megaton weapon is scheduled for completion tonight...."

The Operations Record Book for the Bomber Command Armament School at Wittering had recorded for 26 February 1958 that "owing to heavy falls of snow, a convoy from AWRE was stuck in a snow-drift at Wansford Hill at 1500hr. An officer from this unit was sent to investigate. At 1700hr the vehicle was still unable to be moved. Rations and bedding were sent to the convoy and an officer and a team of airmen were detailed to stand by throughout the night to give help if required. It was not until the following day that vehicles began using the A1. The convoy arrived at the Main Guard Room at 1200hr. Personnel were sent immediately for a meal. Unloading was commenced at 1400hr, when the convoy arrived at BCAS . . .".

This wintry scene may have marked the arrival of Britain's first megaton bomb, but the ORB does not disclose this, saying that "an Historic Document Label has been affixed to the appropriate file regarding stocks of weapons held". Unfortunately the subsequent location of this file[5] is unknown , but the BCAS ORB for August 1958 carried a reference to the second Violet Club, saying that on the 26th "the breakdown of store Violet Club No 2 commenced. This work, to incorporate modifications, is progressing satisfactory".

Service use of Violet Club was marked by its restriction to Vulcans and the subsequent transfer of warheads to Yellow Suns. A minute from DDOR2 to DAWDP on 9 July 1958, referring to this, said:–[6]

---

[1] DCAS 954/58.
[2] XY/246/01 of 3 Apr 58.
[3] XY/246/01.
[4] Minute DDOps(B) to A/DAWDP etc, 7 Nov 58 (CMS.3134/57).
[5] BCAS/TS.1/9/Air.
[6] CMS-2990/56.

Conversion of Violet Club to Yellow Suns

In view of the very small number of Violet Clubs being made available to the Service, and the difficulties of clearing the Victor for the carriage of this weapon, it has now been decided to limit its carriage to the Vulcan.

Vulcan aircraft modified to carry Yellow Sun are now being returned to service and it is desirable to transfer the warheads from all Violet Clubs to Yellow Suns as soon as possible, and at the same time to redeploy the weapons to Scampton and Finningley. . . .

This changeover was confirmed later in the year when it was stated[1] that

Bomber Command wish to get rid of Violet Clubs as soon as possible, but they are anxious to have a number of Yellow Suns in store before they do this. As the obvious time to change over is at the six-monthly inspections, it is suggested that Violet Clubs should start to phase out at the rate of about one a month from April or May, providing the Yellow Suns are not late.

The Violet Clubs are at Vulcan stations and will be dropped from Vulcan aircraft. . . .

Thus by the end of 1958, in its nuclear weapon armoury the V-force had its original kiloton weapons (Blue Danubes) and a small stock of megaton bombs (Violet Clubs – the interim version of OR1136, introduced to give a megaton capability at the earliest possible date, pending the introduction of Yellow Sun, and to be used only by Vulcan squadrons)[2]. These were all, of course, free-falling bombs.

The V-bomber force at that time consisted entirely of Mk 1 Valiants, Vulcans and Victors. As at 31 December 1958 there were 82 V-bombers – 54 Valiants, 18 Vulcans and ten Victors – in 12 squadrons (seven of Valiants, three of Vulcans and two of Victors).

---

[1] Minute from DDOR2 to DOR(C) of 20 Nov 58 (CMS.2990/56).

[2] ". . . the megaton weapon . . . issued to the RAF to provide an interim solution to OR1136 . . . based on the design of an experimental round prepared for Exercise Grapple, with the addition of a nuclear safety device. It consists of an implosion-type warhead Green Grass . . . and the firing circuit developed for the experimental round, assembled in the Blue Danube carcass . . .". (Paper for DOR(C), ref XY/246/01)

CHAPTER XVI

CO-ORDINATION OF RAF/USAF ATOMIC STRIKE PLANS; PROJECT "E" WEAPONS AND TARGET SELECTION

One of the results of possession by Britain of nuclear weapons, and of aircraft with which to deliver them, was closer co-operation with the Americans in this field – leading to the co-ordination of RAF/USAF nuclear strike plans, and the associated supply of American nuclear weapons to the Royal Air Force, under agreements reached in 1957. This meant that in any future conflict the Bomber Command V-force and Strategic Air Command would act in concert from the outset, unlike the informal day/night (US 8th Air Force/RAF Bomber Command) co-ordination of the Second World War, the two strategic bomber arms only operating formally together during the Combined Bomber Offensive of 1943–44.

The supply of atomic bombs to the UK by the United States had been discussed by the Cabinet Committee on Defence Policy, at the instance of the Minister of Supply (Mr Duncan Sandys) on 24 June 1954[1]. A minute from him to the Prime Minister (Sir Winston Churchill) had recorded a conversation during a recent visit to Washington with President Eisenhower in which the latter had "intimated that the Americans intended to allocate a certain number of atomic bombs to the RAF in the event of war", and that planning was going forward on that basis. The Minister of Supply had drawn attention to the need to ensure in advance that British aircraft were capable of carrying these weapons, and the President "had promised to discuss with General Twining, the Chief of the US Air Force, whether there were legal difficulties in disclosing the information" needed for this purpose.

S of S for Air (Lord De L'Isle and Dudley VC) said that General Twining had now informed CAS that the USAF were willing to make available to the RAF "the equipment and technical data . . . required to enable us to modify our aircraft so as to carry and deliver atomic weapons of American design". They were also ready to assist in the re-designing of RAF aircraft and with training, and contemplated "making arrangements of their own in the UK to store, assemble and load atomic weapons of American type for the RAF". These arrangements, he added, "were not dependent on any change in the present terms of the US Atomic Energy Act" – certain amendments to which were likely to be approved by Congress by mid-July, and the Americans might then be able to provide more extensive information. They had asked that any information received from them in the meantime should be treated with the greatest reserve, so as not to prejudice the progress of amending legislation through Congress.

---

[1] DP(54)4th Mtg – Confidential Annex.

After the Minister of Supply had said that US-designed atomic weapons "differed considerably from British ones" and a "considerable range" of modifications would be needed, the Committee took note that the Prime Minister would "take occasion during his forthcoming visit to Washington to put on record his appreciation" of the US offer, invited S of S to "concert with the Minister of Supply the terms of a draft letter to President Eisenhower about the offer of technical information to adapt British aircraft to carry US atomic bombs" and agreed that "detailed arrangements" for such modifications "should be worked out in consultation with the American authorities through Service channels".

The moves towards co-ordination of nuclear strike plans had their origin, on the British side, late in 1954 in a shrewd observation by the then Minister of Defence (Mr Harold Macmillan). The Air Minister (Lord De L'Isle and Dudley VC) had written to him on 14 December about the size of the medium bomber force, saying that he was going to propose that a front line of 240 was "the right figure".

In his reply, on 23 December, Mr Macmillan asked several pertinent questions – the first three of which were: what would be the tasks of the force in the initial phase of war? how would these tasks be integrated with those of the US Strategic Air Command and of the tactical air forces under Saceur? and what size force would be needed to carry out these tasks? The second of these questions, in so far as it concerned the V-force, was taken up by the Air Staff at a meeting a month later. At this meeting, held on 25 January 1955, VCAS (Air Chf Mshl Sir Ronald Ivelaw-Chapman) linked up the factors of American reluctance to release atomic information with the time-scale for the viability of the V-force. Agreeing with the need for co-ordinating the latter's use in war with SAC, he wanted an assurance that a request for release of information was likely to be acquiesced-in by the Americans. What was the biggest stumbling-block – the fact that the V-force was unlikely to be fully built up for at least two years, or the McMahon Act?[1] A point made in discussion by ACAS(Ops) (AVM L F Sinclair GC) was that from contacts he and the CAS had made during their visit to the US early in 1954 it seemed clear that while the Pentagon was ultra security-conscious, General Lemay[2] might be prepared to release information on a need-to-know basis – subject to prior Government-to-Government agreement in principle. A stronger case could be made were the V-force immediately available.

VCAS thought there was a strong case to be made on the time factor: the V-force would start to build up in March 1955 and would reach full strength during 1958; detailed RAF–USAF planning, following the disclosure of information by the Americans, would take a year to complete and need to be phased-in during the build-up – so it was

---

[1] Signed by President Truman on 1 August 1946 and designed to secure a US monopoly of atomic weapons until international control could be achieved.
[2] Commander, SAC, from 19 Oct 48.

important to have the information as quickly as possible. In view of the unique position occupied by General Lemay as Commander, SAC, and of his personal relationship with the US President, it would be best if the approach were made at Prime Minister–President level. A paper should be drafted for CAS, who might be prepared to say that he would follow-up an approach by a visit to General Lemay.

During September 1955 CAS visited the United States, and a brief written for him, on co-ordination of strategic air operations, set out clearly what it was hoped to achieve. Its opening paragraph said that "the primary aim of the defence policy of the United Kingdom is to prevent war" and that "the main instrument for achieving this aim lies in the nuclear capability, together with the means of delivery, which is possessed by the United Kingdom and the United States alone. We should achieve a closer association with the United States world-wide in the field of defence strategy. This is particularly important in strategic air operations, where Bomber Command and the Strategic Air Command will be attacking components of the same vast target complex. It follows that unless there is a full exchange of information and a co-ordinated plan of attack, wasteful overlapping and dangerous omissions will result".

The talks which MRAF Sir William Dickson had in Washington were with his opposite number in the USAF, General Nathan F Twining, and the co-operation which eventually resulted was initiated at a meeting between senior officers of the two air forces at the Air Ministry in August of the following year. This was referred to by Sir William's successor as CAS, Air Chf Mshl Sir Dermot Boyle, in a note for the CoS Committee which they considered at the beginning of 1957 and which set out in detail the proposals for co-ordinated strike plans and for the supply of atomic weapons to the RAF in the event of a general war. (It is worth noting that training for LABS techniques had already gone on, DOR(C) (Air Cdre W R Brotherwood) informing the Head of S6 on 31 October 1956 that 15 officers from squadrons, Groups and Command HQ of Bomber Command and 2nd ATAF had "done a course under USAF instructors on loft and toss bombing and on the qualities and handling of the Mk 7 weapon which is to be carried by the Canberra", adding: "these...officers constitute our instructors for the future". In his letter, which was about a public announcement – or not – on Project E, DOR(C) went on to say that groundcrew would begin training in handling and bombing-up techniques, and that the bomb-carrier manufacturer (M L Aviation Ltd) would be delivering carriers to MUs with the Aero 61B Rack – "the only item likely to give the show away" in terms of security.

Sir Dermot reminded his fellow Chiefs of Staff that he and his predecessors had "been trying for some years to persuade the USAF to begin joint planning for the use of the British and American strategic air forces. Until recently, little progress had been made, mainly because the Americans were not willing to discuss the subject with us until we had a medium bomber force in existence. However, earlier this year the Americans, having realised that the V-bomber force was becoming a reality, sent a team of senior USAF officers to London, to discuss with the Air Ministry the co-ordination of the nuclear strike plans of the USAF and RAF and, also, the provision of American nuclear weapons for the RAF in the event of war. At this meeting[1], outline arrangements for putting these measures into effect were approved, together with a concept of Allied nuclear operations and an outline plan of action for these operations.

"The United States Secretary of Defense and the Joint Chiefs of Staff have now approved these arrangements. Copies of the documents, as agreed by the US authorities, are attached to this note. . . .[2]"

The documents to which CAS referred were three Annexes: the first, Terms of Reference for measures to furnish the Royal Air Force with United States atomic weapons in the event of general war and to co-ordinate the atomic strike force of United States Air Forces with the Royal Air Force"; the second, "Concept of Allied atomic air operations"; and the third, "Brief plan of action".

CAS went on to say that "in his covering letter informing me of American agreement (Annex D), the Chief of Staff of the USAF has stated that he would welcome early notification that these documents have been approved by the appropriate UK authorities. When this approval has been received, he expects that the Joint Chiefs of Staff will direct action to be taken to implement the terms of reference. . .".

Annex 'A' dealt with the co-ordination of atomic strike plans by the two air forces and with the supply of US atomic weapons to the RAF. It drew a clear distinction between that part of the RAF committed to Nato, in which case co-ordination was to be the responsibility of the US C in C Europe and Saceur; and the non-committed part, in which case responsibility was to be that of the RAF and USAF. Operational plans for the employment of all RAF "atomic capable forces" were to be co-ordinated by the US "unified and specified commanders and approved by the Joint Chiefs of Staff". As to the weapons, these were to be kept in USAF custody on RAF operational bases, the RAF providing "physical facilities and normal base support" and being responsible for "operational delivery and loading capability[3]."

---

[1] Held 15/16 August 1956. Unfortunately no record has been traced, though on 13 Dec 56 ACAS (Ops) said in a minute to PS/VCAS that "as regards co-ordination with SAC the latest development was the discussions, under the chairmanship of DCAS, held with a USAF team last August. You have a copy of the minutes of these discussions". Added in pencil is a pointer to the word 'copy' and the comment, "Flagged in 'Encircle' folder attached". It has not proved possible to locate this folder. The ACAS(Ops) minute is in the US/UK Strike Plans folder in 240/16 Co-ord of US/UK Strategic Bomber Force.

[2] These papers are in the folder, Co-ordination of RAF/USAF Nuclear Strike Plans – AHB 1D6/R13, Pt 1.

[3] US atomic weapons were supplied to V-bomber and Canberra squadrons.

Annex 'B', dealing with the concept of Allied atomic air operations, stated the basic premise that in a general war atomic weapons would be used from the outset. It considered that such a war would consist of two phases – an initial one of comparatively short duration, "characterised by an intensive exchange of atomic blows", and a subsequent one of indeterminate duration – a continuation of the initial one, at reduced atomic intensity. It put the case for a co-ordinated RAF/USAF bomber effort by saying that the destructive power of megaton-yield weapons made survival "an issue of primary consideration" – thus it was necessary for the Allied retaliatory atomic air offensive "to be conducted with maximum possible speed and effectiveness, and with its weight of effort unwaveringly exerted against the highest priority targets". In other words, for quick reaction by the two air forces, operating according to predetermined plans which would avoid overlapping and make the best possible use of available resources for successful retaliation.

Annex 'C', the 'Brief of Plan of Action', said that the general strategy of the counter air offensive would begin with "heavy co-ordinated attacks against airfields, logistic facilities, control centres and command headquarters". The resulting contraction of this complex of facilities would force concentrations of surviving enemy aircraft to regroup on remaining airfields, which would then be attacked, "to exploit the vulnerability of such concentrations". Operations would be co-ordinated "to the maximum extent possible" with reconnaissance, fighter, electronic countermeasures and other air support.

In his letter of 12 December 1956 (Annex 'D') General N F Twining, Chief of Staff, USAF, said that "except for minor changes" the annexes were the same as those agreed to by RAF and USAF representatives at their London conference in August.

A paper prepared for the Chief of the Air Staff in advance of the CoS Committee meeting to consider these Anglo-American proposals said[1] that "the arrangements for co-ordination of strategic and tactical nuclear operations . . . are the most important development in recent years in planning for the UK strategic bomber force. They represent further evidence that the United States regards this country, both militarily and economically, as a good investment. This is also shown by the tentative proposal to let the UK have a 1,500-mile ballistic missile, probably in about 1959[2], and the apparent American willingness to make as few difficulties as possible about stockpiling warheads for this missile and for Corporal"[3]. The writer went on to say that he thought it could be justifiably claimed that the major factor leading to these developments

---

[1] ACAS(P), 7 Jan 57.

[2] This was Thor, deployed by RAF Bomber Command 1958–63: see chapters XVII and XXI. American proposals for this deployment were first made at the beginning of 1957.

[3] A surface-to-surface guided weapon.

was "the emergence, even on a small scale, of the UK as a nuclear power with a strategic striking force of its own".

The Chiefs of Staff, at their meeting on 8 January 1957[1], agreed that CAS's paper should be forwarded to the Minister of Defence, inviting him to obtain Ministerial approval of it; and they added two reservations. One was that, provided Ministerial approval was obtained, it should be made clear, when informing the US of UK agreement to the three Annexes, that this agreement "in no way prejudiced our right to determine the future size of the V-bomber force and the number of weapons we should produce". Secondly, the Chiefs of Staff said that, in forwarding this report to Ministers, it should be made clear that co-ordination of plans in no way implied "relinquishment of our national control" of the RAF bomber force.

At the end of January the Minister of Defence (Mr Duncan Sandys) wrote to his opposite number in Washington, Mr Charles Wilson, whose reply on receipt of the approved proposals made it clear that the US Government's agreement to co-ordinated strike plans and the supply of weapons stopped short of the release of any atomic energy information. His letter, marked Restricted Data – Atomic Energy Act of 1954 and dated 1 February, said:–

"I have received your letter of January 30, 1957, with respect to the letter and enclosures dated 12 December 1956 from the Chief of Staff, United States Air Force, to the Chief of the Air Staff of the United Kingdom.

"I agree that it is appropriate for you to authorise the Chief of the British Air Staff to discuss with the Chief of Staff of the United States Air Force and with General Lauris Norstad[2] arrangements for implementing measures:

(1)   to furnish the Royal Air Force with United States atomic bombs in the event of general war; and

(2)   to co-ordinate the atomic strike plans of the United States Air Force with the Royal Air Force.

"You will understand, of course, that with respect to measure No 1 the provisions of United States legislation must govern and that the United States cannot engage in a commitment to transfer custody of such weapons to the Royal Air Force other than by Presidential decision in strict accordance with his constitutional and legislative authority."

Following this correspondence, the chairman of the CoS Committee (MRAF Sir William Dickson) wrote to CAS on 5 February explaining that the Minister of Defence had himself conveyed the UK Government's approval of the proposals (in his letter of 30 January

---

[1] COS (57) 3rd meeting. The Chiefs of Staff had themselves subsequently endorsed, at their meeting on 23 Sep 57 (COS (57) 72nd Mtg), a Strategic Target Policy for Bomber Command, as expressed in a paper by the CAS (Air Chf Mshl Sir Dermot Boyle); and at a later meeting, on 16 Oct 57 (COS (57) 224), their discussions took account of negotitions to furnish the RAF with US atomic bombs in the event of general war, and to co-ordinate the USAF nuclear strike plans with those of the RAF. See file Strategic Target Policy – Bomber Command (AHB ID9/90/22).

[2] Nato Supreme Commander.

1957 to Mr Wilson) and saying that "you are now free to write yourself to General Twining explaining how this happened, and discuss with him and Saceur arrangements for implementing these proposals"[1].

The supply of American atomic bombs to the RAF materialised as Project 'E', which was first discussed by DCAS (Air Mshl G W Tuttle) with two USAF representatives – Major-General R T Coiner, Jr, Assistant Deputy Chief of Staff/Operations for Atomic Energy, and General Wiesanand of the Third Air Force – on 5 March 1957 following an exchange of messages between CAS and General Twining[2]. Project 'E' was in two parts. One applied to RAF Canberras based in the UK and in Germany and assigned to Saceur, equipped to carry US weapons and with crews trained in their use, subsequently applying to Valiants which replaced the UK-based Canberras[3]. The second part applied to arrangements for supplying US weapons to the V-force.

Similar conditions applied to both parts of Project 'E'. The weapons were delivered by USAF transport aircraft; they were not assembled and the fissile material was separated from the HE content in special canisters. Weapons were maintained in storages built under RAF arrangements, the fissile material being stored separately. If it became necessary to assemble weapons for delivery to the RAF, they would be incapable of causing a nuclear explosion until positively armed by crews – a complicated procedure requiring more than one crew member. Training was done with dummy weapons[4].

The supply of atomic weapons and co-ordination of nuclear strike plans were among items discussed at the Bermuda Conference between President Eisenhower and Prime Minister Macmillan in March 1957, as was the provision of IRBMs. This conference was the first meeting between the two leaders since Mr Macmillan had become Prime Minister, and it marked the beginning of a renewal of mutual confidence between the USA and UK, following the deterioration of relations at the time of the Suez operations in October–November 1956. In a letter of 23 March 1957 replying to the Prime Minister's notes on nuclear weapons for the RAF and about Project 'E' the President commented:

"With respect to the item 'Nuclear Weapons for RAF Bombers' I have a couple of additions to the phraseology submitted, merely to make certain that the meaning of the paper conformed to the requirements of United States law. The item as revised would read as follows:

'The United States Government welcome the agreement to co-ordinate the strike plans of the United States and United Kingdom bomber forces, and to store United States nuclear weapons on RAF airfields

---

[1] WFD/94.
[2] DCAS 1336/57, 18 Mar 57. CAS had written to the USAF Chief of Staff on 11 Feb 57: see Co-ordination of RAF/USAF Nuclear Strike Plans ID6/R.13A, pt 1.
[3] Memorandum to accompany the Air Estimates 1959–60.
[4] Brief prepared for the Air Minister (Mr H Fraser), 1 Jun 59.

under United States custody for release subject to decision by the President in an emergency. We understand that for the present at least these weapons will be in the kiloton range. The United Kingdom forces could obviously play a much more effective part in joint strikes if the United States weapons made available to them in emergency were in the megaton range, and it is suggested that this possibility might be examined at the appropriate time.'"

The President continued by saying,

"With respect to the item 'Nuclear bomb release gear for RAF bombers'[1], I agree of course that you shall probably have to make some statement in order to prevent speculation in the press that might prove not only inaccurate but damaging. However, as I explained to you verbally, the United States would prefer not to be a party to a public statement which might give rise to demands upon us by other Governments where we should not be in a position to meet the requests. Consequently I suggest the possible adequacy of a unilateral statement by yourself or by the British Defence Minister to the effect that Canberras are now being equipped to carry atomic bombs[2]."

Following this top-level agreement on co-ordination of nuclear strike plans and the supply of US atomic weapons to the RAF, there was considerable staff discussion during 1957 on a Memorandum of Understanding between the RAF and USAF, negotiated by DCAS (Air Mshl G W Tuttle) at a meeting in Washington on 21 May 1957[3].

The main concern, on the RAF side, was that the Memorandum should be divided into two parts – one dealing with the supply of American nuclear weapons, the other with the co-ordination of atomic strike plans. CAS (Air Chf Mshl Sir Dermot Boyle) explained the RAF standpoint in a letter to the USAF Chief of Staff (General Thomas D White – who had succeeded General Twining) on 24 July, also recalling[4] previous correspondence, when he said that

"In the letters exchanged between Mr Sandys and Mr Wilson on 30 January and 1 February 1957, our two Governments agreed to discussions between us (and also between General Norstad and myself) on the arrangements for implementing measures:–

(a)   to furnish the Royal Air Force with United States atomic weapons in the event of general war; and

(b)   to co-ordinate the atomic strike force of the United States Air Force with the Royal Air Force.

---

[1] Equipment had to be designed and developed to enable RAF jet bombers to carry and deliver American nuclear bombs.

[2] S of S's Memorandum accompanying the 1958–59 Air Estimates, published in February 1958, said that "Canberras in the Second Tactical Air Force and in Bomber Command are being given a nuclear capability".

[3] In view of the Eisenhower–Macmillan talks earlier that year it seems odd that on 16 June 1960 the Prime Minister should have asked the Minister of Defence whether there were "any plans with the Americans for the sharing of bombs . . . should the situation deteriorate" (ID9/194/4 Blue Steel).

[4] CAS.2033/57.

"Mr Wilson drew special attention to the United States legislative difficulties which were bound to affect the arrangements for the first of these two measures."

CAS then went on to discuss the proposed change. "From my point of view", he said,

"it would greatly help from the constitutional and security aspects if you could agree to the Memorandum of Understanding being divided into two parts directly related to the two measures covering the agreement in principle between our two Governments. Morever, there is a practical point in this in that, whilst the Royal Air Force V-bombers already have a growing nuclear capability with United Kingdom weapons, on which planning co-ordination between our two air forces could now go ahead, it will, I think, be at least a year before any V-force aircraft are modified to take United States weapons[1].

"Against this background, I have had the Memorandum of Understanding divided into two parts but so far as possible have retained the original wording. It would greatly help me if you could agree to a division on these lines – subject, of course, to any amendments which are necessary to reflect your special points.

"I am sorry to have to put this back to you but I would hope that the alterations do not pose any major problems from your point of view. . . ."

They did not, in fact, as was clear from the reply by General White of 8 August in which he said:

"I am in agreement with the Memorandum of Understanding as enclosed in your 24 July letter and am forwarding it to the Commander-in-Chief, Strategic Air Command, as the basis of further discussions with the Bomber Command."

This Memorandum, together with the Thor Agreement of 1958, form the bases of RAF/USAF – Bomber Command/SAC collaboration during the existence of the V-force.

The C in C Strategic Air Command said in his reply that when he visited the Pentagon in the near future he looked forward to discussing with the Chief of Staff how co-operation between SAC and Bomber Command could best proceed, and suggested that the two Command Headquarters should get into touch with each other direct, a procedure with which CAS expressed agreement when he wrote again to General White on 11 September[2].

These RAF/USAF discussions on the co-ordination of nuclear strike plans inevitably impinged on the formulation of strategic target policy for Bomber Command, a note on which by the CAS was discussed by the Chiefs of Staff Committee on 23 September[3]. It agreed to submit it to

---

[1] Owing to the modification programme previously referred to.
[2] Correspondence in ID9/240/3 (Pt 3) US/UK Strike Plans.
[3] COS (57) 72nd meeting.

the Defence Committee, emphasising the "likely contingency" of retaliatory action with the USAF. On 21 October DCAS (Air Mshl Sir Geoffrey Tuttle) sent a copy of this CoS-approved paper – Strategic Target Policy for Bomber Command – to the AOC in C (Air Chf Mshl Sir Harry Broadhurst), saying that it had not yet received Ministerial sanction but was sent so that "you may proceed with discussions with Strategic Air Command and also with your own operational planning".

On 20 November the chairman of the CoS Committee (MRAF Sir William Dickson) informed the Chiefs of Staff that the Minister of Defence (Mr Duncan Sandys) had decided not to submit the paper to the Defence Committee at the present juncture – that it was better to wait until more was known of American plans from the joint Air Force talks which were taking place, but in the meantime he approved the paper as the basis for planning. In a subsequent progress report to the Chiefs of Staff, circulated on 20 May 1958, CAS said that two meetings had been held between SAC and Bomber Command with Air Ministry representatives. Examination of separate BC and SAC plans had shown that every Bomber Command target was also on SAC's list and that both Commands had doubled-up strikes on their selected targets to ensure success. A fully integrated plan had been produced, taking into account BC's ability to be on target several hours before the main SAC force from bases in the USA. Under the combined plan, the total strategic air forces disposed by the Allies were sufficient to cover all Soviet targets.

It was in mid-1958 that co-ordination arrangements between SAC and Bomber Command were discussed and implemented, a Co-ordination Conference at Bomber Command HQ (19–22 May) comparing the two Commands' operational plans in detail – including targeting, routeing and timing[1]. As a result (in the words of the report) "potential conflicts were isolated and opportunities for mutual support . . . explored". One purpose of the conference was "to complete the co-ordination of atomic strike plans and combat operations applicable to the period 1 July 1958 to 30 June 1959"; another, "to review the status and progress of the support programme for the supply of USAF nuclear weapons for the strike forces of RAF Bomber Command not committed to Nato". Its main recommendation was that approval be granted to the co-ordinated strike plans.

Subsequently the AOC in C Bomber Command (Air Chf Mshl Sir Harry Broadhurst) visited SAC HQ at Omaha on 4 June to confer with the C in C (General Thomas S Power), the main purpose of his discussions there being – as he reported in a letter to VCAS (Air Mshl Sir Edmund Hudleston) on the 25th –

"to prepare a co-ordinated nuclear strike plan, based on the target directive contained in COS(57)244 dated 16 October 1957, which could

---

[1] Bomber Command/Strategic Air Command Co-ordination Conference Report and Recommendations 19–22 May 1958 in ID9/240/16, Pt 3 US/UK Strike Plans.

be put into effect should combined nuclear retaliation by Bomber Command and Strategic Air Command ever be required. The plan, approved by C in C SAC and myself, is applicable to the period 1 July 1958 to 30 June 1959, is targeted to utilise stocks of British, and after October 1958 USAF, nuclear weapons for the Medium Bomber Force, and includes targets for the first Thor squadron expected to be operational in January 1959 . . .".

Thus, in this practical embodiment of RAF/USAF nuclear strike plans, co-ordination of those plans and the supply of US nuclear weapons to the RAF were inextricably linked[1].

VCAS's reply, on 7 July, presaged some of the difficulties which were to occur over the actual supply of US nuclear weapons, when he commented:

"I note your remarks concerning the custody of US weapons. I shall be very interested to see General Power's proposals, since we have been having some difficulty in the sense of undue restrictions over the access to LABS-fitted aircraft.

"I think the key to the problem is in the interpretation of 'release for employment'. General Blanchard [Commander, 7th Air Division] has agreed verbally with us here that should the need arise to move bombs/aircraft in earnest to dispersal his interpretation would be satisfied if one of his representatives accompanied them. However, it will be better to have the matter tidied up officially by Power"[2].

Project 'E' Weapons

Project 'E', which was the part of RAF/USAF collaboration relating to the V-bombers and the Canberras, lasted until early 1965 as far as Bomber Command were concerned (in RAF Germany it continued until 1969). In the TBF at Marham it went on until the Valiants were withdrawn from service in January 1965, but in the Vulcan/Victor force it came to an end in March 1962. The reasons for its termination in the V-force were twofold: British megaton weapons had begun to be supplied to the RAF in 1958 and became increasingly available after the introduction of Yellow Sun Mk 2 in 1961; and the strict US custodial arrangements made it difficult for the V-bombers to employ dispersal techniques with Project 'E' weapons. This difficulty had early been appreciated; in mid-1958 the AOC in C Bomber Command had had his attention drawn to

"the question of dispersing, in time of tension, that part of the V-force allocated to support Project 'E'[3]. It is clear that refusal to release or delay in releasing the American weapons could make it impossible to

---

[1] Correspondence in ID9/240/16, Pt 3.

[2] See later comments on Project 'E' weapons and V-bomber dispersal.

[3] Acting DD Bomber Ops (Wg Cdr A R Scott)/AOC in C Bomber Command, 13 June 1958.

disperse these aircraft with the rest of Bomber Command . . ."[1].

This point was made at the highest level early the following year when CAS (Air Chf Mshl Sir Dermot Boyle) wrote to the CoS, USAF (Gen Thomas D White), on 16 March 1959 about "one problem" which was "fundamental to our joint plans" and arose directly from "the regulations governing the custody of US atomic weapons allocated for the use of Bomber Command". These meant that these weapons could "neither be flown to dispersal airfields", nor could Bomber Command aircraft "become airborne carrying them under a precautionary landing concept". The result was to frustrate the Command's dispersal and alert plans, and CAS asked the Chief of Staff "how best we might resolve this situation".

In his reply (31 March) Gen White said he had instructed his staff "to seek a method by which your 'V' force could disperse with US weapons". He visualised a method "not involving a transfer of custody but rather temporary possession by the RAF under specific conditions and for specific purposes"; but he warned that "approval of any such interpretation" was "beyond the purview of the Department of Defense".

Subsequently an appreciation of the future of Project 'E'[2] recalled that it had "become technically effective from 1 October 1958, based on the arming of 72 aircraft at three stations with US Mk 5 weapons. The major parts of the SSAs at Honington, Marham and Waddington have been modified to conform to US technical criteria and are exclusively occupied by USAF; the necessary aircraft modification programme is nearing completion; carrier, control, training and handling equipment is being delivered".

What General White said about any change in the custody arrange-ments for US weapons being "beyond the purview of the DoD" implied that a change in US law would be required. As the Appreciation of the Future of Project 'E' put it: "US law requires that US personnel retain physical possession and custody of all US nuclear weapons until authority to release them is received from US Joint Chiefs of Staff, through HQ Strategic Air Command. Bomber Command cannot guarantee to implement their dispersal and alert plans with this element of the MBF unless the US Atomic Energy Act is amended to permit timely release of weapons, or some other effective formula".

There was another operational disadvantage:–

"Because the SSAs on three Class I airfields are committed to Project 'E', UK weapons must be stored on the remaining Class I airfields, and in depots. In consequence, UK weapons are not disposed in the best locations to meet the unilateral strike plan, in which aircraft from 'E' stations must be used. Moreover, Yellow Sun weapons must be held at

---

[1] This and subsequent correspondence are in AF/CMS 255/64, Pt II 'E' Weapons – V-force – Policy.
[2] An Appreciation of the Future of Project 'E' (V-force), by D of Ops (B & R), 8 May 1959.

greater concentration than is desirable from safety aspects."

This D of Ops (B & R) paper suggested that there were alternative courses of action – to continue Project 'E' until 1961/63, or to make a formal approach to the USAF to end or reduce the project. It concluded that the RAF should propose its progressive termination.

Project 'E' had been discussed politically on 4 May 1959 at a meeting between the Secretary of State for Air (Mr G R Ward) and his US opposite number the Secretary for Air (Mr James H Douglas) when the former explained the problem with which the RAF was faced over its bomber dispersal plans "in relation to the movement of Project 'E' weapons" and Mr Douglas "undertook to pursue the matter further with the State Department"[1].

At that time the Project 'E' situation was complicated by the possibility that the RAF would be offered USAF Mk 28 bombs (1,900lb HC) instead of, or in addition to, Mk 15/39 bombs (7,500lb HC). Copies of a feasibility study of equipping the V-bombers to carry the former were circulated in May[2] and subsequently DDOps (B) was asked several questions about it[3] – which aircraft would be required to carry it; in which configuration it would be required; would there be a requirement for dual or multiple carriage; and if it were accepted, would the requirement for the Mks 5[4] and 15/39 weapons be cancelled. Matters reached a higher level when on 4 August 1959 A/ACAS (Ops) (Air Cdre P G Wykeham) minuted VCAS (Air Mshl E C Hudleston) to say that decisions were urgently required on two aspects of Project 'E' – its future status and the programme for phasing it out, and the development of a capability for the medium bomber aircraft to carry a multi-megaton 'E' weapon (the Mk 15/39).

He said that the custody requirement of American law imposed a serious limitation on the usefulness of Project 'E' to the MBF. 'E' weapons could not be dispersed and there was no guarantee that they would be made available in time for the force to get airbone. Three of the Bomber Command SSAs were occupied by these weapons; another station (Scampton) had no nuclear-weapon storage on the airfield; and the only stations on which UK weapons could be held alongside the aircraft were Wittering, Cottesmore and Finningley. "If we consider the case of an enemy attack with a very short period of warning", he commented, "any delay in releasing 'E' weapons could mean that less than half of the MBF could be rapidly brought to readiness".

He advised that UK stocks of both megaton and kiloton weapons were expected to match aircraft by the end of 1959, so that phasing-out of Project 'E' could theoretically start at that time. Because 'E' weapons were more powerful than the equivalent UK ones, the total power of the

[1] AHB file Organisation and Establishment of Thor Units (ID3/90/9/7, Pt 1).
[2] LM DDOR2 (Gp Capt A J M Smyth)/PS to DCAS and others, 11 May 1959.
[3] By DDOR2 – minute of 18 June 1959.
[4] See Appendix 9 for details of US nuclear weapons supplied to the RAF under Project 'E'.

strike would be reduced, but this factor had to be weighed against doubts concerning the release of 'E' weapons.

As to the Mk 15/39 weapons, A/ACAS (Ops) commented that despite a number of approaches at various levels, there was still no assurance that these would be delivered to Bomber Command. In any event they would have the same disadvantages, in respect of weapon release and dispersal, as the other 'E' weapons. If it were decided to terminate Project 'E' fairly soon, there would be little point in proceeding with development to give the medium bombers this capability, since production of the necessary equipment was expected to take about nine months after the confirmation of orders.

He concluded that a lack of decisions concerning Project 'E' was holding up planning, particularly in respect of nuclear weapon storage, while the development effort being devoted to the Mk 15/39 suspension equipment might be wasted.

However, a meeting held by VCAS on 7 August decided that Project 'E' should not be phased-out until sufficient British megaton weapons were available to match the build-up of medium bomber aircraft; so it would be necessary to provide storage to accommodate 144 megaton weapons by April 1962.

Both questions, the provision of storage for nuclear weapons and the possible acquisition of US Mk 15/39 bombs by the RAF, proceeded a stage further in the autumn of 1959; but although the Air Council decided on 22 October that the Mk 15/39 weapon should neither be asked for nor taken it was not until July 1960 that they agreed to the phasing-out of Project 'E'.

When VCAS informed AMSO (Air Chf Mshl Sir Walter Dawson) on 11 August 1959 of the meeting on the 7th he went on to tell him of the storage requirements for megaton weapons – 24 at Honington by 1 July 1961, 24 at Coningsby by 1 November and 24 at Waddington by April 1962 – and said that he would be presenting a paper to the Air Council, meanwhile asking that preliminary planning be instituted for the provision of this storage.

An extremely detailed paper was prepared, asking the Council to approve the addition of nuclear weapons storage and servicing capacity "to complete the long-term requirements for the Medium Bomber Force", at a cost of about £850,000. In effect it outlined the future operational capability of the MBF, for it said that the amount of extra weapon storage capacity required depended on the following factors: weapon policy, aircraft deployment, the status of Project 'E', storage policy and criteria for new warheads, the number of warheads held and production forecasts, and the storage capacity already available.

As to weapon policy, the paper said that the MBF's Mk 2 aircraft would be armed with Blue Steel, for which it was intended·to provide sufficient megaton warheads (Red Snow) for one strike. The MBF Mk1 elements and the Shadow flights[1] would carry free-falling bombs which ideally would also be of MT yield; the possibility of dual carriage of free-fall weapons for these aircraft was being investigated. It was also proposed to set up a reserve of KT weapons for *ad hoc* re-strikes.

On aircraft deployment, the paper said that under draft Plan 'H' the MBF would consist of 144 aircraft based on six Class I airfields – as follows (by squadrons): Coningsby, three Vulcan B.2s; Cottesmore, three Vulcan B.2s; Honington, two Victor B.2s and one Victor B.1; Scampton, three Vulcan B.2s; Waddington, three Vulcan B.1s; and Wittering, two Victor B.2s and one Victor B.1.

Regarding Project 'E', it noted that currently 72 medium bombers were armed with USAF weapons, and that the SSAs at the stations where they were based (Honington, Marham and Waddington) were not available for the storage of UK nuclear weapons. With the exception of Marham, which would continue to be armed with 'E' weapons for operations in support of Saceur, Project 'E' was to continue until UK megaton weapons matched the effective strength of the MBF.

As to storage policy, the paper said that to ensure that the required reaction times were achieved, free-falling weapons and warheads for Blue Steel "must be housed on the same base as the aircraft" which were to carry them. They would be held in SSAs on Bomber Command Class I airfields. Criteria for the storage of the present MT warhead for Yellow Sun Mk 1 (Green Grass) called for the holding of not more than one per building, while "the new warhead for Yellow Sun Mk 2 and Blue Steel (Red Snow) will also have fissile material built in and single storage will apply". As to "the planned KT weapons (Red Beard) the fissile material is removable and is stored separately. Four RBs can be held in the same space as one Yellow Sun. . . ."

Storage capacity available or planned on MBF stations showed that nine of them – Coningsby, Cottesmore, Honington, Finningley, Scampton, Waddington, Wittering, Gaydon and Marham – had buildings designed to house MT and KT weapons.

When the Air Council took its decision on 7 July 1960 that Project 'E' for the strategic bomber force should be phased-out[2] it considered a paper of 14 June by VCAS[3]. This urged that a date of June 1961 should be adhered to, for two reasons: American weapons delivered to Bomber Command had only half the nominal yield they were previously thought to possess, and the advantages of the Mk 5 over the British kiloton weapon (Red Beard) now seemed to be "much smaller than at first appeared"; and existing Project 'E' storage space was needed to accommodate UK weapon production. These proposals, VCAS pointed

---

[1] *Ie*, that would be used operationally if the need arose. This paper, Nuclear Weapons Storage for the RAF – Long Term Requirements Note by VCAS, was sent to ACAS(Ops) by DofOps (B, BM and R) on 18 September 1959.

[2] Conclusions 10(60).

[3] Project 'E' Weapons for the Strategic Bomber Force (AC(60)31), Note by VCAS.

out at the meeting, did not affect the provision of Project 'E' weapons for the force assigned to Saceur. The Council agreed that the phasing-out of these weapons for the SBF should start in June 1961.

Some weeks before this Air Council decision the Prime Minister (Mr H Macmillan) had asked the Minister of Defence (Mr H Watkinson) whether there were any plans for "sharing of bombs with the Americans should the situation deteriorate", and had been told in reply:

"The answer is Yes. Under what is known as Project 'E', they provide us with the balance needed to ensure that all the V-bombers are supplied. This is not just a plan; the bombs are here. The proportion of American bombs will diminish until, about the beginning of 1963, we have enough British-made megaton bombs for the whole force.

"The above applies to the V-bomber force. We see no need to produce British bombs to replace American bombs for the forces assigned to Nato"[1].

In fact the dates subsequently agreed to were 1 July 1961 for Honington and 30 March 1962 for Waddington. On 6 September 1961 D of Ops (B & R) (Air Cdre G R Magill) minuted PS/VCAS to report that arrangements had been made for the phase-out at Honington on 1 July 1961 and that "this operation" had been "successfully completed". The Americans had not yet been informed of a more precise date for Waddington than "the latter half of 1962", and should be given "at least six months' notice" of RAF intentions so as to have sufficient time to make administrative arrangements. A month later (10 October) he wrote to the AOC in C Bomber Command (AM Sir Kenneth Cross) to say that his proposal for an early phase-out of Project 'E' weapons at Waddington had been agreed and a convenient date would be the completion of the SSA extension; also that staff arrangements could be made with the USAF "in order to reach a mutually convenient programme for the phase-out".

On 15 November HQ Bomber Command (Wg Cdr F S Hazlewood) wrote to D of Ops (B & R) to say that a meeting was shortly to be held at Waddington to finalise the date of the completion of works services on the SSA extension. When that date was known it would then be possible to approach HQ 7th Air Division, USAF, with a proposal for phasing-out the 'E' weapons.

The meeting was held on 22 November, and on the 28th Wg Cdr Hazlewood informed D of Ops (B & R) that it had been agreed that the change-over date from American to British weapons was to be Saturday, 17 March 1962, and that all US weapons would be out of Waddington by 30 March 1962[2].

---

[1] Minute M206/60, 16 June 1960 and reply of 22 June in AF/CMS 255/64, Pt III E Wpns – 'V' Force – Policy.

[2] Correspondence in file AF/CMS 255/64, Pt III E Weapons – 'V' Force – Policy.

As to Marham and the time required to make administrative arrangements, the Deputy Commander, 7th Air Division (Col Wilson R Wood), wrote to DDOps(B) on 23 December 1960 to say that the revised date of "around 30 June 1961" quoted at a Project 'E' meeting at HQ USAFE on 27 October for the vacating of RAF Marham by 7th Air Division "fitted in very well" with USAF plans since a large number of their personnel at Marham had overseas tours terminating at that time. He added that owing to the eight months' lead time in programming USAF overseas personnel movements it was a matter of considerable urgency that confirmation of the revised phase-out be received "at an early date".

However, Marham, with its Saceur-assigned squadrons, was a special case in the use of American nuclear weapons by V-bomber aircraft. On 29 December 1960 ACAS (Ops) (AVM T O Prickett) wrote to Saceur and to the Commander, 7th Air Division, about the plan "whereby Valiant squadrons at . . . Marham" were to be "equipped for the dual carriage of Mk 28 weapons". He said it had been agreed that the second and third Valiant squadrons would be transferred to Saceur with effect from 13 July 1961, and the capability for the dual carriage of Mk 28 weapons would also take effect from that date.

He added that the major problems created by the presence of 'E' weapons, which were stored on three airfields, were that since no storage space was available on these stations to permit holding enough British weapons to match aircraft in the National Plan, considerable road movement of these weapons from two maintenance units would be necessary if the plan were put into operation – greatly retarding the rate at which weapon systems could be generated; and since formal approval for the movement of 'E' weapons in aircraft to dispersal airfields had never been given, the reaction capability of the units at the three stations must be prejudiced. For these reasons, it was considerd that American weapons should be returned to the USAF as soon as was practicable.

The timing of this return had to be related to the completion of works services for the storage of Yellow Sun Mks 1 and 2 and Red Beard weapons at Honington and Waddington, the availability of usable British weapons at those stations, and the transfer of the one remaining MBF squadron (No 148) at Marham to the Saceur force in the middle of 1961[1].

Works services at Honington were due for completion in June 1961 and those at Waddington by April 1962, so storage for Yellow Sun and Red Beard weapons should be available from those dates; forecasts suggested that sufficient numbers of British weapons would be available by the time the works services were complete; and the transfer of No 148 Squadron at Marham to the Saceur force in July 1961 would allow the

---

[1] No 148 Squadron was Saceur-assigned from 13 July 1961.

complete withdrawal of all Saceur-assigned 'E' weapons from that station at that time.

Gp Capt A H C Boxer (Gp Capt Plans, Bomber Command) said that the fact that a clearance for the carriage of Red Beard by Victors might be withheld complicated the issue at Honington, where two squadrons of these aircraft were based, the third being equipped with Valiants[1]. It was therefore proposed that the weapon dispositions should be: Honington – July 1961, Yellow Sun Mk 1s to match 16 Victor Mk 1s, and Red Beards to match eight Valiants; and Waddington – April 1962, Yellow Sun Mks 1/2 to match 24 Vulcan Mk 1s and if Yellow Sun availability were inadequate, numbers to be made up with Red Beards.

If this disposition were agreed, he concluded, all SAC Project 'E' weapons could be returned to the USAF by May 1962 instead of December 1962 which it was believed was "the present intention".

In his minute of 6 September 1961 to PS/VCAS (already referred to) D of Ops (B & R) specifically noted the exclusion of Saceur-assigned aircraft from the Air Council decision about 'E' weapons, saying that as a result of the build-up of British weapon stocks the Council had agreed in July 1960[2] that weapons supplied under Project 'E' should be phased out progressively in the period June 1961 – the latter half of 1962, "except, of course, for Saceur-assigned aircraft".

It was not until July 1965 that the last USAF personnel left Marham, the ORB for the following month recording a "nil" return for both officers and airmen. While the TBF had been in existence – up to January 1965 when the Valiants were withdrawn from service – there had been some 70 USAF personnel at the station. Thus in January 1964 there were eight officers and 63 airmen, in June seven officers and 73 airmen, and in December nine officers and 73 airmen. Even in June 1963 there were nine officers and 43 airmen, but by July there was only one officer left and three airmen. The station recorded its last training with 2,100lb (US Mk 43) weapons – *ie* practice loadings – in January 1965[3].

The implications of the Air Council's decision about Project 'E' weapons were conveyed to the Americans during August 1960. On the 2nd, the Commander of 7th Air Division (Maj-Gen C B Westover) had written to ACAS (Ops) (AVM J Grandy) to say that HQ Strategic Air Command had been pressing for "immediate information concerning RAF weapons requirements in order to submit them to the Joint Chiefs of Staff for consideration". SAC had been "tentatively" given "the following data" – 72 weapons, three detachments required until 1 July 1961; subsequently, 24 weapons, one detachment, required until 1 December 1962. These tentative figures would become firm on the

---

[1] The three squadrons at Honington were Nos 55 and 57 (Victors B.1/1A) and No 90 (Valiants B.1/(K)1/(PR)K1).

[2] Conclusions 21(59) Item III, amended by Conclusions 10(60) Item IV.

[3] Figures from RAF Marham ORB.

10th, unless 7th Air Division could furnish SAC with more accurate RAF estimates prior to that date. Gen Westover asked to be advised.

In reply, on the 12th, A/ACAS (Ops) (Air Cdre R J P Prichard) advised him of the Air Council's decision that the need for weapons supplied under Project 'E' to the V-force would be "reduced from the end of June 1961". The requirements, which he understood had been "passed to your HQ by HQ Bomber Command", were confirmed as: existing arrangements for 72 weapons and three detachments until 1 July 1961; subsequently, Honington to be deleted from the programme. As the aircraft at Marham became allocated to Saceur the overall weapon requirement would then reduce, to 24 weapons and one detachment at Waddington by October 1961, continuing at that level until December 1962 when Waddington too would cease to require Project 'E' weapons". In conclusion, A/ACAS (Ops) thanked the Americans for their assistance "both in the past and for the period yet to come"[1].

At the end of 1960 HQ Bomber Command urged the Air Ministry that American weapons should be returned to the USAF as soon as possible, because of storage problems and because they could not be moved to dispersal airfields.[2]

Writing on 2 December to DDOps(B), Gp Capt Boxer suggested that details should be agreed for the withdrawal of Project 'E' weapons "assigned to this Command for use by the Medium Bomber Force in the Co-ordinated Plan". He said that in the past it had been accepted that these weapons should only be withdrawn as British megaton-range weapons became available – a policy based on the belief that 'E' weapons were in the megaton class. But it had been established "beyond all reasonable doubt" that they were in the kiloton range. So the reason for the retention of 'E' weapons was "largely invalidated", and as stocks of usable British weapons increased, the drawbacks associated with holding US weapons "greatly outweighed the advantages".

Target Selection

One other matter affected by the RAF/USAF Memorandum of Understanding, as far as the co-odination of atomic strike plans was concerned, was the selection of targets for the V-bombers. During 1957 work had been done on a strategic target policy for Bomber Command, but this became more urgent when the CAS was due to visit the Chief of Staff of the USAF and the AOC in C Bomber Command was to have planning discussions with the Commander, Strategic Air Command. It was clearly important for the RAF to have a policy approved by the Government, and for its leadership to be in a position to discuss it,

---

[1] Correspondence in AF/CMS 255/64 Pt III 'E' Weapons – 'V' Force – Policy.
[2] Ibid.

before meeting the Americans and learning of their plans. Among the reasons for the co-ordination proposals had been the importance of avoiding overlapping attacks on targets, and of making the best possible use of available bomber resources and weapons.

Before the V-force came into being, the idea of a Targets Committee had been put forward. On 30 September 1954 ACAS (Ops) had minuted VCAS:–[1]

"For the past few years there has been no requirement for a Targets Committee to advise on target selection or decide priorities for target studies, mainly because the Canberra force receives its target information direct from Saceur.

"With the introduction of the V-force, I feel we should have a properly constituted Targets Committee to advise on target selection and to co-ordinate the activities of the various bodies who deal with targets and target material. The Committee should also be responsible for ensuring that Bomber Command knows which targets it is likely to be called upon to attack in war and that all necessary target material to enable the Command to fulfil its tasks is prepared and issued. . . .

"To meet these requirements, I suggest the formation of a Targets Committee. . . . ACAS(I) agrees with my suggestion and if you approve the composition of the Committee and the terms of reference, I will go ahead and get the Committee functioning."

VCAS approved the proposal to re-establish a Targets Committee[2] and ACAS (Ops) minuted D of Ops (2) on 8 October to say that target studies and preparation of target material were at present "limited to those currently under study" – of Soviet airfields and Naval bases facing Western Europe – but that once the committee had been formed and was working he would approach VCAS, who "will then decide whether the time is ripe for an approach to be made to the Chiefs of Staff for guidance on further target studies"[3].

The terms of reference of this Targets Committee were updated during 1957 to bring them into line with current strategic thinking; on 26 November A/ACAS(Ops) (Air Cdre B K Burnett) wrote to VCAS outlining the committee's origins and asking for approval of the change. He explained that its membership consisted of DDOps(B) as chairman, and representatives from JIB, AI5, HQ Bomber Command and "other branches of Intelligence and Operations as required". At its last meeting, on 31 October, "its working was examined and some new terms of reference were drafted to take into account current strategic policy as expressed in the strategic targets policy which has now been approved by the Chiefs of Staff".

---

[1] B Fdr 417/DD Ops (B).
[2] VCAS 1385 of 5 October 1954.
[3] These papers are in VCAS Target Data folder – AHB ID9/90/22 (Pt 1). VCAS was responsible for directing the V-force build-up: see minute, PS to VCAS, 26 April 1955 – "in the general context of your direction of the 'V' Bomber Force build-up and of your approval in October last year of the setting-up of a Targets Committee".

The revised terms of reference, as approved by VCAS, were that
"The Air Ministry Targets Committee is responsible, under
ACAS(Ops), to VCAS.

"The functions of the committee are:–

(a)   To advise on and keep under review the relative importance of
      enemy target systems for strategic air attack.

(b)   To formulate a priority list of targets within the target system
      policy decided by the Chiefs of Staff Committee, to be issued
      by ACAS(Ops) to the Commands concerned.

(c)   To co-ordinate target studies in conjunction with the USAF,
      where appropriate.

(d)   To examine and comment on proposals received from outside
      the Air Ministry involving the attack of strategic targets by
      RAF bomber forces."

VCAS's approval was eventually conveyed to ACAS(Ops) on 9 April
1958, after a delay owing to the papers having been mislaid.

ACAS(Ops) reported to CAS on 19 April on strategic target policy for
Bomber Command; he said that he had received from the Command
their report on the meeting held with SAC to co-ordinate plans, and
that the final progress report would shortly be ready for CAS to see[1].
Subsequently CAS put his memorandum, Progress Report on USAF/
RAF Co-ordination of Nuclear Strike Plans to the Chiefs of Staff
Committee – as subsequently described.

With the forming of V-bomber squadrons from 1955 onwards, target
policy became a matter of urgency, and with the co-ordination of
nuclear strike plans with the USAF Strategic Air Command, one of even
greater urgency. Writing to CAS on 12 September 1957 to send him a
draft paper for the Chiefs of Staff Committee on Strategic Target Policy
for Bomber Command, DCAS (Air Marshal G W Tuttle) commented
that it was "important that strategic target policy is approved before the
C in C Bomber Command can begin co-ordinating planning with
Strategic Air Command"[2].

This paper[3] referred to the CoS Committee meeting on 28 May 1957[4]
when the Chiefs of Staff had "approved a paper by the Joint Planning
Staff and the Joint Intelligence Committee, paragraph 9 of which
advised that broad target policy for Bomber Command should be
decided by the Government on advice from the Chiefs of Staff. Detailed
target selection would remain the responsibility of the Air Ministry and
should cover two eventualities:–

---

[1] LM, ACAS(Ops)/PS to CAS, F.1351/Ops.2562 of 19 April 1958.
[2] DCAS 4211/57 in folder Strategic Target Policy – Bomber Command (AHB ID9/90/2).
[3] Soviet Target Systems and the ability of the Western Powers to attack them.
[4] COS (57) 42nd mtg, Minute 3.

(*a*)   Co-ordinated action with the USAF;

(*b*)   Action on an emergency basis in a situation in which the United Kingdom was forced into unilateral retaliation. . . ."

The paper on Strategic Target Policy for Bomber Command was considered by the Chiefs of Staff Committee at its meeting on 19 September 1957[1] and at the next meeting, on 23 September, was endorsed after being subject to some amendments.[2]

Subsequently, on 15 October 1957[3], the Chiefs of Staff put forward a Memorandum to the Defence Committee of the Cabinet, in which they recommended its endorsement of the paper on Strategic Target Policy "as the basis of Bomber Command's strategic target policy". This paper was subsequently approved by the Minister of Defence and the Chief of the Air Staff was authorised to "initiate appropriate action with the USAF for the co-ordination of nuclear strike plans"[4]. In a Memorandum circulated on 20 May 1958[5] CAS summed-up the situation which had then been reached, on target policy and on co-ordination with the Americans. He recalled that

"in COS(57)224[6] the Chiefs of Staff submitted their recommendations on the broad principles which should govern Bomber Command's Strategic Target Policy. In WFD/256 dated 20 November 1957 the Chairman (MRAF Sir W Dickson) conveyed the Minister of Defence's authority 'for me to begin the co-ordination of plans with the Americans on the basis of this paper and asked me to report progress in due course to the Chiefs of Staff'".

CAS then went on to describe what had happened at the RAF/USAF meetings in mid-November (14-15)1957– two had been held between SAC and Bomber Command, with Air Ministry representation – and what had been planned. He explained that

"Examination of the separate Bomber Command and SAC plans has shown that every Bomber Command target was, understandably, also on SAC's list for attack and that both Commands had doubled-up strikes on their selected targets to ensure success. A fully integrated plan has now been produced, taking into account Bomber Command's ability to be on target in the first wave several hours in advance of the main SAC forces from bases in the US.

"Under the combined plan, the total strategic air forces disposed by the Allies are sufficient to cover all Soviet targets, including airfields and air defence. Bomber Command's contribution has been given as 92

---

[1] COS(57)208.

[2] COS(57) 72nd meeting.

[3] COS(57) 78th meeting.

[4] WFD/256 of 20 Nov 1957.

[5] Copy in 240/22(SAFE) Pt 3 – Co-ordination of Offensive Air Operations.

[6] 16 Oct 57.

aircraft by October 1958, increasing to 108 aircraft by June 1959. 106 targets have been allocated to Bomber Command as follows:—

(a)   69 cities which are centres of government or of other military significance.

(b)   17 long-range air force airfields which constitute part of the nuclear threat.

(c)   20 elements of the Soviet air defence system.

"It is intended that a third meeting should be held this month to co-ordinate the actual routes and timing and ECM tactics of the aircraft attacking the targets selected. Full tactical co-ordination of operations will thus be achieved.

"In addition to the co-ordination of war plans, Bomber Command and SAC are also studying such measures as the use of each other's bases, the integration of Intelligence warning and post-strike recovery. Bomber Command participate in monthly exercises in the UK Joint Co-ordination Centre and in August will take part in a world-wide exercise[1].

"Arrangements have also been agreed between the RAF and USAF to co-ordinate Thor strike capability as this becomes effective. This, of course, is particularly important in view of the very short time of flight of these weapons."

In his conclusions, CAS invited his colleagues "to note the satisfactory progress which had been made in co-ordinating the operational plans of Bomber Command and SAC" and that a joint plan would be in operation on 1 October 1958; adding that he was able to state that "the combined plan produced by Bomber Command and SAC satisfies paragraph 4(a) of COS(57)224[2] and that the target policy for Bomber Command in this . . . plan is based on operational considerations".

CAS's Memorandum was considered by the Chiefs of Staff on 30 May 1958[3]; they agreed that another memorandum, based on it and in the form of a progress report, should be prepared and submitted to the Minister of Defence. This followed a suggestion CAS himself had made during the meeting, that if the Minister wished to discuss further details with the Chiefs of Staff, "it would be desirable to bring in a staff officer from Bomber Command who would be in the best position to give details of the current United States plans".

---

[1] This may have been Operation Tornado, though it has not proved possible to verify this.

[2] Which said that "in the event of co-ordinated action with the USAF, the target policy for Bomber Command should be determined solely by operational considerations of timings, tactics, aircraft performance and weapon availability, subject to the proviso that the combined strike plan should include targets which must be hit in the first strike if the war is to be finished quickly and the damage done to the UK and Western Europe kept as low as possible".

[3] COS Cttee Confidential Annex to COS(58) 46th Mtg on 30 May 1958.

The subsequent CoS Memorandum, of 5 June 1958[1], said that, following the meetings between Air Ministry, Bomber Command and SAC representatives when separate BC and SAC plans had been examined[2], a fully integrated plan had been produced "taking into account Bomber Command's ability to be on target in the first wave several hours in advance of the main SAC force operating from bases in the United States". Under the combined plan the total strategic air forces disposed by the Allies were "sufficient to cover all Soviet targets". Bomber Command's contribution had been given as 92 aircraft by October 1958, increasing to 108 by June 1959. The Command had been allocated 106 targets. It had been agreed that Bomber Command should work through the US Joint Co-ordination Centre at Ruislip, the US Chiefs of Staff agency in the UK for the co-ordination of US atomic strike forces. In addition to the co-ordination of war plans, Bomber Command and SAC were studying other measures such as the use of each other's bases, the integration of Intelligence warning and post-strike recovery. It was also intended to achieve full tactical co-ordination of operations. The memorandum added that arrangements had been agreed beween the RAF and USAF to co-ordinate Thor strike capability as it became effective, and concluded by saying that a fully co-ordinated joint plan would be in operation by 1 October 1958.

In a letter of 7 July 1958 to the AOC in C Bomber Command (ACM Sir Harry Broadhurst), however, VCAS (Air Mshl E C Hudleston) remarked that it was "highly satisfactory" that the combined plan was to be "effective 1st July"; and on the 11th the Minister of Defence (Mr Duncan Sandys) went to Bomber Command HQ for a presentation on it, a brochure containing a summary subsequently being produced[3]. This co-ordinated plan was subsequently re-written annually.

How these Chiefs of Staff/Cabinet Defence Committee/Minister of Defence decisions on strategic target policy eventuated in terms of a directive to Bomber Command, and how the re-constituted Air Ministry Targets Committee was not involved in target selection, was clearly explained in a paper – Notes on UK Target Selection and Co-ordination Developments over the past 10–12 years – dated 26 August 1960. This recalled that

"In January 1957 the Joint Planning Staffs of the Ministry of Defence produced an excellent paper called 'Allied Strategic Nuclear Attack in Global War in 1957 and its Consequences'. The introduction to this paper under the heading 'Action Suggested by the 1957 Study' contains the following paragraph on target selection:—

'The responsibility for the selection of strategic targets is at present

---

[1] COS(58)148.
[2] An examination which had showed that "every Bomber Command target was . . . also on SAC's list for attack".
[3] Bomber Command/Strategic Air Command Co-ordination: Summary of Bomber Command Presentation – 11 July 1958 (copy in file 240/22(SAFE) Pt 3 Co-ordination of Offensive Air Operations).

vested in the Air Ministry. The British strategic air forces are, however, the supreme instruments of national defence policy. We therefore consider that broad target policy should be decided by the Government on advice from the Chiefs of Staff. Detailed target selection would remain the responsibility of the Air Ministry. It would be essential for this target selection to cover two eventualities: —

(a)   Co-ordinated action with the USAF;

(b)   Action on an emergency basis in a situation in which the United Kingdom was forced into unilateral action'.

"At their COS(57)42nd meeting the Chiefs of Staff Committee endorsed this view and invited the Air Ministry to take note that they should be kept informed from time to time of progress on, *inter alia*, target selection.

"As a result of the appearance of the above JIC paper, but also because of the growing need for SAC/BC co-ordination needs and our requests for 'big E' weapons, the Chiefs of Staff met in October 1957 to decide on a strategic target policy for Bomber Command (see COS(57) 224). The conclusions of the CoS Committee were:–

(a)   In the event of co-ordinated action with the USAF, the target policy for Bomber Command should be determined solely by operational considerations of timings, tactics, aircraft performance and weapon availability, subject to the proviso that the combined strike plan should include targets which must be hit in the first strike if the war is to be finished quickly and the damage done to the UK and Western Europe kept as low as possible.[1]

(a)   If the UK should be forced to take unilateral retaliation against the USSR, the target policy of Bomber Command should be to attack the Soviet centres of administration and population. This is the most effective target system for our limited resources.

"As a result of this, Air Ministry, together with JIB,[2] drew up a list of 131 Soviet cities whose population exceeded 100,000; from these 131 cities, 98 were chosen which lay within 2,100nm of UK and they were graded in priority according to population, administrative importance, economic importance and transportation. This list was approved by CAS and put into the C in C Bomber Command's directive as an Appendix in November 1957. This list was last brought up to date in June 1958."

The paper then went on to say, referring to the AM Targets Committee, that though it had approved terms of reference it had not been active since April 1958; that Bomber Command did its own target selection, for both unilateral and SAC co-ordinated war plans, adding: "We, in Bomber Ops, do not know what these specific selections are for

---

[1] This was paragraph 4a, quoted earlier in a footnote.
[2] Joint Intelligence Bureau.

either plan, since the Command does not divulge its plans as it is required to do under the terms of the C in C's directive.[1]

"It is 'self-contained' for all relevant targetting processes, *ie*, production of folders for the medium bomber force. This also includes targetting for Thor and Blue Steel".

Thus operational planning and the organisation of training for the V-force of Bomber Command were guided from 1958 onwards by the strategic target policy approved by the Cabinet Defence Committee and the Chiefs of Staff, by the agreement to co-ordinate nuclear strike plans with the USAF Strategic Air Command, and by the contingency of possible unilateral action should the United Kingdom be involved in unilateral retaliation.

The Memorandum of Understanding between the Royal Air Force and the United States Air Force of 24 July 1957 resulted in a co-ordination conference between Bomber Command and Strategic Air Command held from 19 to 22 May 1958, which completed the co-ordination of combined atomic strike plans and combat operations relevant to the period 1 July 1958 to 30 June 1959. To quote from the report of the conference,[2] one main result was that "the operational plans of each Command were compared in detail to include targetting, routeing and timing. Potential conflicts were isolated and opportunities for mutual support were explored. Procedures for continuing the co-ordination process as plans change with time were considered. . . ."

Writing to VCAS on 25 June 1958 about co-ordination between the two Commands, the AOC in C Bomber Command[3] referred to the Memorandum of Understanding and to "the agreements and recommendations reached at HQ SAC, Omaha, on 4 June 1958 between the Commander in Chief, Strategic Air Command, and myself". He said that the main purpose of the discussions had been "to prepare a co-ordinated strike plan, based on the target directive contained in COS(57)244 dated 16 October 1957, which could be put into effect should combined nuclear retaliation by Bomber and Strategic Air Command ever be required. The plan . . . is applicable to the period 1 July 1958 to 30 June 1959, is targetted to utilise stocks of British, and after October 1958 USAF nuclear weapons for the Medium Bomber Force, and includes targets for the first Thor squadron, expected to be operational in January 1959". The C in C added that "strike details of the Bomber Command contribution to this plan will be lodged with the SAC Joint Centre in UK before 1 July 1958. The plan was completed without the revelation by either participant of details concerning nuclear weapon yields or stock-pile numbers".

This co-operation was between bomber forces which were extremely

---

[1] This remark echoes the wartime relationship between Bomber Command HQ and D/Bomber Ops.

[2] In Co-ord of US/UK Strategic Bomber Force, 240/16.

[3] BC/TS.85397/CinC.

disparate in size; by December 1958, for example, SAC had 380 B-52s and 1,367 B-47s[1] in its bomber force compared with 45 Valiants, 18 Vulcans and ten Victors. But there were other bases of comparision, as CAS pointed out in some notes he sent to the Minister of Defence on 25 July 1958 "indicating the advantages which our Bomber Force possesses in relation to SAC's alert force".[2] He said that, in assessing the value of the British contribution to the Western nuclear deterrent it was misleading to compare the planned size and shape of the V-force with that of SAC and to assume that the British share was insignificant. Not only the size of the contribution was important; factors of time and distance, and the quality and location of forces, were of prime consideration – what had to be measured in terms of deterrence was speed and effectiveness of attack.

As to quality, CAS said that the V-force had aircraft of slightly superior performance in height and speed – though not in range – to those of the SAC, with crews and technical equipment "at least as good". As to quickness of reaction, although the UK was more vulnerable to enemy air attack than the USA, Bomber Command's dispersal plan would give the ability to launch the whole ready force "in ten minutes or less". Further, the location of the UK bomber force, together with the dispersal concept and the performance of its aircraft, meant that in a retaliatory strike RAF bombers would reach their targets ahead of the SAC strike forces based either in Europe or the USA.

Referring to the importance of the British contribution to the protection of Western Europe and the UK, CAS said that no force based in the US, whatever its size or state of alertness, could attack the heart of Russia in time to prevent a second Russian air attack on those areas. He said that the V-force, "far from being a disproportionately expensive and relatively insignificant auxiliary to the SAC deterrent", was the spearhead of, and largest contributor to, the first and possibly decisive Anglo-US retaliatory strike. Though when fully equipped and manned it would be small by comparison with the total size of SAC, its importance would be far greater than such a direct comparison suggested – because of the high performance of its aircraft, because it was nearer to the enemy and because a large proportion of it could be brought to readiness and launched simultaneously from dispersed airfields.

With the formidable destructive power and fall-out of megaton weapons (in the RAF inventory from 1958 onwards), and with the decision to attack "centres of administration and population" if the UK were forced to take unilateral retaliation against the USSR, Bomber Command was reverting to its Second World War policy of area bombing. Should such a situation ever arise, it would be used as a bludgeon rather than as a rapier.

---

[1] Figures from *The Development of Strategic Air Command 1946-1971* (HQ SAC).
[2] Covering letter ref CAS.1971.

During 1960 the AOC in C Bomber Command (Air Mshl Sir Kenneth Cross) told VCAS (Air Chf Mshl Sir Edmund Hudleston) that neither Strategic Air Command nor Bomber Command were prepared to reveal, even to each other, the nuclear yield allotted to each target under the co-ordinated plan. He said that the nominal figure for planning purposes was one megaton "but this varies between kiloton-range yield in the case of our Blue Danube to multi-megaton bombs in the SAC armoury", commenting: "in this area alone there is a barrier to co-ordination, and duplication and wastage is inevitable until American legislation is altered[1]".

---

[1]Letter of 17 May 60 on Target Co-ordination Conference at SHAPE, in VCAS folder Target Information and Data (AHB ID9/90/22 Apl 55–Oct 65).

CHAPTER XVII

THE THOR AGREEMENTS

1958 was a watershed year for Anglo-American co-operation in nuclear strike plans, both as to weapons and their means of delivery; for in addition to the RAF-USAF/Bomber Command-Strategic Air Command co-ordination arrangements there were US-UK agreements on Thor IRBMs, under which they would be deployed to Britain and manned by RAF personnel. The inter-Governmental treaty was published as a White Paper (Cmnd 366) in February 1958 under the title *Supply of Ballistic Missiles by the United States to the United Kingdom*[1]. But the idea of such a project had been mooted some 18 months previously by the Americans[2]. In January 1958 the Air Council were told by DCAS (Air Mshl Sir Geoffrey Tuttle) that a Thor proposal

"had first been mentioned when the US Secretary of the Air Force visited London in July 1956. It had then been envisaged that, in return for the right to station IRBM in this country, the Americans would provide us with *quid pro quo* in the shape of advanced fighters. Following a visit by the Minister of Defence to Washington in January 1957, and the Bermuda Conference in March, it emerged that the Americans were thinking in terms of four squadrons of IRBM, two of them to be manned by the USAF and two by the RAF, to be deployed in this country in 1959. The Prime Minister made a public statement about the project in April 1957, and the Minister of Defence obtained authority at a Ministerial meeting chaired by the Prime Minister on 30 May 1957, to pursue negotiations with the Americans, reporting back to the Defence Committee before concluding an agreement"[3].

As a result of his Washington visit in January 1957 the Minister of Defence (Mr Duncan Sandys, who had just taken over this post) telegraphed the Prime Minister (Mr Harold Macmillan, who likewise had assumed office during that month) to say that "the Americans have explained their proposals for deployment of the 1,500-mile range ballistic rocket to Britain". His telegram[4] continued:–

"They are most anxious in view of progress of Russian ballistic rockets that rocket deterrent should be established in Britain as soon as possible. Their plan provides for bringing into operation by the end of 1960[5] sites manned by British personnel. . . .

"United States would provide weapons and specialised equipment, including anything costing dollars. Nuclear warheads would be held

---

[1] In file on Defence Policy Discussions with Americans (ID6/R.13A, Pt 1, PA Folder).

[2] The implications of basing Thors in the UK were being actively considered by the Air Staff in mid-1956: see Thor Policy (Pt 1), AHB ID/47/298 file.

[3] Air Council Conclusions 3(58), 30 January 1958, in file V/9/220 – American Intermediate Range Ballistic Missiles.

[4] No 187, 30 January 1957.

[5] The first Thor in fact arrived by MATS C-124 Globemaster on 29 August 1958.

under same conditions as nuclear bombs for British bombers. We would undertake site works and would provide general supporting equipment. United States estimate of the cost to us for the four sites[1] is £10 million, apart from costs of personnel and their training and housing[2].

"Proposal would give us a megaton-rocket deterrent in Britain at least five years before we could provide it ourselves[3]. Whatever may have to be cut out of our defence programme, I am sure we must find a place for this project, the deterrent effect of which will be very significant and the cost very moderate"[4].

Two days before this telegram was sent the RAF had been briefed on Thor, at a meeting in Washington on 28 January. Subsequently the Commander, RAF Staff, BJSM (AVM A D Selway), wrote to DCAS to say that

"The first part of the meeting was the presentation to us of Thor. This was done in typically thorough American fashion, with many charts and diagrams, and it was noticeable that some of these were headed with such titles as 'British Training Programme for Thor' and so on. It became very obvious that the Americans are anxious to give us, under certain conditions, Thor as soon as possible. . .[5].

"The original proposal seems to be to set us up with four squadrons of Thor. Each squadron consists of 15 missiles, which involves the employment of 500 men. That is to say, 60 missiles and 2,000 men . . . ."

In February 1957 DCAS was supplied with a note on Thor which said that it was the USAF intermediate-range ballistic missile, a single-stage liquid oxygen/kerosine rocket based on one North American 150,000lb thrust motor. It was 65ft long and 8ft in diameter with a launch weight of 110,000lb, and thus was "basically similar to but a little smaller than Blue Streak". Strategic mobility ranked high in the stated requirements for Thor, and the present concept was "to employ simple trailer/erectors and to locate the weapons in groups of three, to a total of 15, on existing SAC airfields". A Defence Review Costing Exercise in March 1957 outlined the original proposals (later modified) as being for two sites to be entirely constructed by the United States and manned initially by US service personnel; two further sites to be constructed by the United Kingdom, to be brought into operation with British personnel; all four sites to be a UK responsibility as regards manning and operation *wef* December 1960; the US to be responsible financially for all material produced in the US – *ie* missiles, specialised equipment and spares (the US estimate

---

[1] There were eventually 20 Thor squadrons – each site parenting five.
[2] A cost estimate of 19 February 1958 (in file V/9/220) was £1.45m in total for a main station and four satellites.
[3] *Ie* with Blue Streak, then under development.
[4] Mr Sandys' enthusiasm for Thor reflected his pro-missile feelings.
[5] "If we need medium-range ballistic missiles, this is what the British need as their 'intercontinental ballistic missile [due to the United Kingdom's proximity to the Communist empire]. Let's investigate whether they can build their own, and if we can help them, then we won't have to bother" – a summary of US IRBM views in 1954-55 in *The Mighty Thor*, by Julian Hartt (Duell, Sloan & Pearce, 1961).

for the cost of this being £5.7m per site); and the UK to be responsible financially for non-specialist supporting equipment (US estimate £2.9m per site), cost of land and work services. The writer of this minute[1] added: "I have been informed by DOR(C) that each of the four Thor sites would contain 15 missiles deployed in five clusters of three each...".

It seemed also that the Americans were anxious to establish a missile front line with Thors until their longer-range weapons were deployed, and it was the consequent increase in UK vulnerability which later caused the Chiefs of Staff concern. AVM Selway commented that

"Before the meetings took place we met in the Embassy on Sunday night to agree on a line of action, and at that time were rather at sea over the Americans' own policy regarding Thor – especially since they are, of course, much more interested in longer-range weapons. One of the diagrams shown to us on the following day, however, seemed to solve this question as it displayed pictorially how much of the USSR could be covered by Thor shot off within an 80° arc from bases in UK, Turkey and Okinawa".

In 1957, as has been seen, the RAF and USAF were much involved in high-level discussions on the co-ordination of nuclear strike plans and the supply of American atomic weapons for Canberras and the V-force, leading to the Memorandum of Understanding finally agreed in August of that year. During this time, the Thor missile was under development. The possibility that it might be allocated to the RAF had first been mooted in the signal of 30 January from the BJSM about the American presentation. At this time the RAF had its own ballistic missile system, Blue Streak, under development – based on an Air Staff Requirement No OR1139 of 8 August 1955. It was considered that operating Thor might provide some useful advance experience for the deployment of the British MRBM[2], although Blue Streak was intended to be fired from underground[3].

The Americans put their proposals for the deployment of Thor in the UK formally to the Minister of Defence in a Memorandum of US-UK Discussions sent to him on 1 February by the Secretary of Defense. This suggested, "in view of the importance of deploying a ballistic deterrent at the earliest possible date", a "crash program" under which an experimental squadron of· five missiles could be deployed at a USAF base in the UK by July 1958 – paid for and manned by the United States. Then four regular sites would be developed, the experimental squadron being disbanded when these became available. Although this is not what in fact happened, the Memorandum illustrated the urgency which the Americans attached to the deployment of Thor, which at that stage was still an unproved weapon. It was

---

[1] Corres in file on Thor Policy (AHB ID/47/298 Pt 1).

[2] "Should we get Thor, we shall presumably get some fairly early experience of surface sites" (min ACAS(P)/S.6, 1 March 1957).

[3] OR1139, para 13.

acknowledged by the Minister on 18 February 1957[1].

Under the USAF designation SM-75 (WS 315A), designed and built by Douglas Aircraft Co, the missile had then been under development for just over a year. In a paper on Thor – Possible Allocation to the RAF, DD0R9 wrote on 6 February 1957 that it had been "put in hand as a full-scale project just over a year ago, and

"the most strenuous efforts have been made to achieve initial operational capability as quickly as possible. The first test launching has just taken place. A failure resulting in the loss of the round occurred immediately after take-off; . . . but this . . . does not necessarily imply a major set-back.

"The target in-Service date is 1958. If achieved, this will represent an unprecedented rate of development. By comparison, the 'agreed date' for Blue Streak is 1966 and the earliest operational capability might be 1963 or 1964".

In fact the first four launchings from Cape Canaveral, Florida, were unsuccessful[2]; but the fifth produced a flight of 1,100 miles (1,770km) and the sixth one of 1,350 (2,170km), while the ninth test missile far exceeded its design performance by flying 2,700 miles (4,345km), and the weapon was ordered into production[3]. Its planned range was 1,500 miles (2,414km), carrying a megaton-range warhead; this range was "much too small to enable it to be based in the USA" and "the American plan is to locate 15 weapons on a SAC airfield[4]".

During the early part of 1957 there were extensive Defence Review Costing Exercises of items related to the possible deployment of Thor in the UK, ACAS(O) in sending details of these to DCAS on 5 April expressing the "strongest possible opposition" to the USAF plan of having 15 weapons on one base because of the "complete vulnerability to enemy attack"[5]. The manning requirements for ballistic missiles were also considered in detail.

On 18 April a draft agreement on the deployment of US IRBMs in the UK[6] was sent to the Minister of Defence *via* the British Ambassador in Washington by the Secretary of Defense (Mr Charles Wilson). It said that

"Pursuant to the agreement in principle between the Prime Minister . . . and the President . . . reached at Bermuda on 22 March 1957, and in

---

[1] Correspondence in Thor Policy file (AHB ID47298 Pt 1).

[2] Thor 101 failed to lift off; 102 was destroyed by the range safety officer after about 35 seconds' flight; 103 blew up before ignition; and 104 flew for 92 seconds before breaking apart. (*The Mighty Thor*, by J Hartt; Duell, Sloan and Pearce, New York, 1961). Out of 18 Thor R & D firings from January 1957 to October 1958, seven were successful, four partially successful and seven were failures (Min. DCAS/S of S, 12 January 1959 in Organisation and Establishment of Thor Units (AHB ID3/907/7 Pt 1)).

[3] *Jane's All the World's Aircraft*, 1958-59 and 1962-63.

[4] DDOR9 paper.

[5] DOR(C)/TS.4486/8863, in file Thor Policy (AF/CMS814/65 Pt 1).

[6] This was the American draft of 16 April 1957 (see file Deployment of American IRBM in UK May 1957/1958 – AHB ID9/240/17 Pt 1).

support of the purpose of the North Atlantic Treaty . . . , the following arrangements and understandings are agreed regarding the proposed deployment of the United States Intermediate Range Ballistic Missile in the United Kingdom".

It proposed that the US might deploy one experimental squadron of about five missiles at a USAF base in the UK "as rapidly as possible", and that four squadrons of 15 missiles each would be deployed in the UK "as rapidly as practicable"; and it said that missiles, specialised equipment, training facilities and spares would be provided at US expense.

The memorandum on deployment of US-produced IRBMs in the UK, which did not name a specific missile (which could have been Jupiter, the comparable US Army weapon being developed by Chrysler Corp), was closely analysed by the Air Staff and discussed at meetings in the Ministry of Defence on 6 May and at the Ministry of Supply on the 13th. These comments and discussions led to the Minister of Defence suggesting that British representatives should go to Washington to draft a definitive agreement[1], and to the Secretary of State for Air writing to him on 29 May to say that there was much more to be discussed than the Minister had indicated. He agreed that "the main points are those summarised in . . . your paper, but there is a tremendous lot in some of them. The introduction of any new weapon into the Royal Air Force involves a mass of important considerations – technical, operational, logistic and financial – and here we are dealing with a radically new type of which we have no experience".

The Minister of Defence said at a Prime Minister's meeting on 30 May, when his memorandum was discussed, that the draft agreement on the deployment of American IRBMs in Britain was "broadly on the lines which he had discussed with the US Secretary of Defense". Several points – including total cost of the project and division of financial liability between the two Governments – needed further clarification, but the main issue to be settled was the arrangement for controlling the operational use of the missiles.

After its discussion of the issues, the meeting confirmed the principle of joint agreement for operational use of the missles by both US and British units; agreed that the question of the use of American missiles if fitted with British warheads should not be raised in negotiations on the agreement; authorised the Minister of Defence to indicate general acceptance of the US draft agreement as a basis for detailed negotiations – for which he was to arrange for British representatives to go to Washington; and invited him to submit the agreement in its final form to the Defence Committee for confirmation[2].

---

[1] Memorandum GEN.570/4.
[2] Minutes of Prime Minister's Meeting GEN.570/2, 30 May 1957. It is interesting to note that, at a meeting held by the Minister of Defence on 27 May, the possibility of Polaris as an alternative to Thor as an IRBM was raised by the First Sea Lord (Thor Policy file, ID/47/498, Pt 1).

The Secretary of State for Air considered it important that a fact-finding mission should go to the US in connection with the IRBM proposal before any detailed agreement was negotiated, and both the Minister of Supply and of Defence agreed with this. On 15 June, however, the Commander of the US 3rd Air Force (Major-General Roscoe C Wilson) wrote to CAS to suggest a meeting at his HQ to discuss technical aspects of the proposed agreement.

General Wilson explained that, in an effort to expedite planning for the deployment of IRBMs to the UK, the Secretary of Defense had "requested the Air Force to assume responsibility for initiating discussions on a service-to-service level with the RAF". A team from the US, with the latest information on the project, was due to be in UK from 27 to 29 June; the basis for their discussion would be the technical aspects of the proposed US-UK agreement, such as the selection of sites, development of the missile and its preparation, security and training. He suggested a meeting on 27 or 28 June.

CAS told the Secretary of State for Air on 20 June that he thought that this invitation should be accepted, with the RAF team headed by DCAS, and S of S concurred. In a briefing prepared by DDOR9[1], it was pointed out that if the Americans were to site Thor on their bases there would be real danger to the civilian population – for example, if a failure occurred on a firing from Brize Norton with a trajectory passing over the London area. It was suggested that the underground sites on the east coast being selected for Blue Streak might be offered to the Americans, in return for an undertaking that they should develop them to be capable of taking both Thor and Blue Streak.

In the event, a 25-strong Air Ministry/MoS team attended the 27-29 June conference at South Ruislip. From the discussions – which were on a fact-finding basis; the Americans did not attempt to negotiate[2] – it emerged that Thor (with Jupiter still being regarded as a possible alternative) could not be sited underground, and that the Americans were "desperately anxious" to get their IRBMs deployed in the UK, and quickly[3]. Costing was not considered by the conference, and a technical mission to the US was still required.

The Secretary of State for Air expressed concern, in a minute to the Minister of Defence on 15 July, that Thor was not designed to be sited underground – so that its operational and deterrent value were diminished; also that the USAF were determined to locate the first 30 missiles on two sites (15 at each), which must be highly vulnerable, maintaining that "only by this means can the deployment be effected rapidly and cheaply". He thought that an idea of the cost was an essential preliminary to negotiations, and that it was not necessary to

---

[1] 25 June 1957 – ref CMS.3037/57.
[2] Report by DCAS to S of S (through CAS), 1 July 1957.
[3] Ibid. A record of the discussions in Thor Policy file AHB ID/47/298 (Pt 1) shows that joint RAF/USAF organising committees were set up.

send a technical mission to the US in the form originally envisaged–points with which the Minister concurred in his reply of 6 August.

On the 9th DCAS sent detailed RAF replies to questions raised at the South Ruislip meeting in a letter to the Commander of the 7th Air Division, SAC, Major-General W H Blanchard; one of the most important of these answers was that the use of East Kirkby and Sturgate for the deployment of the first two IRBM squadrons could not be accepted, suggesting Hemswell and Feltwell instead. Subsequently DCAS told the Secretary of State for Air[1] that he had discussed the position with General Blanchard, who expected to receive further instructions from Washington "in about two weeks".

According to a meeting which took place in Washington on 17 September, however, there did not appear to be any great urgency on the American side about the deployment of Thor in the UK: for Mr Donald Quarles, Deputy Secretary of Defense, apologised to the British Ambassador (Sir Harold Caccia) for "the delay in replying to the Minister of Defence's letter to Mr Wilson of June 11, enclosing a note of eleven points requiring further discussion on the IRBM project. . . .[2] Mr Wilson's reply to Mr Sandys' letter should be ready within a few days. . . . Meanwhile, there had been certain developments since the Minister of Defence's visit and the Bermuda Meeting".

Mr Quarles said that the Thor and Jupiter projects had been proceeding in parallel, but a committee had recently been set up to consolidate development in a one-weapon project. The US still expected to be ready for initial IRBM deployment in the UK "about the middle of 1959". The original plan had been to site the first two squadrons on US bases, but this had been modified at Bermuda. The UK "had asked to have all four squadrons on United Kingdom bases", and would therefore be responsible for the civil engineering at all four bases, with the US bringing-in special equipment. When asked by the Ambassador whether there was any danger that the overall agreement "was being held up by lack of agreement upon details" Mr Quarles said that to some degree this danger existed; lack of decision on the weapon provided some excuse for not pressing ahead with the details – considerable time would be required for working-out the agreement and the build-up of the bases[3].

[1] DCAS/Secretary of State (through US of S) CMS2960 Siting of American IR Ballistic Missiles in the UK 22 August 1957.
[2] Record of a Meeting in the office of the Deputy Secretary of Defense, 17 September 1957 in file on Thor Policy, AF/CMS 814/65 (AHB ID/47/298 Pt 1). The record included a note of replies "along the following lines" to the 11 points.
[3] In a report of the meeting in a letter of 18 September 1957 to Sir Richard Powell, MoD, Sir Harold Caccia the British Ambassador said there wasn't a great deal of discussion "partly because no-one on our side knew much of . . . what had been going on over the past months. No one here, for example, had received the results of the RAF-USAF meetings held in the UK in June". (AHB file ID9/240/17 Pt 1 Deployment of American IRBM in UK).

Referring to this meeting with Mr Quarles in writing to S of S for Air on 19 December 1957, DCAS said that it was accepted that "we are obliged to finalise the agreement without any precise knowledge of the financial implications" and that it would be examined "between the Ministry of Defence, the Foreign Office and ourselves". On the question of operational control, the draft agreement said that this would be "the subject of joint determination between the two Governments": Mr Sandys had pursued this further on his recent visit to Washington, and had suggested that for political reasons the first squadron to be based in the UK should be under British command – though it was unlikely that the Americans would be prepared to accept this.

The "revised draft agreement on deployment of the United States Intermediate Range Ballistic Missile in the United Kingdom", dated 17 December 1957, spelt out the purpose of this as "pursuant to the agreement in principle between the Prime Minister of the United Kingdom and the President of the United States reached at Bermuda on March 22, 1957, and in support of the purposes of the North Atlantic Treaty . . ." and set down the following deployment plan: four squadrons of 15 missiles each to be deployed in the UK as rapidly as possible; missiles and related equipment of the first two of the four squadrons to be under US operational control, and to be transferred to UK operational control as soon as they were available; the US to undertake to train UK personnel; and sites for the four squadrons to be prepared by the UK. Weapons, materials, equipment and training were to be furnished by the US "pursuant to the Mutual Security Act of 1954, as amended. . .".

It was not until 9 December 1957 that the Chiefs of Staff knew unequivocally that the IRBM to be deployed in the UK would be Thor and not Jupiter, Sir Richard Powell telling the CoS Committee that the Americans "had now decided that the United States Air Force would be the Service involved and the weapon would be the Thor missile". CAS (Air Chf Mshl Sir Dermot Boyle) said that the Air Ministry "had not yet received any details of the project from Strategic Air Command".

Early in 1958, from 20 to 24 January, discussions were held at the Air Ministry between Major-General Blanchard and Air Mshl Tuttle and their staffs and as a result a draft Technical Agreement between the USAF and RAF was formulated – "on the establishment of Intermediate Range Ballistic Missile (SM-75 Thor) Bases in the United Kingdom". This gave the timetable for the first squadron as three missiles by July 1958, three more by September and the remaining nine by the end of 1958.

It said that each squadron was to be deployed on five sites, each one containing three missiles, and gave the following squadron locations: the first, at Feltwell, Honington, Witchford, Marham and Watton; the second, at Hemswell, Caistor, Ludford Magna, Waddington and Bardney; the third, at Driffield, Full Sutton, Holme-on-Spalding Moor,

Riccall and Leconfield; and the fourth at Dishforth, Scorton, Leeming, Marston Moor and Sherburn-in-Elmet. Main base for each squadron would be the first station named. (These did not change, but many of the other locations subsequently differed from this list).

On 27 January CAS told the Minister of Defence that the USAF had agreed with the RAF "that the four squadrons of Thor IRBMs should be dispersed from the start and sited as follows . . ." – naming the four main bases as Feltwell, Hemswell, Driffield and Dishforth. Two days later a note by CAS expressing concern at the "unsatisfactory state of affairs" which existed "regarding the establishment of American IRBMs (Thor) in the country" was considered by the Chiefs of Staff. This note, reproduced as a CoS memorandum and forwarded to Ministers as an expression of their views, said that they were "opposed to being rushed into this commitment", which in their view was "designed to serve American ends more than British".

The Technical Agreement also said that the first squadron would be manned initially by USAF personnel, but that "RAF personnel will replace the USAF personnel as soon as the Royal Air Force is prepared to operate the weapon".

On 29 January 1958 DCAS sent copies of the IRBM Agreements to the Air Council[1] with a recommendation that they be accepted, and at a meeting on the 30th[2] he outlined the steps which had led up to this proposed deployment of American missiles in the United Kingdom, recalling that it had been first mentioned when the US Secretary of the Air Force visited London in July 1956[3]:

"It had then been envisaged that, in return for the right to station IRBM in this country, the Americans would provide us with *quid pro quo* in the shape of advanced fighters.

"Following a visit by the Minister of Defence to Washington in January 1957, and the Bermuda Conference in March, it emerged that the Americans were thinking in terms of four squadrons of IRBM, two . . . to be manned by the USAF and two by the RAF, to be deployed in this country in 1959. The Prime Minister made a public statement about the project in April 1957, and the Minister of Defence obtained authority at a Ministerial meeting chaired by the Prime Minister on 30 May 1957, to pursue negotiations with the Americans, reporting back to the Defence Committee before concluding an agreement.

"Discussions between the two Governments had resulted in the draft documents reproduced as Appendices 'A' and 'B' to DCAS's paper; and Air Force to Air Force discussions, culminating in a series of meetings held during the week 20-24 January, had resulted in the draft technical agreement reproduced as Appendix 'C'"[4].

---

[1] AC(58)5.
[2] Conclusions 3(58).
[3] *Ie* before the Suez operations (October 1956), which upset Anglo-American relations.
[4] These were, respectively, the main agreement, a secret agreement and the technical agreement.

DCAS went on to enumerate the disadvantages of the American IRBM proposals: the weapons would never be within effective British control; they were still essentially in the R&D stage; the deployment would entail a capital expense of about £10 million for the UK and an annual manpower bill of some 4,000 men; the presence of "these highly vulnerable missiles" would make the UK a more attractive target for attack; if the project were to succeed, the danger of pressure to abandon "our independent IRBM deterrent, Blue Streak", would increase; and the way the Americans were handling the project, and remarks Saceur had made about IRBM deployed in Europe, suggested that they "had by no means dismissed the possibility that the weapons in this country might ultimately come under the operational control of Saceur".

In considering these points prior to communicating with the Ministry of Defence, the Air Council followed the advice of the Secretary of State for Air, who suggested that they should not "take too negative a line" on the project – Ministers were "well aware of the disadvantages, some of which they had already accepted". CAS, however, urged that the UK "should not commit itself to any expenditure until we had more convincing evidence that the weapon would become fully operational within a reasonable period of time". On the "extremely complex financial arrangements" envisaged for the project, the Council agreed that these should be examined at official level by the Treasury as well as by the Ministry of Defence. The Secretary of State commented that the agreements as a whole "raised issues on which he thought the Minister of Defence would wish to consult the Defence Committee" – there were notable divergences from the pattern envisaged when Ministers last discussed the project on 30 May 1957. In its conclusions the Council invited PUS to arrange for the MoD to be informed of the substance of their discussion, noted that S of S would write to the Minister of Defence on the wider political implications of the agreements as a whole and on the consequences of accepting the American proposal for an accelerated deployment, and decided that a committee should be set up under US of S to consider problems of works, lands and public relations[1] and to report back to the Council.

The Cabinet considered the deployment of US IRBMs in the UK at its meeting on 12 February 1958[2], having before it a memorandum by the Minister of Defence, to which were annexed drafts of the documents constituting the proposed Agreement with the US Government for this deployment. As a result of their discussion – subject to further consideration of points made during it – the Minister was authorised to continue negotiations with the US authorities on the

---

[1] At the Air Council meeting (Conclusions 3(58)) the Secretary of State had said he "considered that the land clearance and works aspect of the Thor project raised delicate issues of public relations, and that if the scheme were to go through smoothly . . . a very close watch would need to be kept on all activities which would come to public notice".

[2] CC (58) 16th Conclusions.

basis of the draft documents. He was also invited to submit the final draft of the Agreement to the Prime Minister for his approval, and to circulate the draft of his proposed Parliamentary statement about it, "together with details of any further amendments of substance to the text of the Agreement which he might find it necessary to propose".

The Cabinet approved the draft Agreement with the US Government for the deployment of IRBM units in the UK (subject to three amendments which the Prime Minister "had invited President Eisenhower to accept") on 18 February 1958 and "invited the Minister of Defence to announce the conclusion of the Agreement" – the Foreign Secretary being invited to instruct HM Ambassador in Washington to arrange, if possible, the signature on the 24th of the documents comprising it – in Parliament on that date, and to arrange for the simultaneous publications of a White Paper "comprising such parts of it as need not remain secret"[1].

The deployment was also considered two days later by the Home Affairs Committee[2], which invited the Secretary of State for Air to consult the Financial Secretary to the Treasury about expenditure on the first site, and also to submit to the Cabinet his proposals on local consultation and right to object, the financing of the project and the manning of the squadrons. It also "took note that the Home Secretary would at once report the position to the Prime Minister".

On 25 February 1958 the Agreement to deploy American IRBMs in the UK became public knowledge with the appearance of the White Paper mentioned at the outset of this chapter – *Supply of Ballistic Missiles by the United States to the United Kingdom* (Cmnd 366) – and a Parliamentary statement by the Minister of Defence. Referring to the original agreement in principle between President Eisenhower and Prime Minister Macmillan at the Bermuda Conference, the White Paper included a Memorandum – datelined Washington, 22 February 1958 – which laid down the main parameters of IRBM deployment[3]. In particular (in view of the original American plan to man the first two squadrons with USAF personnel), it said that the missiles were to be "manned and operated by United Kingdom personnel" – who would be "trained by the United States Government . . . at the earliest feasible date". A decision to launch the missiles would be a joint one between the two Governments, and references to IRBMs in the Agreement did not include nuclear warheads, which the US Government would provide – warheads so provided remaining "in full United States custody". The Agreement itself was to remain in force "for not less than five years".

[1] CC(58) 17th Conclusions, 18 Feb 58.
[2] HA(58) 3rd Mtg, 14 Feb 58.
[3] The negotiations were also publicised in Treaty Series No 14 (1958) Exchange of Notes between the Government of the United Kingdom and the Government of the United States concerning the Supply to the UK Government of Intermediate Range Ballistic Missiles (together with Memorandum), Washington 22 Feb 58 (Cmnd 406 – April 1958).

In his Parliamentary statement on 24 February Mr Sandys told the Commons succinctly what was in the Anglo-American agreement[1]. He reminded the House that at their meeting in Bermuda the previous March the Prime Minister and President Eisenhower had "agreed in principle that certain guided missiles would be available for deployment in Britain" and continued:

"This was followed by technical studies by the military and scientific staffs of the two countries. These studies having now been completed, Her Majesty's Government and the Government of the United States have concluded an Agreement, setting out the arrangements for the supply and deployment of these weapons.

"The missiles will be manned and operated by units of the Royal Air Force.

"The Agreement provides that the missiles shall not be launched except by a joint positive decision of both Governments.

"The nuclear warheads will remain in American custody and will be kept in an unarmed condition so that there can be no risk of a nuclear explosion; and the weapon is designed in such a way that it would be impossible for it to be launched accidentally.[2]

"The United States will supply the missiles and specialised equipment at their expense and will also pay for the training of British personnel in America. Britain will meet the cost of providing and constructing the sites and supplying certain items of equipment. The British share of this expenditure is estimated at about £10 million.

"The missiles will be deployed in small numbers on dispersed sites, mostly on active or disused RAF airfields. These sites will be mainly in East Anglia, Lincolnshire and Yorkshire."

The only major fact the Minister omitted to mention was that the agreement was to last for five years. It had resulted from the Bermuda conversation of 22 March 1957 between the President and the Prime Minister[3] and formed the political basis for the deployment of Thors in the United Kingdom between 29 August 1958, when the first Thor was offloaded from a C-124 Globemaster at Lakenheath, to 27 September 1963 when the last Thor was returned to the US. During this period, as will subsequently be described, the RAF became the only air force to use Thor – with training and live firings in the US and operational

---

[1] Hansard Vol 583, cols 29–35.

[2] In a letter to *The Times* for 13 September 197? a retired RAF officer, Mr Donald Hofford, referred to the "double-key procedure" used in simulated launches of Thors, an RAF and a USAF officer sitting side by side.

[3] In this conversation (covered by a Memorandum in the report on Anglo-American discussions, 21–24 March 1957) the President had recalled earlier discussions between the UK Minister of Defence and US Secretary of Defense "in which there had been outlined a concept under which United States-developed Intermediate Range Ballistic Missiles (IRBMs) might be provided for deployment in the United Kingdom, when such missiles became available for use. . . . The President said he was glad to be able to inform the Prime Minister that in principle the United States Government was agreeable to working out arrangements for making IRBMs available to the United Kingdom. . . ".

deployment in Bomber Command as part of the Western strategic nuclear deterrent.

Shortly after the Parliamentary statement by the Minister of Defence on the deployment of American IRBMs in the UK, ACAS (Ops) (AVM R B Lees) circulated a minute on 10 April confirming where the first RAF Thor squadron would be sited. It said that Feltwell, near Thetford in Norfolk, would be the main domestic and technical base, with a launching pad of three missiles; associated with it would be four launching pads of three missiles – at North Pickenham, Shepherds Grove, Tuddenham and Mepal. On 20 May ACAS (Ops) reported that the second squadron would be at Hemswell, in Lincolnshire, with associated launching pads at Bardney, Caistor, Ludford Magna and Coleby Grange.

At the Chiefs of Staff meeting on that date the committee concurred with the view of the CAS (Air Chf Mshl Sir Dermot Boyle) that it would be wrong militarily to deploy Thor operationally until they were satisfied that it could function efficiently: a brief was to be prepared for the Prime Minister to take to the United States early in June.

The Thor project in the UK was code-named Emily and on 4 June 1958 a list of officers concerned with it – at the Air Ministry, HQ Bomber Command and HQ 7th Air Division – was circulated. The organisation of missile bases and squadrons was, however, something entirely novel for the RAF. Early in the year AMSO (Air Chf Mshl Sir Walter Dawson) had admitted that "neither the Americans nor ourselves have any practical experience to draw upon for the exact requirements of a unit of this sort".

While the acquisition of sites (former RAF airfields which had been returned to agricultural use) and their development as Thor bases was in progress, CAS again expressed disquiet about "pressure from the Americans to deploy Thor in this country before we can be satisfied that it has achieved a satisfactory operational performance". In a minute of 20 June he reminded S of S (Mr George Ward) that the Chiefs of Staff felt strongly on this subject – early in the year they had expressed "grave misgivings" about the proposed deployment of Thor in the UK – and asked that the Minister of Defence be invited to consider the problem as a matter of urgency before any final decisions were taken. On the 23rd, S of S suggested to the Minister that there should be "an early discussion" to "consider what our next step ought to be".

A Technical Agreement between the RAF and the USAF was signed on the 26th and at a meeting on 2 July the Minister "authorised the RAF to accept the first 15 Thor missiles, starting in August, for the purpose of training . . . and working-up the first squadron". Even after the first one was established in September 1958, however, there were doubts about the formation of further ones beyond a second, for which personnel had already been trained. S of S told the Minister of Defence on 19 January 1959 that "operationally" there were no grounds which justified "our taking weapons for the second squadron". Thor was "still in the development stage. No single missile" had "as yet attempted a full operational test or been tried out over the 1,500nm range". He considered that "in view of the administrative and training factors . . . we should be justified in accepting one more squadron", but recommended that this "should not in any way commit us to taking the third and fourth . . . until we are satisfied that the weapon development programme is proceeding satisfactorily"[1].

Because of such doubts as to 'Thor's operational capability, the Air Staff had stuck to a literal interpretation of the Anglo-US Agreement, that the missiles were being supplied for training purposes, but at a meeting held by S of S on 27 April it was agreed that the position that "the weapon was still only of training value" could no longer be held "indefinitely with the Americans". It was decided to send a team of experts to the US "with the object of reporting to the Air Ministry and the Ministry of Defence whether Thor was now operational".

However, the relevant talks were held in the UK in May with Mr James H Douglas, Secretary of the Air Force, though without prejudice to the proposed visit to Washington, Mr Douglas welcoming "the proposal of an early visit by a British team to consider the operational acceptability" of Thor. But on the political level, the Foreign Secretary (Mr Selwyn Lloyd) felt strongly that "no announcement about the operational state of Thor should be made for the time being as he considered that such a statement could have a harmful effect on the Geneva talks"[2]. Clearly, at a time of international discussions, in which the Russians were involved, about a peace treaty with Germany, it could be prejudicial to acknowledge publicly the operational capability of American missiles in Britain. This point arose at a meeting held by S of S for Air on 16 July, when it was said that "against the background of the Geneva talks it still remained undesirable to make any announcement about the initial operational capability of Thor"[3].

Subsequently DCAS (Air Mshl Tuttle) met General Blanchard, Commander, 7th Air Division, USAF, and on the 20th reported to S of S that the latter "quite understood the problems involved in making a statement about the capability of Thor at the present time"; then, two

---

[1] DCAS had also expressed some environmental and political doubts about the Thor deployment. In a paper sent to S of S for Air on 19 Jun 58 he warned that "about 40 American citizens" would arrive and settle on Feltwell by the end of the month, their numbers increasing progressively until there were about 400 by the end of the year: "you will have seen AMSO's minute regarding the car caravan camp for them". Also he said he had been informed that the Thor missiles for the RAF had "United States Air Force painted on them instead of roundels", which "could be quite embarrassing when they are noticed by the people of Feltwell and the surrounding villages". He was "arranging for re-painting, subject to American agreement".

[2] Minute, PS to S of S/DUSI, 3 Jul 59, in Organisation and Establishment of Thor Units (ID3/909/7 Pt 1).

[3] APS to S of S/PS to DCAS, 16 Jul 59 (Ibid).

days later, DCAS urged S of S that the provision of Thors for the third and fourth squadrons should not be impeded. There was "a constant flow of missiles", he said;

"The Feltwell squadron is fully deployed, all the sites of the second squadron at Hemswell capable of accepting missiles have their full complement, and the Hemswell maintenance facility is also full. Unless we call a halt to the steady flow of missiles from factory to the UK, . . . our only course of action is to start storing missiles at Driffield, the Headquarters of the third squadron. In view of the very encouraging test results, there can be no reason for delaying the receipt of weapons for the third and fourth squadrons, and I have therefore informed Major General Blanchard that he may fly-in missiles ultimately earmarked for the last two squadrons. Had I not done this, we would be forced to suspend the flow of missiles early next week . . ."

Subsequently there were reports in the British press in early August 1959 about the operational state of Thor missiles, based on an article in the 27 July issue of the US magazine *Rockets and Missiles*. On the 7th there was one in the *News Chronicle* alleging that there was a US-UK dispute as to whether or not warheads should be fitted to the Thors; and later – in the 2 November issue of the *Daily Express* – Mr Chapman Pincher averred that political disagreement between the UK and the US had become so serious that it could imperil future military aid, and that "for fear of souring relations with Kruschev, the Prime Minister has ruled that the Thor rockets delivered . . . a year ago cannot be declared 'operational'".

On the 3rd, in answer to a question from the Prime Minister about "how matters stood about the operational capability of Thor", the Minister of Defence (Mr Harold Watkinson) said that they were answering Press questions by saying that the Air Ministry had not "completed all the technical examination needed" before the weapon could be declared operational. Subsequently, with the approval of the Prime Minister and the Minister of Defence, Thor's operational capability was publicly acknowledged on 9 December 1959 when the Secretary of State for Air (Mr George Ward) stated in the Commons, in reply to a Question, that "as a result of the test firings which have taken place in the USA[1] and in the light of the progress made in the training programme, we are now satisfied that Thor is able to take its place as part of the operational front line of the Royal Air Force".

A problem then arose as to the number of combat training launches RAF personnel were to be allowed to do each year. Under the Thor Agreement the US Government were responsible for providing missiles for training, and the Air Ministry and 7th Air Division had agreed that eight were required per year for CTLs; but on 18 December 1959 S of S for Air informed the Minister of Defence that the US Secreatry of

---

[1] The Air Ministry Quarterly Liaison Report for July-September 59 said that a further eight missile firings had taken place from Patrick AFB, Florida, seven had been successful.

Defense had "for economy reasons" halved this number to four, and asked if the Minister would make representations about "adhering to the original programme". In response to a letter of 12 January 1960 from Mr Watkinson, the Secretary of Defense said that he was unable to increase the limit of four launches per year for budgetary reasons, but agreed with the Minister's second point – that the missiles fired would be taken from those deployed in the UK, not supplied direct from the manufacturers. This reply was accepted by S of S with some reservation: he pointed out to the Minister on 23 March that it would not be until December 1960 that a fully modified missile taken from the UK was fired at Vandenberg AFB. This would be alright provided the tests were satisfactory; but only 14 more missiles would then remain to be fired.

The other point raised about the Thors deployed by Bomber Command – the fitting of warheads to them – was resolved on 10 May 1960 when the Minister of Defence gave his agreement to these being fitted. At the end of March, prior to a meeting between the Minister and the US Secretary of Defense, PS to S of S for Air had advised his opposite number in the MoD that "certain American politicians" were aware that warheads were not being fitted to Thors in the UK and that as a result "a certain amount of pressure" was "building up in the USA"[1]

The British Thor deployment was sustained by a massive American airlift: "one of the requirements of the specification was that Thor and its support equipment should be air-transportable in aircraft like the C-124 and C-133, and the 60 Thor supplied to Bomber Command . . . were all delivered by air, representing a total airlift of more than 25m lb (11,340,000kg) of missiles and ground support equipment[2]."

Some idea of what was involved in this airlift can be gained from a book on Thor, where the author thus describes the "means of delivery" from California to the UK[3]:-

"That vital link had been developed to near perfection by the 1607th Air Transport Wing of MATS' Eastern Air Transport Force. They learned the hard way, while hauling nearly 6,000 tons of missiles and materiel for RAF Feltwell alone; that was approximately 300 C-124 flights, usually from Long Beach, California, by way of Dover AFB, Delaware; Harmon AFB, Newfoundland; with possibly another stop at Lajes AFB, in the Azores, depending on the load factor.

"Frequently, the cargo itself demanded tricky flying. Rate of descent, for instance, was restricted to prevent pressure damage to Thor tanks. And when AC Spark Plug guidance units were aboard, take-offs were more exacting than ever.

"Costing thousands of dollars each, the guidance unit gyroscopes were suspended in a lubricant which had to be maintained within

---

[1] Correspondence in Organisation and Establishment of Thor Units (AHB ID3/909/7 pt 1).
[2] *Jane's All the World's Aircraft*, 1960-61.
[3] *The Mighty Thor Missile in Readiness* by Julian Hartt (Duell, Sloan and Pearce, 1961).

exacting temperature ranges throughout the flight. The control of this depended on power from the C-124s after engine start and ground power disconnection. To make sure that there was no drain of that vital power supply, pilots had to keep their outboard engines throttled up to 1,200rpm even while waiting for take-off clearance. That meant they had to keep their brakes set against the pull of the props. Again, to prevent excessive power drain from the cargo, they only checked out the airplane's various power circuits after reaching level-off, and even then checked items but one at a time. Contractors sent along 'birdwatchers', as they quickly came to be known, on such deliveries to watch the gauges for trouble. On landing, a battery system – saved for this moment – was cut in to keep the heat within tolerable range until ground power again could take over".

This airlift had been organised under the aegis of the 7th Air Division, SAC, whose history provides concise summaries of the main stages:–[1]

"Under an early 1958 agreement, the United States and the United Kingdom shared responsibility for the Thor missile program. The United Kingdom agreed to build four bases and to man four Thor squadrons, while the United States agreed to furnish the missiles and provide training for the RAF crews. Effective 20 February, the 705th Strategic Missile Wing (IRBM-Thor) was activated at Lakenheath RAF Station and assigned to the 7th Air Division. It was responsible for monitoring the Thor program and for providing technical assistance to the four RAF squadrons. Thor training for RAF crews began at Vandenberg on 15 September 1957".

Named after General Hoyt S Vandenberg, USAF Chief of Staff 1948-53, this West coast facility – Vandenberg AFB – was constructed primarily as a space base, for the launching of large satellites and space vehicles in orbits which could not be readily achieved from Cape Canaveral. From it, the USAF fired its first ballistic missile – a Thor – on 16 December 1958. A vivid description of the establishment and geographical location of Vandenberg occurs in the book on Thor already been quoted from.

It comments:–

"The keen foresight of Air Force planners . . . was a significant factor in the early 1956 selection of Camp Cooke for transformation into Vandenberg AFB. Just below Point Arguello, the Californian coast turns sharply eastward. From there to the Straits of Magellan and Tierra del Fuego at the southernmost tip of South America, the coast line of the continent slants almost steadily eastward. That geographic fact makes this middle seaward jut of California the one suitable point in the continental United States where rockets can be fired due south without endangering populated communities or friendly neighbors by falling

[1] *The Development of Strategic Air Command 1946-1971* (HQ, SAC, Offutt AFB, Nebraska).

296

boosters or early 'destructs'. Nothing but the sea stretches between Vandenberg-Arguello and Antarctica".

The SAC history recorded that, during 1959,

"on 16 April an RAF crew launched its first Thor from Vandenberg as part of the training program. By the end of the year, three squadrons of Thor IRBMs had been turned over to the Royal Air Force and were operational in the United Kingdom".

Then, in 1960, that

"on 22 April, the fourth and final Thor squadron, which had been trained at Vandenberg AFB, California, was accepted by the Royal Air Force, thus completing the deployment of this IRBM to the United Kingdom".

A detailed description of how the Thors were deployed and operated in RAF Bomber Command occurs in Chapter XXI of this history.

CHAPTER XVIII

EXERCISES AND COMPETITIONS; DISPERSAL TECHNIQUES; LIFE IN THE V-FORCE

By the end of 1958, when Anglo-American co-operation in strategic nuclear warfare roles had been fully established – with agreements on the co-ordination of strike plans, the supply of US atomic weapons to the UK, the deployment of Thor IRBMs in Britain and co-operation on the uses of atomic energy for mutual defence purposes (under a US-UK agreement signed on 3 July 1958) – the V-force of Bomber Command had grown to 15 squadrons. In No 1 Group there were three of Vulcan B.1s – Nos 83 at Waddington, 101 at Finningley and 617 at Scampton; in No 3 Group there were two of Victor B.1s, Nos 10 and 15, both at Cottesmore, and all seven Valiant B.1 squadrons – Nos 7 and 90 at Honington, 148, 207 and 214 at Marham, and 49 and 138 at Wittering. In addition there were Valiants in No 18 Squadron (part of the ECM force) at Honington and they equipped No 543 Squadron at Wyton (part of the Bomber Command Strategic Reconnaissance Wing). At this time, too, guided missile units appeared in the RAF Order of Battle – including the first two Thor squadrons, No 77 at Feltwell, which had received its first missile on 19 September and 13 more by the end of the year, and No 97 at Hemswell, which did not actually re-form until 22 July 1959.

Also in this period the RAF stations used by USAF Strategic Air Command – Fairford and Brize Norton in Oxfordshire and Greenham Common in Berkshire – were crowded with B-47s under the dispersal programme, organised to counter the Soviet missile threat. As the history of SAC described it:

"During the tremendous expansion of the early and mid-fifties, bases had become overcrowded, with some of them supporting as many as 90 B-47s and 40 KC-97s[1]. . . . As the Russian missile threat became more pronounced and warning time became less, SAC bases presented increasingly attractive targets. It was necessary to break up these large concentrations of aircraft and scatter them throughout more bases. . . ."

Later, referring to "termination of B-47 rotational training", the history says:

"The success of the ground alert program and Reflex Action prompted SAC to discontinue the 90-day rotational training program that had characterised B-47 operations since 1953. The 100th Bomb Wing, the last B-47 wing to become combat ready, was the last B-47 wing to perform the 90-day rotational training. This assignment was conducted at Brize Norton RAF Station . . . from early January to early April. Upon departure of the 100th, B-47 Reflex operations

---

[1] Piston-engined tankers, superseded by KC-135 jet tankers.

298

began at Brize Norton. Reflex had already commenced in early January at Greenham Common and Fairford"[1].

These Reflex operations took place in 1958 and involved, rather than complete wings, a small number of aircraft from several wings. The SAC history has recounted that in July 1957

"Reflex Action commenced with four Second Air Force Wings sending five B-47s each to Sidi Slimane Air Base, French Morocco. This new system of operation was based on the premise that a few crews and aircraft on ground alert at oversea bases would be more effective than maintaining entire wings at these bases on 90-day rotational training assignments. If successful, SAC planned to replace the 90-day rotational program at all oversea bases with Reflex Action, with aircraft and crews being frequently rotated from bases in the United States. . .".

The presence of B-47s in the UK, together with the V-bombers and Thors – a very visible presence to anyone flying over England at light aircraft level (2,000-3,000 ft) in the late 1950s-early 1960s and seeing the Oxfordshire/Berkshire airfields crowded with distinctively-shaped B-47s and the white Valiants, Vulcans and Victors on V-force bases and white Thors pointing skywards, meant that greater destructive power was concentrated on UK bases than at any time since the Second World War; and it was to increase, as the number of V-bombers grew and the total of Thors delivered rose to the 60 which had been allotted.

As an indication of the scale of logistics involved in the latter operation, HQ Bomber Command's ORB for May 1959 reported that "since the beginning of the project, the supply Air Movements Section has turned round 178 USAF transport aircraft and handled 2,490 tons of equipment" – in relation to No 97 Squadron at Hemswell; and in June, referring to No 98 Squadron at Driffield, the ORB said that "during the month 21 USAF transport aircraft were turned round, involving 355 tons of equipment. Other USAF equipment received by sea, rail and road totalled 707 tons".

Speaking in the defence debate in the Commons on 26 February 1959 the Minister of Defence (Mr Duncan Sandys) quoted the Commander-in-Chief of the USAF Strategic Air Command (General Thomas S Power) as saying that

"The British V-bomber force, with its high-performance jet aircraft and thermonuclear weapons, is an essential element of the Western deterrent and it has an important place in our joint operational plans, which are now fully co-ordinated.

"Should the free world ever be attacked by the Soviet Union, rapid reaction would be vital. Having regard to Britain's closer proximity, we rely on her V-bombers to provide an important part of the first wave of the Allied retaliatory force. I am therefore particularly glad to observe the steadily growing combat capability and state of

---

[1] Reflex Action, started in 1957, was the deployment of a few B-47s instead of the 90-day rotational assignment of whole wings.

readiness of RAF Bomber Command".[1]

Operational readiness was a matter which was to exercise the Air Staff and Bomber Command HQ during the late 1950s.

For Bomber Command in its V-force period, the readiness was all: training, exercises, maintenance, accommodation and hours of duty all tended to this one end – the ability to get a fully operational V-bomber off the ground in the minimum time possible, so as to give the force invulnerability from attack in order to fulfil its nuclear deterrent role. In this aspect of quick reaction the V-force revived the "scramble" techniques of wartime Fighter Command. For Bomber Command the implications of introducing a 24hr, seven-day-a-week quick reaction alert system throughout the squadrons were far-reaching, particularly as they involved manpower. The AOC in C Bomber Command (Air Mshl K B B Cross) told VCAS (Air Mshl Sir Edmund Hudleston) in a letter of 26 June 1959 that a good deal of progress had been made over readiness; there was an impressive list of re-organisation and action on many items. But "the one stumbling block of manpower shortages dominates all else" – so much so that improvements in actual readiness capability in the squadrons since the previous July had been "lamentably slow".

The C in C referred to a request[2] he had had from the Minister of Defence (Mr Duncan Sandys) to send him a note on the readiness position of the medium bomber squadrons in the Command, the attendant problems not being new ones. "My predecessor in January, and both of us since,[3] have warned the Air Ministry about the effects on our readiness of the shortages in the supply of aircrew servicing chiefs, air radar fitters, and in some of the non-technical trades". He said that the supply of ASCs was "a sorry story", and unless some drastic action were taken he could not forecast the effects after about nine months.

In an enclosed Progress Report on the Readiness of the Medium Bomber Force the historical background outlined made clear the stresses which would be imposed on the available resources of manpower:–

"On 7 July 1958 Bomber Command was directed to introduce a readiness capability into the medium bomber squadrons which would meet the following conditions:–

(a) Strategic Warning: 24 hours' notice, after which 75 per cent of the force should be at readiness, armed and dispersed.

(b) Tactical Warning: 40 minutes, capable of being sustained for one month, and/or 15 minutes sustained for one week.

---

[1] Hansard Cols 1414-1424

[2] Made verbally on 19 June, when the Minister visited Cottesmore and flew in a Victor of No 10 Squadron on an NBS/RBS bombing attack.

[3] Air Chief Mshl Sir Harry Broadhurst relinquished the appointment of AOC in C Bomber Command on 20 May 1959 and was succeeded by AVM K B B Cross, AOC No 3 Group, with the acting rank of Air Marshal.

(c) On notification of an emergency, the generation rate of all medium bomber aircraft on the strength of stations was to be 20 per cent in two hours, 40 per cent in four hours, 60 per cent in eight hours, 75 per cent in 24 hours.

(d) The above conditions were to be met at any time of the day, weekends or holidays throughout the year. Six additional airfields were to be provided to bring the total number, including six operational Class 1 bases, up to 36 airfields.

"These instructions were confirmed at a meeting called by the Minister of Defence with the Secretary of State for Air on 21 July 1958.

"The Command was subsequently directed to submit the revised establishments required at medium bomber bases to the Air Ministry for approval, and an analysis of the manpower requirement for readiness and the introduction of the two-shift/18hr system was completed. This analysis revealed that the dates by which the readiness capability of the medium bomber squadrons would be governed by the supply of manpower, particularly aircraft servicing chiefs and technicians for the servicing of the navigation and bombing systems. . .".[1]

The provision of a limited number of additional personnel at a cost of about £50,000 a year to enable the bomber force to maintain the same state of readiness over weekends and holidays as during the working week was one of the "specific measures to increase the readiness of Bomber Command" approved by the Defence Committee on 21 July 1958. The others were "to assist the Force to maintain a 15-minute readiness to a period of up to seven days by providing sleeping quarters adjacent to aircraft at main bases" and the provision of six additional dispersal airfields.

At the end of his letter to VCAS, the C in C commented that the current position over the readiness of the MB squadrons was that one squadron could meet the requirements then, six more would meet them by the end of the year and a further five by April 1960. For the rest, he could not forecast, but he thought it fair to say that all the medium bomber squadrons

"if warned now during the working week, could meet the aircraft generation rates needed, and some disperse themselves; though they could not all be prepared on arrival in the time required, or be maintained for the full periods needed".

In addition to the manning problems which occupied the C in C Bomber Command during the latter half of 1959 in his correspondence with VCAS, other factors which would help to reduce the MB force reaction time were being dealt with, as evidenced by a minute from DGO to ACAS(Ops) on 22 October, saying that

"A request has been received from HQ Bomber Command for the addition of turning loops at runway ends at dispersal stations Pershore

---

[1] There seems to be a word missing in this last sentence although the sense is clear.

and Leeming. These will enable 'stream' take-offs instead of back-tracking and take-off by individual or pairs of aircraft. The loops will permit a reduction in take-off time of, possibly, five to eight minutes for four aircraft. . . .

"Planning of the works services required at Pershore and Leeming is going ahead . . .".

On 2 November the Director of Bomber, Ballistic Missiles and Reconnaissance Operations wrote to the AOC in C Bomber Command to say that a trial was required

"to determine the minimum take-off time for a dispersed flight of V-aircraft under the following conditions:–

(a) Cockpit readiness awaiting scramble order;

(b) Aircraft positioned on runway or immediately adjacent to take-off point.

"The interval of elapsed time between the executive instructions and 'wheels up' for the first and last aircraft is to be recorded together with such information, stemming from the trial, which you may deem valuable for planning purposes".

In a comment to DGO on his minute of 22 October about turning loops at Pershore and Leeming to help to reduce reaction time, ACAS (Ops) said in his reply of 6 November[1] that the construction of readiness platforms at either end of a main runway was "by far the best method of getting aircraft off in the short interval of time commensurate with the kind of threat we may expect in the future". He added that Bomber Command had been instructed to conduct trials to determine the minimum reaction time for aircraft at cockpit readiness positioned at runway thresholds; and at the end of his minute said he would inform DGO of "any change in Air Staff policy which calls for the planning of ORPs as a general requirement".

Writing to CAS on 9 November about the provision of recreational facilities at Bomber Command stations to alleviate the long periods of duty by personnel there, the AOC in C said that the Alert and Readiness scheme, after initial delays, was now "well under way" – the first two stations had started and others would follow, until by June 1960 eight should be taking part. The scheme required the presence on the station of sufficient personnel to bring to readiness in 24 hours a high proportion of aircraft on the station, and the commitment would continue for 365 days in the year. He commented that "restriction on the liberty of individuals on such a scale, added to the inconvenience of working an 18-hour/two-shift system, particularly against the background of an almost universal five-day week, is bound to become a real hardship as time goes on". Hence the need for recreational facilities, which he went on to outline.

---

[1] Delayed, he explained, "in order that further discussions might be held with Bomber Command". Ref F.110/Ops.

Other aspects of medium bomber reaction times being studied at this period were engine starting times[1] and the provision of dispersal airfields – of which there were to be 30, ACAS (Ops) minuting VCAS on 14 December 1959:

"On the current dispersal plan, work has progressed to the stage where 16 airfields are now ready for use, a further eight on which planning has reached an advanced stage but on which no construction work has yet started would become available during 1960, and the final six for which we have not yet received Treasury approval will not be available before 1961"[2].

He suggested, however, that in view of a possible change in policy to meet a lower reaction time than the 15 minutes currently being planned for, work might be suspended at the remaining dispersal airfields until the policy had been reviewed.

Early in 1960 the AOC in C reported to the Air Ministry that the Medium Bomber Force had from 1 February a readiness capability covering both weekends/public holidays and weekdays, commenting that

"Exercises have indicated that, although initial generation rates are slower than those it was originally hoped could be achieved, the requirement of 75 per cent of the Force to be armed and ready within 24 hours can confidently be expected should it be called upon in an emergency to come to readiness during weekdays.

"In order to achieve a readiness capability over weekends and public holidays, 25 per cent of the available aircraft are held at two hours' readiness during these periods with supporting ground and air crews even though the two-flight/two-shift system is not yet fully operative throughout the Command. . . ."[3]

While these procedures were being brought into practice, a long-term view of future prospects was expressed by ACAS (Ops) (AVM John Grandy) in a letter to SASO, Bomber Command (AVM T A B Parselle), on 15 February.[4] He said that planning for the MBF, in conjunction with the IRBM force,

"must be towards the acquisition of an airborne ballistic missile either in long-endurance aircraft or aircraft with almost instantaneous reaction time based on tactical warning of ballistic missile attack from BMEWS. . . .[5]

"One aspect of the problems which will undoubtedly arise is that of low-level penetration of Russian air defences. This has already been

---

[1] A/DOR(A) on 7 Dec 59 quoted 105 sec for starting the remaining three engines of the Mk 1 V-bombers while taxying on one, 35 sec for those of a Mk 2 Vulcan and 105 sec for those of a Mk 2 Victor.

[2] Facilities required included domestic and technical accommodation, bulk fuel installation, WT masts, ECM storage and electronics centre.

[3] Letter to US of S, Air Ministry, 8 Feb 60.

[4] F.1351 (S)/Ops. AVM Grandy was subsequently to become AOC in C Bomber Command (1963-65).

[5] The BMEW station at Fylingdales became operational in 1963.

referred to by VCAS in his correspondence with your C in C concerning the SAC Bombing Competition, and it would seem to be being tackled seriously by the Americans.[1] Other aspects include technical and organisational requirements to ensure the rapid reaction necessary to make use of the information BMEWS can give us[2].

"While I would certainly not wish to suggest that we should interfere in any way with the responsibilities of the Command in these matters, I feel that considerable benefit would accrue if the problems confronting us could be studied jointly by your Headquarters and the Air Ministry. . . ."

The Minister of Defence had called for six-monthly reports on the state of readiness of Bomber Command, from January 1960 onwards[3], and in the report for 1 July – 31 December 1959 it was stated that the increasing missile threat would make it necessary to reduce the 15-minute readiness capability to about three minutes, which could be achieved with cockpit readiness; also that the introduction of operational readiness platforms was now being planned jointly by Bomber Command and the Air Ministry.

This report also referred to support facilities at dispersal airfields (when General Thomas D White, USAF Chief of Staff, visited RAF Cottesmore on 17 June 1959 he was shown a simulated dispersal camp, with operations caravan, signals and scramble facilities); to the inability to disperse medium bombers armed with Project 'E' (US) weapons, a problem already referred to in this history; to communications, including further facilities which the missile threat would demand – like telescramble direct to aircraft being held at cockpit readiness, and improved conference facilities between the Air Ministry, Bomber Command and Air Defence Operations Centres and between the AOC in C and the two Group Commanders; and to two exercises which had been held during the six-month (July-December) period – Mick, in July, to practise the alert and arming procedures without the dispersal of aircraft; and Mayflight II, in November, to practise all aspects of the Bomber Command readiness plan. ("As you are aware", one of Wittering's wing commanders put it to another in June 1961, "Mayflight is virtually a pre-planned Mick plus the actual dispersing of aircraft".)[4]

Later in 1960 proposals were put forward to increase the reality of Bomber Command alert exercises by carrying-out no-notice dispersal of the MBF under the code-name Micky Finn – an intensification of Mick and Mayflight, the new idea (and its implications) being set out

---

[1] The establishment of seven special air routes over which SAC bombers would fly low-level training missions was jointly announced by SAC and the FAA in November 1959 (*The Development of Strategic Air Command, 1946-1971*).

[2] Fylingdales, the AOC in C stated in February 1963, would increase the warning time to eight minutes.

[3] Minute, DCDS/VCAS, 30 July 59 (RWM/889) in 90/18 Operational Readiness of the RAF.

[4] Minute, Wg Cdr Ops/Wg Cdr Admin, Wittering, 6 June 61 in IIH1/243/2/2 (Pt 2) RAF Wittering Bomber Command Alert and Readiness Plan—Policy).

in a letter to VCAS from the AOC in C on 28 October in which he explained that, so far,

"Alert exercises have fallen into two classes:–

(a) 'No notice' exercises such as Exercise 'Mick' which have been conducted within the Command's resources except for the supply of weapons by Maintenance Command and the USAF. These exercises have necessarily stopped short of dispersal of the Force.

(b) Exercises of the 'Mayflight' type which have included all aspects of the dispersal plan up to and including the scramble but which have been planned for and known about some time in advance.

"Both types of exercise have limitations and the ability of the Force to react within the time laid down can only be properly tested by a 'no notice' exercise of the Mayflight type. Moreover, to obtain a true picture, such exercises should be held both on a normal working day and also during a weekend. It would then be possible to test, *inter alia*, the following vital aspects of the Bomber Command Alert and Readiness Plan:–

(a) The Command's ability to disperse without prior warning.

(b) The plan and procedure for recalling personnel who are away on weekend leave.

(c) Transport Command's ability to find the necessary aircraft at short notice.

(d) The ability of the various dispersal airfields, which belong to the Ministry of Aviation and other Services and Commands, to react rapidly and to provide the necesssary airfield facilities out of working hours and without previous warning.

(e) The ability of the Air Commander, Home Defence Forces, to supply the necessary reinforcements".

The AOC in C went on to say that there were so many agencies involved in no-notice exercises of this scope – Exercise Micky Finn, his letter was headed – that they could only be initiated with special authority from the Air Ministry. He asked for consideration of the proposal, and said that if it were agreed in principle, staff work on the details could begin.

This overriding obsession with operational readiness, to demonstrate the reality of the MBF in its strategic nuclear deterrent role, was reflected in the work of the squadrons in achieving and maintaining combat readiness – both of aircraft and crews. A study of the ORBs (Operations Record Books) of three of the Main Force squadrons, plus personal recollections of former crew members, shows the kind of exercises and training being done during 1960. To give a differential cross-section, and to show that there were common denominators, a squadron of each type of V-bomber has been studied – in fact the first of each type to be formed: No 138 (Valiants) at Wittering, No 83 (Vulcans) at Waddington and No 10 (Victors) at Cottesmore. Certain kinds of exercise were common to all three, and therefore presumably to other squadrons – station exercises, Group exercises (Groupex), Command exercises (for example Exercise Yeoman, a major UK air defence exercise, in May) and Nato exercises (like Fallex, in September). So were the routine training sorties – profiles,[1] Compex (in preparation for Command bombing and navigation competitions), RBS (radar bomb site) sorties and continuation training flights. Common too were the Lone Ranger and Western Ranger flights by single aircraft – the former eastwards, to Wildenrath, Luqa, El Adem, Nairobi, Salisbury or the Persian Gulf; the latter westwards, chiefly to Offutt AFB, Nebraska – designed to prove the mobility and independence from base facilities of the medium bombers and their crews. Other regular exercises were Kingpin[2] and Kinsman, the latter a squadron dispersal as opposed to Mayflight, which was a Command dispersal exercise. In each case the squadrons had their appointed dispersal airfields: No 138 went to Gaydon,[3] No 83 to Leeming and No 10 to Boscombe Down; normally, four aircraft and crews were dispersed. A reference in the last-named squadron's ORB to Exercise Mayflight III in July almost reflects the AOC in C's reference to "exercises of the 'Mayflight' type" in his letter to VCAS, referring to "a BCAR [Bomber Command Alert and Readiness] exercise in which, on receipt of the relevant alert, certain aircraft and crews were detached as rapidly as possible to the dispersal airfield. . . ". Or, in an earlier reference to Kinsman (during June), "the purpose of the exercise was to practise day-to-day operating from Boscombe Down, which is the squadron's dispersal airfield under the BCAR plan".

A full list of 36 medium bomber dispersal airfields approved for Operational Readiness Platforms, circulated in February 1962, showed the following three categories:—

Class 1 Airfields with ORPs and Facilities for Four Aircraft:

Finningley
Coningsby
Honington
Scampton
Wittering
Cottesmore
Waddington
Gaydon
Wyton

---

[1] A staple ingredient of V-force training, these were basically long cross-country flights into which simulated testing circumstances were injected, like emergencies or diversions.
[2] A monthly Command exercise.
[3] Pershore and Middleton St George were also used, but in Sep 61 these were changed to Filton and Yeovilton.

Dispersal Airfields with ORPs and Facilities for Four Aircraft:
Burtonwood
Bedford
St Mawgan
Ballykelly
Kinloss
Dispersal Airfields with ORPs and Facilities for Two Aircraft:
Filton
Leconfield
Leuchars
Lossiemouth
Boscombe Down
Pershore
Cranwell
Middleton St George
Yeovilton
Leeming
Llanbedr
Coltishall
Valley
Manston
Brawdy
Lyneham
Wattisham
Stansted
Elvington
Prestwick
Machrihanish
Bruntingthorpe

In circulating this list, HQ Bomber Command commented:–

"The present Bomber Command dispersal airfields were developed in 1959 to enable the Medium Bomber Force to operate at 15-minute readiness. The threat of ballistic missile attack has now made necessary an organisation to enable the MBF to be launched within the warning period to be expected from the Ballistic Missile Early Warning System (BMEWS) which will be ready at Fylingdales in 1963[1]. This warning period can be as little as three minutes, depending on the type of missile attack. . . .

"To take advantage of reduced warning times, operational readiness platforms and associated equipment have been designed to enable aircraft to stand adjacent to the runway. . . .

"A building programme is now in hand for the construction of ORPs and supporting facilities at 36 airfields"[2].

---

[1] Operational 17 Sep 63.
[2] List and letter in IIH1/243/2/2 RAF Wittering Bomber Command Alert and Readiness Plan – Policy.

In February 1960 the AOC in C Bomber Command (Air Mshl Sir Kenneth Cross) reported to the Air Ministry that the MBF had a readiness capability covering both weekends/public holidays and weekdays. He said that exercises had indicated that, although initial generation rates were slower than those it was originally hoped could be achieved, the requirement of 75% of the Force to be armed and ready within 24 hours could "confidently be expected" should it be called upon in an emergency to come to readiness during weekdays.

He went on to explain that, in order to achieve a readiness capability over weekends and public holidays, 25% of the available aircraft were held at two hours' readiness during these periods with supporting ground and air crews, even though the two-flight/two-shift system was not yet fully operative throughout the Command[1].

It was noted in mid-1960 that daily average serviceability of the Vulcan was about 39% of the MBF, and of the Victor about 33%. The Valiant had a serviceability rate of 57%. In a minute conveying these figures to VCAS (Air Mshl E C Hudleston) on 30 June, S of S for Air (Mr G R Ward) commented that they compared poorly with the standard of 75% or over "which we have assumed for our studies of the future capability of the deterrent force", adding: "In my view it casts doubts on our capacity to mount an effective contribution to the deterrent with 72 Vulcans"[2].

In his reply, on 7 July[3], VCAS commented that the Monthly Summary which S of S had seen did not reflect the Command's true capability to meet the requirement of having 75% or more of the Force serviceable and "combat ready" within 24hr of strategic warning of global war. What the figures did show, he said, was that "we can meet the essential readiness requirement of 20% of the Force available within two hours of receipt of warning". He commented further on 27 July, after Exercise Mayflight III, that the Command's capability to generate the planned proportion of combat-ready aircraft had "considerably improved" since the previous year's Mayflight exercise[4].

In addition to their Western Ranger flights, the V-bombers were also familiar with North American skies through their participation in the USAF Strategic Air Command bombing competitions. The first in which they took part, in 1957, has already been referred to; the next was in 1958, at March AFB, California, from 13 to 18 October, when two Valiant teams, each with two aircraft and four crews, competing in the B-52 class, did well – one coming 7th overall, out of 41 teams, and the other 20th overall. In the overall crew placings, Sqn Ldr R W

---

[1] Correspondence in ID9/90/18 Operational Readiness of the RAF.
[2] Ibid.
[3] Ibid.
[4] Not only the V-bombers were involved in readiness exercises. For example, in 1960 Varsities and Hastings from the BC Bombing School, Lindholme, provided transport support in Mayflight V (7–9 May) and Mickey Finn (20–22 Sep) respectively.

Richardson of No 148 Sqn came ninth out of 164 individual crews, Wg Cdr S Baker (CO, No 138 Squadron) 12th and Wg Cdr F C D Wright (CO, No 148 Squadron) 30th. A remarkable tribute was paid to the Valiant crews from the two Marham-based squadrons in a US newspaper, *The Boston Herald*, which said in its editorial column on 18 October:–

"Out at Riverside, California, a British bombing team placed seventh in this year's 'World Series' of high-altitude bombing, scoring 1379.7 points against the first place 1520 points. In the first of the three runs the Royal Air Force team, under Wing Commander Sidney Baker, came in third.

"Is this good? Well, the Americans had 140 Strategic Air Command crews in the contest, four from each of 35 bases, while the British had just four teams altogether. The Americans were on home grounds; the British in unfamiliar region.

"On each of three nights the crews are sent off on simulated bombing missions. The first target, for instance, was a specified corner of a Butte, Montana, department store. Observers equipped with electronic tracking devices determine the accuracy of the strikes, and other points are added to the score for navigation.

"It is a terrifically exacting test, demanding the utmost in equipment designing, crew training and command skill. Targets are a precise point, like the geometric center of a gasometer in Windsor, Ont. . . .

"The Royal Air Force has more than met the test. . . ."

In London, S of S for Air (Mr George Ward) minuted the Prime Minister on 4 November:–

"In view of your interest last year you may like to have a brief report on the participation by the Royal Air Force crews in this year's SAC bombing and navigation competition.

"41 teams entered, 39 from the United States Air Force and two from the Royal Air Force. Each team consisted of four crews.

"All crews flew the same route, which involved attacking three targets followed by an astro-navigation leg of about 950 miles.

"Our best individual crews came 9th, 12th and 30th out of 164. In the team events our two Wings were grouped with ten B-52 Wings and they came 3rd and 8th in their class and 7th and 20th overall out of the 41 Wings.

"These are very good results, and what is particularly encouraging is the very marked reduction in the bombing and navigation errors as compared with previous competitions. These reductions are doubly pleasing because the conditions under which the competition was flown were much more severe.

"Although they were operating far from their main bases the unserviceability of the bombing equipment of the Valiants was better than that of any of the American Wings. There was no airframe or engine unserviceability".

S of S included a copy of the comments by *The Boston Herald*, and the Prime Minister replied on the 5th: "I am delighted. Well done" – a message which was subsequently sent on to the Valiant crews[1].

There was no RAF participation in 1959, when a flight-refuelling element was introduced into the competition, nor in 1960, when low-altitude navigation and bombing and ECM activity were added[2].

During 1959 (23–30 April) two Vulcans and four Valiants had participated in Exercise Eyewasher, an Eastern Norad (North American Air Defence) Region exercise. Their objective was to penetrate the DEW (distant early warning) line in north-east Canada and their performance earned USAF commendations. The Commander (Major General E H Underhill) wrote on 11 May to the AOC in C Bomber Command (Air Chf Mshl Sir Harry Broadhurst) to thank him for "co-operation and assistance" during the exercise. He said:–

"In view of the great importance of the DEW Line, both to the Eastern Air Defense Force and to the North American Air Defense System as a whole, one of our main exercise objectives was to subject it to a realistic physical test. However, it so happened that no USAF aircraft of suitable range or performance for this task were available to us at the time required. But for the fact that you were able to support us at short notice, much of the value of the exercise would have been lost, and I think it significant that Bomber Command could meet what must have been an unexpected commitment with such promptness and efficiency."

Maj-Gen Underhill went on to make special mention of the performance of the V-bombers, saying that "Wg Cdr Banks and his crews gave a truly professional display of navigation, their time-keeping particularly being impeccable". The ORB of Wg Cdr Banks' No 83 Sqn commented that the BC force under his command in Exercise Eyewasher, "comprising two Vulcans with four Valiants from RAF Marham, were based at Goose Bay, Labrador, and flew on the night of 25/26 April 1959 to exercise the Eastern Air Defence Command of North America". It added that "the sorties by the Vulcans were flown using Grid and Grid Steering techniques and formed a basis for assessment of the G.4B compass in the vicinity of the North Magnetic Pole".

In his subsequent report[3] Wg Cdr Banks said that the Valiants (of No 148 Sqn) were over Frobisher at 42,000ft and the Vulcans at 48,000ft: only one out of the six was formally challenged. However, "any surprise achieved by the first aircraft was not repeated by the following aircraft – which, on revealing themselves to Frobisher, received only laconic acknowledgment". He commented that the heights over Frobisher were "low" owing to high outside air temperatures (–35°C at 48,000ft).

In addition to their UK-based training and exercises, V-force

[1] Corres, PSO, CAS/PSO, AOC in C Bomber Command, 11 Nov 58, in AHB file RAF Participation in SAC Bombing Competition (ID3/921/62, Pt 1).

[2] In a letter to VCAS on 20 March 59 the AOC in C BC (Air Chf Mshl Sir Harry Broadhurst) commented: "I understand that both this year and next year there is a likely to be a flight refuelling requirement in the SAC Competition. This is yet another reason for a speedy decision about our tanker force" (Ibid).

[3] In AHB IIH/272/3/14A Ex Eyewasher.

squadrons had some more exotic activities. Both Nos 83 and 10 Sqns were engaged on Operation Profiteer, a Far East deployment, the former in June and the latter in July. No 83 sent four Vulcans and six crews to Butterworth in Malaysia; its ORB recorded that this was to "exercise crews in the rapid reinforcement of the Far East Air Force and to provide them with operating experience in the Far East theatre". Servicing en route was "carried out by the crew chiefs and aircrews with limited assistance from personnel at the staging posts" – a test of self-help and independence. On 21 June, the ORB also reported, Flt Lt P A Ward and crew dropped six 1,000lb bombs – "thus becoming the first crew to prove the Vulcan in squadron service in the non-nuclear bombing role". Valiants of No 138 Sqn got some Mediterranean and Near East experience during May, with a detachment to Luqa for Operation Sunspot[1] which included bombing trials at El Adem and was interrupted by Exercise Shahbaz II (11–18 May) for which four Valiants went to Mauripur, Pakistan[2].

It can be seen that elements of the squadrons were continually on the move – either out of the UK or, when there, practising dispersal techniques. All the time there were efforts to improve crew standards, which were regularly checked by Group and Command standardisation teams which visited the squadrons: No 138 started to prepare in August for a visit in October; its ORB recorded that all crews had completed training profile sorties, in addition to quarterly ground training requirements, and that lectures and discussion groups, within the various aircrew categories, had been started – the object of these being "to maintain a high level of technical knowledge, in anticipation of the No 3 Group Standardisation team's visit, during October".

All crews were categorised, and their category depended on the lowest common denominator[3]; so if a member were weak in technique or knowledge, he had to be brought up to a higher standard if the crew were to improve their category. No 83 Sqn's ORB for January 1960 recorded that Exercise Compex, consisting of RBS attacks and a scored Astro run[4], had been held – its aim being "to provide squadron crews with practice for this year's Bomber Command bombing competition" – and that in addition the squadron flying task "was mainly devoted to RBS attacks, towards crew classification". One crew held a Select Star classification, six had Select, two Combat and one had none[5].

---

[1] Which the Lincolns used to do in Egypt.
[2] Held in the Cento areas, this air defence exercise was originally code-named Khyber (No 138 Sqn ORB Apps).
[3] Interview with Gp Capt U L Burberry OBE RAF(Ret), on 18 Nov 76.
[4] *Ie*, using astro-navigation.
[5] Select crews could make Western Ranger flights. They had to have a certificate of competence in servicing their aircraft. Western Ranger involved two Atlantic crossings, during which astro-navigation procedures were practised, training in US and Canadian air traffic procedures, RBS bombing and, in winter, experience of Arctic conditions at Goose Bay (No 1 Group history).

The annual competitions held in Bomber Command were comprehensive and exacting. In the 1962 Bombing and Navigation Competition the targets included the south-west corner of a hangar on Ouston airfield in Northumberland, the centre of the footbridge at Hooton railway station in Cheshire and the centre of the road junction in Enford village on Salisbury Plain[1]. Each squadron entered the final round with a two-crew team, each crew making one competition flight, starting with a scramble from their home base, then a high-altitude profile which included an astro-navigation leg and three simulated blind-bombing attacks scored by RBS (radar bomb sites). During these attacks the crews encountered NBS jamming and had to use their ECM against ground radar and make an evasive bombing run.

The flight profile started with a navigation stage which took the V-bombers to a point off the Netherlands coast, then north-eastwards to a point off the Danish coast, northwards over Norway then south-westwards to Glasgow and Northern Ireland and eastwards back to Scotland and Newcastle where the first bombing target was: their attacks were scored by the RBS units at Ouston, Haydock and Larkhill. From the last target a leg ran east by north to a point over south-east London.

The 1963 competition (held 20–24 April) was renamed the Bomber Command Combat Proficiency Competition and was described by the AOC in C (Air Mshl Sir Kenneth Cross) as an "annual stocktaking of our Operational State . . . an opportunity for crews and squadrons to show what they are worth in the most stringent conditions, short of actual operations".

The new title had been introduced, the competition brochure explained, not only because it helped to describe the content of the competition more accurately but to emphasise that there were "factors other than bombing and navigation . . . equally vital to the success of an operational sortie in war".

The competition had a preliminary phase, flown during the first three months of the year, when all the competing squadrons (Nos 9, 10, 12, 15, 27, 35, 44, 49, 50, 55, 83, 100, 101, 139, 148, 207 and 617) had to complete 12 sorties – consisting of a scramble take-off, communications test, navigation stage followed by two bombing runs, and an ECM test – to decide the award of the Medium Bomber Squadron Efficiency Trophy[2].

The final phase of the competition was made up of navigation, bombing and ECM tests like those in the former Bombing and Navigation Competition. Targets were the signpost at the junction of

---

[1] Bomber Command Bombing and Navigation Competitions AHB ID9/982/5 W6-folder to Pt 2.
[2] Presented to Bomber Command by No 460 (RAAF) Sqn Association to commemorate over a thousand aircrew killed in action whilst flying with the squadron during the Second World War.

Emms Hill Lane and East Crane Row in the Ouston RBS complex, and the centre of a school quadrangle on the south-east outskirts of Knighton, Radnorshire. The navigation stage started from a point north-east of the Norfolk coast, went straight up the North Sea between the Shetlands and Norway, then westwards on to a parallel track down through the north of Scotland to Glasgow. A communications test en route required AEOs to record a message consisting of 50 four-letter groups transmitted from the Bomber Command W/T Control Centre at a speed of 22 wpm.

No 83 Sqn also reported a special trial during April 1960 – simultaneous four-engine starting, to reduce the scramble take-off time – and in May Flt Lt M C Hempstead and his crew, who had been doing the trials, got airborne 57 seconds after the scramble order had been given.

Thus were the policies adumbrated at Command HQ and Air Staff levels, to improve the operational readiness of the medium bomber force[1], put into practice by the squadrons in trials, training, exercises and operations.

Significantly also, new equipment – in the shape of Mk 2 Vulcans and Victors – was shortly to be introduced into the V-force. During August 1960 the ORB of No 83 Sqn noted that it was to be located at Waddington (where it had been based since becoming the first Vulcan unit in the V-force) during the conversion of crews and re-equipment with Mk 2s, but was to be redeployed to Scampton from 10 October, subject to the completion of training and equipment with the new type.

This was the shape of things to come, when No 83 Sqn was re-formed at Scampton on 10 October as the first Vulcan B.2 squadron[2]. It was the shape not only of Vulcan and Victor B.2 squadrons but also of the Blue Steel force – the B.2s armed with stand-off weapons.

---

[1] In 1961, when all RAF Commands were asked to report on their Alert and Readiness Plans, the AOC in C Bomber Command (Air Mshl Sir Kenneth Cross) told VCAS (Air Chf Mshl Sir Edmund Hudleston) in a letter of 9 Sep that 76% of his aircraft were expected to be available in 24hr, 86% in 48hr and 91% in 72hr (AHB file ID9/90/18 Operational Readiness in the RAF Jan 61–Nov 62). On 13 Jul 61 the Minister of Defence (Mr Harold Watkinson) had approved proposals for improving the readiness of the Mk 2 V-bombers by giving them simultaneous engine starting. This involved modifying their compressed-air starting system, which had to be done by the manufacturers under the aegis of an R&D project, as opposed to modification of the electrical starting systems of the Mk 1 aircraft which could be done by Service engineering resources on V-force stations, enabling all engines of the Mk 1/1As to be started within 30sec (Ibid).

[2] In 1961, Scampton-based B.2s of Nos 83 and 27 Sqns penetrated US air defences "at a very high level" in Exercise Skyshield, the SAC/NORAD air defence exercise, the former operating from Lossiemouth and the latter from Kindley AFB (No 1 Group history).

CHAPTER XIX

Mk 2 V-BOMBERS AND THE REDUCTION OF THE VICTOR B.2 ORDER

The introduction of Mk 2 V-bombers into the V-force from 1960 onwards – No 230 OCU receiving its first Vulcan B.2 on 1 July and No 83 Squadron its first on 23 December[1] and No 232 OCU (at Cottesmore) its first Victor B.2 on 1 November 1961 and its second on the 7th – did not reflect simply an engineering development of Vulcan/Victor B.1s into the more powerful B.2s, with engines producing almost twice as much thrust (20,000lb as against 11,00lb). Behind this Bomber Command accession of strength lay years of debate at Cabinet and Ministerial level on major issues affecting the medium bomber force – its ultimate size, and the numbers of each type which should form its front line; its viability, resulting not only from numbers and quick-reaction procedures but also from penetrative capability with the B.2s and Blue Steel stand-off bomb; and its cost, in relation to overall defence expenditure. In a word, there was nothing automatic about bringing-in the B.2s, with their respective engine programmes – Bristol Siddeley Olympus for the Vulcan and Rolls-Royce Conway for the Victor. (The Vulcan B.1s also had Olympus engines, but the Victor B.1s had Armstrong Siddeley Sapphires.) Their introduction resulted from Air Staff thinking about the continuing validity of the British independent airborne strategic nuclear deterrent force in an environment of increasingly more sophisticated Soviet missile defences. (On 1 May 1960 the American U-2 pilot F G Powers had been shot down by a surface-to-air missile when flying over the USSR at 65–70,000ft, a higher operating altitude than the V-bombers had been designed for[2].) After the B.2s came into squadron service they formed, from 1962/63 onwards, the Vulcan/Victor Blue Steel force. Had the Skybolt ALBM (air-launched ballistic missile) been put into production by the Americans the Vulcan B.2s would have carried two each, supported by Blue Steel-carrying Victors.

Ministerial discussions on the ultimate size of the V-force had been going on since 1954. At that time the Air Minister (Lord De l'Isle and Dudley VC) had pressed for a front line of 240 medium bombers, and in a memorandum of 4 April 1955 the Minister of Defence (Mr Harold Macmillan – shortly to be succeeded by Mr Selwyn Lloyd) supported him. This memorandum came before the Cabinet Defence Committee

---

[1] Re-equipment of the Waddington Wing with B.2s began on 23 Dec 65 when Wg Cdr J Pembridge, OC No 50 Sqn, flew the first from Woodford to Waddington.

[2] This incident "spelt the end of the high-altitude bomber. The same missile that shot down the U-2 . . . also shot down the XB-70 programme and forced conversion of the B-52 to a low-altitude mission" (*The Wild Blue*, by Steven L Thompson and Walter J Boymen; Century Hutchinson, 1987).

on 2 May, and the Committee authorised the placing of orders for a further 50 aircraft for the Medium Bomber Force, and agreed that crew training should be based on the assumption that the ultimate front line strength of the force should be 240; but it decided to resume consideration of the final figure.

The size of the MBF, and the possible development of the Vulcan and Victor as part of it, were questions that continued to be debated during 1955 and 1956 and were not finally answered until 1957. In October 1955 the Air Minister argued strongly that the number of medium bombers should not be reduced below 200, putting the case for this in the contexts of Nato and the Western strategic nuclear deterrent. Writing to the Minister of Defence (Mr Selwyn Lloyd) on the 5th he said:–

"The sanction behind Nato is not the number of divisions which can be fielded by the Allied Powers. The field forces are inferior in number to the Russian and satellite forces. . . .

"The sanction is the hydrogen bomb and the means of delivery. The American Strategic Air Command was designed to knock Russia out over a period of 30 days. The Americans have admitted in private that they are under-insured for this task. A properly balanced and effective British medium bomber force has an integral and vital part to play in the Deterrent. . . .

"I have given reasons why, in the view of the Air Ministry, this force ought not on military grounds to be reduced below 200 aircraft. It seems to me that whatever else is marginal in our defence plans, including some of the other functions of the Royal Air Force[1], this really essential element must stand".

A decision to proceed with developing the Mk 2 V-bombers was taken at a meeting of Ministers on 31 May 1956, when the whole of the military aircraft programme was considered. This meeting "agreed that the Vulcan development

"should be limited to the Vulcan 2C, that the Victor 2A should be developed, and that both these aircraft should use the Conway engines; agreed that the Bristol Olympus 6 engine should be dropped from the defence programme; and invited the Minister of Supply to discuss with the Chancellor of the Exchequer whether the Bristol Olympus 6 engine should be continued as a civil project and if so what arrangements should be made for financing this . . . work"[2].

---

[1] In *Nuclear Politics – The British Experience with an Independent Strategic Force 1939-1970* (OUP, 1972) Andrew J Pierre comments (p 151) that "as a result of the priority given to bombers the RAF capacity for air transport was woefully neglected for a number of years until Suez exposed its inadequacy".

[2] GEN.514/2nd Mtg. Note of a Meeting of Ministers. Phase 2C Vulcans were those with new engines and re-designed wings: Phase 2A Victors were those with Conway engines introduced and a modified wing enabling the aircraft to reach 56,000ft target height. It was the great increase in thrust available with the developed Conway and Olympus engines that enabled the Air Council on 23 July 59 to curtail the RATO programme (Conclusions 17(59)): see Victor/Vulcan Development and Production – AHB ID3/942/5 Pt 1).

However, subsequently the Treasury expressed doubts, in view of the cost involved, about the wisdom of proceeding with the development of both the Mk 2 V-bombers; and the Bristol Aeroplane Co made a desperate bid to save the Olympus engine, as the Minister of Supply (Mr Reginald Maudling) recounted in a long letter to the Financial Secretary to the Treasury (Mr Henry Brooke) on 11 December 1956. Reminding him of his promise to "look at the question of the two Mk 2 V-bombers and their engines with a view to letting us have a final decision on this vexed and urgent matter in the near future", the Minister said that there had been two developments since the 31 May meeting:—

". . . Bristol's, faced with the cancellation of the Olympus 6, have themselves offered to carry all the development costs over and above that to which HMG were committed by the time their offer was made and to supply engines to us at the same price as Conways, if we place an order for 200 engines. . . . The second development. . . is that as a result of further thought about the level of R&D expenditure, doubts have been expressed by the Treasury about the wisdom of proceeding with the Mk 2 version of both bombers".

Saying that the Mk 2 version of the Victor was going ahead with the Conway engine, the Minister urged that the Mk 2 Vulcan should also proceed:—

". . . I share the view of the Minister of Defence and the Secretary of State of Air that we should now formally decide that the Vulcan Mk 2 should also go ahead with the Olympus engine. The military advantages of keeping both machines and both engines in the programme are very great. . . .

"There are at present 99 Vulcans on order and I am proceeding on the assumption that there is no suggestion that this number should be reduced. . . . We have been re-examining the Vulcan programme since the strike at Woodford[1] and it now looks as if the Mk 2 version can be introduced at about the 45th aircraft[2]. This means that 54 Vulcans should be the new and greatly improved Mk 2 version. . . ."

Two days later, on 13 December, the Secretary of State for Air (Mr Nigel Birch) wrote to the Financial Secretary to add his "strongest support" to the recommendations by the Minister of Supply. He said that it was "essential operationally to develop the Mk 2 versions and to get them into service as quickly as possible". Their better performance, especially in range and height over target[3], "increases the value of our deterrent force and will give the V-bomber element . . . a longer period of useful operational life". S of S added that he did not want to enter into discussion on the ultimate size of the force – the important thing was "to get the improved versions under production as soon as possible"[4].

---

[1] This began on 23 August 1956 and lasted for over two months.
[2] Main modifications were to the wings, necessitated by the more powerful engines.
[3] Also in take-off performance – especially important on dispersed airfields.
[4] CAS[3442] in Victor/Vulcan (B.35) Development & Production (ID3/942/5 (Pt 2)).

Financial constraints on the size of the MBF became evident early in 1957, as far as both the Government and the other Services were concerned. In a memorandum to the Cabinet on the deterrent and the defence budget on 29 May[1] the Chancellor of the Exchequer (Mr Peter Thorneycroft) said that his first consideration had to be "to avoid commitments which might over-strain the economy" and added: "If the Deterrent, even in an expensive form, could be isolated from the rest of the Defence Budget, we could no doubt afford it, though there would still be some awkward problems. . . ." He said he was "very reluctant . . . to agree . . . to firm new commitments until we have examined the costings on which the Service Departments are now engaged".

The Admiralty also had reservations about the amount of money being applied under the Defence Vote to the bomber force. In a Note forwarded by the Minister of Defence to the Cabinet Defence Committee on 29 July 1957[2] the Admiralty, while supporting the principle of the UK making its contribution to the Western nuclear deterrent, expressed the view that this contribution "must not cost so much inside the total resources set aside for defence as to make it impossible to finance the other forces essential to ensure the cohesion of [the] Commonwealth, dependencies and alliances".

The nub of the Admiralty's argument was that "the smaller the manpower of the forces the more important becomes their equipment, and if the Bomber Force and its weapons absorbs an excessive proportion of defence resources, it becomes harder rather than easier to evolve a policy designed to safeguard. . . alliances and worldwide interests". It felt that unless the most specific assurance could be given that the equipment of the conventional forces of all three Services, judged by the Chiefs of Staff to be the minimum, could be afforded "on top of whatever the Bomber Force turns out to cost" the Admiralty could not support "any predetermined Bomber Force having the first call on Defence Votes".

In other words, the Board of Admiralty would not support any unspecified expenditure on the airborne nuclear deterrent force to the detriment of the conventioal (ie, non-nuclear) forces.

This Admiralty view was one of those which came to the CDC before it made its final decision on the size of the strategic bomber force on 2 August 1957, namely that its front-line strength should be 144 aircraft, of which 104 should be Mk 2 Vulcans and Victors. That decision, however, was not reached without a considerable weighing of evidence. A Memorandum by the Minister of Defence (Mr Duncan Sandys) to the Cabinet on the Strategic Bomber Force, dated 27 May[3], had recommended

---

[1] GEN.570/6, in Medium Bomber Force – Size and Composition (ID3/901/6 (Pt 3)).
[2] D(57)18.
[3] GEN.570/2.

that the planned strength of the force should be reduced to 23 squadrons with a front line of 184 aircraft and that of that number of squadrons 15 should be equipped with Mk 2 Vulcans and Victors – a front-line strength of 120. He commented that UK plans, as declared to Nato, had envisaged the creation of a strategic bomber force with a front-line strength of 240 aircraft; but it was now generally accepted that financial considerations made "some appreciable reduction" inevitable. A decision had to be made as to how big this reduction was to be, and how many aircraft of each type the reduced force should contain.

On 30 May the Cabinet Defence Committee considered memoranda by the Chancellor of the Exchequer and the Minister of Defence.

In discussion it was said that 120 Mk 2 V-bombers would provide a front-line strength of 80 aircraft of this type, and that for the time being, staff planning should assume that the front-line strength of the SBF would be not less than 120 and not more than 184 aircraft – but would include, in any case, at least 80 of the Mk 2 type.

The committee authorised S of S for Air and the Minister of Supply, in consultation with the Chancellor of the Exchequer, to place firm orders for further Mk 2 V-bombers and associated equipment up to a total of 120 aircraft in all. It also invited S of S to arrange for detailed costings of the RAF to be completed as a matter of urgency and agreed to resume discussions on the size of the bomber force when these were available, with the aim of reaching a firm decision by the end of July.

Subsequently, before a final decision was due to be taken by the Cabinet at the end of July, the Minister of Defence reiterated his view on the size of the strategic bomber force. In a brief memorandum to the Defence Committee on 26 July he recalled that in his paper GEN.570/2 of 27 May he had recommended that the front-line strength should be 184 aircraft, 120 of them Mk 2 Vulcans and Victors, and added: "Since then I have further studied this question; and, for reasons set out fully in that paper, I am still satisfied that a force of this size is desirable".

The Defence Committee considered the size of the SBF at two meetings, on 31 July and 2 August 1957, in the light of overall defence expenditure and policy. It came to the conclusion, at the end of the latter meeting, that the force's front-line strength should be 144 aircraft – 104 of them Mk 2 Vulcans and Victors. The sort of arguments it had to consider, at the 31 July meeting, were that the demands of defence on "an already strained economy" should not exceed £1,450 million a year; while recognising that the decision to remain a nuclear Power would inevitably impose a greater relative burden on the UK than on the other two nuclear Powers. Again, at the 2 August meeting, it was pointed out that because of the severe strain on the economy and because the UK would never in practice expect to challenge the Soviet Union alone, some reduction in the total cost of the V-force should be accepted – an appropriate compromise would be a front-line strength of 144.

The Minister of Defence recalled that the original plan for it had been 250 front-line aircraft but that this figure had been progressively reduced. The Air Staff now proposed a front-line strength of 184 aircraft, of which 120 would be Mk 2 Victors and Vulcans, as the minimum needed to provide an effective military force in a global war.

It was stated in discussion that the present cost of a Mk 2 V-bomber was about £750,000 and the total cost of providing the force was continually rising. After discussion of the difference in cost between 96 and 120 Mk 2 V-bombers (£54m over a five-year period) out of a total front-line strength of 144 aircraft, it was decided that an appropriate compromise would be to provide for 104 Mk 2s. The committee therefore agreed that the front-line strength of the SBF should be 144 aircraft, of which 104 should be Mk 2 Victors and Vulcans, and S of S and the Minister of Defence – in consultation with the Chancellor of the Exchequer – were authorised to place orders for that purpose.

On 27 September 1957 PUS, Air Ministry (Sir Maurice Dean), informed PUS, Ministry of Supply (Sir Cyril Musgrave), that the Treasury had approved the placing of further orders for 38 Vulcan Mk 2 and 29 Victor Mk 2s, commenting that "we envisage that these will be the final orders needed to form and maintain the Mk 2 V-bomber force approved by Ministers"[1].

However, in a reply of 14 October, PUS (MoS) referred to a "difficulty . . . in relation to the Victor 2". This was, as PUS, AM, put it in a minute to S of S on the 16th, a reference to a cut in the R&D vote – which, by stopping the development of the Victor, might "result in holding up orders for the bomber programme approved by the Cabinet in the summer". He said that the "picture on the ordering of Mk 2 V-bombers" was that even if there was no R&D complication it was not yet possible for contracts for the Victor and Vulcan to be signed, pending settlement of the contractual details now in progress with the firms; and the effect of the R&D complication was that a further delay was likely to be superimposed until the fate of the Victor was known. As it seemed inconceivable that it should be cancelled, he thought that the most promising course of action would be to invite the Minister of Defence to give a decision. On the 17th, PUS wrote in this sense to PUS, MoD (Sir Richard Powell); and on the 23rd, as a result of correspondence with the latter, PUS (MoS) wrote to PUS (AM) to say that he had given instructions that the contract should be placed as soon as possible and that development of the Mk 2 versions should proceed "without restriction".

There were some further difficulties about a fixed-price contract, and further correspondence between the Ministries concerned, but on 5 December PUS (AM) was able to tell the Air Council that the contract for Mk 2 Vulcans had been settled and approved by the Treasury and

<hr>

[1] AHB file ID3/942/5 (Pt 2) Victor/Vulcan (B.35) Development & Production.

was expected to be signed "within the next two days", adding: "Difficulties were being encountered" over the contract with Handley Page, particularly as regards a fixed-price contract, but both Air Ministry and the MoS were "continuing to press for an early settlement"[1].

The first Mk 2 V-bombers had been ordered in June 1956 – on the 1st a contract was placed for eight Vulcan B(K) Mk 2s and on the 14th one for 21 Victor B Mk 2s (although an earlier contract for 33 Victor Mk 1s had been amended to cover eight Mk 2s). In the case of both types, the original Mk 2s were modifications of Mk 1 versions; and the Specification issued by ACAS(OR) on 27 November 1957 – Aircraft Specification No B 129P Issue 2, for the Vulcan B(K) Mk 2 and Victor B Mk 2 – did not "cancel or supersede" (it was clearly stated) the original Specification Nos B.35/46 and B.129P based on the Air Staff's Operational Requirement OR229.

Among the changes included in the 1957 specification, however, were greater take-off weight – to include Blue Steel, weighing approximately 15,000lb; in the case of the Vulcan this maximum design take-off weight was given as 195,000lb – about 30,000lb more than that of the Mk 1 with the 10,000lb Blue Danube bomb aboard. Olympus engines of up to 20,000lb thrust were to be installed in the Vulcan (these were, subsequently, Mk 201s of 17,000lb and Mk 301s of 20,000lb s.t.) and Conways of 23,000lb thrust (at sea level) in the Victor, and all four engines were to be capable of being started within two minutes. The Mk 2 V-bombers were to have a still air range of not less than 3,350nm (excluding the range of an air-launched missile) and an over-the-target altitude of 55,000ft. They were to be capable of carrying not only the original kiloton bomb, Blue Danube, but also the new megaton weapons tested in the Grapple trials – Yellow Sun and Red Beard. The Victor was to be able to deliver up to 35,000lb of conventional bombs or mines, the Vulcan up to 21,000lb, among widely assorted weapon loads. Both types were to be able to carry "a long-range powered bomb of the type proposed in OR1149" – the Air Staff Target for a long-range guided bomb with a range of about 1,000nm. The Standard of Preparation for the Mk 2s, forming an appendix to the specification, said that although no details of this weapon could be given, it would "certainly be heavier" than, and might "also be longer than", Blue Steel, and advised that "consideration should . . . be given to measures" which would "facilitate modifications to the aircraft" which were likely to be necessary in order to carry the weapon. OR1149 was subsequently due to be implemented by the American missile Skybolt (as will be recounted) and the Vulcan Mk 2 was nominated as the carrier, but the cancellation of that project towards the end of 1962 put paid to the development and planning work which had been done.

---

[1]Conclusions of Meeting 27(57), 5 Dec 57 (AHB file ID3/942/5 (Pt 2) Victor/Vulcan (B.35) Development and Production).

These Specifications were issued by the Controller of Aircraft, Ministry of Supply, early in 1958 – for the Vulcan B(K) Mk 2 on 7 January and for the Victor B Mk 2 on 27 February – and major production contracts were placed shortly thereafter: for 39 (originally 40) Vulcan Mk 2s on 22 January and for 30 Victor Mk 2s on 18 March, the latter order later being sharply reduced under controversial circumstances, as will subsequently be described.

The installation of engines of much greater thrust in the Mk 2s meant changes in the wing area to accommodate them. In the case of the Vulcan (to quote from the Standard of Preparation) "the airframe redesign is to include extending and cambering the leading edge of the wing, thinning the outboard portion of the wing and increasing the chord and span". As a result, the Mk 2 had a wing with a span of 111ft and an area of 3,964sq ft compared with 99ft/3,554 sq ft in the Mk 1. In the case of the Victor the S of P laid it down that the airframe redesign was to include an increase in wing span of approximately 10ft, with increased chord and centre section and larger engine air intakes. The Mk 2 Vulcan also had full-span elevons in place of the outboard ailerons and inboard elevator of the Mk 1[1]. Both Mk 2s were to have a radio countermeasures fit – radar and fighter control communications jammers, passive warning receiver and Red Steer tail warning equipment. This resulted from an Air Staff policy decision in 1957 that RCM should be introduced into both Mk 1 and Mk 2 Vulcan and Victor production lines[2]. A report prepared by ACAS(OR) in August 1960 on ECM for medium bomber aircraft[3] enumerated the following equipment being fitted in Mk 1A and Mk 2 Vulcans and Victors[4]: one Green Palm voice communications jammer, two Blue Diver metric jammers for use against ground radars, three Red Shrimp S-band jammers "effective against most ground radars", four Blue Saga passive warning receivers, one Red Steer active defence rearward-looking radar and Window Dispensers "for sowing gravity-launched Window for the confusion of ground radars". Writing to the AOC in C Bomber Command (Air Mshl Sir Kenneth Cross) on 10 February 1961 about "the implications of leaving one of the Victor squadrons without an ECM capability", DCAS (Air Mshl R B Lees) commented that "we cannot afford all that we are asked to provide", adding: "It costs a million pounds to equip a squadron with ECM".

A report issued in 1963 on ECM for medium bomber aircraft[5] said that these were "related to . . . Soviet air defences, on the assumption

---

[1] Because of major differences between the Mk 1 and Mk 2 version, it was decided in 1959 to hold Intensive Flying Trials on the Mk 2s (OS9A files C.11394/Eng Plans).

[2] See AF/CT 1127/75, Pt I ECM in V-bombers.

[3] Ibid, Pt III, with covering Minute to VCAS.

[4] The Mk 1A and Mk 2 modification programmes were contemporaneous.

[5] The Airborne Offensive Sub-Committee of the AM Electronic Warfare Committee Electronic Countermeasures for the MBF 1963–1970 in AF/CT 1127/75, Pt V ECM in V-bombers.

that" these presented "the most formidable opposition" and recalled that in May 1958 the Air Ministry Radio Countermeasures Committee, which became the Electronic Warfare Committee, had confirmed that the aircraft fit should include noise jammers in the VHF, Metric and S-bands, with the addition of an X-band jammer later, a passive warning receiver and an active tail warning equipment (Red Steer). The committee recommended that the long-term ECM policy for the MBF should be based on noise jamming as the primary weapon, and accordingly that a comprehensive noise-jamming system be produced. However, when Skybolt was planned to be introduced, a revised ECM programme was endorsed by the Air Council in October 1961: aircraft armed with the missile would not penetrate organised enemy defences and countermeasures would not be required; until Skybolt was available, however, existing ECM equipment would be retained and the development and production of other installations would continue. After the Nassau Agreement of December 1962 cancelled Skybolt and a low-level attack policy was adopted, a revised ECM policy was approved at Ministerial level and noted by the Air Council on 14 March 1963[1]. The MBF ECM installations were to be Green Palm, Blue Diver and Red Shrimp noise jammers, Window, and Red Steer and Blue Saga warning equipment.

In October 1963 an Air Staff Target (No 3632) for a study of ECM for the protection of aircraft operating at low level was issued; these were to be applied to the Mk 2 medium bombers. An Application Policy for ECM equipment in V-class aircraft, issued in August of the following year[2] with the comment that "no further provisioning of the main ECM equipment is envisaged", showed the following to be standard fitments in the Mk 2 Vulcans and Victors: Red Steer Mk 1, Blue Saga, Window launcher, Blue Diver and Red Shrimp – though there were variations in fit for aircraft employed in different roles, eg free-fall (in the case of the Vulcans) or Blue Steel.

The last free-fall Vulcan squadrons to receive B.2s were the Waddington-based Nos 50, 44 and 101, re-equipped in that order during 1966–67, which meant that the whole of the Vulcan force was operating Mk 2s some ten years after the original contract for this version had been placed[3].

The orders for Mk 2 V-bombers, plus an order for 57 Mk 1 Blue Steel powered bombs which had been placed in December 1960[4], foreshadowed the eventual size and shape of the V-force at its most

[1] Paper No AC(9)63.
[2] Application Policy – ECM Equipment in 'V' Aircraft, 14 Aug 64 in AF/CT1127/75 Pt VIII ECM in 'V' Bombers.
[3] Letter from HQ BC to MoD (BC/S45599/Admin Plans) of 19 Nov 65 detailing re-equipment programme.
[4] The Blue Steel production contract (KF/G/010), placed on 15 December 1960, was for 75 of these powered bombs; but this total was subsequently reduced to 57, which was the number delivered to the RAF.

powerful and in the highest state of readiness – from 1962/3[1] to mid-1969, when the QRA (quick reaction alert) commitment was transferred to the Polaris-armed nuclear-powered submarines of the Royal Navy.

In terms of manpower, its most important component[2], the force had just under half of the total numbers in Bomber Command – some 10,620 out of 23,216. These figures were given by the AOC in C (Air Mshl Sir Kenneth Cross) at a Press conference at Scampton on 14 February 1963 to introduce Blue Steel. They had been remarkably closely anticipated in an Air Ministry forecast made in November 1957 when costings for the medium bomber force were being worked out in order to help determine the Cabinet decision on its size. The prognosis[3] was for Bomber Command manpower of 27,000 in 1962/63 – though this figure was based on an anticipated UE of 184 bombers, so it and the break-down figures should be scaled-down to a UE of 144 bombers. The anticipated total of 27,000 personnel was made up as follows:–

(a)   V-bombers   12,000 on stations and squadrons
(b)   Thor   4,000 approximately
(c)   Other elements   11,000 ("including Command and Group
                       HQ staffs, OCUs, the LRPR force, all the
                       Canberras in Bomber Command and
                       miscellaneous units such as the JARIC")

At the end of 1957, when crucial decisions about its future size and shape had been taken, the V-force consisted of seven Valiant bomber squadrons (Nos 7, 49, 90, 138, 148, 207 and 214), one Valiant long-range PR squadron (No 543) and a Valiant special squadron (No 199)[4]; and two Vulcan squadrons (Nos 83 and 101). These V-bombers were based on six Class 1 airfields – Honington, Marham, Wittering, Wyton, Waddington and Finningley – and were defended by their dispersal (alert and readiness) plans, by the Bloodhound SAGW (surface-to-air guided weapon) squadrons and subsequently by the Fylingdales BMEWS (ballistic missile early warning system) station.

During October 1958 the Secretary of State for Air (Mr George Ward), in a Memorandum to the Defence Board, reaffirmed the need for 104 Mk 2 Vulcans and Victors and for both Mk 1 and Mk 2 Blue Steel. He recalled the Defence Committee's decision of the previous

---

[1] The first Blue Steel squadron, No 617, had an "emergency operational capability" in 1962 but the next squadrons did not begin training with the new weapon until 1963.

[2] When the QRA commitment was transferred to the Royal Navy in mid-1969 the CAS in a signal to the AOC in C BC spoke of "an unsurpassed demonstration of professional skill" in his tribute to the V-force.

[3] Minute, Head of S6/AUS(A) of 6 Nov 57 in Medium Bomber Force – Size & Composition (ID3/901/6 (Pt 3)).

[4] Whose main roles were "to enable Bomber Command to gain experience in the tactical use of RCM as part of the armoury of the main V-force" and "to provide RCM training for the Air Defence systems of Fighter Command, the overseas RAF Commands, RN ships and establishments, and the Army" (Ibid).

year, and reiterated the views expressed by the Prime Minister (Mr Harold Macmillan) earlier in 1958. These statements, and an Air Ministry view on the operational viability of the V-force, were encapsulated in the opening paragraphs of the memorandum[1]:—

"On 2 August 1957 the Defence Committee (D(57) 7th Meeting) 'agreed that the front-line strength of the strategic bomber force should be 144 aircraft, of which 104 should be Mk 2 Victors and Vulcans'. A force of 144 aircraft was approved as an appropriate compromise between military and economic considerations. A plan for a V-bomber front line of 240 aircraft had been declared to Nato. The Minister of Defence had informed the Committee that operationally there were sound arguments in favour of a force of 184 V-bombers.

"On 16 July 1958 the Prime Minister (D(58)33) reaffirmed the purpose of our independent nuclear capability as follows:–

(a) To retain our special relation with the United States and, through it, our influence in world affairs, and, especially, our right to have a voice in the final issue of peace or war[2].

(b) To make a definite, though limited, contribution to the total nuclear strength of the West – while recognising that the United States must continue to play the major part in maintaining the balance of nuclear power.

(c) To enable us, by threatening to use our independent nuclear power, to secure United States co-operation in a situation in which their interests were less immediately threatened than our own.

(d) To make sure that, in a nuclear war, sufficient attention is given to certain Soviet targets which are of greater importance to us than to the United States[3].

"To constitute a minimum deterrent and serve the purposes for which it is intended, the V-force must be operationally viable, ie it must be sufficiently large and well equipped to deliver enough bombs to inflict an adequate measure of destruction in Russia. To be operationally viable the minimum size of the force should be not less than 104 Mk 2 Victors and Vulcans with powered guided bombs".

Referring specifically to Blue Steel, the S of S said that the Defence Committee had "decided a year ago to maintain the Mk 2 element of the V-force at a high level because these aircraft were required to carry first the short-range and then the long-range powered bombs (Blue Steel Mks 1 and 2)". These weapons were required "in order to maintain the capacity of the V-force to attack deep-penetration targets in spite of the expected development of the Russian SAGW defences".

---

[1] DB(58)10, 29 Oct 58.

[2] On 24 Feb 58 the Prime Minister had been quoted in *The Times* as saying in a TV interview that the independent nuclear deterrent "gives us a better position in the world, . . . a better position with respect to the United States. . . ."

[3] Particularly bomber airfields and missile launching sites from which attacks on the UK could be mounted.

As to the cost of the deterrent, S of S said that he calculated that this – for R&D, capital and running costs of the V-force and its weapons over the next five years – would not exceed on an average about £125 million a year or 8½ per cent of a Defence budget of about £1,470 million, including provision of the tanker squadrons and other overseas reinforcement operations. Expenditure on this scale implied the devotion of some £1,300 million a year to other defence preparations – including the defence of the V-bomber and ballistic missile bases; but he estimated that expenditure on UK air defence over the next five years attributable to that role amounted to only £50–60 million a year.

He added that no new factors had arisen during the past year to invalidate the requirement of the V-force, and therefore invited the Defence Board to reaffirm the requirement for a V-bomber force "of the size and composition already planned" and to reaffirm the requirement for Blue Steel Mks 1 and 2.

The fact that successive Secretaries of State for Air had to put up to the Cabinet Defence Committee a closely-argued case for the strategic bomber force resulted not only from the financial constraint of the annual Defence Vote but also from the reservations of the other Services as to the effect upon the conventional forces of the cost of the nuclear deterrent force. This became evident when S of S's Memorandum was discussed by the Defence Board on 30 October 1958[1], as did another matter affecting the V-force – the possible fulfilment of the Blue Steel Mk 2 requirement (OR1149 for a long-range guided bomb) by the American GAM 87 weapon system (Skybolt).[2]

When introducing his memorandum S of S said that if the policy of making a British contribution to the deterrent were to be implemented effectively, an operationally viable bomber force had to be provided; and if it were to be capable of attacking targets inside Russia, despite the expected development in Russian defences, it had to be equipped with powered bombs. Total R&D, capital and running costs of the V-force over the next five years would be on average about £125 million a year – not an unreasonable proportion of defence effort to spend on the prevention of global war, quite apart from the fact that the V-bombers also had cold and limited war roles.

The Navy and Army points of view were put by, respectively, the First Lord of the Admiralty (the Earl of Selkirk) and the Secretary of State for War (Mr Christopher Soames). The former said that while he did not wish to challenge the planned size of the V-bomber force, he was

---

[1] Minutes of DB/C(58) 4th meeting, Conclusions.

[2] A Minute from AUS(A) to PS to S of S and PS to CAS (AUS(A)/5536 of 30 Oct 58) said that a study of a powered guided bomb with 600nm range had been made early in 1957 and was discussed by the DRPC on 16 Jul 57, the MoS then being required to investigate the possible modification of Blue Steel Mk 1, this investigation leading to OR1159 for a guided bomb of 600 miles range. OR1159 was subsequently superseded by OR1187, which in turn was cancelled. OR1149 was an Air Staff Target for a long-range guided bomb with 1,000nm range, issued 7 May 56.

concerned that future weapons for the maintenance of the deterrent were being considered individually, without regard to the cumulative cost to the defence budget in future years; and he asked whether Blue Streak and Blue Steel Mk 2 could be afforded. The conventional forces "must not be starved of equipment owing to any duplication in the provision of weapons for the deterrent". The Chiefs of Staff should examine the deterrent weapons programme as a whole and consider whether it represented the best military means of ensuring the country's security.

Much the same feelings were expressed by S of S for War, who said that expenditure on Army equipment amounted to only 3 per cent of total defence expenditure, compared with 16 per cent in the United States. About £10m a year more should be spent on Army equipment during the next five years. He thought there should be a re-costing of the whole deterrent programme, and a reassessment of the balance of the country's defence effort, before final decisions were taken.

The Minister of Defence (Mr Duncan Sandys) said that the views expressed by the First Lord and S of S for War "in effect, called in question the basic policy of maintaining a British contribution to the deterrent". If that policy were right, the contribution had to be efficient and maintained with up-to-date weapons. The cost of maintaining an effective deterrent would amount to about £300m a year; there were a number of ways in which this could be reduced, but were they consistent with the approved policy? He mentioned several possibilities and said that, as a matter of course, forward costings of the whole programme would be kept under review. If members of the Board wished to suggest alterations to the present policy they should put forward detailed proposals.

The Minister said he was convinced of the need to maintain a British contribution to the deterrent. To this end, the V-bomber force should be built up to the present approved strength and should be provided with the necessary powered bombs to prolong its effective life. He proposed to make a recommendation on those lines to the Defence Committee. He asked CDS (MRAF Sir William Dickson) to arrange with the Chiefs of Staff to consider the points made in discussion and to examine whether the planned programme for the deterrent forces absorbed too great a proportion of the available defence effort – and if so, which elements in those forces could be reduced without destroying the validity of the deterrent.

In a subsequent Memorandum to the Cabinet Defence Committee on 3 November 1958 the Minister of Defence recommended that the Cabinet's decision of 2 August 1957 – that the V-force front line should be 144 aircraft, 104 of them Mk 2s – should be confirmed; that Blue Steel Mk 1, when successfully developed, should be introduced into RAF service; and that, unless there proved to be a better American alternative, Blue Steel Mk 2 should be developed.

The CDC, at its meeting on the 5th, approved these proposals in principle – subject to further review on lines indicated by the Prime Minister (Mr Harold Macmillan): that is, in the course of the comprehensive review of the cost of the deterrent and its defence which the Committee were to undertake. (In a minute on the following day the Prime Minister referred to the possible abandonment of Blue Streak; and at a Defence Board meeting on the 13th the Minister of Defence said that "the difficult question whether to continue with the development of Blue Streak" had "still to be finally decided" – so clearly the MRBM's future was in doubt long before its actual cancellation.)

When the CDC discussed the Memorandum further, at their meeting on the 18th, the proposals were provisionally agreed to – "subject to further review in relation to the level of defence expenditure as a whole". This occurred after the Prime Minister had said, among other comments, that on the understanding that a decision on Blue Steel Mk 2 would be postponed for the time being, the Committee "might provisionally agree that the medium bomber force should not be further reduced".

This decision to have a V-force front-line strength of 144 aircraft held good throughout 1959, the final orders for Mk 2s having been placed early in 1958 – for 39 Vulcan B.2s on 22 January and for 30 Victor B.2s on 18 March. But in the meantime the procurement picture for the strategic deterrent force had changed drastically. While the Mk 2 V-bombers were originally intended to carry Blue Steel Mk 1 initially, and later the Mk 2 version of that weapon, the latter project was cancelled in favour of the American Skybolt – two of which could be carried by a Vulcan B.2. It was therefore estimated that "the same deterrent threat as that represented by the force approved by the Defence Committee in August 1957" – that is, a front line of 144 V-bombers, including 104 Mk 2s – could be "broadly achieved with 72 Mk 2 Vulcans, each carrying two Skybolts". So, the argument continued, this reduced requirement opened-up the possibility of saving money by reducing the order for Mk 2 Victors; for, "if the airborne deterrent is to consist exclusively of Vulcans carrying Skybolt, the need for Victor B.2s will be limited to the number required for the interim Blue Steel force to contribute to the deterrent while the Vulcans are being modified to carry Skybolt, and for photographic reconnaissance". On this basis, the Air Ministry estimated that the Mk 2 Victor order could be cut by 25, from 57 to 32.

A draft note, which though undated appeared under a covering minute of 13 July 1960, referred to the V-force having been "built up to the point where it consists of 96 Mk 1 aircraft, with the necessary nuclear weapons"[1]. A possible reduction in the number of Mk 2 Victors,

---

[1] As at 30 June 1960 the totals of aircraft in the V-bomber squadrons were 104 (authorised) and 106 (on hand) (RAF Monthly Statement).

327

thus eliminating them as Skybolt carriers, had been mooted in the 1960 context of reductions in defence expenditure and of the decisions – the one consequent upon the other – to abandon Blue Streak and to acquire Skybolt.

Although the decision to abandon Blue Streak as a military weapon and to adopt Skybolt as the principal UK deterrent weapon was not formally announced until 13 April 1960 – by the Minister of Defence (Mr Harold Watkinson) in a Parliamentary statement[1] – the Cabinet Defence Committee had made up its mind about Blue Streak on 24 February[2]. At that meeting the committee had considered a memorandum by the Prime Minister (Mr Harold Macmillan); this said that the Minister of Defence considered that "we should abandon the present plan for deploying Blue Streak as a military weapon". The Prime Minister put forward three reasons for supporting this view: the V-force with Blue Steel Mk 1 would be fully effective until 1966; it might be possible to prolong the effective life of the force after 1966 by obtaining supplies of Skybolt from the US "without conditions"; and it seemed likely that, in the 1970s, "some mobile means of delivery of the deterrent will hold the field – whether air-launched, like Skybolt; or launched from a mobile platform on land or on or under the sea, like Polaris". It seemed clear that, early in 1960, the Government was thinking in terms of an American weapon – whether Skybolt or Polaris – to succeed Blue Steel. On 24 February the CDC decided provisionally that the programme for the deployment of Blue Streak as a military weapon should be abandoned. This decision was to be reviewed in the light of an enquiry into whether the development of Blue Streak might be continued for scientific and technological purposes[3].

Subsequently the prospects of Bomber Command having Skybolt as its next major weapon were enhanced by an Understanding (of 29 March) between the US President and UK Prime Minister to co-operate in the development and acquisition of Skybolt, to enable it to be adopted both by the USAF and the RAF.

The Blue Streak decision was confirmed at a Cabinet Defence Committee meeting on 6 April[4] when the Minister of Defence informed it that following a recent further technical assessment and a discussion by the Defence Board on 4 April the general consensus of opinion was that in circumstances other than a surprise saturation attack, V-bombers equipped with Skybolt would have certain advantages over Blue Streak; and the Minister of Aviation (Mr Duncan Sandys) agreed that there would be "certain financial and political advantages in depending on the V-bombers and Skybolt, rather than on Blue Streak", for the

---

[1] Commons Hansard, Cols 1265–66.
[2] D(60) 1st Mtg.
[3] When it was cancelled as a military weapon Blue Streak had cost £84m.
[4] D(60) 3rd Mtg.

strategic deterrent force in the later 1960s. The committee then "took note that the Prime Minister would arrange for the Cabinet to be informed of the decision to cancel the development of Blue Streak as a weapon, and of the terms in which this decision might be communicated to Parliament and to the Government of Australia"[1]. This decision was based on the alternative assumptions that all further work on Blue Streak should cease, or that consideration should be given "to the adaptation of Blue Streak as a space satellite launcher".

After the Blue Streak/Skybolt decision had been made known publicly on 13 April the original Understanding on the latter was reinforced by another one, between the US Secretary of Defense and the UK Minister of Defence, dated 6 June 1960. It was from this time that consideration began to be given to the possibility of reducing the number of Mk 2 V-bombers. On 16 June the Prime Minister minuted the Minister of Defence: "We must be ready to review the strength of the V-bomber force in the light of the decision on Skybolt. Will we want as many Victor Mk 2 aircraft as are at present on order? Might we save money by cancelling some of these? They will after all have a fairly limited life if they cannot carry Skybolt"[2].

When the Skybolt project had been initiated, early in 1959, the joint USAF/RAF requirement was for a 1,000nm-range missile of up to 10,000lb all-up weight which could be carried by and launched from the B-58 and B-52 and the two V-bombers. The original weapon system WS138A – ALBM (air-launched ballistic missile) design would fit into the Vulcan and Victor bomb-bays, but the later designs – Able 2 and 3 – would not go into the Vulcan bomb-bay. Another problem was that the Star Tracker guidance system had to be installed, and as this had to have a reasonable field of view, if it were mounted on the missile itself then the latter would have to be carried under the wings of the V-bombers.

This situation became clear after a visit by British representatives to Douglas Aircraft Co in July 1959; and in a later report, at the end of that year[3] – made at a meeting on 22 December "to review the position on WS138A in USA and its application to the Vulcan and Victor", one of them said that it seemed reasonably certain that the missile could be carried on the Vulcan wing but that "the ground clearance on the Victor being considerably smaller made carriage on it more problematical". He confirmed the need for an under-wing station by saying that, "with the larger missile now proposed and the problem of providing a navigational data-link to the star tracker, fuselage carriage was not the best solution"– adding, "and indeed it may not even be capable of being made an acceptable installation".

It seems that, not long after the meeting at which this report was

---

[1] Because Blue Streak would have been tested at Woomera.
[2] PM Personal Minute, M206/60. Copies were sent to the Minister of Aviation and S of S for Air.
[3] Minutes – ref AV/120/035 in Skybolt Policy file, AF/CMS 813/65, Pt 1.

made, the Air Staff decided against the Victor Mk 2 as a Skybolt carrier (the Vickers VC10 was also considered); for in a minute of 26 February 1960 DOR(A) (Air Cdre T W Piper), writing "in anticipation of approval being given to proced with development of the Vulcan Mk 2 to carry two WS138A weapons", added that "at this stage, it is not the Air Staff intention to carry WS138A on Victor aircraft"[1]. This was later confirmed in a minute of 7 July (AUS(A)/VCAS – R C Kent/Air Mshl Sir Edmund Hudleston)[2] which said that "with Air Ministry concurrence officials who will negotiate the Skybolt agreement in Washington have been instructed that they may accept that only the Vulcan 2 should be developed to carry Skybolt and that Skybolt need only be compatible with the Vulcan 2".

From the early days of the project, when a CA (Controller of Aircraft) Skybolt team visited the USA, it was clear that there were going to be some engineering difficulties in fitting the missile to the V-bombers. At a debriefing meeting on 19 May 1960[3] a member of the team reported on changes made in the missile since a US presentation on 2 March, and said that while it was "still just compatible with the Vulcan, carriage on the Victor could only be achieved by some form of fin-folding". Later, another member reported that if the missile were altered to fit the Victor "the changes would be considerable".

Handley Page Ltd, manufacturers of the Victor, were anxious to claim aircraft/missile compatibility, and in July informed the Ministry of Aviation that their B.2 could carry two Skybolts without modification to either aircraft or missile to improve ground clearance. They claimed that adequate clearance had been obtained by mounting the missiles some 18in further forward, and that this position was satisfactory both structurally and aerodynamically[4]. In a letter to the Air Minister (Mr George Ward) on 21 June Sir Frederick Handley Page said that 50 Victors could be modified as Skybolt carriers at a cost of "well under £1m". However, the Air Staff came to the conclusion that carriage of Skybolt should be restricted to the Vulcan B.2 force. During July 1960, before a final decision that the missile would not be carried by Victors had been taken by the Air Council or the Minister of Defence, DOR(A) explained in a letter to the Air Ministry's Chief Information Officer the reasons for the Vulcan/Skybolt monopoly view[5]. He said that the number of missiles to be purchased – probably about 120–140 – could be carried by the planned front-line force of Vulcan B.2s; the cost of developing and proving an installation on the Victor B.2 would be saved; and the installation of Skybolt on the latter aircraft might be difficult. He went on to explain that the problem was to achieve

[1] Minute to D(RAF)B on Aircraft Development Programme for WS138A (TS5279/DOR(A)) in Skybolt Policy file.
[2] In Blue Steel July/Dec 60 – AHB ID9/194/4, Sub folder 1 of 3).
[3] Minutes, AH/1171/02.
[4] Minute, DOR(A) to D of Ops (B&R) etc, 15 Jul 60.
[5] TS2901/DOR(A).

adequate ground clearance. Initially it had been thought that this could be obtained by folding the missile's fins[1]– which, though technically feasible, was a complication to be avoided as it was unnecessary for the Vulcan or B-52. Handley Page had offered to install a new undercarriage to ensure adequate clearance, and Sir Frederick was doing "extensive 'lobbying' at senior levels to the effect that the Victor could easily be made to operate Skybolt".

In mid-July Handley Page Ltd sent a detailed report to the Ministry of Aviation on the Victor Mk 2 with two Skybolts installed. This was checked at A&AEE, Boscombe Down, but Air Staff policy remained the same – that present plans did not call for carriage of Skybolts by Victor B.2s[2].

The Minister of Defence (Mr Harold Watkinson) had already made up his mind about the Victor B.2s on order. In a minute of 23 June replying to the Prime Minister's questions, he said that after consulting with S of S for Air he had concluded that some of them could be cancelled, explaining: "With two Skybolts in every Vulcan, we can carry 144 bombs without the Victors. Some Victors will still be needed, to carry Blue Steel (which needs one aircraft per bomb), and to maintain the deterrent while the Vulcans are out of service being fitted for Skybolt. The Victors would still be useful for a time without Skybolt, especially if we introduce an improved version of Blue Steel. We shall settle the number to be cancelled when we have more information on the cancellation charges"[3].

Meanwhile, rumours about a possible cut in orders for Victor Mk 2s had begun to reach Fleet Street – in the wake of the Government's cancellation of Blue Streak earlier that year and its efforts to reduce defence expenditure. The *Daily Express* said on 19 July that "another blow to the Government's wilting nuclear defence policy" was on the way – that the "£100,000 half-completed project to strengthen the V-bomber force with 30 faster, higher-flying Victor 2s" was likely to be halted. It commented that the decision, "like the ending of the Blue Streak H-bomb rocket", was being made "to plug a financial drain down which millions have been poured". The paper's air correspondent (Keith Thompson) ended his story by saying that it had been discovered that "the Victor, unlike the Vulcan, cannot easily be adapted to carry the latest planned weapon, the American Skybolt air-launched rocket".

On 23 June the Minister of Defence had replied to the Prime Minister's questions of the 16th as to whether as many Victors were wanted as were on order; after consulting with the Secretary of State for Air, he had concluded that some could be cancelled – "with two Skybolts to every Vulcan, we can carry 144 bombs without the Victors". In the light of this reply the Prime Minister directed that the question of Victor

---

[1] There were eight of these.
[2] Minute, DOR(A)/D(RAF)B, MoA.
[3] ID3/901/6, Pt 4 – Medium Bomber Force – Size and Composition.

cancellations should come before the Defence Committee as soon as possible – which proved to be 25 July, at a meeting for which the Minister of Defence had prepared a memorandum, summing-up the situation on the size of the V-force. This recalled that

"the present plan for the V-force was laid down by the Defence Committee in August 1957, when it was agreed that the front-line strength of the force should be 144 aircraft, including 104 Mk 2 bombers (72 Vulcans and 32 Victors). The Mk 2 aircraft were to carry the Blue Steel Mk 1 guided bomb as this was available, and later Blue Steel Mk 2".

The memorandum then turned to the present situation and its implications: —

"It is now planned that the Mk 2 Vulcans will carry two Skybolt missiles as soon as these are available. 72 Mk 2 Vulcans, each carrying two Skybolts, gives the same deterrent capacity as that approved by the Defence Committee in August 1957.

"If, then, Skybolt goes to plan, we shall clearly not need so many Mk 2 Victors, even if they turn out to be capable of carrying Skybolt. On the other hand, we shall need them for the interim Blue Steel force, to cover the position whilst Vulcans are being modified to carry Skybolt and also for reconnaissance. Also if Blue Steel Mk 1 Star[1] is successful, we might wish to carry a limited number of these weapons in parallel with Skybolt to diversify the deterrent and to retain a completely British-produced element in it. I attach the greatest importance to developing Blue Steel Mk 1 Star if we can find a successful way of doing so, as this would give us some reinsurance against any failure of Skybolt. However, I understand that, even if we decided to go for a mixed bag of Skybolts and Blue Steel Mk 1 Stars, we should be able to provide sufficient carrying aircraft out of a front-line force of 72 Vulcans and some 24 Victors.

"I think, then, that on balance we should be justified in cancelling 25 of the 57 Victor Mk 2s now on order. A reduction of 25 would produce a capital saving of about £14m. . . ."

When the Defence Committee met on 25 July, with the Minister's memorandum[2] before them, he reiterated the position succinctly by saying that, on the basis of the plans for each Mk 2 Vulcan to carry two Skybolts, the number of Mk 2 Victors in Bomber Command could be reduced without diminishing the V-force's deterrent capability. He suggested that 25 of the 57 Mk 2 Victors on order should be cancelled, with a total capital saving of about £14m over the next five years, though this did not imply a commitment to the possible development of an improved Blue Steel for use with the Victors.

The Minister's proposal in his memorandum was approved at this

---

[1] Mk 1A was a development of Blue Steel to give increased range; Mk 1 Star was a more ambitious development to give greater range, speed and height.

[2] D(60)35.

meeting[1], but the decision to cancel 25 Victor B.2s caused a furore since it was not made public in a Parliamentary or Press statement, but leaked out in a casual way – as was later described when the Secretary of State for Air asked for a summary of what had happened. He was told in a minute of 9 August[2] that the meeting – held in the Prime Minister's room at the House of Commons – had ended between 6 and 6.30 p.m., that minutes had been sent to members during the following day (Tuesday, 26 July) and that extracts from them reached officials in the Departments concerned on the 27th. No Minister or official thought in terms of a Parliamentary statement being made, and the news actually leaked out at a meeting of the Airframe Modification Committee on the morning of Thursday, 28 July, when an Air Ministry finance official mentioned the cancellation in the presence of a member of the Handley Page staff. This annoyed Sir Frederick Handley Page when he heard about it, because the previous day he had especially asked (having been warned of the decision in confidence by the Ministry of Aviation) that no public announcement should be made until the following Tuesday – when his employees would return to work after the Bank Holiday.

Not only was the decision to cut the Victor B.2 order by 25 a bitter blow for the company, but the manner in which they learned of the Cabinet Defence Committee decision – without the explanation which would have accompanied a formal announcement – was unfortunate; a double blow in that discussions were going on at that time about a possible take-over of Handley Page Ltd by the Hawker Siddeley Group.

A minute of 26 May 1960 had said that negotiations between Hawker Siddeley and Handley Page for the take-over of the latter company were "on the point of signature"; it added that if there were a serious possibility that the Victor order might be cancelled "in whole or in part, they may be accused of bad faith if they allow the negotiations to be completed without mentioning this. They therefore propose, if we confirm that such a possibility exists, to tell the principals orally in the strictest confidence that the possibility of some reduction in the size of the Victor Mk 2 order cannot be excluded. There would be no reference to the alleged incompatibility of Skybolt and the Victor Mk 2. . . ."

[1] D(60) 7th Mtg.
[2] From DUS II.

CHAPTER XX

THE QRA ERA (1962-69)

During 1961 the AOC in C Bomber Command (Air Mshl Sir Kenneth Cross) decided to extend the 15-minute readiness of the Saceur-assigned Valiant TBF at Marham and the Thor squadrons to the whole of the Medium Bomber Force from 1 January 1962. From 18 September to 14 October the Command held a 15-minute Alert exercise, code-named Macassar, which the C in C told VCAS on 9 October had been "most successful" and had led him to the conclusion that "we must consider maintaining some form of permanent readiness throughout the Command". He thought there were "many reasons for adopting the 15-minute alert posture", among the most important being that the deterrent was strengthened "by having a quick reaction capability between the 24hr strategic warning . . . and the 'bolt from the blue'",[1] and that co-operation with Strategic Air Command would be strengthened by having "strong grounds for closer integration of their Reflex forces in this country".

The C in C's proposal for a permanent alert – starting with one aircraft per squadron, or approximately 15 aircraft from the MBF, which he aimed to increase to two aircraft per squadron (30 aircraft) by the end of 1962 – was first put forward in a letter to VCAS (Air Chf Mshl Sir Edmund Hudleston) on 31 October 1961 following the success of Exercise Macassar. "It seems only military commonsense", he averred, "to maintain a permanent alert concept . . . in the face of the growing Russian threat and the need to build up experience to compete with the greatly reduced warning time during the coming years".

On 17 November he asked permission to hold the first Micky Finn, a no-notice exercise to test his Command's ability to disperse without warning. This involved both the MBF and the Thor force. It was approved by Ministers and held from 5 December, lasting 48hr.

The C in C's permanent alert proposal, which meant considerable increases in establishments, was put to the Air Staff and approved in principle by the Air Council on 7 December. CAS (Air Chf Mshl Sir Thomas Pike) said that it could improve the effectiveness of the MBF, whose state of readiness would be brought into line with that of the Valiants under Saceur, and this would "reinforce the morale of the operating crews and staffs throughout the Command" and improve its "already high standing with Strategic Air Command".

CAS told the C in C on the 13th that the Council supported "the introduction of the first phase of the permanent standby"– "maintaining one aircraft in each squadron at 15 minutes' readiness", to come into force early in the New Year; but it had reserved its position on the

---

[1] Literally, in the form of low-trajectory missiles, giving a much-decreased warning time.

further proposal – to progress to two aircraft per squadron at 15 minutes' readiness, which the C in C had suggested should come into effect towards the end of 1962. This had "wider implications", which CAS thought the Council should "study carefully" before giving a decision.

At the beginning of 1962 the readiness for Saceur-assigned squadrons was increased when, on 1 January, a revised Nuclear Strike Plan came into effect: it meant that four Valiants instead of three were held at 15 minutes readiness at Marham,[1] and eight Canberras instead of four on the squadrons in RAF Germany. On the 19th, SHAPE asked when the RAF would be able to fulfil this requirement. The response was that while the additional Valiant could be made available "without undue cost", the bill for doubling the Canberra B(I).6/8 QRA force was considered by the Air Staff to be "unacceptably high".

After many studies of the financial, aircraft and manpower implications the Air Council Standing Committee decided on 9 April that Saceur's increased QRA commitment, both in the UK and in Germany, should be accepted but that a critical look should be taken at the means by which this was done in Germany. Subsequently the Inspector-General (Air Mshl Sir John Whitley) told VCAS (Air Mshl Sir Wallace Kyle) after a visit to RAF Germany that if it was to fulfil, and to be seen to fulfil, Saceur's QRA requirement, "the aircrew and the corresponding groundcrew bill" that had been put forward "must be met". Then on 21 June the Chiefs of Staff discussed the increased QRA commitment for Saceur-assigned aircraft and agreed with VCAS's view that it should be accepted but that the matter should be reviewed in a year's time; and after the meeting a signal was sent from CDS to Saceur agreeing to the increased capability.

Towards the end of 1962 the AOC in C Bomber Command gave notice to CAS[2] that he would be putting forward proposals to compensate for the loss of Thor weapon systems in 1963 by increasing the number of medium bombers held at immediate readiness. He said that the phasing-out of Thors from the following April would "progressively reduce the number of weapon systems held at immediate readiness (15 minutes) from 68 (54 Thor + 14 aircraft)", unless measures were taken to increase the number of aircraft at IR in the

---

[1] Under the mid-1961 assignment arrangements each of the Marham squadrons was to maintain one fully armed aircraft at 15 minutes' continuous readiness to comply with Saceur's Quick Reaction Alert System (letter from HQ BC to Air Ministry (Ops B3), in Project E – Mk 28 – Saceur-assigned Valiants (AF/CMS 279/64)). Reviewing 1962 with reference to the MBF as a whole, a history of No 1 Group comments: "Earlier in the year an alert system was introduced, known as Quick Reaction Alert (QRA), to improve the deterrent capability. A proportion of squadron crews and aircraft were kept at all times on fifteen minutes readiness to take off, the crews being housed and fed in quarters close to their aircraft and alerted to higher states of readiness by a klaxon. Much could be written on the trials and tribulations of QRA; sufficient to say that it became the most prominent feature in the day-to-day existence of the V-force crew".

[2] Correspondence in V/9/322 Quick Reaction Alert – Medium Bomber Force.

meantime. The effect of such a reduction would mean that the part Bomber Command played in integrated plans with Strategic Air Command would be "correspondingly reduced in size and less easily defined in importance".

On 10 January 1963 the C in C put forward his proposal. From 1 April, he told CAS, "I propose increasing the QRA force to 17 Vulcans and Victors (plus the four Valiants of the Saceur Force)", rising to 20 Victors and Vulcans by 1 July, "when the Blue Steel squadrons will be able to make their contribution". This plan, he added, "will enable me to maintain approximately 20 per cent of the force at permanent readiness and will go some way to compensate for the run-down of Thor"[1].

In comments on the C in C's suggestion, VCAS noted on the 15th that "in view of the possible assignment of part or the whole of Bomber Command to Nato as a result of the Nassau agreement, the time at which this proposal is implemented needs further consideration"[2]. On the 24th AMSO (Air Mshl Sir Walter Merton) noted that the C in C had pointed out, on the question of manpower, that he would be giving up 4,000 men with the phasing-out of Thor, and that no additional technical personnel would be required because Bomber Command were "instituting centralised progressive servicing [introduced in early 1964 after a trial period] which will make for more efficient use of their manpower". Early in March, however, VCAS agreed that no action should be taken to implement the proposals for increased readiness until the final terms of assignment of the V-force to Nato were known[3].

Referring to the costs involved in a QRA commitment, CAS (Air Chf Mshl Sir Charles Elworthy) told the Chiefs of Staff on 19 November 1963[4] that the increase from three to four Valiants and from four to eight Canberras had meant "an addition of 200 men and £500,000 per year". As far as crews were concerned, recurrent QRA duty added to the strains already imposed on them by no-notice exercises to test their readiness. A former AOC No 1 Group[5] thus described the period leading to the introduction of MBF QRA: —

"RAF Commands have traditionally had Alert and Readiness plans, but special significance has always been attached to those for the V-force. In addition to countering raids by manned aircraft, the procedures have needed to take account of the possible threat of surprise attack by low-level trajectory missiles fired from Soviet satellite territories.

"For the V-force to be a credible strategic deterrent, Bomber Command had to demonstrate the ability to generate weapon systems

---

[1] Correspondence in V/9/322 Quick Reaction Alert - Medium Bomber Force.
[2] Minute to ACAS(Ops), Ibid.
[3] Minute, PS/VCAS to PS/CAS, 5 Mch 63, Ibid.
[4] COS 66th Mtg/63, 19 Nov 63.
[5] Air Chf Mshl Sir David Craig, in his RAeS Lecture: see p 151.

very quickly in a period of warning; to disperse widely to reduce force vulnerability on the ground; and to get all aircraft airborne in a matter of 2-3 minutes after a scramble was ordered . . . .

"During the next four years [from 1958] much more comprehensive and detailed Alert and Readiness plans were devised and progressively implemented. There were, however, many hurdles to overcome. The V-force had to be able to generate and disperse at any time of the day or night, including weekends and holidays. So additional specialist ground equipment, dispersals and ORPs, manpower for two shifts, and improved communications, were essential requirements. The 'Bomber Controller' arrangement, whereby changes in readiness states and the scramble instructions could be passed by landline direct to every crew at cockpit readiness (emulating Fighter Command's telescramble arrangements), was introduced.

"By 1962, Bomber Command had been given the necessary resources and had arranged for at least one aircraft from each squadron to be permanently on QRA (quick reaction alert). It was, in the opinion of the then AOC in C Bomber Commnd (Air Mshl Sir Kenneth Cross), only military commonsense to maintain a permanent alert concept in the face of a growing Soviet threat, and because of the need to build up experience in mounting QRA, to compete with a greatly reduced warning time during the years ahead."

Rapid take-off was a crucial element in QRA. On 5 April 1962 a demonstration of Vulcan RTO capability was given at Woodford, the Avro airfield, from rapid engine start through taxying forward through the "snatch disconnect" sequence to take-off.

When Exercise Micky Finn III was held between 13 and 15 November 1963 the AOC in C Bomber Command (Air Mshl Sir John Grandy, who had succeeded Air Mshl Sir Kenneth Cross) sent VCAS (Air Mshl Sir Wallace Kyle) a copy of the report on it, commenting that "a total of 103 aircraft were available for the exercise and 102 of them were combat-ready at their planned main base or dispersal within 24 hours. Because of exercise exemptions and limited ACHDF[1] support we were only able to use 16 of our 29 dispersals but all 47 aircraft planned to disperse did so within 17 hours . . .".

Adding that in general he regarded the results as satisfactory, the C in C continued;–

"There are two aspects of the Alert and Readiness Plan still to be properly tested. The first is to hold a fully supported 'Micky Finn' where the whole Reinforcement Plan can be exercised on a no-notice-basis and this I understand is about to be approved. The second is the carriage of live weapons to dispersal, which has of course been the subject of much correspondence and is being actively pursued. It is most important that approval for this should be given, as I am sure you appreciate."

---

[1] Air Commander, Home Defence Forces.

What was involved in a Micky Finn was well described in a minute CAS (Air Chf Mshl Sir Charles Elworthy) sent to the Minister (RAF) (Lord Shackleton, who had taken up the post on 19 October following the change of Government) on 26 November 1964:-

"You may like to know that Bomber Command recently carried out a major exercise to test the dispersal and readiness of the bomber force. The Command regularly practise various aspects of their alert and readiness plan. Once a year, however, they hold a major no-notice exercise – 'Micky Finn' – which requires the whole force to disperse and be made ready for an operational mission, without any prior warning.

"All home Commands support dispersal, some by manning key sections at the dispersal airfields and others by flying men and equipment from the main V-bomber bases to the dispersal airfields. Hitherto, supporting Commands have been given at least 14 days' warning of dispersal exercises. On this occasion, however, they took part without prior notice so as to simulate realistically the conditions of a sudden emergency. (Some stations had actually been 'stood down' for a long weekend).

"This year's exercise was held from 26th to 29th October. The bomber force began to prepare for dispersal on receipt of the alert message (Alert Condition Two) at 0323Z on Monday, 26th October. The order to disperse (Alert Condition One) was given at 0500Z on the same day. Aircraft dispersed to 25 of the dispersal airfields in the BC Alert & Readiness Plan. The remainder were activated by personnel only.

"The reinforcement of Bomber Command by the supporting Comands worked well, especially considering it was on a 'No-notice' basis. Of the 240 support personnel earmarked, only 28 failed to arrive. The transport support required to move personnel and equipment to dispersals was provided by 17 Transport Command aircraft, all of which arrived at the main bomber bases on schedule.

"Immediately an alert is called aircraft are prepared at their main bases and allocated to crews so that targets are covered progressively in order of priority. This process is called 'initial generation'. When the order to disperse is given, a number of aircraft fly to their pre-arranged dispersal airfields where they are again prepared for their operational sortie; the latter process is termed 'regeneration'. The initial generation rate required by the Bomber Command Alert and Readiness Plan ranges from 30% of available aircraft (*ie* those aircraft not on major servicing or overseas) after four hours to 100% after 20 hours. Regeneration should be completed within three hours of the arrival of aircraft at dispersal airfields.

"The exercise results were briefly as follows:-

(*a*) Medium Bomber Force (Free Fall) and Tactical Bomber Force: Initial generation results showed that of the 61 free-fall weapon systems available for the exercise 46% (28) were ready within four hours, 85% (52) within ten hours and 97% (59) within the planned 20 hours. Of the 35 weapon systems planned to disperse, 94% (33) had been regenerated within 24 hours from the start of the excercise.

(b) Medium Bomber Force (Blue Steel): 30 Blue Steel weapon systems were available for the exercise. 47% (14) completed initial generation within 20 hours and 86% (26) in 40 hours. Of the 12 weapon systems planned to disperse, all were regenerated within 42 hours from the start of the exercise.

"This year's results for the MBF (Free Fall) and TBF forces showed a continued improvement on past exercises. Although widespread low cloud and fog delayed dispersal, 94% of the force had been regenerated within the planned 20 hours. The results for the Blue Steel force were much slower than the target, but this was the first time it had been fully generated. Whilst our aim is to generate all the available weapon systems within 20 hours – and there is no doubt that we will achieve this in time – we have not yet overcome all the problems associated with Blue Steel, which is a complicated system requiring almost as much effort in preparation as the aircraft itself. A further exercise since held to test this element of the Command shows some improvement.

"In sum, we regard 'Micky Finn' 1964 as generally a very satisfactory exercise; the reinforcement plan worked very well in no-notice conditions."

A further reference to QRA, its significance and its implications for Bomber/Strike Command, is made in Chapter XXX (End of QRA) of this history. Referring to the state of readiness achieved by 1963, a history of No 1 Group comments:–

"The V-force was made more efficient by several innovations this year. Operational Readiness Platforms (ORPs) were constructed at the V-force stations. Waddington's was completed in February. These platforms were built adjacent to the take-off runway to facilitate a 'next to no time' scramble by the aircraft in alert conditions. On the same 'alert' theme, a rapid start capability was introduced on the Mk 2 Vulcans and by the end of the year 32 aircraft were fitted. The new aircraft had Olympus 301 engines."

CHAPTER XXI

BOMBER COMMAND'S THORS

Between the beginning of September 1958 and the beginning of December 1959 Bomber Command formed more squadrons – 20 – than at any other comparable period in its peacetime existence. These were the Thor IRBM squadrons, equipped from the United States under the agreement already described, whose sites sowed plantations of white missiles through the East Midlands-East Anglian-Lincolnshire-Yorkshire countryside, from Mepal and Harrington in the south to Driffield and Carnaby in the north. They were based on wartime airfields and had wartime (mainly bomber) squadron numbers[1].

The original plan, following RAF/USAF discussions at the Air Ministry during January 1958, was to have four squadrons, each of 15 missiles, which would be deployed on 20 dispersed sites and come under Bomber Command control. Thus there would be three missiles to a site and each squadron would form a complex with a main base and satellites. The reason for using wartime airfields was that, as a matter of policy, Government-owned land was selected for Thor sites[2].

Defending the Thor sites, V-bomber and SAC bases and dispersal airfields were Fighter Command's Bloodhound air-defence missiles, the first squadron of which – No 264 (ADM) Sqn – was formed at North Coates on the Lincolnshire coast shortly after the first Thor squadron[3]. As the first air-to-air missiles in the RAF, Firestreaks, entered service with Fighter Command Javelins during October 1958[4] this year saw the start of a missile era for the RAF, which during the next five years acquired and operated four different types: surface-to-surface (Thor), surface-to-air (Bloodhound), air-to-air (Firestreak) and air-to-ground (Blue Steel).

Under the original arrangements for Thor deployment[5] the first squadron, No 77, was to be at Feltwell in Norfolk and to have four satellites – Mepal, North Pickenham, Shepherds Grove and Tuddenham. Eventually these four satellites all became squadrons, and this process was repeated at the other three Thor sites, which each produced five squadrons. The genealogy of the first squadron and its protégés was well described in its Operations Record Book:–

---

[1] A "traditional" squadron numbering pattern was decided on by the Air Council in March 1958 (AC Stdg Cttee Conclusions 5(58), 3 Mch 58, Secret Annex 'B'.)

[2] "For reasons of economy paralleling similar solutions by our own military, the RAF elected to build all facilities on government-owned land, and England, in wartime a green checkerboard of airfields, had many sites available" (*The Mighty Thor*, by J Hartt; Duell, Sloan and Pearce, New York, 1961).

[3] North Coates had been re-opened on 1 Jul 57 as the first SAGW station in the RAF, its primary function being to conduct trials of the Bloodhound SAGW system. It was to assume an operational role when these trials had been sufficiently advanced (Station ORB). On 1 Dec 58 the three Fire Units at North Coates were given the number plate of No 264 Sqn, with the title No 264 (Air Defence Missile) Sqn (Squadron ORB).

[4] With No 33 Sqn, which had started to re-equip with Javelin FAW.7s in July 58.

[5] Described in AMQLR (Air Ministry Quarterly Liaison Report) for Jan-Mar 58.

"No 77 (Strategic Missile) Sqn comprises the three missile launch emplacements at RAF Feltwell. Construction of the emplacements commenced in June 1958 and on completion in August 1958 the missile engineers, Douglas Aircraft Co and their associate companies, began the installation of the ground-support and launch equipment".

The squadron was formed at Feltwell on 1 September 1958 with an establishment of 15 Thor IRBMs – 14 of which it had by 23 December – and (the ORB continued)

"the first Thor SM-75 missile was brought to the squadron during November 1958.[1] Functional demonstrations of the missiles and the launching systems by the Douglas Aircraft Co engineers began in January 1959. The three launch emplacements were handed-over to the RAF during March 1959.

"During the six months preceding handover, 77 Sqn assisted the contractors by maintaining watch over the missile guidance section heaters. . . . Considerable assistance was rendered by the squadron missile maintenance technicians to the installation engineers; equipment on the launch emplacements was assembled and fitted.

"In April 1959 launch crew training commenced on the squadron. . .".

From 22 July the establishment of No 77 Sqn was reduced to 3UE IRBMs on the formation of its four associated Thor units – Nos 82, 107, 113 and 220 (SM) Sqns – and (the ORB recorded) "personnel of the five Feltwell squadrons received count-down training and were evaluated as crews".

These Feltwell squadrons were in No 3 Group, and on the same date in July 1959 the first Thor squadron in No 1 Group – No 97 – was formed at Hemswell in Lincolnshire. Its ORB was also quite explicit on the new weapon and its installation:–

"The Douglas Thor missile is a liquid-fuelled rocket, range 1,500 miles, employing an inertial guidance system and carrying a nuclear warhead. The rocket and its associated ground equipment were designed as an integrated weapon system, and the squadron is armed with three of these weapons.

"When all construction work on the launch pads had been completed, the Douglas Aircraft Co installation teams arrived on the site and commenced installing equipment which had been airlifted from the USA. During the whole of this installation and check-out phase, the pads were in the hands of the DAC and associated contractors, and remained so until the USAF Functional Demonstration Requirements were met. . . .

"The pads, and their respective missiles and equipment, were handed-over from the USAF to No 97 Sqn on 20 July 1959, and from

---

[1] There is a discrepancy in dates here with AMQLR for July-Sept 58,which says that "the first Thor missile (less nose-cone/warhead) was offloaded at Lakenheath from a C-124 Globemaster on 29 August. It was delivered to No 77(SM) Sqn, Feltwell, on 19 September." The other airheads were Scampton (for Hemswell), Leconfield (for Driffield) and Cottesmore (for North Luffenham).

this time on, 'bird-watching' shifts[1] were maintained at the site. This entailed operational and servicing personnel keeping continuous watch on the serviceability of various components of the equipment".

As at Feltwell, so at Hemswell, four new squadrons were formed from the original one – the process rather resembling the biological multiplication of cells. The first (September 1959) ORB entry for No 97 Sqn refers under the heading of "Training" to the squadron's three launch pads being "used during the period by Nos 104, 106, 142 and 269 Sqns for IWST (integrated weapons system training)" and says that during the months "launch crews from Caistor, Bardney, Ludford Magna, and Coleby Grange carried out IWST on the site at Hemswell". These stations were where the other four squadrons in the Hemswell complex were based – No 104 at Ludford Magna, 106 at Bardney, 142 at Coleby Grange and 269 at Caistor.

AMQLR for July-September 1958 had announced the "third and fourth" strategic missile squadrons (*ie*, after Nos 77 and 97) as Nos 98 (in No 1 Group) and 144 (in No 3 Group). It said that 98 would be based at Driffield, with satellite launch positions at Carnaby, Catfoss, Breighton and Full Sutton; and that 144 would be based at North Luffenham, with satellites at Folkingham, Polebrook, Harrington and Melton Mowbray.

The ORB for No 98(SM) Sqn noted in November 1959 that "the five Thor missile launching sites which come under command of Royal Air Force Driffield have now been allotted squadron numbers. The launching site which is situated on the airfield at Driffield has been allocated No 98." The other squadrons in the complex were Nos 150 at Carnaby, 226 at Catfoss, 240 at Breighton and 102 at Full Sutton.

No 144 Sqn[2], formed at North Luffenham on 1 December 1959 as the last of the Thor "complexes", had as its associated squadrons Nos 223 at Folkingham, 130 at Polebrook, 218 at Harrington and 254 at Melton Mowbray. Its ORB for December 1959 commented that although the squadron had formed officially on the 1st, "preparation for the formation began some time before this", as it went on to describe:–

"All officers attended a special introductory course on ballistic missiles at RAF Manby in April-May 1959[3]. They then took a further course of training in the USA during July-August-September – one month of classroom training at the Douglas factory at Tucson, Arizona, followed by two months' practical training on the Thor missiles at Vandenburg AFB, California. This training culminated in a live firing of a Thor missile.

"During the same period in the USA, 15 airmen were also

---

[1] No 77 Sqn defined "birdwatch" as "maintaining watch over the missile guidance section gyro heaters" (ORB).

[2] The second Thor squadron was originally announced as No 141 then changed to No 144.

[3] Academic training for Thor personnel had begun in 1958 with GD guided-weapons courses at the RAF Technical College, Henlow, followed by a ballistic-missile lead-in course at the RAF Flying College, Manby (AMQLR, April-June 58).

undergoing similar training as missile fitters, known in the USAF as missile maintenance technicians (MMT), and five NCO aircrew were training as launch monitor console operators (LMCO). At Vandenburg the officers and airmen were divided into launch crews of one launch control officer (LCO), one LMCO and three MMTs."

No 144 Sqn's ORB also noted, at the beginning of 1960, that "the third missile was installed on its pad during January. The three missiles and pads have been numbered 46, 47 and 48, following-on the sequence started in other complexes. . . ." All the missile emplacements were numbered: No 77, as the first Thor squadron to be formed, had Nos 1, 2 and 3. The squadron which had the last numbers, 58, 59 and 60, was No 223 at Folkingham, Lincolnshire, part of the North Luffenham complex, which received its last missile on 1 April 1960.

One of the other North Luffenham squadrons, No 254, described its origin and purpose in a detailed ORB entry after being re-formed in No 3 Group on 1 December 1959 "to operate a Thor intermediate-range ballistic-missile site on a disused airfield known as Royal Air Force Melton Mowbray". Its first task was

"refresher training of the crews while American contractors finished installing the Thor equipment. This . . . took place at RAF North Luffenham and RAF Feltwell, beginning on 18 January . . . and . . . completed by 17 March. During this period the contractor continued the installation assisted, where possible, by squadron personnel.

"On 27 February a protest march by the Campaign for Nuclear Disarmament was staged from Leicester to RAF Melton Mowbray, culminating in picketing the site. The affair was ignored by squadron personnel, on advice from the civilian police, and terminated peacefully after a few speeches by the marchers.[1]

"During March 1960 the squadron took partial control of the equipment from the contractors and 24-hour watch-keeping com-menced on 8 March. On 5 May the squadron was represented . . . at the official handing-over ceremonial parade at North Luffenham to celebrate the completion of the North Luffenham complex. . . .

"July 11 to 13 saw the annual Bomber Command exercise known as Exercise Mayshot in which the squadron took part on a simulated basis only. . . ."

In the following year, however, "between 10 and 12 May the squadron took an active part in Exercise Mayshot, . . . completing eight successful countdowns".

With the installations and activation of the 20 Thor squadrons, Bomber Command had acquired the equivalent of 60 more V-bombers,

---

[1] There had been demonstrations against the deployment of Thor since 1959. On 24 August a "ban the H-bomb" protest march had been made to RAF Mepal, near Ely, where No 113 Sqn – part of the Feltwell complex – was based. As the Thors were 65ft in length, were painted white with RAF roundels on them, and were sited above ground, their locations could hardly be disguised.

for each of the IRBMs represented the delivery on to a target of a megaton-range warhead. The Thors were therefore phased-in to the Command's major exercises during the QRA period.

Indeed they were phased-in completely. An announcement early in 1959 about Bomber Command Signals plans – "Support Communications for Thor Weapon System"[1] – said unequivocally: "the Thor intermediate-range ballistic missiles are operationally and administratively part of the deterrent force under Bomber Command". When in mid-1959 an initial operational capability was announced for Thor, SASO, Bomber Command, said that ". . . the force is currently established to meet this requirement. . . . On the introduction of an IOC, Thor weapon systems already accepted by the RAF and the appropriate Operations Wing, Operations Rooms are to be manned continuously."[2] A percentage of Thors were to be maintained at T.15 readiness[3] 24 hours a day, 365 days a year; targetting was to be controlled through the Bomber Command Operations Centre, and the Medium Bomber Force alert and readiness plan was to be amended to include a section on the Thor Force. In other words, the Thors were operated on the same QRA basis as the V-bombers, though without the element of dispersal. Exercise Respond was a no-notice testing of the readiness of the Thor Force.

For their crews – approximately 39 men (six officers, 15 SNCOs and 18 NCOs/ORs) to a squadron of three missiles – life at their sites resembled that advised for soldiers of antiquity: "Let them be constantly employed either in field days or in the inspection of their arms. . . . They should be frequently called by roll and trained to be exact in the observance of every signal"[4].

There were two Thor centres in each Group of Bomber Command – Hemswell and Driffield in No 1 Group, Feltwell and North Luffenham in No 3 Group – and on or linked to each parent station were five squadrons. From the ORBs of the squadrons based on Hemswell and Feltwell (Nos 97 and 77 respectively – the first to be formed) it is clear that there were four main lines of activity: crew training; missile serviceability; readiness exercises; and security.

In mid-1960, when all 20 Thor squadrons had been formed and had received their complement of missiles, Bomber Command laid down a readiness policy for its strategic missile force – which, it said,[5] was to be "regarded as constituting the equivalent for Bomber Command of the Strategic Air Command Alert Force". It was to "maintain a capability to react within tactical warning at all times".

This directive went on to say that the Thor SMF was "to maintain 60

---

[1] HQ BC Signals Plans No 1/59 in HQ 1 Group file Project Thor Operations – Policy.
[2] Thor Weapon System – Operational Policy, 15 July 59 (BC/S.91560).
[3] That is, 15 minutes' readiness.
[4] Vegetius: *De Re Militari*, tr by Lt John Clarke (Mil Service Pub Co 1944).
[5] Thor Strategic Missile Force – Readiness Policy: SASO, Bomber Command, to HQs No 1 and 3 Groups, 25 July 1960 (BC/S.91519).

per cent of the force at 'standby' or 'available'", and that this figure had been set up as an initial target while experience was being gained; it was hoped to work up to a final readiness capability of 75 per cent. This readiness requirement was "effective throughout the year, including public holidays" – in other words, the SMF, like the V-bomber force, was being run in peacetime on a war footing; otherwise it would have been impossible to claim a QRA capability for the deterrent force. But the Command directive did relent so far as to say that it was "desirable, consistent with the readiness requirement, to arrange for the maximum number of personnel to take advantage of public holidays".

In a historical note in its last Operations Record Book entry before being disbanded[1], No 77 (SM) Sqn provided a useful description of the organisation of the Thor sites. Recalling that the squadron had been re-formed at Feltwell on 1 September 1958 as "the first Strategic missile squadron in the Western alliance", it said that the Thors were "designed to carry a megaton nuclear warhead to a maximum range of 1,500 miles with a CEP (circular error of probability) of two miles"; they were powered by a Rocketdyne MB-3 liquid-propellant sustainer of 150,000lb thrust and two liquid-propellant Vernier rockets of 1,000lb thrust each. The missiles were "housed in a horizontal position in a retractable shelter and were maintained in a 'ready-to-launch' configuration. On turning a key[2] each . . . was designed to lift off its launch pad after 15 minutes – during which time the inertial guidance system would be run up, the shelter retracted, the missile erected, fuel (kerosine-type) and liquid oxygen loaded into the missile and the engines ignited. The entire process, known as the 'count-down', was automatic, being controlled and monitored by electronic equipment housed in mobile (but normally static) trailers".

The ORB described squadron HQ as being in a converted aircraft hanger known as the RIM (receipt, inspection and maintenance)

---

[1] On 10 Jul 63, having become non-operational on 30 June.

[2] Actually two keys – turned by the RAF missile controller and USAF authentication controller. Referring to the Douglas Aircraft Co handover to the RAF on 5 May 60 ("Project Emily's official conclusion") and to various farewell functions which preceded it, Julian Hartt says in his book *The Mighty Thor* (Duell, Sloan and Pearce, '61) that on 27 April the company "threw a traditional military-style 'beer bust' for all the troops of the RAF and USAF units. Among these was the Ninety-ninth Support Squadron, the new designation of what once had been the USAF's 672nd Technical Training Squadron." He adds:–

"In its new and continuing role the Ninety-ninth would be smaller in manpower but ever more important in its duties. These were the officers and men now charged with custody of the nuclear warhead. So long as Thor remained operational, there would be an officer of the Ninety-ninth on duty at all times, in every blockhouse. On a chain around his neck would be a key. An RAF launching control officer beside him would have a similar, but different, key. One was marked 'War'. The other was marked 'Peace'.

"On the consoles there were two locks with similar nomenclature stamped above them. The RAF officer's key, on decision of the Prime Minister, can initiate the countdown for combat launching. But it cannot release the nuclear warhead. The USAF officer's key, on decision of the President of the United States, can bring to life that nuclear warhead. But it cannot launch a missile.

"On such a simple, straightforward arrangement, founded in the mutual understanding and trust of two great nations, rested control of the free world's first nuclear-tipped ballistic missile force . . .".

building, which had offices and an operations room – subsequently renamed the Missile Control Centre – permanently manned by a Royal Air Force squadron leader (the Missile Controller) and a USAF Authentication Controller of lieutenant-colonel or major rank. A large floor area in the hanger was used for servicing missiles and GSE (ground support equipment), most of which was in self-contained mobile trailers, and to provide servicing bays for special equipment (such as guidance sets, control electronics assemblies, LOX and gaseous nitrogen pipelines).

The 77 (SM) Sqn missiles were on 15 launch pads in groups of three at five locations or sites, where there were flights – "A" at Feltwell, "B" at Shepherds Grove, "C" at Tuddenham, "D" at Mepal and "E" at North Pickenham – which subsequently became squadrons. In addition to the flight commanders (all squadron leaders) there were in the RIM building a Wing Commander Operations with four Operations Officers – later re-titled Missile Controllers – under him, and a Wing Commander Technical, controlling technical officers in charge of servicing personnel.

No 77's ORB recounted that all the squadron personnel "had received a crash training programme at the RAF Flying College at Manby for two weeks and from six weeks to three months at the Douglas Aircraft Co plants at Tucson, Arizona, Los Angeles and Sacramento, California". It continued:–

"In August 1958 they started work at Feltwell, where the installation of the weapon system had begun, and later at the dispersed flights. Douglas Aircraft Co were experiencing difficulty in meeting their schedules and RAF personnel were attached to their working teams to assist . . . .

"'A' Flight, which had been started first, was the first flight where the installation was completed; and the weapon system, despite many teething problems, became sufficiently workable for practical count-down training to commence in April 1959, although it was still far from operational. All launch crews were cycled through the training machine which had been set up, with instruction gradually passing from the Douglas technical representatives to the RAF launch crews . . . .

"On 1 September 1959 an organisational change took place – the flights were upgraded to squadrons. 'A' Flight retained the number 77 and the others became 82, 107, 113 and 220 respectively. The squadrons became part of Operations Wing with the squadron commanders responsible to Wing Commander Operations rather than directly to the Station Commander as before . . . .

"During 1959 and early 1960 steady progress was made towards becoming fully operational. Procedures for different types of count-down (*eg*, dual propellant flows) were devised and tested at 77 Squadron and were subsequently published as . . . the standard operational procedures which have been used ever since[1].

"In May 1960 warheads were fitted to the missiles, which completed the weapon system and finally gave it a no-notice strike capability. [By January 1961] the squadron had been fully operational for eight months and subsequent activities [were] confined to the 'Consolidate' modification programme (which reduced the countdown time from approximately 19 minutes to less than the original planned time of 15 minutes)[2] and a continuous process of training of personnel and improvement of procedures . . . .

"The squadron remained operational until 2359hr(Z) on 30 June 1963. During these years it was continually manned by a crew consisting of at least one launch control officer (Flight Lieutenant, GD), one authentication officer (Major or below, USAF), one launch control console operator (NCO aircrew), three missile servicing chiefs (fitters), one electrical fitter/mechanic and four RAF Police.

"There were five of these launch crews . . . working a round-the-clock shift roster. They were exercised frequently, on a no-notice basis, the missiles being counted-down to launch minus eight minutes state (known as a Phase 2 hold). Other pre-planned exercises were also held when the missiles were counted-down to launch minus two seconds — having first been rendered safe. Each missile was in a 'ready to launch' (standby) state for over 90 per cent of the time and the squadron formed an important part of the Western nuclear deterrent force . . . ."

This description of the operational activity of No 77 Sqn could be read-across to the other Thor squadrons. Early in 1963, when Bomber Command held a Press conference at Scampton on Blue Steel, the AOC in C (Air Mshl Sir Kenneth Cross) said that from 1959 to 1961 the RAF Thors had been "the only strategic missile system in use" and that since 1959 they had been at constant readiness. At the time of the Cuban missile crisis (October 1962) 59 out of 60 had been serviceable — the 60th being used for training[3].

This 60th missile was probably the one at Feltwell used by the Command's Strategic Missile School there, which trained new entrants to the Thor force, training also being done on the squadrons[4]. Like the V-bomber crews, the launch crews were categorised[5], and there was a special categorisation test for launch crews who went to the United

---

[1] No 77 had been given the task of standardisation of procedures for the Feltwell Wing squadrons, and these consisted of check-lists for "Preparation for Dry Countdown", "Reset to a Ready Condition" and "Standard Operating Procedures for Setting-in Target Data" (ORB, Sep 59).

[2] In its ORB for Feb 61 No 144 Sqn, noting that "Operation Consolidate" began on the 16th, said that it consisted of "a series of modifications to the missiles and ground equipment to speed the countdown sequence".

[3] Report in *Flight* for 21 February 1963.

[4] Launch crew training began on the first squadron, No 77, in April 1959 and was given to personnel of all the eventual five Feltwell squadrons.

[5] At Feltwell in December '59 officers of No 77 Sqn prepared examination papers to be used in categorising launch crews in the Wing.

States for a live firing of Thor — known as a CTL (combat training launch)[1]. At the same time, each squadron aimed to keep its missiles at the highest possible state of serviceability. In January 1961, Bomber Command had reviewed its readiness policy for SMF and upgraded the requirements: a total of 80 per cent of the missiles were to be at Standby or Available and 60 per cent of them at Standby. These were monthly average readiness requirements — stated as percentages instead of in numbers because at least one squadron was likely to be non-operational during the greater part of 1961 owing to modification[2].

During October 1961 the Thor Readiness Policy was again revised. A directive from SASO, Bomber Command, to the Groups stated that

"The readiness commitment of the Thor force which was given in this Headquarters letter . . . dated 20 December 1960 was stated against the background of the '24hr strategic warning' concept. However, since it is clearly advantageous to make full use of the high readiness capability of the Thor weapon system, it has been decided to revise the readiness policy to place greater emphasis on immediate readiness, rather than on potential readiness over a monthly period.

"In future therefore, a minimum of 65 per cent of the force (ie, 39 missiles) is to be held at 'Standby' at all times. Stations within No 1 Group will be expected to hold a minimum of 20 missiles at Standby, but because one missile at Feltwell is in full use by the Bomber Command Strategic Missile School, the commitment for No 3 Group stations will be 19 missiles. Normally, the minimum Standby force by stations will be nine missiles for Feltwell and ten each for the other staions . . . .

"The remaining 21 missiles are to be held at the highest state of readiness consistent with the requirements of maintenance and training . . .".[3]

Thor training in a pragmatic sense – that is, producing crews who were combat-ready – was done on the squadrons[4], and training in the academic sense at the Bomber Command Strategic Missile School, formed at Feltwell in January 1961. Subsequently a subsidiary element of the school moved from Hemswell to Feltwell, during March. This followed the ruling in Bomber Command's Organisation Memorandum setting-up the school[5], which said that initially there would be a subsidiary element at Hemswell, but that this was to be "absorbed into

---

[1] Eg on No 97 Sqn in October 1961 the month's training included numerous count-downs completed for the purpose of categorising launch crews proceeding to the USA.
[2] Readiness Policy for the Thor SMF, reviewed by BC and re-issued (1G/S.452/AIR) on 31 Dec 1960.
[3] Thor Readiness Policy (BC/S.91519), 19 Oct 61.
[4] Thus the 97 Squadron ORB noted in March 1962 that "'D' crew under the command of Flt Lt D A Helsby successfully completed their categorisation test during a seven-day course controlled by Station Training Flight".
[5] 3/61 of 6 January 1961.

the School at Feltwell at the earliest possible date"[1]. In April 1961 the ORB for RAF Feltwell reported that the Strategic Missile School was "fully established" there; that during the month 43 personnel had successfully completed their training, and 56 students had arrived to begin training. On 4 May there was a parade at Feltwell to mark the handing-over of Thor missile training from Air Training Command, USAF, to RAF Bomber Command.

Several different types of course were run by the Missile School – for launch control officers, technical officers, authentication officers, missile servicing chiefs and missile, general and electrical fitters. The last course – No 25 Launch Control Officer – completed its training on 15 November and at the end of that month the school was closed down, shortly before an announcement by the Minister of Defence that the Thor deployment in the UK was to end. It had thus been giving training courses at Feltwell for a year and ten months.

The apogee of training for Thor crews was, of course, a live firing – but the opportunity for this only occurred in the USA, at Vandenberg AFB (170 miles north-west of Los Angeles), either at the end of training or when crews returned for a combat training launch. The first live launch of a Thor by RAF personnel, code-named Lion's Roar, was achieved on 16 April 1959 by a four-man crew – Sqn Ldr P G Coulson, MPlts A E Cover and M H Sloan and Chf Tech R M Carpenter – and it was observed by AVMs W Sheen (Commander of the RAF Staff at the British Joint Services Mission in Washington) and G A Walker (AOC No 1 Group, Bomber Command). Thereafter seven launches by RAF crews under training in the US took place – on 16 June 1959 (a previous one, on 22 May, went to within three seconds before lift-off before being cancelled); on 14 August and 17 September; three more "in the last quarter" of 1959[2] – two of them being successful but the third Thor breaking-up after two minutes' flying; and a last one on 2 March 1960. The combat training launches by RAF crews also started in 1959 and continued until 1962. A team from Feltwell, formed of personnel from all the squadrons in the complex, launched the first CT Thor from Vandenberg on 6 October 1959 – a firing described as "an outstanding success, both technically and operationally". The second was fired by a crew from Hemswell on 4 December 1959. During 1960 there were four more CTLs: on 2 March, watched by ACAS (Training) (AVM J Worrall); on 22 June, when the missile fired was the first to come from RAF stock, brought out of the Driffield complex and fired by a crew from there; on 11 October, when one of Hemswell's missiles was launched by one of its

---

[1] The Feltwell ORB for March 1961 recorded that "the Hemswell element of the Bomber Command Strategic Missile School, consisting of 71 personnel, moved to Feltwell between 3rd March . . . and 8th March", adding that "it has now been decided to adapt one of the missiles of No 77 Squadron for training purposes and the implications of this are now under consideration".

[2] AMQLR for October-December 1959.

crews; and on 13 December – witnessed by the AOC in C Bomber Command – when the launching was by a North Luffenham crew. There were also four CTLs in 1961 – on 29 March by a Driffield crew (the first RAF night launch and the first using fast count-down procedures); on 20 June by a crew from North Luffenham; on 6 September by a Feltwell crew; and on 6 December by one from Hemswell. The 11th launch in the CTL programme, on 19 March 1962, was a failure, the missile having to be destroyed after 28 seconds; but the 12th and last – on 19 June – was described as "successful in all respects".

An important development in Thor squadron training in the UK was the introduction early in 1960 of the flow of liquid oxygen – which, with RP-1, fuelled the Thors – into the missiles as a normal squadron training exercise[1]. These "wet" countdowns were first done on 2 June by 77 Sqn, which drew up the standard procedures[2]. All previous training count-downs had been "dry" (ie, unfuelled)[3].

The next step in this aspect of Thor training was the achievement of "double propellant" flow – that is, fuelling the missile with LOX and RP-1 simultaneously, as No 77 Sqn did for the first time at the beginning of July 1960. Its ORB for that month recorded, under the heading "Standard Operating Procedures":-

"A double propellant flow count-down, the first in the UK controlled by RAF personnel only, was conducted successfully on 1 July on Emplacement No 1 to verify a procedure produced at No 77 Squadron".

No 77 noted later that year, in its December 1960 ORB entry, that

"For the first time at this squadron a single fuel flow count-down and a dual propellant flow count-down were carried out on 21 December, the RP-1 being flowed into a mobile tank. Henceforth this type of count-down will be carried out once per quarter on each launch pad and will replace the single LOX flow count-down which has been carried out previously to prove the system"[4].

The routine nature of much of the Strategic Missile Force training was exemplified by comments made by the two squadrons in their ORBs at the end of 1960/beginning of 1961. No 77 recorded in their December 1960 entry under "Training" that "the double-flow, five-day period of

---

[1] AMQLR for Apr-Jun 60.

[2] Squadron ORB for Jun 60. The Thor's Rocketdyne MB-3 rocket engine operated on liquid oxygen and RP-1 fuel (*Flight*, 5 Dec 58 and 22 May 59).

[3] In its ORB for March 60 No 144 Sqn (North Luffenham) noted that "practice countdowns can be of two types: wet or dry. In the wet type either one or both propellants, liquid oxygen or RP-1 fuel, are flowed into the missile in much the same way as in a live firing. In the dry countdown no propellants are flowed from their storage tanks". On 7 Dec 60 there was a major incident at No 104 Sqn, Ludford Magna, when a full load of liquid oxygen was spilled over the pad. The squadron CO was replaced and Hemsell's station commander handed-over his command.

[4] No 98 Sqn at Driffield had remarked, in its Dec 59 ORB entry under "Fire Fighting Drills": "This is as important as count-downs when the operation of missiles using potentially dangerous propellants is considered".

350

simultaneous periodic inspections and operational exercises have afforded practical training to launch crews, while improved availability of up-to-date technical manuals has facilitated theoretical continuation training"; and No 97 remarked on the same subject in January 1961:-

"Routine training was carried out in accordance with the Operations Wing Syllabus, a total of 12 count-downs being initiated. Two of these were conducted simultaneously, as an Operational Readiness Exercise for the training of a replacement LCO. A dual propellant flow scheduled during the month was cancelled because of a temporary restriction imposed for this type of exercise. Categorisation of launch crew personnel in accordance with the HQ Bomber Command Categorisation Scheme was started during the month. . .".

Side-by-side with crew training, as a second main element in Thor squadron activity, was missile serviceability; it was each squadron's task to have as many as possible of its missiles serviceable and ready to launch, in order to conform to Bomber Command's Thor Readiness Policy. As has been seen, when revised in October 1961, this required at least 65 per cent of the SMF – that is, 39 missiles, or two per squadron – to be held at 'Standby' at all times. Such a requirement represented a severe commitment in terms of both manpower and serviceability.

What 'standby' meant to individual squadrons had been exemplified in a brief but significant entry in the ORB of No 144 Squadron at North Luffenham for June 1960. This recorded, under the heading "Weapon State", that live warheads were mated to the missiles on the 25th and 27th; that on the 29th the first missile on the complex went into a 'standby' condition – on emplacement No 48 – and that on the 30th "missile No 46 went to standby". The compiler commented that "the assumption of an operational role, with missiles in a standby configuration, was an historic event for the squadron".

Serviceability of the missiles, as with aircraft, could only be adequately proved in flight; and No 98 Sqn at Driffield, one of whose Thors was – as has been mentioned – the first to be taken from RAF stock for firing at Vandenberg, had the satisfaction of seeing its serviceability proved. The squadron ORB noted in June 1960, under the heading "CTL", that "missile 31, which was removed from the site in May, was fired from Vandenberg on 22 June. The shoot was a complete success in all respects. After a flight of 1,375 miles the impact of the R/V (re-entry vehicle) was ½-mile left and 1½ miles short. Valuable training on propellant transfer was gained by the crew during many single and double flows. . . . Crew co-ordination during the period of the six-week stay was greatly improved."

No 97 Squadron at Hemswell had a similar firing experience in October 1960 and recorded it briefly in their ORB: "Sqn Ldr R Tate (the CO) and five members of the Combat Training Launch Detachment returned from Vandenberg AFB, California, on 21 October. The detachment successfully launched Missile No 186 on 11 October. This missile had been taken from Pad 16, where it had been installed since June 1959."

The Thor fired by the Driffield crew had not been "on site" as long as the one from Hemswell, as No 98 Sqn did not re-form in its missile role until November 1959. But the read-out, as far as serviceability was concerned, was that a Thor could stand out in an English winter, and for a period of six months or a year, then be flown to California and successfully fired. This says much for the inherent engineering worth of the weapon system and for the soundness of RAF maintenance. Out of eight Thor launches by u/t RAF crews from Vandenberg, and 12 combat training launches by selected crews from Driffield, Hemswell, North Luffenham and Feltwell – a total of 20, only two were unsuccessful – one training launch when the missile broke up and one CTL when it had to be destroyed. This represented a 90 per cent success rate.

Thors later became extremely reliable launchers for space vehicles, as first-stage boosters. Referring to the firing of missiles sent back from England to California, Julian Hartt says in his book *The Mighty Thor* (previously quoted from) that "Thors would be chosen at random from among those on station in England and returned to Vandenberg with RAF crews for proficiency firings" – which "proved out, incidentally, the high reliability of these long-alerted missiles as well as of the British crews".

The third main line of Thor squadron activity was quick reaction to Bomber Command readiness exercises. During December 1960 the Command Headquarters announced three types of Thor Operational Readiness Exercises: Respond (of which there were to be six per year); Reclaim (four per year); and Redouble (two per year).[1] On the 6th of that month the HQ issued Exercise Instruction No 13/60 – Exercise Nightcheck. This was a "paper and telephone exercise", to take place once a month, and its purpose was "to exercise launch control officers, station operations room and Bomber Command operations centre personnel in passing and displaying count-down information". In addition to these Command exercises, designed to achieve the aims of the Thor readiness policy, the SMF squadrons were also exercised at Group, Wing, station and squadron levels. They were as subject to these constant disciplines as were the Roman legions to their commander who "must frequently drill them . . . to try their skill and strength, and to see whether they perform their evolutions with proper regularity and are sufficiently attentive to . . . his . . . orders and signals. If deficient in any of these particulars, they must be instructed and exercised till perfect".[2]

Certainly the Thor squadrons were exercised with regularity by Bomber Command (in addition to the lower-level exercises), Responds, Reclaims and Redoubles figuring frequently in their ORBs from

[1] 1G/S.452/Air.
[2] Vegetius: *De Re Militari*, Bk III, translated by Lt John Clarke (see page 344).

mid-1960 until early in 1963 when they became non-operational. The Responds were "no notice" exercises, and the SMF was also involved in the annual Mayshot – "a planned Bomber Command exercise held in conjunction with the aircraft forces . . . designed to test the ability of the missile force to react to the various stages of Alert placed upon it".[1] These Alert states, as applicable to the aircraft forces, were Alert Bravo – MBF ordered to disperse; readiness state Blue – aircraft forces to come to 40 minutes to take-off; readiness state Red – aircraft forces to 15 minutes to take-off; and Scramble – the scramble order "may be given at any time after Alert Alpha. It will indicate to the missile units that the launch order is imminent". Alert Alpha, ordered on the authority of the AOC in C Bomber Command during a period of political tension, was applicable to all the Command's forces, both aircraft and missile, and designed to bring them on to a war footing. For the SMF, it meant that the maximum number of missiles were to be prepared to the "Ready" configuration.[2]

ORBs of the squadrons at the main Thor centres — Nos 97 and 98 at Hemswell and Driffield, and Nos 77 and 144 at Feltwell and North Luffenham — show that in their operational period (from mid-1960 to the spring of 1963) they were involved in up to 28 major Bomber Command readiness exercises, in addition to those initiated at lower levels; so the RAF strategic missile force was certainly kept on its toes. In addition to Mayshots, Responds, Reclaims, Redoubles and Nightchecks there was also Triplox[3] – which No 144 Sqn described in April 1962 as "a single Lox flow on all three pads simultaneously". What these exercises involved for the squadrons can be gauged from occasional descriptions in the ORBs. Thus on 11 July 1960 No 77 Sqn represented the Feltwell Wing in Exercise Mayshot, all three emplacements being in Standby configuration for the start. The Command

"twice ordered simultaneous count-downs of the three missiles to the end of Phase 2. Two changes of target were also ordered. A final triple count-down was ordered on the 13th . . . resulting in three simulated launches, thus concluding the squadron's participation in the exercise. In all these exercises the equipment performed without malfunction".

The squadron commander (Sqn Ldr S D Baldock) commented that Mayshot had "proved successful from the squadron's viewpoint and all personnel involved gained in experience from the various exercises performed. There is, however, a need for target change procedures to be revised and reissued". He also commented, on July 1960 as a whole, that "on eight days of the month all three emplacements were in

---

[1] No 144 Sqn ORB for May 1962, which went on to say: "Alert 3 condition called at 0800Z on 7 May 62 – all three emplacements in Exercise Ready condition four minutes later".

[2] Bomber Command Operation Instruction No 17/60 Alert and Readiness Procedures – Missiles gives these Alert and Readiness Measures Applicable to the Aircraft Forces.

[3] "...designed to test the capability of Strategic Missile Squadron launch crews to complete propellant loading into all three missiles simultaneously" (HQ Bomber Command Exercise Instruction No 8/62 Exercise Triplox).

Standby with war reserve re-entry vehicles for the full 24hr period. On 11 further days two of the emplacements were in Standby. These figures are an eloquent tribute to the efforts of the squadron personnel and to the support given . . . by the Technical Wing".

No 77 Sqn also described an Exercise Respond, on 27 October that year:—

"The three emplacements in 'Standby' were brought to an 'Exercise Ready' condition and counted-down to a planned Phase 2 hold without malfunction. Each emplacement was returned to the 'Standby' status. The average times for each stage in the exercise were

'Standby' to 'Exercise Ready' – 17 minutes
Countdown start to long-range theodolite acquisition – 10 minutes
Reset from countdown to 'Standby' – 17 Minutes".

In his comments, the squadron commander said that considerable value had been gained from Respond — "the first Command truly no-notice exercise". It had "afforded the opportunity to assess the reaction time and readiness of the launch crew and to some extent the readiness of the systems".

Exercise Reclaim was described at a Bomber Command Air Staff meeting on 27 September 1960, when plans for different types of alert and readiness exercises were discussed, as "recovering all missiles at Available to the Exercise Ready conditions, and subsequently counting-down those missiles to the end of Phase 2"; and Exercise Redouble as involving the whole missile force.

During the Thor squadrons' operational deployment period, great emphasis was placed on security, because of possible attempts to enter the sites and damage the installations. There was some public hostility to the missiles, because of their nuclear warheads and because they were American weapons, and this hostility was shown in the form of marches and demonstrations organised by the Campaign for Nuclear Disarmament. There was also the possibility of espionage or sabotage, because the Thors were the only IRBMs in the Nato armoury[1]. For these reasons the sites were ringed with security fencing, patrolled by RAF Police with their guard dogs, and all squadron personnel were constantly alerted to the need to watch and deter any unauthorised entry.

To test these arrangements, the squadrons practised their burglarious skills on each others' locations, and no ORB is without its record of attempts to get into another squadron's area. Thus, in the Hemswell complex, on 31 December 1960 "Sqn Ldr Tate, Sgt Harding (Police) and Cpl Newport (Police) successfully penetrated vital areas of No 269 Squadron" [at Caistor]. But this success by No 97 Squadron was counter-balanced by a breaching of their own security; for on 8 January

---

[1] During 1959 the US Government concluded agreements with Italy and Turkey for the deployment of Jupiter (US Army) IRBMs; but the introduction of ICBMs into Strategic Air Command in 1958 (Atlas and Titan) gradually rendered these deployments obsolete, both types of IRBM being phased-out during 1963.

1961, Sqn Ldr Keatley and Flt Lt Hammond of No 106 Squadron successfully penetrated their site, "having concealed themselves in a missile checkout trailer prior to it being moved from Bardney on to this site" – *ie*, Hemswell. The ORB compiler noted: "The lesson has been learned and remedial action has been taken to prevent a recurrence of this type of intrusion." Sometimes a break-in had unfortunate consequences, as on 7 November 1961 when five members of No 2 Police District and Wg Cdr R S Perry, Wing Commander Operations at RAF Driffield, gained entry to No 98 Squadron's site, compromised the launching pads and LCA area and captured the guardroom before two of them were apprehended. "The team's success", the ORB noted, "was due mainly to the dog handler who was in the S and I area for a period of at least one hour and had allowed his dog to run loose and not under his control. He was dealt with by the squadron commander." By contrast, No 223 Squadron at Folkingham reported in its ORB for May 1961 that "two security checks were carried out against the squadron during the month: the first on the 13th when the whole team was arrested within the security fence; the second on the 29th when all intruders were arrested prior to attempting to scale the security fence"

A history of No 98 Sqn (1958-63),[1] referring to security measures, described how their site at Driffield was originally provided with

"a so-called 'unclimbable fence', but security teams of No 2 Police District mounted mock raids and soon proved this to be a fallacy. A roll of barbed wire was mounted atop the fence round the entire perimeter, and a triple roll of wire was coiled to a height of 4/5ft inside the fence. This slowed-down the speed of entry into the site, and our police were successful in foiling the majority of 'raids'. Each launch crew had a sergeant and two corporal policemen, augmented at night by an establishment of five dog handlers. They also had a radio-equipped Land Rover and two pack-sets, and continuous patrols were mounted throughout the 24 hours. There were periodic threats from 'nuclear disarmers', but the squadron site was never approached, and the police continued their lonely vigil with commendable enthusiasm".

The squadron chronicler also referred to the stringent safety precautions – against fire or nuclear fallout – which were presumably characteristic of all the Thor sites. He said that No 98 had been established with one tender and four firemen, but this was considered inadequate; so during 1960

"plans were developed for a so-called ring-main system to be installed, and this . . . became operative in July 1961. A central 20,000gal tank provided water *via* an underground system of pipes to strategic points on each emplacement. The system was pressurised by an electric pump which could be turned on at any of the hydrants. This action also triggered an alarm point in the squadron guard room and at the main

---

[1] ORB, Appendix "H".

Driffield site. Hoses were pre-positioned at each hydrant, and on receipt of a fire alarm the crews were very quickly in position with charged hoses. A monthly practice for each crew was mandatory. . .".

As to the possibility of an accident involving nuclear material,

"the crews were. . . trained in special safety drills associated with the warhead. In the event of an accident each man had a specific task to perform, and these were practised regularly, both on a squadron and on a station basis. The exercises involved an evacuation of the site, followed by a radiac monitoring of the exercise area. Area cordoning and decontamination drills were also practised. . .".

The Thor squadrons proved that RAF Bomber Command could operate strategic missiles; they were keen and efficient units; they added the equivalent of seven-and-a-half squadrons to the destructive power of the V-force; and their swift retaliatory capability was likely to make a potential enemy think hard about the deterrent response to a nuclear attack on the United Kingdom.

After so much work had gone into siting these IRBMs, bringing-in the hardware and technical backing from the United States and training crews in the launch procedures, it was reasonable to consider the possibility of extending their deployment beyond the five years stipulated in the 1958 agreement. In a paper considered by the Air Council in September 1961[1] the Vice-Chief of the Air Staff (Air Chf Mshl Sir Edmund Hudleston) pointed out that Thor represented the only Allied IRBM in the Aircent region; that it was "a proven and efficient weapon" representing a large investment, and should not be discarded lightly – particularly in view of the possibility that technical improvements might be introduced which would bring the count-down time "within the limits of the future early-warning system".

He said[2] that total count-down time for Thor, incorporating the latest modifications, was 13 to 14 minutes; and that current practice was to keep about 40 missiles in the SMF at about 30 minutes' readiness, to have ten available within six hours and the remainder within 24-28 hours. On receipt of an alert the maximum possible number – usually 50-55 missiles – were brought to the 'Ready' condition, at which they were prepared for immediate initiation of the count-down.

It might be possible to increase readiness by holding the forces at a certain point in the count-down, but there would be penalties. Keeping missiles in the vertical unfuelled condition, about seven minutes from launch, meant that a large number of expensive components would be needed for this state as some sub-systems of limited life would be running continuously. It might be possible to keep the Thors in the vertical fuelled position, about 1½ minutes from launch; but this would raise a number of problems, apart from the need for additional components

---

[1] The Future of Thor: Note By VCAS (AC(61)44). Air Council Conclusions of Meeting 15(61), 7 Sept 61.

[2] The paper was written in August 1961.

and manpower. The missile was designed to be kept in the fuelled state for only two hours, after which certain components became frozen through contact with liquid oxygen.

When that occurred, the propellants had to be unloaded and a six-hour recovery period was needed; in those circumstances, a maximum of a quarter of the force would be available at any time. Modifications to the system meant that a higher state of readiness could probably be maintained without additional components or manpower. A trial at Vandenberg was showing that the force could be kept at eight minutes' readiness without extra running cost. A further modification was to change to hypergolic[1] storable fuels; this had been done to Titan (Martin-built ICBM) with little engineering difficulty and had helped to reduce the count-down time from 15 minutes to 60 seconds, but taking full advantage of this would involve an increased demand for components and manpower.

VCAS said in his paper that since it was impracticable to put Thor underground, the missile "must remain very vulnerable" and would have to be fired before coming under attack. For the RAF to retain it after 1964[2] would require US agreement and entail considerable extra cost, and also involve "the probable continued acceptance of under-manning in certain trades[3]". But even in its present form it represented "a positive addition" to the UK deterrent force, and he recommended that an approach should be made to the US to determine their attitude towards the continued deployment of Thor.

When this paper was discussed by the Air Council on 7 September 1961[4] PUS (Sir Maurice Dean) pointed out that the arguments being adduced in favour of an extension of Thor "were almost exactly the converse of those which had led (with the concurrence of the Air Ministry) to the abandonment of Blue Streak as a military weapon". He doubted whether the continued availability of an above-ground, fixed-site missile would be regarded as "filling a hypothetical gap in [the UK's] deterrent capability". No decision was reached, and the Council resumed their discussion on 21 September.

At that meeting the pros and cons of Thor were again discussed; it was described as an "efficient and proven weapon" and PUS thought it "not impossible" – though awkward – to reverse on its behalf the arguments used to end Blue Streak's military career. The Council thought it desirable to discuss with the USAF the terms on which the IRBM force might be maintained for a further period, and S of S (Mr Julian Amery) was asked to discuss the matter with the Minister of

---

[1] Hypergol is a rocket fuel which ignites when in contact with an oxidising agent; hypergolic, 'of two or more liquids spontaneously explosive on mixing'.

[2] VCAS had explained that a supplementary Thor agreement provided that the deployment should be supported for five years from Nov 59, so maintenance was covered up to Nov 64.

[3] The Thor force employed 3,500 RAF personnel and 670 civilians.

[4] Conclusions 15(61) Secret Annex.

Defence (Mr Peter Thorneycroft)[1].

No decision on an extended Thor deployment was in fact reached by the Air Council in 1961. At the 5 October meeting S of S said he had not had an opportunity of speaking to the Minister of Defence and intended to write to him, and at the meeting on the 26th said he had written but had not yet received a reply. There was no further development until the spring of 1962, when at the 9 April meeting CAS (Air Chf Mshl Sir Thomas Pike) said that the position had altered significantly since the Council's decision of 21 September last to explore the possibility of extending the Thor agreement. He considered there was a real danger that the proposal to keep the SMF on "might make it all the more difficult for us to resist attempts to cut down the deterrent, as well as increasing our financial and manpower estimates" – and that it ought therefore to be abandoned. But he thought that, before a firm decision was taken, it should not be made known outside the Air Ministry "until we could make the most effective use of it in discussions about the future size of the deterrent". If in the interim the Americans asked officially for this information, they could be given it – views with which the Council agreed.

The "firm decision" was taken on 31 May 1962 when the Council approved a proposal by VCAS that the suggestion by the Minister of Defence – that expenditure on Thor should end as quickly as possible – should be accepted, and that the run-down should begin in the spring of 1963, being completed by the end of the year. There was tacit agreement that, if there were to be any public announcement, it should be made in Parliament – which occurred, in an almost casual way, on 1 August during Question time in the Commons. Mr Patrick Gordon-Walker (Lab) asked the Minister of Defence what the Government's policy was "regarding the period for which Thor missiles are to be retained in this country", and Mr Thorneycroft replied that it had been decided that the arrangements under which they were stationed in the UK "should be brought to an end during the course of next year". Behind this announcement lay a Cabinet Defence Committee decision on 31 July that RAF Thor bases should be run down, the meeting "taking note" that the Minister of Defence would make the decision known in Parliament on the following day. It was formally conveyed to the RAF by the Air Minister (Mr Hugh Fraser), who wrote on 2 August to the AOC in C Bomber Command (Air Mshl Sir Kenneth Cross):–

"The Government's decision announced yesterday by the Minister of Defence, to bring to an end during the course of next year the arrangements under which Thor missiles are stationed in this country, foreshadows the close of a memorable chapter in the history of Bomber Command.

[1] An unofficial US view at this time was that in 1965/66 Thor would make "little or no contribution to the deterrent", and that if the UK wished to continue with it they would be asked to take over the logistic support (letter to VCAS from the Commander, RAF Staff, Washington (AVM R H E Emson), 5 Dec 61.

"I should like to take this opportunity of expressing the Air Council's appreciation of the very efficient manner in which this system has been maintained and operated by your Command on behalf of the Royal Air Force. The Air Council are also deeply appreciative of the assistance given by members of the United States Air Force who have been associated with the Royal Air Force in this operation and who must share the credit for your achievement.

"Thor was the first strategic ballistic missile system deployed in the free world. You may well be proud that you pioneered the introduction of these weapons into military service. The high state of readiness at which the Thor force has been maintained, the record of serviceability sustained and the success achieved with Combat Training Launches reflects the greatest credit on all concerned."

On the 3rd the AOC in C issued the following Order of the Day to all Thor squadrons and stations:—

"The decision to phase-out the Thor Force of Bomber Command in no way detracts from the vital role which the force played in the past, and the significant part it will continue to play in future, until the very last missile is withdrawn.

"Thor was the first strategic missile system operational in the West. At a time when the threat to this country came almost entirely from manned aircraft, you were the most formidable part of the defence of the United Kingdom, and the Western Alliance.

"You in the Thor force have maintained a constant vigil day and night for almost four years. You have maintained a higher state of readiness in peacetime than has ever been achieved before in the history of the Armed Forces of the Crown. I am well aware of the sacrifices, so willingly accepted, that this constant readiness has imposed on the officers and airmen of the force.

"I am content that history will recognise your devoted service in the cause of peace. I know that I can rely on you for the same devotion during the run-down phase as you have shown since the birth of the force in 1958".

The Minister of Defence had been informed by the US Secretary of Defense (Mr Robert McNamara) on 1 May 1962 that the United States would not provide support for the Thor programme after 31 October 1964, and at their meeting the Minister "indicated that the system would be phased-out". This was reported on 9 July 1962 in a letter to the AOC in C Bomber Command from the Commander of the 7th Air Division (SAC), Major-General Edwin H Broadhurst, who asked how the phase-out was to be accomplished, whether the UK intended to maintain an operational capability during it and whether US assistance was required during that period, and when "warhead and custodial personnel and nuclear components" could be returned to the US. On 1 August the Minister announced that the Joint US/UK Agreement under which the Thor IRBM system was deployed in the UK would be brought to an end during 1963[1].

These matters were subsequently discussed at an Air Ministry/ Bomber Command meeting on 10 August, when it was decided that the operational run-down of the SMF would begin on 1 April 1963 and was to be completed not later than 30 September, the final technical/ equipment aspects of this run-down being completed by the end of the year. A date for the ending of the combat training launch programme was still to be decided, but the Command Strategic Missile School was to close at the end of November 1962.[2] At a subsequent meeting[3] it was stated that the phase-out would be by bases, at consecutive intervals of 45 days. The order of phase-out was then[4] decided as Driffield, Hemswell, Feltwell and North Luffenham — each complex to be declared non-operational on the first day of the run-down period. So, with a 45-day interval between starting dates, Driffield would be declared non-operational on 1 April 1963, Hemswell on 15 May, Feltwell on 1 July and North Luffenham on 15 August.

The Thor run-down procedure was officially communicated by Air Ministry to the 7th Air Division in a letter of 21 August 1962[5] which said that the run-down was to begin on 1 April 1963, that the force was to be run down operationally by 30 September, and it was hoped that the logistic aspects of the withdrawal would be completed by 31 December. From 1 April to 30 September it was intended to maintain a diminishing operational capability. General training was to cease in November but combat training launches were to be discontinued "immediately".[6]

In a reply to the Air Ministry letter, concurring with the proposed run-down arrangements, 7th Air Division pointed out[7] that it was "to the mutual advantage of both our countries that the highest possible operational capability be maintained in each complex at each stage of the phase-down. The United Kingdom would thereby retain the Thor as a positive deterrent force until 1 April 1963, at which time one entire complex of 15 missiles would be released from operational responsibility, the last complex of 15 missiles phasing-out effective 15 August 1963". The USAF letter also called for the early return of 11 Thor boosters – three of them in November/December 1962. All the relevant plans were discussed at a joint UK/US Co-ordination Group Meeting at Bomber Command HQ on 2 October 1962, followed by a Working Group meeting three days later. Each of the RAF stations concerned produced its own Disposal Plan for the Thor System, following detailed guidance from Bomber Command HQ.[8] The run-down involved not only the air-transportation back to the USA of missiles, warheads and

---

[1] In BC/S.97198 Thor Phase-out Policy.
[2] Minutes C.130585/60/Pt II/DDOps(B).
[3] Minutes BC/S.200084/Ops BM, 31 Aug 62.
[4] 27 Aug 62 (BC/S.99005).
[5] C.130585/60/Pt II.
[6] Thor Phase-out policy II-H/272/27/10 Pt I.
[7] Letter from Col N H Van Sicklen, USAF, Deputy Commander.
[8] Thor – Phase-out Plan (BC/S.99005/Plans), 30 Oct 62.

associated equipment, but the disposal of surplus items and the re-allocation or closure of the Thor bases, the transfer of personnel to other duties and the withdrawal of liaison officers from US training programme posts. The Thor Phase-out Plan issued by Bomber Command at the end of October 1962 consisted of four pages of concise instructions. Details were later issued of the "level of preparation" to be reached for missiles being returned to the US, and a list of "shipping dates" for all 53 of them,[1] from 1 April 1963 onwards.

In order to "prove the system" a prototype dismantling was ordered – of launch emplacement No 40 at No 240 Sqn at Breighton. This order was dated 28 November 1962; the exercise was to be "in the nature of a trial" – "to be utilised to provide detailed information on which final dismantling plans for all Thor stations can be based".[2] It was recorded in the squadron ORB in the sparsest terms: on 1 December, at 0800hr, "Launch Emplacement 40 was taken out of Standby Status and dismantling commenced prior to shipment back to the United States". At 1030hr, "the warhead was removed from the unit on this day". Then on 2 December, at 1013hr, "Launch Emplacement 40. Missile No 43 was removed to Royal Air Force Driffield at this time". The next day, "the dismantling of Launch Emplacement 40 continues in absolutely foul weather". Then, on 5 December, at 1140hr, "all power was removed from the emplacement at this time". The end of this "operational exercise" was recorded on 20 December, when at 1300hr "Launch Emplacement 40 ceased to exist . . . all equipment having been removed from the emplacement except the liquid oxygen tank, the dismantling having taken 13 working days".

At the beginning of 1963, on 3 and 4 January respectively, missiles Nos 44 and 45 were removed from launch emplacements 41 and 42 at Breighton to Driffield; and in the 37-page Thor Force Run-down Programme issued by Bomber Command these Breighton missiles, together with three from Catfoss and one from Carnaby, made up the seven being returned early to the United States. No 240 Sqn therefore, with its three missiles removed and its official disbandment recorded on 8 January 1963 – "while the final run-down continues", became the first squadron in the RAF Strategic Missile Force to lay down its arms. The other 19 did so from February 1963 onwards, No 226 Sqn at Catfoss (also in the Driffield complex, like No 240 at Breighton) being the second, its three pads – Nos 34, 35 and 36 – being dismantled during that month, the missiles prepared for shipment then despatched to the US by air from Leconfield.

The last RAF Thor complex to close down was North Luffenham, whose ORB recorded that "Nos 144, 130, 218, 223 and 254 Sqns became non-operational on 15 August, and were disbanded on

---

[1] *Ie*, 60 less seven whose early return had been requested by the USAF.
[2] HQ BC (BC/S.97198/CMEO) to RAF Driffield.

23 August 1963". At that latter date, Bomber Command's strategic missile (IRBM) era officially ended. The Command's ORB recorded that the last Thor missile was returned to the US on 27 September 1963.

Both the Air Minister (Mr Hugh Fraser) and the CAS (MRAF Sir Thomas Pike) paid tribute to Bomber Command for its handling of Thor. In letters[1] to the AOC in C (Air Mshl Sir Kenneth Cross) the former commented that

"Thor was the first strategic ballistic missile system deployed in the free world. You may well be proud that you pioneered the introduction of these weapons into military service. The high state of readiness at which the Thor force has been maintained, the record of serviceability sustained and the success achieved with Combat Training Launches reflects the greatest credit on all concerned".

CAS said that

"When Thor came into service we knew that we would be faced with many new and complex technical and administrative problems and we fully expected that one of the greatest of these problems would be the task of maintaining the morale of the officers and men allocated to the missile sites. In the event, the problems were met and solved with a degree of enthusiasm, skill and resourcefulness which was in the finest traditions of Bomber Command and the Royal Air Force. The high morale which was a feature of the Force from its inception has never flagged, and Thor's fine record of serviceability and state of readiness over the years is a remarkable tribute to the loyalty and sense of duty of all the personnel who played a part. They will be able to look back with pride on a most valuable contribution to our deterrent force. . . ."

---

[1] Organisation and Establishment of Thor units (1D3/090/7 Pt 2). The letters were dated 2 Aug 62 and 12 Aug 63 respectively.

Flight Refuelling and
Strategic Reconnaissance

All photographs are Crown Copyright

Early days: single-point Valiant-to-Valiant refuelling by two B(K).1s of No 214 Sqn, which pioneered the technique for RAF jet fighters and bombers

An underside view of the same pair of Valiants, showing the bomb-bay tank, which held 4,500lb of fuel

At the receiving end: pilot's-eye view of the probe-and-drogue refuelling system, from the cockpit of a Phantom

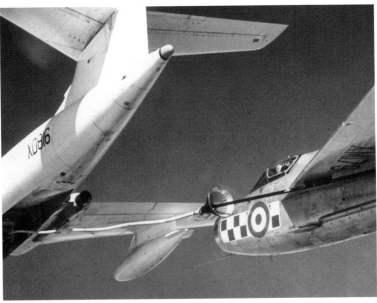

Lightning F.1A of No 56 Sqn refuelling from Valiant B(K).1 of No 214 Sqn, whose tankers - with those of No 90 Sqn - supported oversea deployments by RAF fighters in the 1962-64 period

Another angle on Valiant-Lightning refuelling, showing the bomb-bay tank and the hose reel system

Initial Victor conversion to the FR/AAR role was as two-point tankers, one of which - a K.1A of No 57 Sqn - is seen here replenishing two Buccaneer S.2Bs

The ultimate Victor tanker conversion - a three-point K.2, XL233, of No 55 Sqn

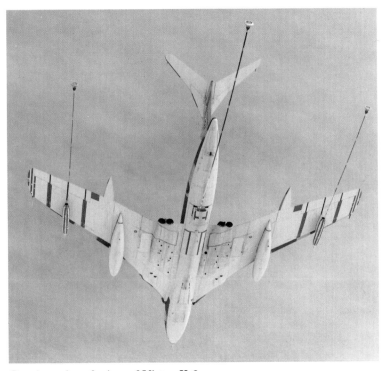

Receiver aircraft view of Victor K.2

The strategic reconnaissance role: two views of a Valiant B(PR)K.1 of No 543 Sqn, showing the underside of the aircraft with photographic installation and bomb-bay into which the camera crate capable of holding eight F96s and four F49 survey cameras was loaded

Victor B (SR).2 of No 543 Sqn, strategic reconnaissance successor to the Valiant B(PR)K.1

V-force Aircrew/Groundcrew Activities

Valiant of No 138 Sqn being serviced at RAF Wittering

Night marshalling of a Vulcan B.1 by torchlights

Inspecting the stowage of a Victor's braking parachute

"Scramble" aboard a Valiant . . .

. . . Victor . . .

. . . and Vulcan. The aircraft entrances were also designed as emergency exits

Valiant of No 138 Sqn and Vulcan of No 617 Sqn, from Wittering and
Waddington respectively, at Pinecastle AFB, Florida, for the 1957 USAF
Strategic Air Command bombing competition

Servicing a Vulcan B.2 of the Strike Wing at RAF Akrotiri, Cyprus, in 1969

Victor B(K).1A XH588 of No 55/57 Sqns over Malaya in 1965

Vulcan B.1s from Waddington at RAAF Butterworth, Malaysia

Victor B.1A of No 55 Sqn, on Far East detachment, being loaded with 1,000lb bombs

Vulcan B.2 of the Akrotiri Strike Wing merging with the landscape at low level over Cyprus

Prototype British Aircraft Corporation TSR.2, the tactical strike/reconnaissance aircraft which was to have succeeded the TBF Valiants and Canberra B(I).8s, but the project was cancelled in April 1965

A "squadron" photograph that never was: the second TSR.2 prototype to be completed, XR220, at A&AEE Boscombe Down with RAF personnel for trials which never took place

CHAPTER XXII

VALIANT ASSIGNMENT TO SACEUR: THE TBF

At the beginning of 1960 one of the Valiant squadrons, No 207, was assigned to Saceur (Supreme Allied Commander Europe). As the squadron Operations Record Book put it: "With effect from 1 January 1960, No 207 Squadron is operationally at the disposal of Saceur, but for training and administration will continue to come under the control of Bomber Command". This "dual control" arrangement was succinctly described in a minute of 4 April 1962 from ACAS (Ops) to VCAS, which said that "operational control of the assigned Valiant force is exercised by Saceur. C in C Bomber Command is responsible direct to him for operational readiness and efficiency of the force. Bomber Command Operational Centre is linked by direct telephone lines with SHAPE Operational Centre. Saceur's orders are passed direct to BCOC by this line and from there to Marham on the Bomber Command network".

No 207 was the first of three Valiant squadrons to be assigned to Saceur in the tactical bomber role; in 1961 two more were so assigned – Nos 49 and 148, on 1 and 13 July respectively. No 49 moved to Marham from Wittering in June 1961 to become part of the Saceur-assigned bomber force, and No 148 (like No 207, already at Marham – so the whole 24-bomber force was concentrated there) noted in its ORB: "The squadron was assigned to Saceur from 13 July and is now committed to keep one aircraft and one crew at 15 minutes' readiness in the QRA dispersal".

This decision to assign three Valiant squadrons to Saceur, approved by the Air Council on 15 May 1958[1] and subsequently agreed to by Saceur, was based on several different factors, formed part of a larger discussion on the uses to which surplus Mk 1 V-bombers could be put and was implemented only after careful consultation with Saceur.

The origins of the Valiant Tactical Bomber Force dated from towards the end of 1957, when at their 20 December meeting the Air Council[2] considered a paper by VCAS (Air Mshl E C Hudleston) on the Deployment of Valiants in 1961 and the Provision of Flight Refuelling Capability after 1961[3]. In this he suggested that three squadrons of Valiants should be formed in 1961 to replace the Saceur-assigned Bomber Command Canberras[4] - as part of a long-term plan "to make the best use of the Valiants that will become surplus to the front line in 1961"[5]. VCAS went on to comment that Saceur

---

[1] Conclusions, 11(58), Top Secret Annex 'B'.
[2] Conclusions, 28(57), Top Secret Annex 'A'.
[3] Paper No AC(57)92, 6 Dec 57.
[4] "All the light bombers are committed to the support of Saceur and... constitute the main part of his striking force" (British Bomber Policy – note by CAS (Slessor), 1 Mar 52).
[5] A front line of 144 V-bombers.

"Has repeatedly stated his requirement for a blind-bombing capability and also his dislike of ground-based aids to achieve this capability. The Canberra force assigned to him is being modified for LABS[1] but to meet the requirement for a blind-bombing capability additional provision must be made. Refurbishment of the existing Gee-H and the provision of Decca or ASV-21 have been suggested . . . . None of these is really satisfactory and the best solution would undoubtedly be to re-arm the Bomber Command Canberra squadrons with surplus V-bombers. Since the medium bombers are more expensive to run than Canberras, it is likely that this would not be acceptable financially other than, say, on a 1 for 3 basis[2]. As Saceur has an adequate fair-weather strike capability and is pressing now to improve his blind-bombing, all-weather capability, it is considered that a re-equipment programme on this basis might be acceptable to him".

At the outset of the 20 December discussion VCAS advised the Council that the Valiant force "would become surplus to the provisional Plan 'L'[3] front line of 144 medium bombers in the first quarter of 1961" and it was necessary to consider the use to be made of Valiants after that date. His paper contained two separate proposals:–

(i)   for the replacement of some of [the] Canberra squadrons with a smaller Valiant force in order to overcome certain long-term operational deficiencies of the Canberra;

(ii) for the long-term use of Valiants for the flight-refuelling tanker force which would continue to be required after 1961.

He proposed a replacement on the basis of 24 Valiants for 64 Canberras, and considered that two Valiant squadrons should be retained for flight refuelling.

The first of the Council's decisions at the 20 December meeting, relating to the Saceur-assigned bombers, was that "subject to a detailed examination of comparative running costs which VCAS would initiate, Saceur should be asked to agree that Bomber Command Canberras assigned to him should be replaced in due course by a smaller number of Valiants". Its second decision was that "the number of Valiants to replace the Canberras should be considered in the light of the detailed assessment of running costs".

Although the use of Valiants in the tanker force was considered by the Council on 9 January 1958, the assignment of Valiants to Saceur was not considered again until 15 May 1958[4], when a Note by VCAS and PUS (Sir Maurice Dean) – "Valiant Tanker and Tactical Bomber Force" – came under discussion. This invited the Council "to agree that 24 Valiants should be substituted for 64 Canberras assigned to Saceur,

---

[1] Low altitude bombing system.
[2] At the 20 Dec meeting VCAS suggested 24 Valiants for 64 Canberras.
[3] Drawn up in 1958, this forecast 144 Vulcans and Victors by 1962-63.
[4] Conclusions 11(58), Top Secret Annex 'B'.

subject to the latter's agreement"[1]. It was at this meeting that the main decision about assigning Valiants to Saceur was taken, when the Council "took note of the logistic and financial implications of maintaining two Valiant tanker squadrons and of assigning Valiant squadrons instead of Canberra squadrons to Saceur" and "agreed that 24 Valiants should be substituted for 64 Canberras subject to Saceur's agreement". VCAS was invited "to make enquiries of Air Mshl Constantine[2] as to Saceur's likely reaction to" the latter proposal; and DCAS (Air Mshl Sir Geoffrey Tuttle) was invited to check whether or not the Valiant could carry two Red Beards[3].

Saceur's reaction – a somewhat grudging acceptance of the idea – was conveyed to the Air Council at its meeting on 3 July when VCAS reported[4] that Air Mshl Constantine "had consulted Saceur informally about the proposal to replace 64 Canberras by 24 Valiants". Saceur had "recognised the value and all-weather capability of Valiants but regretted the numerical reduction in the force assigned to him and anticipated difficulty in convincing other Nato countries that this would not amount to a reduction in the British contribution. . . ."

One consequence of the assignment of Valiants was that Canberra B.6s could be transferred to the Middle East to replace B.2s, and VCAS said that he felt it would be better to clear this with the Defence Committee before approaching the Americans, as had been suggested by the Council at their meeting on 15 May.[5] He was "revising the draft paper for the Defence Committee".

This paper, by the Secretary of State for Air (Mr George Ward), on Employment of Surplus Valiant Aircraft,[6] was again referred to at the 22 July 1958 meeting of the Air Council, when VCAS said that "the draft paper for the Defence Committee was now being examined at staff level and should be ready for submission to the Secretary of State in the near future".[7] The recommendation at the end of this paper set out clearly the Valiant/Canberra situation at that time, S of S inviting his colleagues on the committee "to agree that the surplus Valiants available as a result of the Defence Committee decision of 2 August 1957" – that is, that the front-line strength of the strategic bomber force should be 144 aircraft, 104 of them Mk 2 Vulcans and Victors, resulting in a surplus of Mk 1s (*ie*, Valiants) – "should be used as described above, subject to the acceptance by Saceur of the substitution of Valiants for Canberras". "As described above" referred to the proposed uses for surplus Valiants – "to provide 16 aircraft for flight refuelling, and to provide Saceur with

---

[1] AC 58(28).
[2] Deputy Chief of Staff, Plans and Policy, at SHAPE.
[3] 2,000lb tactical atomic bombs. Saceur's agreement (it subsequently transpired) was given on the assumption that the Valiants would each be capable of carrying two nuclear weapons.
[4] Conclusions 15(58), Item II(e).
[5] Ibid.
[6] Appendix to AC (58) 28.
[7] Conclusions 16(58), Item I(b).

an assigned force of 24 Valiants in replacement of 64 Canberras in Bomber Command at present assigned to him. . . ."

Referring to the replacement of Canberras, the paper said:–

"Because of the probable limitations of their fatigue life, it is doubtful whether present holdings of Canberras of various marks would be enough to support the front line as at present planned (64 in the UK, 48 in Germany, 32 in MEAF and eight in FEAF) until a Canberra replacement became available. Low-level flying with nuclear bombs for which some of these aircraft are, or are being, adapted produces airframe fatigue very much more quickly than flying at the Canberra's designed height. . . .

"In addition the Canberras assigned to Saceur suffer from the disadvantage that they have no self-contained blind bombing aid. Saceur has an adequate fair-weather strike capability, but is anxious about the capacity of his Command to retaliate at night, and in bad weather. The ground-based navigation aids on which the Canberras at present rely are not an effective substitute for a proper blind bombing system.

"Replacement of the Bomber Command Canberras assigned to Saceur by Valiants would help to solve both these problems. The Valiants are independent of ground-based navigation aids. . . ."

There is no record, in the Defence Committee Minutes and Memoranda for the latter half of 1958 and the first part of 1959, of this paper being put to it; and it was not until 9 July 1959 that the Air Council[1] implemented its decision of 15 May 1958 to assign Valiants to Saceur, by saying when this should come into effect. At this mid-1959 meeting the Council considered a paper by VCAS on the Assignment of the first Valiant squadron to Saceur,[2] in which he proposed that "the first of the three Valiant squadrons should be assigned to Saceur at the end of this year in place of one of the B.6 squadrons". He asked for the Council's agreement – "subject to Saceur's acceptance and formal American approval of our proposed deployment of B.6s to MEAF" – and this was given. On the basis of this decision, No 207 Squadron at Marham was assigned to Saceur from 1 January 1960 onwards.

At that date, however, no decision had been taken about Saceur-assigned Valiants having dual weapon-carrying capability; this matter came up at an Air Council meeting on 4 April 1960[3] when a paper by VCAS was discussed.[4]

In this paper – the purpose of which was "to consider the need and the practicability of giving a dual carriage capability to the Valiant squadrons assigned to Saceur" – VCAS recalled that the assignment of three squadrons of Valiants (24 UE) to Saceur in place of the assigned

[1] Conclusions 16(59) Secret Annex 'A'.
[2] AC(59)57.
[3] Conclusions 5(60) Top Secret Annex 'A'.
[4] Dual Carriage for Saceur Valiants: Note by VCAS AC(60)15.

366

Canberra force (64 UE) had been agreed to by the Council at their meeting on 15 May 1958 and had subsequently been approved "in general terms" by Saceur. But it had become clear "towards the end of last year" (*ie*, 1959), VCAS added, that Saceur's approval was "not unqualified". It appeared to have been given "on the assumption that the Valiants would have a multiple-carriage capability and that one Valiant would replace two nuclear-capable Canberras". This requirement had been re-affirmed in a letter from the Assistant Chief of Staff (Air and Special Operations Division) (Major-General R T Coiner, Jr, USAF) at SHAPE on 6 November 1959 to AVM J Grandy, ACAS (Ops), in which the writer had said that it was understood that the Valiants would be substituted "with a ratio of one Valiant for two atomic-capable Canberras, but . . . with the multiple delivery potential of the Valiant the loss in numbers of aircraft in this particular instance is acceptable".

VCAS's paper went on to say that the practicability of giving the Valiant a dual carriage capability depended almost entirely on the nuclear weapon chosen. There were three possible bombs: the Mk 5 (6,000lb) with which the Valiants were at present armed under Project 'E'; the Mk 7 (1,650lb) currently carried by the Canberras; and the Mk 28 lightweight weapon, not presently supplied under Project 'E'.

The Mk 28 was "the most suitable weapon to provide the Valiant with a dual carriage capability". A modification programme, including clearance trials, to enable the three squadrons to carry it could be completed in about 12 months from the decision to go ahead. The cost would be between £150,000 and £250,000. VCAS invited the Council to agree that CAS "should inform Saceur that we intend to provide a dual carriage capability for the assigned Valiant force", but for this, weapons supplied under Project 'E' were required to be replaced by Mk 28 weapons on the same terms.

Having discussed this paper, the Air Council agreed on 4 April that the Valiants assigned to Saceur should be adapted to carry two nuclear weapons each — "provided that Mk 28 bombs could be obtained under Project 'E' on the same terms as the present weapons, and that satisfactory financial arrangements for the adaptation of the aircraft could be made". Saceur was not, however, to be informed of this decision until it had been established how the cost of the modifications could be met.

On 17 May DCAS (Air Mshl S C Elworthy) informed CA(Sir George Gardner) that the Valiant force to be assigned to Saceur would be "provided with the capability of dual carriage of the United States Mk 28 bomb, to be supplied under Project 'E' terms", adding: "We have been told by SHAPE that the weapon can be made available, and I am writing to ask you to accept the task of providing the carriage capability". Preliminary feasibility studies had been initiated in October 1959 and CA staff had indicated that it would be technically possible to achieve an IOC by April 1961, building-up to a total of 24 aircraft by June. He asked for confirmation that the project could be accepted.

Although this confirmation is not recorded, the implication is that it was, for on 29 December 1960 ACAS (Ops) (AVM T O Prickett) wrote to Saceur and to the Commander, 3rd Air Force, to say that it had been "agreed that the second and third Valiant squadrons will be transferred to Saceur *wef* 13 July 1961 and that the capability for the dual carriage of Mk 28 weapons will also take effect from that date".[1]

Some of the operational changes affecting the first Saceur-assigned Valiant squadron, No 207, were evident in its activities during 1960. In July, its ORB recorded,

"the squadron took part in another alert and readiness exercise, code-named Mayflight 3. During previous exercises of this nature, part of the squadron has been deployed to a diversion airfield in accordance with the Bomber Command Alert and Readiness Plan. Now that operational control of the squadron has been transferred to Saceur, this deployment is no longer required, and for Mayflight 3 all No 207 Squadron aircraft operated from Marham".

Scramble take-offs were still the order of the day, however, and on 21 July "a visit by Imperial Defence College students . . . gave the squadron a chance to demonstrate their improved 'scrambling' ability, made possible by the introduction of the simultaneous starting eqipment. To open the flying display, four suitably modified aircraft were parked immediately alongside the active runway, with the crews seated and strapped in at 'cockpit' readiness. The signal to 'scramble' was given by the visiting Commandant, and the last aircraft was airborne within 1min 50sec of the Very being fired. . .".

In September of that year No 207 was involved in Nato exercises:–

"Exercise Flashback and Exercise Swordthrust II represented two phases in the Nato Fall exercise. Exercise Flashback commenced at 1200hr on 20 September, when the six crews participating were brought to 45-minute readiness. 'Scramble' was given by Saceur, through HQ Bomber Command, at 0715hr on 21 September. . . . Flashback involved the simulated attack on targets in southern Europe and . . . Swordthrust II the search for, and simulated attacks on, the aircraft carriers of No 2 Carrier Strike Group in the Lofoten Islands sea area, and simulated attacks on selected Norwegian and UK targets".

Later in 1960, on 10 October, the squadron was incorporated in Saceur's QRA system, which necessitated (the ORB recorded) "the maintaining of one aircraft and crew at 15-minute readiness at all times, in addition to the normal generation standby system. Each tour of duty as Quick Reaction Alert crew is for 24 hours, starting at 0900hr.

---

[1] AF/CMS 279/64 – Project E – Mk 28 – Saceur-assigned Valiants. The Mk 28 was "a lightweight weapon which embodies the latest design features for efficient and safe operation. It . . . can be supplied in a retarded version". (VCAS Note on Dual Carriage for Saceur Valiants, 16 Mch 60).

The crew is housed during the day in a suitably equipped rest room in the Operations block and at night in a five-berth caravan; meals are provided in the aircrew buffet".

On the 13th of that month Saceur himself visited Marham "to review those Bomber Command squadrons assigned to Nato" – all of them, at that date, Canberra squadrons apart from No 207. "After inspecting the aircraft and crews of Nos 207, 9, 12, 35 and 58 Squadrons and four aircraft and crews representing the Medium Bomber Force" – Nos 9 and 12 having come from Coningsby, No 35 from Upwood and No 58 (a PR squadron) from Wyton – "General Norstad watched a demonstration and simultaneous start and scramble take-off by four Valiants of No 207 Squadron . . . all aircraft being airborne within 1min 25sec". Later, in a letter of thanks to the AOC in C Bomber Command (Air Mshl Sir Kenneth Cross), General Norstad said that the scramble was "tremendously impressive and without doubt the best I have witnessed".

The implications of operating V-bombers armed with US nuclear weapons were clearly shown in an Operational Plan sent by Bomber Command HQ to Air Ministry on 16 January 1961, relating to the 1,900lb (Mk 28) bomb.[1] This said that the Saceur QRA aircraft would be "held in readiness in an alert parking area which, with the exception of a removeable barrier across the access taxiway, will be entirely enclosed by a 6ft chain-link fence. Permanent security lighting to the same standard as at present in use at supplementary storage areas will be provided to illuminate the area during the hours of darkness. This parking area will be able to accommodate up to four aircraft. . . .

"Aircrew and groundcrew at readiness will be accommodated in buildings within 250yd of the alert parking area. . . ."

Subsequently (on 3 March 1961) Bomber Command issued security regulations, which said that the US Custodial Detachment – presumably at Marham, but the station was not specified – would

"retain custody of special weapons being transported to the alert site from the storage area, retain custody of all special weapons on QRA and those additional weapons brought to a QRA status and provide a minimum of one US custodial with each weapon on alert status. When two weapons are loaded on an aircraft, an additional US custodial will not be required".

Wg Cdr R D Alexander, who was on No 148 Squadron at Marham until he was posted to No 3 Group HQ in February 1962,[2] has recalled in an interview with the writer that he and his Nav/Radar, Flt Lt K Alport, went on a course at RAE Farnborough on the Mk 28 weapon, which had a warhead variable in destructive power from 60 to 100KT. Only the QRA aircraft, however, were armed with live bombs: two Valiants were in the QRA area, a wired compound, and the crews did a 48hr standby duty.

---

[1] In file Project E – Mk 28 – Saceur-assigned Valiants (AF/CMS 279/64).
[2] He had an Exceptional rating and his crew were Select Star.

Each crew had two targets per aircraft in their Saceur role, and one or two in their National role. The Mk 28 weapons were later replaced (in early 1964) by Mk 43s. None of the crews knew each other's targets, and when they went off on an exercise sortie (Edom – which tested the crews' reaction times, Mick or Checkmate) carried 'Go' bags which contained their flight plans – updated according to the latest Intelligence information. Another exercise was Titton, in which No 148 Sqn was involved in September 1961: its object, explained the No 49 Sqn ORB for that month, was "to give crews a more realistic experience of what a possible operational sortie would contain". The "Bomber Command Alert and Readiness Plan is followed, the aircraft is flown in combat conditions with simulated electrical failures". In its June 1962 ORB No 49 Sqn further described it as "a maximum-range training profile with a scramble start made as operationally realistic as possible".

Dual carriage by Marham Valiants was of the high-level Mk 28 bombs, to be dropped from about 45,000ft; the change-over to low-level, lay-down Mk 43 weapons occurred during 1963. On 15 March of that year D of Ops (B & R) (Air Cdre A W Heward) minuted ACAS (Ops) (AVM D G Smallwood) to say that "the Valiant Saceur-assigned force is shortly to become operational with an American lay-down weapon, the Mk 43, which is RAF-designated the HE 2,100lb HC bomb, in place of the high-level weapon, the American Mk 28 or HE 1900lb HC bomb", adding: "The planned date for the operational change-over to the new weapon is 1 April and for a Tactical Evaluation by SHAPE is 25 March. The necessary agreements were signed yesterday by VCAS and the Commanding General Third Air Force, which will enable the Americans to release operational weapons to us for loading on to the Valiants to meet the requirement of the Tactical Evaluation and the QRA commitment. . .".

A fortnight later, on 29 March, ACAS (Ops) wrote to all AOCs in C to inform them that arrangements had been concluded with the Americans "for the operational use of the HE 2,100lb bomb with the Saceur-assigned Valiant force". Referring to the loading of operational weapons of this type on to Valiants, under conditions laid down in an Air Ministry letter of 6 December 1962, he quoted an amended instruction as now reading: "Two bombs aircraft HE 1,900lb HC or two bombs aircraft HE 2,100lb HC". Thus it was clear that the Valiants were to carry two of the Mk 43 weapon, as of the Mk 28[1]. In its ORB for April 1963 No 207 Sqn recorded that "on the very first day of the month the squadron, with the other Saceur squadrons at Marham, received the Mk 43 weapon from the USAF and so operationally has a true low-level capability, being able to attack targets at low level. For National targets, however, we are still committed to the 'pop-up' attack".

---

[1] This correspondence is chiefly about the loading and flight carriage of nuclear weapons; it occurs in AF/CMS 22/64 Pt IV Nuclear Weapons Operational Policy. The Mk 43 weapon was "bedevilled...by problems of US custodianship" wrote D of Ops (B & R) to ACAS (OR) on 9 Aug 63.

When the three Valiant TBF squadrons (Nos 49, 148 and 207) had been established at Marham in 1961 there were still three Valiant squadrons in the Main Force, and at the beginning of 1962 the AOC in C Bomber Command (Air Mshl Sir Kenneth Cross) asked the Air Ministry to approve the modification of these aircraft for low-level operations. In a letter to VCAS (Air Chf Mshl Sir Edmund Hudleston) on 26 January[1] he said that the build-up of Soviet defensive systems had grealy reduced the Valiants' chances of survival at high level. Having no ECM and being too slow to be routed in company with ECM-equipped Vulcans and Victors, they were vulnerable not only to missile defences and the latest Soviet fighters but also to the older Fresco aircraft[2] which still formed the bulk of the Soviet fighter force. There was now no area within range of Bomber Command aircraft not defended by numbers of supersonic fighters and no worthwhile target not defended by SAMs.

The only practicable alternative for the operation of the Valiant force, therefore, was to avoid a high proportion of these defences by "sending the Valiants at low level". This could be done with "relatively minor modifications" to the aircraft, on the lines described in an attached paper. A new co-ordinated plan was due to come into effect on 1 July, and it would be unrealistic to expect the Valiants to continue in the high-level role until July 1963. Work on the new plan had already started and it was important that agreement to operating the Valiants at low level should be given as quickly as possible, and that the necessary authority for converting them "should follow at an early date".

Low-level operations by the Valiants, the AOC in C was told by VCAS on 13 February, depended on Saceur making retarded weapons available. But he added that "unfortunately there appears to be no practicable means of providing similar weapons, either British or American, for use during the life of the one remaining MBF Valiant squadron following the disbandment of No 138 Squadron". On present plans, he said, No 7 Squadron was to be taken out of the front line before the end of 1963. In view of this, he did not believe that the advantages to be gained by converting it to the low-level role were sufficient to justify doing so. As to the long-term (*ie* TBF) Valiant squadrons, subject to suitable assurances that retarded weapons would be made available for the assigned force, VCAS agreed in principle to the AOC in C's proposals and staffs were being instructed to progress his requirements in consultation with Bomber Command HQ.

In the event, the Valiant contribution to the MBF came to an end during 1962. At the very beginning of that year No 90 Squadron at Honington was switched to the flight-refuelling role, which it performed until its disbandment there on 2 February 1965 when the Valiants were phased out of service. Nos 138 and 7 Squadrons at

[1] Correspondence in Bombers – Valiant Modifications (ID9/B.3-30).
[2] *Ie*, MiG-17.

371

Wittering disbanded there respectively on 1 April and 1 October: in a signal to the latter on their disbandment day the AOC No 3 Group (AVM B K Burnett) referred to No 7 as "the last of the Main Force Valiant squadrons".

The phasing-out of Valiants from Bomber Command service during 1965 is described in detail in Chapter XXVII of this history.

CHAPTER XXIII

BLUE STREAK AND BLUE STEEL MK 2

In the mid-1950s, when the V-force was coming into being, the Air Staff issued requirements for new weapons which would improve Bomber Command's capability for strategic nuclear retaliation: OR1139 (8 August 1955) for a ballistic missile (Blue Streak) with a megaton warhead (OR1142) and a range of 1,500-2,000nm; OR1149 for a flying bomb with a 1,000nm range (7 May 1956); and OR1159 (28 May 1958) for an extended-range (600nm) version of Blue Steel. The purpose of these projected weapons was to extend the viability of the British deterrent force into the late 1960s, following the Mk 2 V-bombers armed with Blue Steel. As a Defence Research Policy Staff paper put it in June 1957, reviewing current defence research and development[1]:–

"As Soviet defences improve, the range of the powered bomb must be increased. This may be achieved by developing Blue Steel or embarking on a new project – OR1149. OR1149 may have a range of about 1,000 miles. . . .

"The ballistic missile, . . . of all the projects of which we have knowledge, has the longest life as a deterrent".

On 22 July the Air Minister (Mr George Ward) had written to the Minister of Defence (Mr Duncan Sandys): "I consider the early development of an operational British ballistic missile and its deployment – in underground sites – as the single most important military project in this country"[2].

A similar view about the importance of a ballistic missile deterrent had been expressed by VCAS (Air Chf Mshl Sir Ronald Ivelaw-Chapman) a year previously[3], when he said that "the development by the United Kingdom of a ballistic missile to replace the manned bomber as a deterrent must be given the highest priority". The idea of missiles entirely replacing bombers never became accepted doctrine, however, the 1957 Defence Statement[4] referring to the V-bombers being "supplemented by ballistic rockets" – that is, the Thors to be supplied by the United States; and Blue Streak was envisaged as "sharing the responsibility" for the deterrent with the V-force, under the concept of a "balanced deterrent". But because it operated from fixed sites, both types of delivery system were needed:–

"Inflexibility is an inherent characteristic of ballistic missiles, both in mode of operation and deployment. The converse is true of a manned bomber weapon system. Flexibility is a prime requirement in war

---

[1] "Review of Defence Research and Development", 4 Jun 57 (File No 125/07/05).
[2] ID6/R.36 (Pt 3) Defence Research and Development Estimates and Priorities.
[3] Note of 7 Jun 56 on the Future Size and Shape of the RAF.
[4] "Defence – Outline of Future Policy" (Cmnd 124).

operations. Therefore, it is logical to assume that for this and other cogent reasons the RAF must maintain a manned bomber weapons system. If, however, the capability of our offensive forces is to remain at a fairly constant level, as dictated by financial considerations, then clearly a balance must be struck between the parts to be played by the missile and manned bomber weapons systems within our offensive striking force...[1]".

In the event, apart from the Thor period (1958-63) the RAF never deployed a mixed (surface-to-surface missile/aircraft) strategic nuclear deterrent force, nor operated Blue Streak, which was abandoned as a military rocket on the promise of the US Skybolt to fulfil OR1149; and a Mk 2 version of Blue Steel was never developed.

The Air Staff Requirement for Blue Streak – "a medium-range ballistic missile system" – stressed its complementary, rather than replacement, character vis-à-vis the bombers. "Although the ballistic missile may eventually replace the manned aircraft as the major component of the strategic deterrent, it is likely that the greater flexibility of the latter will continue to be required for many years. The primary requirement is . . . for a missile system complementary to the bomber force, to serve both as a deterrent and as an effective means of delivery in war". However, since "future enemy defensive systems are likely to include ground-launch guided weapons of increasing range, speed and lethality . . . it may be impossible to reach the major target areas by either subsonic or supersonic bomber aircraft without prohibitive losses. If we are to maintain a medium-range strategic bombardment threat, the ballistic missile offers the best chance of delivery of nuclear warheads. . . ."

The missile envisaged was to be capable of being fired at targets up to 2,000nm distant, and of subsequent development to reach ranges of 2,500nm, though the Air Staff would accept a minimum range of 1,500nm; it was to be designed to carry a nuclear warhead, and intended for use from prepared sites in the UK and the Middle East initially, though ultimately in any part of the world. It was required to be in service "as soon as possible", and the ASR was forwarded to the Ministry of Supply on 8 August 1955. Later that year, and early in 1956, several Air Staff papers were written, and meetings held, on the operational employment of Blue Streak.

The issuing of this ASR had followed some two years' preparatory work, for "in August 1953 the Air Staff called for an evaluaton of all possible solutions to an Air Staff target for a strategic bombardment missile", and "the industrial organisation for the development of [the] project was settled in April 1955" – the de Havilland Propeller Co being "nominated as the firm responsible for the co-ordination of the weapon system and design". The de Havilland Aircraft Co were to be

---

[1] A Preliminary Study of a Balanced Deterrent in the period up to 1970 (file on Guided Weapons - AHB IIA/11/2/26).

responsible for the airframe, Rolls-Royce for propulsion, Sperry Gyroscope Co for inertial guidance and Marconi for ground radar and communications link, while a special re-entry test vehicle was required for experimental work: this was Black Knight – to be designed and flown by RAE and produced by Saunders-Roe. Other possible main contractors considered by the Ministry of Supply were Bristol Aeroplane Co and English Electric[1]. A Ballistic Missile Division was created at RAE to exercise technical supervision and assist the project.

Reporting to S of S for Air (Mr Nigel Birch) on progress early in 1956[2], ACAS(OR) (AVM H V Satterly) said that full-scale missile design was under way, and it was hoped to begin firing some full-scale missiles in 1959 or 1960.

The Air Ministry meetings held on Blue Streak during 1956 discussed such questions as launching sites in the UK and deployment overseas; the maximum range ultimately required; the type of site needed (with respect to vulnerability); the warning period and the time needed for launching; and the need for air transport for components of the missile.[3] On 20 April there was a meeting at RAE Farnborough when the Ballistic Missile Division gave a presentation on the present stage of development of Blue Streak, when assurances were offered that, provided no major problems arose, the in-service date of 1965 should be achieved "or even improved on".[4] However, the Air Staff had to find answers to several questions about the missile's operational employment – for example, how many would be required? Should the launching sites be under or above ground? What was the optimum number of missiles per site? Was there to be a requirement for rapid re-alignment to a new target? These and many other questions formed the subjects of Air Staff operational studies during 1956. At the end of that year, on 14 December, there was a high-level presentation on Blue Streak at the Air Ministry, under the chairmanship of CGWL (Controller, Guided Weapons and Electronics), Dr Robert Cockburn. So far, everything seemed to be going according to plan, although there were many problems still to be solved – particularly those peculiar to a fixed-site missile system. But the overwhelming problem, that of the cost of a large, complex and entirely new kind of weapon, was never to be solved and finally brought about the abrupt ending of the programme early in 1960. Financial considerations had, indeed, begun to affect it as early as 1957 – when two of the associated contracts were cancelled.

Reporting to the Air Council in July, DCAS (Air Mshl Sir Geoffrey Tuttle)[5] said that "recent economy measures" had "necessitated a

---

[1] DCAS Note, 26 Jan 56, to S of S.
[2] The Medium Range Ballistic Missile: Note on Development Programme and Progress (Development of British Medium Range Ballistic Missile (Blue Streak) (AHB ID3/946/9 Pt 1)).
[3] Record, 27 Jan 60 meeting at Whitehall Gardens, in Guided Weapons – Surface to Surface. Blue Streak/Thor (AHB IIA/11/2/26) file.
[4] Loose Minute, OR14/GW (NP)1, 2 May 60.
[5] Progress Report for quarter ended 30 June 57, prefaced by DCAS Note of 17 July.

readjustment of the Blue Streak R&D programme, resulting in cancellation of the contracts for the Marconi radar guidance system and the English Electric insurance inertial guidance system". The R&D time-scale had been extended, so that the first firing was scheduled for November 1960 and the first operational capability date was 1965.

When DCAS next reported on the missile to the Air Council, in a paper considered on 13 February 1958[1], he again emphasised the financial constraints on the programme but urged that it should be more strongly based.

He recalled that when his last Progress Report on New Weapons had been considered, he had been asked to present "a separate and detailed progress report on Blue Streak" – with special emphasis on the extent to which the programme had been retarded "by lack of funds and enthusiasm". Referring to its present status, he said that in August 1957 a revised development programme had been submitted to the Defence Research Policy Committee which limited the total cost of development to about £80 million, and added:

"It was stated that, providing there were no subsequent financial cuts, the revised programme would provide missiles of unestablished reliability to meet the Air Staff's relaxed accuracy requirements by the end of 1963, and a limited number of missiles to meet the full operational requirement by 1965. The DRPC accepted the revised programme but expressed concern that the total cost contained no allowance for contingencies.

"The issue by the Ministry of Supply in December 1957 of a detailed development programme confirmed our fears that the revised pro-gramme was unlikely to provide a limited operational deployment in 1963 nor, probably, a missle developed to the full Air Staff requirement by 1965".

DCAS went on to express the view that, at that time – early 1958, the Blue Streak programme was "planned at too low a rate"; it was an "austerity programme" and "under-financed" – the missile's develop-ment was proceeding at "a dangerously slow pace". Under the arrangement at present envisaged, 23 test firings were proposed for completion by the end of 1963 and only the last ten would have the thrust-controlled motors required for full-range operational missiles. He considered that the number of test firings should be stepped-up to least 35. He understood that the Ministry of Supply had recently reviewed the austerity programme and concluded that not only was it under-financed but that insufficient technical insurance was incor-porated. This review had culminated in a paper to the Ministry of Defence which had

"strongly represented these views and concluded that the total development bill might reach £160 million – double the present

[1] Blue Streak Progress (Note by DCAS, AC(58)8).

programme. The new programme recommends an increased rate of firing, further spending on the test beds at Spadeadam,[1] and certain technical insurances. MoD agreement and Treasury approval have not yet been given to this revised programme and, as a result, it has not yet been possible to take action in industry. The development of Blue Streak is therefore proceeding at what I believe to be a dangerously slow pace, and I regard it as of the utmost importance that the Air Council strongly endorse the new programme recently submitted to the Ministry of Defence by the Ministry of Supply".

DCAS invited the Council to note "the serious position" regarding the current Blue Streak programme, and that MoS had presented a revised and more satisfactory one to the MoD; and to agree that the MoD should be urged to endorse the MoS programme as soon as possible.

The Council "took note" of the Blue Streak position as DCAS had outlined it and agreed that the Secretary of State (Mr George Ward) should impress upon the Minister of Defence (Mr Duncan Sandys) the importance of "establishing a firm and realistic programme" for the weapon – bearing in mind the points S of S had made in discussion: that the Defence White Paper about to be published[2] "stated that a British ballistic rocket of . . . advanced type was being developed on the highest priority in . . . co-operation with the United States"; and that this,

"combined with the provision of £17m for this project included in the 1958/59 R&D estimates, should encourage industry to believe that we were sincere in our intention to press on with Blue Streak".

When the Council next considered Blue Streak, at its meeting on 6 March[3], DCAS produced some comparative costs which he had received from the Ministry of Supply: for developing the V-bombers and their propelled bombs, £160.5m, excluding any intra-mural expenditure; for Blue Streak, £160m, including intra-mural expenditure. Just over two months later, when he gave the Council his quarterly Progress Report on New Weapons[4], DCAS had discouraging news about the missile: a Ministry of Defence working party was looking into how its development and its introduction into service could be accelerated, but the prospects of quicker progress were "not great". VCAS (Air Mshl Sir Edmund Hudleston) pointed out that if the weaon were to be received in 1962, underground construction should begin in mid-1959.

But, in mid-1958, the Government decided that plans for accelerating Blue Streak should be held in abeyance, and set in motion an assessment of how much would be saved if it were not developed as an operational weapon: these were the consequences of meetings of the Defence Board

---

[1] The Ministry of Aviation/Supply missile testing establishment at Spadeadam, Gilsland, Cumberland.
[2] Cmnd 363, Feb 58.
[3] Conclusions 6(58).
[4] Conclusions 11(58), 15 May 58.

on 31 July[1] and of the Cabinet Defence Committee on the following day[2].

The Defence Board came to the conclusion that Britain must continue to maintain an independent element of nuclear deterrent power, a policy which involved providing a ballistic rocket to succeed the medium bomber "in due course". While this rocket had to be under British control, it need not be of British manufacture; and if it were possible to obtain Thor without political restrictions, together with design information about its warhead, this would provide an acceptable interim solution. In that event, dropping Blue Streak and switching resources to the development – with the Americans – of a Polaris-type solid-propellant rocket should be considered. In view of these possibilities, plans for accelerating Blue Streak should be held in abeyance; but nothing should be said to the contractors.

When the Minister of Defence (Mr Duncan Sandys) reported to the Cabinet Defence Committee on 1 August about the Defence Board's discussion he confirmed the views on possible closer collaboration with the United States on a ballistic missile, and that "it now seemed less necessary to accelerate the rate of development" of Blue Streak – views which the CDC endorsed, with the proviso that a detailed assessment should be made of the financial savings obtainable if the missile was not developed as an operational weapon.

The Minister went further when he told the CDC on 10 September[3] that the desirability of stopping the development of Blue Streak should be investigated following "successful discussions" held recently in the US and "the new prospect" of Anglo-American co-operation in the exchange of nuclear information. If a missile/warhead programme were inaugurated, with American help, it might result in a better weapon than Blue Streak; but it would take longer to complete, and in order to maintain the independent deterrent the effective life of the V-force should be extended by developing Blue Steel Mk 2. If there still seemed to be a gap in capability before the new rocket became available, a supply of Thor or other medium-range rockets might be acquired without "strings" and equipped with nuclear warheads, though a decision on such a purchase need not be taken for several years.

During the committee's discussions the points were made that, from the strategic standpoint, the abandonment of Blue Streak could only be accepted on certain conditions: that an assurance was obtained from the US that, if a medium-range rocket of more advanced type were to be developed, their full co-operation – in terms of information – would be forthcoming; that the US would be willing to make supplies of Thor (or similar rockets) available "without strings"; and that the development of Blue Steel Mk 2 was continued in order to prolong the effective life of the V-force to about 1969.

---

[1] DB/C(58) 1st Conclusions.
[2] D.(58) 16th Mtg.
[3] Minutes, D.(58) 18th Meeting.

When the implications of such actions were discussed it was pointed out that, if Blue Streak were ultimately abandoned, it should be made clear that Britain intended to continue participation in the development of long-range rockets; and when a decision to stop Blue Streak development was made public it should be represented not as an abandonment of interest in that field but as a result of new co-operation with the United States. The committee invited the Minister of Defence to "examine in greater detail" the feasibility of adopting the revised policy outlined in his memorandum[1] and the Minister of Supply (Mr Aubrey Jones) to arrange for work on Blue Streak to be "unobtrusively retarded", pending a final decision on the project.

DCAS reported on the Blue Streak situation to the Air Council on 24 September.[2] He said that the Defence Board had instructed the Minister of Defence to examine whether it would be possible to obtain Thor "in a form which would provide an independent British deterrent", and to collaborate with the Americans in developing a second-generation ballistic missile. Pending an answer to these questions, the Board had decided not to proceed with the Minister's plan for accelerating the development of Blue Streak to provide an initial operational capability by the end of 1962. If satisfactory arrangements could be made with the Americans, it might be decided not to proceed with Blue Streak as an operational weapon at all.

The present position, DCAS said, was that the Air Ministry, Ministry of Supply and the contractors had agreed to an accelerated technical programme to give an IOC by 1963, but the Treasury had not sanctioned this. On top of it, the Minister of Defence had asked for the "even greater acceleration" referred to, which in turn would cost more.

As to the stage reached with the project, DCAS reported that development progress continued satisfactorily but slowly[3]. Tests of full-scale motors at the Rocket Propulsion Department, Westcott, had "exceeded expectations". The Director-General of Works was setting-up a team to work on the design of underground launching sites, in collaboration with the de Havilland Propeller Co. On this aspect of the project the most urgent task would be the construction of an operational prototype site in the UK.

At the Cabinet Defence Committee meeting on 10 September, when the Minister of Supply had been "invited to arrange . . . for work in progress" on Blue Streak "to be unobtrusively retarded", the Prime Minister said that during his forthcoming visit to Washington the Minister of Defence "should endeavour to obtain satisfactory assurances on the degree of United States assistance which his proposals assumed". This visit was

---

[1] Memorandum by the Minister of Defence on ballistic rockets (D.(58) 47).
[2] Conclusions 21(58), Top Secret Annex.
[3] When the Air Council Standing Cttee considered this Progress Report on New Weapons on 15 Sep (Conclusions 14 (58)) CGWL said he thought the words "but slowly" might be misunderstood: development was continuing according to schedule.

made on 22-25 September, and he reported on it to the Defence Board on 16 October,[1] the gist of his conclusion – supported by the Minister of Supply – being that there was no practical alternative to continuing with Blue Streak.

He reminded the Board that their previous discussion[2] had "inclined him to the belief" that the best course would be to persuade the Americans "to let us have Thor without political strings", to abandon Blue Streak and to develop in its place a solid-fuel intermediate-range rocket, possibly based on an American design. This had been his approach to the problem when he began his discussions in the United States: these were held at the Pentagon and the State Department and were extremely comprehensive and wide-ranging, co-operation in missile development being one of the subjects discussed.

The Americans, he said, had agreed to a purchase of Thor without political strings; but since they were not going to develop a successor to it in the IRBM range, and since there was small prospect of anything of value to the UK emerging from a European missile project, it was clear that if the UK were to have its own independent nuclear deterrent in the late 1960s it would have to make its own successor to the V-force and to Thor – if that were acquired. Blue Streak "should be ready by 1965"; the V-force with Blue Steel should remain effective until then and could be followed immediately by Blue Streak,without the need to buy Thors, which "would not have an effective life of more than three years after 1965". The alternative would be to decide to buy Thors, to abandon Blue Streak and start afresh with the development of a solid fuel rocket. But this would have disadvantages: it was doubtful whether a solid fuel rocket would be ready for deployment by 1968; if Thors were bought, they might cease to be effective before a solid-propellant missile was ready for deployment; and the large sums already invested in developing a liquid-fuelled motor would be wasted because the development of a solid-fuel motor would mean starting afresh. If Blue Streak were continued with, taking advantage of the smaller and lighter American warhead, anti-defensive devices and other improvements could be incorporated. Known solid fuels, the Minister added, "would have . . . less powerful thrust than contemporary liquid fuels and . . . be insufficiently powerful for launching space satellites". On balance, he had "regretfully come to the conclusion that there was no practical alternative to proceeding with Blue Streak".

The Minister of Supply (Mr Aubrey Jones) concurred; the First Lord of the Admiralty (the Earl of Selkirk) expressed doubt about "the wisdom of investing so large a sum in the development and deployment of so inflexible a weapon as Blue Streak" – a view with which the Secretary of State for War (Mr Christopher Soames) concurred; and the

[1] DB/C(58) 2nd Conclusions.
[2] 31 July.

Board agreed to resume the discussion at their next meeting.

This was held four days later[1], and at it the various options to succeed the V-force were discussed – a land-based ballistic rocket, a new manned aircraft and a sea-launched missile. For the first of these alternatives, the choice was from a developed version of Thor, Blue Streak, or some new rocket using a solid-propellant motor. Although a new manned aircraft would be more flexible, as it could be used for limited- and cold-war purposes, it would be less effective than a ballistic rocket for the primary role of deterring Soviet aggression. Sea-launched missiles would provide greater mobility and probably make an effective defence more difficult, thus increasing the credibility of the deterrent; but the solid-fuel missile of the Polaris type, capable of being submarine-launched, had a much smaller warhead than a land-based rocket: this would "entail a degree of accuracy . . . it might . . . be difficult to achieve from a ship"; also, the cost of nuclear-powered submarines would limit the number which could be provided.

As to the alternative forms of land-based rocket, the Americans did not intend to continue the development of intermediate-range ballistic rockets, but had concluded that it would be technically feasible to develop Thor so that a heavier payload (allowing some room for counter-countermeasures) could be carried and the effective range extended to just over 2,000 miles with a more powerful warhead: they might be prepared to undertake this development in response to a sufficient order, but its cost would probably be heavy, and the adoption of a developed Thor would only be attractive if its costs were much less than that of continuing with the development and production of Blue Streak. The solid-fuel rocket was not yet in sight, and the UK would not be able to develop one in future years if it abandoned all work on rocket development. In the recent Washington discussions the Americans had expressed doubts as to whether solid fuels were better than liquid ones; they were concentrating their efforts on storable liquid fuels. The capabilities of Blue Streak were well known: it would have the right combination of range (up to 3,000 miles), warhead and capacity to carry counter-countermeasures; it could be deployed by 1965. Its development should continue.

The First Lord of the Admiralty said he would regret an irrevocable decision being taken "at this stage" to rely entirely on Blue Streak for the maintenance of the deterrent after the mid-1960s: further consideration should be given to the question of using other means of delivering a nuclear retaliatory counter-attack, particularly with seaborne weapons, and to the possibilities of developing suitable solid-fuel rockets to give greater mobility. "Land-based fixed-site rockets", he averred,

---

[1] On 20 Oct 58 (DB/C(58) 3rd Conclusions). It was clear from these discussions that the Admiralty and the War Office were seriously concerned at the effects of the costs of the deterrent upon the conventional forces: see papers and minutes in The Effect of Nuclear Sufficiency (ID6/R.12A).

"were inflexible and could be used only as a deterrent against a Soviet attack on the UK". But he agreed that it would be imprudent to stop work on Blue Streak, though the position should be reviewed in 12 months' time.

In his summing-up the Minister of Defence said that the discussion had shown general agreement that a land-based rocket would be required to maintain an independent British deterrent in succession to the V-force – without excluding the possibility of either a new manned aircraft or a sea-launched rocket. He added that, unless the cost of providing developed versions of Thor was considerably less than that of continuing with Blue Streak, work on the latter should be continued with a view to its deployment in 1965.

In conclusion he asked the Minister of Supply to prepare an analysis of the cost of providing developed versions of Thor to meet UK requirements, either by purchasing complete weapons from the US or by undertaking the necessary further development and production in the UK; and also to prepare detailed proposals for further R & D on solid-fuel rockets.

When the Cabinet Defence Committee met on 5 November[1] to consider both defence expenditure and ballistic rockets, the Chancellor of the Exchequer (Mr Heathcoat Amory) suggested that the development of Blue Streak should be abandoned; he had expressed concern at the rise in defence expenditure, from £1,465m currently to an estimated £1,650m in 1960-61. But the Minister of Defence pointed out that abandoning Blue Streak meant abandoning the IRBM, since Thor "would only last for another eight or nine years" and the Americans did not intend to develop another intermediate-range rocket. The committee expressed concern that a concentration of effort on the deterrent and its defence might leave insufficient resources available for conventional forces; and in his summing-up the Prime Minister (Mr Harold Macmillan) stressed the agreement on this point, and said that the two main possibilities for significant economies were in relation to the deterrent and its defence.

In its discussion on ballistic rockets the committee had before it a memorandum by the Minister of Defence[2] in which, having recapitulated the options considered by the Defence Board at its meeting on 20 October, he reiterated the conclusion that, if the Government wished to maintain an independent British contribution to the nuclear deterrent after the mid-1960s the development of Blue Streak had to be proceeded with, with the aim of deploying the weapon in 1965. This conclusion had been reached after discussions in the US following his earlier proposal[3] to stop the development of Blue Streak.

---

[1] D.(58) 24th Mtg.
[2] D.(58) 57.
[3] In D.(58) 47.

The committee, however, had reservations: in conditions of nuclear sufficiency[1] it might become less important to have all three elements of the British deterrent as currently envisaged – bombers, Thor and Blue Streak. The Treasury estimated that expenditure on the development and deployment of Blue Streak would amount to between £400-£600m, that the final cost might be appreciably higher and that if underground sites were constructed their cost might be considerably greater than originally estimated; the cost involved in buying Thor and developing a later British rocket should be analysed; and Polaris, in whose development the UK were participating with the US Navy, "might at a later date be developed for installation in British ships or submarines".

When he summed-up this discussion the Prime Minister said that he felt further consideration was required before decisions were taken on future policy. An alternative to the proposals by the Minister of Defence would be to plan on the assumption that the bomber force and Thor would provide an adequate British contribution to the deterrent for about ten years, and that a decision on the development of other British projects could be deferred for the time being. He said it would be helpful if the committee could have an indication of the cost of these two alternatives; and the Minister of Defence, in consultation with the Chancellor of the Exchequer, was invited to circulate a memorandum on the lines suggested by the Prime Minister.

On the same date as this CDC meeting a draft Air Council paper by DCAS on Blue Streak was circulated[2]. This sought the Council's formal approval of the principle of underground siting for Blue Streak and outlined a deployment plan based on the assumption that the missiles would be housed in, and launched from, underground sites. It estimated that the first firing of a Blue Streak from an R&D underground launcher could probably take place in Australia between January and March 1962. It said that 1/6th scale firing tests were currently being done at Westcott, and full-scale tests from a representative firing tube were to be made at Spadeadam. A study was also under way of an alternative design of site in which the prepared missile was housed underground and raised to the surface immediately before firing. DCAS considered that it would be necessary to build in the UK an engineering prototype of the operational site: this would serve to prove some of the civil engineering problems and purely Service requirements; it should be completed by late 1961 and would be RAF-controlled, but for the first 12 months the Ministry of Supply, the contractors and the RAF would all be concerned in conducting engineering and launch procedure trials there. The operational sites would need to be at least six miles apart, and about 70 were required for the missile force to be

---

[1] As described by the Prime Minister in the discussion on defence expenditure – a situation in which the US and USSR could destroy each other.

[2] Draft AC Paper, Blue Streak, Note by DCAS, in file Guided Weapons – Blue Streak/Thor (AHB IIA/11/2/26 Pt 1).

effective. DCAS asked the Air Council for approval of the use of underground sites for Blue Streak; to authorise the construction of a prototype operational site in the UK; to endorse the proposal to conduct a preliminary design study on a "lift" type of underground site (*ie* where a missile was raised to the surface before firing); and to endorse the proposal to base future plans on the deployment of approximately 70 twin-shaft (*ie* two-missile) sites. At the outset of his paper, DCAS referred to the Council's "acceptance in principle" of 4 April 1957[1] that the case for underground sites was "very strong", a decision having been deferred until firm and detailed cost estimates were available.

However, while the Air Staff could make plans for the eventual deployment of Blue Streak, it was still one of the options being considered by the Government to succeed the V-bomber/Blue Steel/Thor era; and when the Cabinet Defence Committee again discussed ballistic rockets at its meeting on 18 November[2]. the question of the costs of future strategic nuclear weapon delivery systems loomed large. The committee had before it a memorandum by the Minister of Defence[3], in which he argued that the development of Blue Streak should go ahead, while at the same time the progress of Polaris should be watched. He said that the cost of this development was estimated to be about £200m (including about £50m already spent or committed), spread over the next eight years. The missiles would begin to come into service in 1965 and a deployment of 100 would be completed by 1970. The cost of production and deployment would be about £280m, so the whole programme would cost about £480m[4]. He said he had given further thought to the proposal to buy Thor "without strings", to stop the development of Blue Streak, to concentrate on research and then "decide what course to adopt"; but the more he looked at it the less he liked it: it had serious disadvantages, which he enumerated. He thought that a submarine-based deterrent offered certain "very important theoretical advantages" over a land-based system, but the feasibility of Polaris had been "by no means" fully proved, nor was it possible to forecast what its cost would be. In sum, the Minister believed that the choice could be narrowed-down to two alternatives – Blue Streak or Polaris. If the UK were starting from scratch, there might be a case for waiting until the Polaris prospects became clearer. But £50m had already been spent or committed on Blue Streak; and he concluded that, while the progress of Polaris should be watched, the development of Blue Streak should go ahead as planned.

---

[1] Conclusions 9(57).

[2] D.(58) 26th Mtg.

[3] D(58)63 – Ballistic Rockets.

[4] The memorandum noted that the development, production and deployment of the V-bomber force and its weapons (excluding the fissile component) would have cost £570m. Running costs of the V-force were about £50m p.a.; those of "the rocket project" would be about £10m p.a.

During the committee's discussion on the memorandum the point was made that the effective life of the V-bomber force and of Thor would be much the same, and that thereafter there would be a need to rely on Blue Streak or a new manned aircraft or a weapon of the Polaris type. While a submarine-based deterrent might offer certain important advantages, the feasibility of the Polaris system had not been fully proved and its cost could not be forecast; and from the military point of view it would be desirable to plan for a combined static and mobile deterrent: the best course might be to continue the development of Blue Streak, without commitment as to its operational deployment and without prejudice to the possibility of adopting Polaris when further information on it was available from the United States.

It was pointed out that current expenditure on Blue Streak was largely attributable to the provision of capital facilities, such as test gear and instrumentation, at Spadeadam and in Australia. These were urgently needed for test purposes and their construction could not be deferred without delaying the weapon's development. Further, abandoning Blue Streak would have adverse effects on industry in the UK and on Anglo-Australian relations in the context of the test facilities at Woomera.

In summing-up the Prime Minister said that despite the arguments in favour of proceeding with Blue Streak's development it was important to achieve, if possible, some economy in defence expenditure. If the bomber force were to constitute the main UK contribution to the deterrent for some years to come, it was for consideration whether decisions on the "scale and form" in which the subsequent stage of the deterrent should be developed might be deferred. It would be helpful to the committee to consider in greater detail the possibilities of making savings in respect of Blue Streak and Blue Steel during the next two financial years – not excluding the former's complete cancellation, to determine whether some reduction could be made in present plans during the interim period, before final decisions were taken on later developments. An analysis of the expenditure attributable to these projects in that period should be prepared; and if it proved impossible to reduce that expenditure significantly, it might be necessary to reconsider the possibility of achieving some economy in the V-force itself.

The committee invited the Minister of Defence to arrange for MoD, MoS and Treasury officials to prepare for it a detailed analysis of expenditure attributable to R&D in connection with Blue Streak and Blue Steels Mks 1 and 2 during the 1959-60 and 1960-61 financial years, together with an estimate of the net saving which would be achieved by the cancellation of Blue Streak, after allowing for cancellation charges. The Minister was also invited to examine, in the light of the result of this analysis, the possibility of making further economies in the main items constituting the nuclear deterrent, including the MB force.

When the CDC again discussed the costs of Blue Streak and Blue Steel Mk 2[1], in the context of reducing expenditure in the 1959-60 Defence Budget and on the basis of memoranda submitted by the Ministers concerned[2], the view was expressed that it might be unwise to decide to abandon Blue Streak until further consideration had been given to the form which the UK deterrent should take from the late 1960s onwards.

In pointing out that "drastic action" had been required to reduce defence expenditure to £1,530.45m – as against the £1,510m budget limit for 1959-60 postulated by the Chancellor – the Minister of Defence said that a further reduction could not be achieved without re-opening "major issues of policy" which the committee had reviewed during the previous months, commenting that it could not be accepted that the defence of the UK by the nuclear deterrent was less important than the discharge of overseas commitments by conventional forces; and a Ministry of Supply submission showed that if a proposed saving of £5m on Blue Streak in 1959-60 were to be increased to £10m, industrial development would be reduced by about 50%, design teams would have to be dispersed and a 12 months' postponement at this stage would mean that the weapon would not be operational until 1969 or 1970.

The committee faced a choice, in the Prime Minister's view, in coming to a decision on the defence estimates for 1959-60, between taking drastic policy decisions, particularly on the deterrent, and deferring such decisions for a further period, provided that defence expenditure was reduced to "a tolerable level" by other measures. In the event, the CDC "took note" that the Prime Minister "would arrange for further consideration to be given to the issues involved in deciding the level of defence expenditure". Thus the future of Blue Streak, as a major item in this expenditure, was uncertain at the end of 1958.

On 16 December S of S for Air (Mr George Ward) had proposed to the Minister of Defence (Mr Duncan Sandys) "a study of future weapon requirements for the deterrent, both airborne and submarine"; and this was reflected in a Minute of the 22nd from the Minister to the Chief of the Defence Staff (MRAF Sir William Dickson), which said that the Chiefs of Staff had "no doubt been considering the respective advantages and disadvantages ... of basing our nuclear deterrent underground or under the sea" and suggesting that "we ought to have a discussion of this matter at an early meeting of the Defence Board". CDS responded by putting a Minute to the CoS Committee[3], which it considered on 1 January 1959 in a discussion on missile systems, as to the best means of studying "the respective advantages and disadvantages

---

[1] D.(58) 31st Mtg, 22 Dec 58.

[2] *Eg*, by the Minister of Defence on Defence Expenditure 1959-60 (D.(58)86), on Blue Streak (D.(58)87) and on Fighter Command (D.(58)88); and by the Chancellor of the Exchequer and the S of S for Foreign Affairs on the size of the armed forces (D.(58)79 and D.(58)82).

[3] WFD 534.

from the British standpoint" of basing the nuclear deterrent underground or under the sea[1].

The chairman (Lord Mountbatten) said that the Minister had called for the committee's views "in time to consider them before the next meeting of the Defence Board", but it was not possible to give a considered view until more technical knowledge of the two systems' characteristics was available, and he considered that some months would be needed to carry out the necessary study. Although the Joint Planning Staff could set down the known facts in a report, he did not believe they were qualified to prepare the kind of report needed: this should be done by a small high-level working party, of which the Vice-Chiefs of Staff should be members, and which could co-opt other experts as necessary for assistance and advice. He suggested that Sir Richard Powell (PS, MoD) should be the chairman.

The CoS endorsement of a special study led to the setting-up by the Minister of Defence in mid-1959 of the British Nuclear Deterrent Study Group, whose subsequent reports had a powerful influence on strategic policies. But VCAS (Air Mshl Sir Edmund Hudleston), representing the CAS, expressed reservations: he thought that the proper body to assemble and set out the known facts was the Defence Research Policy Committee. When that had been done, a separate body might "adjudicate between the alternatives", so that the Chiefs of Staff could then advise Ministers as to the best system to choose.

Sir Richard Powell, however, said that the Minister of Defence accepted that the proposed study would take about six months. The investigation could not be confined to a simple comparison between Blue Streak and Polaris; it had much wider implications, and he did not consider that either the Joint Planning Staff or the DRPC were best qualified to make such a review: an independent body would be preferable. It might consist of five or six members, including scientists and representatives of the Chiefs of Staff, Foreign Office and Treasury. He himself would accept the chairmanship, if the Minister of Defence agreed, as he considered this to be "the most important single defence policy problem" that had to be decided.

The Chiefs of Staff invited Sir Richard to discuss his proposals for making the study – which it was agreed would take about six months – with the Vice-Chiefs of Staff, before submitting them to the CoS Committee, which on 13 January [2] invited him to propose the composition of and terms of reference for a working party. The terms proposed were "to examine future policy for a British-controlled contribution to the deterrent". However, after being approached about it by his PS on 23 March the Minister decided that this study – which had "to some extent...become an argument about the relative merits of Polaris and Blue Streak" (commented to DCDS on 30 Apr) – should be deferred *sine die*.

[1] COS (59) 1st Mtg, 1 Jan 59.
[2] COS (59) 4th Mtg.

In the interim, DCAS (Air Mshl Sir Geoffrey Tuttle) reported at length to the Air Council on the status of Blue Streak, presenting a lengthy Note for their consideration on 30 April[1]. In summarising what he called "the first comprehensive report" on the weapon, he said that progress was satisfactory within the financial limitations imposed. The organisation for its development – with de Havilland Propellers as prime contractor, co-ordinating de Havilland Aircraft (main structure), Rolls-Royce (propulsion) and Sperry Gyroscope (guidance) – seemed to be working well. Comprehensive test facilities were already in use at Hatfield and major static-test facilities, for full-scale testing of propulsion and ground systems, were well advanced at Spadeadam. All test launchings would be done at Woomera, where it was planned to launch the first Blue Streak in 1960. DCAS sought the Council's endorsement of the use of underground sites, as "the only worthwhile method" of ensuring the weapon's credibility. This was needed because the Treasury did not consider that "statements so far made" constituted "explicit Ministerial acceptance of the principle of underground deployment". (The February 1958 Report on Defence, for example, had spoken of an "advanced type" of British ballistic rocket "designed for launching from underground".)

In the discussion on the status report, DCAS recalled that the intention to site Blue Streak underground had already been publicly announced; he did not believe that the question of how many weapons precisely would be required need affect the principle of underground siting. CGWL (Controller of Guided Weapons and Electronics, MoS) (Dr R Cockburn) said that the Ministry of Supply were in full agreement with the idea of underground launching. The Council, too, concurred – deciding that "Treasury approval to the principle of underground launching should be sought as a matter of urgency".

The Council had noted "with satisfaction" the progress in Blue Streak development which DCAS had set out in his report, which detailed the Governmental and industrial ramifications of the project – technical direction of R&D aspects being vested in the RAE (subject to MoS policy decisions) and the Rocket Propulsion Establishment at Westcott providing R&D facilities for "important aspects of propulsion system development". There had been "very close liaison" from the start with related American projects through the US/UK Ballistic Missile Advisory Committee, and firm-to-firm agreements had been completed between DH Propellers and Convair (Convair Division of General Dynamics Corp)[2] on structure and overall systems and between Rolls-Royce and North American Aviation on propulsion systems. It was intended that the Air Ministry Works Department should be responsible for building

---

[1] Blue Streak – Status: Note by DCAS, 22 Apr 59 (AC(59)37). AC Conclusions, 10(59), 30 Apr 59.
[2] Prime contractors for the Atlas ICBM, the first inter-continental ballistic missile to reach production status outside the Soviet Union (*Jane's All the World's Aircraft*, 1958-59 edition).

the operational underground facilities, including the engineering prototype K.11[1], while "purely R&D developments elsewhere" were being built by the Ministry of Works as agents for the MoS. A Joint Design Team of AMWD, MoW and DH Propellers had been formed in September 1958 to co-ordinate the design of the prototype and "to ensure the successful integration of the missile and its system with the launcher".

Thus there was progress with Blue Streak on a broad technical and industrial front; but progress on the political/military front, in deciding whether the United Kingdom should go ahead at all with a land-based strategic nuclear deterrent weapon, was much slower and more complicated. It was the strategic and national implications of the latter decision which were to come within the purview of the British Nuclear Deterrent Study Group.[2]

What DCAS asked the Air Council for was an endorsement of the principle of underground deployment for Blue Streak, and this was given at the 30 April 1959 meeting, when it was agreed[3] that the missiles should be sited underground and that Treasury approval to the principle of launching from such sites "should be sought as a matter of urgency".

However, Treasury approval was not forthcoming, and the main lines of the final battle over Blue Streak – between the Minister of Defence and the Chancellor of the Exchequer – began to be drawn during 1959.

Shortly after the Air Council meeting at the end of April, the Air Ministry sent a paper to the Treasury on the deployment of Blue Streak.[4] In a cost comparison, this said that the Ministry of Supply had estimated that "the total R&D cost of a below-ground Blue Streak (including money already spent) would be £160-200 million, and that the savings effected by accepting above-ground deployment would be in the region of £3.5 million". The conclusion drawn was that the choice of an above-ground deployment would reduce R&D costs by approximately 2 per cent and deployment costs by about 10 per cent, and that this "marginal difference in cost" represented the difference between "an effective and an ineffective system".

Another Government Department involved in Blue Streak deployment was the Home Office, for the missiles – of which there were likely to be 100[5] – would not be sited on disused RAF airfields like the Thors.

---

[1] The "best choice" for which – "subject to confirmation by on-site checks of satisfactory geological factors" – appeared to be RAF Duxford, "because of . . . close proximity to the main assembly factory and . . . adequate domestic accommodation and the technical services . . . when the site is taken over by the RAF".

[2] Which the Minister of Defence decided on 16 June 1959 should go ahead with its examination of "the future of the British-controlled contribution to the nuclear deterrent".

[3] Conclusions 10(59) – TS Annex.

[4] Deployment of Blue Streak (R H Melville/D R Serpell), 8 May 59, in file Development of British Medium-range Ballistic Missile (Blue Streak) (ID3/946/9 Pt 1).

[5] The figure used for planning purposes in 1959 (LM, ACAS(Ops)/VCAS, 26 May 59) (ibid).

"For strategic reasons", the Minister of Defence wrote to the Home Secretary (Mr R A Butler) on 5 June 1959, "wide dispersal throughout the country will probably be necessary, geological conditions permitting. But on present information much of the eastern half of England appears to be geologically unsuitable".[1] He added that survey work had still be to carried out "to determine which areas of the country are suitable for extensive underground construction".

By the end of July 1959 (when the BNDSG held its first meeting – on the 27th) the Treasury had still not been convinced about the justification for the cost of Blue Streak deployment, on top of the costs of the development programme, which had risen. An Air Staff paper of 29 July[2] said that although the Minister of Defence had reiterated in the defence debate[3] that the missiles would be put underground, and the Air Council had approved this requirement in April,[4] "we have not yet brought the Treasury finally to accept this thesis. . . ."

The rise in costs was a double one. During August the Air Ministry reported to the Treasury[5] that the cost of underground deployment had risen from £2 million to £2.88 million per site – excluding the cost of the missile; and development costs also rose. At the beginning of September the Minister of Supply (Mr Aubrey Jones) wrote to the Minister of Defence to report that "De Havilland Propellers have just told us that their work on the agreed Blue Streak programme will cost substantially more in this financial year than they have previously estimated...", sending a copy of his letter to the Chancellor of the Exchequer (Mr D Heathcot Amory).

In his reply, of 8 September, the Chancellor pointed out sharply[6] that the £6 million excess expenditure which "seemed to be in prospect" contravened a directive by the Prime Minister and a collective Ministerial decision:–

"The basis on which we agreed that the Blue Streak programme should be proceeded with during this financial year was 'one year's deliberate and unobtrusive retardation'; and in his Minute of 27 December 1958 the Prime Minister directed that the estimate should be reduced by £1 million in addition to the reductions previously agreed between your Ministry and the Treasury. It is indeed surprising to learn that the Prime Minister's direction has not been implemented.

"I make every allowance for the difficulties of financial estimating and financial control in a major project of this kind.... But I must say quite frankly that I take a very serious view of the situation which

---

[1] Rock masses 300-500ft thick were required (paper in Guided Weapons – Surface to surface Blue Streak/Thor (IIA/11/2/26).)

[2] AMSO/S of S (through US of S).

[3] 29 Feb 59.

[4] 30 April meeting.

[5] Letter Melville/Serpell, 12 Aug 59.

[6] Finance was a major, though by no means the over-riding, factor in the decision to abandon Blue Streak as a weapon.

appears to have developed. When, on a matter of major financial importance, Ministers take collectively at Estimate time a difficult and carefully considered decision, I am entitled to expect that all possible steps will be taken to ensure that that decision is adhered to. I must warn you that I shall be most unwilling to sanction any considerable increase over the Estimate figure in this year's expenditure on Blue Streak...".

Copies of this letter were sent to the Air Staff (CAS, PUS, DCAS, etc), as were copies of the Minister's reply, in which he told the Chancellor that MoS officials had increased their efforts to secure economy in the programme; they had carried out a detailed review of work in hand and to be put in hand, but this scrutiny had not resulted in the savings looked for – "on the contrary, we are faced with the increase of the order of £6 million". He nevertheless thought that it was "desirable to continue to finance this existing programme".

The Minister's letter was written on 15 September, and on the following day the Minister of Defence wrote to the Chancellor to urge the continued funding of the Blue Streak project:–

"Much though I regret the apparently inevitable overspending . . . during the current financial year, I should like to express my strong support of the Minister's view that we must continue to finance the existing programme for the time being, and defer any decisions on our future course of action until we know precisely what the issues are. . . ."

In addition to the cost of development referred to by the Minister of Supply there was a further big item of expenditure, the cost of building the prototype underground launching site (K.11). On 15 October there was a Blue Streak presentation at the de Havilland London office, attended by Air Ministry, MoD, MoS and Treasury representatives, to describe the system's engineering features and the timing of plans for its deployment. An Air Ministry minute describing this meeting[1] commented that "the Treasury reserved their position, but we believe that their misgivings now relate not to the technical concept but to the mounting cost of the . . . R&D programme . . . and the possibility that the British Nuclear Deterrent Study Group under Sir Richard Powell, which is considering possible deterrent weapon systems in the period from 1965 onwards, may recommend the abandonment of Blue Streak".

When DCAS reported to the Air Council on 9 November[2] he referred to excess expenditure in the current financial year (1959-60) of £2 million and also to the prototype underground site, for which Treasury approval was required. This site had yet to be chosen, although construction was scheduled to begin in the following January; its cost was estimated to be £4.7 million. The Council "invited DCAS to keep

---

[1] DUS1 to VCAS (through DCAS), 22 Oct 59.
[2] Progress Report . . . on Weapons Systems . . . (AC(59)88, 30 Oct 59).

[them] informed of any major developments".[1]

Meanwhile the Chancellor of the Exchequer had again expressed concern, in a letter of 4 November to the Minister of Defence (now Mr Harold Watkinson) about the rising costs of Blue Streak, and his verbal duel with Mr Duncan Sandys (now Minister of Aviation following the Government changes) was to be continued in correspondence between them about the programme. The Chancellor reminded the new Minister of Defence that the previous Minister of Aviation had "urged that the existing programme should continue to be financed, at any rate until policy questions could be put and answered"; but

"the development of Blue Streak is now expected to cost £6 million more than the total fixed, with the concurrence of the Prime Minister, for 1959-60, and £11 million more than the last estimate for 1960-61 . . . . Further, the Treasury are being asked to agree to substantial new commitments, such as K.11, and certain works projects in Australia. . . .

"The whole situation is the reverse of satisfactory. I understand that the Working Party under the chairmanship of Sir Richard Powell, which is considering the future of the UK deterrent,[2] expects to be able to make an interim report, covering Blue Streak, by the middle of November. After that date Ministers should be able to decide whether Blue Streak shall continue and, if so, on what terms".

The Chancellor added that in the meantime, until the report was available, he was "reluctantly prepared" to accept the financial implications of allowing work now in progress to continue and to defer decisions on major new commitments.

Clearly, by November 1959 there was a question mark over the Blue Streak programme; but the Minister of Aviation, who had been sent a copy of the Chancellor's letter, made a strong plea to him for its continuance. Writing on the 25th, he said he was "content that decisions should await a study of Sir Richard Powell's report" but added that he must make it plain that the project had reached a stage at which "hesitations which have bedevilled progress need to be removed". He put Blue Streak into the context of the nuclear deterrent force; whatever was done,

"the maintenance of an independent British nuclear deterrent is bound to be a costly business.... But the military power, security and influence which it gives us is out of all proportion greater than anything we could hope to obtain by devoting a similar sum to forces of any conventional kind. It may, of course, be argued that we should scrap Blue Streak and change over to some other form of nuclear deterrent.... Whether we go in for rockets launched from the ground, from the sea or from the air, the next generation of nuclear deterrent is likely to cost something of the order of £500 million. We have already spent £50

---

[1] Conclusions 23(59) – TS Annex.
[2] This was British Nuclear Deterrent Study Group.

million on Blue Streak and it would cost a large sum of money to wind it up…".

"In all the circumstances, I hope that an early decision may be taken to go ahead with Blue Streak at the full planned speed…".

At the beginning of 1960 there was an Air Staff meeting on the siting of Blue Streak, under the chairmanship of the Secretary of State, when papers and maps relating to possible deployment of the weapon were discussed – with particular reference to the first installation. The meeting agreed that a paper should be prepared setting-out possible deployments; for, as S of S pointed out, the view of the Minister of Defence was that any discussion on deployment should await completion of the Powell Committee report – which was "likely to recommend continuation with Blue Streak in underground sites", so the Air Ministry "would shortly be asked to state their plans for deployment and in particular for the first site".[1]

Meanwhile the Minister of Aviation continued his duel with the Chancellor over the programme. Writing on 8 January 1960 to ask for £2 million more for installations at the Woomera range in Australia, he reiterated his theme that "unless we decide… to do without Blue Streak we must not fail to do all that is necessary to ensure that [the] programme proceeds efficiently".

The Chancellor, however, refused categorically to sanction expenditure on the proposed facilities at Talgarno, impact area for the Woomera range, and so informed the Minister of Aviation on 21 January; but the latter was not to be put off and returned to the attack. Leaving for a visit to South America, he dictated a minute when on his way to London Airport on the 25th, having just received the Chancellor's rebuff:–

"One thing I wish to emphasise is that, unless and until we decide to cancel Blue Streak, development should be allowed to go ahead at the full planned rate. To go on with this costly project at a rate so reduced that the weapon would come into service late would be to get the worst of both worlds.

"Therefore, unless the Defence White Paper contains an announcement that Blue Streak is to be abandoned, which I . . . would . . . strongly resist, I must ask you to give the 'all clear' so that further serious delays can be avoided".

No argument or persuasion, however, would move the Chancellor – who in a reply of 4 February ("at a time", as he said, "when the future of the weapon is the subject of a searching review as a major question of defence policy") referred to the Prime Minister's directive of the previous December that all steps which could be taken to reduce expenditure on Blue Streak, without giving an impression that the programme was being abandoned or retarded, should be taken.

---

[1] Minutes in Guided Weapons – Surface to Surface Blue Streak Thor (IIA/11/2/26).

The Chancellor's reference to "a searching review" of Blue Streak comprehended the work which had been done by the British Nuclear Deterrent Study Group and the contribution made by its report to influencing the Government's final decision on the weapon. This work had been going on since the middle of the previous year.

Although CDS had made his suggestion for a study of a land-based or undersea nuclear deterrent at the beginning of 1959 and the Chiefs of Staff had approved this idea, the BNDSG did not start work until late in July that year. This was because the Minister of Defence (as already mentioned) had directed that the study should be deferred;[1] the reason for this, it subsequently transpired[2], being that he did not wish to cast doubt on the future of Blue Streak. After a Chequers meeting in early June, however, the Minister agreed to the terms of reference which had been proposed for the study and to the membership of the group[3]. Its task was "to consider how the British-controlled contribution to the nuclear deterrent can most effectively be maintained in the future and to make recommendations"; and its composition reflected the permanent heads of Government Departments concerned with defence, and the leaders of the Services, under the chairmanship of Sir Richard Powell (MoD): Sir William Strath (MoA), Sir Frederick Brundrett (MoD), Sir Patrick Dean (FO), Mr B D Fraser (Treasury); the three Vice/Deputy Chiefs of Staff – Vice-Admiral L G Durlacher, Lt-General Sir William Stratton and Air Mshl Sir Edmund Hudleston – and Sir William Cook (MoA).

During five months' work before its report was produced at the end of 1959 the BNDSG held 13 meetings and in its research consulted not only the Service Ministries but also specialist bodies like the Joint Global War Study Group and the Air Ministry Strategic Scientific Policy Committee (whose members were Sir Solly Zuckerman and Sir William Cook and Professors M J Lighthill and W R Hawthorne and which produced its own report, *The Nuclear Deterrent – 1970 and After*, 5 October 1959). The BNDSG conclusions, as far as Blue Streak was concerned, were that until the Soviet Union had deployed an efficient system of defence against ballistic missiles the weapon "would not be vulnerable once it had been fired and had successfully got away from the launching-point"; but that "whether deployed underground or on the surface" it would be "vulnerable to pre-emptive attack". It would therefore be effective only if it were fired first, for example, in reply to a Soviet attack with conventional weapons. Because Blue Streak missiles could only be successfully fired before a Soviet nuclear attack on the UK, it would not strictly be necessary to deploy them underground, although such a deployment would "considerably complicate the task of

---

[1] Minute from CDS to DCDS, 30 Apr 59, in file Possible Future Nuclear Deterrent Weapon Systems (BND Bnd – TS407/101/024/63 Pt1).
[2] Minute, 8 May 59, Powell/Minister (ibid).
[3] Minister's office to Powell, 16 Jun 59 (ibid).

the Soviet forces in return for a proportionately small increase in cost". In its recommendations, the Study Group said that if a "fire first" weapon were acceptable, the development of Blue Streak should continue (pending decisions on certain questions which it posed); and in the light of factors set out in its conclusions, Ministers should consider whether further work to enable Blue Streak to be fired from underground sites should proceed.

The report went on to recommend that Ministers should consider whether it would be acceptable for the UK to be seen to be wholly dependent between 1965 and 1970 upon the United States for the weapons (apart from the warheads) used by the British contribution to the nuclear deterrent. If the answer to this was "yes" an approach should be made to the US Government with a view either to ensuring that the V-bombers were armed with WS138A (Skybolt) by 1966, or to obtaining a number of Polaris-firing submarines by a comparable date. If, again, the answer was "yes" and when satisfactory arrangements had been made on the lines proposed, then Blue Streak should be cancelled. If the answer was "no", or if satisfactory arrangements on either of the lines proposed (ie, Skybolt or Polaris) could not be negotiated, a "thin period" for some time after 1965 would be "inevitable"; and the choice would then lie between accepting the limitations of Blue Streak and continuing with its development and deployment, or cancelling it, and accepting whatever gap there might be in the continuity of the British-controlled contribution to the nuclear deterrent, in order to develop an effective mobile weapon system as soon as possible. The Study Group, it was added as a final recommendation, "should complete its investigtion of the most suitable form of long endurance mobile ballistic missile systems"[1].

Copies of its Interim report, setting out the options for the Government on strategic nuclear delivery systems – Blue Streak, or either Skybolt or Polaris – went to Ministers, including the Prime Minister; and early in 1960 the latter drew up a memorandum on deterrent policy which was considered by the Cabinet Defence Committee on 24 February[2]. It said that in the 1960s a position of nuclear equipoise would be reached, which might affect the shape and size of Britain's contribution to the Western nuclear deterrent; but he was satisfied that, in order to maintain an influence in world affairs, she must remain "in the nuclear business".

The Prime Minister set out certain principles – including making "a significant effort in the field of the strategic nuclear deterrent" and maintaining an ability to provide British warheads for "whatever weapons systems" might be adopted – and said that, on the basis of these, the Minister of Defence considered that "the present plan for

---

[1] This second study by the BNDSG was begun in April 1960.
[2] D.(60) 1st Mtg. The Prime Minister's memorandum on deterrent policy was D(60)2.

developing and deploying Blue Streak as a military weapon" should be abandoned. He supported this recommendation, for the following reasons: the V-force, with Blue Steel Mk 1, would be fully effective until 1966; it might be possible to prolong its effective life for several years after 1966, by

"obtaining from the United States, without conditions, supplies of the air-launched, rocket Skybolt"; and it seemed likely that, in the 1970s, some "mobile means of delivery" of the deterrent would "hold the field" - air-launched, like Skybolt; or launched "from a mobile platform on land, or on or under the sea, like Polaris".

The committee agreed with the deterrent philosophy outlined in the memorandum, and the Minister of Defence said that he had the support of the Chiefs of Staff in favour of the development of mobile weapon systems and the abandonment of Blue Streak. Attended by all the main protagonists — the Chancellor of the Exchequer, the Ministers of Defence and Aviation and the Secretary of State for Air — this meeting preceded by a day one of the Air Council when members learnt from DCAS that development of Blue Streak continued to be satisfactory; that telemetry and instrumentation cabling had been delayed and the firing date for Round F.1 was scheduled for October 1960. This information was contained in his Progress Report to 31 January 1960 on Weapons Systems not yet fully released[1].

The Minister of Aviation, while continuing his advocacy of Blue Streak — he thought that mobility would not in practice provide any military advantage for the strategic nuclear deterrent force; the Russians would have to launch an attack on the UK of such a scale to neutralise 60 underground Blue Streak sites that it would involve "the virtual certainty" of US retaliation, said that he would not dissent from the recommendation to abandon Blue Streak as a weapon if development of it continued as part of a UK programme of space research.

In the Chancellor of the Exchequer's view the issues before the committee should not be determined solely on financial grounds; he did not wish to see all UK efforts in strategic nuclear deterrence abandoned, but limited resources would call for some reduction in present plans — he had "never accepted any commitment for expenditure of the order of £500 millions on the deployment of 60 Blue Streak missiles" and "could not escape the conclusion that further expenditure . . . would be wasteful and would only provide a weapon system that was out of date when it became operational".

When the Prime Minister summed up he said there were three main reasons for aiming to develop a strategic nuclear force of the greatest possible mobility: the Chiefs of Staff had concluded that there would be no military value in a static missile and that development of Blue Streak as a weapon should be cancelled; mobility had political advantages — it

---

[1] AC(60)9

made the UK deterrent more credible; and deployment of missiles on fixed sites had an adverse effect on public opinion, and there would be "particular problems" in siting Blue Streaks in the west country.

Pointing out that about £60m had been spent on Blue Streak, and that an effort must be made to get every possible advantage from this expenditure and to try to preserve the scientific and technological skills acquired in the development of ballistic missiles, the Prime Minister proposed that the Ministers who were directly concerned "should put in hand an urgent study of the means of mitigating the consequences" of not proceeding with Blue Streak as a military weapon.

These were conclusions with which the committee – with the Chiefs of Staff in attendance – concurred: it decided provisionally that the existing programme for the deployment of Blue Streak as a military weapon should be abandoned, while agreeing that this provisional decision should be reviewed in the light of the results of the study which the Prime Minister would arrange, of the way in which the development of Blue Streak might be continued for scientific and technological purposes.

A report of this study[1] came before the Defence Committee on 21 March[2], but the Prime Minister said that a final decision could not yet be taken about the future of the Blue Streak project; and in the event the committee agreed that the 1960/61 estimates should be reduced by about £10m on account of Blue Streak, "provided that the reasons for the reduction were not revealed", and to give further consideration to the project's future at a later meeting.

The Defence Committee's provisional decision of 24 February – that the deployment of Blue Streak as a weapon should be abandoned; a decision to be reviewed in the light of an enquiry as to continuance of the rocket for scientific purposes – was confirmed at its meeting on 6 April.[3] At the latter date the committee considered a Report by Officials on the adaptation of Blue Streak for space research, and its previous provisional decision to abandon the missile's development as a weapon; and the Prime Minister said that there were two main issues to decide: whether it would be militarily acceptable to rely on the V-bombers with Skybolt, rather than on Blue Streak, as the UK strategic nuclear deterrent force from about 1965 onwards; and whether it was reasonable to assume that Skybolt and eventually Polaris (if it were needed) would be made available by the Americans on reasonable terms. In other words, he was warning the committee that Blue Streak should not be cancelled unless there were reasonable reserve options.

On these two points, the Minister of Defence said that after recent technical assessment and in the light of a Defence Board discussion on 4

---

[1] Interim Report by Officials (GEN 709/1) about the possible development of Blue Streak for scientific and technological purposes.
[2] D.(60)11.
[3] D (60) 3rd Meeting, Minutes.

April[1] the consensus of opinion was that, in circumstances other than a surprise saturation attack, V-bombers with Skybolt would have certain advantages over Blue Streak. The bomber force had qualities of mobility and flexibility which were useful for conventional operations as well as for nuclear deterrence; and it had the advantage that it could be launched on a radar warning "without an irrevocable decision being taken to launch [a] nuclear attack". The Minister of Aviation "agreed that there would be certain financial and political advantages" in depending on the V-bombers and Skybolt rather than on Blue Streak for strategic nuclear deterrence in the later 1960s. He thought that, from the military point of view, there was no marked advantage one way or the other; in these circumstances he would concur in the decision that the development of Blue Streak as a weapon should be abandoned.

As to the terms on which missile systems might be obtained from the United States, the committee considered the outcome of talks which the Prime Minister had had with President Eisenhower on 28-29 March 1960 at Camp David to be "very satisfactory". The Americans had indicated their willingness to make Skybolt available, and it should be possible to reach a similar understanding as regards Polaris. In summing up that part of the meeting (that is, before considering the future of Blue Streak) the Prime Minister said that the committee's discussion "showed that their provisional decision to abandon Blue Streak as a weapon could now be confirmed".

The decision was made public in a Parliamentary statement a week later when the Minister of Defence said in the Commons[2]:–

"The Government have been considering the future of the project for developing the long-range ballistic missile Blue Streak and have been in touch with the Australian Government about it, in view of their interest in the joint project and the operation of the Woomera range.

"The technique of controlling ballistic missiles has rapidly advanced. The vulnerability of missiles launched from static sites, and the practicability of launching missiles of considerable range from mobile platforms, has now been established. In the light of our military advice to this effect, and of the importance of reinforcing the effectiveness of the deterrent, we have concluded and the Australian Government have fully accepted that we ought not to continue to develop, as a military weapon, a missile that can be launched only from a fixed site.

"Today, our strategic nuclear force is an effective and significant contribution to the deterrent power of the free world. The Government do not intend to give up this independent contribution and, therefore, some other vehicle will in due course be needed in place of Blue Streak to carry British-manufactured warheads. The need for this is not immediately urgent, since the effectiveness of the V-bomber force as the

---

[1] DFB(60)3rd-Conclusions, when a paper by the Minister of Aviation, "Vulnerability of the V-bomber Force", was discussed.
[2] Commons Hansard, Vol 621, Cols 1265-6, 13 April 1960.

vehicle for these warheads will remain unimpaired for several years to come, nor is it possible at the moment to say with certainty which of several possibilities or combinations of them would be technically the most suitable.

"On present information, there appears much to be said for prolonging the effectiveness of the V-bombers by buying supplies of the airborne ballistic missile Skybolt which is being developed in the United States. Her Majesty's Government understand that the United States Government will be favourably disposed to the purchase by the United Kingdom at the appropriate time of supplies of this vehicle.

"The Government will now consider with the firms and other interests concerned as a matter of urgency, whether the Blue Streak programme could be adapted for the development of a launcher for space satellites. . . ."

So ended Blue Streak – for military, financial (it had cost £84m) and logistic reasons – less than five years after it had begun as Air Staff Requirement OR1139. It was to be succeeded, as the proposed next strategic nuclear weapon for Bomber Command, by OR1149 – for a flying bomb with 1,000nm range, a requirement planned to be fulfilled by Skybolt, whose hoped-for acquisition and subsequent cancellation form the themes of the next chapter. Because of plans to purchase Skybolt, and because of delays in getting Blue Steel into service, the Mk 2 version of the latter weapon was not put into development, being cancelled on the authority of the Minister of Defence (Mr Harold Watkinson) at the beginning of 1960[1].

Blue Steel Mk 2 was cancelled three months before the cancellation of Blue Streak. On 1 January the Minister of Defence had written to the Minister of Aviation[2] about a minute he had had from S of S for Air on Blue Steel Mk 2, saying that he had "agreed with the Chancellor that this project should be dropped from the programme" – and would the Minister therefore "proceed with the formal cancellation of Blue Steel, Mk 2".

The reasons for the cancellation of this developed version of the Avro stand-off bomb were threefold, and resulted from discussions which had been going on in the Air Staff, the Defence Board and the British Nuclear Deterrent Study Group for several months: first, it was felt that design work on Blue Steel Mk 2 was proving detrimental to the development of Blue Steel Mk 1 and TSR.2; secondly, it seemed likely that by the time the Mk 2 version entered service its effective operational life would be only about two years; and thirdly, there was a prospect of obtaining supplies of the American air-launched bomb WS138A (subsequently known as Skybolt), which promised greater

---

[1] Minute to Minister of Aviation, 1 Jan 60, in file Blue Steel (OR1132) Financial Aspects (ID/47/296, Pt1).

[2] This and other Minutes quoted are in the 194/4 Blue Steel file – ID9/194/4 18-1, sub-folder A.

range and effectiveness than Blue Steel Mk 2. There was no doubt that a long-range powered guided bomb was required for the V-bombers in the face of increasingly effective Soviet missile defences and counter-measures – hence the Air Staff Operational Requirements OR1149 and OR1159; but the question was, whether the weapon decided on was to be British or American[1].

On 24 June 1959 S of S for Air (Mr George Ward) had written to the Minister of Defence (Mr Duncan Sandys) to say that in December 1958 the Prime Minister had

"agreed that work should continue on Blue Steel Mk 2 (OR1159) until 31 August this year. During the intervening period, we were to examine the possibility of certain alternative American projects.

"This has now been done but it is certain that we shall not be able to come to a final decision by the end of August. We must, therefore, take stock now of where we are going or . . . we shall be in . . . danger of having no long-range weapon at all".

S of S went on to say that the only firm project under development was OR1159; the development of an American weapon had not yet been approved by the US DoD, whose final decision was not expected before October, so it would be "the end of the year before we . . . have sufficient knowledge to make a choice". He recommended that work on OR1159 should continue until the end of 1959, "by which time we should take a final decision between the adoption of this or the American project"[2].

The Minister of Defence, in a minute of 14 July to S of S, concurred in this decision[3].

Later in 1959 a study was made in the Air Ministry of the credibility of Blue Steel Mk 2 as a deterrent system. Prepared by the staff of the Scientific Adviser[4], it concluded that the weapon introduced "a step-functon in invulnerability" compared with the Mk 1 version and that alterations in its flight profile could extend its credibility further, at the expense of "some delay" in its introduction into service.

Towards the end of that year it was becoming evident that development work on the Mk 2 was affecting progress with the Mk 1 and with TSR.2. On 1 December VCAS (Air Mshl Sir Edmund Hudleston) put a series of blunt questions to the PS, MoA (Sir Wiliam Strath), asking him to confirm if effort had been diverted from Blue Steel Mk 1

---

[1] The Defence Research Policy Committee had on 17 Dec 57 agreed in principle to the development of a longer-range version of Blue Steel (Blue Steel Mk 2): see Bombers – Powered Bombs Blue Steel – Effect of curtailing the programme (ID9/B. 18-1). The idea of a long range (1000-mile) guided bomb had been mooted in 1956 as a means of maintaining the deterrent "long after the V-bombers might otherwise have become obsolete" (Science 2 Memo No 258 On the Value of a Long Range Guided Bomb, 14 Mch 56 in ID6/476 (Pt 3) Bombs, Weapons, Explosives and Ammunition).

[2] In Nov 58 the USAF/RAF Task Group had concluded that the USAF proposals "more than meet the requirements of OR1159" (Note by CA – Paper for DRPC, 20 Dec 58 (DRP/P(58)103).

[3] Development and Production of Power-guided Bomb (Blue Steel), ID3/946/8(S), Pt 2.

[4] J E Henderson, Sc 2/955, 17 Nov 59.

to the Mk 2, that consequently the Mk 1 would be late, that resources at RRE (Royal Radar Establishment) were insufficient to deal with the Mk 2 and TSR.2[1] and that if the Mk 2 were proceeded with, TSR.2 "could not be produced by 1965".

In his reply, on 3 December, the Permanent Secretary said that in his Ministry's view the effort which A V Roe had been applying to OR1159 had been detrimental to the progress of Blue Steel Mk 1, and that there would be "a serious clash" at RAE Farnborough between the Mk 2 and equipment for TSR.2 if both the latter projects were to proceed in parallel. They believed that "complete cancellation of Mk 2 work at A V Roe would assist . . . in obtaining delivery of the Mk 1 system at the earliest possible date".

Reporting on this letter to S of S on 15 December, DCAS (Air Mshl S C Elworthy) said that in the light of it "CAS, VCAS and I have reluctantly concluded that we should be prepared to agree to the cancellation of Blue Steel Mk 2, because of the threat to Blue Steel Mk 1 and the TSR.2". But he did not think that any formal acceptance of cancellation should be volunteered until Ministers had had an opportunity of considering the recommendations of the British Nuclear Deterrent Study Group – which VCAS was "still endeavouring to convince . . . that the V-force, if equipped with WS138A (Skybolt), could continue to pose an effective deterrent up to about 1970".

S of S subsequently had a meeting with the Minister of Defence about future deterrent weapons, and a discussion with CAS, PUS,VCAS and DCAS (on 22 December), when they came to the conclusion that a "tactical advantage" seemed to lie with offering to drop Blue Steel Mk 2 in return for firm conditions – that assurance would be given that this step would remove obstacles to the development of the Mk 1 and of TSR.2; and that the need for a deterrent weapon for the V-force to succeed Blue Steel Mk 1 should be firmly accepted.

As an outcome of this discussion, S of S minuted the Minister of Defence on 30 December 1959 to say that he was prepared to agree to the discontinuance of development of Blue Steel Mk 2, subject to two provisos – that assurances would be given that this "would remove any obstacles to the development of Blue Steel Mk 1 and TSR.2"; and that the need for an effective long-range guided missile to succeed Blue Steel Mk 1 should be firmly accepted. This could be WS138A or "another weapon": the importance of WS138A had been stressed in the report by the British Nuclear Deterrent Study Group (as will subsequently be shown in the course of the account of Skybolt negotiations).

It was on receipt of S of S's minute that the Minister of Defence wrote to the Minister of Aviation on 1 January 1960 (as already quoted)

---

[1] "...the resources of the RAE and RRE were insufficient to achieve two Marks of Blue Steel . . . as well as the TSR.2" (Sir Frank Cooper, former PUS, in Foreword to T C G James' *Defence Policy and the RAF*).

to say that he had agreed with the Chancellor of the Exchequer that the Blue Steel Mk 2 project should be dropped, and asking him to proceed with its formal cancellation.

CHAPTER XXIV

PLANS FOR SKYBOLT: THE EFFECTS OF ITS CANCELLATION: THE LOW LEVEL ROLE

As has been seen, the Air Ministry agreed to the cancellation of Blue Steel Mk 2 at the end of 1959 on condition that the need for "an effective long-range guided missile to succeed Blue Steel Mk 1" was firmly accepted.

The weapon envisaged as fulfilling this need was WS138A, Skybolt; and in his minute of 30 December to the Minister of Defence conveying agreement to the termination of Blue Steel Mk 2, S of S for Air went on to ask the Minister to write to the US Secretary of Defense "to explain our need for WS138A, to emphasise the importance of its development in a form in which it could be carried by the V-bombers and to express the hope that the United States will be in a position to negotiate the terms of a joint project at an early date". S of S added that he could also explain RAF interest in Skybolt during his forthcoming visit to the United States.

It was, therefore, at the beginning of 1960 that British interest in Skybolt was formally conveyed to the US Government; and as it was in December 1962, at the Nassau Conference, that President Kennedy formally gave Prime Minister Macmillan the news of the weapon system's cancellation, this British interest in the American air-launched long-range missile lasted exactly two years, and its demise had profound effects as far as the V-force was concerned: for with the Polaris submarine-launched ballistic missile system being offered to Britain as an alternative, and accepted, the days of V-force responsibility for strategic nuclear deterrence were numbered.

At the beginning of 1960, however, means were being considered of extending the credibility of V-bombers armed with Blue Steel Mk 1 into the 1970s. The possibility of providing them with a Mk 2 version of this powered guided bomb (to OR1159) came to an end with its cancellation at the beginning of 1960. The two alternatives then were WS138A and the ground-launched ballistic missile Blue Streak; but as has been seen, the future of Blue Streak was under consideration at the beginning of 1960, and by February of that year a decision had been taken to abandon it as a military weapon. So effectively, the only realistic prospect of continued viability for the V-force after Blue Steel lay in Skybolt – the only air-launched ballistic missile in the armoury of the Western world. Towards the end of 1959 the British Nuclear Deterrent Study Group wrote of the prospects for this system, and of its possible acquisition for carriage by the V-bombers:–[1]

---

[1] British-controlled Contribution to the Nuclear Deterrent: Interim Report by the British Nuclear Deterrent Study Group, 31 Dec 59 (BND(SG) (59)19(Final)).

"We understand that the United States authorities have decided to develop a ballistic missile, WS138A, for launching from aircraft. This ... system is as yet unproven. The US Air Force claims that the weapon would have a range of about 1,000nm, a warhead yield of about half a megaton and an accuracy of 1½ to 2nm. . . . There is a possibility that the warhead yield will be increased to one megaton. . . . The plan is to start production in 1964 or 1965.

"Because the weapon would be developed in the United States, the only direct R&D cost to the United Kingdom would be about £15m in respect of installation, trials and proving flights in the V-bombers. While it is much too soon to make any firm estimate of price, the cost of acquiring missiles (less warheads) from the US would probably be of the same order of magnitude as the cost of producing the same number of Blue Steel Mk 2 in this country.

"Although the US authorities are at present willing to design the WS138A so that it can be carried by the V-bombers as well as by the USAF B-52 . . . , we can as yet have no assurance that this will in fact be achieved. The date by which we could obtain any weapons from US production would be for negotiation, but it would be most unlikely to be before 1966 at the earliest. It will not be possible to sustain the planned V-bomber front line beyond about 1970 and some new carrier would have to be introduced by about that date.

"WS138A, being a ballistic missile, would be invulnerable to Soviet defences once it had been launched; we do not expect that any effective system of defence against ballistic missiles will be developed in the period covered by our study. It is also a more accurate weapon than Blue Steel Mk 2, although its warhead may be smaller. . . . The vulnerability of the V-bombers on their bases in the UK would be the same as when they are armed with Blue Steel Mk 2, but their vulnerability en route to the launching areas would be less, to be the extent that the range of WS138A exceeds that of Blue Steel Mk 2".

British interest in Skybolt, as a future weapon for the V-bombers, led to its development being observed from the beginning by the British Joint Services Mission in Washington. A résumé by DCAS (Air Mshl S C Elworthy) in early 1960 said that the programme had its origin during 1958 when

"ARDC (Air Research and Development Command) invited proposals to meet their Staff Requirement SR168 for a high-performance air-to-surface missile with a range of 300nm. A study of the 13 proposals submitted indicated that a ballistic missile was more likely to achieve the CEP (circular error of probability) required and would also weigh less than a cruise missile. Accordingly in November 1958 the USAF wrote draft GOR177 for a 1,000nm ballistic or boost glide vehicle, with a speed of more than M5.

"In the meantime the USAF were conducting three full-scale experiments, each with different contractors, to test the feasibility of launching high-performance weapons at both subsonic and supersonic speeds. . . .

"Early in 1959 the USAF invited industry to make proposals for meeting the new GOR177 and in view of the UK interest in the weapon included instructions that it must be compatible with the Victor and Vulcan. . .".

The RAF had known all about WS138A since mid-1959, with the receipt of a long "status as of 20 July 1959" report (nine pages) from Group Captain S H Bonser, dated 10 August 1959, which was considered at a DAArm meeting at St Giles Court on 7 September. In his report Gp Capt Bonser detailed the development of Weapon System WS138A – Air Launched Ballistic Missile, from January 1959 when a joint USAF/RAF requirement for a 1,000nm missile "capable of carriage and launch from the B-58, B-52 and the two V-bombers" was put to the American industry. In June 1959 representatives of Handley Page and A V Roe visited the Douglas Aircraft Co at Los Angeles with MoS representatives "to assess the task of installing the American project stand-off bomb known as WS138A in the Mk 2 versions of the Vulcan and Victor. The Douglas Co had just been selected as the prime contractor for the project from a tender competition. . .". The joint USAF/RAF requirement, GOR177, was dated January 1959.

During the first half of 1959 the procedures for selection of a contractor – conferences, bids and presentations – resulted in the choice of Douglas Aircraft Co; subsequently the Weapon System Project Office nominated sub-contractors. Late in 1959, however, there was a reappraisal of the whole project – for various reasons, as DCAS described them:-

"During the early autumn . . . the B-58B (developed version of the Convair B-58A Hustler) was cancelled and the B-70 (North American Valkyrie, whose development as a full weapon system was cancelled in 1961) programme . . . severely cut. This left the B-52 as the prime and virtually sole American carrier of the weapon. This change and the fact that the Weapons System Evaluation Group were not completely satisfied with the Douglas proposal caused the Secretary of Defense to ask the USAF to reappraise GAM87A[1] and to consider Advanced Hound Dog and a number of low-alitiude supersonic air missile proposals as alternatives . . .[2]. By November these alternatives had been rejected . . . and the Secretary . . . directed that a detailed technical examination of the Douglas proposal should be made.

"Accordingly a mixed team . . . from the USAF, Douglas, Nortronics,

---

[1] USAF designation for Skybolt.
[2] At a meeting in St Giles Court on 7 Sep 59, to discuss the report by Gp Capt Bonser and Mr E I Campell (previously mentioned), the chairman (Air Cdre R H E Emson) said that he had received a letter from BJSM telling him that the B-58B had been cancelled: he now thought that arguments in the US would be between "the developed Hound Dog . . . and WS138A".

Aerojet and GE[1] was assembled . . . to assist the Weapon System Project Office. After about four weeks of intense study this group expressed doubt about several aspects of the Douglas proposal and suggested a design of their own. After considerable discussion . . . Douglas . . . agreed that the . . . design offered a better chance of success by 1963, the date the weapon is required in service".

This alternative design was presented on 14-15 January 1960 to an "ad hoc" group of experts set up by the USAF, its chairman reporting his views to the Air Force and the Department of Defense, and a final presentation being made to the Director of Research and Engineering, DoD (Dr Herbert F York), on 29 January. Three days later the Secretary of Defense (Mr Thomas Gates) approved the development of GAM87A but imposed some technical and managerial reservations. Changes to technical specifications, other than necessary design changes, were not to be made without approval of the office of the Secretary of Defense; management like that successfully employed in ballistic missile development was to be used; and the Director, R&D, DoD, was to review the programme once every four months for at least two years. The Air Force had to provide increased funding out of its own resources; and range requirements were to be limited.

The USAF accepted these reservations on 3 February 1960; and thus (as DCAS commented) it appeared that "after numerous vicissitudes GAM87A is firmly on the road, at least until 1 May when the first of Dr York's reviews is due".

A report dated 8 February, by Gp Capt G V Fryer, the RAF Requirements Interchange Officer at HQ, USAF[2], said in its summing-up of the latest position on XGAM-87A that "following the presentation to the Fletcher Committee on the 14th and 15th January 1960, HQ USAF and Dr York were briefed in turn on the Delta II missile. . .: both were received with favour and on 1st February the Deputy Secretary of Defence approved the XGAM-87A programme. His letter of approval listed certain minor provisos, all of which were acceptable to the USAF, whose endorsement of the programme was given two days later. Thus, after a series of ups and downs, XGAM-87A has finally earned a clean bill of health: it has been funded to the tune of $95m through FY 1961 and should lead to the production of a devastating addition to the West's deterrent inventory some four years hence".

It is important to note, however, in view of its eventual cancellation, that the Skybolt programme was hedged about from the beginning with many restrictions and qualifications, appertaining both to the design and to the management of the project. Also that, in parallel with the possibility of the RAF acquiring this weapon, the alternative of

---

[1] Douglas Aircraft was prime contractor for Skybolt, Nortronics Division of Northrop was sub-contractor for guidance, Aerojet-General for the propulsion system and General Electric for the re-entry vehicle (*Jane's All the World's Aircraft*, 1962-63).

[2] ID9/194/4 Sub Folder A (of three) Blue Steel, March 1959 to 1960.

acquiring Polaris was being considered; it did not spring unexpectedly out of the Nassau conference.

In its report of 31 December 1959 the British Nuclear Deterrent Study Group had recommended that Ministers should consider whether it was acceptable for the United Kingdom to be seen to be dependent between 1965 and 1970 on the United States for weapons to be used in the British contribution to the nuclear deterrent; and that if so, an approach should be made to the US Government with a view to ensuring that the V-bombers should be armed with WS138A by 1966, or to obtaining a number of Polaris-armed submarines by a comparable date. If satisfactory arrangements on either of these lines were negotiated, Blue Streak should be cancelled.

After its cancellation the BNDSG was re-activated to look at the relative merits of seaborne or airborne long-endurance mobile platforms for the launching of ballistic missiles. In a note of 12 April 1960 its chairman[1] summed-up its task against the background of the abandonment of Blue Streak as a military weapon by saying that the Americans had "indicated their willingness" to make Skybolt available "at the appropriate time", but that it had not been expedient "to seek a similar understanding as regards Polaris". In discussing UK deterrent policy, Ministers had "recognised the possibility of a gap in the continuity of the British-controlled contribution to the nuclear deterrent", but there had been "no substantive decision that such a gap would be politically acceptable". The group's task was "to consider what long-endurance system or systems should be adopted and when".

By the spring of 1960, to use Roman terminology, the omens were propitious for Skybolt to be acquired for the RAF as successor to Blue Steel. The Mk 2 version of the latter had been cancelled and Blue Streak, the alternative deterrent weapon, was about to be cancelled, the Skybolt programme was under close DoD control and the Secretary of State for Air, after visiting the United States, expressed his enthusiasm for the weapon:

"I am convinced that we must have it or something like it to ensure that the V-bomber force, in which we have invested so many millions of pounds, remains a worthwhile and effective contribution to the deterrent in the years after 1965.

"During my visit . . . I had the opportunity of discussing WS138A with the Secretary of the Air Force, with Strategic Air Command and the Commander of the 1st Missile Division, and also with the manufacturers. It is quite clear now that the Americans are continuing with the project, and also that it will be compatible with carriage on the V-bombers"[2].

---

[1] Sir Edward Playfair, who had replaced Sir Richard Powell. The other change in membership was that of Sir Solly Zuckerman for Sir Frederick Brundrett.
[2] Draft minute, 27 January 1960.

The Prime Minister (Mr H Macmillan) suggested that 100 Skybolts should be ordered, as an earnest of British intentions. "I am sure we should not leave the Americans in any doubt", he wrote to the Minister of Defence on 10 May[1], "that we shall want at least a reasonable number of these weapons.

"Should we not consider putting a provisional order for, say, a hundred? This will ensure that in making the design they will take account of the need to make it compatible with the V-bomber. Have you discussed this with the Chancellor? We must not be straddled between Polaris and Skybolt and getting neither one nor the other.

"I reckon a hundred would cost a sufficiently substantial sum to make the Americans take it seriously. It might be possible to call it a provisional order. My object is to achieve the design that is in accordance with our needs. If you wish I will speak to the President[2] about it next week and ask him how I am going to ensure that we get what he, I know, wants us to have".

But the Chancellor of the Exchequer (Mr D Heathcoat Amory) was decidedly more cautious. "I very much hope," he told the Prime Minister on the 11th, "that we shall not find it necessary to put in an order for this weapon at this stage"[3].

The CAS (Air Chf Mshl Sir Thomas Pike) was single-mindedly enthusiastic about Skybolt, describing it on 16 May as the project which, "in conjunction with the V-bombers, is the cheapest of all the possible courses of action open to us to maintain the effectiveness of the deterrent"[4].

Some scepticism was expressed, however, as to whether it was right to continue with the V-bombers as carriers of deterrent weapons. The case for adopting Skybolt, wrote the Minister of Aviation (Mr Duncan Sandys) to the Prime Minister on 25 February 1960,

"is that it would provide us with a mobile deterrent invulnerable to attack. However, this depends upon the ability of our bomber force to get off the ground within the short warning period available, or to maintain a substantial standing patrol in periods of tension which may be prolonged".

The Minister added that he was not suggesting that they should "go back on the provisional decision reached yesterday" — that is, the Defence Committee decision of 24 February 1960[5] to abandon Blue Streak as a military weapon, which implied reliance on Skybolt or Polaris; but he thought that the Committee "should satisfy itself on this very crucial point".

On the same date as the Defence Committee meeting the Foreign

---

[1] PM's Personal Minute, Serial No M150/60.
[2] *Ie* President Eisenhower.
[3] ID9/194/4 Blue Steel.
[4] Minute to PUS.
[5] D(60) 1st meeting, Minutes.

Office had initiated an approach to the Americans about Skybolt and Polaris; for in a message of 24 February the British Joint Services Mission in Washington had been told[1] that the plan for deployment of Blue Streak was being reconsidered, on the assumption that satisfactory agreement could be reached on two alternative missiles, the air-launched WS138A and the submarine-launched Polaris. A new weapon system was wanted from about 1965, when Russian defences would be getting too effective for the short-range air-launched missile "about to be introduced" (ie, Blue Steel). The V-bombers "could remain effective with WS138A at any rate for 1965–70". The requirement was to buy the missiles ready-made, to use with British warheads and with no conditions attached to the purchase. BJSM was asked whether the US Government would say what the prospects were for making WS138A "technically suitable" for use with the V-bombers, and if the acquisition of these weapons by 1965 could be counted upon; whether it would be possible at a later stage to make the Polaris system, and perhaps the submarines, available; and whether these missiles could be made available unconditionally, if Britain provided the warheads. These weapon systems were to form part of "a co-operative effort in developing the total deterrent forces of the West".

In just over a month the availability of these American missile systems to Britain became the subject of conversations between President Eisenhower and Mr Macmillan — at Camp David, Maryland, on 28–29 March — which resulted in a Memorandum of 30 March. Thus, in what might be described as a cart-before-the-horse situation, Skybolt was authorised to be supplied to Britain long before it had any viability as a practical weapon system[2].

A record of the Camp David discussion[3] shows that the Prime Minister conveyed to the President the British Government's view on future deterrent systems – that it had come to the conclusion that Blue Streak was no longer a suitable weapon and its development for military purposes would stop. He hoped that the President "would be able to give him some assurance about the possibility of supplying Skybolt and/or Polaris missiles, if on examination these proved to be what the United Kingdon needed to replace Blue Streak". Owing to Australian involvement in Blue Streak, with the provision of range facilities at Woomera, there was some urgency about a decision – the Prime Minister explaining that "because of Mr Menzies' timetable in connection with the Commonwealth Conference" he wished "to secure

---

[1] Foreign Office to Washington, No 762 (Appendix B to Minutes of Defence Committe, 24 Feb 60).

[2] Reviewing George B Kistiakowsky's *A Scientist at the White House: The Private Diary of President Eisenhower's Special Assistant for Science and Technology* (Harvard University Press) in *The Times Literary Supplement* for 18 Nov 77 Prof Margaret Gowing wrote: "Skybolt is a familiar name to the British because Kennedy later promised to supply this missile to Macmillan but then had to cancel it; Kistiakowsky tells us that although in 1959 it was energetically promoted by both the contractor and the Air Force it had little substance except on paper".

[3] PM(W)(60)4th Mtg Item 5.

President Eisenhower's agreement to an announcement about the possibilities of securing Skybolt or Polaris missiles . . . before 13 April 1960".

As a result of the Macmillan-Eisenhower conversations of 28–29 March both "a form of words which UK Ministers could use before 13 April about Blue Streak and its possible replacement"[1] and a memorandum on the supply of Skybolt and Polaris emerged in an exchange of minutes on 29 March. In the first, the Prime Minister expressed his gratitude to the President

"for what you told me today about our decision against a fixed rocket site and in favour of mobility. I am sure this was the right decision. . . .

"I was also grateful to you for expressing your willingness to help us when the time comes by enabling us to purchase supplies of Skybolt without warheads or to acquire in addition or substitution a mobile MRBM system in the light of such decisions as may be reached in the discussions under way in Nato. As you know, either I or the Minister of Defence must make an announcement about Blue Streak before 13 April, and I was glad to have your confirmation that the following form of words would cause you no difficulty:-

"'The effectiveness of the V-bomber force will remain unimpaired for several years to come. The need for a replacement for Blue Streak is not, therefore, immediately urgent, nor is it possible at the moment to say with certainty which of several possible alternatives or combinations of alternatives would be technically the most suitable. The Prime Minister, after discussion with the President, understands that the United States Government will in any case be favourably disposed to the purchase by the United Kingdom at the appropriate time of supplies of a suitable airborne vehicle for the delivery of a British warhead. We shall also be considering the acquisition of a mobile MRBM system. . .'".

A minute containing the US offer of Skybolt and Polaris, handed to the Prime Minister,[2] said of the former:–

"In a desire to be of assistance in improving and extending the effective life of the V-bomber force, the United States, subject only to United States priorities, is prepared to provide Skybolt missiles – minus warheads – to the United Kingdom on a reimbursable basis in 1965 or thereafter. Since Skybolt is still in the early stages of development, this offer is necessarily dependent on the successful and timely completion of its development programme. . . ."

Of Polaris, the minute said:–

"As the United Kingdom is aware, the United States is offering at the current Nato Defence Ministers' meeting to make mobile Polaris missiles – minus warheads – available from US production to Nato countries in order to meet Saceur's requirements for MRBMs. The United States is also offering to assist joint European production of

---

[1] PM(W)(60) 4th Mtg Item 5.

[2] It came from the Hon Douglas Dillon, Under-Secretary of State.

Polaris if our preference for United States production proves unacceptable.

"It does not appear appropriate to consider a bilateral understanding on Polaris until the problem of Saceur's MRBM requirement has been satisfactorily disposed of in Nato".

Approval in principle by the President for the supply of Skybolt to Britain was followed-up later in 1960 by a Memorandum of Understanding signed on 6 June in Washington by the US Secretary of Defense (Mr Thomas S Gates Jr) and the UK Minister of Defence (Mr Harold Watkinson) and by a Technical and Financial Agreement of 27 September between the US Department of the Air Force and the UK Ministry of Aviation. The latter followed an Anglo-American planning conference on Skybolt, held in the Pentagon between 11 and 20 September[1].

The Memorandum of Understanding of 6 June followed closely in spirit and terminology the Camp David exchanges between the President and the Prime Minister. It said that the Secretary of Defense and the Minister of Defence

"express their determination that the two countries shall co-operate in the development of the Skybolt missile to permit it to be adopted both by the United States Air Force and the Royal Air Force.

"Mr Gates affirms the intention of the United States Government to make every reasonable effort to ensure the successful and timely completion of Skybolt development and the compatibility of the missile with Royal Air Force Mk 2 V-bombers[2]; and agrees that Her Majesty's Government intends to place an order with the United States Government for about one hundred missiles and their associated equipment. The warheads would be provided by Her Majesty's Government.

"Mr Gates reaffirms on behalf of the Government of the United States the sale of the Skybolt missile, minus warhead, to Her Majesty's Government shall be as outlined by President Eisenhower in his memorandum to Prime Minister Macmillan on 29 March 1960, as amended[3].

"Mr Gates welcomes Mr Watkinson's offer to provide the services of selected scientific staff to maintain liaison with the US development agency and to co-operate in the development program.

"Mr Gates and Mr Watkinson authorise their staffs to proceed with the negotiations of a technical and financial agreement in accordance with the foregoing".

The Cabinet approved the Minister of Defence proposals for the

---

[1] See ID9/B.19-130 Long Range Powered Guided Bomb – Skybolt – Anglo-American Conference.

[2] Later, Skybolt became applicable only to the Vulcan B.2: see references in an earlier chapter to a reduction in the Mk 2 Victor order, as a result of the anticipated Skybolt/Vulcan force.

[3] See p 410.

acquisition of Skybolt when it discussed them on 20 June 1960[1]. In speaking about his Note[2] on the missile the Minister said that by acquiring 144 of them, with spares and associated equipment,

"we should be able in the later 1960s to maintain with the Vulcan Mk 2 bombers a deterrent force equivalent to that previously planned for Blue Streak. The Victor Mk 2 bombers would not be adapted for Skybolt, but could be a complementary component of the deterrent with a developed version of the British powered bomb Blue Steel, if necessary. It would be in our interest to respond without delay to the American desire to expedite the joint development of Skybolt, in order to ensure that it would be fully compatible with our requirements".

Mr Watkinson added that, "on present estimates", the cost of the British requirement would be between £76 million and £115 million (depending on the unit cost of the missile), with a dollar content of up to £108 million.

The US Department of the Air Force/UK Ministry of Aviation Technical and Financial Agreement of 27 September linked itself, in its introductory paragraph, to the earlier agreements of that year. "Pursuant to the Understandings reached", it said,

"between the President of the United States of America and the Prime Minister of Her Majesty's Government in the United Kingdom on 29 March 1960, and the further Understandings reached between the United States Secretary of Defense and the Minister of Defence of Her Majesty's Government on 6 June 1960 relative to the air-to-surface missile known as Skybolt, the United States Department of the Air Force and the United Kingdom Ministry of Aviation agree to co-operate in the development of the Skybolt missile to permit it to be adopted both by the United States Air Force and the Royal Air Force. This Agreement provides for the co-operative development of the missile, re-entry vehicles and associated equipment, and deals with technical and financial arrangements appertaining thereto. It is understood that at this time this is purely a Research and Development program, no production having been authorised by higher authority".

After this international fanfare – with its reservation that Skybolt was currently "purely an R&D programme" – the Agreement stated three objectives for the Department of the Air Force: that it would make every reasonable effort to ensure "successful and timely completion" of Skybolt development; that it would at all stages "take fully into account" UK requirements for the missile and its associated equipment; and that "provided the missile [was] successfully developed, its compatibility with Vulcan Mk 2 bombers assured and a production programme established and maintained" the Department would make available to the MoA on a reimbursable basis missiles and associated equipment, spare parts and

---

[1] C.(60)97.

[2] Extract from CC(60)35th Conclusions, in ID9/194/4 Blue Steel (including Skybolt).

modification kits and operating data, schedules, etc. Referring to compatibility, the Agreement said that the MoA would make "every reasonable effort" to proceed with a development programme for adaptation of Vulcan Mk 2s – there was no mention of Victors – to carry Skybolt, and that a British warhead, "compatible with a US entry vehicle", would be "selected and provided by the appropriate authorities of the United Kingdom after consultation with the United States Air Force". Under the heading of "exchange of information" the Department agreed to furnish the MoA, after the Agreement came into effect, with a "full disclosure of the progress made in connnection with the development work on the project". Finally, either party was entitled to "terminate its interest in the project at any time" – though neither was to do so without prior consultation with the other.

Thus before the end of 1960 the Royal Air Force was firmly linked to the future supply – though no date or numbers were mentioned in the Agreement, which limited itself to the R&D programme – of an American air-launched ballistic missile for the V-bomber force, to succeed Blue Steel[1].

The possibility of this American ALBM failing to materialise was also considered before that year was out, the British Nuclear Deterrent Study Group deciding on 9 September that a Blue Steel Mk 1A might have some validity[2] and producing a draft report for the Minister of Defence on the 13th. He had asked them to consider "to what extent a developed Blue Steel Mk 1 and/or the TSR.2 would provide until about 1968 a reinsurance against the failure of Skybolt and an independent contribution to the Western nuclear deterrent force". In the case of Blue Steel, the Study Group's report[3] said the choice would lie between "a comparatively simple development", the Mk 1A, increasing the range to 250nm, and a higher-performance variant, the Mk 1*D, which would have a range of 350-440nm but would not be in service until 1965/66. BNDSG did not recommend developing any version of the latter; as to the former, they were awaiting a further paper from the Air Staff[4]. As to TSR.2, it could be regarded as an insurance against the failure of Skybolt in the sense that "if Skybolt were to be cancelled we could say

---

[1] The Minister of Defence also asked the BNDSG to consider whether, in addition, an improved version of Blue Steel and a missile for launching from TSR.2 should be developed (Chairman's Memorandum, 6 Sep 60, in TS 407/101/024/63, Pt III – Possible Future Nuclear Deterrent Weapon System (British Nuclear Deterrent BND)).

[2] Minutes, BND(SG)(60) 2nd Mtg in Development & Production of Power-guided Bomb (Blue Steel) ID3/946/8 (S) (Pt 2). However, on 10 May 60 the BNDSG concluded that there was no justification on any grounds for ordering a Blue Steel Mk 1A system (BND(SG)(60) 4th Mtg (Ibid)).

[3] BND(SG)(60)10.

[4] The Air Ministry view, in a subsequent Note (circulated on 19 Sep 60), was that the Mk 1A would offer "certain advantages" over the Mk 1 though it would be "subject to serious limitations". Even its "marginal advantages" from an operational standpoint would be desirable, "provided that achieving them did not further delay the development of Blue Steel Mk 1" (TS 407/101/024/63, Pt II – Possible Future Nuclear Deterrent Weapon System (British Nuclear Deterrent BND)).

that we were producing a British contribution to the deterrent which should outlast the Blue Steel system".

However, on 10 November the BNDSG concluded that there was no justification on any grounds for ordering a Blue Steel Mk 1A system, and on the 24th the Minister of Defence (Mr Harold Watkinson) approved this recommendation in a minute to the Minister of Aviation (Mr Peter Thorneycroft), saying he was sure that "all the firm's effort should be concentrated on getting the Mk 1 into service as quickly as possible". This followed a meeting with his Departmental officials on the 22nd[1] when they discussed the BNDSG report, the Minister saying that he accepted its findings[2]; the main thing was "to get Blue Steel Mk 1 into service as quickly as possible and not to divert the firm's resources from this task".

CDS (Lord Mountbatten) said he was "deeply concerned" about the BNDSG recommendation "that no further action should be taken at present in respect of American weapons" – which he took to mean that "we were to rule out altogether the purchase of Polaris submarines as a possible alternative to Skybolt". The group's secretary (Sir Edward Playfair) pointed out, however, that this recommendation had been deliberately qualified by the words "at present". In his summing-up the Minister asked the Chief Scientific Adviser (Sir Solly Zuckerman) "to prepare questions on the possibility of the independent operation and deployment of Polaris submarines, if we acquired some from the Americans".

Subsequently the BNDSG looked into different categories of weapon system which might be used by the UK for maintaining a nuclear deterrent in the 1970–80 period, and in a report of 27 July 1961 its Technical Sub-committee came down in favour of the Polaris submarine system as against the Skybolt airborne system[3].

The successive Skybolt Understandings, leading to the US/UK Technical and Financial Agreement of 27 September 1960, have already been described. On 24 November the first Skybolt Weapon System Steering Group meeting was held at the Air Ministry. But although at the first Anglo-American conference on Skybolt (held at Wright-Patterson AFB, Ohio, HQ, Air Research and Development Command, from 12 to 20 September 1960) the British delegation had been assured that the programme was being given, and would continue to be given,

---

[1] MM 51/60 (TS 407/101/024/63 Pt III – Possible Future Nuclear Deterrent Weapon System (British Nuclear Deterrent BND)).

[2] On 5 Dec the Minister of Aviation (Mr P Thorneycroft) said he welcomed the Minister of Defence's decision about Blue Steel Mk 1A and Mk 1S and had arranged for the firm to be told immediately (ibid).

[3] BND(TSC)(61)(Final) in MO.26/10/1 Pt I British Nuclear Deterrent Study Group. On 16 Nov 60 the Air Staff had sent to the MoA ASR No 1182 A Long-range Air-to-Surface Weapon. This was to have a range of up to 1,000nm; it was to be in operational service by 1966 and was to serve as an insurance against the non-delivery of Skybolt (AHB file ID9/194/4 Sub-folder 3 of 3 - Blue Steel July/Dec 1960).

top development priority[1] some doubt about its future had become evident before the end of that year. In London during December 1960 the US Secretary of Defense told the UK Minister of Defence that the programme was being slowed down, and by early the following year the seed of cancellation was in the air: during January 1961 the Strategic Weapons Panel of the US President's Science Advisory Committee recommended that Skybolt should be cancelled[2].

Development progressed satisfactorily, however, and the programme continued to receive DoD funding. When the Secretary of Defense (Mr Robert McNamara) visited the Douglas Aircraft Co on 26 September 1961 and learnt that this funding was "marginal" he called for a new budget plan by 10 October – "to reflect all the cash [needed] for the job"[3]. During a courtesy call on the Secretary of State for Air on 3 October the Secretary of the US Air Force (Mr Eugene Zuckert) said he was pleased with the progress of the programme, which he felt was going well, though it was bound to have its ups and downs[4].

1962 proved to be the climacteric year for Skybolt – though at its outset the auguries seemed favourable for the RAF, the Treasury on 24 January having approved an establishment of 28 officers and 193 airmen for the British Joint Trials Force at Eglin Air Force Base in Florida: set up from June 1962 onwards, the BJTF was commanded by Wg Cdr C E Ness[5]. The ALBM was now an Operational Requirement for the Royal Air Force: Air Staff Requirement No 1187, issued on 26 April 1961 and to be reissued on 29 August 1962, had stated that

"To maintain an effective deterrent in the face of the expected improvement in Russian air defence by 1964, the Government of the United States and Her Majesty's Government have agreed to co-operate in the development of the Skybolt weapon system. The weapon is to be compatible with both the USAF B-52 and the RAF Vulcan B Mk 2 installations. . . ."

The aim of the ASR, and the time-scale for the weapon, were specifically stated:–

"The Air Staff require an air-launched ballistic missile to be carried by and launched from a Vulcan B Mk 2 aircraft; the weapon system to be as stated in US GOR177 and its performance to be at least equal to that accepted for the Skybolt/B-52 weapon system. The weapon system is required to be in Royal Air Force operational service in the last quarter of 1964."

The warhead was to be British, the subject of a separate Operational Requirement:–

"The warhead for the Skybolt/Vulcan weapon system will be of British

---

[1] Report to MoD by DRS (Gp Capt Fryer).
[2] Aide memoire, Thorneycroft–McNamara meeting, 11 Dec 62.
[3] Telegram, DRS to MoD, 2 Oct 61.
[4] Minute, PS to S of S/PS to CAS, etc.
[5] Later, Air Mshl Sir Charles Ness.

design and is specified in OR1179. . . ."

There was to be an initial purchase of 100 missiles and 90 warheads[1].

But despite British plans for the acquisition of Skybolt, and for its introduction into Bomber Command, there were signs on the American side that all was not well with the programme. The Secretary of Defense had indicated to the UK Minister of Defence in December 1961 (as became clear subsequently, from an *aide-memoire* presented just before the project was cancelled) that there were reservations as to whether all the technical problems could be solved. Certainly it was a very complex system, containing more than 150,000 component parts, and 60,000 components had to function to accomplish the launch of a missile. The first four live launches, during 1962, were not successful; and these failures, added to development difficulties and rising costs, must have contributed to the decision to end the programme. In the first live launch, from a B-52 on 19 April, the second stage motor failed to ignite; in the second, on 29 June, the first stage motor did not ignite correctly and the missile was destroyed by the range safety officer; in the third, on 13 September, it was destroyed after veering off course; and in the fourth, on 25 September, the second stage burned for only 15sec.

When the British Nuclear Deterrent Study Group, at its meeting on 26 October 1962[2], considered possible alternatives to Skybolt, it envisaged either a British hybrid submarine force (that is, of submarines combining the hunter/killer with the missile-firing role) plus an extension of the V-bomber/Blue Steel combination; or a British hybrid submarine force, though meanwhile hiring or buying a small number of Polaris submarines from the United States.

In the wake of the BNDSG meeting, and at the behest of VCAS (Air Mshl Sir Wallace Kyle), a paper was produced in November 1962 on the Implications of an American Decision to Cancel Skybolt[3]. This said that "current plans" envisaged "the initial introduction of Skybolt in 1964/65, building-up to an effective operational capability during 1966". Prior to that, the deterrent would be maintained by Mk 1 and Mk 2 V-bombers armed with free-falling bombs and by Mk 2 V-bombers carrying Blue Steel Mk 1, all operating from a ground alert posture in an emergency[4]. In the event of Skybolt being cancelled, the paper considered that there were six possible alternative weapon systems: Hound Dog; Blue Steel variants; Bristol X-12; a momentum bomb; Minuteman; and lay-down bombs. Hound Dog was the stand-off cruise-type missile currently in USAF service; it could not be used by the V-bombers or TSR.2 on account of its size. There were two possible developments of Blue Steel Mk 1 – the 1A with a range of up to 250nm,

---

[1] S of S Progress Meeting, 16 Jul 62 (S of S/M (62)6).

[2] BNDSG/M(62)6.

[3] Sent as a draft to VCAS on 21 Nov 62 (in AHB file ID9/B.19-190 Bombers - Long Range Powered Guided – Skybolt – Nassau Conference 1962).

[4] The paper averred that from about the time when the Skybolt force would be operational, enemy resources would demand an airborne alert capability.

a climb to 70/75,000ft and a Mach 3 cruise; and 1S with a 400nm range, peak altitude of 85,000ft and Mach 3.5 maximum cruising speed. The possibility of reviving the Blue Steel Mk 2 project[1] had not been considered because it would be in the same time-scale as the X-12 missile, a ram-jet project by BAC to OR1182[2]: this had a predicted maximum range of 1,150nm, a climb to 70/76,000ft and a Mach 4 cruising speed. The momentum bomb "would be unpowered but would take advantage of its own aerodynamic qualities and the high speed and upward direction of the launching aircraft to achieve its range". Minuteman, the paper suggested, could not pose an effective deterrent unless ordered in very large numbers; although it was "a harder target" than Blue Streak, its vulnerability to a pre-emptive attack was not "significantly different". Suitable lay-down bombs could be developed by 1966–67 and could be delivered both by TSR.2 and by the Mk 2 V-bombers in the low-level role.

The paper enumerated the "main advantages" of the Skybolt system: it posed a ballistic missile threat to targets well inside the Soviet Union; attacks could be launched from outside the range of Soviet air defences[3]; two Skybolts could be carried by each V-bomber; and an airborne alert could be maintained without flight refuelling because of the missile's long range.

On 11 December the US Secretary of Defense and the UK Minister of Defence met to talk about Skybolt and other projects, Mr McNamara presenting Mr Thorneycroft with an *aide-memoire* setting-out the reasons which had led the US Government to a "tentative conclusion" that the Skybolt development programme should be abandoned as far as the United States was concerned. It referred to the technical complexity of the weapon, particularly in respect of its guidance system and potential reliability in service: while it was "by no means impossible" for Skybolt to be successfully produced, Mr McNamara felt that neither the time-scale in which this could be done, nor the missile's expected reliability, were such as to make it "a really worthwhile weapon". The US Government were not contemplating abandoning Skybolt because it was a complete technical failure but because, in view of the difficulties which had surrounded its development and the progress of various other nuclear delivery systems, they did not feel that continuing the programme would be an advantageous expenditure of money.

Reviewing the history of the programme, the *aide-memoire* said that [early in 1961] the Strategic Weapons Panel of the President's Science Advisory Committee had recommended that it be cancelled. Cancellation had subsequently been "seriously considered" at the time of the

---

[1] This (to OR1159) had been cancelled on 1 Jan 60.

[2] BAC's brochure described this as "a long-range air-launched ramjet-powered deterrent weapon"; it was to be in operational service with the V-force by 1966.

[3] A sketch map of Skybolt Release Areas (Appendix "B" to BF/S605/DD Ops(B)) shows these over the UK, Scandinavia and Southern France/Northern Italy.

FY1963 budget review, in the autumn of 1961, but was rejected – "as a result of balancing hopes for timely resolution of technical problems against doubts about the availability of other systems". It was still believed that Skybolt could be made to work; but questions as to when it would work, and how well, were "receiving increasingly discouraging answers".

The *aide-memoire* recalled that the original US offer of Skybolt was made "in a desire to be of assistance in . . . extending the effective life of the V-bomber force"; that in the USAF/MoA technical and financial agreement of September 1960 the project was referred to as "purely a research and development programme, no production having been authorised"; and that in December 1960 Secretary Gates had met Mr Watkinson in London and told him the programme was being slowed down because of technical doubts among US scientists.

Mr Watkinson (the *aide-memoire* continued) acknowledged that his Government had always understood that Skybolt was a research and development project, subject to the uncertainty associated with such projects. In subsequent Parliamentary debates he had made it clear that the US commitment to provide Skybolt to the British was contingent on a successful US development, and stated that the Government had made "other plans" in the event of Skybolt not being successful. In December 1961 Secretary McNamara, in talks with Mr Watkinson, indicated that the United States still had reservations as to whether all the technical problems of Skybolt could be solved; in May 1962 he pointed out that no production programme had been outlined "as of that time"; and in September 1962 talks with Mr Thorneycroft he referred to further increases in Skybolt costs. After mentioning the double R&D costs over three years, the *aide-memoire* said that of the five live test launches conducted so far, all five had been unsuccessful. It referred to the complexity of the system: approximately 60,000 components had to function to accomplish the launch of a single missile, and the weapon had more than 150,000 components parts. It went on to suggest three possibilities:–

(1) the United Kingdom Government might wish to continue the Skybolt programme, either through a cut-back production programme in the United States, or UK production employing US technology; (2) Hound Dog might be adapted to British aircraft; or (3) the UK Government might wish to participate in a sea-based MRBM force under multilateral manning and ownership.

In the record of the 11 December 1962 meeting between the heads of the American and British defence departments the point was made that it was by no means impossible for the Skybolt system to be successfully produced; but Mr McNamara felt that neither the time-scale within which this could be done, nor the expected reliability of the system, were such as to make it a really worthwhile weapon. Mr Thorneycroft described Skybolt as central to British defence policy[1]: agreement on it had formed part of a complex of decisions which included the grant to the United States of facilities at Holy Loch[2]. He said that, of the three possibilities mentioned, only the first was a starter; and added after some more exchanges that the cost of taking over the Skybolt programme would be very great. Although it was the only starter among the alternatives, it still seemed unsatisfactory since Mr McNamara himself had indicated that he had little faith that Skybolt would ever be a really satisfactory operational weapon system: it seemed therefore that the best alternative might be Polaris.

Mr Thorneycroft went on to enquire about US reactions to a suggestion that the UK should build its own submarines and manufacture its own warheads, but should purchase from the US the Polaris missiles, with their associated control systems. There would be a gap in time between when Blue Steel ceased to be a credible deterrent and when the British Polaris force could become operational; this could be about four years, and to fill it he suggested that the UK might hire from the US some submarines complete with missile systems. (When Mr McNamara emphasised the costs, and legal difficulties over the sale of Polaris because of certain nuclear information in their firing systems, Mr Thorneycroft said that the system was probably the only workable alternative and it might be better to spend more money in order to get a really effective and credible deterrent.)

It was believed in the Ministry of Defence that the technical difficulties of Skybolt had been overstated, and that its development could be completed successfully; however, if the US Government could not be persuaded of this, the alternatives were (1) to acquire Polaris, (2) to pay for completion of Skybolt in the US, (3) to complete Skybolt in Britain, or (4) to join with the French in producing a ballistic weapon. A draft paper prepared for the Minister of Defence estimated that to complete a missile based on Skybolt in the UK and to get it into service would take about eight years (*ie* to 1970) and cost £250 million for R&D with a further £60 million for production. If a new carrier were required – probably a long-range subsonic aircraft to replace obsolescent Vulcans – some £150 million would be added to the costs. One MoD view on the US *aide-memoire* explaining the Skybolt decision was that it was a dishonest paper, attempting to justify a conclusion already reached for other motives[3]. Another, pragmatic view of the future of the British strategic nuclear deterrent force[4] was that the arguments used to support the claims made for the V-force armed with Skybolt (*ie*,

---

[1] A phrase almost echoed in 1967 by the then Minister of Defence (Mr Denis Healey) when he described the Anglo-French (BAC-Dassault) variable-geometry project as "the core of our long-term industrial and aircraft programme". Like Skybolt, the AFVG was cancelled.
[2] *Ie* for USN Polaris submarines.
[3] CMS 3515/DOR(C), 14 Dec 62.
[4] VCAS.7452, same date.

penetration of, and immunity from, Soviet defences) proved that, short of continuing with the development of Skybolt, the only weapon system of comparable effectiveness would be the Polaris submarine.

According to messages from Washington to London at the time of the McNamara–Thorneycroft talks, Skybolt had its supporters in the United States. On 14 December a telex from DRS Washington to the MoA quoted from a memorandum to the Secretary of Defense from the Secretary of the Air Force, following the latter's meeting with Douglas, Aerojet and Northrop principals[1] to examine the status of the programme. This memorandum said that "no basic technical problem" had appeared in the programme, and that if the expected success with the guided launches was achieved, development would be on schedule. The view was expressed that there were "no grounds for cancellation on technical considerations". But the message added: "Rubel[2] reported to be exploring possible alternatives, including three separate Polaris submarine concepts submitted recently to him by the Chief Scientific Adviser, MoD". Another message, on the following day[3], said that the USAF, in the person of General Curtis LeMay, its Chief of Staff, were in favour of continuing with Skybolt – otherwise their manned deterrent ended with the B-52/Hound Dog combination.

These meetings and messages were all preparatory to the decisive President Kennedy – Prime Minister Macmillan talks of 18–21 December 1962 at Nassau in the Bahamas. A brief prepared for the Prime Minister by the MoD had said that none of the three alternatives proposed by Mr McNamara in his talks with Mr Thorneycroft were acceptable; it urged that a strong case should be put to the President for continuing with Skybolt, or making available an alternative weapon system, a submarine-based rocket. The alternative of Hound Dog had been considered but turned down by the RAF, mainly on two grounds: that major modifications would be required to fit it to Mk 2 Vulcans and Victors, and that it could not be introduced into service in less than four or five years.

The Nassau decisions – to cancel Skybolt while offering to continue its development on a US/UK 50/50 basis (an offer which was not accepted) and to provide Polaris instead – were embodied, with a US alternative offer of Hound Dog and a British proposal to assign forces to Nato, in a joint Statement on Nuclear Defence Systems. This was one of the *communiqués* issued after the talks, and of the ALBM it said:–

"The President and the Prime Minister reviewed the development programme for the Skybolt missile. The President explained that it was no longer expected that this very complex weapon system would be completed within the cost estimate or the time-scale which were

---

[1] With Douglas as main contractor, Aerojet-General were responsible for the propulsion system and Nortronics Division of Northrop for guidance.

[2] Dr Rubel, deputy to Dr York, DoD Director of Research and Engineering.

[3] Emson, RAFS Washington, to AM, 15 Dec 62.

projected when the programme was begun.

"The President informed the Prime Minister that for this reason and because of the availability to the United States of alternative weapon systems, he had decided to cancel plans for the production of Skybolt by the United States.

"Nevertheless, recognising the importance of the Skybolt programme for the United Kingdom, and recalling that the purpose of the offer of Skybolt in 1960 had been to assist in improving and extending the effective life of the British V-bombers, the President expressed his readiness to continue with the development of the missile as a joint enterprise between the United States and the United Kingdom, with each country bearing equal shares of the future cost of completing development, after which the United Kingdom would be able to place a production order to meet its requirements"[1].

The Prime Minister, "while recognising the value of this offer", decided not to avail himself of it "because of doubts that had been expressed about the prospects of success for this weapon system and because of uncertainty regarding date of completion and final costs of the programme". When Hound Dog was offered as an alternative he could not accept "in the light of technical difficulties".

When the possibility of the US providing Polaris was discussed, the two leaders agreed that any decision "must be considered in the widest context both of the future defence of the Atlantic Alliance and of the safety of the whole free world"; that the issue "created an opportunity for the development of new and closer arrangements for the organisation and control of strategic Western defence". The Prime Minister suggested, and the President agreed, that a start could be made "by subscribing to Nato some part of the force already in existence. This could include allocations from US strategic forces, from UK Bomber Command, and from tactical nuclear forces now held in Europe. Such forces would be assigned as part of a Nato nuclear force and targeted in accordance with Nato plans".

British submarine forces developed under the Polaris agreement were to be "assigned and targeted" in this way; the agreement itself said that the US would

"make available on a continuing basis Polaris missiles (less warheads) for British submarines. The United States will also study the feasibility of making available certain port facilities for such submarines. The United Kingdom Government will construct the submarines in which these weapons will be placed and they will also provide the nuclear warheads for the Polaris missiles".

The agreement added that

"these forces, and at least equal United States forces, would be made available for inclusion in a Nato multilateral nuclear force".

---

[1] Cmnd 1915. The Air Staff Requirement No 1187 for an Air-launched Ballistic Missile System was eventually cancelled on 22 Feb 63 (ID/47/297 (Pt 4) Skybolt Policy).

The Skybolt programme was officially terminated by the USAF on 31 December 1962. Thus the end of that year was a watershed for the Air Staff and for Bomber Command: responsibility for strategic nuclear deterrence, held by the RAF since the mid-1950s, was to be handed-over to the Royal Navy. A note of 28 December 1962[1] perhaps summed-up current feelings: "Most unfortunately Skybolt is gone. Attacking Polaris will not bring it back. . . . [We] must accept that and turn all our energies to building-up the Royal Air Force to fill a 'limited war' role". The Minister of Defence, reporting on 2 January 1963 to the Defence Board on the Bahamas talks[2], made the cogent point that the UK would have to ensure the credibility of its deterrent in the interval before Polaris became available.

On the day the Nassau talks concluded the Minister of Aviation (Mr Julian Amery) wrote to S of S for Air (Mr Hugh Fraser) to put to him[3] the alternatives as far as the RAF were concerned. He said that the "decision to take Polaris instead of Skybolt" implied that the credibility of Bomber Command's deterrent force would "decline between 1965 and 1970/72", and if this were correct it was important to take decisions as soon as possible. He asked the Air Minister to consider five questions:–

Would more Blue Steels be wanted, either the present or the stretched versions? Could TSR.2 be used in a strategic deterrent role, and would a lay-down bomb be wanted? Should the development of a weapon such as Pandora (OR1182)[4] be considered as an insurance against delay or defection in the Polaris programme? Would more advanced ECM be wanted to extend Bomber Command's penetrative power? Would more tankers be wanted?

He proposed a meeting in the New Year (1963) to discuss "these and any other suggestions" S of S might wish to raise.

One critic of the Nassau decision was MRAF Sir Dermot Boyle, who in a letter to the *Financial Times* of 1 February 1963 complained of a "disquieting aspect of the whole business" – the way in which a major military decision seemed to have been taken without proper prior consultation with, or agreement of, the three Chiefs of Staff. This point was further taken up by another ex-CAS, MRAF Sir John Slessor, who in a letter to *The Times* of 6 February 1963 complained of the Government's not making proper use of the Cabinet Defence Committee, and of dichotomy between foreign and defence policy.

The CAS himself (MRAF Sir Thomas Pike) asked some pertinent questions about RAF responsibility for strategic nuclear deterrence up to 1970: What improvements could be made to Blue Steel? What

---

[1] DCAS 7111/62.
[2] At which neither the CNS nor CAS were present.
[3] Correspondence in file Bombers – The Deterrent: Maintaining the Deterrent beyond 1970 (ID9/B.1-60).
[4] ASR1182 was for a long-range air-to-surface missile (see later references).

measures could be taken in the ECM (electronic countermeasures) field to improve the V-force's capability to penetrate Russian defences? What would be the implications and time-scale of developing a lay-down bomb with a megaton warhead to enable the force to operate at low level? And could anything be done to improve TSR.2's strategic potentiality in the late 1960s?[1] He also asked about measures to give TSR.2 a valid strategic capability in the 1970s if a fully independent Polaris force did not materialise, and what could be done to create a valid airborne deterrent in any other form in the 1970s?[2]

Air Staff thoughts on these questions were as follows: there would be no value in getting more Mk 1 Blue Steels (100nm range if launched at high altitude); a stretched Mk 1 (250nm) would not give value for money; the Mk 2 (750nm) version, in service by about 1969, would be too late to give value for money; while Pandora (a BAC ram-jet missile project)[3], costing £100 million and taking not less than eight years to develop, was too late to be relevant to the 1960s. TSR.2 was considered to be "only . . . a longer-term possibility". Possible low-level operations by the V-bombers, carrying a lay-down bomb of megaton-range yield, would improve their chances of survival over Russia. Views for the 1960s therefore included the following: not to increase the Blue Steel order, or to develop it further; not to attempt to maintain an airborne alert capability; to develop a lay-down bomb for the V-bombers and to study further the possible merits of wider dispersal by the V-force[4].

On 31 December 1962 CAS minuted the Secretary of State on The Deterrent 1965–1970[5] to say that he had undertaken to provide a summary of measures needed to improve the V-force's capability in the later 1960s, and an initial survey had suggested the following:–

(a) maintaining a front line of 72 UE Vulcans and 16 UE Victors. 48 UE would be armed with Blue Steel and the remaining 40 UE with free-falling bombs;

(b) giving high priority to the development, for the "free-fall" V-bombers, of a lay-down bomb with a yield in the megaton range. (The same weapon could be used later with TSR.2);

(c) making minor modifications to the navigation and bombing fit of the V-bombers to enable them to operate at low level;

(d) probably needing, in order to improve the chance of penetration, to augment the V-bombers' ECM fit – with a view particularly to low-level operation;

(e) possible provision for wider dispersal, including perhaps the use of overseas bases.

---

[1] Minute, PS to CAS/ACAS(OR), recording discussion on 27 Dec 62.
[2] A development contract for TSR.2 had been placed in Oct 60.
[3] This proposal (to OR1182) was for a ram-jet missile of 900nm range.
[4] Air Staff note sent to CAS by S of S as briefing for his meeting with the Minister of Defence, 28 Dec 62.
[5] CAS, 3860.

On New Year's Eve 1962 – a day when times past and things to come are traditionally celebrated – the Ministers of Defence and Aviation and the Secretary of State for Air met, with CAS in attendance, to consider the situation created by the cancellation of Skybolt and the proposed provision of Polaris[1]. The Minister of Defence said there were two problems to consider: measures which could be taken to close any gap in the British strategic deterrent before 1970, and the question of a reinsurance against the risk that the Americans might not supply Polaris missiles.

In discussion of the gap it was pointed out that from about 1965 the credibility of the deterrent would diminish; bombers would find it increasingly difficult to get through and this problem would be very serious from 1967 – when the Skybolt force would have been completed – until 1970, when the Polaris system would be in service. Among the more promising means of improving the deterrent during this period were (i) an improvement in electronic countermeasures; (ii) a greater degree of dispersal of aircraft – which would involve the lengthening of runways and provision of new buildings, but not the construction of new airfields; and (iii) the development of a lay-down megaton bomb which would enable the V-bombers to make low-level attacks and the TSR.2 to contribute to the strategic deterrent.

Another possibility was to increase the range of Blue Steel – "to 250 miles in about four years, at relatively small cost" – but aircraft carrying it had to be flying at 40,000ft or more when it was released and would therefore be vulnerable. Or, as low-flying V-bombers would be vulnerable to guided weapons of the PT.428 or Mauler type[2], it might be useful to develop OR1168 – a tactical air-to-surface guided weapon for TSR.2 – to carry a megaton warhead.

When the Ministers discussed reinsurance against the risk that Polaris might not become available, the Minister of Aviation said that – subject to confirmation after further study – a British Skybolt or Polaris-type missile could be developed by 1971/72; it might be possible to develop a Pandora-type missile with a total range of 1,250 miles, of which 550 could be at low level; and the possibility that Black Knight[3] might be developed into a ballistic missile was mentioned.

At the end of the meeting the Minister of Defence asked Sir Robert Scott and Sir Solly Zuckerman[4] to arrange for a paper to be presented to him by 15 January, recommending what action should be taken to extend the credibility of the deterrent from 1965 to 1970. On reinsurance, he thought it not possible to build and buy Polaris and also to develop an alternative.

The main operational advantages of Skybolt, it had been pointed out

---

[1] MM(62)31.
[2] Cancelled BAC and US (GD) surface-to-air missiles.
[3] Ballistic research rocket.
[4] Respectively PS, MoD, and Chief Scientific Adviser to the Minister of Defence.

in an Air Staff paper on the future of the deterrent[1], had been its range of 1,000 miles and the fact that two could be carried on one Vulcan – which meant that an airborne alert could be maintained reasonably economically without resort to flight refuelling, and the fact that all its flight would have been ballistic – making it immune to the growing SAM defences which were expected to make penetration by aircraft and cruise-type missiles at high altitude impossible during the era under consideration (1965–70). Any substitute weapons, therefore (the paper concluded), "must be judged by the extent to which they reproduce these capabilities".

The Air Staff said in December 1962 that the V-force front line planned for the later 1960s was 72 (UE – unit establishment) Vulcans and 16 (UE) Victors, a total of 88 (UE) V-bombers. There were enough Blue Steels to equip 48 (UE) of them, leaving 40(UE) to use free-falling bombs. This force would not be able to pose a threat as large as the planned Skybolt force would have done.

The Skybolt programme, as far as the RAF was concerned, formally ended on 3 January 1963 – when the Ministry of Defence stated that "the decision not to proceed with Skybolt should be regarded as taken in the statement issued at the end of the Nassau discussions". Accordingly, action to "wind up. . . the programme" was to "proceed forthwith"[2].

Easier said than done, for the programme had international and widespread implications, and the immediate problem was how to extend the credibility of the airborne deterrent in the pre-Polaris period. As for the immediate effects on the RAF, when the Air Council Standing Committee had considered these on 31 December they dealt with the "phased withdrawal of Service and other staffs in the United States" – *ie* those in Washington and the 200-odd personnel plus dependents at Eglin AFB, Florida, forming the British Joint Trials Force; cancellation of the Skybolt course at RAF Newton; the possibility of restoring cuts made under the Defence Review economies; unfavourable publicity about future prospects of the RAF, resulting from the cancellation decision, which could affect recruiting adversely; and whether the USAF might give up any of their bases in the UK as a result of the cancellation, thereby affecting the proposal to allocate Gaydon to Transport Command. These were housekeeping matters; and there were industrial effects: on 28 December a list had been issued of 15 development contracts which had been terminated[3]: these included, for example, a main contract with the USAF for missiles and equipment for R&D trials of Skybolt/Vulcan; a main development contract with A V Roe for adapting Vulcans to the Skybolt role; and another with A V Roe

---

[1] Future of the Deterrent, Pt I 1965–1970 – DCAS 629/63 in Bombers – The Deterrent Future of the Deterrent (ID9/B.1 65, Pt 1).

[2] Minute, AUS(A)/PS to CAS, AMP, AMSO and others, 3 Jan 63.

[3] US/AirB, 28 Dec 62.

for trial installation of an improved heading reference system[1]. The value of these contracts amounted to over £15 million. Thus the abrupt termination of Skybolt development resulted in a violent jar not only to RAF plans but also to commercial arrangements.

The problem of how to extend the credibility of the airborne deterrent so as to cover the time before Polaris was introduced into service – the so-called "missile gap" – resulted in a flurry of discussions and papers from the end of 1962 until well into the spring of 1963. As has been seen, CAS initiated discussions on 27 December[2] and subsequently provided a brief for the Secretary of State for the latter's meeting with the Ministers of Defence and Aviation on 31 December. The decisions as to what should be done – development of a high-yield lay-down bomb and measures to enable the V-bombers to operate at low level – were made in January 1963 but their practical implications continued to be discussed for several months.

The parameters of this decision-making extended until March, when the Air Council discussed a paper on Bomber Command 1963–70 and initiated the relevant executive actions[3]. Previously the Defence Committee had approved proposals by the Minister of Defence[4], which had been formulated in consultation with the Air Staff. Other bodies which had made contributions to thinking on the post-Skybolt, pre-Polaris deterrent policy were the Defence Research Policy Committee and the British Nuclear Deterrent Study Group; and at the end of January the Government had asked for Parliamentary approval of the Statement on Nuclear Defence Systems issued at the end of the Nassau talks[5].

During January 1963 there were intensive discussions on future deterrent policy and the means by which it could be implemented. On the 2nd the DRPC (AES – atomic energy sub-committee) had recommended the development of a high-yield lay-down bomb[6] on the highest priority; it had asked for the comments of the Chiefs of Staff on this recommendation before it was sent to the Minister of Defence. At an informal CoS meeting on the 3rd the Chief Scientific Adviser (Sir Solly Zuckerman) reviewed the implications of weapons and weapon development following the Nassau agreement. He said that the MoD (though not the Treasury) had approved the development of a low-yield lay-down bomb to ASR1177, for use with the TSR.2 or Buccaneer; this would cost, for R&D on the bomb casing, £10 million. At the cost of a further £1 million the same case could be developed to take a high-yield warhead which could be used by the V-bombers.

---

[1] Heading reference system trials were made during 1962 and a Vulcan B.2 had dropped a dummy Skybolt for the first time on 1 Dec 61 (Summary of Progress, No 1/62).

[2] Minute, PS to CAS/ACAS (OR) (CAS.3830) in file Bombers – Long-range Powered Guided Bombs – Skybolt – Long-term Effects of Cancellation.

[3] Conclusions, 14 March 63 (4(63)).

[4] Memorandum D(63)2, considered at 23 Jan 63 meeting.

[5] Commons Hansard, Cols 955-1074 and 1139-1260, 30-31 Jan 63.

[6] A low-yield lay-down bomb was already under development.

CSA went on to say that the remaining cost of the Skybolt warhead programme had been estimated in the previous March as £24 million, and that at a cost of a further £1 million the same programme could be adapted for the development of the proposed high-yield lay-down bomb/warhead. The net extra cost of the proposed high-yield lay-down bomb would therefore be about £25 million, less some saving to be expected on development of the low-yield lay-down warhead. Some part of the £24 million would already have been committed since last March.

This CSA proposal was to be subsequently endorsed at a CoS meeting on 15 January[1], when it was considered in the context of a draft memorandum by the Minister of Defence on the future of the deterrent[2], of which the committee "took note". This paper was subsequently endorsed by the Defence Committee on 23 January and became the basis of future strategic nuclear deterrent policy in the period before the introduction of Polaris submarines.

The Minister of Defence memorandum had first been circulated in draft form on 10 January[3]; its main assumptions were that the credibility of the V-force equipped only with Blue Steel and free-falling bombs and operating at high altitude would diminish beyond 1965; that it was impossible to have an adequate Polaris deployment before 1969 with 16-missile submarines, or before 1971 with the eight-missile type; and that the current UK defence burden required that expenditure on deterrence should be restricted to the minimum level consistent with credibility.

The draft memorandum said that additional measures in the defence field could have one or more objectives – improving the capability, and therefore the credibility, of the V-force between 1965 and the date of Polaris entering service; and reinsuring, from within UK resources, against a failure to obtain Polaris. The Minister added, however, that he did not consider it would make sense to work on any other assumption than that detailed negotiations with the Americans would give the UK a Polaris force, and that this would provide an adequate deterrent "with the TSR.2 as a useful back-up". If the best course had been to proceed with a separate development, the right choice would have been to complete Skybolt, but this had been rejected. His recommendation was that UK efforts should be limited "to such additional measures in the deterrent field as will show worthwhile results within two or three years after 1965". The steps he proposed related to the V-force and TSR.2; they were based on the Air Staff assessment that, beyond the mid-1960s, the V-bombers must go in at low level if they were to penetrate the Russian defences. Trials by Bomber Command and experience with the training of the Valiant squadrons assigned to Saceur had convinced the

---

[1] 3rd mtg 63.
[2] COS1082/14/1/63.
[3] At their meeting on 15 Jan the CoS Cttee referred to the speed with which it had been produced and the limited opportunities they had had to consider it.

Air Staff that low-level attack by the V-bombers was practicable operationally.

The Minister said that he proposed to leave current plans for the run-down of Bomber Command unaltered; this meant that the front-line strength of 120 would decline to 88, made up wholly of Mk 2 Vulcans and Victors, which would remain in service until the advent of Polaris. TSR.2 would come into service towards the end of the decade, and although intended for a tactical role, could "provide useful strategic support". There would be no change in plans to operate on ground alert from 36 dispersal airfields.

Referring to the implications of low-level operations by the bomber force, the memorandum said that a decision was required on adapting the low-yield lay-down bomb being designed for TSR.2 to carry a high-yield warhead and to arm both the V-bombers and TSR.2. It might also be feasible to convert Blue Steel Mk 1s for release at low altitude – if so, weapons on order should be modified on high priority.

The Minister suggested that as a first step towards achieving the ability to bomb from low level, Mk 1 V-bombers should convert to a low-level role during 1963, using existing weapons – though these would not be satisfactory in the long term, but dropping height might be reduced "by a comparatively simple modification". The number of weapons required needed to be studied further: instead of the warheads approved for Skybolt[1] there would be the same number of high-yield warheads for lay-down bombs; in addition, of the warheads for lay-down bombs approved for TSR.2, about half would be provided in the high-yield version. He added that navigation equipment for the low-level role being provided for Valiants assigned to Saceur should be provided for the whole of the V-force, and that further study was required of the possibility of equipping the force with additional ECM equipment for low-level operations. As to the costs, he considered that capital and running costs of the strategic bomber front line in the 1960s and its deployment should remain broadly unchanged, since there were no proposals to change the size of the front line, the number of airfields or the peacetime rates of training. About £100 million would be saved through the cancellation of Skybolt; the main item of additional new expenditure would be on the high-yield version of the lay-down weapon being designed for TSR.2 – the cost of this proposal being estimated at about £5 million for R&D and £10.5 million for production.

In conclusion, the Minister of Defence invited the Cabinet, "subject to the normal processes of inter-Departmental consultation, to approve a programme limited to the measures proposed in this paper for the improvement of the deterrent capacity of the V-bomber force and for the arming of the TSR.2 to enable it to operate in the strategic deterrent role".

---

[1] Under the agreements, these were to be British-made.

On 11 January, the day after the Memorandum had been circulated, the Defence Research Policy Committee met to consider V-bomber low-level capability[1]. The committee had before them a Note by DCAS (Air Mshl R B Lees) suggesting a number of measures to enable the V-bombers to operate at low level. DCAS took the chair at the DRPC meeting: at its outset he referred to the DRPC (AES) meeting on 2 January and its recommendation to the Chief of the Defence Staff that a high-yield lay-down bomb should be developed with the highest priority. ACAS(OR) (AVM C H Hartley) said that the DCAS paper was a companion to that considered by DRPC (AES) on the high-yield bomb; it had been prepared as a result of a directive given to the Air Ministry to consider means by which the credibility of the V-force might be maintained in the period before the Polaris force, and the Air Ministry's considered view was that the only possible course was to operate the V-bombers at low level. In considering the implications of this they had examined the question of fatigue life of the aircraft at low level,[2] looked into the need for improvements to the navigational fit and studied what could be done to increase survival capability. The DCAS paper said that bulk penetration of Soviet territory at low altitude required that the following capabilities should be investigated and proved in the V-bombers: overcoming mechanical factors peculiar to low-level flight (eg, airframe strength at high speeds and in turbulence), overcoming navigational problems like position-fixing and terrain clearance, survival in a low-altitude defence environment and accurate and safe (ie, avoiding weapon effects) weapon delivery.

When the DRPC discussed the paper the point was made that the practicability of operating the V-bombers at low level in the way envisaged was a matter on which only the Air Staff – who were convinced that if the V-bombers were to penetrate into Russia in the period under consideration, this was the only way in which they could do it – could express an authoritative view. The committee agreed that, if it were decided that the V-force should operate at low level in the deterrent role, they endorsed the need to take the measures proposed. They noted that insufficient information was available on which to estimate the cost and time-scale of the proposals and recommended that these should be examined further before Ministers took decisions.

Four days later, on 15 January, the Chiefs of Staff discussed the draft Minister of Defence memorandum, the Chief of the Defence Staff (Lord Mountbatten) saying that it had been discussed by the Minister with the three Chiefs of Staff on the previous day: as a result, certain amendments had been made to the memorandum, which was in course of production as a Defence Committee paper – so it would not be possible for it to be amended should the CoS Committee have any

---

[1] Minutes, DRP/M(63)1.
[2] The V-bombers had been designed to operate at 50,000ft.

comments to make on it. CDS referred also to the minute by the Chief Scientific Adviser on the development of nuclear warheads suitable for lay-down weapons; he believed the committee would wish to endorse these recommendations.

In the CoS discussion on the memorandum, the speed with which it had been produced was explained by the need for Ministers to reach decisions before Parliament reassembled the following week, on measures to be taken to maintain the credibility of the deterrent in the pre-Polaris period. The committee "took note" of the memorandum, endorsed the minute by the Chief Scientific Adviser and took note that he would forward his recommendations – about the high-yield warheads for the lay-down weapons – to the Minister of Defence.

The British Nuclear Deterrent Study Group also contributed to the formulation of deterrent policy in this critical post-Nassau period; at a meeting on 21 January 1963 it discussed arrangements for giving the deterrent as much credibility as possible in the pre-Polaris years[1]. Its view was that the main expedient was to ensure the possibility, by developing a high-yield lay-down bomb and by "adopting various other measures", that the V-bomber force would be able to penetrate into the Soviet Union at low level. It thought that consideration should also be given to the development of "some form of stand-off weapon" for use at low level, and agreed that there would be an advantage in diversifying the deterrent force, "particularly with the TSR.2, even after the advent of Polaris". But "a careful assessment of the cost implications and time-scale would be necessary before any decision was taken on a stand-off weapon".

This BNDSG meeting – held "to take stock of the present position on matters arising out of the Nassau decisions, following the visits of Sir Solly Zuckerman and his team to the United States and of Mr Nitze and his team to the United Kingdom"[2] – was advised that the Minister of Defence "had it in mind that, once the terms of assignment to Nato had been worked out, all British deterrent forces, including those of the RAF, would be assigned to Nato, while retaining at the same time a national deterrent role for which there would be separate targetting arrangements"[3].

It was the Minister of Defence memorandum on the deterrent in the pre-Polaris period which was to be the keystone of future defence policy, however, subject to its approval by the Defence Committee of the Cabinet – which endorsed the proposals on 23 January[4]. At that meeting the Minister (Mr Peter Thorneycroft) introduced his paper by saying that

---

[1] Minutes, BNDSG/M(63) 1.

[2] The Zuckerman visit to the US was mainly to discuss the Polaris options. Mr Paul H Nitze was Secretary of the US Navy 1963-67.

[3] At the Nassau conference Mr Macmillan had suggested to President Kennedy that British strategic nuclear deterrent forces – ie V-bombers – be subscribed to Nato.

[4] D(63) 1st meeting.

from about 1965 the ability of the V-bombers to penetrate Russian anti-aircraft defences would gradually diminish, so that the credibility of the British contribution to the Western strategic nuclear deterrent would fall for a time below that which would have been achieved if Skybolt had been available. He was convinced that any attempt to devise a British weapon to take the place of Polaris – should the American undertaking to supply Polaris not be fulfilled – would be financially and politically unjustifiable. The question therefore was, what measures might be taken which could be effective by – say – 1967, for the period of about two years before British Polaris-firing submarines could mount an adequate deterrent?

The Minister said that the Air Staff had concluded that, for this purpose, it was necessary to enable the V-bombers to deliver their attack at low altitude – which would involve strengthening the Victor airframes and fitting both Victors and Vulcans with additional navigation and bombing equipment. It would also be necessary to continue the development of the lay-down bomb designed for TSR.2, so that it could be dropped with a warhead in the megaton range from either the V-bombers or TSR.2s. The full cost of a programme on these lines would be £27-30 million over the next five years.

It was pointed out during discussion that although current plans provided for a reduction in the V-force front line, and although each bomber would carry only one lay-down weapon instead of two Skybolt missiles, Bomber Command could still destroy a substantial number of major targets. With the expected development of Russian anti-aircraft defences, this capability would be reduced; but the deterrent effect of the V-force would continue to be substantial, up to 1970.

The further point was made that, for security reasons, it was undesirable to suggest publicly that a low-level bombing capability had been specially developed to compensate for the loss of Skybolt. In any announcement of measures to be taken to fill the "missile gap" it would be important to emphasise the wide diversity of methods available to the RAF for the delivery of nuclear missiles.

Also, in working-out particular measures, normal procedure for inter-departmental consultation would be followed. If examination showed that further modifications to Blue Steel, or the development of another rocket weapon, might help to improve the position during the 1967-69 period, proposals on those lines would be brought before the committee separately.

The committee agreed, subject to the normal processes of inter-departmental consultation, to the proposals in the Defence Minister's memorandum for modifications to the V-bombers and for development of a high-yield lay-down bomb; and took note that the Prime Minister, in consultation with the Minister of Defence and Secretary of State for Air, would consider the terms of a public announcement about "measures to be taken to continue the effectiveness of the British strategic deterrent forces in the period before the full deployment of Polaris".

Because of changes made in the memorandum between its draft form and that finally approved by the Defence Committee on 23 January, and because this document – The Deterrent in the pre-Polaris Period – is seminal to the last six-and-a-half years of the V-force's existence, the whole text[1] is given here:–

"I have been considering, in the light of the Nassau agreement on Polaris, what additional measures should now be taken to improve the credibility of our nuclear deterrent during the period before our Polaris force becomes operational. My main assumptions are that, in the absence of Skybolt, the credibility of the V-force equipped solely with Blue Steel and free-falling weapons and operating at high altitude as at present must inevitably diminish to some extent beyond 1965; that we cannot have an adequate Polaris deployment before 1969 if we go for submarines equipped with 16 missiles, or 1971 if we go for the eight-missile type of submarine; and finally that the defence burden that we face demands that we restrict expenditure on deterrence to the minimum level consistent with credibilty.

Possible Objectives

"Additional measures in the deterrent field could have one or more of the following objectives. Firstly there are those measures which will improve the capability and therefore the credibility of the V-force between 1965 and the time when we expect to have Polaris in service. Secondly there are measures directed to re-insuring, within our own resources, against a failure to obtain Polaris from the Americans.

"I do not believe that it would make sense either politically or financially for us to work on any other assumption than that the detailed negotiations with the Americans will give us a Polaris force and that this will give us an adequate deterrent, with the TSR.2 as a useful back-up. If the best course was to proceed with a separate development on our own, the right choice would have been to complete Skybolt. This we have rejected, and I am sure rightly. My recommendation is that we should now limit ourselves to such additional measures in the deterrent field as will show worthwhile results within two or three years after 1965. . . .

"The steps that I propose relate to the V-force and the TSR.2. They are based on the Air Staff assessment that, beyond the middle of this decade, V-bombers must go in at low level if they are to penetrate Russian defences. Trials by Bomber Command and experience with the training of the Valiant squadrons assigned to Saceur have convinced the Air Staff that low-level attack by the V-bombers is practicable operationally. . . . The following are my proposals:–

---

[1] D(63)2, dated 15 Jan 63.

The Front Line

"Subject to further consideration when we know more clearly what are the Defence Budget prospects as a whole in the new situation, I propose that we leave current plans for the run-down of Bomber Command unaltered. This will mean that by 1965 the current strength of 120 front-line aircraft will decline to 88, made up wholly of Mk 2 Vulcan and Victor aircraft, which will remain in service until we have our Polaris force. Towards the end of the decade, the TSR.2 will come into service and, though . . . intended for a tactical role, it can provide useful strategic support. It may be that we shall have to consider purchasing further TSR.2s for this purpose . . .[1].

Deployment

"There should be no change in existing plans to operate on ground alert from a total of 36 airfields in this country.

"In last summer's discussions in the Defence Committee on the Skybolt programme, great importance was rightly attached to providing part of the V-bomber force with the capacity to operate on airborne alert. At present, however, the Air Staff do not believe that it would be possible to mount an effective airborne alert with weapons of a lesser range and greater degree of vulnerability than Skybolt, at any rate without appreciable additional expenditure on tankers. . . .

Method of Operation and Associated Weapon Requirement

"To enable the bomber force to operate at low level, high priority should be given to developing the lay-down bomb being designed for carriage by the TSR.2 and Buccaneer to carry a high-yield warhead (in addition to one of low yield) and using it to arm both the V-bombers and TSR.2. A decision to do this is required now.

"In addition, I understand that it may be feasible to convert the existing Blue Steel Mk 1 weapons for release at low altitudes, or to develop a considerably lighter and simpler rocket weapon, of which two to four could be carried by each aircraft.[2] Either weapon would greatly improve the chances of successful penetration of the heavily defended target areas. However, costs would be appreciably higher than those for the lay-down bomb[3] and neither weapon could be available in quantity before 1967 or 1968, by which time any low-level penetration by the V-bombers will be getting increasingly difficult. I have instructed that these possibilities be examined quickly. Should either prove a worth-

---

[1] It is possible that feelings in the Labour administration which took over in October 1964 and cancelled TSR.2 in April 1965 were exacerbated against the aircraft by Conservative proposals to use it as a strategic bomber.
[2] There were more than 20 proposals for alternative weapons following the demise of Skybolt, listed in Bombers – The Deterrent – Future of the Deterrent (DCAS/B1-65, Pt 1).
[3] In the list just mentioned, this was described as "cheap".

while proposition, I will make proposals separately about it, but I would emphasise that in any event it is not a substitute for the lay-down bomb.

"As a first step towards achieving the capacity to bomb from low level, the Mk 1 V-bombers in the existing plan should convert to a low-level role this year, using existing weapons. Existing weapons would not be satisfactory in the long term, since their use requires the bomber to climb to a minimum safe height, which may be as much as 26,000ft, for the actual release of its bomb. At this stage of its sortie the bomber would be vulnerable to high-level defences, though for a relatively limited period. I understand, however, that the miminum dropping height might be somewhat reduced by a comparatively simple modification, and I recommend that this should be pursued.

Number of Weapons Required
"The number of weapons required must be studied further. For the moment, it has only been possible to make some arbitrary assumptions for the purpose of costing the associated warhead programme. The assumptions are as follows:

(a)   Instead of the warheads approved for Skybolt, there will be high-yield warheads for lay-down bombs.

(b))   In addition, of warheads for lay-down bombs already approved for the TSR.2, about half will now be provided in the high-yield version. (Previously all were to be of low yield.)

Other Requirements
"Navigation equipment for the low-level role should be provided for the whole V-bomber force.

"Further study is required of the possibility of equipping the force with additional electronic or other countermeasures for operation in the low-level role. This study is being concentrated on equipment that can be in service with the V-force within two or three years after 1965: preliminary examination shows that this will rule out major expenditure in this area.

Costs
"A detailed re-costing of the airborne deterrent is not possible pending further study. In principle, however, the capital and running costs of the front line in the 1960s and its deployment should remain broadly unchanged, since there are no proposals to change the size of the front line, the number of airfields, or the peacetime rates of training effort.

"For the rest:

(a)   The additional new expenditure involved in developing a high-yield version of the lay-down bomb is estimated at about £5 million for research and development, and £10.5 million for production....

(b)   The only other firm requirement which can be costed at this stage is the provision for the whole of the V-bomber force of improved navigation equipment for the low-level role now being fitted to the Valiants. In addition, there is likely to be expenditure on an airframe modification for the Victor Mk 2 and on improving the electronic countermeasures capability of the V-force. A provisional first estimate of the cost of these measures is £1.25 million for research and development and £11 million for production, a total of £12.25 million.

"It seems therefore that for a relatively modest additional expenditure of about £30 million spread over the next four or five years, we can do a good deal to maintain the credibility of the deterrent in this decade. Some of the improvements proposed, for example those in low-level navigation equipment, can be made in the next two years: others will take rather longer, but the general pattern will be one of successive steps, all giving value in the pre-Polaris period. I am sure that these measures must be taken...".

In conclusion, the Minister invited the Defence Committee,

"Subject to the normal processes of inter-Departmental consultation to approve a programme limited to the measures proposed in this paper for the improvement of the deterrent capacity of the V-bomber force and for the arming of the TSR.2 to enable it to operate in the strategic deterrent role".

The committee's approval of these proposals meant that the memorandum formed a blueprint for Britain's airborne strategic nuclear deterrent force in the 1960s: its RAF implications were spelt out in a paper, Bomber Command in the period 1963–70, which was approved by the Air Council on 14 March. Before that, however, the Government sought Parliamentary approval for its new defence policy in a two-day Commons debate (30–31 January) and secured this despite an Opposition motion of no confidence, which was defeated by 337 votes to 234, the main motion ("That this House approves the Statement on Nuclear Defence Systems issued following the Bahamas Meeting in December 1962") being subsequently carried by 330 votes to 236.

The Prime Minister (Mr Harold Macmillan) was chiefly concerned to justify the Polaris agreement and to exculpate the Americans from any blame for the ending of Skybolt, which had "the full and enthusiastic support" of the US Services and Government, but during 1962 the Americans "developed serious doubts" about the system. He said that the decision to stop it might mean for the UK "a short period in this decade when our V-bombers may find it more difficult to penetrate". Once an agreement on an effective contribution to Nato's nuclear forces had been worked out, "we should be ready to assign our V-bomber force for the defence of the Western Alliance".

The Minister of Defence took up the latter point, of a British contribution to Nato nuclear deterrence, when he spoke later in the debate. Mr Thorneycroft said that while independence was important, interdependence mattered too: the problem of a Nato deterrent had been a major matter of discussion on both sides of the Atlantic, and there were many unsolved problems about control and deployment. The British suggestion was that "we should subscribe or allot or assign V-bombers to strengthen the alliance", while being "free to use them ourselves". While working closely with Strategic Air Command, the V-bombers would be kept in Bomber Command. The whole of "this formidable deterrent strike force" was available to Nato; talks could start at once with Nato and Saceur as to targetting and planning[1].

Meanwhile the Air Staff had been making plans for the continuance of airborne strategic nuclear deterrence without Skybolt, on the lines approved by the Defence Committee; and these plans were outlined in a paper put before the Air Council on 14 March by VCAS (Air Mshl Sir Wallace Kyle)[2]. In his Note – Bomber Command in the period 1963–70 – VCAS said that the cancellation of Skybolt had made it necessary to review the method of operating the V-force until 1970, when British Polaris submarines should be operational. Referring to the 23 January Defence Committee meeting, he said that Ministers had approved certain measures which would help to preserve the effectiveness of the force in the period under review; the council would wish to take note of those measures and to consider them in great detail. He also referred to the offer by Ministers to assign the whole of the V-force to Nato, saying that discussions were taking place with the US on the problems involved. It was the Government's intention that assignment should be on the following terms: the Government retained the right to order the use of British forces at discretion, if supreme national interests were at stake; forces must be available to meet national commitments outside Nato, in conditions of lesser emergency; and states of readiness, deployment and dispersal, logistics and support of the assigned forces must remain a national responsibility.

Describing the defences against which the V-force would have to operate, VCAS said that they had become increasingly effective against high-flying aircraft, and by 1966/67 were expected to include an effective system against high-level cruise-type missiles. For these reasons, deep penetration at high level was not feasible – it would require an airborne ballistic missile with stand-off qualities, and no such British weapon existed or could be developed in time. On the other hand, Intelligence had indicated that the Russians had had no greater success than the Americans or the British in developing effective low-level defences other than a possible SAM key point defence system, which would provide the only serious opposition to the V-bombers operating in a low-level role.

VCAS affirmed that in the absence of Skybolt, therefore, low-level

---

[1] Commons Hansard, 31 Jan 63, Col 1164.
[2] AC(63)9.

attack was the only method offering a reasonable chance of penetration. The V-bombers would fly out at high level, descend while still outside early-warning radar cover and go to their targets at low level. Bomber Command trials, and experience gained with the Saceur-assigned Valiant force, had shown that there was little difficulty in locating targets while at such levels – given the appropriate navigation equipment.

He next detailed the weapons required for low-level operations: there were no British ones in existence, but Ministers had agreed that high priority should be given to increasing the yield of the warhead for the lay-down bomb being designed as a low-yield weapon for the TSR.2 and Buccaneer. The resultant high-yield bomb should be available for V-force use by mid-1966 and would also be valuable for TSR.2 in the strategic deterrent role. Additionally, the Minister of Defence had instructed the Ministry of Aviation to see whether it would be possible to modify the existing version of Blue Steel for low-level launch – which, if it could be done within the next few years, would "clearly increase the striking power of the V-force".

Dealing with modifications required for low-level operations, VCAS said that Victor Mk 2 airframes would need some strengthening; a programme to do this had been approved in general terms by Ministers. Assuming an effective fatigue life of over 5,000hr, and that crews were allowed 32 hours' low-level training a year[1], the V-force would not become life-expired until about 1970.

Until the lay-down bomb and/or low-level Blue Steel became available, he believed that the V-force would have the best chance of penetrating to its targets by operating as follows:

(a)   Mk 1 aircraft would fly a high-low-high profile and be armed with Yellow Sun Mk 2 – release height for which required an aircraft to climb, in the target area, to about 20,000ft; during this climb it would be vulnerable to SAM defences. It was hoped that the dropping height of Yellow Sun Mk 2 could be reduced: the Minister of Defence had decided that this possibility should be pursued.

(b)   Initially the Mk 2 aircraft, which would include an element with free-fall bombs as well as Blue Steel, would operate at high level against fringe targets; but it was proposed, as soon as possible, to operate Mk 2 aicraft with free-fall bombs in the low-level role. Blue Steel aircraft would be converted to the low-level role as soon as the missile had a low-level capability.

The other parameters for the V-force of the 1960s described by VCAS were: low-level training – either actual, along routes already available in Germany or to be provided in the UK, or simulated; continued acceptance that it was "neither economical nor effective" to mount an airborne alert, although the possibility would remain open to

---

[1] The amount of training done by crews of the Saceur-assigned Valiants.

review; an emphasis on the 36 dispersal airfields already planned being provided for ground-alert purposes, with facilities for 100 aircraft on operational readiness platforms – the minimum for 88 UE in the front line and 24 tactical bombers assigned to Saceur; installation of additional navigation and electronic equipment (to which Ministers had given their approval) in the V-bombers, including modified Sidescan radar and Green Satin[1] aerials to give better low-level performance, topographical moving maps – as developed for the Saceur Valiants – and radar altimeters; and an ECM fit to counter continuous-wave (CW) radar, "the only effective radar for SAM systems and fighters operating against low-flying aircraft".

VCAS said in conclusion that an accurate costing of the improvements needed to enable the V-force to operate at low level was not possible, pending further study; but in principle the running costs should not be significantly different from those of the ground-alert force approved for the pre-Skybolt period. He invited the Air Council to take note of the measures which had been approved, "subject to the normal processes of inter-departmental consultation, to preserve the effectiveness of the V-force pending the introduction of British Polaris submarines". The Council took note, and invited VCAS to institute the necessary action – also noting that he would be preparing a separate paper on weapons requirements. Thus the way in which the V-force would operate, for the last six years of British airborne strategic nuclear deterrence, was laid down in the spring of 1963.

The AOC in C Bomber Command (Air Mshl Sir Kenneth Cross), who was present at the meeting, said that the improvements mentioned in the paper would not be necessary until 1965 – Skybolt would not, in any case, have been available before then. After that date, the lay-down bomb and low-level operations would give a good chance of making successful attacks. It would be an advantage if the in-service date of the lay-down bomb could be brought forward, and low-level Blue Steel would be a valuable alternative weapon. When asked by S of S (Mr Hugh Fraser) whether the Skybolt cancellation and the need to employ low-level tactics was having any effect on morale, the C in C said that the need for low-level tactics had been appreciated before the decision to cancel Skybolt, and to date there had been no morale problem[2].

On 11 April S of S wrote to the Minister of Defence to recommend to him "some comparatively simple and inexpensive modifications" which, he said, would enable Blue Steel to be launched "at a height of no more than 1,000ft up to 50 miles from the target". Estimated cost of this would be "up to £4½m" and the modified weapon should be ready for operational use in less than two years[3].

[1] A self-contained navigation aid, giving continuous information on track, groundspeed and distance flown.
[2] As an ex-member of the V-force put it to the author, "Skybolt or no Skybolt, we'd have had to get down among the weeds anyway".
[3] ID9/B.1-65 Bombers – The Deterrent – Future of the Deterrent.

A week later, on the 18th, OR1 initiated Standard of Preparation No 54 – for modifications to the V-bombers to give them a low-level capability, explaining that "the decision to cancel . . . Skybolt . . . has much reduced the future credibility of the V-force deterrent in the face of expected Soviet air defences against medium- and high-flying aircraft", but that "in view of the lesser Soviet capability likely to exist during the next few years against aircraft flying at low level, it has been decided that the medium bomber force will operate in the low-level role". So, improvements were required to the aircraft mechanical standards "to enable them to withstand flights at high speed/low level, and to the navigation/attack systems to permit low-level penetration and weapon delivery".[1]

This Standard of Preparation was issued on 3 May and is referred to subsequently in Chapter XXVI on Low-level Blue Steel and Lay-down Bombs. It was later to be superseded (on 5 May 1964) by ASR No 380 Medium Bomber Force Aircraft – Low-level Role.

On 23 April the Minister of Defence directed that low-level Blue Steel should be considered by the Defence Research Policy Committee. "I think it essential", he minuted S of S for Air, "before this project is submitted to the Defence Committee, for it to be considered by the DRPC and the Chiefs of Staff. I realise the urgency, but special arrangements can be made to complete these necessary processes as quickly as possible".

At the DRPC meeting, on 8 May, the War Office opposed approval of the paper[2] requesting endorsement of the proposal to provide Blue Steel with a low-level launch capability, on the grounds of weapon system vulnerability, and subsequently DCIGS (Lt-Gen Sir John Hackett) suggested the setting-up of a small body to consider this; but in reply DCAS said that as the War Office seemed to have doubts about the wisdom of filling the gap resulting from the cancellation of Skybolt, the best course of action would be to refer the matter to the Chiefs of Staff.[3]

The Chiefs of Staff considered modifications to Blue Steel to give it a low-level launch capability at their meeting on 14 May 1963[4] when they endorsed a note by the Air Ministry for use by the Defence Research Policy Committee: this note had proposed to the DRPC that a project study on the necessary modifications should be carried out, at a cost of £60,000. The cost of the actual modifications would be £20m to give the missile a low-level trajectory, or about £3m to give it a low-level launch and an "up and over" trajectory. The DRPC agreed to such a project study being undertaken[5] and in October of that year approved proposals

---

[1] ID9/B.1-65 Bombers The Deterrent – Future of the Deterrent.
[2] DRP/P(63)31.
[3] DCAS 2191/63 (9 May).
[4] 33rd Mtg/63: extract from Minutes in ID9/194/4 – Blue Steel Jan 61-Jun 64.
[5] Minute from S of S to the Minister of Defence, 24 May 63 (Ibid).

to enable Blue Steel to be modified for low-level launch. As DCAS (Air Mshl Sir Christopher Hartley) reported to S or S (Mr Hugh Fraser) on the 16th, "the modification is a relatively cheap one. It will cost only £3.5m in development. . . . The production costs will be about £7,000 per missile with £0.4m for modification to the test equipment".[1] The Minister was further told, in a letter from the AOC in C Bomber Command (Air Mshl Sir John Grandy) after he had visited Scampton, that the first low-level trials weapon had been successfully launched at Woomera that morning (19 November) from a Vulcan flying at 300kt at 2,000ft.[2]

Towards the end of 1963 S of S and the Minister of Aviation asked the Minister of Defence (Mr Peter Thorneycroft) for a long-term decision on Blue Steel low-level modification, and on 20 December he told them he had decided to approve an extension of the holding contract for a further three months.[3]

One other consequence of the Nassau Agreement during this year was that the whole of the V-bomber force was assigned to NATO – a decision formally conveyed, "in implementation of paragraph 6 of the Nassau communiqué", by the Chief of the Defence Staff (Earl Mountbatten) to Saceur on 23 May, with the proviso that "bearing in mind . . . the dual role of the force and the UK commitments outside Nato for the defence of the free world, HMG had decided that they must retain the right to order the use of British forces at discretion, if they decide that supreme national interests are at stake; forces must be available to meet national commitments outside Nato in conditions of lesser emergency . . .; and states of readiness, deployment and dispersal, logistics and support of the assigned forces must remain a national responsibility . . .".

During 1964 the Blue Steel modification programme began to show positive results. The Air Ministry Quarterly Liaison Report for January-March said that "missiles, modified for deployment at either high or low level, have now been developed and firing trials completed. Acceptance firings are now in progress and the programme will be complete before the end of 1964". The next (April-June) issue noted that "acceptance firings are going well and should be completed before the end of this year. Meanwhile the modification programme to give

---

[1] Minute of 16 Oct 63 (in ID9/194/4 – Blue Steel Jan 61-Jun 64).

[2] Letter of 19 Nov 63, in which he went on to state that "whether the missile is to be launched from high or low level, its basic structure will not be altered and the problems of generation, recovery from generation and maintaining a high state of readiness will remain" (Ibid).

[3] Minute to the Minister of Aviation, copied to the Chief Secretary to the Treasury and S of S for Air (Ibid). The changes to Blue Steel required by the Air Staff had been embodied in ASR 1132, Issue 4, retaining the original specification and introducing new low-level launch requirements (LM of 18 Sep 63, ACAS(OR)/DCAS in ID9/B.18-100 Bombers – Powered Bombs Blue Steel – ASR 1132 (Issue 4) Low Level).) Issue 4 was dated 16 Sept 62 and a revised Issue 4 was circulated on 26 May 65. All 57 missiles were to be modified (T/MoD minute of 13 Apr 64 in ID/47/296 Pt 2 Blue Steel (OR1132) Financial Aspects).

Blue Steel a low- and high-level capability is in hand and all the missiles should be modified by the end of this year". Acceptance firings seem to have been completed earlier than expected, for the October-December AMQLR reported: "Acceptance firings of the Blue Steel Weapons System were successfully concluded in October. The Blue Steel Force now has both a high-level and a low-level capability".

During 1966-67 a post-acceptance launch programme for Blue Steel, code-named Operation Fresno, was mounted: it consisted of two launches each from Victors and Vulcans. The first was from Victor Mk 2 XH673 of No 100 Sqn over the Aberporth Range on 27 May and reported as being completely successful; the second was from Victor B.2 XH675 of No 139 Sqn on 26 August, the ORB noting that the weapon was "launched at maximum range and landed 640yd from the target." The first launch from a Vulcan took place on 31 May 1967, when (in the words of AMQLR for April-June 1967) "the missile was released 47 miles from the target and the impact error was 1,065yd", adding: "Three Blue Steel missiles have thus been fired successfully, with the fourth and final one of the series yet to be launched". This last firing was recorded in the AMQLR for July-September 1967:—

"The second Blue Steel missile to be launched from a Vulcan was fired successfully on 7 July 1967. The missile was fired at low-level and flew as planned for a distance of 35 miles with an impact error of 515yd.

"The programme of four in-service Blue Steel firings has now been successfully completed".

These Vulcan B.2 firings were both from a Scampton Wing aircraft, XL390, that on 31 May by a No 27 Sqn crew and on 7 July by a No 617 Sqn crew.

CHAPTER XXV

V-BOMBERS' FAR EAST DEPLOYMENTS

The original specification for the Vulcan and Victor medium bombers[1] stressed that they were to be "for world-wide use in the Royal Air Force"; and the accompanying operational requirement likewise said at its outset that the type envisaged was to be capable of attacking a target "from a base which may be anywhere in the world". Thus the ubiquitous nature of V-bomber operations was assumed from the beginning, and individual aircraft were constantly flying westwards to SAC bases or eastwards to the Mediterranean area, Africa, the Gulf and beyond to Australia and New Zealand.

During the 1957-60 period, at the end of the Malayan Emergency, detachments of V-force aircraft were sent to the Far East. No 214 Sqn was the first to provide one; on 29 October 1957 three of its Valiants left Marham for Changi, Singapore, on Exercise Profiteer – decribed in the squadron ORB as "an operation designed to enable V-force crews to gain experience in operating in climatic conditions peculiar to the Far East".

Although Profiteer is listed among "temporary detachments of UK-based units available for Firedog operations" in the official history of the Malayan Emergency[2] there is no evidence in the records of the V-bomber squadrons which sent aircraft out that these participated in any way in support of the ground fighting. Indeed, the history makes the points, in summing-up offensive air support during the campaign, that jet aircraft were "too sophisticated" for that type of warfare, and that the introduction of jets into the Malayan theatre "coincided with a decline in calls for this type of support". The most effective support aircraft during the campaign, it says, were the Lincoln and Hornet.

The No 214 Sqn ORB makes very brief reference to its Far East excursion, which "went without a hitch", training flights from Changi including one to Vientiane in Laos by two Valiants – "the first time jet aircraft had been seen in Laotian skies", according to the compiler – which landed at Bangkok on their return trip. No 90 Sqn, however, which sent two Valiants to Changi on 2 March 1958, was much more forthcoming in its ORB about its detachment. This had been authorised by Operation Order 1/58 (Profiteer) – based on Bomber Command's Operation Order No 34/57 of 10 October 1957 – which said that "two Valiant aircraft, three aircrews and ground servicing personnel will be detached to FEAF from 4 March 1957 for approximately 14 days". The purpose was to exercise squadron crews in Far East operations; the

---

[1] B.35/46, issued on 24 Jan 47 and based on OR229 of 17 Dec 46.
[2] *The Malayan Emergency 1948-1960* (AP3410), Appendix I to Annex M (MoD June 1970).

aircraft were to be "fully equipped to operate in the conventional role"; and during the detachment operational control was to be exercised by C in C FEAF (Air Mshl the Earl of Bandon).

The ORB gives a vivid account of the sort of training done by the Valiant crews, and of the weather encountered. Normal sorties from Changi "consisted mainly of simulated first-run attacks on certain specified airfields to collect target information for HQ FEAF". Return flights were routed so as to "give maximum practice to the radar defence and fighter intercepters in the Singapore area". Referring to meteorological conditions, the ORB says that on two occasions "aircraft flew through cumulo-nimbus cloud; during a first-run attack on an airfield in North Borneo, severe turbulence was encountered at 48,000ft and the attack was abandoned; on return to base [it was discovered that] a considerable amount of resin paint had been stripped from the radome. . . . On the second occasion, during a let-down at Changi the aircraft entered cloud at 20,000ft; again there was very severe turbulence . . . followed by an immediate extensive clear-ice build-up. On further reduction of height the icing disappeared".

Another Valiant squadron, No 148, sent four aircraft to Malaya in early 1959, a detachment lasting from 3 to 24 February and based at RAAF Butterworth. The ORB's concise description not only says what was achieved but also indicates the logistics involved: "The Valiants, supported by a Comet, went *via* El Adem, Nairobi, Karachi and Katunayake. A separate party of groundcrew flew in a Hastings *via* Luqa, El Adem, Khartoum, Khormaksar, Karachi and Katunayake. . . . Flying commenced on Tuesday, 10 February, with familiarisation flights around Malaya. All crews then completed two long sorties over Borneo and Malaya, taking radar photographs of airfields and towns at the request of HQ, FEAF. . . ."

Three Vulcan B.1 squadrons, Nos 617, 101 and 83, also participated in Profiteer detachments: No 617 sent one aircraft to Butterworth on 14 October 1959; while there it did what the ORB crisply described as a Navex – Thailand, and also visited Clark AFB at Manila in the Philippines, before returning to Scampton on 4 November. No 101, while not mentioning Profiteer in its ORB, records that four aircraft went to Butterworth on 15 January 1960: they did fighter affiliation with RAAF Sabres, profile flights over Thailand and sorties to Clark AFB, returning to Finningley on 7 February. No 83 sent four aircraft and six crews to Butterworth "to exercise crews in the rapid reinforcement of the FEAF and to provide them with operating experience in the Far East theatre".

Thus although the Profiteer exercises were contemporaneous with the last three years of Firedog operations, they did not have any direct relationship to them.

443

During the 1963-66 Indonesian Confrontation period[1], however, V-bombers were regarded as part of the forces capable of being deployed by FEAF. In one of the plans drawn up[2], to come into operation should the Indonesian Air Force attack targets in Malaysia and/or Singapore in riposte for Commonwealth action against para-military bases whence infiltrations were being mounted[3], the V-bombers were to take part in operations designed to eliminate Indonesian air strike capability. These operations would either be carried out with the assistance of Australian and New Zealand forces, using RAAF Darwin as a strike base[4]; or with those forces in a defensive role, Darwin being unavailable and the V-bombers from RAAF Butterworth operating out of Labuan[5]. As far as V-force squadrons were concerned there were three aspects to their task during Indonesian confrontation: rapid deployment to the Far East; detachment at Tengah or Butterworth; possible operations against Indonesian targets.

During November 1963 HQ Bomber Command had issued an Operation Instruction[6] that under Operation Chamfrom four medium bomber aircraft and five crews were to be detached from their parent stations to RAF Tengah or to RAAF Butterworth[7]; and the Bomber Command ORB for December 1963 recorded, under Special Commitments, that arrangements were made to airlift servicing parties and spares pack-ups from RAF stations Honington and Cottesmore in support of four Victor Mk 1As from each of these stations. In the latter month four Victor B Mk 1As of No XV Sqn flew out from Cottesmore to Tengah in Exercise Chamfron, then early in January 1964 this detachment moved from Tengah to Butterworth, and in February the crews were rotated. The detachment continued until 30 September 1964 when it was handed-over to Vulcan B Mk 2s, of No 12 Sqn, RAF Coningsby. It was paralled by another Victor B Mk 1A detachment, of four aircraft from No 55 Sqn at Honington, this commitment being taken over from 17 October 1964 by No 57 Sqn, also Honington-based. The latter squadron's ORB noted that "the first flight made by each crew was a familiarisation with the local area, including the circuits of RAAF Butterworth and RAF Changi. There was only one profile, and the majority of the other flights were bombing at Song Song and China Rock ranges". No 12's record, however, was more picturesque – as perhaps befitted a Vulcan B Mk 2 squadron:–

"On Friday, 2 October, Wing Commander J R Tanner, Flight Lieutenants D H Hulse and N G Steel and their crews flew from Gan to Butterworth, bringing the squadron detachment to four aircraft and

---

[1] Dec 63-16 Aug 66.
[2] Code-named Addington.
[3] Operation Mason (FEAF Op Order 10/65).
[4] Addington One.
[5] Addington Two.
[6] No 14, 23 Nov 63.
[7] HQ Bomber Command Op Order No 4/63.

five crews. No 12 (B) Sqn had arrived and took over the Chamfrom commitment from No 15 Squadron, Victor B Mk 1s. At midnight in the Officers' Mess bar No 15 Sqn's plaque came down and the fox's mask of No 12 Sqn took its place".[1]

An illustration of the rotation of crews during Chamfrom detachments was given in the No 55 Sqn ORB for May 1964,which said that this rotation began during that month "with Flt Lt Farlam and his crew leaving Honington on the 12th. Flt Lt Gallienne and his crew returned on the 21st. Wg Cdr Houston left Honington with his crew on the 20th to take over command from Sqn Ldr I C B Brettell. . . ."

During March the squadron was involved in an alert exercise, the supposition being that hostile aircraft would make a dawn attack on the airfield on the 12th. "To counter this, two Victors were prepared for take-off before dawn on 6½hr flights so as to be off the airfield during the strike. The two other Victors were loaded with 21x1,000lb HE bombs and put on 20-minute readiness. The four aircraft were dispersed about the airfield. The exercise was terminated at 0900hr on 12 March. . . ." But in September there was a real alert:–

"At the beginning of the month relations between Indonesia and Malaysia deteriorated. . . . Night flying was cancelled and a day training sortie recalled. Operational generation of aircraft was started. No 55 Squadron Victors and other Tengah-based aircraft were dispersed on the airfield. Victors 649 and 594 were prepared with 14x1,000lb bombs and fuel and given Combat Ready checks. They were allocated to Flt Lt E J Randell and crew and Flt Lt R J Russell and crew, who had completed briefing on targets and were flight-planned for rapid dispersal to Gan. Victors 645 and 646 were prepared for dispersal without bomb loads. All crews were brought to one hour's readiness".

From 5 to 8 September crew readiness was maintained at one hour; air raid shelters – sited on large monsoon ditches – were constructed with timber and sand bags near the dispersed aircraft, barrack block and squadron offices. From 10 September crew readiness was relaxed to three hours; on the 13th the squadron commander and specialist leaders went to HQ FEAF for a conference and were introduced to a new plan, for which target study and flight planning then began. On 16 September "Flt Lt R J Russell and crew in Victor 594 and Flt Lt Bissell and crew in Victor 594 were dispersed to RAAF Butterworth with target Go-Bags and side arms".

The alert lasted nearly all the month. From 22 to 26 September, "the readiness was relaxed to 17 hours . . . bombs were removed from the aircraft. Limited training sorties were flown by all crews during this period, in order to regain flying efficiency. . . ." Then on 27 September, "the readiness was relaxed to 48 hours and the dispersed aircraft

---

[1] Commemorating the fact that it had been a Fairey Fox squadron 1926-31.

returned to Tengah. It was now possible for normal air and ground training to be resumed".

Another aspect of Chamfrom operations was illustrated by No 57 Sqn's participation in Exercise Hot Squirrel from 3 to 5 February 1965 – "to test the fighter defences of Northern Australia and to familiarise crews with operating from Darwin".

It is worthy of note that the transit flights to this exercise took place under cover of darkness. "The aircraft took off from Tengah at midnight", the ORB recorded, "arriving at Darwin at dawn". Four Victors were involved, an extra crew and groundcrew flying to Australia in a Transport Command Britannia. Having left Tengah on 1 February they returned there on the 8th, "again at night".

The No 12 Sqn detachment to Butterworth in fact lasted only just over two months; by 13 December, as the result of a high-level change of policy, all the aircraft and crews were back at Cottesmore. Operating in a tropical climate, far from the support facilities enjoyed in the UK, had brought new experiences and some problems. "Generally the aircraft flew well", the ORB reported for October 1964. "The main troubles were caused by dampness in the electrical systems, due to heavy monsoon rain and an unexpected rash of hydraulic defects. Second-line support facilities were not as good as those enjoyed in the UK, but these shortcomings were generally overcome by ingenuity. The line accommodation was inadequate for a long detachment".

Early in 1965 the rapid reinforcement of the Far East by V-bombers was practised. On 11 May the CAS (Air Chf Mshl Sir Charles Elworthy) minuted the Minister of Defence for the RAF (Lord Shackleton[1]):–

"On 7 April you approved a practice reinforcement of the Far East by eight Vulcans. The exercise has now been completed and you may like to know how it went.

"The exercise was initiated by a request for reinforcements from the Commander in Chief, Far East[2], at 1400hr on 26 April. The Air Force Department[3] issued a warning to the Commands concerned and, after a simulated interval for political release and initiation of diplomatic clearances to overfly Turkey and Iran, the executive order was given at midnight.

"The first Vulcan took off 1½hr later and reached Gan in 26 hours[4]. The complete force of eight Vulcans reached Gan within 32 hours – that is, 42hr after the C in C Far East initiated his request for reinforcements.

"Bomber Command simulated the bombing-up of all eight aircraft before departure from their base. The Vulcans were supported by

[1] CAS 2526.
[2] Admiral Sir Varyl Begg.
[3] Since 1 April 1964.
[4] 0045hr on 27 April to 0601 on 2 May were the Cottesmore-Gan departure and arrival times in the F540.

servicing crews carried in two Britannias and a Comet.

"All Vulcan crews had a ten-hour rest at Bahrain, and after a quick turn-round at Gan, they could have been on target in Indonesia within 48hr of the C in C's request.

"The Air Commander FEAF[1] then deployed the Vulcans forward to Butterworth and Tengah, and they could have operated from bases in the Malaya peninsula within 72hr of the C in C's request.

"This exercise was well worthwhile, and has demonstrated once again the efficacy of the V-bomber reinforcement arrangements for Plan Addington".

Exercise Spherical, as it was called, had been reported on to the Chiefs of Staff by CAS on 27 April, before it had been completed. He told them[2] that, after receipt of the C in C's signal and the AFD warning to the Commands concerned at 1600Z on 26 April,

"after a built-in delay to simulate bombing-up time, the first aircraft had been declared combat-ready at 2100Z that day and the eight at 0320Z on 27 April. The executive order to go had been delayed until 2300Z; this allowed time for securing political release and catered for time needed to initiative diplomatic clearance to overfly Turkey and Iran. The first aircraft had been airborne at 0045Z and the eighth at 0623Z on 27 April.

"At noon on 27 April, six Vulcans were en route between El Adem and Muharraq and the two remaining ones were about to leave El Adem. Route transport support, consisting of one Comet and three Britannias, was proceeding according to plan; the Britannias were programmed to reach Gan early on 28 April.

"The Vulcan force was due to be complete in Gan at 0845Z on 28 April; this meant that the force, operating from Gan, could be on target within 48hr of the C in C calling for reinforcement. . . ."

The squadron which did this rapid reinforcement exercise was No 35, based at Cottesmore with Vulcan B Mk 2s. Their ORB for May 1965 summed it up by saying on the 6th, when the last two aircraft returned: "Exercise Spherical was completed this month. This was a 'no-notice' exercise to check the feasibility of reinforcement of FEAF by Bomber Command at short call. Seven aircraft were flown by crews of 35 Sqn, who also supplied two extra crews. A total of eight aircraft double-staged out to RAAF Butterworth or RAF Tengah. The crews then flew back to RAF Cottesmore in single stages". The Vulcan specifically mentioned by CAS, XM600, flown by the squadron commander, Wg Cdr D B Craig,[3] and his crew, took off from Cottesmore at 0045 on 27 April and landed at El Adem at 0418hr. It left there at 0728hr, reaching Muharraq (Bahrain) at 1151hr. That was the end of the first double stage, the crew having their ten-hour rest and taking off at 2151hr for

---

[1] Air Mshl P G Wykeham.
[2] COS 21st Mtg/65, 27 Apr 65.
[3] Later ACM Sir David and CAS, then CDS.

Gan, which they reached at 0230 on 28 April; then at 0745hr on 29 April XM600 took off for RAAF Butterworth, where it landed at 1212hr – in other words, being in the Far East a couple of days after leaving the UK, with a 6½hr gain in time.

It seems quite clear that the V-bombers' presence in the Far East, and the fact that they could be got out there so quickly, had a deterrent effect during the Indonesian Confrontation period. In a report on Operations in Malaysia, 1 April-31 December 1965, the Commander in Chief, Far East (Air Chf Mshl Sir John Grandy, who had succeeded Admiral Sir Varyl Begg in May), said that "four reinforcement medium bombers (Victor or Vulcan) were retained in the Command throughout the period. This ensured that all principal targets under contingency plans were covered with forces immediately available. There is little doubt that this force has provided a valuable deterrent to confrontation being conducted on a larger scale. . . ."

On 13 August 1965 No 9 Sqn (Vulcan B Mk 2s) had taken over the detachment at Tengah from No 57 Sqn (Victor B Mk 1As); then early in March 1966 another Vulcan B Mk 2 squadron – No 35, making another visit to the Far East, this time to stay – took over the "Matterhorn Medium Bomber Force commitment" at Tengah, maintaining it until August 1966. During that month the squadron had detached three aircraft to RAAF Darwin for Exercise High Castor, a test of the Australian SAM and fighter defences, the Vulcans finding the RAAF Mirage III-Os "formidable"; when on the 14th, while the Vulcans were still on the exercise, "orders were received" – to quote from the squadron ORB – "covering the withdrawal of the medium bombers to the United Kingdom. This followed the signing of the Bangkok agreement by Malaysia and Indonesia, ending the confrontation between these two countries. The aircraft returned to Tengah on the 17th. . . ." Confrontation was over, and the V-force had played its part.

The first Vulcan B Mk 2s to be withdrawn from the Far East following the end of confrontation, XM657 and XM645, captained by Flt Lts J M Morgan and B Dorrington respectively, arrived back at Cottesmore on 26 August 1966; and the last arrivals, XM610 and XM612 captained by Flt Lts P G Franklin and A M Mitchell, came in on the 30th: their return "completed the withdrawal of the Medium Bomber Detachment from the Far East".[1]

---

[1] Cottesmore ORB.

V-BOMBER BASES
&
OPERATIONAL
CONVERSION
UNITS

THOR
LOCATIONS

CARNABY
FULL SUTTON
DRIFFIELD
CATFOSS
BREIGHTON

FINNINGLEY
CAISTOR
HEMSWELL
LUDFORD MAGNA
SCAMPTON
BARDNEY
WADDINGTON
CONINGSBY
COLEBY GRANGE

FOLKINGHAM

MELTON MOWBRAY
COTTESMORE
NORTH LUFFENHAM
WITTERING
MARHAM
NORTH PICKENHAM
POLEBROOK
FELTWELL
HONINGTON
HARRINGTON
MEPAL
SHEPHERDS
WYTON
GROVE
GAYDON
TUDDENHAM

CHAPTER XXVI

LOW-LEVEL BLUE STEEL AND LAY-DOWN BOMBS

Three events weakened RAF Bomber Command's capability in the 1963-65 period: the cancellation of Skybolt, with the resultant decision early in 1963 that the V-force should operate at low level; the loss of its Valiants at the beginning of 1965; and, only a few months later, the Government's announcement that the TSR.2 project – for an aircraft which was regarded as having strategic as well as tactical value – was being terminated.

The policy decisions which followed the loss of Skybolt have already been referred to, as was the comment made by the AOC in C Bomber Command (Air Mshl Sir Kenneth Cross) at the Air Council meeting on 14 March 1963 when it discussed Bomber Command in the 1963-70 period – that the need for low-level tactics had been appreciated before the decision to cancel Skybolt[1]. This may well have carried the brave implication that every possible operational eventuality had been considered; but in fact, changing-over a force whose equipment had been designed to operate at 50,000ft so that it could operate at near ground level involved many technological and training factors: modifying the aircraft to endure the greater stresses and hazards they would encounter at, say, 2,000ft or below; changing the navigation equipment to include height-above-ground and terrain-avoidance instrumentation, and adapting electronic warning and countermeasures devices to cope with defences likely to be encountered in a low environment; developing new weapons to suit low-level delivery or changing techniques in order to use existing bombs at the end of a low-level penetration of enemy defences; and training crews to become efficient under the new circumstances, by the arduous practice of low-level navigation and weapon delivery.

In fact, the V-force adopted a low-level training policy early in 1963, only a few months after the Nassau communiqué. There was an irony about this timing, since Blue Steel was being introduced then, so the two kinds of operational philosophy were overlapping: low-level, to give the force a credibility until the advent of Polaris; and high-level, in order to provide Blue Steel with its launching environment. Moreover, low-level training was thus preceding the modifications to equipment which were being considered in order to make low-level operations possible; these modifications were under consideration by the Air Staff and the Ministry of Aviation during 1963 and '64. There were in fact five different kinds of role being performed by the V-bombers during 1963, which could be described as a transitional period: Blue Steel, low-level,

---

[1] In a letter of 25 Feb to CAS (MRAF Sir Thomas Pike) he had urged that Blue Steel should be modified (ID3/901/6 Pt 4 Medium Bomber Force – Size & Composition).

tactical bomber, tanker and strategic reconnaissance; and it is quite clear, from the squadron Operations Record Books, how these roles were allocated. The new low-level role was given to the Vulcan and Victor Mk 1A squadrons – at Waddington (Nos 44, 50 and 101 with Vulcans), Cottesmore (Nos 10 and 15 with Victors) and Honington (Nos 55 and 57 with Victors). Training for it began in March 1963 – the weather during January and February had been exceptionally severe, with snow and ice all over Britain[1], No 44 Sqn recording that "training for the low-level role" began on the 12th, the CO (Wg Cdr F R Lockyer) and the two Flight Commanders flying "the first of their required five low-level exercises. Each crew" – the compiler noted – "will fly four low-level sorties at 1,000ft *agl* and will then be checked by the squadron or flight commander at 500ft *agl*". On 25 February four No 57 Squadron pilots (Flt Lts L S Ketcher, P G Lawson and J D Ward, and Fg Off E J W Gregory) had given a briefing on low-level operations to No 139 Squadron (Victor B.2s, later that year to convert to the Blue Steel role) and on 1 March No 57 Sqn themselves received a briefing: a lecture on low-level flying techniques, given to the aircrew by a team from RAF Marham, where the Valiant Tactical Bomber Force was based[2]. In April No 101 Sqn ORB noted that low-level training sorties had been flown by Wg Cdr A Griffiths (the CO), Sqn Ldr A M Laidlay and Flt Lts E H Macey, J O H Lewarne and A Shepphard and their crews, while during May "all crews carried out one or more low-level sorties". Similarly in June and July, when training flights included low-level flight-refuelling sorties.[3]

No 55 Sqn recorded in its ORB for April 1963: "This month was the start of low-level sorties. On 29 April Flt Lt D Mobberley and crew flew on the first with success. The squadron was, by the end of June, to be fully trained in low-level flying to be able to meet the Command's new policy". Also in April one of the Vulcan squadrons at Waddington, No 50, noted that "during the month the squadron commenced to train in earnest for the low-level MBF role . . ."[4]. Then in May one of the Victor

---

[1] No 27 Sqn at Scampton recorded in its ORB for January 1963 that "the whole of Britain spent most of January covered in ice and snow. Intense frost, freezing fog, snow and high winds made mock of scheduled flying... ", though "the extremely cold weather did not hinder the readiness exercises involving the Alert crews, although much anti-freeze and sweat was expended in keeping QRA aircraft at full readiness".
[2] The Waddington ORB for March recorded that "a major change of policy came with the introduction of low-level profile flight by Vulcan Mk 1A aircraft, thus giving the force alternative operational techniques. A presentation on the subject was given by a briefing team from RAF Marham on 5th March...".
[3] The Honington ORB for Apr 63 mentions Trial No 467 – Low Level In Flight Refuelling: "To avoid the need to penetrate enemy early-warning radar cover at high altitude it might be desirable to extend the low-level range of certain MB aircraft by means of IFR. The object of Trial No 467 was to determine the feasibility, by day or night, of IFR as a means of extending the low-level range".
[4] On 12 Jun 63 the squadron lost an aircraft, XH477, which crashed in hills near Aboyne in Aberdeenshire on a low-level training flight.

squadrons at Cottesmore, No 10, commented in its ORB that "it can be seen that the squadron has now undertaken a low-level attack role. Due to aircraft fatigue limitations the majority of sorties are now undertaken at 1,000ft *agl*, with every third sortie at 500ft *agl*. Low-level training took priority over all other flying during the month . . .".

"Due to aircraft fatigue limitations . . .". This was one of the factors which had to be taken into account in planning for the new role, which inevitably lagged behind its implementation at squadron level with existing aircraft and equipment, designed for high-level operations. Commenting on 1963 operations, the history of No 1 Group says that "a major policy change" in that year was "the declared intention to operate the Vulcan 1A free-fall squadrons in the low-level role from 1 June. The Mk 2 force followed suit and actually changed roles from 1 May 1964".

The major policy decisions and their formulation have already been referred to: the Minister of Defence memorandum on The Deterrent in the pre-Polaris Period, approved by the Cabinet Defence Committee on 23 January; and the VCAS paper Bomber Command in the Period 1963-70, approved by the Air Council on 14 March. In sum, these documents authorised the use of the V-bombers at low level and the development of applicable weapons – modified Blue Steel and a lay-down bomb. The technical implications of these decisions, however, took very much longer to work out – during the remainder of 1963 and into 1964. They concerned the aircraft themselves and the modifications to them which would be necessary, and the weapons they were to carry; the former were the subject of a Standard of Preparation and the latter of Air Staff Requirements.

Standard of Preparation No 54, which had the title Medium Bomber Force Aircraft – Low-level Role and was issued on 3 May 1963[1], showed in its 63 paragraphs and three appendices just how complicated was the business of converting a high-level force to low-level operations, its four opening paragraphs spelling-out the new situation and what the Air Staff considered was necessary to meet it:–

"The decision to cancel the Skybolt long-range air-to-ground missile system has much reduced the future credibility of the V-force deterrent in the face of expected Soviet air defences against medium- and high-flying aircraft. However, in view of the lesser Soviet capability likely to exist during the next few years against aircraft flying at low level, it has been decided that the Medium Bomber Force will operate in the low-level role.

"The operational aim is to evade organised defences as much as possible; this may be achieved by flying as low as possible en route, avoiding ring defences by the use of stand-off weapons where available.

"The Victor Mk 1/1A and Vulcan Mk 1/1A will be withdrawn from

---

[1] Over the signatures of ACAS(OR) and DOR(C).

bomber service by mid-1965, but the Saceur-assigned Valiants are planned to continue in service until the late 1960s[1]. Modifications to these aircraft systems are required to give them a low-level capability commensurate with their planned lives in the bomber force.

"The Mk 2 V-bombers are required to pose a measure of deterrence until at least 1970, and as such must be modified to enable them to operate in the low-level role against an increasing Soviet defence capability".

The SoP said that since weapons releasable at low level, or at pop-up height[2], would be available for the whole MBF by the third quarter of 1963, modification to aircraft systems to give them low-level capabilities were required "as soon as possible". All marks of Vulcan and Victor free-fall aircraft were required to have a capability appropriate to pop-up weapon delivery by the third quarter of 1963; and in the case of Mk 2 aircraft, major modifications were to be applied where possible in production or during retrofit programmes.

Hard on the heels of Standard of Preparation No 54 came the draft Air Staff Requirement No 1132 (Issue 4) – a new version of the original Blue Steel OR – which was circulated on 13 May 1963 and said that "the Air Staff requires the further development of the Blue Steel missile to enable it to be launched from Mk 2 V-bombers flying at the lowest possible level". The modifications necessary were to be "the minimum compatible with the requirements" – launch from the lowest possible level in the height band 250ft–1,000ft – and the requirements would apply to all the Blue Steel missiles in service. This ASR, dated 26 May 1965 in its final form, contained 56 paragraphs covering every aspect of Blue Steel low-level operations.

The SoP, which was to be superseded on 5 May 1964 by Air Staff Requirement No 380 with the same title[3], detailed the weapons to be carried by the different marks of V-bomber in the low-level deterrent role:–

Valiant	Mk 43 lay-down bomb, and possibly Red Beard[4] pop-up delivery
Victor Mk1/1A	Yellow Sun Mk 2 pop-up delivery[5]
Vulcan Mk1/1A	ditto
Pre-retrofit Victor Mk 2	ditto
Vulcan Mk 2/Free Fall	ditto
	High-yield ASR 1177-type lay-down bomb, when available
Post-retrofit Victor Mk 2	Blue Steel low-level release when available
Vulcan Mk 2/Blue Steel	ditto

---

[1] In the event, the Valiant force was withdrawn from service in January 1965.
[2] *Ie* following a rapid climb after a low-level approach to a target.
[3] Both are in Bombers – The Deterrent – Future of the Deterrent (DCAS/B.1-65 Pt II).
[4] Red Beard was a tactical atomic bomb.
[5] During 1963 BCAS teams modified YS Mk 2 weapons for low-level delivery (BCAS ORB).

The V-bombers' operational mission was described as having a high-low-high profile, with "a low-level phase of up to 1,000nm in the extreme case". In training, this phase would normally be of the order of 350-500nm. A capability to operate in all weathers was required, the height at which aircraft would fly varying at the discretion of the captain, according to prevailing conditions: it might be as low as 50ft in good visibility or up to 1,000ft in poor visibility. Pop-up manoeuvres were required for delivery of Yellow Sun Mk 2 and possibly for Red Beard. In these, the SoP stated, "the aircraft will climb to a weapon release height of the order of 12,000ft, and it is accepted that the speed of entry . . . might have to be less than the ultimate cleared speed of the aircraft, so that the operational manoeuvre may be properly simulated in training".

This type of training was to be conducted over the UK, North America and possibly North Africa, and the SoP pointed out hazards peculiar to low-level flying – turbulence, impact damage (from hailstones and bird strikes), visibility and temperature. Pilot's Notes were to be amended "to include advice on handling the airframe/engine combination at high speed/low level, including the pop-up manoeuvre where appropriate".

Referring to modifications to the V-bombers for low-level operations, the SoP said that their equipment standard for that role should not affect their capability in the high-level role in limited war, using either HE or nuclear weapons, nor equipment incorporated for other specific purposes – for example, rapid start and take-off and autoland systems. As to the strength of the aircraft, modifications to the Valiant and the Vulcan/Victor Mk 1/1As were not required; strengths of the Mk 2 types were to allow all-up weights of 225,000lb for the Victor and 220,000lb for the Vulcan.

Flying so close to the ground in their new role (weapon launch was to be "at the lowest practical height") the V-bombers were to have the maximum possible self-defence through electronic equipment and camouflage. For low-level operations the Mk 2s had to carry four types of ECM (electronic countermeasure) fit – ARI 18105 passive warning receivers, ARI 5919 active tail-warning equipment (to be replaced by ARI 5952), rapid-blooming window and infra-red decoy flares. They were additionally to have, for pop-up manoeuvres and high-level (limited war) operations, ARIs 18074 VHF communications jammer, 18075 metric radar jammers, 18076 centimetric radar jammers, 18205 L-band radar jammer, 18146 X-band jammer (in the Victors) and 18051 window (gravity-launched). As to camouflage, the Valiant and Vulcan/ Victor Mk 2 metal upper-surfaces were to be "coloured by a variegated pattern of greys and greens", while under-surfaces could remain in the white anti-flash standard. The first Waddington Vulcan to be so camouflaged, XH505, was flown to HSA at Bitteswell on 24 March 1964 to be painted in the new colours.

Then there were modifications to the navigation/attack systems. Sidescan radar installations (ASR 3600) were required in all Mk 2 aircraft, which were also to have Decca Mk 4 roller maps. For dead reckoning, Green Satin Mks 1 and 2 were to be modified "to function down to the lowest possible height", and all Mk 2 aircraft were to be equipped with the GPI (ground position indicator) Mk 6. Also for the Mk 2 V-bombers, a terrain-avoidance/clearance radar was "highly desirable". (They were subsequently fitted with General Dynamics terrain-following radar.)

The SoP added, in referring to maintenance and reliability, that MBF aircraft had to be "capable of reverting to their full performance in high-level operations, when required for limited-war situations". The Air Staff accepted that pre-flight changes would be necessary in some cases, but the required servicing effort was to be minimised. Further, the effect of high-speed/low-level flight on the serviceability of the entire aircraft weapon system was to be considered.

It was clear that the change-over to a low-level role for the V-force during 1963, both with Blue Steel weapons and free-fall bombs, involved considerable planning and logistic problems. It is clear also, from the Standard of Preparation issued by the Air Staff in May of that year, that flexibility of operation was to be retained for the force – for low-level, high-level and limited-war roles.

Serious concern was expressed by the AOC in C Bomber Command (Air Mshl Sir Kenneth Cross) during 1963 about the reliability of Blue Steel. Writing to CAS (MRAF Sir Thomas Pike) on 30 July[1] he said that he had recently had its reliability, and the associated problem of maintaining it at readiness, examined by his Research Staff; and although their studies had only been based on R&D firings in Australia and limited experience gained from the Joint Service Trials at Scampton, their conclusions were "far from reassuring".

As to reliability, the chances of a missile being fit for powered launch at the launch point were no better than 40%, while the probability of a missile reaching its target after launch was about 75%. This meant that "of, say, six weapons on readiness, two or at the most three would be launched and the remainder will have to be carried over the target and dropped free-fall. Of those launched, one will probably fail to reach the target." He added that although there was as yet no experience of maintaining Blue Steel aircraft on Readiness, "the frequency of changing the aircraft/missile system will be appreciably greater than with a free-fall weapon"; and he came to the glum conclusion that "considered in the context of a full-scale generation of 75% of the Blue Steel force during an alert, the low reliability implies that on present assessment only 14 missiles out of 36 could actually be launched and 11 would reach the target".

[1] BC/S. 6400/CINC.

The AOC in C was equally concerned about the problems of generating missiles:–

"It is already evident that the time to generate a Blue Steel weapon system cannot be reduced much below seven hours even when no defects arise, and may take between ten and 15 hours. We are therefore taking steps to maintain permanently some missiles in a partly generated state. What concerns me more, however, is the time it will take to recover from either a full-scale exercise or an emergency generation of weapons. Owing mainly to the need to dry out missiles after draining the HTP (one drying unit only is scheduled for each station), the time could be as long as 15 days for a station to recover its normal peacetime preparedness. We shall obviously have to be very careful before mounting a full-scale exercise, if in fact we can ever risk doing so."

CAS replied in placatory terms, saying that he shared the C in C's concern about the shortcomings of Blue Steel[1],

"but as you say we are basing our conclusions at the moment on a small sample of R&D firings and the experience gained . . . from the trials at Scampton. We can expect to learn a great deal about the deficiencies of the weapon – and the way to correct them – from these trials, and we must hope that when the appropriate modifications are embodied in the production missiles we shall see a noticeable improvement in performance and generation time.

"Similarly, we can certainly hope for improvements in the method and the time taken to dry out the weapons . . .".

Blue Steel had perforce become from the outset both a high- and a low-level weapon – *ipso facto*; for its acceptance into service coincided with the introduction of a low-level role for the V-force, and the trials by the JSTU (No 4 Joint Services Trials Unit in Australia, which did the Blue Steel acceptance trials, for which the V-bombers flew out weapons[2]) reflected this dual capability. Remarks in the opening chapter of No 4 JSTU's final report, on the operational background to the trials, summarise admirably the whole course of tests of this air-to-surface weapon and the sea-change to which it was subjected in the course of development:–

"The Conception

"The operational requirement for an air-to-surface stand-off weapon system was the subject of discussions in both Air Ministry and the Ministry of Aviation in the early 1950s. From these studies emerged a firm operational requirement (OR1132) which was issued in late 1954. The first contract on Messrs A V Roe called for a design study of a stand-off bomb suitable for carriage by Royal Air Force V-bombers.

---

[1] CAS.2392, 9 Aug 63.

[2] These flights were called Blue Rangers, No 83 Sqn (the third Vulcan squadron to get Blue Steel) doing its first in November 1963. The BS Vulcan squadrons' base, Scampton, housed the other Blue Steel trials unit, No 18 JSTU.

"Work on the project by the newly constituted Weapons Division of A V Roe started shortly afterwards and from these preliminary studies came the proposal for a missile which, in substance, is . . . Blue Steel. . . .

"The Operational Climate
"It was originally envisaged that the missile should be employed solely at high level, with release heights in the order of 50,000ft, and all the early design and development work was to this end. The operational conception was of a force of V-bombers standing outside the enemy defensive network and launching missiles travelling at speeds between M1.5 and M2.5 and attaining an apogee of 70,000ft, whilst covering a range of approximately 100nm. At a later date it was planned to replace the Blue Steel system with the American weapon Skybolt.

"Following the cancellation of Skybolt, to ensure that the period of credible deterrent offered by the V-bombers could be extended, it was decided to use the main V-force in the low-level role. A feasibility study revealed that only minor modifications were required to adapt Blue Steel to the low-level environment and contracts were placed on Hawker Siddeley Dynamics Ltd, Woodford, for design and development of these modifications in mid-1963.

"The Australian Trials
"This then was the background to the Australian Blue Steel trials. Following the launching of 2/5th scale models from Valiant aircraft, full-scale test vehicles approximating to the final operational missile were launched during 1960. The W100 series of Blue Steel missiles, however, were not launched until 1961 and it was February 1962 before the first W100A Blue Steel missile (virtually the production operational round) was released at Woomera.

"All the missiles launched before November 1963 were released at high level, the first low-level launch being made at 2,000ft from a Vulcan on 19 November 1963. The final trial of the series was, in fact, at high level – on 16 October 1964 to prove the dual capability of the system; whilst the final low-level release was made at 1,000ft above ground level, at 350kt IAS, from a Victor aircraft on 19 August 1964"[1].

On 16 October 1963 DCAS minuted S of S for Air to say that the DRPC had approved the proposals to enable Blue Steel to be modified so that it could be launched at low level. This modification was "a relatively cheap one": it would cost "only £3.5m in development, though this would be reduced by £1.25m if a decision were taken quickly because certain work at present planned on high-level Blue Steel development need not be done". Production costs would be about £7,000 per missile with £0.4m for modification to the test equipment. To modify Blue Steel in this way "would be very much cheaper than equipping the 48 Blue Steel aircraft with laydown bombs".

[1] Blue Steel Acceptance Trials – Australia No 4 Joint Services Trials Unit (Pts 1-4).

When, a month later, S of S visited RAF Scampton to see Blue Steel for himself the AOC in C Bomber Command (Air Mshl Sir John Grandy) wrote to him on the following day (19 November) to say that "the first and most important requirement" was to get Blue Steel into the low-level role as quickly as possible"; he had heard that day that the first low-level trials weapon had been launched that morning from a Vulcan flying at 300kt at 2,000ft. But there were certain requirements, like an efficient heating system for the HTP and gyros when the missile was at readiness on an aircraft; authority to fuel missiles at readiness on aircraft with warheads fitted; authority to fit thermal batteries to readiness missiles and leave the batteries on them; and authority to fly missiles with warhead loaded, from main bases to dispersals in order to test the capability of the weapon systems. When these problems had been overcome, the C in C said, "Bomber Command will have an excellent and viable deterrent and strike capability".

He had sent a copy of his letter to VCAS, who on the 26th wrote to S of S answering several of the points raised. Thus, the HTP heating problem had been resolved by adopting a method of ducting warm air into the missile; the problem of gyro heating had been to provide a suitable and reliable ground power source: twelve generators were being ordered on an interim basis to cover QRA commitments; Bomber Command had "the dispensation, in an emergency, to load fuelled missiles with warheads fitted"; fitting the thermal batteries to missiles on QRA aircraft was "specifically excluded" by the terms of the CA Release: however, the matter was being re-examined in an attempt to meet the Command's requirements; and the carriage of Blue Steel when fitted with an operational warhead raised special problems – because of the complexity of the missile, and in particular because of the presence of some 400 gal of HTP and the tendency of the missile to leak: he felt that "we should not try to extend the authority to carry free-falling weapons to Blue Steel until we have had a reasonable amount of experience on the behaviour of the missile, and its general handling characteristics".

There were still delays in the Blue Steel modification programme, however, and in December 1963 the Ministers of Aviation and Air wrote to the Minister of Defence to request an early decision. The former said that the RAF could be given a low-level operational capability within six months of a decision to go ahead on the full project; the latter that he fully supported the Minister of Aviation's request for an early decision to go ahead with the modification of Blue Steel for the low-level role. On the 20th the Minister of Defence (Mr Peter Thorneycroft) gave a qualified approval for work to proceed – an extension of the holding contract for low-level Blue Steel for another three months, at an estimated cost of £0.65m; and initial production expenditure over the same period of time amounting to about £0.1m. These decisions had in fact been conveyed to the MoA and the Treasury by the MoD on the 16th.

On 1 July 1964 the Controller of Aircraft (Mr Morien Morgan) sent DCAS (Air Mshl Sir Christopher Hartley) a CA Release "for the carriage, and launch in an emergency, of Blue Steel in the low-level launch role from Vulcan B Mk 2 and Victor B Mk 2 aircraft". He said that Blue Steel firing trials were due to be completed by the end of the year and he expected to offer DCAS "a final CA Release, covering weapon effectiveness, accuracy, etc," in about March-April 1965. He also included a clearance "for flights to dispersal airfields in peacetime with live warheads (less thermal batteries) fitted to weapons on Vulcan B Mk 2 aircraft"[1]. On the 14th the Nuclear Weapon Safety Committee had endorsed a joint MoA/RAF paper on the mounting of a Blue Steel QRA, subject to the thermal batteries not being held in the partially or fully inserted position. Subsequently, in November of that year, the CA Release was amended to include the Blue Steel Victors – giving clearance for filled and fuelled QRA, including flights to dispersal with operational warhead pods, by Victor B Mk 2s[2].

Also during 1964, major endorsements of the programme of modifications required for the V-bombers' low-level role were given, by the Chiefs of Staff on 14 May, by the Weapons Development Committee on 24 June and by the Minister of Defence (Mr Peter Thorneycroft) on 27 July[3]. The programme as finally agreed showed some changes from the original one: it was not thought necessary to undertake work to improve the Victor's fatigue life, requirements for navigation system improvement were reduced, and it was concluded that it would not be possible in the time available to obtain the special low-level ECM equipment at first envisaged. On the other hand the programme proposed took account of extensive low-altitude flying trials, ground trials on the effect of bird strikes, work on the engines to give protection against bird strikes and to assess the effects of sustained low-level operations, the installation of a terrain warning equipment and the development of long-range fuel tanks. The total estimated R&D costs were £2.2m and the estimated production cost about £11m. The estimated production costs of the connected project for modifying Blue Steel for the low-level role had gone down from £0.8m to £0.25m[4].

Serious problems arose with the handling of Blue Steel missiles while they were in service, particularly on Quick Reaction Alert (QRA) aircraft: these related to the HTP (high test peroxide) and kerosine propellants in the missiles, the thermal battery supplying electricity to the warhead and the incompatibility of aircraft de-icing fluids with HTP.

[1] ID9/B.18-90 Powered Bombs – Blue Steel CA Clearance.
[2] Minute, DCA/RAF to DCAS, 25 Nov 64 (Ibid).
[3] AHB ID9/B.6-80 'V' Bombers Low Level Role and ID3/946/8 (Pt 1) Development of Blue Steel.
[4] Submission to Secretary of State, 24 July 64 (Ibid). The Air Ministry Quarterly Liaison Report for Jan-March 1964: "Blue Steel Missiles, modified for deployment at either high or low level, have now been developed and firing trials completed. Acceptance firings are now in progress and the programme will be complete before the end of 1964".

On 30 July VCAS (Air Mshl W H Kyle) wrote to the Minister (RAF)[1] to point out the risks involved in converting the Blue Steel QRA commitment to the powered role: the presence of HTP and kerosine within the weapon inevitably increased the potential risk of fire; on the other hand, the absence of propellants meant that the weapon could only be used as a free-fall bomb, which was quite unacceptable. He said that HTP was readily soluble in water and its activity could be reduced quickly by dilution. Special handling and monitoring procedures had been introduced, designed to ensure that the condition of the propellant during fuelling and while on QRA was regularly scrutinised; and a fire tender, water tender and crews were constantly on duty at the QRA site. The Nuclear Weapons Safety Committee had considered these safety proposals and endorsed the handling procedures for QRA aircraft carrying Blue Steel, and had confirmed that – given these safeguards – the fire hazard was in their view acceptable.

The other problem VCAS mentioned was that of the thermal battery, which provided the only source of electrical energy to the warhead: it could be inserted after the weapon was in position on the aircraft, but this took ten minutes or more, while QRA V-bombers could become airborne in two minutes; so to match this capability the aircraft should be held on QRA with the thermal batteries inserted – which the MoA opposed, but they had devised a scheme whereby the batteries could be located in a semi-installed position. Tests were to be held to see what happened if a missile were accidentally dropped while on standby, or crushed under its parent aircraft. Meanwhile, CA clearance had been given for the mounting of QRA by Vulcan aircraft with ready-to-use Blue Steel missiles, but without thermal batteries installed, and similar clearance for the Victor was expected shortly. VCAS added that he would approach the Minister separately on the question of the thermal batteries when this had been cleared with the NWSC, and meanwhile, clearance had been given to insert the batteries on standby in the event of an emergency. On the following day (31 July) PS to the Minister informed PS/VCAS that in view of the special precautions referred to by VCAS, and the conclusions reached by the NWSC, the Minister (RAF) agreed that this form of QRA might be introduced.

The other problem, that of HTP/de-icing fluid incompatibility – mixing HTP with DC2A aircraft de-icing fluid resulted in an instantaneous explosion, came to light in November 1964, and on the 26th ACAS(Ops) (AVM D G Smallwood) wrote to DCAS to say that as an immediate action, the use of de-icing fluid on aircraft fitted with powered missiles had been forbidden. Then on 11 December the AOC in C Bomber Command (Air Mshl Sir John Grandy) wrote to DCAS (Air Mshl C H Hartley) referring to this "belated discovery" and

---

[1] AF/B18-93 DCAS Powered Bombs – Blue Steel – Use on QRA Aircraft ID9/B.18-93.

459

saying that a working party had looked into de-icing methods on the Vulcan and Victor and had concluded that provided commonsense precautions were taken – "including keeping the working areas clear of catalytic material" – the probability of HTP and de-icing fluid "combining in combustible quantities" was remote. There was currently a total ban on using de-icing fluid on aircraft armed with fuelled Blue Steel and he understood that this could not be lifted until the situation had been considered by the NWSC. The C in C continued:–

"We have already had some freezing temperatures and slight snow, and we must expect more. Unless the ban on the use of de-icing fluid is lifted very soon, therefore, I may have to use unpowered missiles in order to maintain Blue Steel QRA aircraft in a flyable state."

He added that he was extremely reluctant to take this step and would be most grateful if DCAS would do all he could to bring the problem before the NWSC as quickly as possible.

A Memorandum of 22 December from the Ordnance Board to MoD – D of Ops (B&R) RAF, signed by the chairman, OB/AAEE Blue Steel Safety Committee, said:–

"The OB AAEE Blue Steel Safety Committee are satisfied that the proposed precautions [*to be taken when de-icing Victors and Vulcans with DC2 when fitted with Blue Steel operational missiles*] are adequate and reduce any risk of fire to a minimum compatible with maintaining the state of readiness necessary for QRA aircraft".

On the matter of the insertion of thermal batteries, in February 1965 VCAS (Air Mshl B K Burnett) informed the Minister (RAF)[1] that a modification had been produced which permitted the batteries to remain in a partially inserted position during standby with absolute safety; when they needed to be fully inserted, during an emergency or when a 'scramble' signal had been given, a simple action taking some ten seconds was required to complete the sequence. So, if this modification were incorporated into all Blue Steel missiles, Blue Steel reaction time would be comparable with that of Yellow Sun. The NWSC had endorsed these proposals, technical clearance had been given and the Minister's covering approval was now sought for the partial insertion of thermal batteries into Blue Steel missiles on standby alert, which was subsequently given[2].

The RAF purchase of 57 Blue Steel missiles had included four which were specifically for in-service proof firings by Bomber Command after the weapon's entry into service, the firing programme allowing for launches over the RAE Aberporth range in April, July and October 1966 and in March 1967. The missiles were to be fuelled with kerosine and HTP but would carry inert warheads.

---

[1] VCAS 788, 10 Feb 65.
[2] PS/VCAS to PS/Minister (RAF), 22 Feb 65.

The first of these proof firings in fact took place on 27 May, a Blue Steel being launched from a Victor B.2 flying at 1,000ft *asl* at 350kt IAS. Its components functioned properly and it impacted within 1,000yd of the 25nm range target[1]. The first Vulcan launch was on 31 May 1967, described as being "from an angle-off of 68° from the 43-mile target, from a height of 1,000ft AMSL and at a speed of 350kt"[2].

Blue Steel began to be phased-out of service during the last quarter of 1968[3]: the two Victor B.2 squadrons at Wittering, Nos 100 and 139, were disbanded on 1 October and 31 December respectively; the Vulcan B.2 squadrons at Scampton went on in the Blue Steel role until 1969-70 – No 83 being disbanded on 31 August 1969, No 27 ceasing operations as a Blue Steel unit and reverting to a free-fall role on 31 December 1969[4] and No 617 making its final training flight carrying a Blue Steel missile on 21 December 1970, its ORB recording for that month that "all squadron crews have now been converted to the free-fall role and as from 31 Dec 70 there will be no further Blue Steel training commitment".

The aircraft were converted as well as their crews: from September 1969 there was a steady feed-in of Vulcan B.2s from RAF Scampton to HSA Ltd at Bitteswell for conversion, this programme going on until late 1971. The Blue Steel missile holdings at Scampton were gradually decreased until the end of 1970 – beginning of 1971, and the Missile Engineering Squadrons were disbanded – that at Wittering by the end of March 1969 and at Scampton by the end of March 1971.

Thus Blue Steel, conceived as a high-level weapon but adapted for low-level use also[5]. The new weapon to be used in the low-level role, by the Mk 2 free-fall Vulcans, was the high-yield[6] ASR 1177-type lay-down bomb. This resulted from a Joint Naval/Air Staff Requirement (NASR 1177) for "a general-purpose nuclear bomb", the introduction to this requirement clearly setting the scene for the new weapon – as far as the RAF were concerned – in the pre-Polaris period. It said that

"Because of envisaged enemy countermeasures and the need to change aircraft approach and delivery tactics, the existing British nuclear bombs Yellow Sun, Blue Steel and Red Beard will be unsuitable as primary weapons beyond 1975[7]. Moreover, with the cancellation of

---

[1] ID9/194/4 Blue Steel June 64-Oct 1969.

[2] Ibid – Minute, ACAS(Ops)/VCAS, 21 Jun 67.

[3] AF/CT 3415/65, Pt I Blue Steel – Operational Use and Phase Out.

[4] Its ORB had earlier commented with some bitterness that on 1 July at 0001hr "Quick Reaction Alert (QRA) ended without fuss at midnight. A congratulatory signal was received from the C in C, thus marking the end of one of the most important chapters in the squadron's history. It seemed a pity that there was no greater recognition for a job well done".

[5] The Blue Steel Vulcan and Victor Mk 2 squadrons had a low-level role like the free-fall squadrons (see *The Times* for 21 Sept 64, describing a low-level sortie in Victor XL190 of No 100 Sqn from Wittering).

[6] The low-yield version (600lb) was to be used in the Canberra B Mks 15 and 16.

[7] Yellow Sun was the megaton bomb, Red Beard a tactical atomic weapon.

Skybolt as the planned replacement for Yellow Sun and the introduction of Polaris unlikely to become fully effective before 1970, an urgent need exists for a new bomb to maintain the United Kingdom independent deterrent during the interim period and as supplementary capability thereafter.

"By 1966, the manned bomber aircraft may survive enemy defences in the European theatre and deliver a successful strike only by flying at high speed at very low level. Yellow Sun and Blue Steel are designed for release at medium/high altitude[1] where the delivery aircraft and/or bomb is vulnerable to interception, whilst Red Beard cannot withstand the low-level flight environment, is limited in method of fuzing and delivery, and possesses some undesirable safety restrictions when held at readiness in an operational state[2]. Early replacement is essential.

"The replacement bomb must be multi-purpose by design. It must satisfy joint Naval and Air Staff requirements for carriage and delivery in current medium-bomber aircraft and planned high-performance aircraft, to exploit fully their low-level strike capability against strategic and tactical, hard and soft targets . . . , with corresponding different warhead yields. . . .

"Research and development studies show clearly that such a bomb can be produced fully within the time-scale. However, to maintain an effective United Kingdom nuclear deterrent during development of the Polaris weapon system, priority is to be given to production of the high-yield version for the RAF medium bomber force. . . ."

The object of the Requirement, as far as the Air Staff were concerned, was a bomb (WE 177 Type B) "for delivery in the laydown mode by June 1966 and capable of modification for delivery in the ballistic, loft and retarded modes". It was to be "as small and light in weight as possible"; including the tail fairing, the weight of the Type B version was not to exceed 1,000lb. Dimensions of the Type A (600lb) and Type B bombs were similar: 144in long, with a carcass diameter of 16.5in and tail fin span of 24in.

WE 177, for which the civilian contractors were Hunting Engineering Ltd, was on trials during 1965 and expected to be in service by the first half of 1966. A progress report of 20 July 1965[3] forecast "approval to the Service of the type 'B' weapon for lay-down delivery in temperate climates by mid-February 1966, plus or minus nine weeks. . .". Another progress report referred to Service trials being held between 28 February and 6 July 1965: one of the trials vehicles was at Cottesmore and was loaded into, and flown in, a Vulcan. A report on this trial said in its Introduction that

"RAF Cottesmore was tasked . . . with flying trials on the ASR 1177

---

[1] Blue Steel was to be capable of release at heights between 30,000ft and 60,000ft (OR1132).
[2] Red Beard had no provision for in-flight loading.
[3] Minute from OR30(RAF)/150 headed "WE 177 Progress".

weapon system, to establish its compatibility in a Service environment, prior to a general release to service. A total of 50hr flying was required for Store No 2, involving simulated bombing runs at high and low level in a Vulcan B Mk 2 aircraft.

"The trials vehicle was a type 'B' 950lb weapon. . .".

Although it had been hoped that the WE 177 'B' weapon would be in service by mid-1966[1], deliveries did not begin until September of that year. A report to the Air Force Board in October[2] said that these deliveries were two months later than forecast and eight months behind the target date. The final delay had been caused by "warhead modifications, a safety requirement and the need to obtain the Prime Minister's approval for road movement". But Bomber Command was now – that is, in October 1966 – "able to operate QRA with this weapon". The Ministry of Aviation was increasing the output of WE 177Bs so that the order would be completed by May 1967. Meanwhile, Service Handling Trials were continuing at Cottesmore and Akrotiri, and the question of "limited environmental trials" in the Far East was under discussion with the MoA. The trials at Akrotiri, held from October 1965 onwards, were those originally scheduled for FEAF – that is, tropical trials – but not held in that theatre because of political circumstances at the time, during the 1963-66 Indonesian Confrontation period[3].

---

[1] An Aide-Memoire for a meeting at RAE on 1 Dec 65 on CA Clearances of WE 177 said that the Air Staff had hoped to achieve an operational capability of the Vulcan/WE 177 'B' system by February 1966 and that the latest forecast date for delivery was February 1966.

[2] Annex to AFB(66)35.

[3] "VCAS has accepted the Air Commander FEAF's request that, for the time being, the trials rounds of WE 177 should not be deployed to FEAF. . ." (Minute, D of Ops (B&R) to DOR3(RAF), 23 Aug 65).

CHAPTER XXVII

LOSS OF THE VALIANTS; VICTOR SR AND FR

The cancellation of Skybolt and the after-effects which have just been described were followed by the two events which, as already suggested, weakened Bomber Command: the loss of its Valiants and the cancellation of TSR.2.

Vickers Valiants, referred to previously in this history in their various manifestations and achievements – as the first V-bombers, in strategic reconnaissance and ECM roles, as pioneer jet tankers, on nuclear weapon tests and in low-level tactical bomber operations, provided the foundation and original backbone of the V-force. To have them suddenly removed from service in 1965 was a big blow not only to the Command – which lost six squadrons, comprising its flight refuelling and strategic reconnaissasnce capabilities and its TBF assignment to Saceur – but to all the personnel who flew and serviced Valiants. The AOC in C (Air Mshl Sir John Grandy) issued an Order of the Day following their official withdrawal from service on 27 January 1965; this said:–

"Personal from Air Officer Commanding in Chief for AOC 3 Group, CRE and Station Commanders.

"It is a bitter blow that the outcome of the Valiant troubles[1] has had to be their withdrawal from service. As the first of the V-bombers the Valiants, and the air and ground crews who have flown and maintained them, have played a major role in the nation's defence for nearly ten years.[2]

"Valiants were the aircraft from which the first British nuclear weapons were tested and they were the spearhead of our nuclear strike force until the arrival of the Vulcan and the Victor. They have been flown in the Medium Bomber, Tactical Bomber, Photo Reconnaissance, Tanker, Electronic Countermeasures and Associated Training Roles. Valiants took part in active operations in 1956[3], a Valiant flew the first non-stop flight in 1960 from the United Kingdom to Singapore and return, and Valiants have been used on innumerable occasions for goodwill visits to many distant countries throughout the world.

"Since last August when the spar troubles were first detected we have had a period of uncertainty during which exhaustive tests have been carried out. During this time I have been much impressed by the high morale and spirit with which this setback has been faced by you all; your

---

[1] Which started on 6 August 1964 when Flt Lt J W Foreman of No 232 OCU, Gaydon, "was giving instruction to a student pilot in Valiant WP217 when a loud bang was heard associated with a pronounced airframe shudder. The exercise was abandoned and on return to base it was found that the starboard flap would not come down. A flapless landing was carried out. . .". The engineers found the rear spar of the starboard mainplane cracked and the starboard flap drive sheared." (No 232 OCU ORB).

[2] The first Valiant squadron, No 138, had formed at Gaydon in February 1955.

[3] Ie The Suez Operation.

example has been in the best tradition of the Royal Air Force.

"The Valiant is now to be retired. I send to all ranks of the Valiant Force past and present my congratulations on the excellent record that has been maintained with this fine aircraft throughout its service in the Royal Air Force".

News of the Valiant troubles had reached the Air Staff after the precautionary inspection of a percentage of the force, and was then conveyed by CAS to the Chiefs of Staff and by the Minister (RAF) to S of S, who on 23 September 1964 asked to be informed[1] of the results of inspections and of the effect on QRA and on target coverage for Saceur. On the 30th the AOC in C Bomber Command (Air Mshl Sir John Grandy) wrote to CAS (Air Chf Mshl Sir Charles Elworthy) to tell him it had become clear that few aircraft were going to be available for normal flying and that the majority would be grounded, except for emergency operations, until they could be repaired[2]. He suggested, as an insurance that two of the Valiants' roles would be fulfilled, an acceleration of both the Victor tanker conversion programme and the Victor Mk 2 PR re-equipment programme for No 543 Squadron.

At this time there was confident reference to a "repair scheme", when ACAS(Ops) (AVM D G Smallwood) reported on the situation to S of S and the Minister (RAF) on CAS's behalf on 2 October. The latter, in a reply to AOC to C Bomber Command on the 6th, said that it was clear that it would be mid-November at the earliest before an accurate assessment could be made of the effect on the TBF; meanwhile, he did not propose that Saceur should be told officially about the problem.

On the same day, Saceur was informed by the UK NMR (National Military Representative) at Shape HQ that a fatigue fault had been discovered in the Valiants; and DCAS (Air Mshl Sir Christopher Hartley) wrote to the Controller of Aircraft, MoA (Mr M B Morgan), pointing out that the Valiant failures had occurred at between 35% and 75% of the assessed safe fatigue life and the special inspection had shown that only four out of 60 aircraft were free of fatigue cracks – which was evidence that the existing formulae and factors used to assess aircraft fatigue lives could be unreliable, and that therefore their validity should be re-examined, especially because of "immediate concern" for the Victor and the Vulcan in the low-level role.

In order to keep the strategic reconnaissance capability in being, as No 543 Squadron at Wyton had been reduced to two flyable Valiants – only one of which was useable in the SR role, C in C Bomber Command suggested to CAS on 12 November that the first two Victor PR Mk 2s should go to the squadron instead of to A&AEE for their trials. The RAF would therefore get the aircraft earlier and No 543 crews would have the benefit of flying them. CAS agreed (on 27 November) that the

---

[1] PS/S of S to PS/Minister(RAF) and PS/Minister(RAF) to PS/CAS, 29 and 23 Sep 64.
[2] Correspondence in ID9/B.3-40 (Pt 1), Bombers, Valiant – Fatigue Life.

squadron should undertake the equipment clearance trials, though these would be under MoA direction.

On 26 November 1964 VCAS (Air Mshl B K Burnett) advised the Minister (RAF) about the implications of the Valiant repair programme – involving 40 aircraft over a period of five months at a cost of about £250,000, according to the Ministry of Aviation. He said that, subject to the Minister's comments, he intended to give instructions for this to proceed as quickly as possible; and on 30 November the Minister signified his approval.[1]

But in early December the Valiant fatigue problem took a turn for the worse: inspection had revealed a crack in the front spar bigger than that in the rear spar; as a result, a signal was sent to Bomber Command on the 9th ordering the cessation of flying in the Valiant force, except in a national emergency.[2] Saceur, to whom the three TBF squadrons at Marham were assigned, was advised of this new development on the 11th. At the end of December VCAS told the Minister (RAF) that he hoped that "sufficient evidence and analysis" would be available by mid-January 1965 "to permit objective decisions on the future of the Valiant fleet".[3]

A note prepared for the Prime Minister early in the New Year on the Valiant[4] said that its R&D costs were difficult to identify because a good deal of its equipment and its engines were common with other aircraft; development of its airframe had cost about £10m, and 100 Valiants had been bought by the RAF at a cost of £57m. At one time there were 72 Valiants in the RAF front line, but since 1959/60 their numbers had been: 24 assigned to Saceur as a TBF, equipped with 48 American nuclear weapons; 16 converted for use as tankers; and eight in the SR role. The total number of Valiants, including those used for training and research, was currently 61.

On 15 January VCAS told S of S and the Minister (RAF) that investigations had shown that 60 out of these 61 RAF Valiants were suffering from fatigue damage, and that it was the opinion of the MoA, Vickers and the RAF that none of them "could be cleared as fully safe to normal design standards for flight". He intended to put it to the Air Force Board Standing Committee that there was "little alternative to withdrawing all the Valiants from service" – a view with which the committee concurred at its meeting on the 18th, and which the Chiefs of Staff discussed the following day, primarily with reference to the Saceur commitment.[5] Subsequently, Saceur was informed personally of the decision by the AOC in C Bomber Command on the 25th.

---

[1] LMs in ID9/B.3-40 (Pt 1) file Bombers, Valiant – Fatigue Life.
[2] LMs, ACAS(Ops)/VCAS and VCAS/Minister (RAF), ibid (Pt 2).
[3] VCAS.7750, 31 Dec 64, ibid.
[4] Subsequently incorporated in an annex to a minute from S of S to the PM (who agreed with the proposals on the Valiants) on 20 Jan 65.
[5] COS 4th mtg/65.

While the decision to ground the Valiants – announced in a Ministry of Defence statement on 26 January 1965 – was received with equanimity at No 232 OCU, Gaydon, which had its Victor training commitment, the noble phrases of the AOC in C received a cynical echo at Marham, where the TBF and tanker squadrons were based.

The OC Gaydon (Gp Capt A H Chamberlain) said in his ORB remarks that "the end of January (1965) brought the decision to withdraw all Valiant aircraft from service and saw the end of Valiant training at Gaydon". He recalled that the first course had started there on 1 February 1955 and that "since that time, 1,475 aircrew of all categories" had been trained on Valiants, "in addition to many hundreds passing through on refresher courses". A decision was awaited on the disposal of the station's remaining Valiants (there were four still on the strength).

Marham's comments were much longer, more detailed and quite bitter in tone; a long entry in the January 1965 ORB was headed "The Valiant Story". It said:

"The story of the decline and fall of the Valiant force began on 6 August 1964 and ended, for the RAF at any rate, on 26 January 1965. Between these dates there had been a period of restricted flying and another in which the grounded aircrew drew on their experience alone for the ability to deliver their weapons in war.

"Inspection of WP217 after landing at Gaydon on 6 August showed only too plainly that the aircraft had suffered major damage. The fuselage skin below the starboard inner plane had buckled, popping the rivets; the engine door had cracked and on the top surface of the mainplane between the two engines the rivets had been pulled and the skin buckled. The primary cause of the damage was a broken rear spar on the starboard side. All Valiants of a similar age and life pattern were grounded forthwith.

"By 25 August a manufacturer's working party had been set up to discover the extent to which the Valiant fleet was affected by metal fatigue, and on 17 September XD818[1] was given an 'A' category, and by the 21st 15 other Valiants had been categorised. Eventually all the Valiants were divided into three categories:–

   a.   Cat A   –   Flyable to 5% of remaining fatigue life –12
   b.   Cat B   –   Flyable in an emergency – 19
   c.   Cat C   –   Grounded – 5

"For a time only the Valiants in Cat 'A' flew again but eventually some Cat 'B' aircraft were also cleared for limited flying. Each aircraft was fitted with recorders and a most assiduous watch was kept on the readings in order, if possible, to relate fatigue co-efficients to heights flown and weather conditions. The Saceur-QRA commitment was maintained throughout.

---

[1] This was the aircraft which had made the first live drop of a British thermonuclear weapon in Operation Grapple and which was subsequently preserved.

"In the meantime two aircraft in Category 'B' were given to teams from 19 MU who literally hacked out with axes sections of the spars for further examination by metallurgic experts. After further inspection of these parts all the aircraft were grounded on 11 December 1964, from which date until 26 January 1965 the QRA force continued but no flying took place.[1] Aircrews embarked on a period of intense and varied ground training and interest visits.

"On 26 January 1965 the long-awaited and much-postponed announcement was received at Marham – by permission of BBC radio and television. Not until 1730hr, when most personnel had gone home for the night, was an official signal received. This authorised the disbandment of No 214 Sqn, cessation of QRA and the ending of all Valiant training.

"The official news and the MoD announcement was numbing in both its effect on Marham and its matter-of-factness. Marham's contribution to Nato, which was by far the most powerful and reliable of any RAF station, was dismissed and great play was made of the loss of tankers. There was no doubt at Marham or at Shape which was the greater loss.

"It is understood that one Valiant is to be preserved for historic purposes, but the future of the rest is not finally known".

This unusually frank and bitter comment, over the signature of the station commander (Gp Capt P A Kennedy), was understandable in view of the fact that Marham had been a Valiant station for nearly nine years: No 214 had been formed there on 15 March 1956 as the second of the Main Force squadrons in the V-force, followed on 1 May by No 49 and on 1 July by No 148, and Valiants had operated continuously out of Marham since that year. Now they were to be broken up there – with one exception, XD818, which dropped the first British megaton bomb in the Grapple trials in May 1957 – and the crews re-deployed.[2]

With the withdrawal of its Valiants Bomber Command was unable to fulfil the three roles they had performed – strategic reconnaissance, flight refuelling and TBF contribution to Saceur's forces – until they were either replaced or an alternative arrangement made. In the case of SR and FR the Valiants were replaced by Victors; in the TBF role there was no replacement – as a matter of policy the medium-bomber

---

[1] The times of each practice alert during January, and the times of the last aboard crew member of each of the three TBF force squadrons (Nos 49, 148 and 207) were given in the ORB, and Marham described as "an operational base . . .up to 26 January".

[2] Marham linked-up the preservation of this Valiant with the arrival of its first Victor tankers in a ceremony on 25 May 1965 attended by Gp Capt K G Hubbard who captained XD818 when it dropped the megaton weapon on 15 May 1957. A plaque to commemorate this aircraft and Valiants in general was unveiled; it recalls that the first prototype flew on 18 May 1951, that the Valiant was the first of the V-bombers, was designed to deliver nuclear or conventional bombs and that "originally intended to be a high-altitude bomber, . . . was also employed in the reconnaissance role, as a tanker and latterly as a low-level tactical bomber". It says that the "world-wide capability" of the V-force is typified by XD818, in which No 49 Sqn crews flew nearly 600 sorties, accounting for most of its 2,560 flying hours, and the names of 22 overseas bases it visited are commemorated. The inscription ends: "Together with the rest of the Valiant force,XD818 was taken out of service on 26 January 1965".

commitment to Saceur was allowed to lapse. These changes will be described in turn, beginning with the least-complicated one, the re-equipment of No 543 Sqn at Wyton with Victor SR Mk 2s from May 1965 onwards.

This had been decided upon well before the first symptom of trouble with the Valiants occurred; it had been discussed in the Air Ministry during 1960[1], and on 23 April 1964 there was a progress meeting at Wyton to discuss the introduction of Victor 2s and the conversion of crews. No 543's ORB recorded that it was expected that the first would be delivered in March/April 1965 and thereafter new aircraft would arrive at the rate of one a month. After the acceptance of the second Victor it was proposed to phase out the Valiants on a one-for-one basis. Central Reconnaissance Establishment (under whose aegis the squadron operated) proposals for aircrew training during the re-equipment phase included the recommendation that three squadron crews, including that of the CO (Wg Cdr A W Tarry), should be converted to Victor 2s.

No 543 had had a foretaste of Valiant troubles in July 1964, during Operation Pontifex[2], when four crews and three aircraft were positioned at Salisbury Airport, Southern Rhodesia, and WZ394 "developed a crack in the rear spar which necessitated [it] being returned to base for repair". However, the detachment completed its task successfully by 12 August and the last Valiant to return – leaving Salisbury on the 20th and routed *via* Duala in the Cameroons "to carry out a special task" (as the ORB enigmatically noted) – reached Wyton on the 26th. But there was nothing enigmatic about the spar troubles which were revealed during September. As the ORB put it:–

"Early in the month Valiant WP223 was taken out of 1st Line pending a spar inspection. Later in the month under special Technical Instruction No 122B all aircraft were taken out of 1st Line for inspection of the rear spar inner plane, by CWP (contractor's working party). The results of these inspections revealed that only one aircraft was fit to fly a limited number of hours. Six of the remaining seven – WP223, WZ380, WZ389, WZ392, WZ394, WZ397 and WZ391 – were available for use in emergency only. These aircraft were to be serviced and combat-readied as required".

The squadron comment on this situation was that "after the results of the rear spar inspections were known there were serious policy discussions on the subject of the future crew requirements and the

---

[1] At a technical progress meeting on 11 Apr 60, when the chairman explained that "the Victor Mk 2 in the long-range PR role should be in squadron service commencing the third quarter 1961" (files on Development and Introduction of Victor Aircraft – Pt III, C 127845/60).

[2] An air survey of Northern and Southern Rhodesia and Bechuanaland, to be carried out by a 543 Sqn detachment under the control of CRE. Covering approximately 400,000 square miles of territory, meaning that 66,000 miles of successful flight lines needed to be flown, it was believed to be the largest task of this nature ever undertaken by the RAF.

future flying programme . . . By the end of the month these problems were still not resolved".

No 543 in fact went through a very difficult seven-month period – marked by aircraft being inspected, limited in flying hours, grounded and finally withdrawn from service, and crews being reduced in number – until May 1965 when the first of the Victor 2s arrived. The bad news had broken at the beginning of October 1964, when, after the squadron's nine Valiant B(PR).1s had had their rear spars inspected during September, only two were found fit to remain in first-line service, and that under strict limitation:–

"WZ391 and XD826 are to be flown to achieve 12 hours per month for each of the squadron's five crews. It is expected that, at this rate of use, the aircraft will remain in first line until the re-equipment of the squadron is complete.

"Valiants WZ380, WZ389, WZ392, WZ394 and WZ397 are to be kept fully serviceable for emergency use only.

"WZ223 is to be semi-stored in a fully equipped condition and recovered once a month and fully serviced.

"WZ382 is to be stored and only deterioration servicing carried out".

So much for the engineering implications. On 1 October the crews were told that

"following the inspections of the rear mainplane spars, the Valiants were to be withdrawn from 1st Line with the exception of one aircraft, which was limited to 40 hours' flying per month. Therefore the policy was to retain five crews to meet the War Role in the case of National Emergency, when four of the Valiants, taken out of 1st Line, would be recovered. The intention was to keep the remaining pilots in current flying practice and for their crews to fulfil a limited classification commitment. The three crews earmarked for training on the Victor 2 PR aircraft, plus two other crews, were nominated to remain on the squadron. In case any member of these crews was taken off flying permanently, a reserve crew was selected to remain in a non-flying capacity. The crews not selected to remain on the squadron were told that postings would be found to meet, as near as possible, their individual requests".

Later that month limitations were introduced on duration of flights and manoeuvres which could be performed:

". . . flying training for pilots was further reduced by a restriction limiting circuit flying to 40 minutes during a particular sortie. Other limitations were restricting the aircraft to 30° angle of bank, 0.5G and 250kt indicated airspeed. The arrival of Valiant XD826 from Gaydon[1] on 14 October improved the flying prospects and it was agreed that selected crews should fulfil their classification tasks as far as possible, with an average of 12 flying hours a month".

---

[1] This aircraft had had Category B repairs and a unit refit at Gaydon (No 232 OCU ORB).

During November the squadron had two aircraft available for flying, and five crews; priority was given to training for the classification commitment, and two half-yearly crew checks and an instrument rating test were completed.

RAF Wyton, parent station of the UK reconnaissance and special duties force (Nos 51, 58 and 543 Sqns), noted in its ORB for December 1964 that 543's six-monthly classification requirements had been fulfilled before its last two Valiants had been grounded. These hitherto serviceable aircraft, WD391 and XD826, were grounded on 10 December so that checks could be done on their rear spars. The squadron were supplied with a pair of Canberra T.4s to keep the pilots and navigators in flying practice. At the very end of the year, on 31 December, the first crew to convert to the Victor 2 (Sqn Ldr J A Holland, Flt Lts R A Norman and D Christison and Fg Off K Smith) began their course at No 232 OCU, RAF Gaydon.

The "word from on high" about the future of the Valiants – that they were to be withdrawn permanently from RAF service – was received at Wyton (as at Marham) in a signal from HQ Bomber Command on 26 January 1965; but there was none of the bitter reaction there had been at Marham: at CRE, the station and the squadron the announcement was noted without comment. CRE's documentation of the decision was brief and factual: "the decision not to repair Valiant aircraft spars", its ORB noted, "was received from Headquarters Bomber Command by Signal on 26 January 1965. No 543 Sqn has meanwhile been relieved of its war plan commitment pending the introduction into service of the Victor B (SR) Mk 2 aircraft".

During February the squadron's Valiants ("categorised as Cat 5 components by HQ Maintenance Command on 26 February", as CRE's ORB recorded) were dismantled and in March they were scrapped. Meanwhile four crews – three of them "old hands", one a new crew – were training on Victors at No 232 OCU.

Sqn Ldr J A Holland and his crew, who had been the first to convert at Gaydon, delivered the first of No 543's new aircraft – Victor B/SR Mk 2 XL230 – from Radlett to Wyton on 19 May 1965, CRE noting in its ORB that this marked "the start of re-equipping . . . No 543 . . . with the Victor" and that further scheduled deliveries between then and November would "bring the squadron back to full operational status by the end of 1965".

The acquisition of Victors by No 543 Sqn – two had arrived by June 1965, three by August, four by September, five by November (although in that month XL230 had to be returned to Handley Page for wing strengthening) and six by January 1966 – meant that RAF strategic reconnaissance capability was greatly improved: its new SR aircraft had both a better performance and more efficient photographic equipment than their predecessors. A description of No 543's enhanced effectiveness, referring to the Victors' range, speed and height advantage over the Valiants, went on to appraise their qualities thus: —

"The range of the Victor is at least 40 per cent greater than that of the Valiant, while its capability for photographic coverage is more than double. With its improved radar equipment the new Victor can map with radar an area of 750,000 square miles in six hours. Five Victors could cover the whole of the Atlantic in less than seven hours, and on a single sortie could produce radar photographs for a mosaic of the whole of the Mediterranean which would enable a count of every ship to be made.

"The Victor carries over three times more photoflashes for night photography than the Valiant, and is also fitted with improved navigational equipment enabling a higher standard of accuracy to be attained. A new Rapid Processing Radar Unit is carried which provides in-flight processing of a continuous strip record of the radar picture obtained by the aircraft.

"The F96 reconnaissance cameras carried in the Victor have a superior performance to the cameras carried in the Valiant and Canberra PR.7 aircraft. The cameras can also be fitted with lens cones of various focal lengths, thereby providing operational flexibility. Forward coverage is three times more than before because more film can be carried in the magazines, and lateral cover on each flight-line is increased by mounting a fan of up to eight cameras so that the area covered overlaps on each camera. All the equipment is designed to provide intelligence at the largest possible scale with high resolution and minimum distortion for detailed photographic interpretation.

"The squadron is supported in its role by a team of photographers and photographic interpreters".[1]

With its re-equipment No 543 were also involved in trials, not only of the camera fit but also of the aircraft: HQ Bomber Command, the RAF Wyton ORB recorded in June 1965, "have directed that a Priority A is to be carried out to confirm that the Victor B/SR Mk 2 in the Radar Reconnaissance role is able to carry out the operational tasks previously undertaken by the Valiant (PR) Mk 1 in the maritime search role". That the new aircraft had this capability seems to have been soon confirmed, for in September the ORB noted that 543 had flown three maritime co-operation exercises during the month and that this task was becoming "a regular and increasingly important part of the squadron's role". Its aim was "to combine the advantage of the high, fast search capability of the Victor with the low-level capability of the long-range maritime patrol aircraft, to achieve an efficient and economical coverage of shipping movements".

No 543 appears to have become operational again in the SR role (albeit with only three aircraft – two in full operational service and one undergoing an acceptance check) in mid-August 1965; for when

---

[1] Extract from an article on No 543 Squadron in *Air Clues* for July 1966.

officers from the Joint Services Staff College course were shown round one of the SR/B Mk 2s on the 12th they "were also shown photographs" – the squadron ORB recorded – "taken on the previous day's sorties, the first by a No 543 Sqn Victor".[1]

The type's reconnaissance qualities were comprehensively detailed in a history of Handley Page aircraft[2], which said that "in addition to having highly developed radar mapping and sideways scanning capability,

"the Victor SR.2 carried a day-reconnaissance camera crate which was compatible with the two large bomb-bay fuel tanks giving 40 per cent longer range than that of the Valiant B(PR).1; for night reconnaissance, 108 photo-flashes could be carried in the bomb bay in three canisters with one bomb-bay tank, or 36 photo-flashes in one canister with two bomb-bay tanks. The cameras used were F96 Mk 2 for day photography, F89 Mk 3 for night work and F49 Mk 4 for surveying and mapping. Each 8in photo-flash was of several million candle-power, but since most of the SR.2's operations were maritime it carried less comprehensive ECM equipment than the B.2R[3]. One Victor SR.2 could photograph every ship in the whole Mediterranean in a single seven-hour sortie, bringing back 10,000ft of exposed film for processing either at Wyton or at the Joint Air Reconnaissance Centre nearby at RAF Brampton; infra-red and 'false-colour' infra-red photography was particularly valuable and successful".[4]

No 543 Sqn establishment was for eight aircraft, and this total was achieved in April 1966. Unfortunately one of the Victors, XM716, was destroyed in an accident which occurred on a demonstration flight during a Press visit to Wyton on 29 June 1966. It was being flown by Sqn Ldr J A Holland, who had captained the first of 543's crews to convert to the Victor (as already recorded). However, despite this sad loss, the aircraft strength remained at eight and the squadron was therefore in full working order again from early 1966 – just over a year after it had been withdrawn from operations.

In the case of No 543's re-equipment, although it took a long time to accomplish, leaving the RAF with a significant gap in strategic reconnaissance capability, there were no political or military complications; as has been noted, plans to re-equip the squadron with Victors had been made before the Valiant troubles began: the Central

---

[1] The only sortie recorded for 11 August was Navex and PR C/T (4hr 30min)by Flt Lt J G Marmam and his crew.

[2] *Handley Page Aircraft since 1907*, by C H Barnes (Putnam & Co Ltd, 1976).

[3] B.2R was the retrofitted version, resulting from "a second retrofit production line for B.2s to modify and extend their ECM installations, to install Conway Co17 engines and rapid take-off equipment, aimed at reducing 'scramble' time to one minute per aircraft, to provide for carriage and launching of Blue Steel, to introduce fixed-droop leading edges . . . and to provide increased stowage for 'Window' dispensers . . . ." (ibid).

[4] False-colour infra-red gave "a more effective penetration of camouflage than infra-red black-and-white film" according to the *Air Clues* article already quoted.

Reconnaissance Establishment[1] said in its ORB for March 1964 that notification had been received that No 543's re-equipment with Victor Mk 2s would start "in the second quarter of 1965". But in the case of the Valiant tanker squadrons there was a military need to maintain a flight-refuelling capability, and in the case of the TBF force the politics of the British contribution to Saceur.

A decision to re-equip the tanker force with Victors, and to have three squadrons in this role, had been taken in 1962; its implementation was hastened by the Valiant troubles. During 1961 the Air Staff had considered the possibility of Victor tankers; a minute of 25 May 1961 (D of Ops (B & R)/D Air Plans), referring to the latter's minute of 18 April), expressed the view that there was "no technical reason . . . why the Victor 1 should not be used as a tanker"). Then in the spring of 1962 the Air Council endorsed the ideas of a third squadron (in addition to Nos 214 and 90) and the use of Victors for flight refuelling: on 1 March 1962[2] it gave approval in principle to the third squadron proposal and invited VCAS (Air Mshl Sir Wallace Kyle, who had just assumed this post) to initiate a design study of the Victor 1 in the tanker role. VCAS subsequently reported to the Air Council in a paper dated 20 November 1962 on the The Re-equipment of the Tanker Force with Victor Mk 1/1A Aircraft: this recommended that the Council should confirm the introduction of the Victor as a replacement for the Valiant as a tanker, and also confirm the requirement for a third tanker squadron. The Council agreed to these proposals at its meeting on 22 November and invited VCAS – who had said that he was "satisfied that three tanker squadrons were essential to support fighter reinforcement along all the routes we might be required to use" – to initiate the necessary action.

The proposal to make Victor B.1/1As into tankers received further endorsement early in 1963 from both the Chief Scientific Adviser, MoD (Sir Solly Zuckerman), and the Chiefs of Staff. On 3 January CSA minuted the Chief of the Defence Staff (Earl Mountbatten) to say that at their meeting on 12 December 1962 the Defence Research Policy Committee had considered a proposal that a development contract should be placed for the conversion of Victor B.1/1As to the tanker role – a proposal based on the results of a project study which had been approved the previous May. CSA's minute, summarising this study, said that the development cost of the conversion was estimated to be £850,000, and the estimated cost of converting 27 aircraft was £7m. It ended by saying: "The DRPC endorsed the proposal for a development contract to be placed. I should be grateful, therefore, for the

---

[1] Which had become an operational Group on 1 Apr 63, assuming full responsibility for the tasking, control and training of the UK Reconnaissance Force (Bomber Command Org Policy file AF/CT 3127/65 Pt II).

[2] Conclusions 3(62).

[3] Conclusions 16(62).

CoS's comments on this proposal".

In response, the Chiefs of Staff gave their approval on 24 January 1963[1] to a development contract to be placed for converting Victor B Mk 1/1As to the tanker role, instructing their Secretary to inform CSA accordingly. But complications – both financial and industrial – then arose, and continued throughout 1963 and 1964.

The financial complication sprang from Treasury reluctance to agree to expenditure on a third tanker squadron or to approve the cost of modifying Victors for flight refuelling, and the industrial complication from Ministry of Aviation reluctance to give Handley Page a new contract: these difficulties became evident in mid-1963.

On 23 May the CAS (Air Chf Mshl Sir Thomas Pike) gave the Air Council[2] some disquieting news about the tanker proposals which had been approved at the beginning of the year: he said that the Treasury were withholding agreement to the modification of aircraft for a third Victor FR squadron until they knew the results of the Defence Review and the deliberations of the Oversea Policy Committee.[3] He added that he understood that the Treasury had also withdrawn their agreement to the modification of Victors for the first two squadrons, commenting that these squadrons were vital to RAF operational plans. AMSO (Air Mshl Sir Walter Merton) said that an early decision was necessary to avoid a general hold-up of work, and PUS (Sir Maurice Dean) offered to raise the matter personally with the Treasury to see what could be done – an action which the Council asked him to take, and to report back on as soon as possible.

The industrial complication came to light when at an Air Ministry/MoA meeting on 13 August the Ministry of Aviation expressed reservations about giving a contract to Handley Page because of doubts about the company's financial soundness; and subsequently, negotiations between Handley Page and Hawker Siddeley Aviation on a possible merger reached deadlock.

But at the end of 1963 came the news that the Air Council wanted to hear. "You will wish to know", VCAS (Air Mshl Sir Wallace Kyle) was told on 19 December,[4] "that the Treasury have agreed in principle that 24 Mk 1 Victors should be converted to the tanker role. . . . It is unfortunate that . . . the price of this project has risen. . . . The original estimate was for £7m and covered 27 aircraft. The latest information from the MoA [is] that the conversion of 24 aircraft will cost £8m".

However, there still remained an industrial problem, as to which company was to do the work. Summing-up the situation on 16 March 1964, PUS (M T Flett, who had succeeded Sir Maurice Dean) told the Secretary of State for Air (Mr Hugh Fraser) that as a result of the "18

---

[1] 6th Meeting/63.
[2] Conclusions 10(63).
[3] On overseas commitments.
[4] AUS(A) (F Cooper)/PS to VCAS.

months' battle with the Treasury" full financial authority had been given for the necessary R&D expenditure and for the first 16 sets of flight refuelling equipment; but "the division of the embodiment task between HSA and HP" still had to be sorted out as well as a final examination of the two firms' quotations.

This uncertain situation continued throughout 1964. On 27 May the Minister (RAF) (Mr Fraser – whose title had been changed with the advent of the Ministry of Defence and the Air Force Board on 1 April 1964) was told by PUS(RAF) that an estimate had been obtained from Hawker Siddeley and a quotation from Handley Page that had made it possible to draw up "a soundly based estimate of the cost of the project". At a meeting on 12 June held to agree on arrangements for a Victor tanker conversion programme the chairman (Gp Capt R R Goodbody, DDE9 (RAF)) explained in his opening remarks that the Treasury "had given limited financial approval to the conversion of Victor B.1/1A aircraft to the tanker role. The approval was limited to 12 aircraft and the conversion of a further 12, to make up the establishment, would be the object of further financial negotiations". Then on 9 July the Minister was told by AUS(S) (Air) (B Humphreys-Davies) that the Treasury had "authorised the completion of the manufacture of all the modification sets and the flight-refuelling equipment, and the feed-in of the 15 aircraft[1] which the Ministry of Aviation now propose to allocate to Handley Page for conversion". But the Treasury had "refused to authorise the allocation of any aircraft to Hawker Siddeley until they have been given a more convincing explanation . . . of the necessity for incurring an extra £1.3m by sub-contracting part of the work to Hawkers". However, this question seems to have been resolved during the next two months, for on 15 September the Minister was told that the Treasury had authorised the balance of the nine tankers planned to have embodiment work done by HSA.

In the meantime the Valiant spar failure troubles had occurred and further complicated the tanker situation. On 17 September VCAS informed DCAS (Air Mshl C H Hartley) that although the outcome of the current investigation into Valiant fatigue life was not certain, at least it was known that the life of the tanker force would be "considerably less than . . . expected". He asked DCAS to press the MoA to "speed up the administrative work" and to bring pressure to bear on HSA to carry out the technical work as quickly as possible. "In this way", he added, "we may relieve what is bound to be a difficult situation with our tanker force".

It seemed from DCAS's reply that work had already begun on the conversions; he told VCAS on 14 October that though contracts with Handley Page and HSA had still not been let, "we have been repeatedly assured that work has not so far been held up for want of full contracts".

---

[1] The other nine being converted by HSA.

It also looked as though all the work would go to Handley Page: on 27 November PUS (MoA) (Sir Richard Way) asked PUS(RAF) if he would agree that all 24 Victors should be converted by their original manufacturers; there had been labour difficulties at HSA's Armstrong Whitworth division and Handley Page had been "very resilient in the face of their problems". Commenting that estimates of the costs of the conversions were an average of £108,000 per aircraft or £2.592m in total, compared with an estimate of £3.7m "under the present plan"[1], Sir Richard added: "I understand that owing to recent fatigue troubles with the Valiant, you are now more anxious . . . to complete the build-up of your Victor tanker squadrons immediately. . . ."

The Air Force Board agreed that the conversions should be done by Handley Page: on 9 December PUS(RAF) wrote to PUS(MoA) to say that they were "only too anxious to give the whole job" to the company "in view of the savings which would result". However, there were two qualifications: an assumption that the MoA no longer felt it necessary to give some of the work to Hawker Siddeley, in order to insure against "the virtual disappearance of Handley Page from the aircraft industry"; and if that assumption were correct, PUS(RAF) said that it was necessary before the Air Force committed itself to Handley Page for the whole order for the company to provide firm proposals as to delivery dates and prices which were acceptable to the two departments.

However, with the complete withdrawal of Valiants from service in January 1965[2] the provision of alternative tankers became an urgent matter, encapsulated in a proposal put to the Air Force Board on 8 February 1965 for a force of six two-point Victor tankers – as opposed to the full three-point conversion – which would become available from June onwards. This proposal, approved by the AFB,[3] had been put forward in a joint paper by VCAS (Air Mshl B K Burnett) and DCAS.[4]

In this, they stated quite bluntly that the withdrawal of the Valiants had "left the Royal Air Force without a flight refuelling capability", and said that under present plans – ie for the conversion of Victors as tankers, which (as just described) had been under discussion since 1961 – this capability would not be restored until the first of the Victors came into service in the last quarter of 1965. With the first due to be delivered in August and to enter service in October, and an initial one-tanker-per-month production rate, only five would have been produced by the end of the year and the first squadron would not be complete until the end of February 1966.

The paper went on to say that before any flight-refuelling tasks could be resumed Victor B.1/1A bomber crews would have to be converted to the tanker role, and that following this, fighter aircraft crews in both the

---

[1] *Ie* the HP/HSA division of the task.
[2] Announced by the Ministry of Defence on 26 January.
[3] Conclusions 3(65), 8 Feb 65.
[4] Victor Mk 1/1A Tanker – Crash Programme (AFB SC(65)5).

UK and Cyprus would have to be trained in refuelling from the Victor's wing-mounted refuelling points.[1] Six tankers were the minimum number required for this training task, and also for mounting a limited reinforcement operation. Even that limited capability would not be achieved until early 1966, and with current political tensions in the Middle and Far East, such an operational limitation was unacceptable. It was therefore essential to get six tanker aircraft into service "as rapidly as possible".

Three alternative ways of achieving this were considered in the paper: borrowing or buying American tankers; speeding-up the existing Victor three-point tanker conversion programme; or producing six partially modified Victor tankers. The first two alternative courses were rejected. If there were a loan or purchase of American aircraft, air and ground crews to operate them "would hardly have completed training before re-training on the Victors became necessary". This option was therefore not considered further, though the paper said that the possibility of assistance from tankers operated by the USAF was being investigated. As to the second course, the paper noted that for a Victor to be converted to a three-point refueller – two points in wing-mounted pods for fighters, one in the fuselage for bombers and transport aircraft – took eight/nine months; and a study had shown that acceleration of the first six aircraft incorporating the modifications was not possible because there was insufficient time to advance the delivery of the long-dated materials required for the modification kits and some sub-contracted equipment.

The third alternative, producing six partially modified Victors, could be achieved in one of two ways – either by fitting only the central fuselage refuelling point, or by fitting only the wing pod installations. The supply of components for the latter was further ahead than for the former, and the latter presented a simpler modification and permitted a much quicker turn-round time. The fact that wing-pod installations "would not provide a capability of refuelling V-bomber aircraft" was "acceptable" since it was "not vital to current reinforcement plans".

Describing the implications of the Victor two-point tanker crash programme, the paper said that a Handley Page study had shown that six of these aircraft could be produced by the end of August 1965, deliveries starting with two in June. Clearance flying could be completed on the prototype tanker which was already flying. As Victors already being converted by the company were "in an advanced state of strip-down and re-build", it was proposed to feed-in six fully serviceable Victor Mk 1As into a special conversion line and to embody "only those modifications essential to give them the two-point refuelling capability". To produce the first of these tankers by June, the first of the six Mk 1As had to be fed into the conversion line early in February and the last early

---

[1] By contrast with the Valiant's FR equipment in the fuselage centreline.

in March. Under present Victor squadron run-down patterns it would be possible to provide aircraft to meet this programme without affecting the planned V-force front-line strength.

The paper then went on to describe the capabilities of the two-point tanker, the effect of their production on other Victor programmes, and the financial implications.

The two-point tankers (it said) would be Victor Mk 1A bombers fitted with two podded hose drum units – one on each wing, a hose drum unit control panel in the cabin, a slightly modified fuel control panel in the cockpit and "minimum wiring and piping modifications". Standard bomber-type overload fuel tanks would be carried in the bomb-bay, giving a total of 81,000lb of fuel, of which 48,000lb would be capable of being transferred through the wing-mounted installations. This would give "a similar capability to that of the Valiant tanker, with the added advantage of two refuelling points".

As to the effect on other Victor production, the paper said that as the two-point tankers would use components and manpower destined for the full specification tanker programme, the latter would inevitably be delayed: indications were that it would yield the first two full-standard tankers by December 1965, but only one month's delay would be incurred in completing the whole programme. Starting a two-point tanker programme would affect the Victor Mk 2 (SR) retrofit production line by a diversion of labour, but it was believed that the requirement could be drawn from the centre of this line and that no delay would occur on the first three SR conversions.

Setting-out the financial implications, the paper said that the approved plan for the Victor tanker programme had envisaged a conversion line divided between Handley Page and Hawker Siddeley – on the advice of the Ministry of Aviation, because of the former's uncertain future, in order to safeguard the tanker programme and also industrial backing for the Victor generally. Total estimated cost of the project on that basis was £7.75m, which had been approved by the Treasury. The MoA had subsequently "taken a more favourable view of Handley Page's prospects" and proposed to give them all the work, with an estimated saving of about £1m. The paper commented that with the withdrawal of the Valiant the urgency of the Victor programme again became predominant and fully justified the application of part of that saving to the crash programme – the cost of the latter depending on whether or not the six two-point tankers were subsequently returned to the firm for retrofit to the full specification. On the assumption that they were, the best "broad estimate" available from the MoA for the extra cost of the programme was about £0.5m. This included the costs involved in interfering with the main contract, subsequent retrofit of the six two-point tankers, and disturbance to the Victor Mk 2 (SR) programme. Treasury approval would not be required, and the first two aircraft could be "fed into the firm next week".

479

The paper then went on to make a subtle point about the need for careful selection of Victors for two-point tanker conversion.

It pointed out that to offset the sudden loss of the Valiants meant that in addition to regaining a flight refuelling capability as soon as possible the Victor tanker force had to be maintained at as high a level as possible during the time it was building up to its ultimate strength of 24. It therefore suggested that a significant benefit would be achieved if the aircraft for two-point tanker conversion were selected not from those which would otherwise have been fed into the full tanker conversion programme but from those destined for the OCU (one), long-term storage (two) and "in use" reserve (three). The main programme would then be uninterrupted. Towards the end of it, wing pods from the two-point tankers would need to be withdrawn, but by that time at least 18 three-point tankers would be in service and the former two-point tankers would then revert to their original planned roles.

The paper went on to say that although this proposal would bring "significant operational benefits" in 1966 it would involve some extra cost and a temporary change of role for six Victors, and would therefore need to be submitted for Treasury approval, but added: "It would suffice, however, for the Committee[1] to approve the crash programme on the assumption that the two-point tankers would ultimately be converted to the full tanker specification. This would enable aircraft to be fed into the programme immediately, thereby permitting the earliest possible re-introduction of an in-flight refuelling capability".

The Committee were invited to endorse the proposed crash programme to produce six two-point Victor tankers at an extra cost of about £0.5m, on the assumption that these would ultimately be brought up to the full tanker specification, and to agree that the question of whether these tankers should be retained in the front line for some months longer by the expedient suggested should be considered urgently at staff level. On 8 February 1965 the Committee approved[2] these proposals and agreed that action should proceed immediately. They also invited VCAS to inform the Minister (RAF) and the Secretary of State for Defence.

In explaining the situation to the Minister on 11 February, VCAS told him[3] that Handley Page had said they could produce six two-point tankers by the end of August 1965, the first two being delivered in June. To do this they needed to feed the first aircraft into the conversion line "early this month"; and this could be done "if we make available, as we propose to do, serviceable Victor 1s rather than diverting aircraft which are already being stripped-down for the full conversion programme".

In fact Handley Page managed to get the first two Victor two-point

---

[1] AFB Standing Committee.
[2] AFB SC Conclusions 3(65), 8 Feb 65, Secret Annex B.
[3] VCAS.810 Victor Tanker Crash Programme in Use of V-bombers in Tanker Role (ID3/901/11 (Pt 1)).

tankers to the RAF by May, and earned themselves a Parliamentary plaudit at the start of the crash programme, when the Minister (RAF) (Lord Shackleton) said in the House of Lords on 17 February '65[1]: "It rather looks now as if the Victor tankers will be available a good deal earlier than . . . originally planned. There is a good prospect that the first two . . . will be in service, in a partly modified condition,[2] in early April and four more at the end of August. . . . If this improvement in the programme is achieved we should take note and say that Handley Page have earned some compliments".

At the company's Radlett factory the scene in early 1965 must have been as busy as at any time since Victor production began. As their historian described it:[3]

"Concurrently with the conversion of the nine Victor SR.2s for No 543 Squadron, Colney Street[4] began a day-and-night programme to convert six Victor B.1As, returned to Radlett from Cottesmore by Nos 10 and 15 Sqns after disbandment in March and October 1964, into two-point tankers using the wing-mounted Flight Refuelling FR20B hose-drogue pods already under trial on XA918. At first it was intended to make these units interchangeable with under-wing tanks or 'Red Neck'[5] on the standard strong points, but this was found to bring the trailing drogues dangerously near the tail unit, so a position further outboard was chosen. . . . The first B(K).1A to fly was XH620 on 28 April 1965; all six went to No 55 Sqn at Marham, which became operational as a tanker unit in May and was employed in refuelling fighters after satisfactory trials with the Lightnings of No 19 Sqn in August. . . ."

No 55 Sqn, which was to be the first operator of Victor two-point tankers, had become non-operational as a Medium Bomber Force squadron at Honington on 1 March 1965 and moved to Marham on 24 May to begin its new task. As the ORB put it, "A change of role occurred simultaneously with the move, the squadron being converted from medium-bomber to in-flight refuelling role. The first two aircraft arrived at Marham on . . . 25 May. . . ." These were the first Mk 1A two-point tankers, XH602 and XH648, and by the end of May the squadron had received two more – XH667 and XH620.

In the meantime, arrangements had been made to keep the fighter pilots in flight-refuelling practice through US Air Force co-operation with its KC-135s. On 19 March VCAS had explained in a note to the Air Force Board[6] that one of the results of the Valiant fatigue failure had been that there were now no pilots in Fighter Command who were in

---

[1] Lords Hansard, Cols 568-569.
[2] Ie, as two-point tankers.
[3] *Handley Page aircraft since 1907*, by C H Barnes (Putnam, 1976).
[4] HP's Radlett factory.
[5] A reconnaissance radar housed in wing pods.
[6] Annex C to D371/31.

current FR practice, and if nothing were done to remedy this situation the position would deteriorate – to the extent that 25% of RAF fighter pilots would need refresher training and the remainder would be untrained. Six Victor tankers would be insufficient to dispose quickly of this training commitment.

In reporting on the tanker situation to the Chiefs of Staff on 23 February[1] VCAS (representing CAS) had said that the crash programme was being achieved "at the expense of a slight delay to the availability of the Victor reconnaisance squadron", but from July/August there would be "a small tanker capability", sufficient to meet Fighter Command's training requirements and to provide limited support for overseas reinforcements. He added that, as an interim measure, negotiations were under way with the United States for the loan of two KC-135s to be stationed at Upper Heyford to maintain the Lightning F.2 and F.3 squadrons and for one KC-135 to be based in Turkey to perform a similar function for the Cyprus-based No 29 (Javelin) Sqn. This programme was not yet finalised; the USAF was willing to help, but Treasury approval was still awaited, though not expected to be withheld.

VCAS informed CAS on 23 March[2] that these negotiations had been successful. On the same day the latter told the Chiefs of Staff[3] that Treasury approval had been given for the use of three KC-135s and VCAS told the Minister (RAF) that the first one, with an advanced planning party, was to arrive at Upper Heyford the following day and both tankers would be "in place" and ready to start training on about 5 April.

This RAF/USAF flight refuelling training was known as Operation Billy Boy, and a Fighter Command/NEAF Operation Order of 2 April[4] explained what it involved;

"Due to the temporary lack of in-flight refuelling tankers in the Royal Air Force an alternative tanker source is needed to maintain the in-flight refuelling proficiency of the fighter squadrons of Fighter Command until the situation is restored by the introduction of the Victor tanker into RAF service towards the end of 1965.[5] The USAF has agreed to provide sufficient KC-135 tanker support to meet the training requirements of Nos 23, 56, 74 and 111 (Lightning) squadrons of Fighter Command and No 29 (Javelin) Sqn of NEAF for a period of six to nine months. Training for Fighter Command squadrons will commence on 5 April. Training for No 29 Sqn will commence on 26 April subject to the successful completion of negotiations with the Turkish Government".

Two KC-135s would be based at RAF Upper Heyford "to provide one

---

[1] COS 10th Mtg/65.
[2] VCAS 1708.
[3] COS 15th Mtg/65.
[4] FC/NEAF Joint Op Order No 5.
[5] The estimated in-service date for the two-point tankers, however, was mid-1965.

sortie per working day for Fighter Command squadrons from 5 April until further notice. At approximately two-monthly intervals one of these aircraft would deploy to Adana/Incirlik to provide one sortie per day for six days for continuation training of No 29 Sqn. . . . During the initial period of training of No 29 Sqn a separate, additional tanker will be provided for a period of up to ten days".

Leuchars-based No 74 Sqn recorded in their April 1965 ORB that pilots had "started on Exercise Billy Boy, which is in-flight refuelling from KC-135 tankers based at Upper Heyford – the initial training being 1½hr sorties refuelling with 3,000lb each sortie. By the end of the month nine pilots had completed a minimum of three refuelling sorties".

Then in May "several sorties were again flown on Exercise Billy Boy, the flight profile being one hour with the tanker followed by 40 minutes' PIs".[1]

Meanwhile No 29 Sqn at Akrotiri had made their Billy Boy contacts: on 23 April their Javelin FAW.9s had been fitted with refuelling probes and under-wing tanks, and from 26 April to 1 May they achieved 406 engagements with a KC-135 of the 611th Air Refuelling Sqn, USAF, detached to Adana from Seymour-Johnson AFB for this exercise. Each morning during this five-day period (No 29's ORB recorded) the tanker was on station for four hours and eight or ten Javelin sorties were flown on to it, four of the fighters daily filling up their tanks and flying three-hour cross-countries. "No major difficulties were encounterd, although the boom and hose system was new to all crews.[2] Everyone was impressed by the accuracy and professional attitude of the USAF crew, who did a flypast on the last day to let the groundcrew see the aircraft".

No 56 Sqn at Wattisham, which had just converted from Lightning F.1As to F.3s in April 1965, did their Billy Boy training during May and their ORB for that month made some interesting comments on it – particularly regarding the USAF equipment and method for flight refuelling, noting that the KC-135 "has a rigid refuelling boom to which is attached a seven-foot flexible hose and drogue", which called for "a different receiver technique to that used on the hose-and-reel-equipped Valiant". In the 24-28 May period five tanker missions were allotted to the squadron with three pairs of Lightnings on each tanker. Although only one sortie was cancelled owing to Lightning unserviceability, "two were lost when the tanker was forced to return to base with a probe end stuck in the drogue. Four probes were lost in the 27 sorties achieved, which is about the rate expected from the results of other squadrons".

Leuchars-based No 23 Sqn also suffered from broken probes on its Lightning F.3s during tanker training with the USAF. Its April 1965 ORB, noting that 22 conversion and 25 continuation training sorties

---

[1] Practice interceptions.
[2] RAF fighter pilots were used to the hose and reel system.

had been completed during Billy Boy, commented that the loss of probes on 15% of those sorties had been "unacceptably high"; and the CO (Sqn Ldr J McLeod), while recording proudly that since 75% of No 23's pilots had had previous experience of in-flight refuelling and the squadron "had initially the lion's share of the KC-135" it was now "in the position of being the most experienced one on in-flight-refuelling the Mk 3 Lightning", it had also "broken the largest number of probes" – a weakness which would be "largely eliminated by a current modification".

No 111 Sqn, also with Lightning F.3s and like No 56 based at Wattisham, made the interesting comment in its ORB for April that "initial contacts on the 'boomed' KC-135s proved relatively easy compared with the Valiant tanker". But the CO (Sqn Ldr G P Black) noted in his remarks on the 1hr 45min refuelling sorties flown with the tankers of 919 Sqn, SAC, that "the kinking and shortness of the KC-135's hose and drogue (9ft)" had "proved more strenuous on probe rivets", and that remaining in contact for prolonged periods of up to five minutes had been "more exacting and tiring than Valiant refuelling".

During May, as has been recounted, No 55 Sqn moved to Marham to start their new role; and once they had become operational with their Victor tankers they would give the RAF fighter pilots the opportunity of renewing contact with familiar flight-refuelling equipment. Their ORB for that month had recorded that the squadron would be "equipped initially with six Victor Mk 1A two-point tankers" and would have an aircrew strength of eight crews, and had commented: "The re-equipment with two-point tankers is an interim measure only and at a later date these aircraft will be withdrawn and replaced with the more versatile three-point tankers. Possession of the two-point tanker does not permit Victor-Victor refuelling operations and is a severe limitation to the squadron's long-range capabilities". In this first month of their new role No 55 began a No 3 Group trial to ascertain the two-point tanker's fuel consumption; this was to be flown in two phases, in the first with the refuelling hoses stowed and in the second with them trailed, the Victors being flown at a steady 270kt RAS (rectified airspeed).

In June the squadron got up to a strength of five aircraft and Handley Page received Ministerial congratulations for having supplied them; the Minister for the RAF (Lord Shackleton) informed the Minister of Aviation (Mr Roy Jenkins) on 3 June that at a recent Air Force Board meeting "great appreciation" had been expressed at the way the company had "helped us over a rather critical situation in regard to tankers following the grounding of the Valiants". Their "speedy conversion of the Victor tankers" was "meeting a most important operational need . . . which indeed might be crucial in providing us with a capability to carry out urgent reinforcement operations overseas. . . ."[1]

During July the No 3 Group trial was completed, a Tanker Training Flight was formed at Marham[2] and No 55 "got down to the day-to-day business of training the pilots of No 74 Sqn" – which would supply the receivers in the forthcoming Tankex to Cyprus – "in the techniques of in-flight refuelling", nine successful sorties being made with nine pairs of Lightnings. This exercise, which occurred in August, marked the reinstatement of the RAF tanker force; or, as the Victor squadron's ORB described it,

". . . the culmination of two-and-a-half months' training and effort on the part of both air and ground crews in the shape of Exercise Forthright 22 and 23.

"This exercise involved the redeployment of four Lightning aircraft of No 74 Sqn to Royal Air Force Akrotiri. . . . [It] was completely successful although a one-day delay was incurred by a double pod failure on the return phase when four Lightnings of No 19 Sqn were refuelled back to Leconfield".

No 74 endorsed these comments, their ORB recording that conversion to the Victor tankers of No 55 Sqn had begun on 20 July and had "progressed smoothly"; by the end of the month "all previously IFR-qualified pilots had flown at least one sortie each on the new tanker". As to the Victor-supported detachment in the following month: "Exercise Forthright 22 saw the deployment of four F.3s with six pilots and a ground support party to Cyprus. The aircraft left Leuchars for Wattisham on 13 August and took off from Wattisham on the 14th, flight-refuelling to Akrotiri. All . . . arrived on schedule, after an average flight time of 4hr 10min. This marked the first occasion that the Victor tanker has been used for an operational overseas deployment. . . ."

In preparation for their flight-refuelled return to the UK, six No 19 Sqn pilots converted to receiving from the Victors during July, and found no undue difficulty in the change from the Valiant. The squadron's flight refuelling officer (Flt Lt E J Scott) also investigated low-level tanking, finding it possible but extremely difficult – reactions which were to be borne out, after No 19's return to Leconfield in early August, by a demonstration described with some vivid comment in the ORB:–

"Low-level tanking has . . . been a feature of the month – for Exercise Unison[3] at the RAF College, Cranwell. Flt Lts Scott and Wratten, the pilots involved, have found that this sort of display flying is possible only if the 'plug-in' is carried out over the sea – where conditions are relatively smooth. The Victor's wing is particularly prone to flexing in

[1] AFB Conclusions 9(65), 27 May 1965.
[2] Formerly the Victor flying element of No 232 OCU (RAF Gaydon Org Policy file – AF/CT4063/65 PtI).
[3] The fourth in a series of biennial gatherings organised by the CoS Cttee for senior officers and defence officials of Britain and the Commonwealth countries.

turbulence, and the whip effect at the basket end of the drogue is quite frightening if a Lightning is not on the end to tone it down."

By October No 55 Sqn had its full strength of six Victor Mk 1A two-point tankers, and that month went further afield than Cyprus – to Tehran, refuelling four Lightning F.3s of No 74 Sqn which were to participate in an IIAF (Imperial Iranian Air Force) Day on the 17th. Exercise Donovan, as this was called, involved supporting the Lightnings from Akrotiri to Iran and on their return flight. With it and other exercises No 55 were well "in business" from August 1965 onwards, and at the beginning of December were joined at Marham by No 57 Sqn, albeit in an interim phase with Victor Mk 1/1As but changing its role for re-equipment as a tanker squadron with three-point Victors. As its ORB explained, the remainder of its aircraft had "gone either to Radlett for tanker conversion or to St Athan for major inspections". As the latter were completed the aircraft would be used to replace those on the squadron, which would then themselves go for majors or tanker conversions.

No 55 Sqn had been "at home" to the Press on 9 August 1965, before its supporting role in the deployment of Lightnings of No 74 Sqn to Cyprus, and one of the reports which resulted (in *Flight* for 19 August) gave a useful summary of the flight-refuelling situation to that date and of the prospects when Bomber Command acquired Victor three-point tankers. It said that

"with the premature retirement of the RAF's Valiant tankers last February due to fatigue problems, the Service was temporarily deprived of operational air-to-air refuellers. Following a prototype conversion last year, the RAF accepted an offer from Handley Page to convert Victor B.1As to tankers much more rapidly than would otherwise have been done. Now, after only six months, including a two-month work-up, 55 Sqn based at RAF Marham has five Victor tankers operational, with more to come. On 14 August they took part in an exercise in which four Lightning F.3s flew to Cyprus non-stop in 4½hr.

"The first Victor tankers have two refuelling points; the hoses and drogues are unwound from two underwing pods which can be used simultaneously. When the 'customer' has made contact, he edges forward until the yellow part of the hose has wound back to the pod and he is then in the optimum position for accepting fuel, which starts to flow automatically. The Victor captain flies the tanker while the co-pilot manages the 31-cell fuel system and keeps a check on tanker *cg* movements. The navigator/radar works the pod and hose-trailing controls. Most fuel transfers are performed in stable air above 30,000ft; it takes about four minutes to refuel a fighter and about ten minutes for a bomber. The Victor B.1A tanker conversion carries 52,850lb of transferable fuel.

"The present two-point tankers will not be converted to the three-point standard to which later Victor conversions will be made.

The three-point refueller will have an additional hose/drogue unit on the fuselage underside. This will be a tremendous advance on the old single-point Valiant tanker on which failure of the hose/drogue equipment meant the complete waste of the sortie. The RAF will subsequently form two more Victor tanker squadrons at Marham".

Although one of these two more squadrons, No 57, had gone over to its new role with its arrival at Marham in December 1965 (as just noted) it was starting from scratch and was far from being operational either in terms of equipment or training. Its first three-point tanker, XA937, did not arrive until 14 February 1966 and went straight into the Aircraft Engineering Squadron so was not available for flying until March. The aircrews concentrated on continuation training in their existing Victors and did ground training courses – on the three-point tanker at Finningley and on the Mk 20B/Mk 17 HDU (hose drum unit) equipment at Marham, and the squadron set up a tanker trials cell to co-ordinate the trials flying required under a No 3 Group directive.[1] This was designed to confirm performance data for the Victor three-point tanker and to establish a Tacan/Collins rendezvous procedure and flight-refuelling procedures prior to the planning and execution of FR exercises or operations. It was in four phases: a performance trial to confirm climb data and cruise consumption, both in a "clean" condition and with hose/hoses trailed; Tacan/Collins RV procedure; FR procedures with Lightnings; and tanker-to-tanker FR procedures.

In March, No 57 Sqn was able to start the No 3 Group trial with its first three-point tanker (XA937) and to begin crew conversions, Lightnings of Fighter Command taking the opportunity of "prodding" on six of the familiarisation and handling sorties. But the change-over to flight refuelling was a gradual process, as evidenced by the ORB for April, which recorded that crew strength had been raised to 12, which "gave the opportunity to release another crew to the tanker role"; it also noted some technical difficulties – unserviceabilities with the Mk 17 HDU[2], which caused curtailment of the tanker trial early in the month. On 4 April one of the Victors had lost the drogue from the end of its Mk 17 hose and 11 days later two of the squadron's aircraft had had similar occurrences, these incidents causing doubts about the stability of the hose. A restriction on the trailing and use of the Mk 17 HDU remained in force throughout May, the tankers operating in a two-point role; and it was during this month that XA930, one of the four Victors flown over Marham in formation on 1 December 1965 to signal No 57's arrival there to take up the new role of flight refuelling, was delivered to Radlett by a squadron crew for modification as a three-point tanker.

---

[1] Victor Mk 1/1A Three-point Tanker Performance – Rendezvous, Flight Refuelling and Procedures Trial (3G/S12370/6/ Ops; No 57 Sqn ORB, Feb '66, Appendix 1).
/2 The three-point tankers had two Mk 20B wing pods and two 2,000 gal tanks in the bomb-bay (file on Victor B.35/46 Instruments – AF/CT 761/65 Pts I & II).

June 1966 saw the emergence of No 57 as an operational three-point tanker squadron, for by then eight of its crews had achieved the classification Operational (Tanking), it had six aircraft modified for the role (though one was on loan to Boscombe Down) and it did its first operational tanking exercise, with Lightnings to and from Cyprus, in conjunction with three crews from No 55 Sqn. The ORB commented that since this exercise (Forthright 46/47) was a "first" for No 57 the initial briefing and preparation were "of necessity very thorough and comprehensive", and that "because of this the whole exercise was completed successfully with tankers and Lightnings arriving at their allotted destinations on time". The last day of the month had arrived "with one crew at Akrotiri and two . . . at Wheelus AFB" (Tripoli, Libya), "having by now completed five Forthright sorties with all rendezvous and transfers completed as planned".

With two Victor tanker squadrons thus "in business", a third was formed in August 1966 to bring the flight-refuelling force up to its planned strength: this was No 214, which had been the original Valiant tanker squadron. It was officially re-formed at Marham on 1 July with an establishment of eight Victor B (K) Mk 1/1As and effectively re-formed there on 1 August, after the crews of Wg Cdr D Mullarkey (the CO) and Flt Lt G R Barrell had finished their courses at the Tanker Training Flight. Then on 8 August three crews (those of Flt Lts E J Longden, E F Smeeth and W L Thompson) were posted in from No 57 Squadron. Initially No 214 borrowed aircraft from No 57, but the first of its own (XA938) was delivered to Marham on 27 September.

By the end of 1966 No 214 had seven Victor K.1/1As[1] out of an establishment of eight, and in February 1967 – in what its ORB described as "the most eventful month so far for the squadron" – had four crews involved in Exercise Forthright 59/60, taking Lightning F.3s to Akrotiri and returning with F.6s; this meant that it was by now fully operational as part of the tanker force. At that date too No 55 Sqn, which had initiated the Victor flight-refuelling role with the "crash programme" two-point tankers, had started its conversions to, and re-equipment with, the three-point version: in January aircrew had completed the three-point refuelling course and the Engineering Flight went on a one-week course at the Flight Refuelling School for electricians, airframe and engine fitters, to familiarise them with the operation and servicing of the Mk 17 HDU of the three-point tankers, the first two of which were delivered to No 55 during January. By the following month it had two two-point and three three-point tankers, against an etablishment for five two-point and three three-point Victors (K.1As).

Thus the three-squadron Victor tanker force at RAF Marham (Nos 55,

---

[1] The designation K.1 referred to the three-point Victor tankers.

57 and 214 Sqns) was operational from the beginning of 1967[1] and it continued in that form for the next ten years, sustaining and improving the RAF flight refuelling capability. When on 12 June 1967 command of No 55 Sqn was handed-over by Wg Cdr P B McCorkindale, CO since 25 May 1965, to his successor Wg Cdr R A Harvey it was recorded in the ORB that "much of the credit for speedily converting the Victor into an operational tanker after the demise of the Valiant must go to him". This squadron activity had been the fulfilment of the "crash programme" decided on by the Air Staff in early 1965, followed by the industrial activity of Handley Page in converting B.1/1A Victor bombers into two-point tankers. The combined result had been that the gap in RAF flight refuelling capability had been limited to ten months – from October 1964 when Nos 214 and 90 Sqns had done the last Valiant tanker operations to August 1965 when No 55 Sqn had first operationally demonstrated the Victor's flight refuelling capability.

Thus Victors had taken over the Valiants' strategic reconnaissance and flight refuelling roles, but neither they nor Vulcans were destined to take over the tactical bomber role in support of Saceur. By decision of the UK Government, as will now be described, the three Valiant TBF squadrons at Marham – Nos 207, 49 and 148 – were not replaced after the Valiants were withdrawn from service. The Valiants themselves had succeeded Canberras in assignment to Saceur (as described in an earlier chapter), but a 1965 proposal that the Valiants should be replaced by Vulcan B.1/1As was rejected by the Government.

This proposal had been made by Saceur (General L Lemnitzer), as reported by CAS (Air Chf Mshl Sir Charles Elworthy) to the Air Force Board on 8 February 1965[2], when he said that Saceur "had suggested that the squadrons assigned to his command should be replaced by Vulcan 1 aircraft". CAS went on to comment that although there was a view that this proposal should be resisted, on the ground that the financial saving represented by the Valiants' withdrawal was badly needed, "it could also be argued that we had certain obligations to Saceur which we could not easily ignore". He added that a paper was being prepared "examining the problem in detail".

This situation, in which the question was whether or not to replace the TBF Valiants, had been reached after four months' uncertainty of which Saceur had been kept regularly apprised. He was originally told of the fatigue troubles, which were more widespread than had at first been thought, by UK NMR Shape[3] (Air Commodore C B E Burt-Andrews) on 6 October 1964. Then, when towards the end of November it was thought that 40 out of the total 61 Valiants were repairable by a simple modification and would last at least to the end of 1968, UK NMR was instructed on 1 December to report this latest position personally to

---

[1] In June of that year it successfully flight-refuelled 13 Lightning F.6s of No 74 Sqn from RAF Leuchars to RAF Tengah, Singapore, and back in Operation Hydraulic.
[2] Conclusions, Meeting 2 (65).
[3] National Military Representative, Supreme HQ, Allied Powers Europe.

Saceur. But, after further inspection of a Valiant on 9 December had revealed more extensive cracks than had hitherto been found and all flying was suspended pending further examination, UK NMR was again instructed (on 11 December) to tell Saceur the latest position. The final decision came on 19 January 1965 when the Chiefs of Staff agreed that the whole Valiant force should be withdrawn from service immediately, the Prime Minister (Mr Harold Wilson) and Secretary of State for Defence (Mr Denis Healey) agreeing with this conclusion on the following day and the Chief of the Defence Staff (Earl Mountbatten) informing Saceur briefly by telephone on 22 January. Then on the 25th the AOC in C Bomber Command (Air Mshl Sir John Grandy) called on Saceur to explain the position personally.

General Lemnitzer, who was "most concerned" at the news, which was "graver than he had expected from his brief conversation with CDS"[1], pressed the AOC in C to say whether there was "any possible alternative solution" to restore the coverage of targets. With the loss of 48 strikes[2] he was in danger of having a number of uncovered targets in Europe.

Sir John Grandy said that some Vulcan 1s would be going out of service during the year and the possibility of retaining them "certainly existed"; but this had to be subject to decisions by the Chiefs of Staff and the Government. Saceur indicated that he was considering an approach to CDS to ask whether the UK could not find an alternative to the Valiants.

On the following day (26 January) the Ministry of Defence issued a statement about the withdrawal of the Valiants, and the Chiefs of Staff Committee[3] considered the replacement of the Saceur-assigned Tactical Bomber Force. The statement made no comment about replacing Valiants in the latter role; it said:

"Some of the Valiants are assigned to Saceur in a tactical role and Saceur and the North Atlantic Council have been informed of our decision. But the British strategic force of Vulcans and Victors is unaffected. This country makes a contribution to the strategic forces of the Alliance in the shape of the V-bomber force assigned to Saceur. This contribution to Nato remains unchanged by the decision about the Valiant tactical bombers. . . ."

CDS told the CoS Committee that Saceur was anxious to retain the target coverage provided by the TBF Valiants and so would welcome a proposal to replace the Valiants by Vulcans. As bases for their discussion the Committee had before them an Air Force Department paper which examined the means of re-equipping the TBF with 24 Vulcan Mk 1s and a draft submission to the Secretary of State for Defence. CDS said that re-equipment of the force with Vulcans would please Saceur and would enable the UK to take credit for having made special efforts to maintain

---

[1] Report by NMR (Shape) UK to MoD London, 25 Jan 65.
[2] Each of the 24 Valiants in the TBF carried two nuclear weapons, at Saceur's insistence.
[3] COS 5th Meeting/65.

the level of its assigned forces. But, although this re-equipment could probably be achieved without incurring expenditure additional to what was already budgeted, he wondered if there were a real military need to replace the Valiants: he was not convinced that the targets could not be equally well covered without the TBF. Withdrawal of the Valiants presented an opportunity of realising a potential saving of £5.9m, which could be spent on other projects.

CAS took up this financial theme, saying that it had been estimated that the TBF could be re-equipped with Vulcan Mk 1s without exceeding expenditure already budgeted; if this were not done, he was sceptical about the prospects of money saved being allocated to the RAF for other projects. The financial position was complicated by the fact that the TBF base, Marham, was partially funded by infrastructure[1] and a number of projects there had been pre-financed. He added that he was reluctant to see a decision on the problem deferred, for two reasons: Saceur had enquired about the feasibility of using Vulcans in the TBF when he spoke with the C in C Bomber Command on 25 January; and the Valiant crews had been grounded since 9 December 1964[2] and he was concerned about their morale.

In his summing-up of the ensuing discussion, CDS said he considered that the TBF could be withdrawn from Saceur's EDP (Emergency Defence Plan) without affecting the validity of the deterrent. While recognising the political advantages to be gained from re-equipping the force with Vulcan Mk 1s,[3] he thought the money saved by not doing so could be spent on projects more essential to the RAF.

CDS added that Saceur had raised the question of replacing the Valiants on the previous day (25 January), and while he accepted that an early decision was required he felt that further study was needed. Detailed costing should be carried out to establish the exact savings which would be achieved if the TBF were not re-equipped with Vulcans, and suitable projects examined on which the RAF might spend these savings. He and the CAS would make arrangements to brief the Secretary of State for Defence, who should also be formally informed of their views. In endorsing what the CDS had said, the Committee took steps to investigate the financial alternatives: it invited the Air Force Department, in consultation with the Defence Scientific Staff, to examine alternative projects upon which money not spent in re-equipping the TBF with Vulcans might be used; and it invited the Defence Secretariat, in conjunction with the AFD, to calculate the cost of re-equipping the TBF with Vulcans and to determine the savings if this action were not taken.

---

[1] *Ie* as part of Nato expenditure.
[2] Nos 49, 148 and 207 Squadrons each did their last training sorties on this day, but maintained the QRA at Marham until 26 January 1965.
[3] Which the AFD paper had suggested should initially carry one British weapon but be modified for dual carriage of US weapons.

On the following day the Secretary of State for Defence himself took up the matter of the Valiants with the Air Staff. In a minute sent to VCAS[1] he said that the Prime Minister had asked whether Saceur had been "kept in the picture from the start about the fatigue failure in the Valiants". He had also asked when Saceur had first been told and whether three other points had been brought out: the effect on 2nd TAF and on RAF capacity to refuel strategic bombers, and the possibility of re-assigning the latter to a tactical role. The minute asked for answers to these questions as soon as possible.

They came the next day[2], in a resumé of the situation up to the CoS meeting: this assured the Ministers that Saceur had been "kept fully informed throughout about the Valiant fatigue problem"; he had first been told on 6 October that

"a fatigue fault in the Valiants had been discovered and that an urgent technical investigation was being carried out; he was subsequently kept informed of developments and eventually advised by CDS by telephone on 22 January that we were having to disband the Valiant force. No mention of a possible replacement of the Tactical Bomber Force was made. On the instructions of the Chiefs of Staff . . . this was followed up by a personal visit from the AOC in C Bomber Command on 25 January to explain the detail of the Valiant decision. In the course of the C in C's discussion with Saceur, he was asked whether it might be possible to replace the Valiant TBF with some Vulcan 1s which are . . . planned to go out of service this year. When pressed, the AOC in C said he thought that this would be possible but that it would be a matter for consideration by the Chiefs of Staff and HM Government. The Strategic Bomber Force is, as you know, already assigned to Saceur[3]; to re-assign a part of it in the tactical role would merely be 'robbing Peter to pay Paul'".

The minute added that the points about the effect on 2nd TAF and the RAF capability to refuel strategic bombers had not been mentioned to Saceur.

On the same day (28 January) CDS brought S of S comprehensively up to date on the situation and asked for a decision. Recalling that on the 20th he had sought approval for the Valiants to be withdrawn from service and for the "necessary action to be taken to inform Saceur" – approvals which had been given, he reminded the Minister that he had told him that a study was being made of various alternative ways of meeting the TBF commitment to Saceur, "using some of the other V-bomber squadrons". This study had been completed and was considered at "our meeting on Tuesday, 25th January".[4] CDS added that

---

[1] APS/SofS to Secretary to VCAS, 27 Jan 65.
[2] VCAS 510, 28 Jan 65.
[3] As from 23 May 1963, under the Nassau communiqué Statement on Nuclear Defence Systems.
[4] This date should be 26 Jan (the CoS Cttee meeting already referred to).

he was attaching a copy of an Air Force Department paper "from which you will see that it would be a practicable proposition to replace the Saceur-assigned Valiants with an equivalent number of Vulcan Mk 1 aircraft, which we had planned to phase out of service later this year".[1] He went on:−

"At our meeting, we took into consideration the fact that the withdrawal, without replacement, of the 24 Valiants would undoubtedly meet with a bad reception in Nato circles, particularly as we had had to withdraw certain other assigned and earmarked aircraft. . . . We further took into account that an uncompensated withdrawal would discredit us in Saceur's eyes, since to abandon this capability in circumstances which he knows it is within our power to redress is to imply that we have hitherto assigned to him a force which, in our view, has little military significance. Our action could also cast doubt in the minds of our other Nato allies on the worth of our offer to contribute the Medium Bomber Force to an Atlantic Nuclear Force.

"On the other hand, it could be argued that there is no good military case for the Tactical Bomber Force because Saceur already has at his disposal far more nuclear weapons than he requires and because his longer-range targets could be better dealt with by the external nuclear forces of the Alliance. As a consequence, the TBF could be withdrawn without affecting the credibility of the deterrent. This argument does not, however, take into account that the TBF provides Saceur with his only all-weather capability for reaching his more distant tactical targets. A refusal to replace the force would thus strengthen Saceur's hand in his demands for IRBMs. . . .

"At official level the Foreign Office favour the proposal for re-equipping the TBF, both for the general effect on the Nato alliance and because of the many other withdrawals in Nato-assigned forces currently being made.

"You may feel that it would be prudent to defer a definite decision until we have received the official reactions of Shape and the Nato Council. However, because Saceur has already raised the question of re-equipping the TBF with Vulcans and because the Valiant crews have been grounded since 9 December 1964 . . . we should welcome an indication of your initial reaction to this problem".

Saceur's own view, that the replacement of TBF Valiants by Vulcan Mk 1s should be considered by the UK Government, was conveyed to CDS by CAS on 28 January, with some observations on possible consequences if they were not. In a minute headed "Future of the

---

[1] The recommendation at the end of this paper was a double one: that S of S be asked to approve the offer to Saceur of 24 Vulcan 1s as replacement for the TBF Valiants and that authority to proceed with modification and supply programmes be given as a matter of urgency. Modification to the Vulcan 1s was for dual carriage of US weapons, to give Saceur the same delivery capability as he had had with the Valiants. Cost of the modification programme was roughly estimated as about £0.5m, and of operating the Vulcan force until 1968/9, £5.4m compared with £5.9m for the Valiant force.

Saceur-assigned Tactical Bomber Force"[1] CAS said that CDS "might like to know" that he had had a message from Deputy Saceur (MRAF Sir Thomas Pike) "in the following terms":–

"There is a letter in the post from Saceur to CDS acknowledging the removal of the Valiant Force from his EDP (Emergency Defence Plan) and requesting that the UK Government should consider the replacement of the Valiants by available Vulcan Mk 1 aircraft as soon as possible. I feel it important that you should not lose sight of the effect that a serious reduction in the UK contribution to ACE (Allied Command Europe) Air Forces could have upon major OF-6 posts in ACE. It could well occur that our tenure of Comaircent and ComTwo-ATAF and other essential posts might be jeopardised. Other nations, . . . I am sure, will not be slow to take advantage of the situation if the Valiants are not quickly replaced."

However, as will be seen, they were not to be. On 8 February the Air Force Board were brought up to date on the situation, CAS reporting that Saceur "had now been informed of the decision to withdraw the Valiant force from service and had suggested that the squadrons assigned to his command should be replaced by Vulcan 1 aircraft". He then went on to comment that "although there was a view that this proposal should be resisted, on the grounds that the financial saving represented by the withdrawal of the Valiants was badly needed, it could also be urged that we had certain obligations to Saceur which we could not easily ignore. A paper was being prepared examining the problem in detail"[2].

Three days later the Secretary of State for Defence expressed the view to CDS that the Valiants should not be replaced. Giving the reaction requested on 28 January, S of S said that the Valiant force "was not one that was available for worldwide use" and that as CDS had said in his minute, Saceur already had at his disposal far more nuclear weapons than he required, and longer-range targets could be better dealt with by external nuclear forces. S of S went on:

"The Valiants were due for replacement about 1968 by TSR.2s. In discussions on the aircraft programme, our revised planning now envisages a reduction in our European capability. My inclination is to use the withdrawal of the Valiants as a convenient opportunity of reducing our contribution in Europe. The resources saved could be regarded as a contribution either to the reduction that must be secured or towards items which now seem to me to require higher priority. . . ."

S of S added, however, that he would "wait for the result of" CoS studies "before taking a final decision".

By now it was clear that replacement of the Valiants "hinged upon political and financial, rather than on military, considerations" – as the

---

[1] CAS 616A (in State of Readiness of V-bomber Force – MO 3/5/1, Pt 2).
[2] This was the AFD/DS note which the Chiefs of Staff considered on 23 Feb 65 – see p 495.

Acting CDS (Admiral Sir David Luce) put it to the Chiefs of Staff on 23 February, when they discussed[1] an Air Force Department note putting the financial alternatives: the cost of re-equipping the TBF with Vulcan 1/1As, and the saving which would be made if the force were not re-equipped.

Acting CDS, who was in the chair, said that the AFD costing showed that if the TBF were not replaced the savings stemming from the withdrawal of all Valiants would be £13.8m. The force could be re-equipped with Vulcans at a total cost of £0.5m over and above what the cost would have been had the Valiant remained in service. He apprised the committee of what had happened since they considered the Valiant TBF replacement on 26 January: that S of S had told CDS on 11 February that his initial reaction was not to replace the Valiants, and that Saceur had urged that serious consideration be given to re-equipping the TBF, in view of its importance as an element of his "already inadequate all-weather strike capability".

VCAS (Air Mshl Sir Brian Burnett), representing CAS, took up this latter point: he said that the TBF was "the only strike force with an all-weather capability directly under Saceur's control". There was no problem about replacing the Valiants with Vulcans, which could readily be modified to carry two American weapons each. From the purely military point of view it made good sense to replace Saceur's all-weather bomber force for such a small outlay, but the decision was "clearly a political one".

This aspect was emphasised by Mr E J W Barnes of the Foreign Office, who said that re-equipment of the TBF had implications "considerably wider than those affecting Saceur". Although it could be argued that the UK were under no legal obligation to maintain elements such as the TBF which were included in the North Atlantic Council Annual Review, there was a strong moral obligation to do so, particularly as it had been maintained that the Valiants made a valuable contribution to Saceur's nuclear strike plan. He had accepted the loss of Canberras on a temporary basis[2] but was clearly unhappy about the prospect of no replacement being found for the Valiants, when he knew this could be obtained at little cost. Further, the TBF required no expenditure of foreign currency, and abandoning it could weaken the UK's position in Nato, as well as undermining the claim to certain major posts.

A further financial point made in subsequent discussion was that, although it was obviously cheaper to allocate 16 rather than 24 Vulcans to the TBF, station overheads would remain the same and savings would be

---

[1] CoS 10th Meeting/65.
[2] The Saceur-assigned Valiants at Marham (three squadrons of eight aircraft each, *ie* 24 Valiants each carrying two weapons and therefore covering 48 targets) had replaced three squadrons of Canberra B.6s (16 aircraft each, with one weapon per Canberra, therefore also covering 48 targets).

achieved only in operating and modification costs. A rough estimate of the order of cost was £12m for 16 aircraft and £7m for eight, compared with £14.3m for 24.

In his summing-up, Acting CDS referred to both financial and political aspects. Noting that the Secretary of State's initial reaction to the Valiants' replacement had been unfavourable but that he had deferred a final decision until after studies on the subject had been completed, CDS suggested that he should be informed of the cost of replacing the Valiants, of the savings which would be realised if they were not replaced, and of the importance which the Foreign Office and Saceur attached to the UK continuing to assign a TBF to Nato. This submission to S of S should include a costing figure for the compromise solution of re-equipping the force with 16 instead of 24 Vulcans, and Acting CDS considered that it should be prepared in consultation with the Foreign Office and the Defence Secretariat.

The committee agreed with these remarks, "took note" of the AFD paper and instructed the secretary to prepare a draft minute to S of S in the way suggested.

Subsequently the matter of whether or not to replace the Valiants of the TBF with Vulcans moved into higher political spheres of decision; in a minute of 4 March the Minister of Defence set out the pros and cons for the Foreign Secretary and then put his own view. There were four arguments in favour of replacement:–

"Saceur knows about the Vulcans and has already pressed us to make these available to him to compensate for the loss of the Valiants. If we do not replace them, Saceur will lose 48 long-range all-weather strikes (two bombs to an aircraft), the major portion of such forces as are wholly under his control.

"We are already unpopular with Saceur and, to a lesser extent, with the Nato Council for the extent of temporary withdrawals of forces that we have had to make to meet our inescapable commitment elsewhere. Failure to replace the Valiants may lead to increased difficulties with the Council when we wish to remove other forces temporarily or permanently. . . .

"The French may well get to hear that Saceur is objecting to our withdrawals and, in particular, to our position on the Valiants, and they may use this against us, possibly in connection with the negotiations for the ANF[1].

"It may also be more difficult to counter German attempts to gain additional senior posts, and thereby influence, in Nato at our expense."

But there were "strong arguments", S of S said, "on the other side":–

"Whatever Saceur may say, I do not believe that we need worry too much about this reduction in his own forces, given the strength of the external American nuclear forces. In any case, he still has assigned to

---

[1] Atlantic Nuclear Force.

him the rest of the V-bomber force.

"The targets covered by the Valiants could only be attacked in circumstances of general war; and the targets whose potential destruction deters the Russians are covered several times over by American nuclear forces.

"Although replacement by Vulcans would cost only £0.5m more than we had planned to spend on the Valiants, the possibility of not replacing them and so saving nearly £14m over the next few years is attractive when we are considering savings by 1970 of the order of hundreds of millions of pounds. This is an unexpectedly favourable opportunity of making an economy which is unlikely to occur again."

S of S added that the UK had "no reason to be ashamed" of the temporary withdrawals from Nato; it had "a perfect right" to withdraw forces in the event of an acute overseas emergency. As for longer-term reductions, he doubted whether the continued assignment of 24 Vulcans would "much affect the popularity" of any proposals the UK might make. A decision not to assign the Vulcans would be "evidence of our firm intention to take a realistic view of Nato strategy" and to "reduce defence expenditure wherever we can". His conclusion was that the UK "should decide now to tell Nato that we find ourselves unable, with the pressures on our defence programme, to replace the Valiants for the few remaining years of their planned service life. . . ". He hoped the Foreign Secretary (Mr Michael Stewart) would agree.

But the Foreign Secretary disagreed. He understood, he said, the financial attraction of not replacing the Saceur-assigned Valiants, and that the military case was "questionable"; but he considered the political arguments for the UK continuing to fulfil its commitments were "overriding". The removal of the Valiants from Saceur's command was of "quite a different order" from the temporary withdrawals of forces which had had to be made. He recalled that

"we freely entered into a commitment at the time of our last Annual Review to raise and maintain certain forces and assign these to Nato, including a tactical bomber force of 24 Valiants. Although this is not a legal commitment . . . it is an obligation which we ought to fulfil if we possibly can. The fact that replacement aircraft exist, that Saceur knows they are available, and that the additional cost over the estimated expenditure of maintaining the Valiants is so small, all argue for making the replacement. Moreover, as the Vulcans will be based in England, we have the opportunity to make a significant contribution to Nato without any detriment to our balance of payments position."

The Foreign Secretary further averred that a decision to replace the Valiants "would be a timely mark of our loyalty to Nato and help to mute criticism of our other withdrawals". He advised S of S that he was sending copies of his minute to the Prime Minister, Chancellor of the Exchequer and Minister of Aviation; and when the Prime Minister (Mr Harold Wilson) saw his copy on 12 March he asked that the subject should be put on the agenda of the Defence and Oversea Policy Committee. At a meeting of the latter on 19 March 1965 the question of the TBF replacement was finally decided[1].

The committee considered minutes by both the Secretary of State for Defence and the Foreign Secretary and both Ministers put their points of view verbally, the former proposing that the Government should tell Nato that it was unable, with the pressure on the defence programme, to replace the Valiants, the latter emphasising that if they were not replaced, the effect on the UK's relations with its Nato allies and with Saceur might well prejudice its case if it subsequently wished to press for further withdrawals or reductions of its Nato forces.

In his summing-up of the subsequent discussion the Prime Minister said[2] there was general agreement on the committee that the Valiants should not be replaced and that the Government's reply to Nato should be "on the lines suggested by the Secretary of State for Defence", adding that it should be "prepared to reconsider the matter if there were strong adverse reactions, particularly from the United States Government, which might prejudice the case for a subsequent reduction of ground forces". The committee invited S of S "to be guided by the Prime Minister's summing-up in informing Nato in the sense he proposed".

However, S of S subsequently challenged the Prime Minister on his summing-up as recorded in the minutes, saying that it had been agreed that "the caveat should be omitted". It would, he averred, "place the Chief of the Air Staff in an extremely difficult position because it would be quite impossible to keep the TBF at Marham in limbo until the decision had been ratified". He added: "the position of the crews would be particularly difficult since they have been in enforced idleness for three months already. For this reason I strongly recommend that the final sentences should be deleted".

But the Prime Minister stood his ground. On reconsideration, he told S of S[3], he still thought the sentence represented "the right balance of advantage" – that the initial reply to Nato "should be to the effect that we do not intend to replace the Valiants, but that we should . . . be ready to reconsider the matter" if there were a strong adverse reaction. He added that he appreciated the difficulty with which "this tactic" confronted CAS, in so far as it involved keeping crews in limbo "until we reach finality". But, he asked, need that take very long? And was it not preferable to trying to force a premature decision which might turn out to be wrong?

On 25 March the Foreign Office advised the UK Delegation to Nato that Ministers had decided that Nato should be informed that they

---

[1] OPD(65).
[2] Minutes, DS17 (Cabinet), 22 March 1965.
[3] PM's personal minute, M.25/65, 24 March.

found themselves unable, with the pressure on the defence programme, to replace the Valiants previously assigned to Saceur and saw no overriding military justification for doing so.

The Foreign Office advised that it would be necessary to inform Saceur "at an early date", and it was proposed to do this "by a message from the Defence Secretary communicated through you", adding that "in view of Parliamentary interest, and of the need to redeploy the RAF personnel now at Marham, the Defence Secretary will have to make a statement soon".

In a letter to Saceur on 26 March, delivered personally by the Permanent British Representative to the Nato Council in Paris (Sir Evelyn Shuckburgh) on 29 March[1], S of S said that the Government had been giving urgent consideration to the possibility of replacing with modified Vulcan Mk 1s the Valiant bombers which had been withdrawn from service, adding:–

"We have given full weight to the concern which we know that you feel about the diminution of the nuclear strike forces assigned to you, as a result of the withdrawal of the Valiants. But, after taking most careful account of all the operational and other factors involved, we have come to the view that the proposed replacement of the Valiants for the few remaining years of their planned service with Nato cannot be justified by military or other considerations sufficient to override the counter-vailing need to deal with the serious pressures on our defence programme. You may be assured that this does not diminish our intention to maintain the fullest possible support for Allied Command Europe, or our understanding of your problems."

S of S finally told Saceur that he intended to inform Parliament on 1 April, and his statement there was as follows:–

"After most careful consideration of all the operational and other factors involved, the Government have formed the view that replace-ment of the Valiants for the few remaining years of their planned service with Nato cannot be justified by military or other considerations sufficient to override the countervailing need to deal with the pressures upon our defence programme. Saceur and the North Atlantic Council have been so informed".[2]

This was the last public word about the TBF Valiants, but the Air Staff had to wait a little longer before getting final authority to disband the force: until 14 April, when VCAS was told, in a minute from PS/S of S for Defence, that "the decision of the Defence and Oversea Policy Committee about the Valiants[3] was such that we have had to await the reaction of our allies to our announcement before finally disbanding the force at Marham". Reactions had been received from Saceur and

---

[1] Message from UK Del to Nato to FO (No 82), 29 Mch 65.

[2] Hansard (Commons), Written Answers, Cols 275–276.

[3] ODP(65) 16th Mtg, item 2.

the Americans[1] and there had been "no pressure on us from our allies to replace the Valiants". The minute concluded: "In these circumstances, the Secretary of State agrees that you should now act on the decision that the Valiants will not be replaced."

Thus ended the third act in the 1965 saga of the Valiants: after their replacement in the SR and tanker roles by Victors, their non-replacement in the Tactical Bomber Force.

---

[1] UK Del tel No 82 and Washington tels 751 and 759, respectively.

CHAPTER XXVIII

TSR.2

In his arguments against replacing the Saceur-assigned Valiants with Vulcans the Secretary of State for Defence (Mr Denis Healey) had referred to the Government's "firm intention" to reduce defence expenditure wherever it could, in his minute of 4 March 1965. Just over a month later, on 6 April, the Chancellor of the Exchequer (Mr James Callaghan) announced during his Budget speech in the House of Commons that the British Aircraft Corporation TSR.2 – the tactical strike/reconnaissance machine ordered for the RAF to replace its Valiants and Canberras – would be cancelled. He made reference to it against the background of defence expenditure, especially overseas, saying that the Government had had to consider the future of the project and that the S of S would make a full statement about the decision to cancel it.[1]

In his statement,[2] S of S said that the Government had been "wrestling continuously with this problem" since they took office some six months previously, commenting that it had "always been obvious" that the cost of continuing the TSR.2 programme was "likely to impose an intolerable burden" on the national economy in general and the defence budget in particular. He went on to say that on coming into office the Government had discovered that the programme planned for TSR.2 would have cost about £750m for research, development and production. An order for 150 would have meant that each one would have cost £5m; an order for 100 would have meant that each would have cost over £6m. He suggested that a programme "of this order" was not one which " could be held to represent value for money". He said he did not believe that the Government would have been justified in taking a decision to cancel TSR.2 when they decided on other changes in the military aircraft programme two months previously[3]: "we needed better information than we then possessed on the probable cost of the TSR.2 and on the cost and performance of possible alternative aircraft". The Government now had enough further information to take a decision.

After several interruptions, S of S went on to say[4] that the House had been informed that "we should seek a fixed price for" TSR.2, but that in view of all the complexities of the programme the manufacturers[5] had not been able to give one. The best arrangements they had been able to offer "would have given no assurance that the Government's ultimate

---

[1] Commons Hansard, 6 Apr 65, Cols 279-280.

[2] Ibid, Cols 318-319.

[3] Among these were the cancellation of the P.1154 and HS681 projects, announced early in February.

[4] Commons Hansard, 6 Apr 65, Cols 325-326.

[5] British Aircraft Corporation, a consortium formed in February 1960 by the Bristol Aeroplane Co, English Electric Ltd and Vickers Ltd.

501

financial responsibility would have been limited". Every week the programme continued it was costing the taxpayer something like £1m. The Government had decided "with deep reluctance" that they must now cancel it.

S of S stated that "the fundamental reason for the cancellation" was "the stark fact that the economic implications of modern military technology" ruled out "British development and production of this type of aircraft for a purely national market". But he added that the Government had no intention of requiring its forces "to forego the aircraft at present planned to replace the Canberra towards the end of this decade without making certain that they can carry out their operational tasks by other means" – though it would not be possible to define those tasks precisely until the defence review was completed later in the year. That review might show that the number of aircraft required "with TSR.2 performance characteristics" might be "substantially below the existing TSR.2 programme", adding that "on certain hypotheses about long-term commitments it might even be possible to reshape our defences in such a way as to dispense with this type of aircraft altogether".

This comment provoked an intervention by the member for Harwich (Mr Julian Ridsdale, Con), pointing out that the Minister had said that "under certain circumstances" he envisaged the RAF without a strike aircraft and asking: "Surely the only circumstances in which he can envisage the RAF without a strike aircraft would be the complete withdrawal of our forces from the Far East, the Middle East and Cyprus. Is that the Government's policy?"

"No," S of S replied. "I myself think it most unlikely that these hypotheses would be fulfilled. They would, indeed, require such a radical change in our commitments as to imply tremendous changes not only in the RAF weapons programme but the weapons programme for the whole of our forces". He then added: "In order to make quite certain that, whatever happens, our Services will have appropriate aircraft in sufficient numbers, Her Majesty's Government have secured from the United States Government an option on the F-111A aircraft at a price per aircraft which, even on a full-scale programme, would represent less than half the estimated total TSR.2 research, development and production cost".[1]

In the event, not only was TSR.2 cancelled – to the accompaniment of bitter controversy in political, military and aviation industry circles – but by the end of the decade the UK had withdrawn from its bases east of Suez, and the RAF never acquired F-111As. But this chapter is only concerned with TSR.2 – in recording its demise, looking at its origins, to

---

[1] Commons Hansard, 6 Apr 65, Cols 326-341 cover the remainder of the statement by S of S which was frequently interrupted. As he was speaking it was put out as a Press release by the Ministry of Defence (see *Flight International* for 15 Apr 65, where it is reproduced in full).

establish what kind of an aircraft it was intended to be and what sort of roles it was expected to perform.

TSR.2 originated in an Air Staff General Operational Requirement, No GOR.339, issued in March 1957, for a tactical strike/reconnaissance aircraft, to be in service by 1964 "or as soon thereafter as possible" as a replacement for the Canberra. It was to have an all-weather capability with a self-contained bombing system, and minimum take-off and landing requirements; its radius of action was to be 1,000nm; it was to operate mainly at low level (1,000ft or less above the ground) and to be able to deliver its main (nuclear) weapon by loft manoeuvre at low level or in a dive toss attack from medium level.

When this GOR was circulated on 29 October 1957 an introductory note by DOR(A) said that it stated "the broad, though tentative, outlines of the project". It had been forwarded to CA (Controller of Aircraft, Ministry of Supply), who had issued it to industry for "examination of the technical problems". Industry was "required to report" by the end of January 1958.

The GOR emphasised the Canberra replacement character of the aircraft envisaged: it was to be able to deliver its tactical nuclear weapon (the one developed to OR1127 – Red Beard) by day or night either visually or using blind-bombing techniques, or alternative weapons – HE bombs or rockets – visually; it was also to have PR and electronic reconnaissance capability. It was to use as little runway as possible, through improved take-off and landing performance. It would have a two-man crew – pilot and navigator.

The introductory note to GOR.339 when it was circulated added a new, strategic dimension to its proposed capabilities: "such an aircraft", said the last of six paragraphs summarising Air Staff thinking on the project, "with range increased by flight refuelling, would pose a low-level threat to Russia and thus augment the primary deterrent". No word about strategic deterrent capability occurred in the operational requirement itself, nor in the subsequent Air Staff Requirement, No OR343.

Nine companies responded with design proposals to GOR.339 after it had been sent out in the autumn of 1957: A V Roe and Co (who sent in a heavy brochure describing the Avro 739); Blackburn and General Aircraft (who proposed a development of the NA.39 Naval strike aircraft designated B.103A); Bristol Aircraft (who submitted the Bristol Type 204); Fairey Aviation (who were sent GOR.339 for study though no record exists of their proposal); English Electric (who "made a thorough study of the requirement and . . . probably expended more effort than any other firm currently engaged on the GOR.339 exercise"[1]); Handley Page (who produced a detailed study but said that

---

[1] LM, DDOR1/DDOR4, 22 Jan 58.

they were not proposing to tender[1]); de Havilland Aircraft (who proposed the P.1129); Short Brothers (who proposed a VTOL low-level strike aircraft) and Vickers (who sent in a brochure).

Copies of GOR.339 had been sent to the companies by the Controller of Aircraft, MoS (Air Mshl Sir Claude Pelly), on 9 September 1957 with a request for proposals by 31 January 1958; and on 16 September the Secretary (Sir Cyril Musgrave) met company representatives and explained that the contract "would only be awarded to a group of firms".[2]

On 24 September the DRPC (Defence Research Policy Committee) gave the TS/R aircraft project a UA (under assessment) classification, at a meeting when they "took note of" a 1,500-word Air Ministry Note setting-out the case for such a new type. This Note, dated 26 August, put the requirement into a strategic context with its opening reference to the advent of the hydrogen bomb – which had so "enormously strengthened the power of the deterrent" that the immediate danger of "deliberate global war" had receded. But there was an increased risk that Russia might seek to gain her ends "by resort to cold and limited war by proxy". If such wars were not contained there was a grave risk that they might lead to global war by accident. Forces were therefore needed which were "capable of using conventional and if necessary nuclear weapons" as a sanction against local aggression, or as a means of preventing its extension and defeating it.

The Note went on to say that by 1965 a new aircraft would be required in the RAF for tactical strike/reconnaissance "in situations of this kind", for which no aircraft already planned would be suitable. It also added a strategic aspect by saying that a type suitable for this role would possess added value "by enabling us to maintain an effective contribution to Saceur's forces on the Continent" – a contribution made by Canberras, and subsequently by Valiants of the TBF – "and to augment the main deterrent by posing a low-level threat to Russia itself".

Two aspects of the TSR.2 story were therefore in existence from 1957: possible use of the aircraft to supplement the strategic nuclear deterrent force; and a re-grouping of the aircaft industry to provide the programme contractor. The possibility of TSR.2 being used to "augment the primary deterrent" had been mooted in the covering note to OR.339 which went to the Air Staff, the Admiralty, the War Office and the Ministry of Defence, so the idea had wide circulation; and the Ministry of Supply view on industrial integration had been described in the letter from Handley Page (Gp Capt R C M Collard, sales manager) to ACAS(OR) (AVM W H Kyle), already quoted, in which he went on to say that the Ministry of Supply "encourage some sort of amalgamation" but adding that "one cannot amalgamate on the basis of

---

[1] On the ground that MoS had "made it clear" they would place the order "with a concern having very large resources" (letter, Gp Capt Collard/ ACAS(OR), 17 Dec 57.)
[2] TSR.2 Significant Events and Policy and Financial Decisions (PE document).

one chance in, say, four of getting business. Therefore the work must inevitably go to one of the large combines existing already".

In fact, it went to a new combine, as accurately forecast by ACAS(OR) in a minute of 11 February 1958 to DCAS (AVM G W Tuttle).[1] Noting that the "detailed studies of GOR.339 completed by the aircraft industry" had been "received recently", he went on to say that "the principle of rationalisation within the aircraft industry suggested by the Minister of Supply"[2] had been accepted and firms were "prepared to strengthen their individual design and production facilities by working together on GOR.339". He then added: "To give but one example, Vickers, English Electric, Rolls-Royce, EMI and Elliotts are willing to form an associated group. The manpower and technical effort which such a group could devote to GOR.339 is far beyond anything that has been concentrated on a single project in the past . . . ; in particular, it covers the equipment requirements".

This minute, headed "NA.39 and GOR.339", was in response to one from the Secretary of State for Air (Mr George Ward) of 5 February, in which he had suggested that an aircraft to GOR.339 might not come into service before 1968 at the earliest and that the only solution to the Canberra replacement problem was to go for an existing type like the Blackburn NA.39,[3] or an RAF version designated B.103 by the company and described in their brochure of January 1958. In DCAS's view, the NA.39 only improved the quality of the existing RAF tactical bomber aircraft "by virtue of its superior speed".

Subsequently (on 13 February) the whole question as to whether the RAF needed a new tactical strike/reconnaissance aircraft to GOR339 was discussed by the Air Council.[4] Its conclusion was that such a new aircraft was required and that the NA.39 should not be considered.

The Council had before it a note circulated by DCAS "comparing the main features of the Canberra, the NA.39 and Blackburn's proposals for an RAF version of the NA.39", with a view to assisting it to decide whether "a new tactical strike/reconnaissance aircraft to GOR.339" was required. DCAS recalled that in July 1957 the Council had agreed that this requirement should be issued to industry for design studies; in his view, the study he had circulated confirmed the need for a new aircraft.

Putting the point whether the NA.39 "would do" instead of the aircraft to be built to OR.339, DCAS referred to the role to be performed by the new type and the particular features it would have to embody: it would have to be supersonic and to operate from runways of not more than 1,000yd; it would have to incorporate an adequate blind bombing/navigation system and needed considerable range. He said that the NA.39 could never be supersonic, would need a 3,000yd

[1] In VCAS Operational Requirements Committee – Papers and Minutes (ID9/49/9 Pt 1).
[2] Mr Aubrey Jones.
[3] Which first flew on 30 April 1958.
[4] Conclusions 4(58) Secret Annex, 13 Feb 58.

runway in the tropics and had an inadequate blind bombing system and inadequate range. Referring to factors affecting a Canberra replacement, DCAS said he doubted whether this would be needed very soon, for three reasons: its fatigue life "looked like increasing"; Valiants might be used instead of Canberras in support of Saceur; and a lack of work in the aircraft industry meant that "immense resources could be deployed on any new project" – a view which CA (Air Mshl Sir Claude Pelly) supported. DCAS's conclusion was that, even if the RAF were not allowed to have the aircraft to GOR.339, it was doubtful if having the NA.39 could be justified. It seemed desirable to avoid being forced into a decision until more information was available about the expected life of the Canberra, and until the MoS and the Air Staff had completed their evaluation of industry's proposals to meet GOR.339 – "as they would do early in April".

PUS (Sir Maurice Dean) said he felt it would be "disastrous" if the Air Staff were not allowed to go forward with GOR.339 – which it might not get if consideration of the NA.39 were opened up; and in summing-up the discussion the Secretary of State (Mr George Ward) said his main concern was the gap, and whether this would not have to be filled by an interim aircraft. New factors revealed by DCAS's study held out hope of extending the Canberra's life and of bringing forward the delivery date of the new type to GOR.339. It seemed to be the Council's view (he said) that it would be a mistake to order the NA.39, and he suggested that DCAS should prepare a minute for him to send to the Minister of Defence saying that while the Council was not yet in a position to confirm its forecasts about the life of the Canberra and arrival date of the aircraft to OR.339, its studies were far enough advanced to justify the view that the latter was required and the NA.39 would not be considered – views which the Council endorsed.

The NA.39 had been referred to in the 1958 *Report on Defence*, published during February[1], in the section dealing with Sea Power. This said that a low-level tactical bomber was being developed for the Royal Navy; that the prototype would fly later in the year and that "its adoption by the Royal Air Force" was "being considered". On the 20th of that month VCAS (Air Mshl Sir Edmund Hudleston) advised[2] that the Admiralty would "very soon be compelled to place orders for the NA.39", but that they would be "unlikely to be able to do so" unless the RAF accepted the aircraft, which it was "not prepared to do". He thought that as a consequence there was "every possibility" that the issue would be "forced up to the Defence Committee" and would "inevitably go to the Minister of Defence", and that in anticipation of these events a paper should be prepared "setting-out our arguments

---

[1] Cmnd 363.
[2] Minute to Head of S.6 on NA.39.

506

against the NA.39 and for GOR.339".

Thus by early 1958 two further aspects of the TSR.2 story – in addition to the industrial and strategic implications already mentioned – were in existence: a difference of opinion between the Royal Navy, which wanted the RAF to have the NA.39, and the Royal Air Force, which wanted to have GOR.339, as a low-level tactical bomber; and the escalation of a matter of military aircraft procurement into a major political issue – bound up, as the requirement for a type to come into service in the mid-1960s inevitably was, with future British defence policy.

The Air Ministry's views on the Canberra replacement were not in fact put to the Minister of Defence by S of S until 16 April, but in the meantime the latter had referred to it during his speech in the Air Estimates debate on 10 March.[1] Saying that the Canberra had "several years of useful life before it" he added: "but we see a clear and continuing need for a strike and reconnaissance aircraft in overseas theatres. We are, therefore, considering the performance which could be offered by types already under development or by the designs put forward by industry in reply to the general operational requirement issued last year". His deputy, the Under-Secretary of State for Air (Mr Charles Orr-Ewing), was more expansive on the subject at the end of the debate when he said,[2]

"We were asked what we intended to do about replacing the Canberra, and in particular whether we were to use the NA.39. My right hon friend explained that we were giving much thought to this. Naturally, we cannot reach very quick conclusions. As regards the NA.39, speed is only one of many factors we must take into account before a choice is made. For example, range, and the ability to operate from short runways, also matter greatly. Any successor to the Canberra must be able to find and attack its target by night and day, without ground aids. In fact, it must have 'built-in' flexibility. Besides this, we must consider when we shall want the replacement, and when various possible candidates will become available. . . ."

During March the assessment group at the Ministry of Supply[3] reported that the draft OR339 (little changed from GOR339) was "feasible" and could best be met by a twin-engined aircraft of conventional pattern, estimating that CA Release could be achieved by mid-1965; and on the 28th the DFS[4] there recommended placing a contract with English Electric (as leader), Vickers-Armstrongs (Aircraft) and Short Brothers.

Then, on 16 April, S of S put the Air Ministry's case to the Minister of Defence (Mr Duncan Sandys). He said that it was clear there was an

---

[1] Commons Hansard, Col 44.
[2] Ibid, Col 191.
[3] TSR.2 Significant Events and Policy and Financial Decisions (PE document).
[4] Directorate of Future Systems.

essential requirement for a successor to the Canberra; that if it was to do its job and have a useful length of life it must have "greatly improved performance" over the Canberra; that the NA.39 did not measure up to the requirements in certain important respects; and that designs submitted by industry in response to GOR.339 suggested that "we can get a very good aircraft which will fully meet our operational requirement".

S of S added that the MoS and Air Ministry had "almost completed" their examination of the submissions by industry in response to GOR.339 and would shortly be putting forward their recommendations to the DRPC[1], which had classified the project as "under assessment", money having been allowed for it in the 1958/59 R & D Estimates.[2]

During April 1958 the difference of view between the Admiralty and the Air Ministry, on a common aircraft to meet their requirements, sharply intensified. S of S told the First Lord (the Earl of Selkirk) on the 22nd that the NA.39 fell so far short of RAF requirements for a Canberra replacement that "it would be quite wrong" for him to advocate its selection, even though he still held to the view – expressed in letters and discussions earlier in the year – that it would be in the interests of both Departments "to make common cause in the field of future aircraft whenever possible".[3]

He said he was satisfied that GOR.339 was " a realistic specification" based on a sound analysis of military requirements for the 1960s, and was one that industry could meet. He was equally sure that the NA.39, "even if all the developments that Blackburns offer were to be successful", could not fulfil GOR.339: for example, it could not achieve supersonic speed in level flight and this was "a fundamental drawback". The only alternative way in which the Air Ministry could help the Admiralty was by taking the NA.39 as an interim aircraft between the Canberra and GOR.339, but the Canberra could be "made to last" until the RAF got the latter; and in the light of "the considerable cost of the NA.39" S of S did not feel he would be justified in pursuing this alternative.

The Ministry of Supply, he concluded, had advised him that the Air Ministry "ought to come a firm decision about the GOR.339 this summer", adding: "in view of the remarks made by the Minister of Defence in his White Paper I . . . felt it necessary to send him a note giving my firm recommendation that the RAF should go for an aircraft to GOR.339 for their Canberra replacement". He enclosed copies of papers forwarded in support of this recommendation – an analysis of the Air Staff case for a Canberra replacement, and a table giving comparative performances of the Canberra, NA.39 and GOR.339.

On 13 May the First Lord put the Admiralty case for NA.39 to S of S.

---

[1] Defence Research Policy Committee.
[2] A copy of this minute was sent to the Minister of Defence.
[3] Correspondence in Requirement for a Tactical Strike/Recce Aircraft (ID3/945/2 Pt1).

First, it was expected to be in service by 1961 while GOR.339 would not be available "until at least four years and probably five or six years later", and while not "a direct substitute" it seemed to be "a great step towards" what was required. Secondly, NA.39 surpassed the Canberra's capability in all respects and was "remarkably close" to GOR.339 in most of them. He suggested that, on the timing of the introduction of NA.39 and its "marked superiority over the Canberra", S of S should "look once again at the Blackburn project", adding: "If during . . . the next six months you were to decide to associate your Ministry with production orders for this aircraft, we would be delighted to form a joint RN/RAF Development Unit from the Admiralty pre-production allocation".

Subsequently S of S rejected the Admiralty arguments: in a letter of 2 June to the First Lord he said that CA had assured him that GOR.339 could be in service in 1965 if an order to proceed were given immediately. He added that NA.39 was inferior to the Canberra in two "very important respects" – radius of action (25 per cent less) and airfield performance (needing a 3,000yd runway in the tropics as against 2,400yd). Much though he appreciated the offer to form a joint RN/RAF Development Unit, his decision "to go for the GOR.339" as a Canberra replacement was "inevitable", nor did he feel justified in recommending the NA.39 as an interim aircraft.

It was clear that there could be no Air Ministry-Admiralty meeting of minds on NA.39, and the First Lord accepted this with regret. In a further letter to S of S on 26 June he said (in words which, in view of subsequent events, had a prophetic ring) that he had hoped that "the considerable effort" which had been put into the development of this aircraft "would have a made a useful contribution to the strength of the RAF as well as to that of the Navy".

Having warded off an Admiralty challenge to GOR.339 the Air Ministry then secured its endorsement by the DRPC, which (as already related) had given the project an "under assessment" classification in the previous September. Subsequently, as the minutes recorded[1], "a detailed investigation of the technical problems involved had . . . been made by the aircraft industry and by the research establishments . . . . The committee was now" – at its meeting on 17 June – "required to decide whether this project should proceed or not, and at what priority".

DCAS (Air Mshl Sir Geoffrey Tuttle) said he would not apologise for presenting "one of the longest and most detailed cases ever put before the committee", but he was anxious to emphasise four points: the issue, "one of the most important ever considered by the DRPC", was vital to the three Services, to the aircraft industry, to the UK's balance of payments and to its position in Nato; it was vital to the Army in its

---

[1] DRP/M(58)8, 1958.

strike/reconnaissance role, to the Navy to strike against submarine bases and to the RAF abroad, was important to the aircraft industry in helping to keep it in being, and would demonstrate to Nato that the UK "intended to assist in other ways than maintaining a deterrent"; it would probably be "the last military fighting aircraft developed in the UK"; and a quick decision by the committee was vital if the 1965 date were to be achieved.

The DRPC endorsed the need for the development of an aircraft "of the type described" and agreed that GOR.339 should be entered on the R&D programme with an importance grading II and an agreed forecast date of 1965[1]; but some dissentient views were expressed in discussion.

Vice-Admiral M L Power suggested that while "this would be a very desirable aircraft if money to develop it could be made available, both the cost and the time-scale were optimistic". The later and expensive stage of NA.39 development would coincide with the earlier and more expensive stage of GOR.339 development, and there might be a case for delaying the latter for perhaps two years to take advantage of technical advances during that period. The gap "could be covered by the NA.39". CA (Air Chf Mshl Sir Claude Pelly) said that the estimate of £35m as the cost of development, including the provision of ten prototypes, was "realistic" and should not be exceeded.

The chairman (Sir Frederick Brundrett) was concerned that one aircraft was being developed to meet two distinct requirements. While GOR.339 would certainly meet Army requirements, NA.39 could do so four or five years earlier. He thought there was merit in considering whether GOR.339 could not be developed further[2]. In subsequent discussion the point was made that logistically it would be unsound to develop two different aircraft when one "could do the whole job": experience had shown, it was said, that the more specialised aircraft was "in the wrong place when required".

Once OR.339 had been endorsed by the DRPC it was submitted to the R&D Board with requests for its entry on the R&D programme; the

---

[1] Which upset the Air Staff, VCAS minuting DCAS on 4 Aug 59: "In view of the fight we had to get OR.339 accepted, any slippage in the agreed forecast date is deemed to prejudice the further arguments we shall certainly have about retaining this aircraft in our programme".

[2] Sir Frederick expressed further reservations about OR.339 in a minute to the Minister of Defence early in July, and in forwarding a copy of this to CAS (Air Chf Mshl Sir Dermot Boyle) on 14 July DCAS advised that he would find it "a very useful piece of background" but added: "I . . . would be very glad if you would ensure that no quotation is ever made from it nor that its existence is ever known". Referring to the reservations expressed at the DRPC meeting, Sir Frederick said he was "by no means happy that the OR.339" was "necessarily the aircraft that we ought to have". While he was convinced that there had to be a successor to the Canberra, he had two serious doubts. The Air Ministry were correct in arguing that they would have to carry out independent operations under various treaties, but taking the OR.339 in-service date of 1965 and considering what bases and responsibilities the UK was likely to have then, he wondered whether the Air Staff were "planning on a realistic basis". If it was not necessary to plan for such operations there would only be the Army support requirement, and for this an aircraft a good deal less sophisticated could be accepted.

choice of Vickers-Armstrongs (in the lead) and English Electric to design and develop the aircraft with support from Shorts; and an approach to the Treasury for approval of an interim contract up to £150,000 for the first six months. This submission was made on 2 July and some 12 days later the Board recommended the design and development of OR.339 by Vickers and English Electric, subject to satisfactory negotiations. The two companies were immediately asked by the Ministry of Supply for details of their association. During July also, S of S wrote to the Minister of Defence advising him of the DRPC conclusion on OR.339 and asking for his agreement to issue the OR to the MoS and to the industry[1].

In his minute (dated 2 July) S of S recalled that he had told the Minister on 16 April that he would report back as soon as the DRPC "had considered the Air Ministry case for a new strike/reconnaissance aircraft". He went on[2]: "No doubt you will have...been informed that at their meeting on 17 June the committee agreed that the Operational Requirement should be entered on the Research and Development programme with an importance grading II and an Agreed Forecast date of 1965. I hope you will now agree that the approved Operational Requirement should be issued to industry, but if you wish I should welcome the chance of discussing the matter further with you, together with our professional advisers. I am sending a copy of this minute to the Minister of Supply".

The latter (Mr Aubrey Jones) subsequently put his own case for OR.339 to the Minister of Defence. Writing on 11 July, he pointed out that it was "likely to be the only new military aircraft for some time", and added: "without it my efforts to retain a strong...industry to meet military and civilian requirements will probably fail, with the grave economic and Service consequences which must follow".

Meanwhile the Air Staff continued to refine their requirement: "in view of the favourable progress being made in obtaining a new aircraft work was commenced to prepare the draft OR in final form[3]. The first draft was circulated to branch and staffs and final comments and amendments prepared".

However, a Middle East crisis in mid-July 1958, involving a large airlift of British forces into Jordan, diverted the attention of the Minister of Defence from domestic affairs; and the Ministries involved in the OR.339 discussions were advised on 16 July[4] that he hoped to be able to discuss "the requirement for a new strike/reconnaissance aircraft ... as soon as the immediate trouble in the Middle East" was over.

On 1 August the Air Staff were advised[5] that the Minister of Defence would be holding a meeting on the 5th to discuss OR.339 and that the

---

[1] From chronology in RAF Buccaneer ASR343 – Historic Diary (AHB II/129/2/2).
[2] Minute in Requirement for a Tactical Strike/Recce Aircraft (AHB ID3/945/2, Pt 1).
[3] RAF Buccaneer ASR343 – Historic Diary (II/129/2/2).
[4] PS to PUS.
[5] By PS to SoS.

Ministry of Supply would be represented at it, and in preparation for it a brief on the new type was prepared for S of S and CAS, summarising views which had already been expressed and enlarging on aspects which might come up in discussion. But there is no record of such a meeting being held; instead, on 7 August all the Departments involved – the Admiralty, Air Ministry and War Office – were sent a long questionnaire by the PUS, Ministry of Defence (Sir Richard Powell), who in his covering letter said that the Minister was "considering urgently whether he should authorise the production of the NA.39 and the development of OR.339". To help him in reaching a conclusion PUS had been asked to obtain the answers to the questions (there were seven, with many sub-questions) as quickly as possible.

The questions about the two aircraft were summarised in PUS's covering letter: they asked what the operational tasks were which the NA.39 and OR.339 were intended to fulfil in police actions (or other situations short of limited war), limited war and global war; what the requirements were for reconnaissance/strike in support of the Army in police action, limited war and global war; if the Royal Navy were not equipped with NA.39s what tasks would there be in police action, limited war and global war which could not be performed by the RAF with Canberras, V-bombers and fighter-bombers and later with the OR.339, or by the Royal Navy with other naval aircraft or later with Sea Slug used as a surface-to-surface weapon; if the RAF were not equipped with the OR.339 what tasks would there be in police actions, limited war and global war which could not be performed by the Royal Navy with NA.39s and other aircraft or the RAF with Canberras, V-bombers and fighter-bombers, and later with the NA.39 operated from land and a modified version of it with radar and other equipment of a comparable performance with that to be installed in OR.339; what differences in performance there would be between a Naval version of the NA.39 and the previously-mentioned modified version and OR.339; what was the operational importance of those differences in police action, limited war and global war; and could a version of the NA.39, modified as mentioned, be in service with the RAF sooner than OR.339 – and if not, what were the limiting factors?

Although the Minister of Defence seemed to be trying to determine whether the OR.339 requirement could be met by a modified NA.39, the Air Ministry did not consider that this was an "either or" problem. As the DUS (Mr R H Melville) put it in forwarding the replies to the questionnaire to PUS, MoD, on 22 August:–

"The NA.39 is a shipborne aircraft, subject to the physical limitations in terms of weight and size suffered by all aircraft whose design is restricted by deck strengths and lift capacity. It is . . . designed to a specification governed by conditions as evaluated some six years ago, for maritime purposes.

"The OR.339 is a land-based aircraft, designed to incorporate the scientific knowledge and experience now available to us, translated into a requirement directly related to the known and appreciated political and military developments we may expect to encounter in the mid-60s." He added that "neither the NA.39 nor the suggested derivative" would survive in the operational conditions that OR.339 was designed to meet, that for RAF purposes the NA.39 would be "obsolescent" by the time it was produced and that neither the NA.39 nor its derivative would meet the military requirement.

Meanwhile (on 28 July) the Ministry of Supply had written to the Treasury[1] giving £35m as an in-office estimate for OR.339 up to CA Release and seeking aproval for placing a design study contract, at an estimated cost of £150,000, immediately after Ministerial approval of the requirement had been given.

The War Office had submitted their replies to the questionnaire on 20 August[2] and the Admiralty put in theirs – with an introduction entitled Production of the NA.39 and Development of the OR.339 – on the 28th. The latter strongly advocated the Naval need for the NA.39, operating from a mobile base, and stressed that it was not in competition with OR.339 – either in character or in time. The NA.39 prototype was already flying; OR.339 was "intended for different roles and for operation from land bases, in seven years' time, at least".

So many different hypotheses had been postulated in the Minister of Defence's questionnaire to the three Services that a computer would have been needed in Storey's Gate to give an accurate read-out from the answers. While they were being studied by the MoD staff some new questions were posed – for example, DCAS was asked whether consideration had been given to any foreign aircraft to fulfil the OR.339 requirement[3] – and the Ministry of Supply suggested that the requirement might be elaborated to include a variable-geometry wing based on the Barnes Wallis Swallow project[4]. Then, on 10 September, one issue in the controversy was clarified – the Minister of Defence authorised a production order for NA.39s for the Royal Navy's aircraft carriers. He told the First Lord that he was satisfied that a case had been made out for this requirement, and although the number required had still to be settled, it would be greater than the 50 for which Treasury approval had been sought to order long-dated materials.

This step was interpreted by the Air Staff to mean that there was "a determination to introduce the Blackburn NA.39 into the Royal Air Force"[5], and in mid-September the Minister of Defence, who was shortly

[1] TSR.2 Significant Events and Policy and Financial Decisions (PE chronology).
[2] "The War Office was asked to contribute some of the answers to the questionnaire. Their reply. . . [was] submitted about 20th August" (RAF Buccaneer ASR343 Historical Diary (AHBII/129/2/2)).
[3] "Towards the end of August the threat of foreign contenders to OR.339 reappeared. MoD asked DCAS if we had given consideration to any suitable foreign aircraft" (ibid).
[4] "Meetings were held at MoS, RAE and Vickers Armstrong Ltd at which the Swallow technique of variable geometry was studied in relation to OR.339" (ibid).
[5] Minutes, DUSI/CAS of 11 Sep and DCAS/S of S of 17 Oct.

leaving for a visit to the United States, was pressed to give a decision on OR.339. "As you know", he was told by the Parliamentary US of S (Mr Ian Orr-Ewing) on the 16th, "we regard this as a matter of vital importance and want the earliest clearance to enable development work to start"[1]. However, the Minister's reply (transmitted by telephone) was that he could not reach a decision on a matter of such importance before leaving for the US, particularly as his talks there "would cover interdependence, development and so on". He would consider the matter, "in the light of his discussions", as soon as he got back[2].

The Air Ministry were then asked by the Ministry of Defence whether there was any reason why the NA.39 could not enter RAF squadron service shortly after production aircraft were available, but the latter were told on 30 September[3] that if "regardless of operational or financial considerations the NA.39 were introduced into RAF service in 1961, it could be flown by RAF pilots", but there were "strong operational reasons" – explained in the Air Ministry reply to the Minister of Defence's questionnaire on 22 August – why it should not be chosen for this purpose[4].

In the meantime, while the crucial decision by the Minister of Defence was awaited, there had been some movement on the procurement front: on 10 August a second draft of OR.339 had been issued and on 16 September the two main contending companies, English Electric and Vickers, gave details of their collaboration if either were chosen to take the lead on the project; and both companies and the Ministry of Supply were given copies of a table of comparative performances of all likely foreign aircraft contenders, to be used for briefing purposes if necessary[5].

On 17 October and again on the 30th S of S pressed the Minister of Defence to come to a decision, recalling in the earlier minute that he had written on 2 July about the new aircraft, "in the light of the decision taken in June by the DRPC to approve such a requirement", and that the case for it had been "elaborated . . . in some detail" in reply to the Minister's questionnaire. On the 30th he told the Minister that since the project had been considered by the DRPC further examination by the Air Staff, MoS and industry had shown that it was possible to get an aircraft of "even better performance than was thought a few months ago". In take-off particularly, "not more than 1,300yd to 50ft would be possible even under tropical conditions"; low-pressure tyres "would enable the aircraft to operate from a runway with a LCN[6] of the order of 16 to 20 for the 500-mile sortie"; and the aircraft could be designed to

---

[1] Corres in Requirement for a Tactical Strike/Recce Aircraft folder (ID3/945/2 Pt 1).

[2] Ibid, minute PS/US of S to PS/PUS, 22 Sep 58.

[3] AUS(A) (R C Kent) to F W Mottershead, MoD.

[4] In what was "a fairly blunt reply" (RAF Buccaneer ASR343 – Historic Diary (AHB II/129/2)).

[5] TSR.2 Significant Events and Policy and Financial Decisions (PE chronology).

[6] Load Classification Number.

exceed M2 while retaining its "essential low-level and short-take-off features". He said that an aircraft of such performance was in advance of any being currently designed in the UK or even in the US, and that "a significant step forward" could be taken "by going for this OR"[1]. (Following references in Parliament and the Press to TSR.2 as a "bomber", DCAS emphasised to S of S on 5 December[2] that what the Air Staff wanted was "a strike/reconnaissance aircraft, not a supersonic bomber".)

S of S and CAS discussed OR.339 with the Minister of Defence on 11 November[3] and two days later the latter gave his decision. "After very full consideration", he told S of S on the 13th[4]. "I am now satisfied that you have made out the case for replacing, in due course, the Canberra with an aircraft which would comply with the general specifications defined in OR.339. The way is therefore clear for you to ask the Ministry of Supply to approach the Treasury for authority to place a development contract for this aircraft". Copies of this minute were sent to the Chancellor of the Exchequer and the Minister of Supply.

On 15 December the Treasury gave its approval to the placing of an initial design contract for OR.339 at an estimated cost of £150,000, at the same time asking to be kept informed "and, where appropriate, consulted, on the measures to be taken to control the progress of the programme, to check on the estimates and the costs of the firms engaged on it and to limit the introduction of improvements and modifications". So the approval – later extended to cover an increase up to £600,000 in 1959 – was hedged about with considerable reservations[5].

Meanwhile the OR.339 requirement had been continuously under review: on 17 November a third draft had been issued and on 29 December a fourth was circulated. By this time much was known about it publicly[6] and on 1 January 1959 – appropriately, as if marking the beginning of a new era for the RAF and the British aircraft industry – a Press statement about it was made by the Minister of Supply. This said that, subject to satisfactory negotiations, the development of the new RAF aircraft, the TSR.2, would be "undertaken jointly by Vickers-Armstrongs and English Electric, the work being shared . . . on a

---

[1] This correspondence is in both Requirement for a Tactical Strike Aircraft (AHB ID3/945/2, Pt 1) and VCAS Operational Requirements Committee – Papers and Minutes (AHB ID9/94/9 (Pt 3)). In the former is a minute by DCAS making these new points about OR.339 which was sent by CAS (Air Chf Mshl Sir Dermot Boyle) to the CDS (MRAF Sir William Dickson) on 30 October.

[2] Minute, Tuttle/S of S, CAS and others in ID9/B.20-1 Bombers – Tactical/Strike Reconnaissance Aircraft – Comparison of OR.339 and NA.39.

[3] Minute, 11 Nov 58, ACAS(OR)/CAS, in Requirement for a Tactical Strike/Recce Aircraft (AHB ID3/945/2, Pt 1).

[4] Ibid, and in VCAS folder, Operational Requirements Committee – Papers and Minutes (AHB ID9/94/9, Pt 3).

[5] Ibid, D R Serpell, Treasury/F J Doggett, MoS.

[6] "The topic of OR.339 was a hot one and both the Press and MPs showed much interest. Much of the content of the draft OR had been disclosed by Government officials...".(RAF Buccaneer ASR.343 – Historic Diary).

fifty fifty basis". A joint project team drawn from both companies was being established at the Vickers' works at Weybridge. The statement continued:

"Subject equally to satisfactory negotiations, the development of the engine for the new aircraft will be undertaken by Bristol Siddeley Engines, the new company formed out of Bristol Aero-Engines and Armstrong Siddeley Motors . . . .

"The TSR.2 is a tactical support [*sic*]and reconnaissance aircraft. The specification was originally based on General Operational Requirement No 339. In the course of study it has been found technically possible to incorporate in the final operational requirement modifications which will greatly increase the usefulness of the aircraft in limited operations and for close support of the Army. . . . While the TSR.2 will be capable of performing the roles of all the various marks of Canberra, it will by reason of its greater flexibility and higher general performance be far more versatile and more in the nature of a general-purpose tactical aircraft."

When the new aircraft was thus announced by the Minister of Supply the name TSR.2 was used for the first time to describe what had hitherto been referred to as OR.339[1] and before that (up to mid-1958) as GOR.339. TSR.2 was a specification number given to the project by the MoS; the Air Staff had originally expected that it would have a number similar to that given to the V-bombers (B.35/46) – *eg*, B.-/58[2], but TSR.2 was the designation applied to it and by which it became universally known. Its operational requirement number, however, changed – the Air Staff deciding in February 1959 to call it OR.343; and this Requirement, for a "tactical strike and reconnaissance weapon system", was issued on 8 May 1959. It had been based (said the Introduction to it) "upon analysis by the Air Staff and Ministry of Supply of the studies of GOR.339 made by the aircraft industry and the research establishments". The aircraft required in OR.343 – which had 114 paragraphs, compared with 48 in GOR.339 – was to be twin-engined, to have a radius of action of at least 1,000nm without in-flight refuelling or overload fuel tanks, to be able to obtain reconnaissance information for tactical purposes by day and by night under all weather conditions, to deliver tactical nuclear weapons from low altitude or high-explosive weapons as an alternative, to be able to operate in any part of the world and to be flown by a two-man (pilot and navigator) crew. The Air Staff required a CA Release for the

---

[1] The OR reference seems to have persisted, for on 5 Aug 60 A/ACAS(Ops) minuted DLFP: "Would you please note that VCAS wishes the future MR Tactical Strike Aircraft to be referred to . . . as the TSR.2 and not GOR.343. The former name is now known to Ministers and reference to GOR.343 creates confusion" (ID9/940/10). "The MoS . . . referred to it as TSR.2 and explained that this was an unclassified description popular with the politicians" (RAF Buccaneer ASR343 – Historic Diary AHB II/129/2/2).
[2] APS to S of S/MoD, 31 Dec 58 (Reqt for a Tactical Strike/Recce Aircraft (ID3/945/2, Pt 1)).

weapon system which would enable a squadron to be fully equipped with it by the end of 1965.

The change of OR number to OR.343, announced on 18 February[1], aroused some suspicions in the Treasury as to whether the requirement had been changed "to the extent of demanding a whole new weapon system"; however, these suspicions were somewhat allayed by information showing how the OR in its new form had evolved from its predecessors. The Ministry of Supply and the Air Ministry also proposed a timetable and plans for getting contracts placed[2]; and after the draft ASR No OR.343 had been considered by the Operational Requirements Committee on 8 May 1959[3] and the OR issued, the first TSR.2 contract was placed – on 3 June. This covered preparatory work in connection with design and development planning. Then on 14 July the DRPC awarded OR.343 an In-Service Priority II classification and an Agreed Forecast Date of 1965–67, which alarmed the Air Staff, who insisted on first priority for the strike version while agreeing reluctantly that release in the reconnaissance role could be given at a later date[4].

While OR.343 went through the initial states of acceptance in mid-1959[5] and a development contract was placed for its powerplant, the Bristol Siddeley Olympus 22R[6], the major problem that was to dog the project – its cost – had occurred before the end of the year. On 15 October the retiring CA (Air Chf Mshl Sir Claude Pelly) had advised CAS (MRAF Sir Dermot Boyle) that development cost estimates for TSR.2 were likely to amount to "something between £70 and 80m" – about twice the original estimate made in 1958. Then in November the Ministry of Aviation (which had been formed in October, taking over the aviation functions of the former Ministries of Transport & Civil Aviation and Supply) prepared a submission to the Research and Development Board asking for three things: acceptance of the TSR.2 development programme; Treasury approval being sought for this at an estimated cost of £62m up to initial CA release; and an extension of the existing contract with Vickers, together with a letter of intent.

On 30 November the R&D Board accepted the TSR.2 development as had been outlined and approved an approach to the Treasury for the programme, estimated at £62m up to initial CA release, with the warning that a further £15–25m might be needed to complete development. As a result of this authority a letter was sent from the MoA to the Treasury on 9 December seeking authorisation for an increased programme (£62m plus possibly £15–25m), proposing that

---

[1] By ACAS (OR), who said it had been decided that "the project which originated under the number GOR.339 will in future be dealt with under the number OR.343".

[2] RAF Buccaneer ASR343 – Historic Diary.

[3] Minutes in VCAS folder Operational Reqts Cttee – Papers and Minutes.

[4] RAF Buccaneer ASR343 Historic Diary.

[5] In August DOR(A) wrote to PS to CA asking for confirmation that OR.343 had been received and was acceptable to MoA; receipt was acknowledged but he was told that it was still being studied in detail.

[6] On 18 Dec 59. Treasury approval for this development had been given on 17 Aug 59.

the initial contract (which expired at the end of December) should be extended for a further six months while a development contract was negotiated and suggesting that a Letter of Intent be sent to Vickers for nine development-batch aircraft.

Treasury reaction to this request was sharp and unfavourable: the MoD was asked on 16 December to reconsider the whole project and the NA.39 possibility; concern was expressed about the great increase in estimated costs; the letter of intent suggestion was not agreed to – rather, the Treasury suggested a limited commitment to keep work going while the whole situation was reviewed.

The MoA rejoined by saying that the case for the NA.39 could hardly have been pressed more strongly than it was, and the reasons why the aircraft would not meet the RAF requirement had been fully established. They suggested that the TSR.2 programme should not be slowed down and asked for an extension of existing arrangements to an estimated cost of £1.85m while consideration was given to confirmation of the requirement. In response, on 31 December 1959 the Treasury authorised a further six months' work up to £1.85m, in addition to the existing authority of £0.6m.

This authorisation came as the result of a lengthy appraisal of the TSR.2 programme sent to the Treasury by the MoA on 9 December 1959[1], from which it is clear that – even at an early stage – the technical complexities and the time-scales were going to be difficult to meet.

The Ministry commented that, from Vickers' first assessment of the programme and costs involved on the airframe side, and for items of equipment being developed under sub-contract, and from their own assessment of what was involved in the development of equipment under MoA contract, it was evident that "the effort needed to develop the weapon system" was "far greater than was originally expected". Further, to meet an initial CA Release date of September 1965, and the CA Release dates of end-1965 in the full strike role and 1966 in the reconnaissance role, "coupled with the late start on the project", the effort had to be "very concentrated".

Provided that authority to proceed was given by the end of 1959, that the build-up of effort took place as intended and that the programme could proceed without hindrance, the Ministry were confident that the CA Release dates could be met. But this would not be possible if any major changes were required by the Air Staff during the period of development; and the achievement of the dates would only be possible if the requirement were "frozen from the outset" – except in so far as technical progress might show that relaxations in the requirement were needed, which could be accepted by the Air Staff.

---

[1] F J Doggett, MoA/D R Serpell, Treasury in ID9/B.21–10 (Pt 1) Bombers – Tactical Strike/ Reconnaissance Aircraft TSR.2 – Development and Costs.

Before the authorisation was given the Treasury expressed great concern at "the enormous increase, from £35m to £62m – really to £90m, in the estimated development cost of this aircraft" and commented bleakly that if the current estimates "had been before Ministers a year ago" it seemed "not impossible that the question of meeting the RAF requirement with a version of the NA.39 would have been more strongly pressed"[1]. Early in 1960 AUS(A) reminded CAS of TSR.2's potential roles:–

"Since in certain quarters in the MoD there appears to be a tendency to tie the future of this aircraft almost entirely to limited war requirements, it might perhaps be useful if I were to remind CAS that in our plans the TSR.2 also features in Bomber Command, where it is required in due course to replace the tactical Valiants assigned to Saceur, and in RAF Germany where in due course it is required to replace Canberra B(I).6/B(I).8 and reconnaissance squadrons[2]."

While the industrial base for the TSR.2 programme was being laid in 1960 with the formation of British Aircraft Corporation, alarm was already being expresssed at the cost of the project and a battle was being fought in Whitehall for its acceptance by the Ministry of Defence, with the Treasury stubbornly refusing to approve funding until MoD agreed that the new aircraft should be developed.

BAC's creation proceeded quickly and smoothly because it accorded with Government policy towards the aircraft industry and because of the spur of the TSR.2 contract which would only be awarded to a collaborative project by two major companies. Agreement had been reached in principle on 18 December 1959 on a merger of the Vickers, English Electric and Bristol Aeroplane aviation and guided-weapon interests, participation being respectively on a 40:40:20 basis;[3] on 12 January 1960 the intention to set up a new company was publicly announced; then on 10 June a merger agreement, resulting from months of legal negotiations, was formally executed and enabled BAC to come into operational existence on 18 June[4].

But while BAC was being created the new RAF weapon system which was the new corporation's *raison d'être* had still not been authorised by the Government and its cost continued to rise: revised estimates discussed with MoA, AM and MoD representatives at the Treasury on 8 February showed that the original estimate of £35m for development up to CA release had risen to £62m. The Minister of Defence (Mr Harold Watkinson), who had attended an Air Staff presentation on TSR.2 on 2 March, told the Chiefs of Staff on the 7th that he was not yet convinced of the need to develop TSR.2 in view of its cost; he would like to have

[1] D R Serpell, Treasury/R C Chilver, MoD, 16 Dec 59 (Ibid).
[2] AUS(A) (R C Kent) minute to PS/CAS, 12 Feb 60.
[3] *Vickers Against the Odds 1956–77*, by H Evans (Hodder & Stoughton, 1978).
[4] Ibid.

their views on the project[1]. This lack of confidence in it was reflected in the view of the Treasury, who on 25 March told the MoA[2] that it was difficult for them to give unqualified approval "to a contract of this size (some £54m excluding the engine)"[3] when the MoD were "not ready to say . . . that the project should go forward" – adding that "the cost, both development and production, of the TSR.2 has increased enormously since the 1959 'forward look' costings"[4]. In a confidential letter to Sir George Edwards on 1 April CAS (Air Chf Mshl Sir Thomas Pike) referred to "the astronomical cost of the aeroplane" – quoting a MoA estimate of £1.7m per aircraft.

What the Minister of Defence asked the Chiefs of Staff to do at their meeting on 7 March, in order to help him to make up his mind, was to examine the need to develop an aircraft with the characteristics of TSR.2, "bearing in mind the cost of such a highly sophisticated and versatile type". The Joint Planning Staff were to make a study of the tactical roles of aircraft in both limited and global war; and the Air Ministry, in consultation with the Admiralty, was to make a report based on this study on the types of aircraft needed to fulfil those roles. Their report was considered by the CoS Committee on 5 April and subsequently re-drafted; when it was re-considered on the 26th[5] the CDS said that it had "originated from the anxiety expressed by the Minister of Defence at the very high cost of TSR.2"[6].

The Chiefs of Staff decided at this meeting to ask the Air Ministry, in conjunction with the Admiralty and the War Office, to embody the amended report in a comprehensive paper "considering both the roles of tactical strike and reconnaissance, and close-support aircraft[7], and the more detailed specifications of the aircraft types required". As a consequence, on 12 May an Air Ministry paper with the title Aircraft Requirements for Tactical Strike, Reconnaissance and Offensive Army Support was sent to the Admiralty and the War Office for their comments.

A fortnight later, at a meeting with the Chiefs of Staff, the Minister of Defence emphasised his wish to "give the earliest possible consideration" to the paper which was "in the course of preparation on the TSR.2". He said he was "most anxious . . . to consider this immediately upon his return from the United States" (where he would try to "interest the Americans in the acquisition of this aircraft for their own use"); and in a minute to CDS on the same day (26 May) he added a new aspect to

---

[1] Minutes of meeting (MM/COS(60)1st Mtg) in Bombers Tactical Strike/Reconnaissance Aircraft TSR.2 Development and Costs (ID9/B.21-10 Pt 1).

[2] Ibid.

[3] On 18 Dec 59 a contract had been placed with Bristol Siddeley for development of the Olympus 22R.

[4] Bombers Tactical Strike/Reconnaissance Aircraft TSR.2 Development and Costs (ID9/B.21-10 Pt 1).

[5] CoS(60)27th, Mtg.

[6] In a minute of 3 Mch 60 AUS(A)(R C Kent) said he was "horrified" by a quotation of "£1½-2m per aircraft" (ID3/945/2 Pt 2 Reqt for a Tactical Strike/Recce aircraft).

[7] OR345, ie the Hawker P.1127 proposal.

thinking about the proposed type's operational use, when he said that he was "attracted by the idea" of giving TSR.2 "an increased strategic capacity by fitting it with some kind of missile". In his view "a very high cost aircraft like this" had to be given "all the capacity that we can". As the Air Staff noted,[1] the Minister "asked that a study for giving the TSR.2 a strategic capability should be put in hand". His comment, however, caused some puzzlement in the MoA. The suggestion that he meant "a weapon like Bullpup . . . appeared to be news"[2].

On 28 June the Chiefs of Staff approved the Air Ministry/Admiralty/War Office report, which CDS was to forward to the Minister of Defence as an expression of their views, while the MoD in conjunction with the Air Ministry were to prepare a fuller explanation of the financial implications. The Committee noted that the Air Ministry were studying the problem of developing a cruise-type missile for use with TSR.2; it seemed that "neither Skybolt nor Blue Steel could be made compatible with this aircraft".

Exactly a month later, on 28 July, the Minister gave his approval to the project: he agreed that there was a Royal Air Force requirement for TSR.2 and invited the Ministry of Aviation "to seek early Treasury approval with a view to concluding negotiations for the full development contract." He also invited the MoA and the Air Ministry "to consider the possibility of giving TSR.2 the capability of launching a stand-off missile"[3]. Alternatives subsequently examined included not only Blue Steel and Skybolt but also a modified version of Blue Water – originally a surface-to-surface weapon.

On the 29th the Air Ministry (AUS(A)) told the Treasury that a full re-examination had been made to decide whether a developed NA.39 "or some American or other foreign aircraft" could meet the OR.343 requirement, but "we are satisfied there is no other aircraft which could do the job".

However, the Prime Minister (Mr Harold Macmillan) and the Chancellor of the Exchequer (Mr Selwyn Lloyd) considered that TSR.2 should be discussed by the Defence Committee; and on 16 September the committee endorsed the need to develop this aircraft for the RAF and agreed that a full development contract for the airframe should be placed. It also invited S of S for Air and the PS, MoA, to ensure that R&D costs and "the probable final unit cost, were kept under strict control"[4].

The Minister of Defence had previously met the Chiefs of Staff, on the 13th when they had before them a note by Sir Solly Zuckerman "reviewing the case for the TSR.2 in the light of time and cost and also in terms of a comparison with the NA.39". He told them that the Prime

[1] RAF Buccaneer ASR343 – Historic Diary (II/129/2/2 – AHB).
[2] Radio-command weapon for use from any kind of aircraft, developed for the US Navy and USAF. Later (1 Sep 60) AUS(A) commented that "the Minister of Defence's enthusiasm for the TSR.2 seems likely to be considerably influenced by our assessment of its potentialities as a contribution to the strategic deterrent."
[3] This was the outcome of a meeting at the MoD between the Minister, S of S for Air and PS, MoA, and their officials (minutes in AHB ID9/940/10 – TSR.2).
[4] Minutes, D(60) 9th Mtg (ID3/945/2 (pt 3) – TSR.2). A Minute of 27 July from AUS(A) to PS/S of S had noted: "Vickers, as I understand it, said that the TSR.2 could penetrate low level and deliver a ballistic missile of 100 miles' range based upon the existing Blue Water with a warhead of the Skybolt type".

Minister had "re-opened the whole issue" of TSR.2 and had directed that it should be decided by the Defence Committee on the 16th. This issue, he said, had "been in the melting-pot" for over a year; he wished to put an end to any further vacillation. Moreover, the present development contract was due to run out on the 30th. There were "three primary questions" that needed to be answered, and on which he was seeking the advice of the Chiefs of Staff: was a Canberra replacement needed? did the operational requirement, OR339, still stand? and would it be possible to compromise by accepting an aircraft that did not meet OR339, *eg* the NA.39? He did not wish the issue to be confused by consideration of a possible contribution by TSR.2 to the strategic deterrent.

In his summing-up after the discussion the Minister said that he "accepted the agreed views of the Chiefs of Staff" that the operational requirements for TSR.2, "which had been reached as a result of most careful inter-Service examination", could not be reduced; and that an aircraft with these capabilities was necessary, to fulfil certain specific RAF and Army roles. He did not subscribe to the proposal "to attempt to develop the NA.39" and accepted that in its present form it would not meet the requirements. On the assurance that the Air Ministry "would arrange for a steady production programme" he agreed to support the proposal to go ahead with the TSR.2[1].

On 22 September the Minister informed his US opposite number (the Hon Thomas Gates) that the Government had decided to place a development contract for TSR.2 with BAC: this followed a meeting he had had on 8 September with Mr Dudley Sharp, Secretary of the US Air Force, whom he had informed about TSR.2. The Secretary had said that the Americans were interested in an aircraft with STOL and terrain-following capability and thought there would be an advantage in a full exchange of information. Mr Watkinson's letter to Mr Gates resulted from this discussion[2].

Thus development of the TSR.2 had been approved by the Government[3] three-and-a-half years after the original operational requirement had been issued and after discussions involving the Air Ministry, Admiralty, War Office, MoA (which came into existence at a crucial stage), DRPC, Treasury, Chiefs of Staff, Minister of Defence and finally the Cabinet Defence Committee. No wonder that, after the Government's decision had been made, CAS (Air Chf Mshl Sir Thomas Pike) wrote to the British Aircraft Corporation managing director, Sir George Edwards, to say "how delighted" the Air staff were at the outcome of the TSR.2 discussions", adding: "we shall now watch the development of the aircraft with the greatest interest"[4].

---

[1] Minutes, MM/COS(60)9th Mtg in ID3/945/2 (Pt 3) TSR.2.
[2] Correspondence in ID9/940/10 TSR.2. (VCAS Branch Folder).
[3] Cabinet Defence Committee minutes (D(60) 9th Mtg) in TSR.2 file – AHB ID3/945/2/Pt 3).
[4] Ibid, personal note, 21 Sep.

In the autumn of 1960 the financial and industrial implications of the TSR.2 decision were fulfilled: on 23 September the Treasury gave its approval to an expenditure of £61.7m up to CA Release, and on 6 October the main development batch contract was signed[1]. TSR.2 was now therefore not only Governmentally authorised but also funded and ordered into development. Its strategic capability was endorsed when the British Nuclear Deterrent Study Group – having considered TSR.2 in the deterrent role at its 9 September 1960 meeting – at its 5 October meeting "invited the Air Ministry to prepare a paper on the use of the TSR.2 in the deterrent role"[2].

Development of the aircraft was, however, to be dogged by difficulties – principally rising costs – and delays over the next four-and-a-half years. A continuous increase in expenditure seems to have been endemic to the project. Revised estimates by BAC on 16 June 1961 showed an increase in estimated costs, from £41.7m to £48.5m; and in March of the following year an examination was made of possible economies in the programme, which a senior Air Ministry official described as "expensive by any reckoning"[3]. He told CAS that the Treasury had "experienced great difficulty in getting any up-to-date estimates out of the MoA", and that their "main anxiety" had been "generated" by reports... suggesting that" TSR.2 would be "very late into service".

On 27 March 1962 the Minister of Aviation (Mr Peter Thorneycroft) warned the Minister of Defence that estimated costs of development – for airframe, engine and equipment – were now "about £137m"[4]. He said that the major part of this increase had been attributable to "a wide variety of equipments" for which design studies had not been completed and whose development costs were "necessarily in some degree uncertain", and also to "a serious increase in the engine cost". The third quarter of 1966, he considered, was a realistic target date for initial release in the nuclear strike role – subject to a satisfactory outcome of the review of the forward-looking radar. (This review was to recommend a choice of British-made Ferranti FLR, with which there had been considerable delay, or US Texas Instruments equipment.)

The Minister of Aviation, who in November 1961 had expressed concern that the development of "most of the electronic equipment" for TSR.2 was "lagging behind the aircraft programme"[5], concluded by saying that a paper on the revised programme and cost estimates was

---

[1] This was KD/2L/02/CB42A (PE information).

[2] At a later (10 Nov 60) BNDSG meeting two kinds of weapon were to be investigated for this role – a retarded/lay-down bomb and a missile (minutes, BND(SG)(60)4th Mtg in AHB file ID9/B.21-10 (Pt 1) Bombers – Tactical Strike/Reconnaissance Aircraft TSR.2 Devlt and Costs). On 13 Jan 61 BNDSG "noted that a laydown weapon could be developed for use with the TSR.2 in the strategic role" (BND(SG)(61) 1st Mtg).

[3] Minute, AUS(A) (R C Kent) to CAS on 5 March, in TSR.2 file AHB ID3/945/2 Pt 3.

[4] Ibid.

[5] Minute, 15 Nov 61, in ID3/945/2 (Pt 3) TSR.2 file.

being prepared for the Defence Research Policy Committee, and that he would advise on the outcome of the FLR examination as soon as it had been completed; but the reaction of the Minister of Defence, on 6 April, was that the programme would have to be submitted to the Defence Committee again – "as they originally approved the project on the basis of much lower estimates of cost"[1].

When the DRPC considered a joint Air Ministry/Ministry of Supply paper on TSR.2 on 18 April it approved continued development at £137m with an agreed target date for Service release in the nuclear strike role of the third quarter of 1966, and in the conventional and reconnaissance roles within the following year[2]; but continuation of the project was to be subject to future review when forward costings became available[3]. Just before this meeting, in a minute of 17 April[4] the Minister of Aviation had told the Minister of Defence that he agreed with his proposal of 6 April that a memorandum on TSR.2 should be put to the Defence Committee "as soon as possible after the DRPC has considered the project".

Early in May the important decision was taken to continue with the Ferranti FLR equipment: on the 2nd the Minister of Aviation told the Minister of Defence of this decision; on the 10th S of S for Air wrote to the former agreeing with it but asking if it were possible to get contractual guarantees on performance and delivery dates; and on the 15th the Minister of Defence also concurred, adding that it was "probably right" that he should put in a paper on TSR.2 to the Defence Committee, "in view of the large demand which the project is making on the defence budget".

The Minister's memorandum was a long one, with two appendices. It said that when the Committee had endorsed the need to develop TSR.2 on 16 September 1960 it was expected that its development would cost about £90m; now, full development was expected to cost £137m, a "large increase in costs" which was "most unwelcome". Nevertheless the Government was "fully committed to the TSR.2" and it was "an essential element in our plans for the RAF". He recommended that, pending the outcome of the Defence Review, its development should go ahead – a recommendation with which the Defence Committee concurred on 23 May[5]. It agreed that development "should continue for the present" but invited the Minister, "in the light of the costings provided for the annual Defence Expenditure Review, to seek a final decision" on TSR.2 development and production "before the summer recess".

However, before this pre-summer recess decision was taken there were

---

[1] Minute in TSR.2 file ID3/945/2 (Pt 3).
[2] PE chronology.
[3] RAF Buccaneer ASR343 Historic Diary (AHB II/129/2/2).
[4] TSR.2 file ID3/945/2 (Pt 3).
[5] Minutes of D(62) 9th Mtg, 23 May 62.

approvals for BAC to buy long-dated materials and some discouraging news from the corporation as to time-scale and costs. The Defence Committee had "only approved £2m for long-dated materials until the Defence Review Costing was available"[1] and during June the Treasury approved this expenditure on these materials for the second batch of aircraft[2], an ITP (instruction to proceed) being issued for long-dated materials for 11 pre-production aircraft on 22 June[3]. These approvals and ITP represented a limited, modest confirmation of the future of the TSR.2 project.

But at a Management Board meeting in June it was disclosed that the first flight would be in August 1963 and that this lag in the programme would have been made up by the eighth development batch aircraft. The board said it would not accept a first flight date later than June 1963 and directed BAC to produce a new plan to meet this date[4]. This slip-back in the TSR.2 first flight date was reported to S of S for Air by DCAS (Air Mshl R B Lees) on 9 July. He said that it had resulted from a failure to produce the correct number of detailed design drawings, which meant that certain parts of the aircraft were not being manufactured; the company had been "instructed to produce a revised programme with a view to the first flight being made in June 1963"[5]. Then, on the 23rd, revised estimates from BAC showed an increase in costs from £48.5m to £59.7m.

Nevertheless the project received further Governmental approval before the summer recess: when the Cabinet considered the whole of the current defence procurement programme on 3 August, and decided to cancel the tactical guided missile project Blue Water (being developed by BAC), it agreed that the development and production of TSR.2 should go ahead[6], although there had previously been an attempt by CDS to re-open the whole issue – the Minister saying that this was "politically and industrially out of the question"[7].

Thus by mid-1962 the project had been confirmed once again, at a cost estimate of £137m to the completion of development, but by the end of the year its cost had risen further and dissatisfaction had been expressed with BAC's management of the programme. These matters came to a head at a Management Board meeting on 12 December, when the estimated cost was said to be £175m and the board recommended changes in the corporation's management of the programme[8]; then, in

[1] RAF Buccaneer ASR343 – Historic Diary (AHB II/129/2/2).
[2] Ibid.
[3] PE chronology.
[4] Historic Diary.
[5] TSR.2 file ID9/940/10.
[6] The relative merits of TSR.2 and Blue Water as close-support weapons led to an exchange of notes between CIGS and CAS in July 62 (TSR.2 file ID3/945/2 Pt 3).
[7] Minute, AUS(A)/PS to S of S, 2 Aug 62, in ID9/B.21-40 (Pt I), Bombers – Tactical Strike/Reconnaissance Aircraft COS Review – requirements for TSR and Offensive Support (TSR.2 and Buccaneer).
[8] PE chronology.

the same month, Treasury authority was sought to commit a further £5.875m on materials for the 11 pre-production aircraft[1]. Early in 1963 the problems of TSR.2 programme costs, time-scale and management continued to intensify, as reflected in papers and meetings at Ministry and Ministerial levels[2]. CA (Sir George Gardner) told the MoA Research and Development Board, in a Note of 4 January, that the total project cost should be increased from £137m to £175m, that the confidential policy date for initial CA Release should be set back from the first to the fourth quarter of 1967 and that some changes had been made in BAC's technical management organisation with the aim of "strengthening their control of the programme"[3]. The Board, apprised of these developments on 7 January, agreed that the Minister of Aviation (Mr Julian Amery) should discuss them with BAC; and subsequently (11-16 January) the Ministry's PS (Sir Henry Hardman) told the corporation's managing director, Sir George Edwards, of MoA dissatisfaction over the management of the TSR.2 programme – which the latter put forward proposals to remedy, also informing the MoA that BAC's revised estimates were likely to reach £72.7m, an increase of £13m[4].

On 21 January the R&D Board approved the continued development of TSR.2 at £175/200m and resolved to consider management arrangements in the light of further discussions with BAC[5]; and on the following day the Minister of Aviation reported to the Minister of Defence (Mr Peter Thorneycroft) on the current situation, in advance of a Defence Committee meeting. He recalled that in April 1962[6] the cost of developing the weapon system was expected to be £137m, with initial CA Release in the third quarter of 1966 and full CA Release in late 1967. Since then, he said, there had been setbacks to the development of both the airframe and the engine, and it now looked as if initial CA Release would have to be put back to late 1967 and full CA Release to late 1968. The present estimate for airframe development was £62m but he was advised that this was likely to rise "to £80m or so". Additional work resulting from the loss of the Vulcan flying test-bed[7], and from the

---

[1] Historic Diary.

[2] "I am very concerned, as I know you must be, about the latest rise in the cost of the TSR.2", wrote the Air Minister (Mr H Fraser) to the Minister of Aviation (Mr J Amery) on 22 Jan 63. "I am afraid this is bound to bring the aircraft under attack again" (ID9/940/10 Pt 3). Also from early 1963 the use of TSR.2 in the strategic role was being considered: see correspondence in AHB ID9/B.21-80 Bombers – Tactical/Strike Reconnaissance Aircraft TSR.2 – In the Long Range Strike Role.

[3] MoA R&D Board TSR.2 Development Programme and Costs (Note by CA) in Bombers – Tactical Strike/Reconnaissance Aircraft TSR.2 Devlt and Costs AHB ID9/B.21-10 (Pt 2).

[4] PE chronology.

[5] Ibid.

[6] AHB ID9/B.21-10 file.

[7] ID9/B.21-10 file, report of MoA meeting on 12 Dec 62 to consider failure of Olympus 22R development engine in Vulcan Mk 1 XA894 during a ground run at Filton on 20 Nov 62. The flying test-bed was completely destroyed but was later replaced.

delay in CA Release, would increase engine development cost from an original £34m to "around £45m". Estimates for equipment now included the cost (£2m) of a ground station for a radio link; and in the light of all these figures, he concluded, it now looked as if total development costs to full CA Release would be "not less than £175m". He added that on the production side it looked as if unit costs might rise by about 10% above the present £2.1m figure.

The Minister of Defence was informed by the Minister of Aviation on the following day (22 January) of the increase in estimated development costs and delay in CA Release date, and on 6 February the latter confidently told the Prime Minister (Mr Harold Macmillan) that he had no doubts about the technical validity of TSR.2, that there should be less room for error in the estimates (of £175-200m) and that BAC had made management improvements and were willing to accept incentive clauses in their contract[1]. However, a rather more cynical view was expressed in an official's minute on that date[2] which commented that "the cost increases of this project continue to break all records" – comparing the total cost estimates in April 1962 with the latest ones. The former showed R&D costing £137m and the production of 138 aircraft £295.8m – a total of £432.8m; the latter, R&D costing £175/200m and production £325/340m – a total of £500/540m.

In mid-February, however, the DRPC (Defence Research Policy Committee) approved the continuation of the project – though with some considerable reservations, which echoed criticisms which had already been made[3], and suggestions for economies. On 12 February, the day before the DRPC meeting, the Minister of Defence had suggested to S of S for Air that TSR.2 production should be limited to 50 or 60 aircraft, the remainder of the 138 total being made up by Buccaneer Mk 2s; but on the 25th S of S rejected this suggestion and was supported in this view (on 4 March) by the Minister of Aviation, though the Admiralty continued to press it energetically[4], emphasising that a comparison should be made with "a logical development" of the Buccaneer "with significant improvements" in navigation equipment and weapon delivery capability.

The DRPC endorsed the continuation of the project on 13 February[5] "at a revised estimated development cost of £175-200m, with a Confidential Policy Date for initial release in the nuclear strike role of the fourth quarter of 1967", subject to "further consideration by the

---

[1] PE chronology.
[2] S.6 to DRPS (Air) in file Bombers – Tactical Strike/Reconnaissance Aircraft TSR.2 – Devlt and Costs (ID9/B.21-10 Pt 2).
[3] On 7 Feb ACAS(OR) (AVM C H Hartley) in a minute to DRPS(Air) had questioned "the competence of the MoA . . . either to manage a major project or to offer any valid advice about it" (ibid).
[4] Correspondence in file Bombers – Tectical Strike/Reconnaissance Aircraft CAS Review – requirements for TSR.2 and Offensive Support (TSR.2 and Buccaneer) (AHB ID9/B.21-40 Pt 1).
[5] Minutes – DRP/M(63)3.

Committee of the implications of the R&D programme of continuing the project when the 1963 costings became available" – that is, in the context of the whole defence expenditure programme – and "an examination by the Air Ministry and the Ministry of Aviation, in consultation with the DRP staff, of the possibility of achieving economies in the project". The committee also noted that some of its members "had expressed concern about the management of the project".

On 26 March the Chiefs of Staff considered and approved a report by the Joint Planning Staff on the military implications of replacing a proportion of the planned TSR.2 force with Buccaneer 2s[1], and subsequently the Chief Scientific Adviser to the Minister of Defence, Sir Solly Zuckerman, was asked to investigate how the Buccaneer's effectiveness might be "maximised"[2].

When on the 27th the DRPC considered possible economies Lt-Gen Sir John Hackett commented that "in view of the huge cost of the TSR.2, on which the army were bound to rely for tactical support and reconnaissance, he had serious misgivings about the extent to which it would be possible to meet the Army's needs from manned aircraft resources." He recalled that when Blue Water was cancelled "the current (1962) estimate of the cost of developing the TSR.2 was £137m; it was now £200m".

In a subsequent note on the CoS meeting of 26 March the Secretary of the Committee said (on the 28th) that in approving the report "the Chiefs of Staff concluded that our ability to meet certain essential commitments in our strategy, for which the TSR.2 is designed, would be seriously prejudiced by TSR.2's being replaced by the Buccaneer 2, even with the contemplated improvements. From the military point of view, therefore, the TSR.2 programme should proceed as at present planned"[3].

Its cost, however, continued to horrify members of the Government: thus the Minister of Defence (Mr Peter Thorneycroft) commented in a letter of 3 April to CDS, Sir Robert Scott and Sir Solly Zuckerman[4] that what struck him was that "the cost of the present planned programme of 138 TSR.2s is of the same broad order of magnitude as the aircraft carrier replacement programme or the strategic nuclear deterrent programme", adding that this was "a remarkable figure for a light bomber replacement". He said he had "from time to time upon professional advice" described TSR.2's role "as anything from a substitute for Blue Water to a substitute for a V-bomber"; it seemed to him that some aspects of its role required an aircraft with capabilities of the order of those proposed for TSR.2, while others could be

---

[1] COS 21st Mtg/63.
[2] "... to enable it to discharge... some portion of the roles of the TSR.2".
[3] COS. 126/63, 28 Mar 63, in ID9/940/10 Pt 3.
[4] In ID9/940/10 Pt 3.

performed by an aircraft with capabilities "far short of these". He suggested that other existing or potential types should be considered as to the possibility of their being able, "with or without some adaptation", to discharge portions of the role intended for TSR.2 – for example, the Buccaneer, the P.1154, "or any other aircraft which might be developed as a successor to the Hunter or the Lightning or the Sea Vixen".

On the following day Sir Solly Zuckerman wrote to CA (Sir George Gardner) asking for an examination, in the context of the Minister's letter, of "the Buccaneer Improved Weapon System, sometimes referred to as the Buccaneer III" and of "modifications to the Buccaneer undercarriage to widen the range of airfield conditions from which it could operate"[1].

If the development of TSR.2 were to be extrapolated in the form of a graph, one line – depicting costs – would rise steadily upwards, while another – representing time – would continue steadily along horizontally. Once the project had been launched it became like the genie let out of the bottle, steadily increasing in size and incapable of being controlled, despite the number of bodies charged with monitoring it. Writing to PS/DCAS in October 1963 ACAS(OR) (AVM R H E Emson) commented: "there are now four committees overseeing the project as a whole: the Progress Review Committee, the Development Progress Committee..., the Management Board... and the Steering Committee"[2]. Earlier that year, on 24 April, the Prime Minister (Mr Harold Macmillan) had bluntly and briefly minuted the Minister of Aviation: "Can you give me the latest position about the TSR.2? What will it cost? Will it ever fly?"[3] On 1 May the latter was at least able to reply positively about cost, confirming the current estimate of £175/200m.

Even while this forecasted expenditure was being approved, however, forebodings of higher costs were being expressed; and while one time-scale was being considered at official level, another was being implemented in industrial terms. Thus whilst Treasury approval was given on 25 October to the continued development of TSR.2 at a total estimated cost of £175m, noting that this might rise to a possible £200m, the DRPC had already been told on 17 June that the overall cost of the programme was likely to be £197/222m – the chairman (Sir Solly Zuckerman) saying in his summing up that "he proposed to inform the Minister of Defence that in the light of the latest information the overall cost of the TSR.2 programme was likely to be £197/222m"[4]. And while the committee was given October 1966 as an Agreed Target Date for initial CA Release, S of S for Air was advised by DCAS (Air Mshl C H Hartley) on 3 October of a further slippage, the build of the first

---

[1] In ID9/940/10 Pt 3.
[2] File Bombers – Tactical Strike/Reconnaissance Aircraft TSR.2 – Devlt and costs (AHB ID9/B.21-10 Pt 2).
[3] PM's personal minute, M161/63 (ID9/B.21-1 Pt 2).
[4] Minutes, DRP/M(63)11.

development batch aircraft being "two months behind schedule".

The first orders for TSR.2s were placed during 1963. On 12 June the Treasury gave authority for 11 pre-production aircraft, then subsequently agreed to an announcement being made about production aircraft, though without specifying how many (the Air Ministry had asked for 30). At the same time a RAAF evaluation mission visited the UK to consider a possible purchase of 24 TSR.2s but later in the visit (24 October) an Australian Government decision to buy TFXs was announced. In August the Air Minister asked the Chief Secretary to the Treasury (Mr John Boyd-Carpenter) to give "sympathetic consideration" to his Ministry's case for ordering 30 TSR.2s "to the production standard". On the 27th the Chancellor agreed to a form of words about "a development batch order for nine and a pre-production order for 11 aircraft". The actual announcement, made on the 30th by the Ministry of Aviation, was in guarded terms: "In addition to the orders already placed for the TSR.2... for development and for introductory flying by the RAF, British Aircraft Corporation have now been authorised to acquire long-dated materials[1] to enable production of TSR.2s for squadron service to begin".

On 28 October the Air Ministry gave the first public details about its new tactical strike/reconnaissance aircraft, at a briefing for air correspondents, held "to dispel some current misconceptions in the Press about the role and operational uses of the TSR.2"[2]. In a summary of the subsequent reports the Chief Information Officer (Air Cdre J Barraclough) said that, with one exception, coverage received had been "extensive and favourable", adding: "inevitably there was a tendency to dwell upon the cost, which was generally put at £500m"[3]. On the 30th the first meeting of the TSR.2 Steering Committee, one of the four committees "overseeing" the project, was held: its membership represented the MoA, the RAF and the manufacturers. The others were the Progress Review Committee, Development Progress Committee and Management Board.

Thus by the end of 1963 the project had officially become public knowledge, and earlier in that year the Air Council had approved plans for the initial deployment of the new aircraft, from late 1966 onwards. These had been outlined in a paper by DCAS and Acting AMSO (Air Mshls R B Lees and Sir John Baker-Carr) on TSR.2 training, considered by the Council on 23 May. Their Note[4] suggested that the

---

[1] On 29 Aug an ITP was issued to BAC for the purchase of long-dated materials for 30 production TSR.2s up to £1m (PE chronology).

[2] Letter, MoA/Treasury (P Brightling, AS/Air A.3 to F R Barratt) in TSR.2 file ID9/940/10 Pt 4.

[3] Or even more; for in a leading article on TSR.2 in its 14 Nov 63 issue *Flight International* said that "Mr Denis Healey, Labour Party spokesman on defence matters", – who was to be the Minister of Defence at the time of the project's cancellation – "stated that TSR.2 is becoming 'the biggest scandal in British politics since the South Sea Island Bubble'", calculating that each aircraft cost £20m, "basing his arithmetic on a programme cost of £1,000m".

[4] Paper No AC(63)21.

most suitable site for the Operational Conversion Unit, where the first crews would be trained on the six pre-production aircraft[1], would be Coningsby. As for low-flying training by these crews, and subsequently by crews of TSR.2 squadrons in Bomber Command and RAF Germany, the most suitable area would be Libya – in conjunction with Hal Far airfield, Malta, which was to become surplus to Royal Navy requirements in 1965. The three TSR.2 squadrons due to be based at Akrotiri, Cyprus, would do their low-flying training over Turkey.

The Council were asked to agree that Coningsby should be developed as a TSR.2 OCU, that training requirements of TSR.2 squadrons in NEAF and FEAF should be met within those Commands, that low-level training by TSR.2 crews from the OCU and squadrons in north-west Europe should be done in Libya, and that Hal Far should be developed (at an estimated cost of £0.2m – the development of Coningsby being estimated to cost £0.1m) as a base from which low-flying training in Libya could be done. Approval was given to these proposals, with the proviso that the Foreign Office should be consulted about those which concerned Libya[2].

Whatever long-term plans were made for TSR.2, however, its progress as a project was dogged by delays. DCAS (Air Mshl C H Hartley) reported "a further slippage" in the programme to S of S on 3 October. He said that BAC had admitted at the last Development Progress meeting that the build of the first development batch aircraft was now two months behind schedule; it was also "virtually certain" that the first flight would have to be made from Boscombe Down instead of from Wisley, which would add a month to the first flight date, so that TSR.2 could not now be expected to fly before April 1964[3].

A confidential note on TSR.2 costs prepared by the MoA towards the end of 1963[4] said that the current commitment was about £90m and the current estimate of production cost per aircraft was £2.3m, "including a sizeable contingency margin". Air Ministry long-term costings, it said, provided for 138 aircraft, of which 11 were pre-production. The first 30 of the 129 production aircraft had been ordered.

On 4 December *The Times* commented, in a long article referring to the previous week's adjournment debate in the Commons on TSR.2, that for many weeks the air had been "thick with inflated estimates of cost on one side and exaggerated claims of performance on the other", and that "dark rumours of cancellation" had been followed by official denials "strenuous enough to spread panic through an arms industry still groping fearfully about in the ruins of Blue Streak and Blue

---

[1] Of the 11 pre-production aircraft, five were to go initially to the MoA to be used by A & AEE for Service clearance trials and six to the RAF in early 1966 to form the initial squadron (Brief for CAS for his visit to Weybridge in Sep 62, in ID3/945/2 Pt 3).
[2] Conclusions 10(63).
[3] ID9/940/10 Pt 4.
[4] Ibid, Air B.3(a), St Giles Court, 25 Nov 63.

Water". It went on to aver that the suggestion that TSR.2 "was to carry the main weight of the strategic nuclear strike task between the decline of the V-bomber and the introduction of the Polaris missile" had aroused suspicions that the Air Staff "had contrived an extension of the airborne deterrent by the simple expedient of calling it something else".

This last point (and other criticisms) prompted a response from the Air Minister, in a speech drafted for delivery in his constituency on the 6th, when he said that the possible use of TSR.2s in the strategic role was "a bonus – nothing more, nothing less", emphasising that the design of the aircraft had been frozen "long before there was any question of cancelling Skybolt"[1]. On the 12th the Chiefs of Staff approved a brief which had been produced by the Air Ministry for use by the Minister of Defence in the event of there being a debate on TSR.2 before the Christmas recess[2].

1964 was a climacteric year for TSR.2: not only did the recriminations between customer and contractors continue[3], costs continue to rise[4] and engine troubles continue, leading to first flight delays, but the project as a whole came under sharp scruitiny as soon as a new (Labour) Government was returned to power on 15 October, less than three weeks after the prototype aircraft had successfully made its first flight from Boscombe Down.

During the year the programme had continued with the same kind of jerky rhythm which had characterised it since 1961 – a pattern of increased costs, delays and dissatisfactions with the project management leading to crisis meetings, then to Government approval of continued development, albeit at a higher cost and over a longer time-scale.

This pattern was epitomised in the early months of 1964, leading to a mid-year situation in which development costs had risen to £240m and the first flight was unlikely to take place before the end of July. In January, BAC had told the Management Board that the first flight date would be set back to the end of April; the Aviation Council[5] had advised that the estimated cost of development had risen from £175/200m to £240/260m and the production price from £2.3m to £2.8m per aircraft;[6] and at a meeting on the 31st between the Minister of Aviation and the heads of BAC and BSE the former said that since he took office the estimated cost of airframe development had increased from £60m to £85m and of engine development from £22m to £30m, and there had

---

[1] ID9/940/10 Pt 4, minutes and drafts.
[2] COS 70th Mtg/63 Pt 1 (in AHB ID3/945/2 (Pt 4) Requirement for Tactical Strike Recce Aircraft (TSR.2)).
[3] In a personal minute of 17 Jan 64 to DCAS (AM C H Hartley), ACAS(OR) (AVM R H E Emson) commented: "I have no confidence in the ability of the management of BAC to give us the aeroplane we want, when we want it and at the right price".
[4] In a minute to DS9 on 8 May DOR3(RAF) (Air Cdre A D Frank) said that "at the WD Staff meeting there were the inevitable expressions of horror at the increase in cost but no sign of any attempt to . . . cancel the project".
[5] PE chronology.
[6] Ibid.

been an increase in the estimates for equipment: S of S for Air said he thought these figures were "optimistic", and it was admitted at the end of a long discussion that the costs were "uncontrollable".

Subsequently the Minister of Aviation reported on these costs to the Minister of Defence, Mr Amery telling Mr Thorneycroft on 5 February that they now totalled £216m, but with a contingency allowance amounting to a "confidential policy estimate of £240-260m"[1], and the Chief Secretary to the Treasury (Mr John Boyd-Carpenter) commenting when he saw the figures on the 12th that he found them "very disturbing indeed". By April, the latter figure had become an officially accepted one: the MoA advised the Management Board that estimates of R & D costs had increased from £175-200m to £240-270m, and on the 20th the R & D Board approved the continued development of TSR.2 at a revised estimated cost of £240/260m[2]. On 8 May, Treasury approval was sought for a total of £240m[3], and on the 13th the Weapon Development Committee endorsed the continuation of TSR.2 development at a revised cost of £240/260m, Treasury authority for £240m being received on 24 June.

The prototype TSR.2, first of the development batch aircraft, had left BAC Weybridge on 4 March for Boscombe Down for re-assembly and flight test; it was due to fly for the first time in mid-May. However, development troubles with the Bristol Siddeley Olympus 22R engine led to postponements in the first flight date, initially to the end of June. But on the 24th of that month the Minister of Aviation advised S of S for Defence that this flight would not take place before the end of July, then on the 16th of that month told him that an engine modification to make it suitable for the first flight had been successful and that TSR.2 should fly in the second half of August.

It had been hoped that the aircraft might make its first public appearance at the SBAC Farnborough Show in September 1964, but a further engine setback – fatigue failure of part of the main shaft of an Olympus during a test-bed run on 24 July – largely put paid to that hope. The Minister (RAF) (Mr Hugh Fraser) was advised on 11 August that the prototype TSR.2 should be ready to start taxying tests in the following week, and that at the relevant stage in those tests it should be ready to fly, but that the chances of its appearing at Farnborough were "poor". In the event, taxi trials did not begin until 2 September, and on the following day the Minister of Aviation advised the Controller of Aircraft (Mr Morien B Morgan) that despite the pressures there must be to authorise the first flight so as to enable TSR.2 to fly over Farnborough during the SBAC Show, and the "strong reasons of industrial national prestige involved", the Government would not wish him or his Department to agree to such a flight in any circumstances

[1] AHB file ID9/B.21-10 Pt 2.
[2] PE chronology.
[3] Ibid.

where "the safety of the aircraft, the crew or the public might be jeopardised" – views with which CA concurred, in a minute of 4 September. The possibility, however, of flying over Farnborough during the SBAC Show did not arise as it was not until 27 September that TSR.2 made its first flight – a successful one of 14 minutes' duration – from Boscombe Down.

On 14 September the Air Force Board Standing Committee had approved comprehensive plans for TSR.2 aircrew training and requirements for ground training and servicing; but within less than three weeks the Government which had authorised TSR.2 development had been swept away in a General Election; and shortly after taking office on 15 October the new Labour administration began taking a close look at the military aircraft procurement programme with a view to possible reductions in defence costs, through the purchase of alternative types – including the American TFX, a two-seat multi-purpose tactical aircraft with variable-geometry wings, being developed for the USAF and US Navy by General Dynamics as prime contractor[1]. From 13 to 19 December a team led by DCAS (Air Mshl Sir Christopher Hartley) "visited Washington on a fact-finding mission vis-à-vis F-111, F-4C, C-131, C-140 and Orion. A report was submitted to the Minister of Defence (Mr Denis Healey), when the team returned"[2].

This mission, and another one to the US to study TFX avionics, were referred to at an Air Force Board Standing Committee meeting on 1 March 1965 when measures to contain TSR.2 costs were discussed[3]. A paper of 25 February by DCAS, with the title TSR.2 Costing Exercise[4], was considered; and in introducing it ACAS(OR) (AVM R H E Emson) said that "Ministers had asked for a report on the comparative merits of the TSR.2 and the TFX, including cost", by 1 April. He went on to say that "a Minister of Defence team was leaving that day for America to examine the avionics of the TFX Mk 2 and a second team, led by DCAS, was leaving next week for America to investigate the general progress of development of this aircraft. In the meantime, the Ministry of Aviation had been given the task of re-examining the progress of the TSR.2 and of attempting to negotiate a maximum price contract for it with the British Aircraft Corporation". For this purpose, he added, "it was necessary to have an up-to-date specification which took account of actual flight experience with the aircraft so far".

The Standing Committee, which DCAS himself was unable to attend, expressed concern at the apparent degradation in performance represented by the proposed revised specification and decided to resume its discussion of the proposals at an early date; and a meeting of

---

[1] "The return of a Labour Govt . . . resulted in numerous comparisons being made between TSR.2 and F-111 (TFX), Buccaneer 2* . . ." (ASR343 – Historic Diary).
[2] ASR343 – Historic Diary.
[3] AFB Stdg Cttee Conclusions 6(65).
[4] AFBSC(65)10.

the Air Force Board later that day, attended by DCAS, invited him to consider urgently the points raised in discussion – principally, that if the specification represented "a realistic assessment of what the aircraft might now be capable of achieving", it could go forward to the MoA as a basis for obtaining a fixed-price quotation from BAC – and report back to the Standing Committee[1].

In the event, CAS (Air Chf Mshl Sir Charles Elworthy) minuted the Minister for the RAF (Lord Shackleton) on 3 March to say that the Service members of the AFB and PUS/(RAF) were satisfied that "the specification and guarantee points" set out by DCAS represented "a proper and acceptable basis for the fixed-price contract examination". He recommended that the Minister approve the proposals – which he did on 4 March[2].

The new Government, in asking the Air Staff to report on an alternative to TSR.2 and the MoA to look at its progress and attempt to make new contractual arrangements with BAC, was at the same time having the structure and purpose of the British aircraft industry examined: on 9 December 1964 a committee under Lord Plowden had been appointed to consider the industry's "future place and organisation" in relation to the country's economy, "taking into account the demands of national defence" and other fields of activity.

Earlier – in fact on 2 November 1964, only a fortnight after having assumed office – the Government had decided to look closely into defence expenditure with the intention of reducing it. At a meeting of the Cabinet's Defence and Oversea Policy (Official) Committee on that date[3], the first step was taken in a sequence of meetings and memoranda which was to lead over the next five months to decisions to cancel three major RAF aircraft projects – the TSR.2, P.1154 and HS681. The committee "invited the Ministry of Defence, in consultation with the Ministry of Aviation, to prepare a paper listing questions which would have to be examined in any detailed study of the possibility of reducing expenditure on defence". This paper was to be considered on the 11th, together with "the revised report of the Long Term Study Group and the paper by the Treasury and the Department of Economic Affairs on defence costs". Clearly the investigation was to be wide-ranging and thorough.

A Memorandum dated 6 November, on Defence Expenditure, by PUS, MoD (Sir Henry Hardman)[4], showed the three largest costs in the 1965/6-1974/5 period to be:

---

[1] AFB Conclusions 3(65).
[2] Minutes, CAS 1339 and PS/Minister to PS/CAS, 3 and 4 Mch 65 respectively: see ID9/940/10 Pt 7 TSR.2.
[3] OPD(0)64. The Official Committee consisted of Departmental PUSs, the Defence and Oversea Policy Committee of Ministers.
[4] OPD (0) (64)11.

		R & D	Capital	Operating	Total
(i)	BAOR	—	250	1295	1545
(ii)	Carrier force with aircraft	120	435	850	1405
(iii)	Strike and Tac/Recce aircraft	195	490	690	1375
	(including TSR.2)	195	490	465	1150

A list of the same date, headed Largest R & D Projects Now in Hand, Cost in Period 1965/6 to 1974/5, showed the following:

		£ million
(i)	TSR.2	182
(ii)	P.1154	166
(iii)	HS681	70
	etc	

On 13 November the Defence and Oversea Policy (Official) Committee had before it[1] "memoranda by the Ministry of Defence . . . on defence expenditure". These and other papers were to be circulated to Ministers "for their discussion on British defence and oversea policy at Chequers during the weekend of 21/22 November".

Whatever the specific decisions taken on defence expenditure at the Chequers talks, two parameters quickly emerged – its limitation to £2,000m a year at current prices, and the possibility of replacing TSR.2 by the US TFX.

Thus on 27 November the Secretary of the Cabinet circulated "a draft submission to Ministers on the further study of defence policy and expenditure to be undertaken in the light of the Ministerial discussions at Chequers", and it clearly spelt out the proposed restriction on defence expenditure and the implications of this for the equipment programme. It said that the purpose of this study would be to review in detail the UK's

"complex of commitments and capabilities in order to secure substantial economies in defence in real terms. For this purpose the 'target' of the review should be a level of defence expenditure in 1969/70 not exceeding £2,000m at 1964 prices, provided it is clear that such a target can be achieved on a realistic basis, ie consistently with the continuing discharge of such external commitments as we may retain. . . ."

In order to achieve economies, alternative possibilities should be examined, including

"equipping our forces with alternative weapon systems (whether of our own manufacture or by purchase from other countries) which will enable them to continue to discharge an effective role in the

---

[1] OPD(0) (64) 12.

Meditterranean and east of Suez but will be less costly than existing programmes"[1].

One alternative weapon system already being considered was the TFX: as mentioned earlier, an Air Staff team went to Washington in December 1964 to look at it and other US types. A brief on defence expenditure, prepared in advance of this visit and headed Possibility of Buying US Aircraft, commented on an alternative to the TSR.2:–

"The US F-111A – the TFX – appears likely to meet the United Kingdom requirement in all significant respects although it is the American custom to build separate versions for strike and reconnaissance. The United States has been very chary of releasing information about this aircraft. There is some reason to believe that there are difficulties about aerodynamics, weight growth and rising cost.

"Research and development costs of the TSR.2 are currently forecast as £272m and production costs for 158 aircraft as £469m. A total of £741m. About £160m has so far been spent or committed.

"The TFX[2] will not cost less than £2m. 158 aircraft at £2m would, with spare engines, cost £332m. Cancelling the TSR.2 and substituting the TFX would therefore save about £250m".

This was the Government's arithmetic – that if defence expenditure were to be contained within a £2,000m a year limit, some of the more expensive weapon-system programmes would have to be cancelled; and its logic – that if alternative weapon systems which were not only cheaper but would fulfil RAF requirements were available elsewhere, then they should be purchased.

On 28 December a note advising members of the Defence and Oversea Policy (Official) Committee as to how "the Defence Studies agreed by the Committee" at its meeting on 1 December were to be carried out was circulated[3]. It reminded the officials that the committee had considered how these "further studies of defence policy and expenditure, requested by Ministers after the discussion at Chequers", were to be implemented; and recalled that it was agreed that, as a first step, the Ministry of Defence "should prepare a paper covering the whole range of defence expenditure and indicating the various ways in which economies might be achieved in order to hold expenditure in 1969/70 at not more than £2,000m at 1964 prices". It went on to give the terms of reference, agreed in correspondence with the departments mainly concerned, for the committee's "remit to the MoD", who had been invited – consulting other Departments as appropriate – "to set out the various ways in which defence expenditure might be reduced, in 1969/70, to alternative figures down to £2,000m at 1964 prices – with a description of the military implications of the different possibilities".

---

[1] OPD(O) (64)27. The examination of equipment alternatives was to be made so as to enable Ministers "to take very early decisions on . . . the TSR.2, P.1154 and HS681."

[2] TFX was the project designation, F-111 the USAF/USN designation.

[3] OPD(0) (64)29.

The note added that the MoD would "not be able to avoid some consideration of the political and economic implications of the results of their studies", and that these should be circulated to the committee "not later than the end of February". But there was a particular urgency about some aircraft projects: "special studies" were being carried out on the TSR.2, HS681 and the Shackleton Mk 2, and it was hoped that these would be completed "by about the end of the year".

When the Defence and Oversea Policy Committee met on 15 January 1965[1] to consider defence economies it considered two memoranda on the aircraft programme – one by the Secretary of State for Defence on The RAF Aircraft Programme[2] and one by the Minister of Aviation called Review of the Aircraft Programme[3]. It was at this meeting that the first Ministerial view that TSR.2 should be cancelled was expressed, when in opening the discussion S of S for Defence said that his proposals "involved four major projects. He recommended that the TSR.2, the P.1154 and the HS681 should be cancelled and replaced by the F-111A (TFX), the Phantom, a developed version of the P.1127 and the C-130E." Referring to individual aircraft capability, he said that the TFX was "broadly equal" to the TSR.2.

In discussion the Chancellor of the Exchequer (Mr James Callaghan) said that he accepted S of S's recommendations, and averred that from the point of view of the MoD as a customer "the case seemed unanswerable" – the US aircraft "were available at fixed prices and with fixed delivery dates; they would cost much less and be in operation earlier". But the committee decided to seek further information: it asked S of S, in consultation with the Minister of Aviation, to circulate a paper on "measures which might be taken to deal with the difficulties which the aircraft industry would face in the event of a Government decision to cancel certain of the current aircraft projects", and also invited the two Ministers "to review the figures concerning costs and savings in relation to the TSR.2 and TFX".

Memoranda by not only S of S for Defence and the Minister of Aviation – respectively on The TSR.2 and The TFX and TSR.2 and TFX[4], with joint ones on TSR.2 and TFX Costs[5] and The Aircraft Industry and Future Defence Needs[6] – but also by the Chancellor of the Exchequer on the Aircraft Programme[7] were considered when the Defence and Oversea Policy Committee resumed its discussions of defence economies on 22 January, the Prime Minister commenting that in his meeting at Chequers with leaders of the aircraft industry they had not "seriously challenged the financial and economic arguments for the

[1] OPD(65) 2nd Mtg.
[2] OPD(65)9.
[3] OPD(65)7.
[4] OPD(65)11 & 13.
[5] OPD(65)14.
[6] OPD(65)15.
[7] OPD(65)17.

programme now proposed". Referring to the TFX Mk II they had argued that it "was in an early stage of development, that costs might well rise" and that the UK would be "at the mercy of the United States aircraft industry". Again no firm decision was reached; the committee agreed to resume its discussion in the following week, the Secretary of State for Defence and the Minister of Aviation being asked in the meantime to produce a paper elaborating proposals for the new projects[1].

When the discussion was resumed, on 29 January[2], with further memoranda by the Secretary of State for Defence on The RAF Aircraft Programme[3], by the Minister of Aviation on Cancellation of HS681 – Effect on Short Bros and Harland[4], and by both Ministers on The Aircraft Industry – New Projects[5], the committee reached decisions on all the major aircraft projects except for TSR.2 – a decision on which was deferred, pending "more definite information . . . about its cost and performance" and the report of a study of the social and industrial consequences of cancelling it, to be presented to Ministers by 1 April. It was agreed that the P.1154 and HS681 should be cancelled, that limited development of the P.1127 should be authorised – together with an order for 40 Phantoms (which would have Rolls-Royce engines) and an option on a further 110, that 24 C-130Es should be ordered with an option on a further 58, and that the Comet should be adopted as the Shackleton Mk 2 replacement.

These decisions were confirmed by the Cabinet on 1 February[6], the Chancellor of the Exchequer commenting that while he recognised the force of the argument which had led the committee to recommend that the decision on TSR.2 should be postponed for a short period, the delay "should not be allowed to involve us in a virtual commitment to complete this aircraft since it would then become impossible to achieve our objective of reducing the Defence Budget to £2,000m at 1964 prices in 1969-70".

At this Cabinet meeting the Prime Minister, reporting on the Defence and Oversea Policy Committee's examination of the defence aircraft programme, said that TSR.2 "presented the most difficult problem". It "had originally been estimated to cost a total of £325m (including £90m in respect of research and development), *ie*, an average cost for 158 aircraft of £2.1m. This estimate had now risen to a total of £750m or approximately £5m per aircraft, an increase which illustrated the uneconomic character of the manufacture of military aircraft in the UK. . . ".

The Cabinet agreed that a decision on the TSR.2 should be deferred "for a limited period".

---

[1] OPD(65) 4th Mtg.
[2] OPD(65) 5th Mtg.
[3] OPD(65)20
[4] OPD(65)28
[5] OPD(65)21
[6] OCC(65)6th Conclusions.

In the Commons on the following day the Prime Minister made known publicly the Government's intentions towards the five main military aircraft projects during a debate on an Opposition motion of censure[1]. He said that the P.1154 as a replacement for the Hunter was "not a practicable proposition"; that there was an urgent need for an operational version of the P.1127, that specially modified Comets would be ordered as replacements for Shackleton Mk 2s and that C-130s would be bought instead of the HS681. As to the Canberra replacement, he referred at the outset to what had been called the "nuclear bonus" of TSR.2[2], and said that fewer aircraft had been surrounded with greater controversy – "not excluding passionate controversy over cost estimates". So far as costs were concerned, he commented that the original estimate for R & D was £90m, and went on: "It has now risen to the region of £300m and the most authoritative estimate which I can get today for research, design and production is £750m – which, on an order for 150, would cost £5m per aircraft or 25 times the cost of the Canberra which it is designed to replace. No one can be frivolous about a question of this kind, when each plane is costing about as much as a pre-war battleship".

The Prime Minister referred subsequently to "considerations" which were "in the mind of the Government" as to decisions which would have to be taken. There was to be what he called an "immediate evaluation of the future of TSR.2"; an "authoritative estimate" was needed from the firms concerned as to its final cost, "backed by the strictest contractual conditions as to price, performance and delivery: we cannot go on with estimates; we shall have to have fixed prices, guaranteed, with penalty clauses on delivery and the rest, if we are not to put the time-scale still further back"; and more information was needed about "the certainty, capability and cost of certain possible alternatives". Adding that this information would "take some more months to assemble", the Prime Minister said that meanwhile TSR.2 would go on. When the decision was taken, it would be against a background of operational defence requirements, of the cost to the taxpayer ("£4m a month while it goes on", he subsequently interpolated) and of the future of the aircraft industry.

Earlier in his speech the Prime Minister had referred to the Secretary of State for Defence being "engaged in a round-the-clock examination" of defence policy and commitments – looking to see what this meant in terms of expenditure, and would be "reporting to the House in due course".

This examination, involving defence expenditure as a whole and TSR.2 in particular, continued on 12 February when the Defence and

---

[1] Commons Hansard, 2 Feb 65, Cols 897-1018.
[2] Recalling the 1958 announcement that TSR.2 was to be developed as a Canberra replacement the Prime Minister said: "It was at a later stage – the history of this has inevitably been clouded by nuclear controversy – that what the right hon Gentleman the then Secretary of State for Air called the 'nuclear bonus' concept came into being".

Oversea Policy (Official) Committee discussed the defence review[1] – PUS, MoD (Sir Henry Hardman), pointing out that although it would be possible to consider the possible cancellation of TSR.2 in isolation from the defence review, the TSR.2 decision would be "so significant for the total defence budget" that when Ministers were considering it, it would be helpful for them to have an indication of conclusions likely to emerge from the defence review. The committee invited the Ministry of Defence to circulate their report on possible economies in defence expenditure not later than the middle of March and the Ministry of Aviation, in consultation with the Treasury and the MoD, to circulate by the same time "a paper clarifying the financial aspects of the possible cancellation of the TSR.2".

When the Defence and Oversea Policy Committee met on 29 March specifically to discuss the TSR.2 and TFX[2] it had before it memoranda by the Secretary of State for Defence on The TSR.2 or the F-111A[3] and by the Minister of Aviation on TSR.2 and TFX[4] and a Note prepared by DEA/Treasury Officials on Cancellation of TSR.2: Release of Resources for Exports[5]. In his summing-up of the discussion the Prime Minister said that there seemed to be general agreement that the Government were now in a position to take a decision and that TSR.2 should be cancelled. There had been no change in performance and it had not proved possible to negotiate a fixed price: the manufacturers "had offered a sliding scale by which they would make a profit if the final cost were below a target figure and would accept a degree of loss if the target figure were exceeded. Their loss would, however, be limited and the Government would have to bear the whole excess if costs increased beyond that point" – total cost still seemed likely to be near the earlier estimates made by the Minister of Aviation. As to the TFX, a limited commitment should be made, though even that was to be avoided if possible; the matter was to be brought to the Cabinet on 1 April. The Minister of Defence was invited "to pursue negotiations with the United States Government for an option on the purchase of the TFX".

On 1 April two Cabinet meetings were held – one at 10 a.m. and the other at 10 p.m.[6] – before a final decision was taken to cancel TSR.2. At the morning session, when a memorandum on the TSR.2 or the F-111A by the Secretary of State for Defence was considered[7], the Cabinet agreed to resume their discussion at a subsequent meeting and invited S of S for Defence, "in consultation with the Chancellor of the Exchequer and the Minister of Aviation to circulate the latest information about the terms of the agreement which might be

[1] OPD(0) (65) 4th Mtg.
[2] OPD(65) 18th Mtg.
[3] OPD(65)57.
[4] OPD(65)59.
[5] OPD(65)60.
[6] CC(65) 20th and 21st Conclusions.
[7] C(65)57.

concluded with the US Govt for an option to acquire the TFX aircraft".

The decisive Cabinet meeting on the TSR.2 or F-111A, at 10 p.m. on 1 April 1965, had before it a memorandum by the Secretary of State for Defence – The Need for an Option on the F-111A[1] – and the draft by him of a public announcement about the cancellation of the TSR.2 and the taking-up of an option to purchase F-111As. In his memorandum, S of S warned the Cabinet that there were "grave political and military dangers" in cancelling TSR.2 unless, at the same time, an option was secured on the F-111A. Without such an option, he said, "once we have cancelled the TSR.2 we shall be entirely in the hands of the Americans as to the terms, price and politico-military conditions under which we might subsequently buy the F-111A, if this proves necessary". The memorandum continued:–

"Our objective must be to secure from the United States Government an option to purchase the F-111A which binds them to supply it to us at the best possible price, while leaving us free as to whether we take the option up, and the numbers we purchase if so. This freedom is required until we have completed the defence review".

S of S went on to say that this had been the objective in negotiations with the United States which were still in progress. Their Government had made a "far more attractive price offer" for the F-111A – making the first ten aircraft available at £2.125m and later Mk 2s at £2.32m, these figures including about £335,000 per aircraft for R&D, a charge which the US Govt had said it would waive in full if necessary to maintain the basic aircraft price. This was "as firm and as good an offer" as could be secured and there could be no doubt that "the existence of the TSR.2" had produced it. By comparison, the TSR.2 cost estimate was £2.9m excluding the R&D cost of up to £300m. His memorandum then said:–

"If we secure the option, we would not have to place a small initial order for training aircraft until January 1966. No further orders would need to be placed until two years from now. Thus, we shall have completed our defence review before these decisions are needed.

"The United States Government is expected to confirm specifically today that the terms of the option arrangement do not commit HMG to purchasing F-111A aircraft."

S of S's conclusions were that an option in favourable terms on the F-111A was "indispensable" if TSR.2 was to be cancelled. That day's offer, "coupled with the specific assurance that the arrangement would not commit us to buying any F-111As", provided "a uniquely favourable opportunity". He recommended that the Government should cancel the TSR.2, conclude an arrangement with the US Govt for an option on the F-111A and make an announcement on the lines of his draft.

---

[1] C(65)58.

When he summed-up the first part of the discussion the Prime Minister said that two possibilities could be excluded – a decision to complete the TSR.2 programme or to cancel TSR.2 and replace it with an immediate order for 110 TFXs. The choice, therefore, was one of three courses – to cancel TSR.2 and take no action over a replacement; to cancel TSR.2 and secure an option on the TFX, on the lines described by S of S for Defence; or to postpone any decision until the review of oversea commitments showed whether there was a requirement for this type of aircraft. In his concluding summing-up he said that the balance of opinion was in favour of the second course – to cancel TSR.2 and to secure an option on the TFX on the lines suggested by S of S for Defence; but before such a decision could be taken it would be necessary that the terms of the option agreement should be confirmed by the US authorities – particularly that "it involved no commitment at this stage to purchase any TFX". Subject to that condition, the Government's decision to cancel TSR.2 might be announced by the Chancellor of the Exchequer in his Budget speech on 6 April.

The Cabinet then took the major decisions, at its late-night meeting, which formed the basis of the Chancellor's Parliamentary announcement, recorded at the start of this chapter. It invited S of S for Defence, in consultation with the Chancellor and the Minister of Aviation, "formally to confirm with the United States authorities the terms which they had conveyed orally for the option to purchase the TFX and in particular to confirm that this involved no commitment at this stage to purchase any aircraft"; secondly, it agreed that subject to the previous conclusion being fulfilled "the TSR.2 should be cancelled and an agreement signed with the United States Government for an option to buy the TFX in the terms proposed by the Secretary of State for Defence"; thirdly, it agreed that this decision should be announced by the Chancellor in his Budget speech on 6 April; fourthly, that the announcement of it should be revised on the lines agreed in discussion; and finally, that S of S for Defence and the Minister of Aviation should hold a Press conference on 6 April.

When the cancellation was announced, TSR.2 was grounded on the instructions of the Minister of Aviation, and the question then arose as to what to do with the three aircraft which had been completed. After the Minister, S of S for Defence and the Chancellor had expressed their views on possible research use of these TSR.2s, the Defence and Oversea Policy Committee decided on 2 June[1] that there should be no further programme of test flying; and it invited the Minister of Aviation to "consider the disposal of the three completed aircraft". But although TSR.2 never flew again, some of its development accrued to the benefit of other aircraft – notably the Olympus 22R powerplant which as the Olympus 593 powered the Concorde SST[2].

---

[1] OPD(65) 28th Mtg.
[2] And Optical Linescan for the Buccaneer.

Perhaps the last word on TSR.2 could well be left with the Committee of Public Accounts, which in its Second Report for the 1966–67 Session briefly recounted the history of the project (paras 38–40) and then drew some cost control lessons from it (para 45), as follows:–

"In December 1959 the estimated cost of development of the TSR.2, including nine development aircraft, was £80–90m, covering work up to acceptance for introduction into service in all roles in 1966. This estimate was based on the airframe contractor's first estimate of likely costs, an incentive contract for the development of the engine, and Ministry estimates for many items of equipment for which design studies had not been completed.

"In March 1962, largely as a result of the receipt of development cost plan estimates for the bulk of the ancillary equipment and of an increase in the estimated cost of developing and supplying prototype engines, the cost of the project was revised to £137m, with acceptance for introduction into service by the latter part of 1967. This was the first estimate made on the basis of a substantially complete design. Increases in costs reported by both the airframe and engine contractors caused the Ministry, in January 1963, to revise their estimates to £175–200m with acceptance for introduction into service at the end of 1968, and in January 1964 to £240–260m, the higher figure allowing for a further possible 12 to 18 months' delay in the completion of the programme. No further official estimate was made by the Ministry of the cost of development alone but, after unsuccessful negotiations with the airframe and engine contractors early in 1965, the Chancellor of the Exchequer announced in the House of Commons on 6 April 1965 that the Government had decided to cancel the TSR.2 forthwith. By then £125m had been paid to contractors; further payments were expected to amount to about £70m.

"On both the airframe and engine contracts the increased estimates were attributed to changes in design and specification; to successive delays; and to under-estimation of the costs and of the technical effort required."

Drawing its financial moral from this abruptly terminated programme, the Committee accepted that TSR.2 was "an aircraft of such advanced concept that it created particularly complex problems of management both for the Ministry and the contractors at a time when the latter were in process of reorganisation under the Government's plan for rationalisation of the aircraft industry":

"Nevertheless it seems . . . that all concerned were at fault in not securing the earlier introduction of an adequate system of recording and reporting costs against physical progress to enable policy decisions to be made on the basis of up-to-date information on the financial effect of the technical problems encountered."

The Committee noted "the various steps taken to improve control over expenditure on projects of this nature". They trusted that when future Committees of Public Accounts came to consider the control of expenditure on other projects, the "improved procedures now introduced" would "prove to have been fully effective".

The Government's option to buy the TFX never matured into a purchase of F-111s and resulted in an extension of service for the Vulcans: "following the cancellation of the F-111K programme", it was stated in a draft Air Staff paper of July 1969 on The Viability of the Future Vulcan Force[1], "it was decided to retain the Vulcan force in service. Present plans call for a UK front-line force of 40 free-fall aircraft (from the end of 1970 when Blue Steel is phased out), reducing to 32 UE at the end of 1971, plus a force of 16 UE deployed to Cyprus".

---

[1] In file Vulcan Policy – AF/CT 827/68 Pt I.

CHAPTER XXIX

VULCANS IN CYPRUS

Formal authority for the deployment of two Vulcan B.2 squadrons from Cottesmore to Akrotiri during the first quarter of 1969 was given on 23 May 1968, when an operational policy statement – Operational Policy for NEAF Vulcan Squadrons – was issued for planning purposes[1]. This said that two squadrons of Vulcans, Nos 9 and 35, would replace the four Canberra squadrons of the NEAF Strike Wing (Nos 6, 32, 73 and 249) during the first quarter of 1969[2]. Each Vulcan squadron was to be equipped with eight UE B.2s, and they were to arrive at their new location from the UK in four batches of four – the first four on 15 January 1969, the second four on 5 February, the third on 26 February and the fourth on 19 March. They were both to be based at Akrotiri and to have three operational tasks: to provide the UK nuclear contribution to Cento (Central Treaty Organisation) in accordance with approved war plans; to provide nuclear support as necessary to meet the requirements of UK war plans; and to support UK conventional war plans in the Mediterranean and Gulf areas. In the first two of these tasks they were required to generate 75% of available aircraft within 24hr and the remaining 25% as soon as possible thereafter, 100% of available aircraft being generated within 72hr; and three armed aircraft were to be required to disperse to Muharraq (Bahrain) and six to Masirah Island, maintaining the state of readiness required by NEAF strategic alert procedures for up to 28 days and being capable of flying a single operational sortie: the remaining aircraft would be required to operate from Akrotiri. The squadron's training tasks would be to train to meet their operational role, and in addition to normal day-to-day training they would need to carry out routine long-range training flights to areas in which they would be required to operate, to make regular training detachments to Masirah (assessed as six detachments of three aircraft for three weeks each year), and to take part in Cento exercises – involving approximately one detachment of eight aircraft for up to ten days to a Cento airfield, and three detachments of up to six aircraft for up to ten days to an Iranian airfield each year.

Plans to deploy V-bombers to NEAF became public knowledge on 22 July 1968 when the BBC Overseas Service broadcast a news-item saying that Britain was to send "two squadrons of Vulcan nuclear bombers to Cyprus around the end of the year". They would be stationed at the Sovereign Base on the island and (said the BBC's Defence Correspondent) would be "part of an increased contribution to Nato forces in

---

[1] See file Vulcan Policy – AF/CT 827/68, Pt 1.
[2] See the author's *The Bomber Role 1945–1970* (AHB 1984), Ch 9 Bombers in Cyprus – Canberras (1945–1969) and Vulcans (1969–1975), for the origins of Cento and the bomber commitment.

the Mediterranean".

This statement, that aircraft "capable of carrying nuclear weapons" would be based in Cyprus in support of Nato, inevitably caused a furore both in Nicosia and in London; and under pressure from the MoD the BBC broadcast a retraction on the 24th, saying that the two squadrons of Vulcans which Britain was sending to Cyprus would be the first Vulcan units to be stationed abroad: they would replace four squadrons of Canberras which were being withdrawn because of their age, and would be deploying in support of the Central Treaty Organisation (Cento), not Nato as reported earlier. (The possibility of "double-earmarking" the Vulcans, so that they would be available not only to Cento but also to Nato for conventional operations on its southern flank, had been considered earlier in 1968; but when the Chiefs of Staff examined the proposal they felt unable to support it, largely because of the incompatibility of the different requirements.)

The pending move of Nos 9 and 35 Sqns to Akrotiri was referred to by the retiring AOC in C Strike Command (Air Chf Mshl Sir Wallace Kyle) when he paid a farewell visit to RAF Cottesmore on 31 July. He said that, following the departure of the Vulcans to Cyprus early in 1969, Cottesmore would continue as a flying station – accommodating the Canberra OCU from Bassingbourn and three squadrons from Watton.

On 15 January 1969 the Vulcan deployment to Akrotiri began with the departure of four No 35 Sqn B.2s from Cottesmore. Early in February its four remaining aircraft were deployed and on the 26th the first four of No 9's B.2s left a snowy Britain for the sunshine of Cyprus, its second four arriving at Akrotiri on 19 March to bring the new Bomber Wing up to strength with 16 Vulcans. On the following day the squadron was told that its "primary function" was to be "continuation of the nuclear deterrent role", except that the treaty organisation of which the Vulcans formed a striking force was "Cento and not Nato".

During its five-year existence (1969–75) the Vulcan Bomber Wing did many of the same activities its predecessor the Canberra Strike Wing had undertaken – participation in Cento and Nato exercises, firepower demonstrations, Ranger flights, detachments, alerts, evaluations and standardisations. As an example of what the crews were in for, No 9 Sqn were told at a briefing on 20 March 1969, in the words of their ORB compiler, that they would "be doing Rangers or detachments to Sharjah, Masirah, Muharraq, Peshawar, Teheran, Nairobi and Tengah" – in response to which information (he noted) "the hollow laughter of the cynics rang round the briefing room. However, as if instantly to shame such lack of faith, Flt Lt C Woods and crew were nominated for a Tengah Ranger, and after an abortive attempt on the 19th . . . they left Akrotiri on the 20th and returned on the 26th". Clearly, as from the inception of the V-force, the principles of dispersal, flexibility and self-sufficiency were to be put into practice.

The Vulcans' main commitments were to Cento, to the reinforcement of the Persian Gulf area and to Nato, and in fulfilment of these commitments they participated in various exercises and training flights. Thus supporting Cento meant contributing to the organisation's annual Shahbaz air defence exercises, by flying aggressor sorties, and to the firepower demonstrations put on for the Permanent Military Deputies; in addition, single aircraft flew Rangers to Teheran and Ankara – all these activities helping crews to familiarise themselves with the Cento environment and with the low level routes (the turbulence encountered on which caused the Vulcans to use up their fatigue life at an alarming rate, until procedures were devised to offset this)[1]. Practice for the reinforcement of the Persian Gulf area was achieved by regular Pedigree detachments to Masirah Island (with more low-level flying, in Iran and Oman, over "rugged and featureless terrain of the type likely to be met operationally"), and Nato exercises included Dawn Patrol, Deep Furrow, Deep Express and Epic Battle, some of these involving Royal Navy and US Navy forces, others involving air, land and naval elements. Low flying was also done over Italy, along the Calabrian routes: thus the Vulcans operated to the west, south and east of Cyprus. A difference in this respect between them and the Canberras was that the latter used to do a good deal of training (both bombing and with AS30 missiles) on the El Adem ranges, but these ceased to be available after the Colonel Gadaffi coup of September 1969 had removed the pro-Western King Idris from power.

Apart from the frequent exercises already mentioned, and those designed to test the air defences of Cyprus (Springtrip) and Malta, there were quick-reaction alerts, "generation games" (the generation of nuclear and conventional weapons), followed by a fly-off, MoD weapon standardisation team tests and tactical evaluations. In December 1971 a Vulcan captained by Wg Cdr R Dick made a goodwill visit to the Imperial Ethiopian AF Base at Asmara, and in February 1972 he flew a "One Off" Ranger to RNZAF Ohakea for a Royal New Zealand Aero Club Pageant on 4 March.

The NEAF Bomber Wing also participated in the Strike Command Bombing and Navigation Competition, the best crews being selected from the two squadrons and sent to the UK some weeks beforehand for acclimatisation and training. Crews were also subject to the "trappers" – the No 1 Group Standardisation Unit – and to an MoD Weapons Standardisation Team, which checked their knowledge of the weapons carried. As with the UK-based Vulcan squadrons, there was strong overall emphasis in training and exercises on low-level operations. No 35 Sqn noted in its ORB that on 7 July 1971 the new Italian

---

[1] Including regulating take-off times to avoid low-level flying during the hottest part of the day, and forbidding it until 30,000lb of the normal (76–77,000lb) fuel load had been used up.

low-level routes were flown for the first time and were "thought to be better training value than the all-too-familiar Cyprus low-level route"[1].

After the Turkish invasion of the island at dawn on 20 July 1974 the Vulcan squadrons performed some interesting roles, in maritime reconnaissance and as airborne communications posts – relaying messages between NEOC (Near East Operations Centre), the United Nations controllers in Nicosia and the Turkish authorities in Ankara. Although the Sovereign Base Areas were not affected by the Turkish occupation of the north of Cyprus (except by an influx of refugees), the island's situation as a British base, with its Near East/Cento commitments, had changed for good. The No 35 Sqn ORB for September 1974 noted that "flying over the Republic continues to be prohibited and the majority of training flights have been carried out either in the UK" – where a NEAF detachment had been established at Waddington – "or Malta", although by October more local flying from Akrotiri, and the range at Episkopi, had become available.

In December 1974 the two squadrons were told that they were to be withdrawn from Cyprus to the UK, and this withdrawal occurred in January 1975, No 9 going to Waddington and No 35 to Scampton. These "resident squadrons" of the NEAF Bomber Wing were to be replaced by "detachment squadrons" from the UK: thus four Vulcans of No 50 Sqn arrived at Akrotiri on 20 January, as a Strike Command detachment. The withdrawal of the Cyprus-based RAF bombers marked the end of an era which had begun in 1957 with the commitment of four Canberra B.2 squadrons to the Baghdad Pact forces, these squadrons forming the NEAF Strike Wing until superseded by the Vulcan B.2s of the Bomber Wing.

---

[1] In the 1971 Cento Exercise Shahbaz XVII UK participation consisted of Vulcans and Canberra PR.9s operating from Mehrbad AFB in Iran against Iranian targets, with Lightnings and Bloodhounds in Cyprus. "This region-wide air defence exercise served to improve the operational efficiency of the forces of the member nations and their ability to work together under operational conditions" (Central Treaty Org file V/9/791).

CHAPTER XXX

END OF QRA

Although Quick Reaction Alert was not exclusive to Bomber Command (it was also maintained in Fighter Command and in RAF Germany) it represented in a special way the highest state of efficiency and retaliatory power achieved by the V-force, and its succession by a Royal Navy Polaris force QRA from midnight on 30 June 1969 signified the end of an era for RAF strategic bombing capability.

QRA, having been approved in principle by the Air Council on 7 December 1961, had been introduced in the Medium Bomber Force (as already recorded) from 1 January 1962: from that date, one aircraft in each squadron was maintained at 15 minutes' readiness. When the Thor force was in operation (1959-63) and capable of delivering up to 60 megaton warheads, the number of weapon systems held at an immediate (15-minute) readiness was 68 – 54 Thors and 14 V-bombers; but with the disbandment of the Thor force in 1963 proposals were put forward to increase the number of V-bombers on QRA to 20. "I propose increasing the QRA force to 17 Vulcans and Victors (plus the four Valiants of the Saceur force), rising to 20 Victors and Vulcans by July 1 when the Blue Steel squadrons will be able to make their contribution", the AOC in C told CAS on 10 January 1963[1]. However, although the Air Staff supported this idea in principle, its practical realisation was complicated by Saceur's request during 1961 for an increase in the number of RAF strike aircraft on QRA from four to eight Canberras and from three to four Valiants, a request which was acceded to during 1962: on 21 June CDS signalled Saceur to say that the increased capability was expected to become effective during the last quarter of 1962, that the total number of aircraft on QRA at Marham would be four Valiants, and that the additional facilities there would be completed within six months of the approval to commit funds. In view of this, and until the final terms of the assignment of the V-force to Nato were known and the results of Bomber Command's trials of Centralised Progressive Servicing had been assessed, it was decided in mid-1963 that QRA arrangements in the Command should remain "as currently planned".[2]

This assigment of the Medium Bomber Force to Saceur – for targetting, planning, co-ordination and execution of strikes – became effective from 23 May 1963[3], but the AOC in C Bomber Command retained responsibility for day-to-day control of the force and to the Air Ministry for its overall efficiency and readiness for war. While the Valiant force was fully assigned to Saceur, the UK Government retained a

---

[1] AHB 8/9/322 Quick Reaction Alert – Medium Bomber Force.
[2] DGO/PS to AMSO minute, 12 June 63.
[3] SASO BC Memorandum to Nos 1 & 3 Gps, 19 June 63.

national responsibility for decisions on states of readiness, deployment and dispersal, the number of aircraft available to Nato and their equipment, and logistics and support.[1]

During the mid-1960s there was no diminution in V-force activities, the force being entirely Vulcan-equipped and operating from Waddington, Scampton and Finningley. Thus in April 1966 12 aircraft from Waddington took part in Exercise Co-op, a Nato exercise, when "low cloud on the low-level route over Central and Southern France prevented the aircraft successfully completing this leg. One aircraft captained by Flt Lt K P Clarke of No 101 Sqn was followed by a French Air Force Vautour throughout his climb in solid cloud out of the low-level route. This was the only reported interception by the aircraft of the Waddington Wing. . . ."[2]

Then in Exercise Micky Finn, starting at 0500hr on 9 May 1966, "22 Vulcan Mk 1A and Mk 2 aircraft were generated. . .", then from 2 to 21 June, "eight Vulcan Mk 1A aircraft, with aircrews of No 101 Sqn, flew to Malta to take part in Operation Sunspot. . . .

"The squadron carried out extensive practice of new bombing manoeuvres, type 2J attacks, in which the aircraft climbed from low level to 2,500ft and 2G attacks in which the aircraft climbed to 8,500ft before releasing their bombs.

"For many of the crews it was their first experience of dropping live 1,000lb bombs from a relatively low level, and crews reported the blast effect of the bombs bursting".

Another Exercise Micky Finn was called on 11 July 1967 at 0500hr, nine Mk 1As and nine Mk 2s and weapon systems being prepared in 12hr 55min: two Mk 1As operated from Waddington and the remaining 16 plus two Finningley-based were dispersed – two Mk 2s to Brawdy and two to Filton, three to Honington (including the two Finningley-based aircraft flown by Waddington crews), two to Manston and two to Wattisham; and two Mk 1As to Macrihanish, three to Marham and two to Valley. At 1300hr on the 13th the order to scramble was given and all the aircraft were airborne within one minute.

From the beginning of 1966 the number of dispersal airfields had been reduced. The Waddington-based Vulcans (free-fall B.1As/B.2s) used Finningley and Marham as near dispersals and Wattisham, Filton, Machrihanish, Manston, Valley and Brawdy as distant ones; Scampton's Blue Steel Vulcan B.2s used Coningsby and Bedford as near dispersals and Kinloss, Lossiemouth and Boscombe Down as distant ones; Cottesmore's free-fall Vulcan B.2s used Honington and Leconfield as near dispersals and Pershore, Leuchars, Lyneham, Yeovilton, Ballykelly and Leeming as distant ones – three squadrons operating from each of these main bases; while Wittering's two Victor B.2 Blue Steel squadrons used Gaydon, Wyton and Coltishall as near dispersals and St Mawgan

---

[1] SASO BC Memorandum to Nos 1 & 3 Gps, 19 June 63.
[2] Waddington ORB, as are the following references.

as a distant one. The former dispersals given up by Bomber Command in 1966 were Middleton St George, Cranwell, Prestwick, Llanbedr, Burtonwood, Bruntingthorpe and Elvington[1].

On 17 April 1967 APS/S of S for Defence minuted the MA (Military Assistant) to the Chief of the Defence Staff to say that S of S had approved CDS's proposals of the 12th that the total V-bomber force "need not exceed 63 UE Vulcan Mk 2s" and that the Victor bomber force and the Vulcan Blue Steel capability "should be withdrawn from service by the end of 1968 and the end of 1969 respectively"[2]. Subsequently, in a signal of 7 August, Saceur was informed of the gradual reduction in the number of weapon systems available from the MBF, pending the introduction of the first Polaris submarine. As the latter was due to occur in June 1968, it seemed acceptable (the signal said) to disband the two Victor Blue Steel squadrons later in that year: the effect would be to reduce the availability of weapon systems from the MBF to 72 on 30 September and 64 on 31 December. Further details of the strength and deployment of the remaining V-bombers from 1 January 1969 onwards and of the introduction of the remaining Polaris submarines would be given as soon as possible[3].

When the Chiefs of Staff discussed arrangements for transfer of the responsibility for the strategic nuclear deterrent role from the V-bomber force to the Polaris force at their meeting on 19 June 1969 they agreed that there should be no formal Press release. It was said in discussion that although no public ceremonies were being held to pay tribute to the work of the V-force, the AOC in C Strike Command would be conveying an official tribute to the personnel concerned[4].

The other sea-change which affected the Medium Bomber Force – administratively but not operationally – during its QRA period was the merger of its controlling formation, Bomber Command, into Strike Command on 30 April 1968; and it was the latter's HQ which fourteen months later recorded in its ORB the cessation of the Quick Reaction Alert Force:—

"At midnight on 30 June 1969 the Medium Bomber Force of Strike Command handed-over to the Royal Navy the responsibility for providing the UK permanent peacetime QRA force. Over the past seven years a proportion of the V-force has been held at a high state of readiness to counter surprise attacks whilst, at all times, the remainder of the force has maintained the capability to generate all weapon systems to meet their commitments to Nato. The peace-keeping value of this contribution to Nato and [the] Western cause has been inestimable; the burden has been a very heavy one and has demanded

---

[1] LM AF/W/140/D Ops (B & R) (RAF) 2804 of 27 Aug 65 from D of Ops (B & R) (RAF) containing a dispersal plan for the long-term medium bomber force.

[2] ID3/901/6 Pt 5 Medium Bomber Force – Size and Composition.

[3] Ibid.

[4] Ibid – COS 24th Mtg/69, 19 Jun 69.

dedicated service from air and ground crews alike. The handover of the QRA responsibilities will entail only minor changes in the state of readiness of the V-force and in all other respects it will continue to function and have the same operational commitments as before. The V-force will maintain its unqiue contribution to the long-range Western deterrent and will continue assigned as part of the Nato deterrent force".

By this date the MBF of Strike Command consisted of six Vulcan B.2 squadrons in No 1 Group – three at Scampton (Nos 27, 83 and 617) in the Blue Steel role and three at Waddington (Nos 44, 50 and 101) in the free-fall role. The last two Victor B.2 bomber squadrons – Nos 100 and 139 at Wittering, both in the Blue Steel role – had been disbanded by the end of 1968. The 48 Vulcans were assigned to Saceur in the long-range strike role, carrying British nuclear weapons. The Vulcan OCU at Finningley (ten B.2s) provided a possible source of additional weapon systems, but the total number of aircraft/crews available – say, 50–55 – represented only about half the MBF four years previously, when there were nine Vulcan and four Victor bomber squadrons. In the intervening period the Vulcan B.1As were phased out of the front line (in 1967)[1] and all the squadrons re-equipped with B.2s, two of them (Nos 9 and 35) being deployed to Cyprus – as recorded in the previous chapter – and one of them (No 12) disbanded while the Victor free-fall bomber squadrons were converted to the tanker role.

The MBF QRA force at the time of the hand-over to the Royal Navy, though smaller than it previously had been, had the capability of delivering more megaton deterrent weapons than its successor force – say, 48 with a full complement of aircraft/crew combinations from six squadrons backed-up by the OCU, compared with 32 Polaris missiles if two out of the four nuclear-powered submarines of the Polaris Force were on war stations.

CAS (Air Chief Mshl Sir John Grandy – himself a former AOC in C Bomber Command, from 1963 to 1965) sent a congratulatory signal on 30 June 1969 to the AOC in C Strike Command (Air Chf Mshl Sir Denis Spotswood) on the maintenance of QRA by the MBF. He said he thought it was

"appropriate to remember that this task has meant maintaining, at all times throughout seven years, the highest state of readiness which the Royal Air Force has known in peacetime. The way in which QRA has been performed and the reaction of the Force to the operational demands in our plans and those of Saceur has been an unsurpassed demonstration of professional skill, dedication and tenacity.

"The long hours of arduous duty in cockpits, crew rooms, dispersals, hangars and operation rooms have brought the reward of knowing that

---

[1] See Vulcan Policy file – AF/CT 827/68 Pt 1.

a vital task has been successfully completed. I send my congratulations to you and all under your command who have been connected with this very heavy responsibility over the years.

"But when QRA by the medium bomber force ends it does not presage a general relaxation in our readiness for operations. The future roles of the force will call for the same determination as you have shown in the past and the maintenance of high generation rates. When you set about your new and continuing tasks you can look with justifiable pride upon your past achievements and from them find inspiration for the future".

No 1 Group of Strike Command noted in its ORB that its Vulcans had "ceased to mount a continuous Quick Reaction Alert Force at 2259Z on 30th June, when the third UK nuclear submarine, HMS *Renown*, became operational"; and it went on to comment that QRA had been maintained "at all times and in all weathers since 1st February 1962", and that its passing would

"scarcely be regretted by the Vulcan air and ground crews who have spent many weekends on 'standby'; but QRA provided numerous side benefits which added to the efficiency of the Force as a whole. Groundcrews were regularly exercised in the preparation of operational weapon systems, sometimes at very short notice, and aircrews were practised in the checking and acceptance of such systems. Alert procedures and reaction to changes in readiness states became second nature to crews because of Exercises Edom, which were called every other day for the QRA Force[1]. To replace these side-benefits which ended with the cessation of QRA, HQ Strike Command has devised Exercise Edith, which will exercise selective generation of weapon systems, supporting ancillaries, communications and alert procedures on a 'no-notice' basis".

On 3 July 1969 the Minister of Defence announced the change in British strategic nuclear deterrence, from an airborne to submarine delivery system. In response to a Parliamentary Question, asking if he would "make a statement on the transfer of the United Kingdom's contribution to the North Atlantic Treaty Organisation strategic nuclear deterrent from the Royal Air Force to the Royal Navy", Mr Healey said in a Written Answer[2]:–

"Responsibility for the United Kingdom's contribution to Nato's strategic nuclear deterrent forces was transferred from the Royal Air Force to the Royal Navy on 30 June 1969. Our Polaris force is now able to undertake this task and it is no longer necessary to keep aircraft of

---

[1] "In Exercise 'Edom', aircraft and crews at QRA standby are exercised up to the take-off position . . ." (SASO, BC, to HQs Nos 1 and 3 Gps, 6 Mch 64, in AHB IIH/272/1/26 (Pt 1) Operational Research – Operational Readiness). In his letter, SASO instructed that when an aircraft came off QRA it was, "whenever possible, after weapon unloading and re-crystallisation, to be used immediately on a 'scramble' training flight, operating from the ORP or . . . from the QRA hardstanding".

[2] Commons Hansard, 3 Jul 69, Col 136 (Written Answers).

the V-bomber force at immediate readiness.

"Apart from those aircraft which have replaced the Canberras in the strike role in support of Cento, the Vulcan aircraft remained assigned to Nato, but will now be available for operations in the tactical role.

"I should like to pay tribute to the way in which the officers and men concerned at all levels in the Royal Air Force have discharged their arduous responsibilities for the last 12 years, and to express full confidence in their successors in the Royal Navy".

It was widely felt at the time that this brief and impersonal statement hardly did justice publicly to the role which the medium bomber force had so faithfully performed in maintaining an all-the-year-round alert[1]; and the Government was asked in the House of Lords on 22 July "whether any message of gratitude" had been sent to "the officers and men of the V-bomber force on relinquishing their responsibility for nuclear deterrence; and if not, why not?"

The Lord Privy Seal (Lord Shackleton), who replied to the questioner (the Earl of Cork and Orrery), referred to the "congratulatory signal" from the CAS and added that on 3 July, "in another place", S of S for Defence had "paid a similar tribute". Then the Earl, in a Supplementary Question, asked if he would not consider giving CAS's message "a rather higher degree of publicity . . . so that its contents could be known to the nation at large?"

In response, the Lord Privy Seal said he would circulate it in the Official Report[2]; and, as a former Minister of Defence for the RAF (1964-67), paid his own tribute to the MBF, saying that he had "seen something of the V-bomber crews and they were the most extraordinarily dedicated and efficient body of men, and no praise can be too high for their devotion to duty".

---

[1] Noting in its ORB that "a congratulatory signal" had been received from the C in C, No 27 Sqn commented that "it seemed a pity that there was no greater recognition for a job well done".

[2] Lords Hansard for 22 Jul 69, Cols 761-2, records CAS's signal and the exchanges preceding it. Subsequently (25 Jul, Cols 1205-6) the Earl of Cork and Orrery asked for an explanation of the initials QRA in the signal and this was provided by the Parliamentary US of S for Defence (Lord Winterbottom).

THE REVISED TIZARD REPORT

The Chiefs of Staff conclusions and recommendations arising from the revised Tizard Committee Report were as follows – first, the Chiefs' own main conclusions:–

(a) Given sufficient accumulation in peace and adequate means of delivery, atomic and biological weapons might achieve decisive results with relatively small effort against the civil population of a nation without a clash between the major military forces and too rapidly to permit either the building-up of military forces or the exercise of sea power.

(b) Some five or ten atomic bombs landed on the target, with the prospect of more to follow, might well cause the evacuation of cities to an extent sufficiently seriously to sap the power of waging war by conventional means of any country physically and psychologically unorganised to meet such action. Without the moral backing of adequate military power in being, with which to limit or repel invasion, or to launch an effective counter-offensive, such attack might well lead to collapse. On the other hand, some hundreds of atomic weapons might fail to cause the collapse of a country suitably organised physically and psychologically, and morally reinforced by adequate military power in being.

Although biological weapons have not yet been used in war, we consider that the number of atomic weapons required would be materially reduced if biological weapons were simultaneously used.

(c) There is no firm basis on which to assess the quantities of atomic and biological weapons required by any nation to bring about the collapse of another, and many of the factors involved are imponderable. Nevertheless, our estimate, based on such information as is at present available, leads us to believe that some 30-120 atomic bombs accurately delivered by the USSR might cause the collapse of the United Kingdom without invasion, whereas several hundred bombs might be required by the United States or the United Kingdom to bring about the collapse of the USSR.

The number of bombs required to cause a similar collapse in the United States would probably be somewhat greater than for this country, but the problem of landing them accurately in the United States at the ranges involved is much greater.

(d) The percentage of bombs despatched which could be accurately delivered depends on future developments in the technique of attack and defence, the ranges involved and the relative concentration of targets. Unless defensive weapons and methods can be developed more rapidly and to a far greater extent than the methods of attack already envisaged, there seems to be little possibility of preventing the accurate delivery of a substantial proportion of the weapons launched – perhaps 50 per cent or more.

The most promising form of defence so far conceived is the Guided Anti-aircraft Projectile; and the importance and urgency of its development cannot be over-emphasised.

The Chiefs of Staff also considered that "the following conclusions, substantially as reached by Sir Henry Tizard's Committee", remained valid:–

(a) Until fighters using controlled or guided weapons and reliable ground-controlled weapons are available, the strategic bomber capable of speeds approaching the speed of sound will have a great advantage. In contrast, once the defensive weapons mentioned above are in being, provided the expected advances have been made in radar, deep strategic bombing with ordinary explosives as exploited in the last war is likely to be too costly to be sustained over a long period. Heavy precision attacks on important targets will still be possible despite the loss rate.

(b) Anti-aircraft fire of conventional but improved kind will remain a necessary defensive supplement on land and sea to supersonic fighters. Particular importance attaches to anti-aircraft fire as the defence against fast low-flying aircraft, since against these all forms of wire barrage may well be ineffective, and supersonic aircraft may be unable to intercept in the time available.

(c) The rocket will remain a very difficult form of bombardment to counter, and will be effective at ranges up to perhaps as much as 400 miles, the more so since it can be used in the sustained "dribble" attack uninterrupted by weather and independent of the defender's fighter superiority. Much the same remarks apply to pilotless aircraft, but we think that they are likely to be inferior to rockets at medium ranges.

It is thus of importance, in view of the difficulty of intercepting rockets, that no potential enemy should possess bases within 400 miles of ours.

(d) The development of the rocket may make possible a reduction in the size of the capital ship below that of the present battleship, and at medium ranges on land rockets may become a substitute for aircraft in tactical bombardment.

(e) No adequate proportion of our essential imports is likely to be carried by air within the next twenty years. Foreseeable developments in the range and speed of only slightly subsonic aircraft, and of submarines and torpedoes, will give decisive advantage to a properly equipped enemy attacking our convoys, until carrier-operated supersonic aircraft and methods of nullifying torpedo attack are evolved. We believe both these defensive measures are technically possible, though we cannot forecast when they will be achieved. Fast ships sailing alone will not enjoy the immunity they had in the late war.

(f) A general study is required of the contribution which storage of materials and foodstuffs on a large scale could make to the reduction of imports and, therefore, to the defensive strength of this country, and of the contribution which new methods and techniques could make not only to this problem but to the increase of domestic production of foodstuffs.

(g) Foreseeable developments in bombardment by aircraft and pilotless weapons are likely to force our main naval bases further from those of the enemy. Increasing value will attach not only to the base facilities but to the industrial potential of the major Dominions.

(h) We do not foresee any developments that will lead to successful amphibious operations or independent airborne operations without air and sea superiority sufficient to ensure continuity of supply and build-up. Indeed, the increased range and accuracy of long-range fire we foresee would increase the power of the defence and would in some measure offset the air and naval superiority the attacker must possess.

(i) Much increased flexibility of land power may result from the development of specialised transport aircraft, capable of moving the heaviest military loads into and out of small fields. Similar results would follow if the cross-country performance of heavy vehicles could be greatly improved. Special aircraft can certainly be designed, and we believe that novel methods of moving heavy loads across country may be evolved.

(j) Sources of uranium, thorium and other relevant elements will be of great strategic importance. Natural sources of oil will also remain equally important.

(k) It is of first importance that a reduction in the time interval between research and development, on the one hand, and the availability in quantity of weapons, such as aircraft, can and must be achieved in this country.

(l) Research into earth mechanics might contribute to new methods in land warfare and certainly to the reduction in cost of ARP measures.

(m) The continued and indeed improved integration of military and scientific thought at all levels remains an essential defence requirement, and must ensure in the immediate future that much emphasis is placed on long-term research, and the improvement of the level of technical education in the Services, and indeed in the country as a whole.

(n) The effect of the changes we foresee in weapons may have a great impact on the men who operate them and therefore on their selection and training.

The Recommendations which followed were that, should the Chiefs of Staff accept these conclusions, they should:–

(a) Invite the Deputy Chiefs of Staff Committee (or the proposed Committee on Defence Research Policy) to consider the tasks in respect of naval, land and air weapons given in Annex I, paragraph 51.

(b) Direct that a Joint Inter-Service, Civil and Scientific Staff be set up forthwith, under the Deputy Chiefs of Staff Committee, to maintain a continuous study of future developments in weapons and methods of warfare, and the research and development problems and priorities involved, and to estimate the relative value and cost of various defence measures.

(c) Invite the Home Office to begin, in co-operation with the other Departments concerned, an immediate investigation into the Civil Defence implications of the new weapons and, in particular, into the effect of the sudden evacuation of the principal cities, into the possibilities of controlled dispersion both of industries and civil population, into maintenance of public services and into shelter provision, in respect of the United Kingdom; and invite other appropriate Departments to undertake a similar review in respect of our main overseas bases. The principal problems are given in Annex I, paragraph 50.

(d) Maintain and make use of the deception organisation, which should be conversant with the latest developments in weapons and methods of war.

Eleven further recommendations were put forward, with the introductory note:–

"We further recommend that the Chiefs of Staff should accept the following recommendations substantially as reached by Sir Henry Tizard's Committee":–

(a) Direct that this report be taken into account in any further studies on the Security of the Empire and on the shape and size of our post-war Imperial forces arising out of the report by the Post-Hostilities Planning Staff and the Joint Planning Staff.

(b) Encourage and extend the integration of scientific and military thought at all levels, and in particular ensure a high standard of qualifications in the scientific and technical intelligence services.

(c) Take steps to foster a higher level of technical education amongst the three Services, and such other steps as are open to them to promote a higher level of technical education throughout the country.

(d) Invite

(i) The Service Ministries and Combined Operations Headquarters to examine the effect of both Sir Henry Tizard's and our Reports upon their policies and to review the effects of the Weapon developments we foresee on the men who use them and on the new problems of organisation and training which they will cause.

(ii) Other appropriate Departments to study the effect on our economic and defensive strength of a policy of storage of materials and foodstuffs on a large scale in peacetime, and the problem of the re-distribution and dispersion throughout the Empire of our industries and population.

AOCs in C BOMBER COMMAND, 1945-68*

(giving dates of appointment)

15 Sep 45	Air Marshal Sir Norman H Bottomley KCB CIE DSO DFC
16 Jan 47	Air Marshal Sir Hugh W L Saunders KBE CB MC DFC MM
8 Oct 47	Air Marshal A B (later Sir Aubrey) Ellwood CB DSC
2 Feb 50	Air Marshal (later ACM) Sir Hugh P Lloyd KCB KBE CB MC DFC LLD
9 Apr 53	Air Marshal G H (later Sir George) Mills CB (KCB) DFC
22 Jan 56	Air Marshal (later ACM) Sir Harry Broadhurst KCB CBE DSO* DFC* AFC
20 May 59	Air Marshal Sir Kenneth Cross KCB CBE DSO DFC
1 Sep 63	Air Marshal Sir John Grandy KBE CB DSO
19 Feb 65	Air Chief Marshal Sir Wallace Kyle GCB CBE DSO DFC

*Bomber Command was amalgamated into Strike Command on 1 Apr 68

AOCs No 1 Group
AVM C E N Guest CB CBE   15 Jan 47–
AVM G H Mills CB DFC   24 Jan 49–8 Aug 50
AVM E C Hudleston CB CBE   8 Aug 50–1 Apr 51
AVM D A Boyle CB CBE AFC   5 Apr 51–
AVM J R Whitley CB CBE DSO AFC   27 Apr 53–
AVM G A Walker CBE DSO DFC AFC   3 Oct 56–
AVM J G Davis CB OBE MA   14 Jun 59–
AVM P H Dunn CB CBE   1 Dec 61–
AVM D C Stapleton CB CBE DFC AFC   1 May 64–
AVM M H Le Bas CBE DSO   1 Jun 66–
(Became No 1 (Bomber) Group, Strike
Command–   1 Apr 68)

AOCs No 3 Group
AVM R M Foster CB CBE DFC   9 Jul 46–
AVM A Hesketh CB CBE DFC   14 Dec 48–
AVM W A D Brook CB CBE*   15 Sep 51–
AVM E C Hudleston CB CBE   1 Sep 53–
AVM K B B Cross CB CBE DSO DFC   2 Feb 56–
AVM M H Dwyer CBE   4 May 59–
AVM B K Burnett CB DFC   9 Oct 61–
AVM D F Spotswood CBE CBE DSO DFC   5 Aug 64–
AVM D G Smallwood CB CBE DSO DFC   28 Nov 65–
Air Cdre J T Lawrence CBE   15 Feb 67–
(No 3 Group disbanded–   1 Nov 67)

* Killed in a flying accident on 18 Aug '53, just before he was due to take up the post of VCAS.

CANBERRA SQUADRONS IN ORDER OF FORMATION

Squadron	Where formed	Date	Previous Aircraft
No 101	Binbrook	May 51	Lincoln B.2
617	Binbrook	Jan 52	Lincoln B.2
12	Binbrook	Mar 52	Lincoln B.2
9	Binbrook	May 52	Lincoln B.2
109	Hemswell	Aug 52	Mosquito B.35
50	Binbrook	Aug 52	Lincoln B.2
540(PR)	Benson	Dec 52	Mosquito Mk 34A
10	Scampton	Jan 53	Dakota
149	Coningsby	Mar 53	B-29 Washington
44	Coningsby	Apr 53	B-29 Washington
57	Honington	May 53	B-29 Washington
15	Coningsby	May 53	B-29 Washington
27	Scampton	Jun 53	Dakota
18	Scampton	Aug 53	Dakota
21	Scampton	Sep 53	Mosquito VI
40	Coningsby	Oct 53	York
139	Hemswell	Oct 53	Mosquito B.35
76	Wittering	Dec 53	Dakota
58(PR)	Wyton	Dec 53	Mosquito PR.35
82(PR)	Wyton	Dec 53	Lancaster B.1
90	Marham	Jan 54	B-29 Washington
199	Hemswell	Jan 54	Lincoln/Mosquito
115	Marham	Feb 54	B-29 Washington B.1
207	Marham	Mar 54	B-29 Washington B.1
100	Wittering	Apr 54	Lincoln B.2
35	Marham	Apr 54	B-29 Washington B.1
61	Wittering	Jul 54	Lincoln
102	Gutersloh	Oct 54	Liberator VI/VIII
103	Gutersloh	Dec 54	Lancaster I/III
104	Gutersloh	Mar 55	Lancaster VII
213	Ahlhorn	Jul 55	Vampire
542	Wyton	Nov 55	Spitfire XIX
88	Wildenrath	Jan 56	Sunderland GR.5
59	Gutersloh	Aug 56	York
32	Akrotiri	Jan 57	Venom FB.1
73	Akrotiri	Mar 57	Venom FB.1
6	Akrotiri	Jul 57	Venom FB.4
249	Akrotiri	Aug 57	Venom FB.4
45	Changi	Dec 57	Venom FB.1
69(PR)	Laarbruch	May 54	Mosquito XVI
31(PR)	Laarbruch	May 55	Devon
80(PR)	Laarbruch	Jun 55	Hornet F.3/4
17(PR)	Wahn	Jun 56	Beaufighter TT.10

VICTOR SQUADRONS: AIRCRAFT AND COs

No	10	Cottesmore	B.1	Formed	1 May 58	Wg Cdr C B Owen
						DSO DFC AFC
					15 Feb 60	Wg Cdr R B Phillips DFC AFC
					29 Jan 62	Wg Cdr T C Gledhill AFC
					28 Feb 64	Farewell flypast as MB sqn
No	15	Cottesmore	B.1	Formed	1 Sep 58	Wg Cdr D A Green
						DSO OBE DFC
					1 Apr 60	Wg Cdr J G Matthews AFC
					1 Dec 62	Wg Cdr N G S Marshall
					30 Sep 64	Sqn withdrawn from 1st line –
					1 Oct 64	non-operational
No	57	Honington	B.1	Formed	13 Jan 59	Wg Cdr K C Giddings
						OBE DFC AFC
					19 May 60	Wg Cdr D G Bailey
					8 Jun 62	Wg Cdr J R Mason
					24 Jul 64	Wg Cdr R D A Smith DFC
					26 Nov 65	Final parade prior to move to
						Marham as tanker sqn
		Marham	B(K).1A		Dec 65	
No	55	Honington	B.1A		Oct 60	Wg Cdr R G Wilson DFC AFC
					18 Mar 63	Combined with No 57 Sqn to
						form a Victor Wing under the
						command of Wg Cdr J R
						Mason, No 55 Sqn becoming
						'A' Flt and No 57 Sqn 'B' Flt
					Jun 63	Wg Cdr A J Houston AFC
		Marham	B(K).1A		May 65	Moved to Marham in tanker
						role
No	139	Wittering	B.2		1 Feb 62	Wg Cdr B W Plenderleith MA
					18 Nov 63	Wg Cdr J G G Beddoes
					11 Oct 65	Wg Cdr D S Bell DFC AFC
					28 Oct 67	Wg Cdr F McClory
					31 Dec 68	Sqn disbanded
No	100	Wittering	B.2		1 May 62	Wg Cdr M M J Robinson
					19 Oct 64	Wg Cdr W J Harrington
					4 Jan 67	Wg Cdr H M Archer AFC
					27 Sep 68	Sqn disbanded
No	214	Marham	B(K).1/1A		1 Jul 66	Wg Cdr D Mullarkey MBE
					10 Jun 68	Wg Cdr C D Preece AFC
					Jun 70	Wg Cdr J R Tucker
					12 Jun 72	Wg Cdr A G Springsley
					5 Jul 74	Wg Cdr D Parry-Evans
					11 Jul 75	Wg Cdr J D Lomas
					24 Dec 76	Sqn Ldr G W Wagstaff
					28 Jan 77	Sqn disbanded

VALIANT SQUADRONS: AIRCRAFT AND COs

No 138   Wittering   B.1   W/C R G W Oakley DSO DFC DFM
                                    1955-57
                                    Wg Cdr S Baker DSO DFC 1957-60
                                    Wg Cdr H M Chinnery MVO AFC 1960-62
                                    (Sqn disbanded 1 April 1962)

No 543   Wyton   B(PR).1   Wg Cdr R E Havercroft AFC 1955-57
                                    Wg Cdr R Berry DSO OBE DFC 1957-59
                                    Wg Cdr C G St D Jefferies DFC 1959-62
                                    Wg Cdr B Hamilton OBE DFC AFC 1962-63
                                    Wg Cdr A W Tarry 1963-66
                                    Wg Cdr R H McV Redfern 1966-68
                                    Wg Cdr J A Worrall 1968-70
                                    Wg Cdr G Harper 1970-72
                                    Wg Cdr R F Mudge 1972-74
                                    (Sqn disbanded 24 May 1974)

No 214   Marham   B.1   Wg Cdr L H Trent VC DFC 1956-58
                                    Wg Cdr M J Beetham DFC 1958-60
                                    Wg Cdr P G Hill 1960-62
                                    Wg Cdr K Smith DFC 1962-64
                                    Wg Cdr P B MacCorkindale 1964-65
                                    (Sqn disbanded as a Valiant sqn 28 Feb
                                    1965)

No 49   Wittering   B.1   Sqn Ldr D Roberts DFC AFC 1956
                                    (May-Sep)
                                    Wg Cdr K G Hubbard OBE DFC 1956-58
                                    Wg Cdr R W Payne AFC 1958-61
                                    Wg Cdr A H Chamberlain AFC 1961-62
                                    Wg Cdr J Langston 1962-64
                                    Wg Cdr D J Corbet 1964-65
                                    Flt Lt B D Pettit (Mar-Apr 65)
                                    (Sqn disbanded 1 May 65)

No 207   Marham   B.1   Wg Cdr D D Haig DSO DFC 1956-57
                                    Wg Cdr C P N Newman OBE DFC 1957-59
                                    Wg Cdr W D Robertson 1959-61
                                    Wg Cdr W E Martin DFC AFC 1961-63
                                    Wg Cdr A D Dick AFC MA 1963/64
                                    Wg Cdr J F Stewart 1964-65
                                    Flt Lt B A Sherlock (Mar-Apr 65)
                                    Flt Lt M J A Bryett (Apr-May 65)
                                    (Sqn disbanded as a V-bomber sqn 28
                                    Apr 65)

No 148	Marham	B.1	Wg Cdr W J Burnett DSO DFC AFC 1956-57
			Wg Cdr F C D Wright DFC 1957-59
			Wg Cdr T Helfer DFC AFC 1959(Apr-May)
			Wg Cdr D C Lowe DFC AFC 1959-61
			Wg Cdr H K Rees 1961-63
			Wg Cdr D H Tew AFC 1963-65
			Flt Lt C V Taylor (Apr 65)
			(Sqn disbanded 28 April 65)
No 7	Honington	B.1	Nov 56 Wg Cdr A H Boxer DSO DFC
			17 Oct 57 Wg Cdr C D North-Lewis DSO DFC
			17 Nov 58 Wg Cdr B P Mugford
			17 Oct 60 Wg Cdr B L Partridge
			4 May 61 Wg Cdr J Wilson MBE
			1 Oct 62 Sqn disbanded

VULCAN SQUADRONS: AIRCRAFT AND COs

No 83	Waddington	B.1	Formed 21 May 57	Wg Cdr A D Frank DSO DFC
			Dec 57	Sqn Ldr D R Howard DFC AFC
			Feb 58	Wg Cdr L F Banks DFC AFC
			15 Aug 60	Wg Cdr R J Davenport
		(B.1s transferred wef 10 Aug 60 to re-equip No 44 Sqn, Waddington)		
	Scampton		Re-formed 10 Oct 60	
		B.2	First aircraft (XH563) arrived 23 Dec 60	
			17 Dec 62	Wg Cdr J A G Slessor
			Jun 65	Wg Cdr G L Bonny
			15 Aug 67	Wg Cdr J M Pack
			25 Jul 69	Sqn Ldr W A Mears
			31 Aug 69	squadron disbanded
No 101	Finningley	B.1	Formed 15 Oct 57	Wg Cdr A C L Mackie DFC
			Oct 59	Wg Cdr W J H Roberts
			17 Jun 61	sqn transferred to
				RAF Waddington
			15 Jan 62	Wg Cdr A Griffiths
		B.1A		
			3 Feb 64	Wg Cdr J D Upton
			19 Nov 64	Wg Cdr L C Spargo
			26 Nov 66	Wg Cdr D J Mountford AFC
		(First Mk 2 crews arrived, Mk 1A crews started to depart – Oct 67)		
		B.2		
			9 Aug 68	Wg Cdr G H Burleigh AFC
			21 Dec 70	Wg Cdr E H Macey
			14 Dec 71	Wg Cdr P A Hamill
			3 May 74	Wg Cdr J D N Hopkins
			10 May 76	Wg Cdr A A G Woodford
			13 Jun 78	Wg Cdr M V P H Harrington
			20 June 80	Wg Cdr W M Parker

No 617 Scampton B.1   Re-formed 1 May 58 Wg Cdr D Bower OBE AFC
                     7 May 60   Wg Cdr L G A Bastard AFC
       B.1/1A

	23 May 61	Wg Cdr B A Primavesi
		(OC-designate, 50 Sqn)
		(Wg Cdr Bastard att No 230 OCU, Finningley, 23 May–19 Jul)
	19 Jul 61	Wg Cdr L G A Bastard AFC

(B.1/1As allotted to No 50 Sqn, re-formed at Waddington 1 Aug 61)

B.2   First a/c collected from Woodford 1 Sep 61

	9 Nov 62	Wg Cdr H G Currell MVO DFC AFC
	22 March 65	Wg Cdr D G L Heywood
	23 March 67	Wg Cdr R C Allen
	14 March 69	Wg Cdr C A Vasey
	29 March 71	Wg Cdr F M A Hines
	22 Oct 73	Wg Cdr V L Warrington
	8 Sept 75	Wg Cdr R B Gilvary
	Jul 77	Wg Cdr F Mason (unable to retain command owing to ill-health)
		Wg Cdr J N Stephenson-Oliver
	Jul 79	Wg Cdr J N Herbertson
	31 Dec 81	Squadron disbanded

No 44 Waddington   Re-formed 10 Aug 60 Wg Cdr L F Banks DFC AFC
(On re-equipment of No 83 Sqn with B.2s, bulk of groundcrew and half the aircrew assumed the number 44)

	25 Oct 60	Wg Cdr J A G Jackson DFC AFC

B.1/1A

	1 Aug 62	Wg Cdr F R Lockyer
	21 Oct 64	Wg Cdr M A D'Arcy
	27 Jun 66	Wg Cdr V McNabney GM

1A+B.2 (first appears in ORB for Jan 67 – XJ823, which had been delivered to Nos 44/50/101 Sqns on 1 Nov 66)

	19 Jul 68	Wg Cdr W E Bliss

B.2 (last B.1A – XH475 – flown in Sept 67 on Akrotiri Lone Ranger)

	7 Jul 70	Wg Cdr M D Fenner
	16 Jun 72	Wg Cdr C M King
	29 May 74	Wg Cdr D Haller (temp)
	6 Sep 74	Wg Cdr D J Dawes
	20 Sep 76	Wg Cdr W A Mears
	Aug 78	Wg Cdr A C R Ingoldby
	12 Jul 80	Wg Cdr S A Baldwin MBE

No 27 Scampton   Re-formed 1 Apr 61, Wg Cdr V N Cramer
       B.2   First arrived 20 Apr 61

	20 Jun 63	Wg Cdr J Gingell MBE
	10 Jun 65	Wg Cdr K C D Nixon AFC
	27 May 67	Wg Cdr P J Goodall
	6 June 69	Wg Cdr J S Cresswell
	21 Jun 71	Wg Cdr I Fraser
	29 March 72	Disbandment parade

Reformed 1 Nov 73 in the Maritime Radar Reconnaissance Role – eventually to take over the role of Strategic Reconnaisance and Air Sampling from No 543 Sqn

No 50 Waddington

Re-formed 1 Aug 61 Wg Cdr B A Primavesi (Three B.1s – XH482, 497 and 499 – and one B.1A – XH506 – allocated to the sqn from 617 Sqn and flown into Waddington on 31 Jul. Two more a/c – XH498 and XH505 Mk 1A – flown in from Scampton on 1 Aug).

B.1A

1 Jul 63	Wg Cdr W J Stacey
14 Jun 65	Wg Cdr J F W Pembridge AFC

B.2 (first delivered to Waddington, 23 Dec 65; No 50 fully equipped with B.2s by July 66)

22 Jun 67	Wg Cdr M G Bradley AFC
28 Jul 69	Wg Cdr G T Smeaton
18 Dec 70	Wg Cdr D W Lowe
9 Apr 73	Wg Cdr A Parkes
4 Jul 75	Wg Cdr W Ward
1 Jul 77	Wg Cdr N B Baldwin
9 Jul 79	Wg Cdr T Garden
25 Jun 81	Wg Cdr C P Lumb

No 50 informed by AOC No 1 Group (AVM M W P Knight) on 18 Nov 81 that disbandment would take place on 30 Jun 82 along with that of Nos 44 and 101 Sqns

No 9 Coningsby B.2

Re-formed 1 Mch 62

1 Mch 62	Wg Cdr K Stevens
31 Mch 64	Wg Cdr C G Maughan AFC
20 Jul 64	Wg Cdr K J L Baker (killed in accident to Vulcan B.2 XM601 on 7 Oct 64 with all members of his crew)

Cottesmore

Nov 64	
17 Nov 64	Wg Cdr J E Pollington
17 Dec 66	Wg Cdr A M Christie
27 Jun 68	Wg Cdr J E Sewell MBE

Akrotiri

wef 26 Feb 69

19 Jun 70	Wg Cdr R Dick
19 Jun 72	Wg Cdr A Howie

Waddington

(after withdrawal from from Akrotiri, 9-24 Jan 75)

24 Jan 75	Wg Cdr B J Mather
29 Dec 76	Wg Cdr R E Turner
11 Dec 78	Wg Cdr J A Prideaux
19 Dec 80	Wg Cdr P W Mayes

No 12 Coningsby B.2

Re-formed 1 Jul 62 (First a/c, XH560, arrived 25 Sep 62)

1 Aug 62	Wg Cdr P J Lagesen DFC AFC
17 Jun 64	Wg Cdr J R Tanner
25 May 66	Wg Cdr D H Tew AFC
29 Dec 67	Final dining-in night held to mark the disbandment of No 12 as a Vulcan sqn

No 35 Coningsby		Re-formed 1 Dec 62 – sixth B.2 sqn in No 1 Group and
		third 'V' sqn to form at Coningsby
	5 Nov 62	W/C A A Smailes AFC
	16 Apr 63	W/C D B Craig
Cottesmore	2 Nov 64	
	1 Jun 65	W/C D A Arnott DFC
	19 Jun 67	W/C H S Carver MVO
Akrotiri	15 Jan 69	First five crews departed for
		(sqn posted wef 1 Jan 69)
	2 Sep 69	W/C R K Hepburn
	23 Aug 71	W/C J B Fitzpatrick
	18 Dec 72	W/C K I Watson
Scampton	16 & 23 Jan 75	(with subsequent detachments
		to Cyprus – Ex Forearm)
	Jun 75	W/C A T Atkinson
	Jun 77	W/C R Sweatman
	May 79	W/C I O Junor
	19 Jun 81	W/C N I Hamilton

THOR SQUADRONS: BASES AND COs

No 77 Sqn	Feltwell	Sqn Ldr	S O Baldock	Sep 58-Nov 61
			K Hayes	Sep 61-Jul 63
No 113 Sqn	Mepal	Sqn Ldr	P J Hearne	Jul 59-Jan 62
			P S Cockman	Feb 62-Jul 63
No 220 Sqn	North Pickenham	Sqn Ldr	F R Leatherdale	Jul 59-Feb 62
			R Henderson	Feb 62-Jul 63
No 82 Sqn	Shepherds Grove	Sqn Ldr	B J S Knight	Jul 59-Dec 60
			R Lingard	Jan 61-Sep 61
			W A Young	Oct 61-Jul 63
No 107 Sqn	Tuddenham	Sqn Ldr	P P Flood	Sep 59-Jan 61
			H G Norton	Feb 61-Jul 63
No 97 Sqn	Hemswell	Sqn Ldr	R Tate	Jul 59-Feb 61
			R K F Collyer	Mar 61-May 63
No 269 Sqn	Caistor	Sqn Ldr	T A Dicks	Sep 59-Jun 61
			P Edelsten	Jun 61-May 63
No 106 Sqn	Bardney	Sqn Ldr	R F Keatley	Jul 59-Feb 62
			T C Woods	Feb 62-May 63
No 104 Sqn	Ludford Magna	Sqn Ldr	D H Young	Jul 59-Dec 60
			B A Bourne	Jan 61- 63
No 142 Sqn	Coleby Grange	Sqn Ldr	W A Gill	Sep 59-Mar 61
			J W Abrey	Mar 61-Apr 63
		(Wg Cdr from 1 Jan 63)		
			E S Dodds	Apr 63-May 63
No 98 Sqn	Driffield	Sqn Ldr	P G Coulson	Nov 59-May 61
			S Hudson	Jun 61-Jun 63
No 150 Sqn	Carnaby	Sqn Ldr	E R G Haines	Aug 59-Feb 60
			D H Downs	Mar 60-Sep 61
			R G Milton	Sep 61-Apr 63
No 226 Sqn	Catfoss	Sqn Ldr	E R Morriss	Nov 59-May 61
			P I Hart	Jun 61-Jan 63
		(Last F 540)		
No 240 Sqn	Breighton	Sqn Ldr	R W Steel	Aug 59-Jul 61
			L E A Hacke	Jul 61-Jan 63
No 102 Sqn	Full Sutton	Sqn Ldr	L A Baldchin	Nov 59-Dec 61
			J Slater	Jan 62-Apr 63
No 144 Sqn	North Luffenham	Sqn Ldr	W J Hibbert	Feb 60-Nov 61
			R A Hale	Nov 61-Aug 63
No 223 Sqn	Folkingham	Sqn Ldr	F W Lister	Feb 60-Nov 61
			C M Bruce	Nov 61-Aug 63
No 130 Sqn	Polebrook	Sqn Ldr	W J Hibbert	Dec 59-Feb 60
			D S Lister	Feb 60-Aug 61
			H Millar	Sep 61-Aug 63
No 218 Sqn	Harrington	Sqn Ldr	J C Burch	Dec 59-Nov 61
			F W Slaughter	Dec 61-Aug 63
No 254 Sqn	Melton Mowbray	Sqn Ldr	D E Liddle	Dec 59-Aug 61
			E W Beer	Aug 61-Nov 61
			D A Bailey	Nov 61-Feb 63

NUCLEAR TESTS IN WHICH THE RAF WERE INVOLVED

Test	Date	Type of Warhead and of Burst	RAF Participation/Personnel
Operation Hurricane Monte Bello Islands	2 Oct 52	Kiloton; under water (in HMS *Plym*)	Wg Cdr J S Rowlands, Sqn Ldr P E Mitchell Sunderland (No 88 Sqn)
Operation Totem Emu Airfield (SW of Woomera,	Oct 53	Kiloton; on top of 100ft tower	Canberra for radiation sampling (Wg Cdr G H Dhenin and Gp Capt D A Wilson): a/c specially modified
Operation Mosaic Monte Bello	Jan-Jun 56	Tower detonations	Canberra B.6 (No 76 Sqn); Shackletons (No 269 Sqn): Varsities: air communications; air transport support; obtaining scientific information. Two Hastings (No 53 Sqn)
Operation Buffalo Maralinga	Jul-Nov 56	Kiloton (Blue Danube round); first trial to include an air drop (11 Oct 56)	Valiants (No 49 Sqn); Canberra B.6s (No 76 Sqn); Hastings (Nos 24 and 53 Sqns)
Operation Grapple Christmas Island	May-Jun 57	Megaton; air drops (15 and 31 May and 19 Jun)	Valiants (No 49 Sqn); Canberra B.6s (No 76 Sqn); Canberra PR.7s (No 100 Sqn and No 58 Sqn); Shackletons (No 240 Sqn); Hastings (Nos 24, 99 and 511 Sqns)
Operation Antler Maralinga	Aug-Oct 57	Kiloton weapon bursts – two on towers, one suspended from balloons (for the first time)	Valiants (No 543 Sqn); Canberra B.6s (No 76 Sqn); Varsities and Whirlwinds (No 1439 Flt); Shackletons (No 204 Sqn); Hastings (Nos 99 and 511 Sqns)
Operation Grapple X	Oct-Nov 57	Fourth drop of nuclear device in the megaton weapon range	Valiants (No 49 Sqn); Canberras (Nos 58 and 76 Sqns); Hastings (Nos 24, 99 and 511 Sqns)
Operation Grapple Y	Apr-May 58	Megaton weapon drop from Valiant	Valiants (No 49 Sqn); Canberras (Nos 58 and 76 Sqns); Shackletons (No 240 Sqn); Whirlwinds (No 217 Sqn); Hastings (Nos 24, 99 and 511 Sqns)
Operation Grapple Z	Aug-Sep 58	UK megaton weapon trials completed – two drops from Valiants, two balloon-suspended rounds	Valiants (No 49 Sqn); Canberras (Nos 58 and 76 Sqns); Shackletons (Nos 204 and 269 Sqns); Whirlwinds (No 217 Sqn); Hastings (Nos 24, 99 and 511 Sqns); and a Varsity Flt

NUCLEAR WEAPONS CARRIED BY THE
CANBERRAS AND V-BOMBERS

	Date	*Type*
Canberra B(I).8	1960-66	US Mk 7
	1966-	US Mk 43
Canberra B.15/16	1960-	Red Beard (1,750lb/15kt)
Valiant (MBF)		Blue Danube
		Red Beard
Valiant (TBF)		US Mk 28
	1963-	US Mk 43
Vulcan B.1/1A		Blue Danube and Violet Club (1958-59)
	1960-63	Yellow Sun Mk 1 7,000lb/½mt)
		interim megaton wpn 11,000lb/½mt
	1961-66	Yellow Sun Mk 2 7,250lb/1mt)
Vulcan B.2	1963-70	Blue Steel (Red Snow warhead)
		Yellow Sun Mk 2
		WE.177B 950lb retarded low-level
Victor B.1/1A		Blue Danube
	1960-63	Yellow Sun Mk 1
	1961-66	Yellow Sun Mk 2
Victor B.2	1964-68	Blue Steel (Red Snow warhead)

US NUCLEAR WEAPONS SUPPLIED UNDER PROJECT 'E' AND THE THOR AGREEMENTS

Date	Weapon	Weight	Yield†	Aircraft	Remarks
Oct 58	Mk 5	6,000lb MC		Valiant	To be replaced by Mk 15/39*
	Mk 5 Mod 3				
	Mk 7	1,650lb		Canberra	Free-fall or loft delivery
	Mk 15/39*				
	Mod 0 & 2	7,500lb		Valiant	
	Mod 0	6,700lb			
	Mod 1	6,600lb			
	Mk 28	1,900lb HC		Valiant	Replaced by Mk 43
	Mk 43	2,100lb HC		Canberra	Dual carriage
				Valiant	Dual carriage
Nov 58	Thor	110,000lb at launch	1 Mt		IRBM

†Confirmation or amendment of yield figures was sought before publication from the US authorities, whose view was that they were still Confidential.

CODE NAMES/WORDS

Exercise Alpine	An exercise controlled by No 1 Group (1965)
Exercise Ardent	Annual air defence exercise
Exercise Billion	A new (1965) Group exercise on which aircraft scrambled on orders from the Group Commander
Exercise Bomex	Group exercise
Exercise Buckboard	Nato air defence exercise
Exercise Chamfron	Far East reinforcement (known as Spherical from Nov 64)
Exercise Co-op	Nato air defence exercise involving high/low penetration of Continental air defences
Exercise Dividend	Major UK air defence exercise for 1954
Exercise Edom	Bomber Command no-notice exercise, first held 21 June 62 (called at any hour of the day or night)
Exercise Full Play	Annual major Bomber Command exercise, 1958: attacks of Continental targets; RBS attack of simulated UK target: "penetration of Western and Northern European defence areas . . . interception with fighter aircraft"
Exercise Kingpin	Monthly exercise directed by Command
Exercise Kinsman	"Designed to familiarise air and ground crews with their MBF dispersal areas" (No 617 Sqn ORB, Nov 63: Scampton-Burtonwood)
Exercise Matterhorn	MBF Far East detachment, 1966
Exercise Mandate	Major UK air defence exercise for 1959
Exercise Mayflight	Dispersal, alert and readiness, scramble (described in a Minute of 6 Jun 61 as "virtually a pre-planned Mick plus the actual dispersing of aircraft")
Exercise Mayflower III	Annual full-scale alert and readiness exercise (1960)
Exercise Mick	To practise aircrews and Ops staff in Alert and Readiness procedures (to test ability to generate aircraft and weapons on main bases)
Exercise Micky Finn	Annual no-notice dispersal exercise to test readiness capability (dispersal supported by all Home Commands)
Exercise Maenad	Annual Bomber Command low-level exercise (1964-)
Exercise Momentum	Annual air defence exercise
Exercise Orpen	Autumn defence exercise (1957)
Exercise Phoenix	Autumn defence exercise (1957)
Exercise Profiteer	Vulcan detachments to the Far East
Exercise Respond	Called for the generation of the Thor Force
Exercise Strike Back	Autumn defence exercise (1957)
Exercise Sunray	Shallufa, Egypt, detachment (1953)
Exercise Sunspot	Luqa, Malta detachment
Exercise Tiffow	To give crews realistic experience of what a possible operational sortie might contain
Exercise Topweight	Saceur exercise (theatrewide atomic/air defence exercise for 1959)
Exercise Whipsaw	SHAPE atomic exercise
Exercise Yeoman	Major Command exercise involving simulated NBS attacks on Continental targets and penetration of UK air defences

Operation Bold	Anti-terrorists, Malaya
Operation Hydraulic	First in-flight refuelling of Lightnings to FEAF (1967)
Operation Musgrave	Anti-terrorists, Malaya
Operation Sapphire	Atomic weapons trial, Australia
Operation Tornado	Reinforcement of MEAF (No 7 Sqn – Jul-Aug 58)
Blue Ranger	Blue Steel-carrying flights to No 18 JSTU at Edinburgh Field, Adelaide, for trials over the Woomera range: 18 missiles eventually delivered by Scampton Vulcans
Blue Shadow	A sideways-looking search radar
Green Satin	A self-contained navigation aid, giving continuous information on track, groundspeed and distance flown; measurement of drift and groundspeed
Orange Harvest	Passive radar search equipment for use in the maritime role
Orange Putter	Tail warning equipment (primary tail warning radar)
Red Neck	High-resolution radar reconnaissance system to OR3595: mounted in pods and fitted to wings by underwing tank attachments
Red Steer	Tail warning equipment for B.2 Vulcan and Victor (replacement for Orange Putter)

APPENDIX No 11

OPERATIONAL REQUIREMENTS ASSOCIATED WITH THE V-FORCE

OR No 229	Medium-range bomber 17 Dec 1946
OR No 1001	Atomic bomb (Blue Danube) 9 Aug 1946
OR No 1139	MRBM (Blue Streak) 9 Jun 1953
OR No 1132	Guided bomb (Blue Steel) 3 Sep 1954
ASR No 1136	Thermonuclear bomb (Yellow Sun) 6 Jun 1955
OR No 1142	Megaton warhead for Blue Streak 22 Jul 1955
OR No 1141	Megaton warhead for Blue Steel Jan 1956
OR No 1159	Extended-range air-to-surface guided missile 3 Feb 1958
OR No 1160	Megaton warhead for air-to-surface GM to OR No 1159 11 Jun 1958
OR No 1168	Advanced Tactical Air-to-surface Guided Weapon 14 Aug 62
OR No 3508	Warning device to indicate the approach of aircraft or missiles 1949
OR No 3510	Tail-warning device in bomber aircraft 1949
OR No 1089	Control of Bombs – Television
OR No 3509	H2S Mk 9 (early version of H2S Mk 9A for V-bombers)
OR No 3518	Centimetric radar jammer
OR No 3520	VHF communications jammer
OR No 3521	Metric radar jammer
OR No 3595	High resolution radar for RAF reconnaissance
OR No 5005	Prototype heavy tractor for use with the V-bombers
OR No 5072	Ring-mains conversion unit (converting mains power into forms required for servicing and starting V-bombers)
ASR No 2110	Bomb Plotting Radar
OR No 1081	Bomb-hoisting systems
AR No 2113	Electronic Plotting Table
ASR No 3580	Electronic Positioning System for Flight Refuelling 15 Apr 55
OR No 223	PR version of the B.3/45 High Speed Bomber
OR No 244	Trainer version of the B.3/45
ASR No 1187	Agreement to co-operate in the development of the Skybolt weapon system. Issued 26 Apr 61; re-issued 29 Aug 62; cancelled 22 Feb 63
ASR No 1182	Long-range air-to-surface missile
ASR No 1177	Low-yield Lay-down Bomb
ASR No 1132	Issue 4 – Changes to Blue Steel – low-level launch

APPENDIX No 12

CHRONOLOGY

Political and International Events

1944

Nov 7   Chiefs of Staff (COS) instructed Joint Technical Warfare Committee (JTWC) to carry out investigation into future developments in weapons of war.

1945

May 8   German surrender came into effect.

12   Churchill's "Iron Curtain" telegram to Truman.

Jun 26   United Nations' Charter signed in San Francisco by 50 countries.

Jul 3   Report of Tizard Committee on Future Developments in Weapons and Methods of War.

5   General Election – Labour returned to power
25/26   results announced.

16   First atomic device (containing plutonium) detonated at Alamogordo, New Mexico.

Aug 6   Atomic bomb dropped on Hiroshima.

	9	Atomic bomb (plutonium type) dropped on Nagasaki.
	21	Attlee announces formation of Advisory Committee on Atomic Energy (ACAE) with Sir John Anderson as chairman.
	28	Attlee Memorandum on atomic bomb circulated to senior ministers.
Sep	10	Chadwick sends telegram from USA saying military applications of atomic energy made production plant of our own essential for defence of UK and Commonwealth.
	20	COS instruct JTWC to carry out revision of Tizard Report following dropping of atomic bombs.
Oct	10	COS minute to PM recommending production of A-bomb.
	12	Tizard memorandum advocating appointment of Scientific Adviser.
	16	Gen 75/5th meeting asks for a report by Officials.
	26	COS meeting expresses itself in general agreement with Tizard memorandum.

	29	Attlee tells Commons that a research and development establishment is to be set up at Harwell to engage in research on all aspects of atomic energy. Report by Officials recommends production of atomic bomb.
Nov	1	Gen 75/7th meeting considers Report by Officials.
Dec	10	ACAE Report on Large-Scale Production.
	18	Building of one pile to produce plutonium in UK approved by Gen 75 group of ministers.
1946		
Jan	1	COS report to PM recommending a stock of atomic bombs.
	29	Attlee announces formation of production organisation at Risley to manufacture fissile materials, and the appointments of Cockroft and Portal.
Mar	5	Churchill's "Iron Curtain" speech at Fulton, Mo.
	21	Strategic Air Command (SAC), USAF, created.
May	1	Atomic Energy Bill published.

		SAC given responsibility for delivery of atomic weapons against an enemy.
		Third Draft Air Staff Requirement (ASR) for a long range bomber circulated by DOR (A).
Jul	1	Fourth atomic bomb explosion – Bikini Atoll, dropped from B-29.
	5	Cabinet Defence Committee agreed to setting up of Committee on Defence Research Policy.
	8	Report by COS on Future Developments in Weapons and Methods of War.
	25	Fifth atomic bomb explosion – first under water crater.
Aug	1	McMahon Act signed by US President. Atomic Energy (Official) Committee set up.
	9	ASR (OR1001) issued for an atomic bomb, to be suitable for carriage in bombers whose requirements were stated in 1946 (B.35/46, B.14/46 and OR229/230).
Sep	25	Official Committee on Atomic Energy holds first meeting.

Oct	5	UK Government proposal to create Ministry of Defence announced.
Nov	1	Penney sends Portal proposals for atomic weapon development.
	6	Atomic Energy Act "to provide for the development of atomic energy and the control of such development and for purposes connected therewith."
	7	Draft OR229 for a medium range bomber circulated: speed 500kt; height at target 45,000 ft; radius of action 1,500 nm.
17 Dec		Operational Requirements Committee for OR229 held—and for OR230 for a long-range bomber.
1947		During 1947 HMG and COS adopted for planning purposes the assumption that a Russian attack might come in 1957.
7 Jan		Approved OR 229 issued.
	8	Decision by meeting of Gen 163 Cttee Ministers to develop atomic bomb.

	24	MoS Spec B.35/46 issued.
	24	English Electric, Handley Page, Avro and Armstrong Whitworth invited to tender for the supply of prototypes to B.35/46.
Mar		Text of Yalta and Potsdam Agreements published.
Mar		Foreign Ministers meet in Moscow to discuss drafting of peace treaties with Germany and Austria.
Apr		End of Moscow Conference.
May		Dr Penney told of January 8th decision and to go ahead.
Jun	5	Marshall Plan initiated (European Recovery Programme).
Jul		Marshall Plan Conference in Paris.

28	Tender Design Conference on B.35/46 held at MoS: decided to order the Avro design and that the RAE should undertake high-speed wind tunnel tests on the HP crescent-wing design.
30	Report by Defence Research Policy Committee on "Future Defence Research Policy" published.
Sep 8	Air Council considers four types of bomber R & D projects.
Oct 14	Major Charles E Yeager USAF becomes first pilot to fly supersonically (in Bell X-1).
Nov 19	Victor (HP80) prototype contract (MoS sends HP "Intention to Proceed" (ITP) contract for two aircraft).
27	Agreed that ITP should be issued to A V Roe to cover design of B.35/46 and flying model.
Dec 17	Prototype B-47 (six GE J35s) makes first flight.
1948	
Jan	Vulcan prototype contract for two aircraft.
3	First draft of second issue of OR229 specification circulated.

Feb 22	Communist coup d'état in Prague.
25	Second draft of second issue of OR 229 specification circulated.
Mar 4	Discussions opened in Brussels. Western Union Treaty between Britain, France, Belgium, The Netherlands and Luxembourg.
17	Five-power Treaty signed at Brussels providing for collective self-defence.
3 Apr	CAS Note on "Modernisation of the Strategic Bomber Force".
5	Collision between BEA Viking and Soviet Yak fighter over Berlin – 15 people killed including the pilot of the Yak.
14	COS accept basic assumption that USSR and her satellites the potential enemy.
16	Valiant ITP issued: intention to build two prototypes.

	30	Brussels Treaty Defence Ministers and Chiefs of Staff meet in London to study military equipment needs.
May	12	Minister of Defence (A V Alexander) said in answer to a Parliamentary Question that "all types of weapons, including atomic weapons" were being developed.
1 June		Final published version of OR229 specification circulated.
June	10	Second issue of Specification B.35/46.
	14	COS agreed that the RAF should proceed with training in handling and storing atomic weapons.
	24	Russians stop rail traffic on Berlin-Helmstedt line on pretext of "technical troubles". This action followed the Russian walk-out from the Allied Kommandatur and the delivery of US, British and French Notes of Protest on interruption of communications between Berlin and the West.
	25	Eight Dakotas dispatched to BAFO.

	28	Dakota force augmented by a further eight and airlift by RAF to West Berlin begun (Operation Knicker – subsequently Plainfare).
July	7	Olympic Games opened in London. B.35/46 preliminary mock-up conference at A V Roe.
	16	Air Ministry and United States Embassy in London announce that USAF B-29s had left their bases in America for Britain. During July and August three USAF bomber groups, each of 30 B-29s, arrived and were located at Lakenheath, Marham, Scampton and Waddington.
	19	Spec B.9/48 issued by MoS.
Aug	24	Advisory Design Conference on the A V Roe version of the B.35/46.
Sep	3-5	Exercise "Dagger", first full-scale UK air defence exercise since end of the Second World War, included USAF B-29s.
		During September a military body was created within the Brussels Treaty known as the Western Union Defence Organisation (Field Marshal Montgomery appointed Chairman of Commanders-in-Chief Committee with Head-quarters at Fontainebleau).

Oct 19	General Curtis Le May assumed command of SAC.
Nov	Harry S Truman elected US President.
9	HQ SAC opened at new location, Offutt AFB, Omaha, Neb.
12	CAS wrote to Head of Air Force Staff, BJSM (USA) to ask him to sound out possibility of obtaining some B-29s for the RAF.
22	First meeting of Herod Committee.
1949	
Jan	Atomic energy programme expanded by addition of third pile and low separation plant.
Apr 4	North Atlantic Treaty signed in Washington (Brussels Treaty Powers and Canada, United States, Denmark, Iceland, Italy, Norway and Portugal. Subsequently three other countries invited to join Alliance – Greece and Turkey in September 1951 who acceded to the Treaty on 18 February 1952 and the Federal Republic of Germany in October 1954 who became a member officially on 9 May 1955.

Decision to take up to 300 NS men a year for pilot training.

May	12	Berlin blockade lifted at 0001hr: phased reduction in Operation Plainfare followed.
	13	First Canberra prototype (B.3/45) flies.
Jun-Jul	25–3	Second full-scale Air Defence Exercise to be held since Second World War; personnel of Western Union Air Forces participated for the first time.
Aug	1	First mock-up conference on Avro B.35/46.
	24	North Atlantic Treaty came into force.
	29	First nuclear explosion by Soviets near Semipalatinsk.
Sep	17	First meeting of North Atlantic Council in Washington.
	20	PM states that R & D on atomic weapons and means of delivery are all "projects to which I attach the highest importance."
Oct		B.14/46 (Shorts) cancelled.

587

6   Last RAF aircraft on Berlin Airlift arrives at Gatow – with a cargo of coal.

1950

22 Mar   First Washington (B-29) allotted to RAF arrives in Britain.

Apr 1   Aldermaston taken over for atomic weapons development.

10 Apr   RAF instructors complete conversion course, held by USAF, on B-29 aircraft.

13   No 115/218 Sqn re-formed at Marham for training on B-29s.

25   North Korean forces cross 38th Parallel and invade South Korea.

26   United Nations Security Council meets and orders a cease fire in Korea.

27   President Truman announces "cover and support" for South Korea and orders USAF to assist.

Jul 1	US land forces committed to defence of South Korea.
8	General McArthur appointed Commanding General UN Forces in Korea.
9 Jul	Two Sunderlands of No 88 Sqn flown to Iwakuni, Japan.
10 Aug	First RAF Washington squadron (No 115) completed conversion training.
1 Sep	First RAF Washington squadron formed.
5	Further squadron of Sunderlands requested: No 209 Sqn moved from Seletar to Iwakuni.
Sep 12	HMG announces three-year £3,600m defence programme. (This was later raised to £4,700m).
13/14	Second preliminary mock-up conference on Avro B.35/46.
15	NATO Council, meeting in New York, decided that an integrated force should be created for the defence of NATO European countries and placed under a Supreme Commander.

	Oct 27	Intervention of Chinese troops in Korea reported.
	Nov 8	First jet v jet fighter battle – F-80s v MiG 15s in Korea.
Second RAF Washington squadron formed.	15	
Bomber Command jet conversion flight formed at RAF Binbrook.	Dec	
	17	First MiG 15 shot down by USAF F-86A Sabre in Korea.
	18	Approval by North Atlantic Council of report on Germany's contribution to Western defence, and of creation of an integrated force for Western Europe.
	19	Appointment of General Eisenhower as Supreme Commander NATO.
	20	Merging of military side of Western Union in North Atlantic Treaty Organisation.
	28	COS agreed that an order for 25 B.9/48s should be placed because it was "strategically necessary" to accelerate production of these aircraft.

591

1951

Jan 8 — Production order for 25 B.9/48 Valiants approved by Minister of Defence.

10 — Joint War Production Committee decided "way was clear" to place this order with Vickers.

27 — PM tells Commons production order placed for first British four-engined jet bomber.

Feb 1 — Third RAF Washington squadron formed.

9 — Vickers receive production order for 25 B.9/48s from MOS: estimated cost £8m, with delivery to begin in 1953.

Apr 2 — General Eisenhower assumes command of Allied Armies in Europe.

7 — New plan ('H') for expanding RAF issued.

11 — President Truman announces dismissal of General McArthur as Supreme Commander, Allied Powers and C in C UN Command, Korea.

May	18	Prototype Vickers 660 (built to B.9/48 specification) flew for the first time from Wisley: trials continued at Hurn. Australian Government formally agreed to use of Monte Bello as nuclear test site.
	25	B-47s entered service with SAC, USAF.

First Canberra bomber arrived at RAF Binbrook.

Aug		B-29 crews from Bomber Command took part in SAC Bombing Competition held at MacDill AFB, Fla.
	10	Short SA.4 VX158 (built to B.14/46 Specification) makes first flight from Aldergrove.
Oct	24	Russian nuclear explosion.
Oct	23	B-47 first makes its appearance with 306th Bomb Wing, Col M N W McCoy flying the first operational aircraft from Boeing to MacDill AFB.
	25	General Election in United Kingdom.
	27	Formation of Conservative Government by Mr Winston Churchill.

1	Dec	No 231 OCU re-formed at RAF Bassingbourn for Canberra training.
1952 Jan		Valiant deployment and dispersal plans discussed by Air Council.
12		Valiant prototype crashed: crew escaped but co-pilot killed.
Feb		PM informs Parliament of plans to test an atomic bomb at Monte Bello.
Apr		PM directs COS to make a fundamental strategic review: they produced a Global Strategy Paper which propounded the doctrine of nuclear deterrence. First flight of second Valiant prototype.
May		No 231 (Canberra) OCU opened at RAF Bassingbourn.
Jun 12		Cabinet agrees to orders being placed for 50 B.35s subject to Treasury approval.
Jul 9		Defence Committee approves COS Report on Defence Policy and Global Strategy.
22		First Victor and Vulcan production contracts: first B.1s to be delivered in 1955.

593

Aug	6	Avro B.35/46 first prototype pre-flight conference.
	30	Avro Type 698 (Vulcan) flies for first time: subsequently appears at SBAC Show at Farnborough in September.
Oct	2	Air Council decides that the A V Roe version of the B.35/46 should be named Vulcan. At this meeting CAS referred to his "inclination . . . to establish a 'V' class of medium jet bombers".
	3	First British atomic test, Monte Bello Islands, directed by Dr William Penney (Operation Hurricane).
	12-18	Bomber Command Washingtons participated in SAC Bombing and Navigation Competition at Davis Monthan AFB.
	20	Four No 12 Sqn Canberras and two supporting Hastings left Binbrook on a 24,000 mile Goodwill Tour of South America led by AOC No 1 Group (AVM D A Boyle).
	23	PM announces first British atomic explosion.

Oct	31	First thermonuclear explosion – at surface level: US experimental device exploded at Eniwetok – 10 Mt, equal to 1,000 times the size of Hiroshima bomb "but very far from being a practical deliverable weapon."
Nov	1	
	4	Polling for President of the United States and election of Mr Eisenhower.
	15	US explodes thermonuclear weapon experimentally at Eniwetok (airburst): deuterium-tritium bomb.
Dec	4	Announcement of cutback in UK fighter production.
	5	Air Council agreed on the name Victor for the Handley Page B.35/46.
	24	Handley Page HP80 (Victor) prototype flies for first time.
1953		
Jan	5	Canberras of No 12 Sqn return to UK from tour of South America.
	28-29	Vulcan B Mk 1 inspected for final mock-up conference.
Mar	1	Run-down of RAF Washington force begins.

595

Jun	9	ORC discusses and agrees text of OR 1139 (Blue Streak).
Jul	7	Return of 35 Washingtons to the USA begins.
	10	General Gruenther succeeds General Ridgway as Supreme Commander, Allied Forces, Europe.
	27	Signature at Panmunjon of Armistice Agreement in Korea.
Aug	1	Bomber Command Armament School (BCAS) formed at RAF Wittering.
	12	First Soviet thermonuclear detonation: lithium 6 deuterium bomb.
Sep	3	Second prototype Vulcan (Olympus 100s) made first flight from Woodford.
	9	ACAS (OR) describes development of Victor and Vulcan as "very, very slow."
Nov	7 & 14	First production model atomic bombs delivered to RAF (by No 42 Group from AWRE to BCAS).

Dec	8	President Eisenhower's proposals, before UN General Assembly, for the international control of atomic energy.
	21	First production Valiant flew.
1954		
Feb	18	Statement on Defence includes the words: "We intend as soon as possible to build up in the Royal Air Force a force of medium bombers capable of using the atomic weapon to the fullest effect...The Royal Air Force has major deterrent role....Atomic weapons are in production in this country and delivery to the forces has begun".
Mar	1	US explodes thermonuclear weapon in Marshall Islands: lithium 6 deuteride bomb (experimental device: Bikini: surface, Feb 28). The Bravo test, yielding 15Mt, was "in a form readily adaptable for delivery by aircraft." Authority given for opening up party to take over RAF Gaydon as a station in No 3 Gp.
	26	Second US thermonuclear weapon explosion.
	30	PM's statement in Parliament about the hydrogen bomb.
	31	Last Washington (B-29) leaves for USA.

Jun	16/24	Cabinet Committee on Defence Policy considers a minute by MoS and memoranda by the Chiefs of Staff on Hydrogen Bomb Research and Production and on Defence Policy in the light of the development of the H-bomb: authorised H-bomb production programme.
		Orders placed for a further 32 Victors and 32 Vulcans, bringing the number of each type on order to 57.
Jul	8 & 26	After discussions at two meetings the Cabinet authorised the production of thermonuclear bombs in the UK.
	15	Draft ASR for thermonuclear bomb (OR 1136) circulated.
Aug	3	No 1321 Flight formed at RAF Wittering for the purpose of conducting special trials on the Valiant on behalf of MoS.
Sep	3	Operational requirement for Blue Steel Mk I (ASR OR1132) issued by Air Staff. To be in service by 1960.
Nov		MoS accepted OR for Blue Steel.

18/20	Nov	Air Council considers implications of setting-up the medium bomber force.
1	Dec	Churchill in Commons said that "the advance of the hydrogen bomb has fundamentally altered the entire problem of defence".
	1955	
1	Jan	No 138 Sqn (8 UE Valiant B.1s) authorised to form at RAF Gaydon.
13		Valiant B.1 C(A) Release for Service, clearing the aircraft for use in temperate climates, day flying only.
8		First Valiant B.1 flown from Wisley to Gaydon by CO No 138 Sqn (Wg Cdr R G W Oakley).
17	Feb	Statement on Defence says Britain proceeding with development and production of thermo-nuclear (hydrogen) bombs.
1	Apr	No 543 Sqn (four UE Valiants B/PR) formed at Gaydon.

6   COS decision to develop as first priority a megaton weapon with yield of about 1Mt.

May 2   Orders for further 50 V-bombers approved by Cabinet Defence Committee.

9   Formal admission of Federal Germany as a member of NATO.

14   Signature of Eastern Security Treaty (Warsaw Pact) between USSR and the seven Eastern European satellite states.

26   General Election in United Kingdom. Conservative majority returned.

6 Jun   ASR No 1136 for thermonuclear bomb issued (Yellow Sun Mk1).

15   US-UK Agreement for Co-operation Regarding Atomic Information for Mutual Defence Purposes.

29   First B-52 delivered to the 93rd Bomb Wing, Castle AFB, Calf.

4	Jul	No 232 Operational Conversion Unit – first V-force OCU – formed at Gaydon.
22	Jul	OR 1142 issued for megaton warhead for Blue Streak.
28		MoS accepted OR 1136 requirement (warhead for Blue Steel and Yellow Sun).
29		Valiant WP222 of No 138 Sqn crashed at Wittering killing all four crew members.
8	Aug	ASR OR1139 issued for medium range Ballistic Missile (Blue Streak): to be complementary to the bomber force; to have 2000-2500nm range.
5	Sep	Two Valiant B.1s of No 138 Sqn leave UK on proving flight to Far East.
5-11	Sep	RAF Valiants fly in SBAC Farnborough Display.
26		Valiants of No 138 Sqn leave New Zealand on return from proving flight.
	Nov	Survey visit to Christmas Island began.
6	Nov	Russian nuclear explosion—probable air burst giving output of "hundreds" of kilotons at the usual proving ground near Semipalatinsk.

	22	Largest Soviet explosion so far, above one megaton, burst 5,000 ft above Semipalatinsk.
1956		
Jan		Blue Steel accepted as a requirement; also megaton warhead installation (OR1141).
Mar	9	Development contract awarded to A V Roe for Blue Steel missile (ASR No 1132).
	16	Russian nuclear explosion with output of around 40 Kt.
1 May		No. 49 Sqn re-formed at RAF Wittering to carry out 'F' Series trials.
7 May		Air Staff Target AST 1149 issued calling for flying bomb with 1000-mile range.
	20	First air drop by US of a thermonuclear weapon (burst height 4,320 ft).

Date	Event	Event
	ACAS (OR) signed the Service release for the Vulcan, clearing it for speeds up to M0.98 and flying at up to 167,000lb auw.	
31		Meeting of Ministers (Gen 514/2nd Mtg) decided that Mk 2 version of V-bombers should be developed.
Jun 7		Prime Minister announced in House of Commons that thermonuclear tests would take place in 1957.
19		Third series of British tests of atomic weapons completed in Monte Bello Islands – firing of two tower burst weapons (Operation Mosaic).
Aug	IFT and Operational Reliability Trials with Vulcan begin at Boscombe Down.	
Aug 15-16		RAF/USAF meeting at Air Ministry on co-ordination of atomic strike plans.
Sep 12-19		Final installation conference on Victor B.1 at Radlett.
27		Round 1 fired successfully in Operation Buffalo at Maralinga.
1 Oct	Vulcan accident at LAP on return from Australia: as a result minimum approach height limitation was made 450 ft.	
11		First British atomic bomb dropped at Maralinga, South Australia, in Operation Buffalo tests by a Valiant of No 49 Sqn.
Oct 31-Nov 6		Anglo-French operations against Egypt.

603

31 Oct — Canberra B.2 of No 10 Sqn first aircraft to drop bombs on Almaza airfield. First Valiant to drop bombs XD 815 of 148 Sqn.

Nov — First draft ASR for multi-megaton bomb.

Proposed ASR for Canberra replacement circulated within Air Ministry, for a "tactical strike/reconnaissance aircraft capable of supporting a tactical offensive (possibly nuclear) in limited or global war, to succeed the Canberra…"

Dec 12 — USAF CoS writes to RAF CAS about US agreement in principle to furnishing RAF with atomic weapons in time of war, and to co-ordinated atomic strike plans.

1957

Jan 10 — Mr Harold Macmillan became UK Prime Minister.

18 Jan — No. 230 OCU had its first Vulcans (XA 895 and XA 897) available for flying from RAF Waddington.

Feb	1	US Defense Secretary agrees to authorising discussions on RAF being furnished with US atomic bombs in event of general war, and on co-ordination of USAF/RAF atomic strike plans.
Mar	5	RAF/USAF discussions on co-ordination of atomic strike plans.
		Cabinet decides that additional orders should be placed to provide for a force of 120 Mk 2 Victors and Valiants.
	26	GOR No 339 issued to MoS.
Apr	4	UK Government decides not to go on with development of supersonic manned bomber.
May	15	First British hydrogen (thermonuclear) bomb dropped at Christmas Island.
	21	USAF/RAF Memorandum of Understanding on supply of atomic weapons and co-ordination of atomic strike plans.
		First Vulcan squadron (No 83 Sqn – four B.1s on loan from No 230 OCU) formed at Waddington.
	25-27	Valiants participated for first time in major UK air defence exercise (Exercise Vigilant).

	30	Meeting of Ministers agrees that AM and MoS should be authorised to place firm order for further 42 B.2 V-bombers, giving planned front-line strength of 184.
	31	Second megaton weapon dropped at Christmas Island (Orange Herald).
Jun	19	Third and final test weapon dropped from No 49 Sqn Valiant, completing Britain's first series of megaton weapons trials (Operation Grapple).
	21	RAF/USAF meeting to discuss plans for providing US special weapons for NATO Canberra Force.
Jul	11	First RAF squadron Vulcan delivered – to No 83 Sqn.
Jul	24	CAS sends back revised Memorandum of Understanding to USAF Chief of Staff.
	29	Handley Page Victor B.1 released to the Service by Air Ministry.
Aug	2	CDC decides that V-force should consist of 144 aircraft, 104 of them Mk 2s.

8	Three Vulcans of No 230 OCU left RAF Waddington for Pinecastle AFB to take part in SAC bombing competition.	US Chief of Staff, in letter to RAF CAS, agrees with latter's revised version of the Memorandum of Understanding.
2 Sep		GOR 339 submitted to industry for appraisal.
24	Last Valiant purchased for RAF service leaves the manufacturer's works.	
Oct 4		USSR launches Sputnik.
6		Soviet hydrogen bomb detonated.
9	Victor B.1 (XA 930) arrives at Boscombe Down for operational reliability trials.	Operation Antler series of kiloton trials completed.
30 Oct– 5 Nov	Vulcans and Valiants compete in SAC Bombing Competition at Pinecastle AFB, Fla.	
21	First Victor course began ground school at No 232 OCU, RAF Gaydon.	
8		Operation Grapple – X, second British megaton series of trials, successfully completed.
28 Nov	Victor enters service with No 232 OCU: XA931, first aircraft, delivered to RAF Gaydon.	
1958 Jan	Victor ORTs carried out at Boscombe Down in XA 930 by two-crew detachment from No 232 OCU under Sqn Ldr Ringer.	B-47 Reflex operations began at Greenham Common and Fairford.

Feb	3	Draft OR 1159 – for extended-range Blue Steel – circulated.
	13	Defence White Paper says British megaton bombs in production and delivery to RAF has begun.
	18	Cabinet approves draft Agreement with US Government on deployment of IRBMs in UK.
21 Feb		Memorandum accompanying 1958-59 Air Estimates states that Canberras of 2nd TAF and Bomber Command being given nuclear capability; that satisfactory flight-refuelling trials had been undertaken using Valiant tanker and receiver aircraft: these began tentatively in February and more concentratedly in March (No 214 Sqn, Marham).
	22	US-UK Agreement on installation of 60 Thors (IRBM) in Eastern Britain, to run for five years (subsequently Nov 59 – 31 Oct 64): US to supply missiles and warheads, UK sites and installations.
	24	*The Times* quotes Macmillan in a TV interview as saying that the independent deterrent "gives us a better position in the world…a better position with respect to the United States…."
	25	White Paper on Supply of Ballistic Missiles by the US to the UK (Cmnd 366) issued.

19	First British interim megaton weapon scheduled for completion.
9 Apr	First Victor (XA935) delivered to No 10 Sqn, RAF Cottesmore.
18	Victor IFTs began at Gaydon.
28	Operation Grapple-Y experimental megaton weapon tested at Christmas Island; dropped from No 49 Sqn Valiant.
5 May	Canberras in 2 TAF now have ability to carry nuclear weapons.
6	Conference Prospect held to put RAF views and policies before the public.
15	Air Council agree to assignment of three Valiant squadrons (24 UE) to Saceur in place of Canberra Force (64 UE).
28	OR1159 issued for extended-range (Mk 2) Blue Steel.
Jun 11	ASR No 1160 issued for megaton warhead for OR 1159.
26	USAF/RAF technical agreement on Thor signed.

609

Jul	3	US/UK Agreement for Co-operation on the Uses of Atomic Energy for Mutual Defence Purposes signed.
		Yellow Sun free-falling megaton weapon recommended for limited approval.
	21	Minister of Defence approved proposals for improving the readiness of Bomber Command.
	29	Western Ranger No 1 (Vulcan XA 896 – Sqn Ldr J F Pembridge, No 230 OCU) left RAF Waddington.
Aug		First Thor offloaded at RAF Lakenheath.
Sep	1	No 77 (SM) Sqn formed at RAF Feltwell with 15 UE IRBM. No XV Sqn formed at RAF Cottesmore – received first Victor on 16 Sep.
	2 and 11	Nuclear devices dropped at Christmas Island from No 49 Sqn Valiant.
	23	Grapple 'Z' series of megaton weapon trials completed: two air-dropped rounds and two balloon-suspended rounds fired.
Nov		First Thor SM75 missile brought to No 77 (SM) Squadron, RAF Feltwell.
	18	CDC re-affirmed size of MBF as 144 aircraft.

610

Dec	17	S of S for Air (Mr George Ward) announced decision to develop a new strike/reconnaissance aircraft as a Canberra replacement.

1959

Jan		Vickers and English Electric chosen as joint main contractors for TSR.2 (ASR343).
	22	Joint USAF/RAF requirement for 1000nm range missile (GOR177) put to US industry.
Apr	16	First launch of a Thor missile by u/t RAF crew – from No 98 Sqn RAF Driffield at Vandenburg AFB.
May	8	OR343 (TSR.2) requirement issued.
	20	ACM Sir H Broadhurst relinquishes appointment as C in C Bomber Command: AVM K B B Cross relinquishes appointment as AOC No 3 Group to become C in C Bomber Command with acting rank of Air Marshal.

9	Jul	Valiant XD861 of No 214 Sqn (Wg Cdr M J Beetham) makes first non-stop flight to Cape Town in 11 hr 52 min (11 hr 28 min overhead), flight refuelled twice by squadron aircraft.
22		Nos 82, 107, 113 and 220 (SM) Sqns formed at RAF Feltwell: No 77 (SM) Sqn UE reduced to three Thor IRBMs.
27		Minister of Defence asks for six-monthly reports on state of readiness of Bomber Command.
20	Aug	Prototype Victor B.2 lost over Irish Sea: wreckage recovered and cause (loss of pitot tube) established.
28-	Sep	Final conference on Victor B.2 held.
14	Oct	General Election in United Kingdom. Ministry of Aviation formed.
6		First combat training Thor missile fired by RAF team from RAF Feltwell over Pacific Missile Range.
28		First successful Valiant-Vulcan flight refuelling rendezvous.

4	Dec	Second combat training Thor missile fired from Vandenburg by team from RAF Hemswell.
Dec	21	Strategic Air Command receives first Hound Dog missile.
	31	Assignment of first Valiant squadron to Saceur wef this date.

1960

Jan	1	OR1159 [Blue Steel Mk 2] cancelled.
Feb	17	Government White Paper says that BMEW station will be at Flyingdales in Yorkshire (third in system – others in Alaska and Greenland); also, that "the possibilities of mobile launchers, whether aircraft or submarines, for long-range delivery of nuclear warheads are being investigated".
	24	Decision to abandon Blue Streak taken at CDC meeting. Minister of Defence (Harold Watkinson) says Skybolt "eminently suitable weapon."
Mar	2	S of S for Air (George Ward) says RAF could get four V-bombers airborne from one airfield in less than four minutes.
		RAF team from RAF Feltwell fires combat training Thor from Pacific missile range at Vandenburg: last launch by a u/t RAF crew.

29		Understanding between US President and UK Prime Minister to co-operate in development and acquisition of Skybolt to enable it to be adopted both by USAF and the RAF.
Apr	13	First French atomic explosion in the Sahara.
		Blue Streak abandoned as a military weapon. Skybolt adopted as the principal UK deterrent weapon.
	26	60th – and last – Thor delivered to RAF North Luffenham by MATS C-124.
May	1	F G Powers shot down in a U-2 over the Soviet Union.
	25-26	Valiant WZ 390 of No 214 Sqn (Sqn Ldr J H Garstin) makes first non-stop flight to Singapore: 15 hr 35 min, refuelled twice by Valiant B(K).1s of the same squadron from Akrotiri and Mauripur.
Jun	3	HQ Task Force Grapple disbanded.
	6	Understanding on Skybolt between US Secretary of Defense and UK Minister of Defence.
	18	British Aircraft Corporation came into operational existence.

	1 Jul	First Vulcan B.2 (XH 558) delivered to No 230 OCU, RAF Waddington.
	25	Twenty-five of 57 Victor B.2s on order cancelled by CDC.
	27	First sophisticated W100 bomb (Blue Steel) flown at Aberporth.
	31	End of campaign against CTs in Malaya (Operation Firedog).
Aug	2	Announcement that order for Victor B.2s being reduced.
5-12 Sep		"Scrambles" by four of each type of V-bomber at SBAC Display.
	12-20	First Anglo-American conference on Skybolt held in US.
	15	RAF Germany Canberras start QRA role.
	27	Technical agreement on Skybolt between US Department of the Air Force and UK Ministry of Aviation.

Oct	7	Minister of Defence (Harold Watkinson) announces placing of full development contract for TSR.2.
Dec	15	Order for Blue Steel placed (75 were ordered – subsequently reduced to 57). Secy Gates meets Mr Watkinson in London: tells him that Skybolt programme being slowed down.
1961		
Jan	10	Issue of ASR No 1182 – for a long range air-to-surface weapon.
	29	Forty-four Thor missiles take part in Exercise Respond.
Mar	9-10	First overseas flight-refuelled flights by Vulcans, non-stop to Nairobi; refuelled over Idris.
Apr	26	OR No 1187 for an air-launched ballistic missile system (superseding OR No 1159) issued.
Jun	20-21	Vulcan 1A of No 617 Sqn flew non-stop from RAF Scampton to Richmond (Sydney, Australia): first non-stop UK-Australia flight: refuelled by Valiant tankers of No 214 Sqn, (11,500 miles in 20 hr 03 min).

Jul 1	RAF Hunter ground-attack aircraft, plus troops, sent to Kuwait following request from Ruler for assistance. Canberra squadrons concentrated in Persian Gulf area and V-bombers at readiness in Malta; Valiants on Sunspot training detachment there alerted to take part in Operation Sandaric.
13	Proposal for improving readiness of Mk 2 V-bombers, by giving them simultaneous engine starting, approved by Minister of Defence.
Aug 13	Berlin Wall begun.
17	No 1 Blue Steel course started training at BCBS, RAF Lindholme.
Sep 11	Disbandment of last Bomber Command Canberra bomber squadron, No 35, at RAF Upwood.
18	Victor B.2 given a CA release.
	Macassar – 15 min Alert Exercise – started in Bomber Command: ended 14 Oct.
Oct 5	AST No OR355 for a Tactical Strike/Reconnaissance/Interceptor Aircraft (TSR.2 replacement) circulated.

14   Exercise Skyshield: RAF V-bombers (Vulcans) take part for first time in US national air defence exercise: four from No 83 Sqn, four from No 27 Sqn.

31   AOC in C Bomber Command told VCAS: "I propose instituting the permanent alert early in the New Year".

Nov   Victor B.2 introduced into operational service.

5 Dec   First Micky Finn. Bomber Command readiness exercise – dispersal without prior notice – involving Thors.

1962

1 Jan   Beginning of QRA commitment in Bomber Command – one aircraft per squadron on 15 min readiness. MBF state of readiness thus brought into line with that of Valiants under Saceur. Saceur's revised Nuclear Strike Plan came into effect – four Valiants on QRA.

31   S of S for Air (Julian Amery) announced that Nord AS30 missiles would equip RAF Canberras and help to extend their life until introduction of TSR.2.

1 Feb   First Victor B.2 received into squadron service by No 139 Sqn at RAF Wittering.

	15	Announced that 200 RAF personnel selected to form British Joint Trials Force for advanced testing of Skybolt with Vulcan B.2 at Eglin AFB.
Mar	1	Air Council agreed in principle to the need for a third tanker squadron.
		First Blue Steel training rounds delivered to the Joint Services Trials Unit at RAF Scampton.
	30	No 101 Sqn Vulcan flies non-stop UK-Aden (6hr 13min).
Apr	19	First live launch of Skybolt "partly successful" (first stage functioned satisfactorily, second did not).
Jun	29	Second "hot" launch of XGAM-87 Skybolt, dropped from B-52 over Atlantic Missile Range; first stage propulsion failed to ignite.
Jul		S of S for Air said he had reached an agreement with the late Minister of Defence that there should be an initial purchase of 100 Skybolt missiles and 90 warheads.
	3	Thorneycroft signalled Amery from Woomera to say that he had just witnessed completely successful air launching of production model Blue Steel.

619

Jul	9	Cabinet Defence Committee decided that 100 Skybolts should be ordered.
Aug	1	Minister of Defence announced that the Joint US/UK Agreement under which Thor IRBMs deployed in UK would be ended in 1963.
Aug-Sep		No 617 Sqn "emergency operational" with Blue Steel.
	20-22	Bomber Command readiness exercise: second Micky Finn; 101 out of 112 available aircraft and 59 out of 60 Thors generated.
	25	CA Release given for Blue Steel to be carried on Vulcans with operational warhead in national emergency.
Oct		Advance party of technical staff for British Joint Trials Staff (BJTS) (Skybolt) arrives at Eglin AFB.
	22	US President announces that long range missiles being installed in Cuba and that a naval blockade of Cuba would begin on 24 October.
Nov	14	Three Vulcans (from Nos 27, 83 and 617 Sqns) set out on round-the-world flight.
Nov	22	Air Council confirmed that Victor 1/1A should replace the Valiant in the tanker role and that a third squadron should be formed.
Dec	11	Thorneycroft-McNamara meeting on Skybolt.

620

18-21	Kennedy-Macmillan talks in Bermuda: President's decision to cancel plans for production of Skybolt made known in Statement on Nuclear Defence Systems (21 December). Hound Dog not acceptable to RAF as alternative.
1963	
Jan 2	DRPC (AES) endorsed development of lay-down bomb for use by V-bombers to allow them to operate at low level.
11	DRPC endorses decision by Defence Committee that V-force should operate at low level and approves measures necessary to give the force a low-level capability.
23	CDC approves proposals for modifications to equipment of V-force to improve credibility until Polaris available: agreed to modifications to enable V-bombers to operate at low level and to development of high-yield lay-down bomb.
31	Whole of V-bomber force to be assigned to NATO, but independent use not restricted (see also 23 May).

Feb	14	Press conference held at RAF Scampton to introduce Blue Steel. C in C revealed that Bomber Command had 23,216 men of whom 10,620 were in the V-force.
Feb		The Statement on Defence (Cmnd 1936) said: "Blue Steel is in service".
Mar	13	Draft ASR 1177 (Issue 4) for General-Purpose Nuclear Bomb.
May	3	SOP No 54 MBF Aircraft – Low-Level Role issued.
	5	ASR No 380 MBF Aircraft – Low-Level Role issued.
	6	Valiants of Bomber Command assigned to NATO for the first time in tactical role.
	16	Draft ASR No 1132 for a propelled air-to-surface missile to be launched at high or low level from V-bombers circulated.
23 May		RAF V-force formally assigned to NATO (Saceur) for targeting, planning, co-ordination and execution of strikes.
31		Canberra QRA in Germany increased from four to eight.

Jun	5	Minister of Defence approves project study of modifications for low-level Blue Steel.
	17	Minister of Aviation gives costs of cancelled projects, including Blue Streak (£84m) in written Parliamentary answer.
Jul	30	C in C Bomber Command writes to CAS about shortcomings of Blue Steel.
Aug	15	RAF Thor Force became non-operational.
	25	"No notice" alert exercise initiated by AOC in C Bomber Command.
	28	MoA gives clearance for use of Blue Steel on QRA with Vulcan B.2.
Sep	17	Fylingdales BMEW station declared operational.
	27	Last Thor missile returned to USA.
Oct	1	DRPC endorsed proposals to enable Blue Steel to be modified to operate at low level.
Nov	19	First Blue Steel low-level trials weapon successfully launched from a Vulcan at Woomera at 300 kt/2,000 ft.
Dec		No 139 Sqn (Victor B.2s RAF Wittering) converted to Blue Steel role.
Dec		Operations began in Malaysia and Borneo against Indonesian confrontation.

Dec 16 — Minister of Defence approves extension of holding contract for low-level Blue Steel for another three months and that necessary initial production orders should be authorised.

31 Dec — Run-down of Thor Force expected to be completed by this date.

1964

Feb 4 — S of S for Air (Hugh Fraser) said at press conference at RAF Wittering that V-force now equipped and trained to attack targets from low level.

1 Mar — Centralised servicing introduced in MBF squadrons.

Apr 1 — Unified Ministry of Defence formed, the Air Ministry becoming the Air Force Department, the Air Council the Air Force Board and the Secretary of State for Air, the Minister of Defence for the Royal Air Force.

30 Jun — RAF Christmas Island closed: all Service personnel withdrawn.

6 Aug	Rear spar of Valiant from RAF Gaydon fractured in flight: examination of Valiant reveals evidence of aircraft fatigue.
Aug 19	Final low level Blue Steel release at Woomera, from Victor at 1000 ft/350kt.
Sep 27	TSR.2 makes first flight.
Oct	Change of Government – Labour Administration.
Oct	Acceptance firings of Blue Steel concluded.
26-29	Exercise Micky Finn held – Bomber Command annual no-notice dispersal exercise to test alert and readiness capability.
9 Dec	All Valiants grounded, except for national emergency.
31	TSR.2 makes second flight.
1965	
18 Jan	Air Force Board (Standing Committee) decided to withdraw Valiant force from service immediately.
25	AOC in C Bomber Command informs Saceur that Valiants being withdrawn from service.

Valiant force officially withdrawn from service (wef 27th) due to fatigue failure (MoD announcement 26 Jan).

27

2 Feb   Prime Minister announces cancellation of P.1154 and HS681.

Valiant training element of No 232 OCU disbanded; Nos 90 and 214 Sqns (Valiant tankers) withdrawn from operations.

1 Mar   Nos 90 and 214 Squadrons (Valiant B(K).1) disbanded.

Mar 19   DOPC decides that NATO-assigned Valiants should not be replaced.

Apr 3   380th Bomb Wing returned to US after nearly 12 years B-47 operations at RAF Brize Norton.

6   Cancellation of TSR.2 project announced by Chancellor of the Exchequer (James Callaghan) in his Budget speech.

Air Ministry approves practice reinforcement of Far East by eight Vulcans.

7 Apr

Nos 49, 148 and 207 Sqns (Valiants) disbanded at RAF Marham.

1 May

First sortie by a Victor B(K).1 two-point tanker flown from RAF Honington.

7 May

	25	First two Victor B(K).1 two-point tankers transferred from RAF Honington to RAF Marham.
	26	Progess report of this date says Blue Steel and Victor 1/1A tanker training "virtually complete".
	28	First Victor tanker sortie flown from RAF Marham by Sqn Ldr Alexander, No 55 Sqn.
Jun	30	HQ 7th Air Division, SAC, discontinued.
Jul	1	Control of RAF Gaydon transferred to Flying Training Command. Victor flying element of No 232 OCU at RAF Marham re-named Tanker Training Flight, and No 232 OCU disbanded.
		Order placed for 158 General Dynamics light-weight terrain-following radars for Victor Mk 2 and Vulcan Mk 2.
Nov		Last Vulcan Mk 1 course graduated from No 230 OCU.
Dec	1	No 57 Sqn (eight UE Victor B.1/1As) became non-operational: moved from RAF Honington to RAF Morham to await deliveries of three-point Victor tankers.
	14	500th "Western Ranger" flight flown to Offutt AFB, Neb.

627

	Date		RAF / UK events	World events
		1966		
	14	Feb	No 57 Sqn, RAF Marham, receives first Victor three-point tanker.	
		Feb	22		Fifty F-111s to be ordered from the United States.
	27	May	First Blue Steel launch in Operation Fresno (post-acceptance launch programme for missile) from Victor over Aberforth range.	
		Aug	11		Malaysia-Indonesia Treaty signed in Bangkok.
			16		End of Indonesian confrontation operations.
					Withdrawal of USAF units from France.
			Production problems delay re-arming of Vulcan B.2* (*free fall) squadrons with WE177B lay-down nuclear bomb.	
	26	Aug	Second Blue Steel launch by Victor in pre-acceptance launch programme	
	1	Sep	No 214 Sqn (eight UE Victor K.1/1As) re-formed: second of three squadrons to be equipped with three-point Victor tankers.	
			First lay-down nuclear weapons (WE177B) delivered to RAF Cottesmore.	

1 Oct	Delivery of first three-point tanker to No 214 Sqn.
8 Dec	Bomber Command at this time "making gradual changes in emphasis of attack from the high-level to the low-level mode".
1967	
Feb	Announced in Defence White Paper that Bomber and Fighter Commands would merge in April 1968 to form Strike Command.
May 3	Evacuation of Aden began.
31	First Vulcan launch of Blue Steel in Operation Fresno.
Jun	Arab-Israeli six-day war.
Jul 5	Cancellation of Anglo-French variable-geometry aircraft announced in Commons by Minister of Defence.
7	Second Vulcan Blue Steel firing in Operation Fresno.
1968	
Jan 16	F-111A project cancelled.
1 Apr	Strike Command formed, amalgamating Bomber and Fighter Commands.

Date	Event	World event
1 Jun	Merger of Flying Training and Technical Training Commands.	
Aug 21		Czechoslovakia invaded.
30 Sep	No 100 Squadron (Victor B.2s) disbanded.	
31 Dec	No 139 Squadron (Victor B.2s) disbanded.	
1969		
Jan	ORC (Operational Requirements Committee) agreed that Victor Mk2 should fill RAF requirement to replace present aircraft in tanker force in the early 1970s.	
30 Jun / 1 Jul	Medium bomber force QRA terminated at midnight. UK-based V-bombers transferred to tactical role on RN Polaris force becoming operational.	Apollo 11 on Moon.
28-30	Exercise High Noon (no-notice alert and readiness exercise replacing Micky Finn) held for first time since QRA ended for Vulcans.	
Aug	Factory programme to convert 24 Blue Steel Vulcans to the free-fall role scheduled to begin.	

Nov	SALT (strategic arms limitation) talks begin.
	Following withdrawal of Blue Steel by the end of this year, whole Vulcan force to use low-level free-fall weapon delivery technique.
1970	
1 Jan	No 27 Sqn, RAF Scampton, assumed a free-fall role, No 617 Sqn thus remaining the sole Blue Steel squadron.
19-22 May	No 54 Sqn Phantoms, flight-refuelled, flew non-stop to Singapore in 14 hr 9 min during the five-nation exercise Bersatu Padu.

APPENDIX No 13

SELECTIVE BIBLIOGRAPHY

David A Anderton *The History of the US Air Force* (Crescent Books, New York, 1981)

C F Andrews *Vickers Aircraft since 1908* (Putnam, 1969)

Lorna Arnold *A Very Special Relationship – British Atomic Weapon Trials in Australia* (HMSO, 1987)

C H Barnes *Shorts Aircraft since 1900* (Putnam, 1967)

C H Barnes *Handley Page Aircraft since 1907* (Putnam, 1976)

Denys Blakeway and Sue Lloyd-Roberts *Fields of Thunder – Testing Britain's Bomb* (Counterpoint, 1985)

Andrew J Brookes *Photo Reconnaissance – The Operational History* (Ian Allan Ltd, 1975)

Andrew J Brookes *V Force – The History of Britain's Airborne Deterrent* (Jane's, 1982)

Ronald W Clark *Tizard* (Methuen & Co, 1965)

John Ehrman *The Atomic Bomb – An Account of British Policy in the Second World War* (Cabinet Office, 1953; 68/94 Secret)

Alfred Goldberg *The Atomic Origins of the British Nuclear Deterrent* ("International Affairs" – July 1964 (Chatham House))

Margaret Gowing, assisted by Lorna Arnold *Independence and Deterrence – Britain and Atomic Energy 1945-1952 – Vol 1 Policy Making; Vol 2 Policy Execution* (Macmillan, 1974)

A J R Groom *British Thinking about Nuclear Weapons* (Frances Pinter, 1974)

Julian Hartt *The Mighty Thor* (Duell, Sloan & Pearce, 1961)

Gp Capt K G Hubbard *Operation Grapple – Testing Britain's First H-bomb* (Ian Allan, 1985)

Lord Ismay *Nato – The First Five Years 1949-54*

A J Jackson *Avro Aircraft since 1908* (Putnam, 1965)

Robert Jackson *Avro Vulcan* (Patrick Stephens, 1984)

Robert Jackson *V-bombers* (Ian Allan Ltd, 1981)

W E Jones *Maralinga – Field of Thunder* (unpublished when read)

Maj-Gen S Woodburn Kirby with Brig M R Roberts, Col G T Wards and AVM N L Desoer *History of the Second World War – The War Against Japan Vol V* (HMSO, 1969)

AVM Stewart Menaul CB CBE DFC AFC *Countdown – Britain's Strategic Nuclear Forces* (Robert Hale, 1980)

Ministry of Defence *The Malayan Emergency 1948-1960* (MoD, 1970)

AVM Wilfred E Oulton CB CBE DSO DFC *Christmas Island Cracker – An Account of the Planning and Execution of the British Thermo-Nuclear Bomb Tests 1957* (Thomas Harmsworth Publishing, 1987)

Andrew J Pierre *Nuclear Politics – The British Experience with an Independent Nuclear Force 1939-1970* (OUP, 1972)

R N Rosecrance *Defense of the Realm – British Strategy in the Nuclear Epoch* (Columbia University Press, 1968)

Institution of Royal Engineers *History of the Corps of Royal Engineers* – Chapter X – The Nuclear Test Programme

Dudley Saward *Bomber Harris – The Authorised Biography* (Cassell Ltd and Buchan & Enright Publishers Ltd, 1984)

John Simpson *The Independent Nuclear State – The United States, Britain and the Military Atom* (Macmillan Press, 1983)

William P Snyder *The Politics of British Defense Policy 1945-1962* (Ernest Benn Ltd, 1962)

Ivan Southall *Woomera* (Angus and Robertson, 1962)

Strategic Air Command, USAF *Development of Strategic Air Command 1946-1976* (Office of the Historian, Strategic Air Command, 1976)

Adrian Tame and F P J Robotham *Maralinga – British A-Bomb Australian Legacy* (Fontana/Collins, 1982)

Gordon Thomas and Max Morgan Witts *Ruin from the Air – The Atomic Mission to Hiroshima* (UK publishers, Hamish Hamilton, 1977)

Sqn Ldr K S Tripathi DFC *Evolution of Nuclear Strategy* (Vikas Publications, 1970)

Derek Wood *Project Cancelled* (Macdonald and Jane's, 1975)

Herbert F York *The Advisers: Oppenheimer, Teller and the Superbomb* (W H Freeman & Co, 1976)

Solly Zuckerman *Monkeys Men and Missiles: An Autobiography 1946-88* (Collins, 1988)

Index

Notes: The references in this index do not include the appendices. Ranks and titles are as at first mention.

335, 363, 364, 365, 366, 367, 368, 369,
371, 410, 411, 427, 428, 432, 436, 438,
440, 464, 465, 466, 469, 474, 489, 490,
491, 492, 493, 494, 495, 496, 497, 498,
499, 501, 504, 506, 519, 550, 552, 553,
596, 618
Sacramento, 346
Safety cttees, Br, 220
Salisbury (SR), 163, 164, 306, 469
Salome Cttee, 91, 92
SALT talks, 631
Sandys, D, 102, 199, 230, 252, 257, 259,
261, 275, 280, 281(fn), 287, 291, 299,
300, 317, 326, 328, 373, 377, 378, 386,
392, 400, 507
San Francisco, 3
Santa Monica (photos), 238-9
Saunders-Roe, 375
SBAC Displays, 54, 96(fn), 117, 122, 162,
533, 534
Schneider Trophy, 153
Scientific Adviser, AM, 187, 188, 400
Scott, Sir R, 424, 528
Scott-Hall, S, 46, 47, 49
Sea Slug, 512
SEATO, 85, 158
Second World War, 2, 4(fn), 82, 312(fn)
Selkirk, Earl of, 325, 380, 508
Semipalatinsk, 85, 587, 602
Serby, J E, 48, 50, 55, 68
Serpell, D R, 389(fn), 390(fn), 515(fn),
518(fn), 519(fn)
Shackleton, Lord, 338, 481, 484, 555
Shadow flights, 266
SHAPE, 44, 101, 104, 363, 367, 370, 465,
468, 489
Sharp, D, 522
Shaw, C W, 235
Shoeburyness, 21
Shorts, 47, 48, 49, 51, 53, 504, 507, 511,
539
Shuckburgh, Sir E, 499
Sicklen, Col N H Van, 360(fn)
Sidescan radar, 180, 438, 454
Simpson, Lt-Gen F E W, 17(fn)
Singapore, 40, 138, 165, 166, 442, 443,
444, 464, 489(fn)
Smallboy, 87(fn), 92
Soames, C, 325, 380
Song Song range, 444

South America, 110
South Australia, 170(fn), 180
South Korea, 588
South Pacific, 225, 226
South Sea Island Bubble, 530(fn)
Southern Instruments, 247(fn)
Soviet air defences, 321, 431
Soviet fighter force, 371
Soviet long-range air force, 75
Soviet SAGW defences, 436
Soviet SAM defences, 436
Soviet Union, 2, 3, 9, 64, 82, 83, 84, 85
Spadeadam, 377, 383, 385, 388
Specifications:
B. 3/45, 55
B. 5/47, 69
B. 9/48, 47, 53, 54, 58, 585
B. 14/46, 46, 47, 49, 50, 52, 53, 54, 58,
592
B. 35/46, 47, 49, 50, 52, 55, 56, 58, 59,
61, 581, 584
B. 120P, 56, 320
OR. 3605, 185
PR. 31/48, 69
Spectre/Stentor rocket motors, 191, 192,
193, 200
Springfields, 30, 42, 94
Sputnik, 607
SSAs, 98(fn), 263, 264, 266, 267
Staf, C, 122
Stafford, R S, 47
Staff Reqt SR168, 404
Stalin, 83
Standard of Preparation, No 54, 439,
451, 452, 453, 454
Star Tracker, 329
Stettin, 32(fn)
Stewart, M, 497
Strategic Target Policy, 273-9
Strath, Sir W, 394, 400
Stratton, Lt-Gen Sir W, 394
Suez, 69, 502, 537
Suez Operation, 96(fn), 101, 129-134,
153, 288(fn), 464(fn)
Supply, Minister of, 13, 22, 24, 26, 32, 42,
62, 102, 224, 252, 253, 285, 315, 316,
318, 379, 380, 382, 390, 391, 505, 515,
516
Supply, Ministry of, 11, 14, 15, 18, 25,
29, 31, 42, 45, 46, 47, 48, 49, 51, 52, 53,